Handbook of information management

8th edition

Edited by Alison Scammell

Aslib *imi*

INFORMATION MANAGEMENT

Published by Aslib-IMI

ISBN 0 85142 457 0

©Aslib and contributors, 2001

Information Management International (IMI) is a trading name of Aslib.

Aslib-IMI provides consultancy and information services, professional development training, conferences, specialist recruitment, Internet products, publishes journals (in hard copy and electronic formats), books and directories and provides outsourcing revises to the information community.

Aslib-IMI, founded in 1924, is a world class corporate membership organisation with over 2000 members in some 70 countries. Aslib actively promotes best practice in the management of information resources. It lobbies on all aspects of the management of, and legislation concerning, information at local, national and international levels.

Further information is available from:

Aslib-IMI
Staple Hall
Stone House Court
London EC3A 7PB
Tel: +44 (0) 20 7903 0000
Fax: +44 (0) 20 7903 0011
Email: *aslib@aslib.com*
WWW: *www.aslib.com*

Printed and bound by Bell and Bain Ltd., Glasgow

Listing of editions

First published 1955
Second impression 1956
Second edition, completely revised, 1962
Second impression, with minor corrections, 1963
Third edition, completely revised, 1967
Second impression 1968
Fourth edition, completely revised, 1975
Second impression 1977
Third impression 1978
Fifth edition, completely revised, 1982
Sixth edition, completely revised, 1992
Seventh edition, completely revised, 1997
Eighth edition, completely revised, 2001

Contents

Biographical notes

Barbara Allan

Barbara Allan has worked in information and library services in computing, construction, education and training organisations. Her experience includes project management, and training and development. Barbara has managed a number of projects including: establishing a new resource centre; moving and also closing a library; implementing IT systems; and introducing innovative human resource management processes. Barbara is currently involved in a number of innovative web-based projects in the education and training field.

Mary Ellen Bates

Mary Ellen Bates is the owner of Bates Information Services, a company providing business research to business professionals and research support to special librarians. She is the author of four books, *Mining for Gold on the Internet* (McGraw-Hill, 2000), *Researching Online for Dummies* 2nd edition, with Reva Basch (IDG Books, 2000), *Super Searchers Do Business* (Information Today, 1999), and *The Online Deskbook* (Information Today, 1996). She is a frequent international speaker and writer about the information industry. She can be contacted at *mbates@BatesInfo.com, http://www.BatesInfo.com,* or +1 202.332.22360.

Fiona Bell

Since gaining an MA in Information and Library Studies from Loughborough University in 1995, Fiona Bell has worked for Business Link Leicestershire. Originally she joined as part of the enquiries team but after an organisational restructure Fiona took on sole responsibility for the information resource for the company. The Information Centre responds to business enquiries from both internal customers (colleagues from other departments) and external customers (businesses and members of the public wishing to start a business). The department has grown from one to six employees. Its income has increased more than threefold in the last year, and staff and customers now have access to a suite of products which enable them to tackle a wide range of enquiries with confidence. Fiona has also spent short spells in the libraries of Leicester University and De Montfort University. She also worked at Birmingham University Library.

Paul Blackmore

Paul Blackmore is currently Information & ICT Manager (Deputy Director) at Lancaster University Careers Service. Previously he was Business Intelligence Officer/Customer Liaison Engineer for British Steel Plc and Intranet/Internet Webmaster & Corporate Liaison Manager for Wirral Metropolitan College. He has managed various learning support projects in both industry and education, including the implementation of the first UK FE/HEI delivery of learning environment intranet/extranet services to corporate-based satellite Learning Resource Centres. He was responsible for the development and management of hybrid-technology (WWW-CD-ROM) Virtual Learning Environments for delivery in-house, and to third party organisations nationally. His current interests concern the research, implementation and delivery of Personal & Career Development Learning programmes via Networked Collaborative Learning. Paul is a frequent presenter and author of articles and papers regarding the implementation and operational management of intranets and networked learning environments, and author of *Intranets: a guide to their design, implementation and management* (Aslib, 2001).

Marshall Crawford

Marshall Crawford, BA (Philosophy, University of Illinois), MLS (University of Maryland). Information Services Director at the National Building Specification, a division of the Royal Institute of British Architects Companies Ltd. Throughout his career he has held a number of key positions as technical librarian, consultant and construction information specialist. He has extensive experience in the UK and also worked in the Middle East on major projects. He led the team which developed Uniclass, the classification scheme for the construction industry which was launched in 1997. Member of IIS, CIIG and SLA.

Stella G. Dextre Clarke

Stella Dextre Clarke is an information scientist practitioner and manager turned consultant. Most of her career has been in the information industry, organising production of publicly available bibliographic databases and derived products. She now specialises in the design and implementation of knowledge structures for information retrieval, such as classification schemes, thesauri and taxonomies. She also runs training courses on thesaurus construction. She is a Fellow of the Institute of Information Scientists and a member of the BSI committee on standards for indexes, filing and thesauri.

Tom Dobrowolski

Tom Dobrowolski is a senior lecturer in the Institute of Information Science of Warsaw University in Poland. His main interest is the culture of information. He has published two books about the Internet in Polish, and a few articles in English (with David Nicholas of City University, London).

Elizabeth J. Eastwood

Elizabeth J Eastwood graduated from Manchester Metropolitan University with a BA (Hons) in Library and Information Management. Since then she has held several posts. She has worked as a children's librarian in the London Borough of Havering, and as a scientific information officer at the European Laboratory for Particle Physics (CERN) in Geneva. She became a chartered member of the British Library Association in 1995. Elizabeth spent one year working at the Medical College of Pennsylvania Libraries in Philadelphia, USA, and has recently earned a Masters Degree in Library and Information Science from Dominican University, Illinois, having specialised in health science information work. Recently returning to England, she has taken the position of Information Manager at the charity, Arthritis Care, and is looking forward to helping the organisation meet their goals for the community.

Peter Evans

Peter Evans became an ALA in 1972 and had a varied library career beginning in public libraries then spending 6 years at what is now the University of Hertfordshire where he helped develop some of the first computer applications - cataloguing, circulation, and serials listings. Managing the University's industrial services unit involved him in liaising with a wide variety of local special libraries.

Subsequent special library experience in a computer consultancy led on to working with a number of library automation companies including Dynix, Geac and Oracle.

Four years ago he founded Biblio Tech Review - a web-based library technology news and information resource - www.biblio-tech.com.

Ina Fourie

Ina Fourie is a lecturer in the Department of Information Science at the University of South Africa (Unisa, which is a distance teaching university.) She has 12 years' experience in teaching computerised information retrieval and information organisation to undergraduate and postgraduate students. Before joining Unisa in 1988, she was a senior librarian at the Atomic Energy Corporation of South Africa. She obtained her first degrees at the University of the Orange Free State: BBibl (1981), Honours (1982) and Master's (1987). Her Master's dissertation deals with the need of professional librarians for training in computer-related aspects. In 1994 she obtained a postgraduate Diploma in Tertiary Education (*cum laude*) from Unisa, and in 1995 the DLitt et Phil from the Rand Afrikaans University. Her doctoral thesis investigated a multimedia study package for distance teaching in online searching. Other activities include publishing on distance teaching and various aspects of information organisation and retrieval, designing computer-assisted instruction (CAI) tutorials and web-based instruction programmes, and presenting short courses in various aspects of information organisation and retrieval.

Peter Groves

Peter Groves specialises in intellectual property, competition and information technology law. A solicitor since 1980, he is with the virtual City firm, Davis & Co (Solicitors) Ltd. Peter is the author of several books and many articles on these subjects, and is a prolific lecturer and presenter of training courses, details of which can be found at www.petergroves.co.uk. He has lectured at Essex University, London Guildhall University and the Oxford Institute of Legal Practice, and as a guest lecturer at the University of Seattle. He is the general editor of *The Business Client Handbook* and joint editor of *Motor Law*, the legal newsletter for motor industry managers.

Catherine Hare

Catherine is a Senior Lecturer in the School of Information Studies at the University of Northumbria. She has worked in a wide variety of libraries and information units, including a year in Paris. Before joining the School in 1990, she was head of an information unit in the private sector, working for a firm of economic consultants specialising in European Community affairs. Her professional interests lie in the field of records management, information resource management, information technology and delivery methods for professional education and training in the field of records and information management. She is Course Leader for the MSc in Records Management by Distance Learning and the Advanced Diploma in Lifelong Learning (Records Management), Immediate Past Chair of the Records Management Society of Great Britain, Editor of the Records Management Journal (published by Aslib), and is currently a member of a European research project, E-Term, which is developing a training programme in electronic records management.

David Haynes and Fran Huckle

David Haynes and Fran Huckle work together as information consultants. They are both experienced information professionals with interests in information policy, and information seeking in an electronic environment. David Haynes formerly worked for Aslib as a researcher and then as a partner with The Information Partnership. In 1994 he set up David Haynes Associates, a registered management consultancy firm specialising in library and information management. Fran Huckle has had a varied career having worked for the London Business School, Cirencester Agricultural College and ACRE before she joined David Haynes Associates. Her particular interests lie in Internet access issues and information retrieval.

Susan Henczel

Susan Henczel is the Education and Business Development Manager at CAVAL Collaborative Solutions, an academic library cooperative in Melbourne Australia. She has over 25 years' experience in the information industry in Australian academic, state reference, government, public and corporate libraries. Susan's extensive experience in all aspects of library work has led to her current involvement in continuing professional development activities for librarians and other information workers. She is also involved in the management and coordination of regional, state and national projects related to the information industry and knowledge economy in Australia. Susan is currently conducting information audit workshops in Australia and New Zealand and is developing audit programs for public and private sector organisations. Her forthcoming book entitled *The Information Audit: a practical guide* is the latest volume in Guy St. Clair's Information Services Management Series and was published by Bowker (UK) in February 2001.

Declan G. Kelly

Declan is Research Services Manager at the BBC Information & Archives and has worked for the BBC for 13 years following a spell in health information for the DHSS. During his time in the BBC, Declan has had a number of roles: three years as a science subject specialist doing enquiry work for programmes such as *Horizon* and *Tomorrow's World*, seven years at Bush House working for the World Service as Deputy and then Research Manager during which he was involved in merging of book and press cuttings libraries and planning/building the World Service Research Centre, which brought all their information services together in one 24 hour centre. Two years were then spent looking after intake and acquisitions for all of the London-based libraries and archives, followed by a year as 'Operational Process & Change Manager'. Declan is currently the Research Services Manager in BBC Information & Archives.

Mark Kerr

Mark Kerr has been writing and training on Internet topics since late 1995. He is the author of the Aslib Know How Guide *How to Promote Your Web Site Effectively*, editor of *Tips and tricks for Web site managers* (Aslib, 2001), and writes articles and book reviews for a number of publications in the information sector. Mark works at South Bank University as Centre Manager for London ASPECT, a business advice and training centre in the UK Online for Business network, run as a partnership between the University and Business Link London Central. Eight years owning a courier company, three years driving a taxi in York and five years designing web sites and delivering Internet training inform a clear and entrepreneurial approach to solving marketing, publishing and IT problems.

Amanda McKenzie

After gaining an LLB Hons at the University of Central England, Amanda McKenzie went on to the Guildford College of Law to complete the Law Society Finals. She then worked at the city law firm Herbert Smith, in their Know How department. Amanda moved into the sphere of legal information by joining Olswang in 1996 first as information officer and then in 1999 as Information Services Manager. She is currently Vice Chair of the Legal Information Group committee of BIALL and also a member of the Library Association Copyright Alliance.

Michael Maher

Michael Maher is Head of Information Services for the Birmingham region of the national law firm Eversheds. He has played an active role in law librarianship over the last 15 years. He has been Treasurer (1994-6) and Chair (1998-9) of the British and Irish Association of Law Librarians (BIALL) and held numerous other positions within it. He is also a founder member of the Association of Law Librarians in Central England. He has spoken on many aspects of legal information at numerous law and library courses and conferences within the UK and overseas. He has had several articles published and was a member of the steering committee which produced the extensive BIALL survey 'Law and Order: Trends in Legal Provision'.

Julie McLeod

Julie McLeod is a Senior Lecturer in the School of Information Studies at the University of Northumbria at Newcastle. She joined the School in 1994 after a career in industry-based information, library and records management services, culminating with a management position in the pharmaceutical sector. Her teaching and research interests are in records management, and information storage and retrieval, and she has been involved with a number of records management consultancy contracts. She is also involved in a range of innovative training and education initiatives for records management, including the new Lifelong Learning Award pioneered with BBC staff, and the MSc in Records Management by distance learning. With Catherine Hare she is co-author of *Developing a Records Management Programme* (Aslib Know How Guide) and joint editor of the *Records Management Journal*, also published by Aslib. She is currently a member of the BSI Committee working on the first international standard on records management.

Adrienne Muir

Adrienne Muir is a Lecturer in the Department of Information Science at Loughborough University. She is currently carrying out doctoral research on legal deposit of digital material. Other research interests include preservation (especially digital preservation), digital libraries and the social impact of digital information. Previously she managed Digital Library and Preservation research programmes for the British Library Research and Innovation Centre, and the Library and Information Commission. She has also worked as a researcher in the areas of digital libraries at Loughborough University, and information and cultural policy at the Policy Studies Institute. She started her career at the National Library of Scotland.

Neil Munn

Neil Munn is responsible for developing the internal knowledge management programme for the e-business consultancy, Rubus. Prior to joining Rubus, he spent 12 years as a member of the Knowledge Management programme in the Management Consultancy Services division of PricewaterhouseCoopers holding a variety of positions.

David Nicholas

David Nicholas is Head of Department and Professor at the Department of Information Science, City University. He is also Director of The Internet Studies Research Group, an interdisciplinary association of researchers examining the impact of the Internet on strategic groups and industries and attempting to understand what the Information Wild West means for all of us. Currently he is Project Head of a digital consumer health information project sponsored by the Department of Health.

Sandra Parker

Sandra Parker is currently course leader of the MA/MSc in Information and Library Management at the University of Northumbria at Newcastle. Her teaching interests lie in the management of information services, particularly in the field of human resources management. Her research interests are mainly qualitative in nature, in the field of performance management, with a particular emphasis on user issues. She has been Chair of the editorial board of the Northumbria International Conference on Performance Measurement for five years, and is Editor of *Performance Measurement and Metrics: the international journal for library and information services*, published by Aslib. She has previously worked in public, academic and special libraries and information services. She has been active in the professional associations throughout her working life, and was elected President of the Library Association in 1996.

Paul Pedley

Paul Pedley is Head of Research at the Economist Intelligence Unit. Prior to this, Paul was Library & Information Services Manager at Theodore Goddard. Paul has also worked for the developers of Canary Wharf in London's docklands, and also in government libraries at the Department of Trade and Industry, the Office of Telecommunications (OFTEL), and the Property Services Agency. Paul is a Fellow of the Library Association, and is an active member of a number of professional groups. He is the current chairperson of the Industrial and Commercial Libraries Group of the Library Association, and he is a former chair of both the City Legal Information Group and the Property Information Group. He is a special libraries representative on the Library Association Copyright Alliance. He is the author of three Aslib Know How Guides – *Copyright for Library and Information Service Professionals, Intranets and Push Technology – Creating an Information Sharing Environment*, and *The invisible web*. Paul's book, *Free Business and Industry Information on the Web*, was published by Aslib in 2001.

John Ross

John Ross graduated originally in Cybernetics and started his career in the computer industry with English Electric Computers, later part of ICL. After three years with a computer manufacturer he went back to University to do research, and that was where he first became involved in library automation and information retrieval. Since then, much of his career has been involved with information technology and its application to libraries and information management. He set up his own consultancy, *Infologistix*, in 1980 and has undertaken a wide range of library-related and other assignments around the world since then.

Alison Scammell

Alison Scammell managed the Information Services for both the Building Societies Association and Council of Mortgage Lenders between 1987 and 1994. After spending four years as an independent information management consultant and two years as Aslib's Commissioning Editor, she now works for an IT marketing and communications agency.

Guy St. Clair

Guy St. Clair is Senior Systems Analyst, Knowledge Management and Learning, Dynamics Research Corporation, New York, NY USA. Prior to accepting this position, Mr St. Clair was President of SMR International, a New York-based management consulting firm with a specialisation in information management, knowledge management, and professional and strategic learning. Known for his writings on information and knowledge management, Mr St. Clair is the author of *Customer Service in the Information Environment* (1993), *Power and Influence: enhancing information services within the organization* (1994), *Entrepreneurial Librarianship: the key to effective information services* (1995), and *Total Quality Management in Information Services* (1997), all published by Bowker-Saur. He also authored *Change Management in Action*, published by the Special Libraries Association, in 1999. His newest book, *Beyond Degrees: professional learning in the information environment*, will be published in 2002. He is a Past-President of the Special Libraries Association.

Jan Sykes

Jan Sykes is an independent consultant specialising in information management projects. She has managed large-scale trials of desktop information products, written surveys to analyse information needs of designated user groups, conducted follow-up interviews to refine the survey data, and worked with companies to evaluate and select content to help them meet business objectives. Jan has over 20 years' experience in the information industry. Prior to becoming an independent consultant, Jan was Senior Director of Client Services Consulting for Knight-Ridder Information, Inc. In that capacity, she managed account development and instructional development activities. She also has sales, training, and sales management experience in the information industry. Early in her career, she worked in abstracting and indexing, and later managed a fee-based information service for the Institute of Paper Chemistry. Jan Sykes has an MA from Middlebury College, Middlebury, VT and a BS from the University of Wisconsin. She is a member of the American Society of Information Science and Special Libraries Association. Her consulting company, Information Management Services, Inc. is located near Chicago, IL and she can be reached at jansykes@ameritech.net or +847-583-8337.

Sara Tompson

Sara R. Tompson is the Director of Library Services at Packer Engineering in Naperville, IL. Previously she ran the library at the Fermi National Accelerator Laboratory in Batavia, IL for five years. She has worked in physical sciences or engineering libraries since receiving her MS in Library and Information Science from the University of Illinois in 1987. Sara is Past-President (2000-1) of the Illinois chapter of the Special Libraries Association, and a member of the SLA Research Committee (2000-3). She is one of the co-authors of the 4th edition of *Special Libraries: a guide for management* (SLA, 1997), and numerous peer-reviewed articles and book reviews. Sara is an adjunct faculty member at Dominican University's Graduate School of Library and Information Science, and regularly teaches Special Libraries Administration.

Steve Thornton

Steve Thornton is currently the Improvements Manager for the Information Resources Department of the UK's Ministry of Defence's Defence Evaluation and Research Agency (DERA). He has spent the last 25 years working for library and information services in the defence research arena. A former member of Aslib Council, he also spent 22 years on the Aslib Electronics Group Committee. He is a proponent of meaningful performance measurement of library services, and the creation of easy and effective benchmarking tools and mechanisms.

Introduction

Alison Scammell

I am very pleased to introduce this new edition of the Handbook. Formerly entitled *Handbook of Special Librarianship and Information Work*, this represents the eighth edition of what is generally regarded as Aslib's 'flagship' reference work, the seminal text on modern information theories, procedures and practices since 1955.

The title has been changed to reflect a broader spectrum of managed information services and structures than merely the management of a physical collection of material. Although there are still many references to libraries and librarians throughout the book, by dropping the notorious 'L' word from the title, the intention is to emphasise the diverse nature of information work, in all its myriad forms. We are living and working at a time when 24/7 information availability across a variety of delivery channels is an accepted and routine part of everyday life. We are entering a new era of third generation computing where information will be accessible from multiple devices and electronic service delivery is becoming common place. Information professionals these days are as likely to be knowledge managers, web site editors or systems developers, with little or no responsibility for traditional library tasks.

The role of the information profession is very wide ranging and continues to defy hard and fast definitions. Information management is a complex set of activities involving the selection, organisation, analysis, evaluation and dissemination of information. The intention of the Handbook is to review and update these subjects, providing a comprehensive coverage of current best practice building on a corpus of knowledge and expertise spanning many decades of research, development and practice.

As with previous editions, the focus of the Handbook is on special information services rather than public and academic libraries although the Handbook contains a wealth of information which will be of relevance to information professionals working in all sectors. The contributors – academics, practitioners and consultants – are from a range of backgrounds and fields. Many are well-published authorities in their subjects while others are more recent entrants to the profession whose fresh ideas and experiences provide a particularly valuable contribution.

The content broadly reflects the coverage of the previous edition, with an emphasis on the core theories and principles of information organisation, retrieval and dissemination. Some new chapters appear for the first time. Although the Internet receives prominent coverage throughout the Handbook, there is now a chapter examining the legal issues thrown up by the Internet, many of which are still unresolved. Other new subjects included for the first time deal with freedom of information, project management, digital library research, the hybrid library, the effective web site and the intranet. There is a particular emphasis throughout the Handbook on understanding our clients' needs and two chapters cover this in some depth – information needs assessment and information audits.

Information provision must always be closely tied to the strategic objectives of the enterprise. As Guy St. Clair points out in his chapter, information professionals are stakeholders in organisational success so they must be team players rather than the intellectual arbiters of information provision. This coincides with a shift in power from the information provider to the information consumer. As David Nicholas and Tom Dobrowolski explain in the final chapter of the Handbook, the time is now right to reassess the terminology of information use and how we refer to our clients and indeed ourselves. They propose adopting the concept of the 'information player' instead of 'user' as a more appropriate term to reflect the 'complex engagement that takes place between a person and today's interactive systems.'

It is probably true that we should no longer refer to the 'end use' of information. Does information ever really have a final use? The concept of knowledge management demonstrates the enduring value of information as it continually evolves and reshapes itself.

There has probably never been a more exciting time to work in the information profession but neither has it been more challenging. As a profession we know we are working on or near the frontier but it is not always easy to tell where the boundaries lie. The Handbook provides a basic route map but as individual information professionals we are responsible for navigating our own paths and moving the boundaries forward.

I would like to thank all of the Handbook authors for their hard work, enthusiasm, vision and commitment to maintaining the high standards of information provision.

Chapter 1

Digital library services: an overview of the hybrid approach

Elizabeth J. Eastwood and Sara R. Tompson

'The special librarian is capable of working in the hybrid world of print and electronic media and providing the best mix of information resources in the most appropriate formats for the environment.' From the background to: Competencies for Special Librarians of the 21st Century (*http://www.sla.org/professional/competency.html*)

Introduction

The term 'digital libraries' has been given many varied definitions. Digital libraries exist along a whole continuum of practices, from totally electronic resources with no particular physical space and no human intermediaries for access, to the simplest electronic representation of access points to information, e.g. an online public access catalogue (OPAC). In this chapter, 'digital libraries' and 'electronic libraries' are taken to be synonymous terms.

'Special libraries' and 'information centres' are used to mean information units that are part of parent organisations, and that specialise in certain topics. The Special Libraries Association management text on special libraries notes: 'The mission of special libraries is to provide focused information to a defined group of users on an ongoing basis to further the mission and goals of their parent organisations' (Porter, et al., 1997). These specialised information centres are also sometimes known as 'workplace libraries' in the UK (see the Library Association Press Release on the Web at: *http://www.la-hq.org.uk/directory/press_desk/199926.html*).

Approach

In this chapter, the aim is to provide an overview of the current predominant service architecture in special libraries, which falls in the middle of the continuum: the combination of print and electronic resources. This is termed the 'hybrid' approach to digital libraries. This chapter is not concerned with the consortia and project initiatives of completely digital information resources. Rather, it deals with the practical situation that special librarians and information professionals are working with day-to-day.

The chapter outlines the history of these digital libraries and demonstrates how hybrid libraries are the current workable solution. The concentration is on the digital library services offered by a hybrid library and how this set-up has affected the overall library services, including challenges of collection development, and how these differences concern management, staff, and users. The issues described by Edward A. Fox, et al. will be touched upon. These authors wrote, that for the information professional, the term digital library:

> ...calls for carrying out of the functions of libraries in a new way, encompassing new types of information resources; new approaches to acquisition (especially with more sharing and subscription services); new methods of storage and preservation; new approaches to classification and cataloguing, new modes of interaction with and for patrons; more reliance on electronic systems and networks; and dramatic shifts in intellectual, organisational, and economic practices. (Fox et al., 1995).

Digital libraries

It is necessary to first set the context of digital library resources and services, before today's most common form, the hybrid of print and digital libraries, can be discussed. That is the aim of the definitions, characteristics and history that follow.

Digital library definitions

In general, digital libraries used to be considered, '...as systems providing a community of users with coherent access to a large, organised repository of information and knowledge' (Lynch and Garcia-Molina, 1995). Even earlier, Kenneth Dowlin, in 1984, described an electronic library as incorporating:

- 'management of resources with a computer
- the ability to link the information provider with the information seeker via electronic channels
- the ability for staff to intervene in the electronic transaction when requested by the information seeker
- the ability to store, organise, and transmit information to the information seeker via electronic channels' (as quoted by Collier).

Cherie Noble's 1998 statement that, 'As pervasive and ubiquitous as the term has become, the virtual library is a concept that is still evolving'

(Noble, 1998) is certainly just as true two years later, as can be seen from this sampling of recent definitions from both sides of the Atlantic.

- In his staff's 1999 how-to text, *Creating a Virtual Library*, editor Frederick Stielow defines, simply, the totally electronic library: 'The term virtual library simply means that all services are provided through the Internet, rather then in a building' (Stielow, 1999).

- The editors of one of the reports of the ongoing joint US and European Union Research Agenda for Digital Libraries represent those information professionals who see digital libraries as global enterprises: 'Digital libraries represent a new infrastructure and environment that has been created by the integration and use of computing, communications, and digital content on a global scale' (Schäuble and Smeaton, 1998).

- A technical definition can be found in a recent N.R. Adam, et al. article in *Communications of the ACM*: 'Digital libraries can be viewed as infrastructures for supporting the creation of information sources, facilitating the movement of information across global networks, and allowing the effective and efficient interaction among knowledge producers, librarians, and information and knowledge seekers' (Adam et al., 2000).

- Gary Cleveland, writing for the Universal D T section of IFLA, the International Federation of Library Associations and Institutions, emphasises the library aspect of the phrase 'digital library': 'As a starting point, we should assume that digital libraries are libraries with the same purposes, functions, and goals as traditional libraries — collection development and management, subject analysis, index creation, provision of access, reference work, and preservation' (Cleveland, 1998).

- Donald J. Waters, in writing about the US Digital Library Federation project, quotes the Federation's working definition: 'Digital libraries are organisations that provide the resources, including the specialised staff, to select, structure, offer intellectual access to, interpret, distribute, preserve the integrity of, and ensure the persistence over time of collections of digital works so that they are readily and economically available for use by a defined community or set of communities' (Waters, 1998).

These definitions focus on electronic resources, but it has come to the attention of many that although the reality of digital libraries is strengthening, a library's collection will have to provide both print and electronic materials still for some time and the most important goal is to have seamless access to all formats which will '...provide a coherent view of a very large collection of information' (Lynch and Garcia-Molina, 1995). As these authors describe it, '...the digital library system needs to extend smoothly from personal information resources, workgroup and organisational systems, and out to personal views of the content of more public digital libraries' (Lynch and Garcia-Molina, 1995). Special librarians and information professionals will still need to be able to manage and successfully work with hybrid library collections for a substantial amount of time.

Digital libraries: a brief history

As noted by Stephen Harter (1997), digital libraries can be said to have physically existed in some form since the days of punch card circulation systems. As a concept, digital libraries have existed in science fiction for several centuries, but the idea was seriously launched by Vannevar Bush's 1945 concept of the Memex Machine (Nyce and Kahn, 1991). Digital libraries may be more commonly thought of as beginning with the advent of digitised access tools, that is, online public access catalogues or OPACs, computer databases that replaced traditional card catalogues and augmented them with links between records (e.g. a record for one book on a particular subject could be relationally linked to a list of records for books on that subject). Most OPACs are based on the Machine Readable Cataloguing (MARC) standard and formats, developed in the mid-1960s by the US Library of Congress and other organisations, and currently in use in a variety of flavours: USMARC, LCMARC, UKMARC, UNIMARC, etc. (Furrie, 1998).

During the 1970s and 1980s what can be called 'the information chain' was highly structured. As author Roxanne Missingham notes:

> Search specialists and libraries were central to all components of the information chain. Full-text information was accessible only in the published format, predominantly in libraries. Tools for finding a path to the relevant information were through references from colleagues, or print and electronic indexes ... In the 1990s the creation of electronic information, development of networked access and delivery of new library services has seen a radical transformation in the information chain... (Missingham, 1999).

While F.W. Lancaster's famous prediction of the 'paperless library' in his seminal 1978 text (Lancaster, 1978) has not yet come about, nor is it expected to any time soon, since the days of early OPACs, libraries have continued to move toward more electronic resources. As Noble says, 'With the development of new and emerging networking systems, however, it is likely that the virtual library will become the gateway that integrates access to most, if not all, of the library's resources and services, both traditional and virtual' (Noble, 1998).

Characteristics for consideration of digital library services

Digital in its most basic sense as applied to libraries means electronic format rather than paper. Providing and maintaining documents and resources in electronic format requires an infrastructure or architecture of hardware, software and networks. This chapter will simply touch on some key areas of consideration for the information professional.

Practically, special libraries often combine Internet and intranet resources and access. A 1999 survey of special librarians in Illinois, USA, found Internet/intranet combined access to be a key emerging trend (Tompson, 1999). A special library's user population can drive the architecture of digital library resources. For instance, accessibility within and beyond the parent organisation may necessitate some resources being intranet-only accessible, in a protected subdirectory behind a firewall.

Mel Collier (1997) has listed the main characteristics of a digital library, and they can be used to help describe the digital library services that are part of a hybrid library collection. According to Collier:

1.   'Access to the digital library is not bounded in space or time. It can be accessed from anywhere at any time.

2.   Content in electronic form will steadily increase and content in printed form will decrease.

3.   Content is in textual, image, and sound form.

4.   Usage of electronic information as a proportion of total usage will steadily increase, and usage of printed material as a proportion of total usage will decrease.

5.   Expenditure on electronic material will steadily increase and, relatively, expenditure on printed material will decrease.

6.   Expenditure on information will shift from ownership to subscription and licensing.

7.   Expenditure on equipment and infrastructure will increase'.

[Numbers added by Eastwood and Tompson]

When dealing with a hybrid library collection, compatibility of all resources used by the staff needs to be maintained. The integrated library system, that which houses the circulation and acquisition modules currently used to hold the document location tools to the print collection, will need to be compatible with the digital collection management system. The latter is the system that will have the capacity and technical requirements needed to house the electronic materials of the collection. One illustration is the set up at the Fermi National Accelerator Laboratory: the Library OPAC runs on a DEC Alpha machine (*http://fnlib2.fnal.gov/ MARION*). The Web OPAC includes clickable links to the digitised preprints and technical reports (e.g. *http://fnlib2.fnal.gov/MARION/AAG-0426*), but those documents are actually housed on and served from a UNIX machine (*http://fnalpubs.fnal.gov/archive/2000/*). HTML is the common language that links the two systems. In the future, more integrated systems that deal with both print and electronic will appear in libraries. Until that is widespread, the two or more systems need to be compatible. This is a technical challenge that should not be overlooked.

Recently, the concept of a library or information service maintaining a web site has gone some way to linking access to traditional and digital materials. The web site provides access to information about the services offered, including access to the local print material location tools, as well being the portal to many electronic services available through the library, including bibliographic databases, online union catalogues, and full-text links. The library staff also can author their own digital documents. For example, the guide to using the library collection could be available in print in the library, but it could also have been made into a digital document (scanned or web-authored), so that it would be available to all of the potential users of the library, whether they are locally or remotely located. Having digital library services goes some way to constructing a 'library without walls', so that the user need not be physically present at the library. (See the discussion of the variety of services offered in a hybrid library later in this chapter.)

Having digital materials has also brought up the question of users having 24/7 service accessibility, at some level. This characteristic of digital libraries is one that must be considered by management in light of who their users are, and what is expected and wanted from the service provided. Technical aspects must also be considered if remote access is to be available even when the library is not open. Such considerations to be dealt with include: technical support for malfunctions; open or controlled access to resources; and questions concerning automated payment.

Many special libraries and information centres have built digital material collections to supplement their physical collections. More documents every day are becoming available digitally, largely through consortia and initiative collections. The availability of materials through these means helps to support the delivery of 'just-in-time' materials, which is a relatively recent collection philosophy. This is contrasted with the traditional warehousing of documents 'just-in-case' users need them at some point. However, technical considerations exist if services are to be relied upon to be available remotely and electronically, with a quick response time.

Resources in a digital library can be in a variety of formats and encoding languages, including Postscript, PDF (Adobe's Portal Document Format), HTML (Hypertext Markup Language, still the most common encoding for web browser-readability documents), or one of the newer formats such as

XML, eXtensible Markup Language. Choosing the encoding language to use must be based on the document type, as well as what needs to be done with it. For example, scanning documents to create a PDF file maintains the quality standards of the original, but the capability to search text inside the document is lost.

Deciding what digital resources will be available through the library is another major collection management issue. There is the question of what local, as well as remote, material will be available. For example, an engineering library may choose to link to EI Global Village, a commercial product, and to internal project reports, via the same web interface. Selection decisions must be made in accordance with user needs. Preservation issues are a major concern when dealing with digital resources. One of the most important questions brought up by the question of preservation is 'technical obsolescence' (Cleveland, 1998). He specifies the three main areas of consideration:

- the preservation of the storage medium
- the preservation of access to content
- the preservation of fixed-media materials through digital technology.

This author also mentions the importance of creating more long-term preservation policies, which are usually best supported and work through consortial arrangements. Being a part of a group – e.g. the CEDARS project in digital archives (*http://www.leeds.ac.uk/cedars/*) – will help with standardisation that will aid sharing of information for a substantial amount of time.

This section of the chapter has largely focused on the technical characteristics and challenges of maintaining digital library services. However, the societal considerations also have considerable repercussions on the success of such services. A recent article specifically notes that '…crossing the digital divide demands an approach to the design and evaluation of digital libraries that is both socially grounded and participative' (Bishop et al., 2000). The authors also indicate in what particular areas consideration is most required (these authors draw from another article by Levy et al.). These areas include:

- 'social consequences of digital library use and non-use, especially for traditionally marginalised groups
- social practices associated with system use
- social interactions and relationships that are inextricably woven into system use

- participation of a broad spectrum of potential users – especially those most likely to be left out – in all stages of the system's lifecycle, from design and testing through implementation and evaluation' (Bishop et al., 2000).

All of these points are of great importance if the services offered are to be successful and pertinent to the user community.

The special librarian and information professional's role and overall mission is to aid users in retrieving the most relevant and useful materials for their enquiry. The characteristics of digital libraries should always reflect that mission. The goal of a digital library should be compatibility and transparency. The user should not need to be painfully aware of the hardware and software utilised to access information, but should rather be able to use a workstation as a tool for quick access to a wide range of information easily.

The 'local hybrid library' approach

The term 'local hybrid library,' taken from Judith Pearce's VALA 2000 conference article (Pearce, 2000), illustrates the most common special library model as of this writing – one with both print and digital materials and services. This section aims to define the hybrid library concept and the equipment and people involved.

Hybrid library definition

'Three years ago prognosticators suggested that 90 per cent of top-of-the-line special library operations would be virtual within a short time. That forecast has given way to the reality of hybrid operations, with varying concentrations of virtual and traditional resources and services' (DiMattia and Blummenstein, 1999). Almost all special libraries can be considered as supporting a local hybrid library architecture. In such a library the collection consists of materials in a variety of paper-based and digital formats, and there is an attempt to provide the users an integrated interface, usually web-based, to locate any item in the collection, irregardless of format.

This set-up has become a reality for many reasons. Most importantly, the funding that is required to support a totally virtual collection is high. Other reasons include users' ambivalent attitudes to electronic materials when familiar with the paper-based documents, and the type of documents available electronically which are only now becoming well balanced to incorporate all subject disciplines and document formats. It would not be surprising to see a law firm library totally virtual, as a majority of the databases used by this type of library have been among the first to be digitally converted, largely due to financial incentives. On the other hand, a museum library should wait until sophisticated hardware and software exist to adequately support images. In his digital libraries text, Arms brings out another important reason for a growing number of hybrid libraries as opposed to a completely virtual library: 'New organisations can begin afresh, whereas older organisations often must maintain current services while introducing new services' (Arms, 2000).

Hybrid library architecture

'The hybrid library should not...be seen as nothing more than an uneasy transitional phase between the conventional library and the digital library but, rather, as a worthwhile model in its own right, which can be usefully developed and improved' (Pinfield et al.). The hybrid library architecture warrants explanation and description, as many special libraries are currently supporting this set-up, which will be maintained for a long time to come. The editor's observation in the previous edition of this Handbook holds just as true today: 'The assumption is still that the hard-copy material will continue to be used, in varying degrees for a very long time' (Scammell, 1997).

Judith Pearce writes that the emerging architecture of a hybrid library '...recognises the value of maintaining a holistic view of the library's resources through catalogue-level descriptions as well as providing users with access to more detailed subject- or format-based listings and links to remote resources' (Pearce, 2000). Pearce's description of hybrid library architecture highlights the use of the web interface, which allows access to:

- 'the books and other physical information resources in the library's collections
- digital copies of physical information resources in the library's collections
- CD-ROMs and online information resources which the library is licensed to access on behalf of its users, including full-text databases, union catalogues, indexing and abstracting services; encyclopedias and other reference tools.
- information resources freely available on the Internet.'

A user of a hybrid library should not recognise a difference in formats, especially when searching for relevant materials. A search string should result in a list of relevant documents regardless of format, as opposed to the user needing to search separately for print or electronic resources. Again, the technical architecture and linking of different formats should be transparent to the user. As Stephen Pinfield writes, 'The point of this is to encourage users to look at the *best* source for their needs regardless of its format' (Pinfield, 1998).

In some cases, format of an item has taken priority over informational worth when users access a library's collection. For example, if a library points a user to a bibliographic database that supports full-text articles, it would not have been unusual for the database set up to disregard the library's physical stock, and concentrate the users' search onto the digital full-text documents available. A hybrid library's objective is to support access to both the physical stock as well as the digital materials. As just one illustration, customisation of the OVID ® medical database has gone a long way towards this goal. A list of retrieved articles from a specific search includes links to full-text articles, as well as a 'LOCAL HOLDINGS' field to indicate if the library holds the paper journal. This is a good example of seamless searching, regarding formats, of a collection. This is the goal of the big 'H' hybrid library initiatives currently being studied by a number of institutions.

To aid seamless searching, internal database structure is required. As Lynch and Garcia-Molina note, 'The most urgent infrastructure need is to establish common schemes for the naming of digital objects, and the linking of these schemes to protocols for object transmission, metadata, and object type classifications' (Lynch and Garcia-Molina, 1995). Having a standard document-naming scheme to use for library collections is thought to aid resource sharing, linking between different libraries' integrated library systems, and also to allow for future developments. The growing acceptance and creation of metadata tags will help to make this technical consideration a reality.

As mentioned earlier, the library or information centre can use two types of electronic user interface: the Internet and the intranet. The Internet's architecture is established, more or less, before one begins adding personalised information. However, having an intranet as the interface means that a great deal of thought and time must be put into the design, and usability studies will need to be conducted to make the intranet a success. An intranet is simply a network that stores information behind an organisation's firewall, so no one outside can access it. An intranet typically has the look and feel of the Internet, especially the Web. This is because both use the TCP/IP protocol – Transmission Control Protocol over Internet Protocol (see the Free Online Dictionary of Computing, at *http:// wombat.doc.ic.ac.uk/foldoc/index.html*, for more details).

Today, many companies are using this approach, especially when the library or information centre's audience are the company's employees, and sensitive information not for public viewing may be contained in the database, e.g. internal product reports, case files etc. This brings back the point that the digital library resources and access are shaped by who is going to use the service, local or remote users. This is an important consideration when designing the interface to the collection.

Using Ford Motor Company's Research Library and Information Services (RLIS) as described by Varnum, one can examine how an intranet is integrated and used in a special library environment. Their goal was to provide the employees with access to the best information available on the Web and the company intranet in a customised form. Firstly, they established the user base. There were three distinct user groups:

- 'Library staff. In addition to RLIS staff, librarians at the 20 other libraries within Ford worldwide use the RLIS home page frequently. Members of this group use the site several times a day and tend to know exactly what they are looking for and where to find it.

- Frequent users. This group of individuals – perhaps 750-1,000 Ford employees – uses the RLIS intranet heavily, visiting the site perhaps several times a week each . . . . Members of this group know their way around the site well, and generally know where to look to find the needed information.

- Infrequent users. This is the largest group – the bulk of Ford's 100,000 employees with desktop intranet access. They visit the site weekly or less often, usually to find a specific piece of information, but generally not knowing where to find it' (Varnum, 1999).

Varnum and his team decided that customisation of information provision was desirable, as they knew that many of the employees used only a small proportion of the resources the RLIS made available. However, the team also realised that making every link available through the Library intranet site was an impossible technical task. To overcome this, they created the 'MyRLIS' facility, where employees can maintain their own favourite links as personal bookmarks, accessible through their library account.

Centralising all information in their accounts also allows the users portable accessibility. As noted, 'Not only does this provide extra value to our customers, but it also gives them another reason for people to use our site: convenience' (Varnum, 1999). Realising and assessing the users needs is paramount when dealing with hardware and software considerations. The RLIS example helps to illustrate the organic nature of architecture design in a fast paced, multi-resource information world.

The creation of the World Wide Web browser at CERN, the high-energy physics laboratory in Switzerland in the early 1990s, brought a welcome standardisation of interface, and has encouraged most users of the Internet to choose this method of access to online information. Libraries and information centres have also realised the power of browsers for the users, and many service interfaces are through the Web.

Here is an example to illustrate how a modern day special library user would expect to be able to use the library resources, and what service architecture would be required to successfully fulfill the researcher's enquiry. This describes a physics researcher looking for a particular use of a Monte Carlo Simulation.

1. Search a local OPAC
2. Find a link to a preprint full-text server
3. Preprint server notes that the preprint was subsequently published
4. Researcher needs the final, published article
5. A subscription access is needed to the journal web site: it has been set up via IP access
6. The researcher is off campus and cannot access the journal site
7. However, the researcher notices that the journal site indicated only has abstracts of the articles available electronically
8. The site does note that the library has a paper subscription to the journal
9. The next time the researcher is at the office, he or she goes to the library and photocopies the article.

This description shows that a number of different components are needed to create and maintain a hybrid library environment:

- hardware, software and networking for the OPAC
- link creation by library staff
- annotation of records by preprint server staff (often librarians)
- electronic subscription to journal set up by library staff – IP access chosen by library or assigned by publisher (as noted, this locks out access by organisation users not connected via the local area network)
- annotation of the journal web site (note that library staff could have annotated the link and saved the researcher the step of going to the site and discovering only the abstracts)
- journal site customisation with local print holdings noted
- library photocopier provided (along with copyright and usage warning!).

What are hybrid library components?

It is instructive to give an overview of the components usually supported in a special library's hybrid library environment. The concentration will be on the components needed to support the digital library services of a hybrid library. Chris Rusbridge (1998) has compiled a (non-exhaustive!) list of interfaces that a user would face in a hybrid library environment:

- 'local OPAC (telnet / web)
- COPAC union catalogue (telnet / web / Z39.50 [bibliographic standard])
- regional virtual union catalogue (web / Z39.50)
- stand-alone CD-ROMs
- off-line CD-ROMs and diskettes
- networked CD-ROMs
- full-text services
- electronic reserve systems
- remote datasets at the community data centres (BIDS, EDINA and MIDAS)
- remote datasets at other universities
- remote commercial datasets
- local datasets e.g. bibliographies, pamphlet collections and archives
- local web-based documents, library and institutional
- local web resource gateways
- remote web subject / resource gateways
- remote web resources
- remotely mounted electronic journals (EJs)
- local and remotely mounted e-books
- books: loanable, reference, and available via interlibrary loan (ILL)
- paper-based journals
- special collections, maps, slides, sound recordings and videos.'

Other resources include indexes and finding tools, directories, photographs, and numerical data sets. Rusbridge is using the library at the University of Warwick as his model, but this multitude of resources is also evident in special libraries and information centres. Although these are all services offered by one special library, the user should not be fully aware of all the different types, but should be able to gain the information desired quickly and easily, regardless of format.

Hardware

There are a number of hardware considerations that a special librarian or information professional should include in the physical space. Libraries and information centres offering digital resources must ensure that users can get to the resources. This means providing, within the library and / or throughout the parent organisation, adequate numbers of computer workstations with enough memory and disk space to easily use the applications and resources, and adequate numbers of printers that can handle all the formats in which the digitised information is available. A fast printer is an essential piece of hardware when the special library supports a substantial number of digital services.

Also, due to the various different media that is required in a fully integrated paper and electronic information environment, aspects of the physical environment need to be considered. These could include provision of headphones at all monitors if there are audio documents, screen magnifiers for the visually impaired, or a special keyboard '…for people who have trouble/can't type' (Schuyler, 1999).

The way the library or information centre handles the existence of physical disabilities is indicative of the thoughtfulness and general awareness of the service providers. In addition to hardware considerations, there are a number of software applications that could be utilised to provide full service to all potential service users. For example, the programme JAWS for Windows (*http://www.synapseadaptive.com/henter2/jfw/JFW32.html*) uses speakers to read the materials from the screen. There are several software programmes that magnify text, e.g. ZoomText (*http://www.zoomtext.com/*) (Schuyler, 1999). However, with all of these specific programs, there are known incompatibilities with other software and even hardware.

Frequent enhancement and upgrading of computer equipment must be planned, as compatabilities with hardware and software rely on constant attention. Cleveland (1998) notes that the other main requirements, specifically when dealing with integration of more digital materials, are:

- 'high-speed local networks and fast connections to the Internet
- relational databases that support a variety of digital formats
- full-text search engines to index and provide access to resources
- a variety of servers, such as web servers and FTP servers
- electronic document management functions that will aid in the overall management of digital resources.'

Software
There are a substantial amount of software considerations in a hybrid library. Concerning digital services that require company or organisation affiliation to use, authentification capabilities are required. Deciding whether to use a site licence, IP access or to have individual or group passwords is a major undertaking, and must be made with the knowledge of who uses the services, and from where.

On many different levels, privacy arrangements are required. If the special library access is part of an intranet, and the collection incorporates sensitive documents, then there must be a guarantee that nothing will compromise the sensitivity of that information. If high security is required, there are a number of software options, including a key cryptosystem infrastructure. However, the level of security required needs to be carefully ascertained, as such systems are expensive and restrictive, when there may be a less constrictive system available that secures the information adequately. This will also be an important issue when e-commerce services begin to become more prominent in special information centres.

Similarly, having adequate rights management guidelines and technical provision will help contributors to the collection feel at ease with providing information to the library system. This also concerns the protection of authors' intellectual property. Accessing full-text material digitally has come up against much resistance; particularly resistant are those who do not believe digital protection of their works is adequate. A special librarian or information worker must realise this legally sensitive area, and learn how to comply whilst providing an efficient service. Copyright considerations are a highly sensitive issue when dealing with digital interlibrary loan (ILL) and document delivery (DD) roles.

CDs and DVDs
There is growing discussion on the usefulness of buying and maintaining CD-ROMs and DVDs, mainly due to the increasing access through the Web directly from the vendors/publishers. However, Breeding has explained why many special libraries and information centres will maintain CD-ROM hardware: 'Libraries just need to pay attention to the general trends in the industry and develop data storage and information infrastructures consistent with the world at large, but each needs to do so in a way that is optimised for its specialised needs' (Breeding, 1999). For special libraries, CD-ROM access is an easier method for a small number of subscriptions. DVDs are also coming on the scene and no doubt their superior reproduction qualities will be attractive to many special libraries, especially art and newspaper libraries.

International concerns
The globalisation of information provision has repercussions on digital library services. It is an especially pertinent consideration if the intranet is serving all the global branches of the company, or if the service goal is to reach as many people as possible with the Internet as the interface.
As noted by Peters, '…the question of multilingual access is an extremely complex one. Two basic issues are involved: i) multiple language recognition, manipulation, and display ii) multilingual or cross-language search and retrieval' (Peters et al., 1997). If this is a necessity for the service, time

must be spent to plan for all the different languages to be accessed through the interface. This must be done at the highest level, and normally will require work coordination with information systems staff.

Design and organisation
The look of the web site, or the interface chosen, greatly affects the way the services are used. As shown by the Ford RLIS example, many users prefer customisation of interfaces, and this is mentioned as an emerging trend in the last section of this chapter. As mentioned previously, offering customised access requires hardware and software decisions, and examining the user's interface preferences. Intranet interfaces can be routinely customised, and Factiva (Dow Jones/Reuters, *http://www.factiva.com/index.asp*) is one example of a company that has successfully completed many information services customisations.

The special librarian must take time to decide the most appropriate way to organise the information on the site. The most important requirement is that information retrieval procedures should be intuitive to the majority of users. Often, subject categorisation helps the user refine searches appropriately. Many search engine creators have realised this. For example, Northern Light (*http://www.northernlight.com/*) provides 'folders' of relevant, and subject-specific, materials deemed related to the user's initial search. These folders of materials are displayed alongside the display of the generally related materials, and can help give the user some further ideas to help make her/his search more relevant.

Collection maintenance
Collection management issues exist for digital resources as much for the library's print collections. In particular, special librarians must be familiar with the changing resources available, so that effective and efficient decisions can be made. For example, deciding when to stop a paper subscription and relying on the digital version. All such collection decisions must be driven by user needs. Other considerations concerning the content of the digital library services offered include what remote resources should be linked to, including:

- collaborations
- initiatives
- clumps (union catalogues grouped around subjects, physical geography, or type of institution, e.g. COPAC, OCLC)
- how much the service should rely on full-text databases
- how many secondary resources (access tools) should be used.

Along with this question of remote and local service is the question of offering an e-reference service. Totally virtual library projects such as the Internet Public Library (*http://ipl.org/*) have maintained the reference service, but it obviously has to be digitally provided. However, if a special library offers reference services electronically, this could affect the amount of time staff have to deal with local requests. Electronic reference services require a substantial amount of time to work with, and should not be considered a decision to take lightly.

All of these considerations culminate with the question of preservation. Preservation of all materials, from housekeeping memos to archiving actual information articles, is of paramount importance. The traditional paper-based organisation generated a great deal of paper which many special libraries or information centres still have stored away. Deciding what to preserve when dealing with electronic documents has many problems attached, but, 'the preservation of digital content for long periods of time, across multiple generations of hardware and software technologies and standards is essential in the creation of effective digital libraries' (Lynch and Garcia-Molina, 1995). Therefore, due consideration must be given to this important stage in maintaining efficient service provision.

All the points mentioned above have to be kept in mind when providing digital library services. Special librarians must remember as well that supporting a hybrid library will be more expensive than providing either a paper or an electronic service, but such a service will best serve the informational needs of the special library user.

The impact of digital library services on other services: results of an informal survey

There is not much in the literature about how implementing digital library services, to any degree, affects other areas of library service. Accordingly, the authors queried colleagues on this topic via a set of questions posted to six email discussion lists:

- DigLibn
- e-collections
- lis-elib
- lis-medical
- MEDLIB-l
- SLA-Illinois
- Web4Lib.

The lists were chosen for both their diverse originations (some are UK-based, some US-based; all have participants from all over the globe) and for the likelihood that the list members work in special libraries with a hybrid of print and digital resources. A total of 89 responses was received and are tallied and summarised below. Note that not all respondents answered all questions, and many chose more than one answer, especially for the areas question, where this was expected.

Did the acquisition and provision of digital resources affect acquisition and provision of your other resources and services?

- yes, a great deal – 29 responses
- yes, somewhat – 52
- no, not at all – 7.

In what areas (check all that are relevant) did the acquisition and provision of digital resources affect your library operation?

- funding/budgeting – 79
- staff time available – 67
- staff training focus – 76
- user contact time – 60
- other, please note – 28 – folded into comments
- any additional comments? – discussed below.

The majority of the respondents (~58 per cent) found that acquisition and provision of digital resources within their libraries had something of an impact on their acquisition and provision of traditional, print resources. The greatest impact was felt in the area of funding and budgeting (~88 per cent), followed closely by staff training focus (~85 per cent). Respondents interpreted this point in one of two ways, or sometimes both: training required for staff to be able to use, and to help others to use, digital resources, and/or the larger training responsibility required of library staff with the implementation of digital resources.

About 75 per cent of the respondents reported that staff time available had changed with the addition of digital resources. Most often the comments indicated that staff responsibilities had been increased. About 67 per cent of the respondents noted that user contact time had changed with the addition of digital resources. Most often, as indicated in the comments, staff members were spending MORE time with users than before.

The complete set of comments to the survey is available by request to the authors. The majority of the comments did not shed any new light on the ways in which acquisition and delivery of digital library services is affecting traditional, print resources, but the responses did further support all of the issues covered in recent literature, from pricing to changing staff responsibilities to the greater-than-ever need for human facilitators in special libraries and information centres. Some of the rather different comments are noted below.

For many of the respondents, digital resources were replacing print resources – either electronic counterparts or similar resources were being purchased online (mostly) or on CD-ROM (a trend that seems to be fading) and the print version was being dropped. This was most often due to budget constraints; some respondents explicitly noted they would like to keep both print and electronic, but could not afford to do so.

Many respondents noted that their parent organisations are not funding, or able to fund, all the digital resources they and their users would like. So they are turning toward initiatives, grants, and alternative funding resources, often successfully. However there is concern that the organisations must recognise and properly fund this need if hybrid, let alone digital, libraries are to thrive. New sources of funding are being used, or sought, by many librarians providing both print and electronic resources. Some of the large digital library initiatives on both sides of the Atlantic have afforded libraries access to more digital resources than they could normally have purchased with their budgets – most initiatives include special pricing and/or outright grants.

A number of respondents noted that they and/or their staff are now training users more than ever. Some respondents explicitly noted that staff members seem to enjoy the new role of training users. Another changing role for special librarians and information professionals with the addition of digital resources is that of detailed research. Digital resources often provide direct access to users, so they are doing much of their initial research themselves. However, they come to library staff with very difficult research questions that take more time to answer. This can be an enjoyable challenge, as some noted, but it does require deeper training of staff. There were also comments that digital resources have created totally new roles in libraries and information centres, the two most mentioned being web master and electronic licensor.

One interesting trend noted in two comments was that users were requesting more interlibrary loans than ever before, as they were aware of other organisations' holdings thanks to some digital resources and catalogues. Several respondents noted the plus of space-saving, shelf room gained by utilising digital resources rather than print. Some of the trends, less mentioned in the literature, but noted by these survey respondents, are:

- privatisation of library funding and/or services, even when the library is part of a public institution
- new ways of doing business – new models for provision of service, especially collaborative approaches with other organisations

- the advent of one huge digital library for the planet (a concept that was more frequently mentioned in digital library literature earlier in the 1990s)

- librarians not being the sole decision-makers about library resources – other departments are funding and have input, other organisations are often involved, especially in consortia, and users themselves, especially faculty in higher education settings.

The effects of a hybrid library on people

The information seekers and information providers are both integral to the success of the hybrid library system. However, it has become obvious that users, staff, and management of libraries or information centres have different needs and behaviours concerning digital library services, as opposed to the paper-based collection. These need to be known if an efficient and effective service is to exist.

Users and digital library services

Users' relationships with the collection are of paramount importance to the service: it is the reason services exist. Therefore, the way users react and work with the collection and access tools is indicative of the effectiveness of the service arrangements. Since digital library services have come into being more areas have developed where users are required to use different methods of searching for locating materials. A large number of sociological and cultural issues concerning these behaviours arose in the 20th century that will continue into the next computer-focused century.

User personalities

With a hybrid library system, users have to deal with a combination of old usage habits and the need to acquire new technical skills. At times this can be confusing. Users of digital library services have a number of issues of which the staff and management of the collection must be cognisant, in order to provide an effective and efficient service is provided. As Schatz and Chen write, '…digital libraries are a form of information technology in which social impact matters as much as technological advancement' (Schatz and Chen, 1999). Special library users have a number of different information requirements. For instance, Roxanne Missingham noted that scientists' information needs depend on '…age, stage of career and stage in the research process, and differences in what is available in the information market in different disciplines' (Missingham, 1999). No matter what field of work they are in, special library users' information needs will always be based in a mixture of factors.

In today's society there are many different generations of users. Fast-paced progression of computer use in society has occurred in people's lifetimes. This has produced a cultural digital divide, as well as the more familiar hardware digital divide of the 'haves' and 'have-nots'. There is the 'Net generation', as Noble calls them, the infrequent users, who have limited experience from their work environment, and then there are the older generation who have come up against a new technology that is controlling much of the globe, but regarding which they have no firsthand experience. Depending upon whom the library or information centre is serving, the level of understanding required is different.

Each generation of user that exists today has unique characteristics. The 'Net generation', as the generation who are on the rise, is the most significant to investigate. They are very comfortable with technology, and are the dominant user type in the future. They use computers at work and during their free time for everything. This type of service user expects digital services to be available all the time, 24/7. Noble also notes that they are, '…highly motivated to receive end-user instruction, sometimes in a classroom setting or workshop series, and they are likely to implement what they have learned' (Noble, 1998).

Most of this group of users wants to be able to do things for themselves, but realise there may be a need for education about the techniques beforehand. A high level of service is expected whether they are local or remote users of the digital library services. The growing number of remote users and enquirers has repercussions on how the information services are designed and provided. For example, the user interface will be the first thing that the users see, and so it should be straightforward and informative for all levels of computer comfort. It is as users get deeper into the digital services offered that a varying level of service can be given, e.g. having both basic and advanced searching screens is advisable.

Another interesting situation is when there is, '…the possibility that users may be expert in their chosen area of study but may be relative neophytes in computing technology and computer networks' (Jones, 1999). Again, helping users understand the computer interface with easy-to-understand instructions, and a free-text search engine for user help, will go a long way to make the subject expert comfortable with the unfamiliar technology. As a contrast, those who did not grow up with computer technology may not (though many may) be as comfortable with it or likely to use it as a first choice for information needs. They can also be less demanding of interfaces and other points of access, as they are less familiar with system capabilities.

As indicated earlier, the 'Net generation' lives with computer technology. A study to investigate the users of an inhouse and remote access catalogue (Rout) saw a correlation between the success of users searching the catalogue who also owned a computer. This characteristic must be considered in light of the characteristics of the user community that is being served by the special library or information centre. Arms supports the fact that there are many different levels of users, and stipulates that '...designers of digital libraries must resist the temptation to assume a uniform, specific pattern of use and to create a system specifically for that pattern' (Arms, 2000). The needs of these different users must be reflected in the levels of services offered. As has already been noted, consideration also has to be given to the physical location of users, e.g. internal, external, and international. This affects user interface design, the type of authentication required for access to full-text databases, and how long the databases are accessible e.g. 24 hours 7 days a week, or only during opening hours.

Use of digital library services
There has not been a great deal of research concerning how people use electronic resources. However, the studies that have been done are illustrative of certain characteristics that are important to realise when designing access to such services. The quality of the hardware and software used to support the digital library services dictates the effectiveness of the information provision. As Arms writes, '...major advances have been made in the quality of computer displays, in the fonts displayed on them, and in the software used to manipulate and render information' (Arms, 2000). These advances have meant that document quality can be perfect, especially important concerning picture scanning, but the special library must make a commitment to the users and keep up to date with these hardware and software changes, so the best information in the best quality is available at all times.

In particular, the rise in reading from a computer screen has pushed manufacturers to strive to construct better screen displays, as users' health can be at risk. Better equipment is made every day, so library management needs to keep aware of new products and also make sure enough budget is earmarked to allow additional hardware stock to be purchased when necessary. This situation is noted by Arms: 'It will be a long time before computers match the convenience of books for general reading, but the high resolution displays to be seen in research laboratories are very impressive indeed' (Arms, 2000). It has been noted that people do not like to read more than three screens, or over 500 words, from a computer display, so they choose to print out the document. However, the rise in PDF files has also encouraged printing rather than screen reading (McKnight, 1997). This can become a technical problem if the information centre is too slow to support the increase in amount of printing being done. In all areas, investment in better hardware is essential.

E-books are an important development but are still very much at the experimental phase. There are a number of obstacles to overcome: technological and design features, ergonomic aspects and copyright, pricing and distribution issues. Despite this it seems that real progress is being made on both the technical and commercial front. There are now various models available, and these tend to have common design features such as touch screen functioning and the ability to 'turn pages' so that the user doesn't have to keep scrolling just a few paragraphs at a time. These devices are digital readers or 'metabooks': capable of storing vast amounts of data, ideal for the professional and research end of the market.

A user study (Jenkins, 1997) highlighted the importance users place on having a print copy of an article. Significantly, a paper copy is preferred, as it is a medium on which a reader can mark up and highlight important sections. This annotation feature cannot be easily replicated electronically. As Cliff McKnight writes, even though there are software packages that annotate text on the screen, '…all these methods require far more resources than a simple pencil and all require the development of additional skills' (McKnight, 1997). Document format is important; for example, often PDF files of scanned articles are preferred over HTML web documents, as HTML can give, '…poor presentation of tables and equations' (Morrow, 1999). However, using SGML (Standard Graphical Markup Language, HTML is a subset thereof) to create text may alleviate that problem, as it is more 'friendly' to such graphics.

User preference has also been recorded (see the Tilburg University Report, 1999, on paper vs. electronic journals) concerning the availability to browse the book and journal shelves – serendipity. It is possible to create database search software that allows browsing, putting the located items from a search into the appropriate place in the classification scheme. Generally, in special libraries, more direct research is conducted, and so end-user instruction into the finer art of document searching is a more valuable skill to nurture.

Hans Roes, after drawing from a number of user studies concerning electronic journal usage, concluded that, '…users want easy access through one interface with as little authentication hassle as possible. Not only do they want this at your institution, they also want it at home and while working elsewhere' (Roes, 1999). Roes supports the fact that this user requirement comes up against technical barriers that libraries must tackle.

Portals are appreciated by many digital library service users (Morrow, 1999). Centralising links to subject-specific resources aids precise information retrieval, and provides a 'one-stop shop' for basic reference. However, Morrow does stipulate that even a portal service, '…will still be only one of a portfolio of reference services that any one student or researcher are likely to want to consult, not an answer to all their information needs' (Morrow, 1999).

Searching habits

One of the most interesting and illustrative areas of user studies is researching and assessing searching strategies used by digital library users. Again, not many studies have been written about this area, but those that are available have shown interesting correlations in usage patterns. Also, this issue relates to the previously mentioned design questions concerning types of user interfaces. Arms has put into four categories all the types of different searching methods used, and connects those with the type of information the users are hoping to retrieve (Arms, 2000). The four types of searching are:

- surfing
- introductory information to a subject
- ready reference information seeking
- research information gathering.

The services provided by the special library or information centre must be able to support these four information-searching types.

For users who use the surfing technique, hardware capability is needed to support a possible numerous amount of 'windows', or user sessions, being open at the same time. This information searching technique was noted in the Poynter studies (Nielsen, 2000). Browsing across many open sessions, and using different applications was a common behaviour. Multi-tasking whilst using electronic resources is very common. Then there are the users who want to find basic, introductory information on a topic. In this case, services are needed which support retrieval of good introductory material by easy and obvious navigation techniques. The ready reference user requires a page of relevant links to web sites or databases that hold a great deal of information on specific topics. Also, these users would appreciate access to the usual, and newly available, electronic versions of ready reference resource tools, e.g. *Encyclopedia Britannica* and a dictionary. Lastly, there is the research level category. This requires more specific and detailed information resources, which may only need to include access to research journals and location tools, e.g. Medline through OVID® with full-text capabilities. The type of resources that are needed to support research information gathering should be decided carefully, as usually they are expensive. In a special library environment, the research strategy is prominent.

There is always a need for both a basic and an advanced search screen available to accommodate all possible users. Studies have also shown that users prefer phrase searching, and that many users, '...overly narrow the results...' (Barnett, 1999) unconsciously by using too many words. These studies also highlight what instruction users would find potentially beneficial. For example, Barnett notes that the help pages should be made more accessible, otherwise users do not bother with them, and this results in a higher rate of failure. These are important issues for librarians and their interface designers to consider.

Design of user interfaces
It is also instructive to go into a little more detail about the design of the user interface. Nielsen writes of an eyetracking study that came up with a number of interesting observations. One observation was that users do not respond to graphics until at least the second or third visit: text is more attractive. Also, it was noticed that users practised, 'shallow reading combined with selected depth,' meaning that, '…text needs to be scannable, but it also needs to provide the answers users seek' (Nielsen, 2000). The differing levels of user understanding that often occur in a special library also support this text design.

Another current issue in the information retrieval field involves the design of multidisciplinary user interfaces. The old, but still used, set-up is to have a number of different electronic databases requiring the user to log-in to each one separately. However, the new model is to have a generic search interface that can search all the digital library services at once. Many see the multidisciplinary, generic, interface as essential. As Huwe writes, '…university libraries offer impressive collections of databases to member institutions, but users have to 'make peace' with their menus before they can be sure they're finding all of their options' (Huwe, 1999). Products that search through many databases include Knowledge Cite Library, Database Advisor, and Pharos.

However, the appropriateness of a common interface has been questioned. In a study comparing an 'integrated interface' (HERA) and a 'common interface' (HERMES), a number of mixed reactions were noted (Park, 2000). However, the overall feeling of the participants was that a combination of the two interfaces would be the best solution. The participants did not like having to search all the databases the library had, and would prefer to be able to choose the most relevant databases. After choosing the best databases, the participants would appreciate being able to search them all together. As Park writes, '…some subjects found HERA…easier because they did not have to worry about selecting the right database(s), and it involved fewer decisions than with HERMES' (Park, 2000). This preference indicates that many users may not want to make decisions concerning the information resources that they search, and that the librarian should be able to choose the most appropriate ones for the user community.

Meer states that there is, '…a great need for standardisation among electronic interfaces'. He notes one way that this has been done in some libraries is to use vendors (e.g. OCLC's FirstSearch, *http://www.oclc.org/firstsearch/*), through which different databases can be used. Meer also indicates another way to aid standardisation has been the adoption of graphical user interfaces (GUI), which use the Windows or web interface formats familiar to many people. However, Tinanoff writes that if librarians feel that there is too much difference in databases for standardisation, then at least, '...basic navigational functions such as scrolling, exiting from the databases, printing, or downloading...as well as improved on-screen instructions' can be used to make a general familiar interface (Tinanoff, 1996).

Physical location is seen as less important in a hybrid library, but a sense of community can be even more necessary to impart to users in such settings. Kim Guenther explains that, '...recreating the tangible qualities of the physical library on the web requires blending both product design (web portals and virtual communities) and strategies that assess market viability and quality (customer profiling and data mining)' (Guenther, 2000). Knowing the information retrieval behaviour of clients is essential in developing efficient digital library services. Cultural, social, and technical details should be recognised and acknowledged.

Staff and digital library services

The respondents to the authors' survey noted some key changes for staff in providing a hybrid collection of digital and print resources and services: added responsibilities for the electronic items, with no lessening of print responsibilities; user training as a growing niche; troubleshooting capabilities for hardware as very necessary; carrying out more in-depth or difficult research; creating Web-accessible documents and/or content; and learning about and implementing licensing and other legal arrangements for access to digital resources. All of these topics are discussed in the library and information science literature.

The digitisation of library resources can provide a growth opportunity for staff, as noted throughout the literature (see for example Huntingford on IMPEL2 and Tenopir and Ennis on their survey). Paraprofessionals can and are stepping up to tasks like HTML editing for the creation of library web pages, enhancing their skills and making themselves more valuable in the information marketplace. It is worth noting here a large area of discussion in the literature that was not highlighted by the respondents – staff difficulties in a hybrid library setting. The broadest issue is difficulty in dealing with change: 'What many regard as technostress is really resistance to change' (Clark and Kalin, 1996). There is significant literature on librarians' reluctance to embrace the change that is the only constant in the new century. Much of the literature does focus on public library settings, but doubtless this issue affects many in specialised library settings as well. Many information professionals (managers as well as staff) value order and stability. The rapid pace of change in the digital age can be upsetting and render librarians unable to deal proactively with the myriad of digital services potentially available, as noted by the UK IMPEL2 study (*http://ilm.unn.ac.uk/impel/finalrpt.htm*; see also Huntingford writing in *Ariadne*) and others.

The other staff issue in library settings that are a hybrid of digital and print resources that is covered extensively in the literature (though more so in the early 1990s than nowadays) is burnout due to technology problems. This can often be due in part to the added digital responsibilities with no lessening of print responsibilities, which the survey respondents did mention. As Pitkin notes, 'Librarianship was once a field with well-defined standards, procedures, and objectives, but now it is much more like a business adapting to an ever-changing marketplace. In particular, those librarians who prefer orderly progress to the rough-and-tumble of unpredictable market demands suffer' (Pitkin, 1997). Some authors – for example, Clark and Kalin and Bartlett – have termed this burnout 'technostress'. Again this is discussed more in terms of local (UK) or public (US) libraries, but certainly some special librarians are ill-prepared to deal with daily hardware and networking issues ranging from correcting a printer's postscript settings to allocating dynamic IP addresses for public workstations. Managers can do much to assist staff in dealing with the difficulties of digital resources piled on top of print resources in the current hybrid library setting.

Management and digital library services

Many of the issues facing library staff are of course also facing library managers. In this section, a few additional concerns that have not yet been addressed in detail will be highlighted. Many of the things that library staff in a hybrid setting need – training in support of digital equipment, assistance in prioritising electronic versus print services, training in how to best assist users with the new technologies – are incumbent upon managers to provide. Managers of special libraries need to make certain their staff are, and remain, up to date in all the new as well as the old resources the library provides, the goal being, '...an appropriate skills mix' (Pinfield et al., 1998).

Roy Tennant, the founder of the Web4Lib list and a columnist for *Library Journal*, has said that the most important management decision is '...hiring staff for the new millennium'. In his list of personality traits for librarians in the new century, he notes one in particular for managers: 'Skill at enabling and fostering change – since change is constant, organisations need staff who can guide it, using judgement and communicating well' (Tennant, 1998). Tennant also notes flexibility as a key trait for staff dealing with digital resources and services, adding that they, '...most likely won't be doing the same thing for long'. Flexibility is a theme in many articles on managing libraries in the digital age, including Youngman's for an online-only journal, where he notes: 'Whatever model is developed for managing change, libraries must focus on flexibility in both staffing and structure' (Youngman, 1999).

Managers need to be able to determine what skill sets their staff needs to meet the challenges of a hybrid library setting. A good way to do this, suggested by Youngman, is to assess user needs and then assess the existing skills of staff, and identify gaps in the staff members' skill sets that need to be filled in order to satisfy users' increasingly complex information needs. Empowering staff is a key technique mentioned in the literature as one way to cope with the rapid change of the digital era. Empowerment simply means a participatory environment, where staff are involved in decision-making, and where they can see the broader picture. Some educating and training of staff members can be necessary to advance them to the state where they can truly participate in planning and decision-making, but the most important aspect of empowerment is communication. One author has noted: 'Management style can have a profound influence on technostress. Not surprisingly, participative management gives employees more of a sense of ownership in the organisation' (Bartlett, 1995).

How to equip librarians and information professionals to deal with rapid change that includes many hardware issues? This is a key question for the library profession. Library and information science education is a part of the answer – as much as possible, those studying the profession should be taught broad skills and paradigms that can be flexibly applied in a variety of information provision settings, including hybrid libraries. Also, it may well be that a different kind of LIS professional is needed in this new century – who can appreciate the challenge of connecting people with information, regardless of the settings or formats. Jose-Marie Griffiths, the University of Michigan CIO, also a professor in the School of Information Studies, has identified five characteristics as key to the 'new information professional' the ability to:

- 'guide in the face of an uncertain future
- collaborate
- prioritise and maintain agility and flexibility in the face of changing goals
- empower
- understand the core capabilities of one's organisation, work group and colleagues' (Griffiths, 1998).

Clearly, there is a need for information professionals who are ready and willing to respond proactively to change and are not mired in traditions solely for tradition's sake. The face of the profession is changing.

The big 'H' Hybrid libraries: the elib projects

A note must be made here to the various projects being conducted to research 'Hybrid libraries'. The term, 'big "H" Hybrid libraries' is used so as not to confuse the concept with the local hybrid library service structure that is the main focus of this chapter. There can be a fine line between the local hybrid library and the Hybrid libraries, but Knight highlights the differences:

'...the Hybrid libraries' information systems should provide the end user with a seamless interface that will allow them to locate paper books and journals held locally and at neighbouring sites at the same time as being able to find relevant online resources, electronic publications and digitised material. To do this, the user needs to be provided with a front end that can access information in a variety of databases which are widely distributed and can contain a variety of information in different formats' (Knight, 1997).

'Hybrid libraries' is the term used to describe a research and development initiative as part of the eLib programme in the UK. Largely, the projects are investigating how behind-the-scenes technology can connect physically separate collections to create a broad base of services to users. However, there are connections and future relationships with the local and regional or national hybrid systems. As Pearce notes:

...the full extent of the library's holdings needs to be represented in union catalogues. The library's digital collections need to be accessible as part of regional or national digital library services. Significant holdings in given subject areas or formats need to be declared in directories, union lists, subject gateways, multimedia publications and online exhibitions (Pearce, 2000).

The ramifications of the eLib projects will therefore be felt by the local systems, hopefully with significant benefits for both. The eLib projects are cutting-edge research studies which are unparalleled by any other initiative. The projects involve higher education institutions largely, as this sector has research time and money, and has currently supported over 60 projects. Mel Collier highlights the benefits from the studies as '. . .not only on how libraries will develop, but more fundamentally on how teaching, learning and scholarship will be conducted in the digital age' (Collier, 1997).

Stephen Pinfield, a member of one of the projects, has written that the issues the projects are facing include '. . .authentication, interconnectivity, end-user environment, and cultural and social skills concerning users and information professionals' (Pinfield, 1998). The five projects all have a slightly different focus:

- HyLiFe (Hybrid Library of the Future; *http://hylife.unn.ac.uk/*) and MALIBU (MAnaging the hybrid Library for the Benefit of Users; *http://www.kcl.ac.uk/humanities/cch/malibu/*): user focus
- HeadLine (Hybrid Electronic Access and Delivery in the LIbrary Networked Environment: *http://www.headline.ac.uk/*): authentication
- Agora (*http://hosted.ukoln.ac.uk/agora/*): interoperability and 'information landscapes'
- BUILDER (Birmingham University Integrated Library Development and Electronic Resource; *http://builder.bham.ac.uk/main.asp*): many issues from an institutional angle.

At the moment, these projects are facing slightly different issues than the local hybrid libraries of this chapter. However, it is easy to see how they could soon integrate and work well together for the good of the information seeker and provider.

Challenges associated with digital library services

There are a number of challenges that exist when dealing with digital library services, especially while also supporting paper-based documents. Many of these have already been discussed. The major challenges briefly described here are personality of library, format, funding, copyright, licensing, and staff issues. Cost, format and other issues that affect print collections can affect acquisition of and access to electronic resources, but the methods of overcoming these do not vary significantly from print to electronic. As the Head of the Library at University of Chicago, Martin Runkle, said in a *Library Journal* article: '...I am a digitisation enthusiast, but one can't ignore the practical considerations, such as cost and intellectual property rights, and one must consider the cost/benefit ratio for specific categories of materials' (Oder, 2000).

Personality of library and users

The type of special library may define how flexible and willing the staff are to support digital library services. Each sector has a different focus of user and service. As Arms writes, '...some corporate libraries, such as those of drug companies, already spend more than half of their acquisition funds on electronic materials and services. In contrast, printed materials, manuscripts, and other tangible items will be central to humanities libraries for the foreseeable future' (Arms, 2000). Arms also highlights the fact that digital library services '...depend on people and cannot be introduced faster than people and organisations can adapt them' (Arms, 2000). It should be noted that the people Arms refers to include users, staff, management, and vendors.

Format

Digital library services, perhaps even more than traditional print services, must be very carefully chosen to meet the library users' needs. Everyone is accustomed to dealing with print books and journals. Even though the information in many electronic products is the same as that in print, the format can be an obstacle to user access, so it must be carefully chosen. In some specialised information centres, for example, CD-ROM products accessible on a local area network may work well. In other, perhaps larger parent organisations, web-browser accessible products deliverable to the users' desktops would be the desired format. These decisions are important, as if the formats are not correctly chosen, the users will not benefit from the resources.

Funding/Cost

Arms writes that '...In the short term, the pressure to support traditional media alongside new digital collections is a heavy burden on budgets' (Arms, 2000). Therefore, special libraries will need to make sure that enough of the available budget each year is given to the maintenance and introduction of digital library services. As has been mentioned, hardware and software costs will also rise, and the funding must exist. As can be seen from the survey overview, many librarians have had to make tough decisions concerning cancellations of titles to be able to support digital resources. A special librarian in a hybrid library must be prepared to make such decisions.

Copyright

'Copyright was once seen as a dull and almost irrelevant area of law relating to information provision. It has now become central to all that libraries, archives and information centres wish to do' (Cornish, 1997). Copyright law on both sides of the Atlantic is in a state of flux. However, there are substantial efforts being made to standardise the processes, especially concerning electronic material. For a more complete overview, see, for example, Balas' article on copyright issues (Balas, 1998). Copyright is based on protecting authors' and publishers' rights to a work, ensuring that a work cannot be over-or mis-used without compensation to publishers and/or authors. Clearly it is easier and faster to misuse, e.g. widely distribute, documents in electronic form than with print documents. Ensuring intellectual property rights of web-based and other electronic products is a challenge faced by publishers and authors and is by no means solved. The special librarian or information professional needs to stay cognisant of copyright issues, and ensure that information made available to users does not violate copyright law.

Many professional organisations and institutions of higher education are offering short courses and/or workshops on this topic, and the special librarian will need to avail her or himself of these updates regularly. Gary Cleveland has listed four of the main copyright functions required:

- 'usage tracking
- identifying and authenticating users
- providing the copyright status of each digital object, and the restrictions on its use or the fees associated with it
- handling transactions with users by allowing only so many copies to be accessed, or by charging them for a copy, or by passing the request on to a publisher' (Cleveland, 1998).

All of these considerations need to be faced.

Licensing

Licensing of electronic databases can be considered an aspect of copyright – the purpose of a licence agreement is often to ensure that the publisher's copyright is protected. Electronically available journals and databases are the products most frequently being acquired by today's print – electronic hybrid libraries that may require licensing agreements. As with copyright, the library and information science profession is endeavouring to keep practitioners up to date on licensing issues as much as possible. The special librarian must avail her/himself of these opportunities. The resources of the special or workplace library's parent organisation may well come in useful here – many firms that maintain special libraries or information centres also maintain a legal department. The trained solicitors in those departments can provide assistance with the terms of a licensing agreement from the point of view of protecting the parent organisation.

A major role of the special librarian will need to be ensuring that the agreement will not limit user access to needed information. For example, when some journals first were made available electronically, libraries could only have access through a dedicated IP address, i.e. one terminal or workstation. This proved highly restrictive, and most publishers have now broadened their provision of service, so that all users in an organisation can access the journal from their desktop workstations.

Staff

In the hybrid library environment, the staff has to be a multidisciplinary team. This is a big difference from traditional library roles. Each staff member needs to be able to deal in a basic manner with roles encompassing: computer hardware and software; legal considerations (i.e. licence agreements), and that of educator or trainer. The challenges within this area occur when trying to find people who are willing to add to their responsibilities and skills. Having a mixture of expert workers in these areas as members of the library staff is also desirable, but harder to gather. Therefore, basic training opportunities should be given to all staff in all potential areas of skills required. All of these challenges are important and real considerations that have to be dealt with intelligently for digital library services to be successfully integrated into existing collections.

Emerging trends

Some emerging trends in digital library are summarised below: software, CD and DVD formats, customisation, and applying library expertise in new areas. This is an overview of some interesting trends, and is by no means exhaustive.

Software

The proliferation of Internet services and resources, and similar organisational services on intranets, has required cross-platform or operating system communication and compatibility. While web browsers are functional cross-platform tools, special librarians and information professionals are getting involved in some efforts to better utilise free and / or very versatile Internet tools.

One of these is a proposed markup language that is said to be more robust than the Web mainstay HTML: the World Wide Web (W3) Consortium's proposed XML, or eXtensible Markup Language (*http://www.w3.org/XML/*). On this web page, the W3 Consortium explains XML's utility as:

> …a set of rules, guidelines, conventions … for designing text formats for such data, in a way that produces files that are easy to generate and read (by a computer), that are unambiguous, and that avoid common pitfalls, such as lack of extensibility, lack of support for internationalisation / localisation, and platform-dependency.

Of special note is the last point, platform or operating system independence. There have been some discussions of XML on email discussion lists populated by librarians, e.g. Web4Lib to name just one. A search of the 2000 Web4Lib archives in June 2000 yielded 67 original messages dealing with XML in some manner. The library literature is just beginning to discuss XML. In 1998, Exner and Turner noted the rise of XML for web authoring, and especially its usefulness for adding metadata, secondary data (e.g. subject headings, etc.) about the primary data or document, something librarians do all the time (Exner and Turner, 1998). A recent article on XML from CERN, the high energy physics laboratory where the Web itself was invented, makes a special case for XML as a useful format for easily adding metadata (van Herwijnen, 2000).

The W3 Consortium also supports and promotes open source code and software based upon it. As with XML, discussions about open source architecture are just beginning in the library and information science world. Open source code is nonproprietary computer code – anyone can write in it and applications written in it are freely shared, the philosophy behind such sharing being that the code and its products will thus evolve. There is an Open Source Initiative based in the United States (*http://www.opensource.org/*). The Linux Operating System is an open source product; Linux is a freely available variant of the UNIX operating system written from scratch by Linus Torvalds and a team of programmers over the Internet.

The library world has discussed Linux more frequently than open source. Again looking at the 2000 Web4Lib archives, 50 original messages as of June 2000 were on the topic of Linux. Bascom Global Internet Services (*http://osee.bascom.org/*) is a Linux developer company that is running an Open Source Equipment Exchange (computer parts, and also software) that has been specifically marketed to libraries, as well as others. As noted in a *Library Journal* article by Michael Rogers, the exLibris company is using Linux as their operating system platform for their Aleph 500 integrated library system. (See also the exLibris web site at *http://www.aleph.co.il/products1.html*).

CD and DVD formats

Resources on CD-ROM, especially reference products like indices, proliferated in the 1980s and 1990s and were widely used in libraries. Most CD-ROM products work best on stand-alone workstations, meaning they are only available within the special library or information centre, not via the network. As noted by the INFOWorld Electric Test Center in a 12 February, 1996 column on CD-ROM server software: 'You would think that something so simple, so digitally pure as a CD-ROM would play well on today's LAN, but mixing the two is like trying to blend opera and disco.' Smaller organisations with common computer platforms have successfully provided data from CD-ROM products to users' desktops.

Various versions of CD-ROM writable software and drives emerged in the 1990s, with rewritable CDs (CD-RW) coming to prominence at the end of the decade (Herther, 1998). This new format has made quick and durable storage a viable and fairly inexpensive storage medium. CD-ROMs may well have more utility as a storage medium than as a format for reference services.

DVDs, or digital video discs, came to prominence towards the end of the 1990s, with some conflicting formats and some attempts by broadcast and entertainment companies to imbed monitoring and payment capabilities into DVDs, thus complicating developments. DVDs have a larger storage capacity than CDs, and can more easily store data in a variety of formats (video, data, etc.) As noted by Herther in her overview article on CDs and DVDs, SilverPlatter was one of the first database vendors to offer products on DVD. Whether this trend will continue is difficult to predict. Also in the beginning stages is the use of recordable / writable DVDs. As with writable CDs, this format could be utilised for efficient storage of large amounts of information.

Customisation

As discussed earlier, delivering information via the Internet or an intranet allows for ease of customisation because a document need only be created once to be accessed by any number of people, from those within an organisation (intranet) to millions of people worldwide (Internet). Customisation is also facilitated by the fact that the still-standard markup language for web pages, HTML, is nonproprietary and easy to learn and use.

Many vendors are taking advantage of the ease of customisation with web pages to offer this as a feature of their products to libraries and organisations. Examples include:

- news feed services – for example, Wavo's MediaXpress (*http://www.wavo.com/*), which allows customised feeds to an organisation and also further customisation by individual users; or, the older NewsEdge (*http://www.newsedge.com/offerings/index.htm*) which now offers a range of customisable feeds and products, including content groups
- business publication aggregators (with a newsfeed component) like Factiva's Dow Jones Interactive (*http://bis.dowjones.com/aboutdji/*).

With these sorts of services, the vendors or the librarians select information feeds and resources well suited to the organisation's needs, and that material is made prominent on the intranet. Reuters' Inform service (http://www.reuters.com/inform/) is an interesting variant that provides customised commodities information on the public Internet for customers (i.e. not fed to the intranet).

Most Internet search engines and/or portal sites are offering customisation, for example Yahoo's 'My Yahoo' (*http://my.yahoo.com/*). Most libraries that have web-accessible catalogues already customise the vendor's web product for their local site, and some are beginning to offer further customisation, like the Ford Motor Company's customisable 'MyRLIS' system discussed earlier in the chapter. This trend of libraries providing customised information via digital resources is expected to grow.

Bringing library expertise to new areas

As mentioned earlier, metadata is data that describes other data. Librarians have been creating metadata for centuries, ever since someone created the first set of indices for royal records in an ancient civilisation. As with customisation, the programs and platforms of the digital age are facilitating the easy creation of metadata. All of the mark-up languages used to create web pages, from SGML to the HTML and XML subsets thereof, include the capability for metadata creation.

For example, the HTML structure and function allows for the listing of keywords in a metatag field. Web crawlers and search engines can search these keywords that are not visible in a regular browser window. It is easy for a librarian to add descriptive headings to a web document – hopefully using a standardised set of keywords or a thesaurus for consistency – to ensure that all resources in a collection that is accessed digitally are equally retrievable. A keyword-tagged web document could either be a resource in itself (e.g. full text of a report) or it could be a representation (e.g. a catalogue record) of a printed resource.

The Dublin Core initiative (*http://purl.org/DC/*) is a set of metadata elements that creators (principally librarians and information professionals) and participants have agreed upon; it has become an International Standards Organisation (ISO) standard, ISO/IEC 11179. A more recent Working Group on Dublin Core in Multiple Languages (*http://avalon.ulis.ac.jp:8080/~nagamori/*) has extended the list of metadata elements to a variety of Asian and European languages.

As more and more libraries add digital services, special librarians and information professionals will be using aspects of the creation and layout languages (e.g. HTML) to exploit the information retrieval process. Dublin Core may well be superceded by more advanced metadata developments. As just one example, OCLC is developing a package to allow for web catalogue creation with powerful metadata aspects, MANTIS (*http://orc.rsch.oclc.org:6464/*).

Another area in which librarians are having an organised impact on the digital world is in the concept of 'PURLs', or persistent URLs. A URL is a uniform resource locator, the digital 'address' of a document laid out in a standard syntax so browsers and other tools can retrieve the document.

With the proliferation of web sites, millions of URLs have come and gone. Librarians are interested in providing stable access to information for their users, and thus developed the PURL movement, led and supported by OCLC, the National Library of Australia and other library consortia (*http://www.purl.oclc.org/*). A PURL is simply a URL to an intermediate service, that includes a sort of look-up table, and is guaranteed (up to some point) to be stable – the PURL redirects the browser to the source document. When the source document address changes, the creator notifies the PURL service, but does not need to change the PURL used.

Digital Objective Identifiers (DOIs) represent the PURL philosophy of permanence applied to object oriented systems, which now include some integrated library systems and catalogues. A DOI is a way to reliably identify and access digital objects, using a proxy server that looks up and points to the objects. A key driver behind the development of DOI systems is to provide publishers with a means by which property rights issues can be managed; it was developed by the International DOI Foundation on behalf of publishers (*http://www.doi.org/*).

Conclusion

This overview of the current state of digital library services in special libraries focused on the current prevailing model, the hybrid library. Digital resources are expected to continue to make inroads into special library collections. However, print materials are expected to remain viable for some time. This new century is an exciting time to be a special librarian or information professional. Many of the emerging trends in information access and delivery can provide good niches for information professionals willing and able to step out of more traditional librarianship roles. This chapter is intended in part to provide a beginning road map for those embarking on this journey.

References

[**Note** that all URLs cited were operable as of the time of writing (May 2001)]

Adam, Nabil R. Vijayalakshmi Atluri and Igg Adiwijaya. SI [systems integration] in digital libraries. *Communications of the ACM* (Association for Computing Machinery), **43**(6) June 2000, 64-73.

Arms, William Y. *Digital Libraries*. Cambridge, MA: Massachusetts Institute of Technology (2000).

Balas, Janet. Copyright in the digital age. *Computers in Libraries,* **18**(6) June 1998. Available at *http://www.infotoday.com/cilmag/jun98/story2.htm*

Bane, A. F. Business periodicals on disc: how full-text availability affects the library. *Computers in Libraries*, May 1995, 54-6.

Barnett, Andy. A survey of Internet searches and their results. *Reference & User Services Quarterly*, **39**(2) Winter 1999, 177-81.

Bartlett, Virginia. Technostress and librarians. *Library Administration & Management*, **9**(4) Fall 1995, 226-30.

Bishop, Ann, et al. Socially grounded user studies in digital library development. *First Monday*, **5**(6) 2000. Available at *http://firstmonday.org/issues/issue5_6/bishop/index.html*.

Breeding, Marshall. Does the Web spell doom for CD and DVD? *Computers in Libraries*, **19**(10) Nov/Dec 1999. Available at *http://www.infotoday.com/cilmag/nov99/breeding.htm*.

CD-ROM Server Software: product comparison highlights INFOWORLD Electric Test Center, 12 February, 1996. (Printout from web site, no longer available online.)

Clark, Katie and Kalin, Sally. Technostressed out? How to cope in the digital age. *Library Journal*, August 1996, 30-2.

Cleveland, Gary. Digital libraries: definitions, issues and challenges. UDT Occasional Paper # 8, March 1998. IFLA [International Federation of Library Associations and Institutions] Universal Dataflow and Telecommunications Core Programme. Available at *http://www.ifla.org/VI/5/op/udtop8/udtop8.htm*.

Collier, Mel. Toward a general theory of the digital library. Presented at *ISDL '97*. Available at *http://www.dl.ulis.ac.jp/ISDL97/proceedings/collier.html*.

Cornish, Graham. Copyright. In: Scammell, A. (ed.) *Handbook of Special Librarianship and Information Work*. London: Aslib, The Association for Information Management, (1997, 7th ed.), 303-18.

Dempsey, Lorcan. Scientific, industrial and cultural heritage: a shared approach – A research framework for digital libraries, museums and archives. *Ariadne*, **22** 12 January 2000. Available at *http://www.ariadne.ac.uk/issue22/dempsey/intro.html*.

DiMattia, Susan S. and Blummenstein, Lynn C. Virtual libraries: meeting the corporate challenge. *Library Journal*, **124**(4), 1 March 1999, 42-4.

Dowlin, Kenneth. *The Electronic Library*. Denton, TX: Convention Recording Services (1984).

Exner, Nina and Turner, Linda F. Examining XML: new concepts and possibilities in web authoring, *Computers in Libraries*, **18**(10) Nov/Dec 1998. Available at *http://www.infotoday.com/cilmag/nov98/story2.htm*.

Fox, Edward, A., et al. Digital libraries (Editorial). *Communications of the ACM*, **38**(4) April 1995, 23-8.

Furrie, Betty and the Follett Software Company Data Base Development Department. Understanding MARC Bibliographic: Machine-Readable Cataloguing; Part II: Why Is a MARC record necessary? Washington, DC: The Library of Congress (1998). Available at *http://lcweb.loc.gov/marc/umb/um01to06.html*.

Griffiths, Jose-Marie. The new information professional. *ASIS Bulletin*, Feb/Mar 1998. Available at *http://www.asis.org/Bulletin/Feb-98/griffiths.html*.

Guenther, Kim. Designing & managing your digital library. *Computers in Libraries*, January 2000, 35-9.

Harter, Stephen P. Scholarly communication and the digital library: problems and issues. *Journal of Digital Information* (JoDI), **1**(1) April 1997. Available at *http://jodi.ecs.soton.ac.uk/Articles/v01/i01/Harter/*.

Herther, Nancy K. CD-ROM to DVD-ROM: moving optical storage along a bumpy road into the new century. *Database*, **21**(2) April/May 1998, 26-30+.

Huntingford, Jim. The impact of IMPEL. *Ariadne*, **13** January 1998. Available at *http://www.ariadne.ac.uk/issue13/impel/*.

Huwe, Terence K. New search tools for multidisciplinary digital libraries. *Online*, March 1999. Available at *http://www.onlineinc.com/onlinemag/OL1999/huwe3.html*.

Jenkins, Clare. User studies: electronic journals and user response to new modes of information delivery. *Library Acquisition: practice & theory*, **21**(3) 1997.

Jones, Michael L.W. et al. Project soup: comparing evaluations of digital collection efforts. *D-Lib Magazine* **5**(11) November 1999. Available at *http://www.dlib.org/dlib/november99/11jones.html*.

Knight, Jon. The hybrid library: books and bytes: The Knight's Tale. *Ariadne*, **11, 1997**. Available at *http://www.ariadne.ac.uk/issue11/knight/intro.html*.

Lancaster, F. Wilfrid. *Toward Paperless Information Systems*. New York: Academic Press (1978).

Lynch, Clifford and Garcia-Molina, Hector. Interoperability, scaling, and the digital libraries research agenda: A report on the May 18-19, 1995 IITA Digital Libraries Workshop. Available at *http://www-diglib.stanford.edu/diglib/pub/reports/iita-dlw/main.html*.

McKnight, Cliff. Electronic journals: what do users think of them? Presented at *ISDL '97*. Available at *http://www.dl.ulis.ac.jp/ISDL97/proceedings/mcknight.html*.

Meer, Vander, et al. Are library users also computer users? A survey of faculty and implications for services. *Public Access Computer Systems Review*, **8**(1) 1997. Available at *http://info.lib.uh.edu/pr/v8/n1/vand8n1.html*.

Missingham, Roxanne. Science and technology: a web of information: impact of the electronic present and future on scientists and libraries. Presented at *Information Online & On Disc 99: strategies for the next millenium* (Proceedings of the North Australasian OnDisc Conference and Exhibition). Available at *http://www.csu.edu.au/special/online99/proceedings99/205a.htm*.

Morrow, Terry. Is the customer always right? End-user services in a networked age. Presented at the *1999 IATUL Conference: the future of libraries in human communication*. Available at *http://educate.lib.chalmers.se/IATUL/proceedcontents/chanpap/morrow.html*.

Nielsen, Jakob. Eyetracking study of web readers. *Alertbox*, 14 May 2000. Available at *http://www.useit.com/alertbox/20000514.html*.

Noble, Cherrie. Reflecting on our future. *Information Today*, February 1998. Available at *http://www.infotoday.com/cilmag/feb98/story2.htm*.

Nyce, James M. and Kahn, Paul (eds.) *From Memex to Hypertext: Vannevar Bush and the mind's machine*. Boston : Academic Press (1991).

Oder, Norman. Navigating change at the University of Chicago. *Library Journal*, 1 June 2000, 44-6.

Park, Soyeon. Usability, user preferences, effectiveness, and user behaviours when searching individual and integrated full-text databases: implications for digital libraries. *Journal of the American Society of Information Science – JASIS*, **51**(5) 2000, 456-68.

Pearce, Judith. The challenge of integrated access: the hybrid library system of the future. Presented at the *VALA 2000* conference. Available at *http://www.nla.gov.au/nla/staffpaper/jpearce1.html*.

Peters, Carol and Picchi, Eugenion. Across languages, across cultures: issues in multilinguality and digital libraries. *D-Lib Magazine*, May 1997. Available at *http://www.dlib.org/dlib/may97/peters/05peters.html*.

Pinfield, Stephen. Hybrids and clumps: with so much information out there, users often have difficulty finding what they want. *Ariadne*, **18**. Available at *http://www.ariadne.ac.uk/issue18/main/old/pinfield.html*.

Pinfield, Stephen, et al. Realising the hybrid library. *D-Lib Magazine*, October 1998. Available at *http://www.dlib.org/dlib/october98/10pinfield.html*.

Pitkin, Gary M. Technostress in Libraryland. *Colorado Libraries,* **23** Fall 1997, 58-61.

Porter, Cathy A., et al. *Special Libraries: a guide for management.* Washington, DC: Special Libraries Association (1997, 4ᵗʰ ed.).

Roes, Hans. Promotion of electronic journals to users by libraries – a case study of Tilburg University Library. Presented at UK Serials Group Seminar *Promotion and Management of Electronic Journals,* London, 28 October 1999. Available at *http://cwis.kub.nl/~dbi/users/roes/articles/london99.htm.*

Rogers, Michael. Linux operating system moving into library market. *Library Journal,* **125**(5) 15 March 2000, 26, 28.

Rout, James. A comparative study of inhouse and remote access catalogue users at the Edmonton Public Library. Available at *http://www.slis.ualberta.ca/cap98s/jrout/maindoc.html.*

Rusbridge, Chris. Toward the hybrid library. *D-Lib Magazine,* July / Aug 1998. Available at *http://www.dlib.org/dlib/july98/rusbridge/07rusbridge.html.*

Scammell, Alison. The role of the special librarian in the electronic era. In: Scammell, A. *Handbook of Special Librarianship and Information Work.* London: Aslib, The Association for Information Management (1997, 7ᵗʰ ed., 3-22).

Schatz, Bruce and Chen, Hsinchun. Digital libraries: technological advances and social impacts. *Computer* (the Journal of the IEEE Computer Society), **32**(2) February 1999, 45-50.

Schäuble, Peter and Smeaton, Alan F. (eds.) *Summary Report of the Series of Joint NSF-EU Working Groups on Future Directions for Digital Libraries Research.* 12 October 1998. Available at *http://galileo.iei.pi.cnr.it/DELOS/NSF/Brussrep.htm.*

Schuyler, Michael. Adapting for impaired patrons. *Computers in Libraries,* **19**(6) June 1999. Available at *http://www.infotoday.com/cilmag/jun99/schuyler.htm.*

Stielow, Frederick (ed.) *Creating a Virtual Library* . New York: Neal-Schumann Publishers, Inc. (1999). (How-To-Do-It Manuals for Librarians, no. 91).

Tennant, Roy. The most important management decision: hiring staff for the new millenium. *Library Journal,* **123** 15 February 1998, 102+.

Tenopir, Carol and Ennis, Lisa. The impact of digital reference on librarians and library users. *Online,* November 1998. Available at *http://www.onlineinc.com/onlinemag/OL1998/tenopir11.html.*

Tilburg University Report: *The Use of Paper and Electronic Journals by Researchers: discussion of research results*. Tilburg University Library, January 1999. Available at *http://cwis.kub.nl/~dbi/project/journal/eindrep.pdf*.

Tinanoff, Susan. End-user searching with CD-ROM databases. *Katharine Sharp Review*. **2** Winter 1996. Available at *http://www.lis.uiuc.edu/review/winter1996/tinanoff.html*.

Tompson, Sara. Illinois special libraries, a snapshot and some trends. In: Estabrook, Leigh, Hicks, Betty Lou and Tompson, Sara. *Librarians in the 21st Century*. Panel held at the Illinois Library Systems Directors (ILSDO) Institute, Allerton, IL, 2 September 1999. Available at *http://www.sla.org/chapter/cill/uiucsla/index.html*.

van Herwijnen, Eric. The impact of XML on library procedures and services. *High Energy Physics Libraries Webzine*, **1** March 2000. Available at *http://lhcb.cern.ch/~evh/xmlandlibrary.htm*.

Varnum, Kenneth J. Lessons learned: designing a second generation intranet. *Online*, January 1999. Available at *http://www.onlineinc.com/onlinemag/OL1999/varnum1.html*.

Waters, Donald J. What are digital libraries? *CLIR Issues*, **4** July / August 1998 (Council on Library and Information Resources). Available at *http://www.clir.org/pubs/issues/issues04.html*.

Youngman, Daryl C. Library staffing considerations in the age of technology: basic elements for managing change. *Issues in Science and Technology Librarianship*, Fall 1999. Available at *http://www.library.ucsb.edu/istl/99-fall/article5.html*.

Chapter 2

Staffing the special library

Guy St. Clair

Introduction

If nothing else, managing a special library is an exercise in variety and diversity. One has only to look at what a special librarian is, or think about what a special librarian does, to understand the value of flexibility and change implementation in the professional life of a special librarian. The Special Libraries Association (SLA), well known for it advocacy work on behalf of specialist librarianship, has its own definition of the special librarian, and it, too, reflects the variety and diversity of the special librarian's work. SLA, with some 15,000+ members, defines a special librarian as 'a knowledge professional who provides focused information and service to a specialised clientele having an impact on their success, mission, and goals' (SLA, 1999). The definition continues by noting that the term 'special librarian' is used interchangeably with the term 'information professional', and describes the association as having as members information professionals who work in corporations, media, finance, science, research, government, academe, museums, trade associations, non-profit organisations, and non-traditional enterprises (SLA, 1999).

The definition applies to all specialised librarianship, regardless of where in the world the definition is applied. Although SLA has its headquarters office in Washington, DC and is made up of mostly North American members, its emphasis on variety and diversity clearly positions special librarians as *different*. Special librarians are not only different from others in the workplace, they are different from other librarians and information professionals and, indeed, from others who practise special librarianship. These differences, particularly the differences *within* this branch of information services management, are so pronounced that it is difficult to identify common themes that unite special librarians.

But the themes are there, and as is being demonstrated throughout this book, common interests and the overarching information environment can be considered in order to come to a fair understanding of what the staffing needs are for a special library.

For one thing, special librarians are working in a societal culture in which fundamental ideas about information management and information delivery are being challenged and, in some cases, threatened. As a result, librarianship as a profession is moving from what is generally described as 'traditional' librarianship to the broader spectrum of information management and information delivery. For special libraries in particular, the demands of the workplace require a shift from the general to the specific, for the tenets of 'general' or 'traditional' librarianship do not work in the company or organisation that requires specialised information delivery. They are important to know about, of course, but as a foundation upon which to build a successful special library, they are not – it is generally agreed – very useful.

The reasons are not hard to come by. In the specialised library, the practice of librarianship becomes that of information management and information delivery, and the librarian moves from being a gatekeeper to being a host, from being a protector of resources to being a generous sharer of resources, from being an educator to being a knowledge manager. In doing this work, special librarians turn from traditional library education and professional development to strategic, performance-centred learning (both in their own development and in the learning they bring to their clients). In the process they undertake to acquire skills and competencies in knowledge development and knowledge sharing, and knowledge hoarding becomes a thing of the past.

All of this happens, of course, because the special librarian is at work in an information workplace that is unlike any other. As an information manager, the special librarian participates in an arena that I have referred to elsewhere (and continue frequently to speak of) as the 'splendid information services continuum'.

> Librarianship is but one subset of a multitude of service activities that are more rightly described as information services. Such services are known by a great multiplicity of names but primarily they embody, in addition to librarianship, such information delivery activities as records management, organisational or corporate archives, information brokerage, information resources management, publishing, and consulting. Information technology, the development of software and hardware, telecommunications, and electronic publishing fit equally well into an information services scheme, and the futurists of information services – embodied in such groups as the United States Federal Government in its attention to the development of a National Information Infrastructure, the 'G7' [now 'G8'] nations, the group of leading economic group nations (in that body's attention to the development of a global information infrastructure), the In-

formation Futures Institute, various 'think tanks' and research/ discussion groups, and various professional associations – all come together under one framework which pulls together all efforts to deliver information to the people who seek it.

Information itself is now defined very broadly, and while specific and traditional approaches to information delivery continue, among some information leaders the move to a more integrated perspective is wholly appropriate. In the specialised research and business community, for example, information is anything workers need to know in order to do their work. Thus 'information' can include such items as customer records, information from and about suppliers, information about budgets, financial results, R&D reports and so forth. At the same time, and of special interest for workers in libraries, the list includes external information that workers must have available in order to achieve their workplace objectives, and in most organisations it is the library which is usually charged to provide external information. As a result of this new thinking about how information is defined, many information services managers and consultants, even vendors, have begun to organise their work not around the way the information is stored, or the medium through which it is delivered, but around the end-user and the use to which it will be put. These people are all seeking to achieve one goal: to provide the information their customers seek. Under this framework, information services and information services management, as a discipline and as a specific field of study, is structured. (St. Clair, 1996)

This 'splendid information services continuum' is, for those considering a career in specialist librarianship, an equally splendid challenge. It is a challenge that the smart and ambitious information worker seeks to meet, for it has the unique advantage of giving the specialist librarian an opportunity to work with a product – information – that is literally unbounded in its reach. For those seeking to staff a specialist library, then, the first attribute to look for is an interest in and an enthusiasm for this broader 'playing field', a willingness to move beyond the confinement of traditional librarianship to a broader, more inclusive workplace. In essence, information services can be thought of as any work that has anything to do with the identification, capture, organisation, storage, retrieval, analysis, interpretation, packaging, and dissemination of information, and this is the environment in which the special library staff will work.

Aside from the work environment itself, however, there are other considerations that make the work of the special library different from those of other libraries, or similar information delivery organisations. That broad base from which to work is important (Elizabeth Orna (1990) has defined information as anything that people need 'to know and apply in their work, to achieve their and the enterprise's objectives'), but it is only one attribute of modern society's approach to information that affects the work of the special librarian. Another key consideration is what might be referred to as the 'ubiquitousness of information', a condition that has only been recognised in the last few decades. Previously, information was something that people needed and used, but because technology had not advanced so far, it was possible to organise and implement – relatively successfully – one's access to information; but a few years ago that access and organisation became impossible, and information became something everyone was suddenly aware of, and suddenly willing to offer his or her own unique version for handling that information. As a result, information as a part of daily life became, almost without anyone's noticing, a subject much to be discussed, worried about, and to express opinions about.

Such a state of affairs would not have come about, of course, without the advent of enabling technology, and no one – least of all a special librarian – is going to lament the demise of manual information record-keeping and management and the advent of digital information. In moving to this new information medium, however, the role of the special librarian (indeed, of all information providers) has changed. Today, thankfully, enabling technology enables information providers to seek and to provide seamless information delivery and, as important as anything else, the special library becomes less of a 'place' and more of a resource.

Finally, though, the ubiquitousness of information and enabling technology have led to what, for some librarians, is their biggest problem (and for others, the realisation of their happiest dreams): the advent of an almost-universal understanding of the value of information and its role in the lives (and not just their workplace lives) of the people who use the special libraries. Everyone is now an information expert, and the special library is no longer a repository or collection of materials organised and arranged just in case someone might need them.

In fact, the 'just-in-case' scenario was replaced by the special librarians early in the last century, when under the enthusiastic leadership of such people as John Cotton Dana, the delivery of information was not confined to information collected in one space, but was broadened to include information that could be gathered – from any source – to be of value to those who needed it when they needed it. The early special librarians and their followers replaced 'just-in-case' information delivery with 'just-in-time' information delivery, and it was that important distinction that characterised specialist librarianship for most of the 20th century. But with the

coming of the new century, and with knowledgeable information customers acquiring more and more expertise in information use, the focus of our
services changed again, now to a more customised information environment. As that amazing century moved towards its end, David R. Bender
noted the change:

> We're moving even further ahead now, beyond 'just-in-case' and
> 'just-in-time' information delivery, and that's where I think we're
> going to be as we begin the 21st century.

> We're always listening to the information customers, of course,
> and hearing what they need, but now in addition to mediating
> and consulting, we're analyzing and interpreting, and custom-
> izing, and providing information that I like to characterize as
> 'just-for-you'.

> It's a powerful, very powerful paradigm we're dealing with
> here… We've gone from 'just-in-case' to 'just-in-time' to 'just-
> for-you'. (St. Clair, 1997)

That 'powerful paradigm' is clearly understood (and expected) in the
management community. In fact, among those who employ specialist librarians, understanding the value of information is a particularly
essential attribute, one that is critical to success in today's information-
delivery environment and one that any successful candidate for
employment must exhibit. Martha P.B. Schweitzer, the president of the
Special Libraries Association's largest chapter (in New York) and herself
an executive search consultant to major law firms, financial institutions,
and publishing companies, has commented on the importance of this
attribute for candidates seeking employment in these types of organisations (although she does not, in fact, limit this attribute to those
environments):

> Information makes a crucial difference in decisions made in
> business, in war, in love, and in human relationships. One miss-
> ing piece of data can skew the picture used to navigate an
> enterprise. It takes brains, instinct, organisational skills and in-
> tegrity to effectively connect the dots for an accurate information
> picture. At our organisation, where we've taken the concept of
> 'connecting the dots' so seriously that we've incorporated it into
> our corporate identify [the firm is known as INFOdot, Inc.], we
> look for professionals who understand the nature and power of
> information, who enjoy solving puzzles and who seek to pro-
> vide the service which takes care of the problems their customers
> face. Of course we seek candidates for these positions with gradu-
> ate LIS degrees, for the degree helps the individual hone those

skills and aptitudes, but it does not guarantee them. (Schweitzer, 2000)

The message is clear: to be a successful candidate for employment in a special library, knowing about the capture, organisation and dissemination of information is essential, of course. But far more important, at least from the perspective of the people who are doing the hiring and who have very specific expectations about what a special librarian will provide for the organisation, is an understanding of how information is used and of how the work that these people do, as the organisation's information specialists, contributes to organisational success. The specialist librarian must, above all, value information and be willing to work with information understanding that value.

The special library environment: the organisational relationship

Special libraries are found in all kinds of organisations, as the definition cited earlier makes clear. What is not made clear in most discussions about special librarianship – and the staffing of special libraries – is the extreme importance of the relationships that are established in the organisation between the employees of the special library and other information stakeholders who are also part of (or in some way connected to) the organisation. In many respects, these organisational relationships, an understanding of how they are developed and the implementation of methodologies for their successful development and utilisation, play a far greater role in the success of the special library staff than do the staff's educational and professional development background and activities. Obviously, the attaining of qualifications and the continued development of those qualifications is critical, but it is in understanding the work of the parent organisation and the required attention to mission-specific information delivery that truly ensures the success of the specialised library's staff.

Management expectations

When new special librarians (that is, people who have library work experience, but not in a specialised library) come into their new work environment, one of the first lessons they learn is that their egalitarian approach to information management is out of place in their new workplace. Because every service delivered from a special library must be mission-specific, and because resources made available for the support of the specialised library are uniquely dependent on the level of mission specificity that can be documented and conveyed to those who have resource allocation authority, special librarians are required to understand exactly what their information clients expect from them in the way of library and research services. More important, because of the political nature of organisations – and because every unit manager in the organisation is eager to figure out how to move resources from the special library's allocation to their own (and special library managers are equally eager to do the same thing in reverse) – the question of client expectations is often superimposed over a more telling question: What does management want? It is an axiom of work in today's business community that those who manage the organisation are given various responsibilities (conceptualising and planning, organising, controlling, and evaluating and measuring), and that among these, the primary one is control. There are those who would assert that the only role for executives is to control costs, and while such a superficial reading of the manager's job is open to question, there is no denying that financial control is an essential fundamental for success for any executive. Those who work in a specialised library must understand – first and foremost – that it is their relationship with management that will dictate whether or not they will be successful in their work. If they have the resources to provide the services, products, and consultations they are expected to provide, they will succeed. If they do not, they might make passing gestures at success, but success – in terms of providing the information services that they have been hired to provide – will ultimately elude them.

Such a potentially bleak scenario is not necessarily a foregone conclusion, however, for if those who work in specialised libraries – and those who understand them – can relate to and accept (and even buy in to) the expectations that management has for the organisation and for the information services that the special library provides for the parent organisation, there will not be a 'battle of wills'. These two opposing forces, if they work in collaboration with one another, can develop and sustain an information services operation that provides the benefits that the organisation requires. To work in such a collaborative environment requires, of course, that the employees of the specialised library understand how they 'fit' into the organisational scheme.

In most organisations for which they supply research and information delivery, special libraries are not expected to be profit centres and they are, in fact, usually considered overhead operations in the organisation's management plan (and especially in the financial planning and reporting that the organisation is required to perform on a regular basis). As a result, librarians and other staff employed in these libraries find themselves in something of a circular professional quandary: educated to work in libraries generally, for which there is little promise of 'profit' and in careers which are often fairly uncomfortable because of the constant 'fight' for resources, these librarians develop behaviours and management skills based on the assumption that life will be tough. Then they move into specialised libraries which, for the most part, are found in for-profit organisations, and these same librarians hopefully begin to anticipate that if they demonstrate the value of their work in contributing to the organisation's financial success, funding will be available for managing the special library as the 'taken-seriously' operation that it should be. Alas, such is not the usual outcome, for while there are many special librarians operating in the for-profit community, and while many of the parent organisations show a healthy profit at the end of the financial year, the libraries themselves are expected to be managed and supported as if they were 'fringe' operations, cost centres instead of profit centres. It is not a pretty picture for special library managers, and the only way to move to a satisfactory and successful arrangement is to understand clearly and specifically what the library's customers want and need, and to be able to convey those needs – in mission-specific terms – to the organisation's executives. At the same time, the special library manager must also be able to convince these same executives that client needs match management expectations for the organisation's specialised library.

Those management expectations can be identified. As indicated here, determining and publicising the ratio of the services, products and consultations provided by the special library to the successful achievement of the organisation mission is highest on the list. If there is any single attribute that special library staff must possess, it is a clear understanding of what the parent organisation exists to do, and of how the special library fits into that picture. This is not a difficult assignment, for it simply requires that the library staff read and understand the organisational mission statement and vision statement (and, if there is one, a strategic or operational plan for the larger organisation). Annual reports are also useful for providing this kind of information, but the point is, it does not really matter what resources the staff use to find the information, a good clear reading of the organisational mission and vision statements is essential. When this information is discussed in terms of the mission and vision statements for the specialised library (or, if they do not exist, as they are being developed), library staff will – almost without trying – find the connections between their work and the larger community in which they are involved.

As part of its mandate to control costs and, indeed, as part of the overall control function of any executive, management expects efficiency in information delivery. For some specialist librarians, this simply means that the company or institution which employs them will provide the tools (electronic access, reference and research resources, etc.) that they need to do their work. For others, it means going out into the organisation and determining how other departments and units function effectively and efficiently, and then developing the special library's operations management so that it matches that of the larger organisation.

The term 'quality information management' is now used throughout the information industry with some frequency (even casually with its own acronym: 'QIM'), and the popularity of the concept is based on its relatively high importance to those with management responsibility for the delivery of information. It really doesn't matter if the information being sought by and delivered to the client is internal or external, research documentation from a report, a record of a transaction, or the linking of an expert with someone who needs to make the link, quality information management has become the standard by which information delivery is judged, and staff in a specialised library use QIM as the foundation for their work. As noted in another context, QIM as a subset of organisational management and as a specific management methodology for providing the highest standard of information delivery to an identified user base builds on six 'essentials' of general quality management as practised in the information industry:

- intense focus on customer service
- accurate measurement
- continuous improvement
- new work relationships built on trust and teamwork
- a desire for quality on the part of all information stakeholders
- the commitment and enthusiasm of senior management in the parent organisation (Barrier, 1992; St. Clair, 1999).

Connected to these 'essentials' is another management expectation for the specialised library, and for the people who staff it: enterprise-wide participation. It has become clear in the last decade or so that for information delivery to be truly effective, and to contribute to the successful achievement of the corporate mission, the special library must become a 'library without walls'. Of course many organisations will continue to operate a functional unit known as something like a 'corporate library' or 'information centre' or 'research resources office' but, by and large, those who work in these units are not expected to stay locked within that space. They are expected to move out into the organisation, bringing news and demonstrations of applicable products to those departments that might benefit from such activities. Similarly, they meet on a regular basis with planning staff in the different sections of the organisation, to ensure that the services and materials they are providing are relevant to the work that is being done, and that the best information is being provided. Specialised library staff become expert at product development, particularly in the development of electronic products that are easily accessible at the user's desktop, and the old-fashioned subject bibliographies formerly distributed throughout the company in hard copy, for example, are now captured in an easily accessible database, and available to all who need them. Special librarians as knowledge managers, as noted below, become expert at working with specific projects and programmes, as advisors and as resource providers. Taking this function to its logical fulfillment, the recently recognised concept of the insourced information specialist is now almost expected in some organisations. In this situation, a member of the special library staff is literally moved out of the physical workspace of the library to work in the office or department in which his or her expertise in information management will be reserved for the exclusive use of the member of a particular project or programme (St. Clair and Berner, 1996). This is, indeed, a far cry from working 'in' the specialised library, but it succeeds well in providing the members of the project or programme team with the specialist information delivery that they will need.

Information management in the 21st century

One thing becomes clear as we think about how information is delivered as we move into the new century: there is no longer – at least in specialised librarianship – a 'one-size-fits-all' type of information delivery. The special librarian in this new century must be willing to be flexible, to understand the clients' interests and information needs, and to adjust his or her prior 'thinking' about information delivery to match those interests and needs. Just how important that adjustment is for the specialist librarian can be seen as we review – however briefly – the place of librarianship in society today.

Within the information industry, it would seem that there is general agreement that what we now call 'specialist librarianship' has grown out of the long tradition of library service as practised for many years, probably centuries, but which was first formalised and structured as a profession in the late years of the 19th century. That tradition was one that was seriously, perhaps even strenuously, connected to education and, as a result, librarians were taught that their first role was that of teacher, to be the educator who taught the expectant users how to search for and retrieve the information he or she was seeking. As part of that tradition, however, those who practised librarianship also made a commitment to take care of and, usually, to protect the artefact in which the information was contained (most usually in Western civilisation, of course, in the book or similar printed artefact), so that librarians were warehouse managers as well as educators. Now that situation has changed drastically, and the librarian is called upon not only to continue to do those things, but to become knowledgeable about information as it appears in many other formats as well. So librarianship has moved from 'library work' to information management, and librarians must now understand the concepts of information delivery in many guises. In fact, what was referred to as an information 'continuum' earlier could now be – particularly for special librarians – an information spectrum, for the special library 'tradition' was, and continues to be, quite different from that practiced by other librarians. The specialist librarian is an information worker whose primary job was to get the information the client required, and whether it was contained in a book or document found within the premises of the parent organisation, or whether it was located outside the organisation, the specialist librarian's job was never to teach the user how to find the information. It was to find the information.

So in one respect, the special library of the 21st century combines so-called 'traditional' librarianship (i.e. librarians as educators and/or warehouse managers) with equal attention to the demands of an information-hungry, always-demanding clientele. In fact, it is in special-ised librarianship that we find so much attention (that is, *real* attention) being given to customer service/client relationship management, as noted above in that description of the essentials of quality information manage-ment; and even in traditional librarianship, the role of the librarian and information worker has taken on new dimensions as the influences of today's society bring new interests, better educated customers (with higher expectations) and new and improved methodologies for library service delivery into the workplace.

As a result, the delivery of information by the specialist librarian becomes dependent on the information delivery (and information technology) con-ditions that prevail in the parent organisation. In many organisations (and predictably for most in the future), those librarians are going to be operating in a highly digitised environment, one that is already being studied in other parts of the information industry and one which will, it can be predicted with some confidence, affect the way information will be delivered for those clients who today use a specialised library.

Reflecting this move of the profession into an information-focused and knowledge-based direction, special librarianship is among the many information-intensive disciplines that are moving toward that type of information delivery exemplified by what is called the 'integrated digital environment'. Such an environment does not preclude the printed page, of course, but it is recognised as an environment in which the enabling qualities of modern information management and information technol-ogy combine to create a new work environment in which the network-centric 'framework', so to speak, of the technology permits a dif-ferent way of working with information (and, of course, a different way of thinking about how information is accessed and used).

An integrated digital environment is generally thought of as a workplace or an environment in which there is immediate access to the information needed to do business. In its efforts to migrate its information-manage-ment capabilities to a network-centric integrated digital workplace, the United States Air Force has adopted this definition, and it is one which notes that such a workplace requires digital tools, an information-sharing (as opposed to information-hoarding) work culture, connectivity, and corporate memory. It is also a workplace – it almost goes without saying – in which there is ubiquitous connectivity among knowledge workers (United States Air Force, 2000).

In this first year of the new century, we cannot state unequivocally that such a definition will apply to all specialist libraries. For one thing, an integrated digital environment is generally a much 'broader' information-delivery agency than a special library is expected to be. Many special libraries (particularly those which have evolved from an organisation's traditional paper-based library, a library which is more than, say, 50 years old) exist to provide 'traditional' library services, and while their real role is to be the information nexus for the organisation, that is not always the case. Other information units exist, departments such as records management units, organisational archives, and so forth, and for many of these organisations, the principles on which the integrated digital environment is built are better applied in these more information-focused units. On the other hand, the evolving nature of the integrated digital environment has not been lost on those organisations seeking to move into knowledge management (as discussed below), and attempts to instill the principles and methodologies of the integrated digital environment into the larger organisational sphere are being given serious consideration in many organisations.

There are important differences, of course, between a library and an integrated digital environment, particularly for those special libraries in which the staff is expected to provide primarily information, documents, technical reports, and similar material from external sources. As information providers move more to electronic delivery, however, the differences become less distinct, and specialist librarians employed in organisations providing more electronic information delivery find the principles of the integrated digital environment of value to them.

Nevertheless, some differences must be acknowledged, at least for the foreseeable future. Traditional librarianship – including those special libraries that are managed and provide services as traditional libraries – must, by definition, be about collections. In this larger electronic arena known as the integrated digital environment, the focus is no longer on collections and, indeed, the whole point of the effort is to encourage people to work differently, to understand that information can be made useful without being 'collected'. The principles that were developed in the United States Air Force Digital Environment Project demonstrate these and have serious implications for managers of special libraries, as they seek to establish a framework of information delivery through the services, products, and consultations offered by that library. For example, of the three principles of a network-centric integrated digital environment (at least one as envisioned by the United States Air Force), the creator/owner of the information is the keeper of the information, ensuring that, unless required for some justifiably viable reason, multiple instances of the same data will not exist. Such a principle puts particular pressure on the specialist librarian to understand how his or her work proceeds in the organisation, and, particularly, requires a re-thinking and a reconsideration of such matters as the attribution of ownership, how information is retained and stored and continues to be accessible when personnel changes take place, or when programmes are closed or transferred to another department or agency.

Similarly, the second principle of the integrated digital environment requires particular attention to the role of the specialist library in the parent organisation, for it asserts that reporting is replaced with access to information. Obviously this principle is more applicable in the 'broader' information environment referred to above, in which those who are seeking a particular document or a single fact or 'piece' of information can simply be referred to an electronic resource for the information. Nevertheless, in the specialised library, there will continue to be more and more of these occasions as well, as users contact the library to seek guidance and, in consultation with the specialist librarian, discover that they can access the information directly, simply by using the URL or other 'finding aid' that the librarian offers.

Finally, though, it is the third principle of the integrated digital environment that has particular resonance for specialist librarians. The principle calls for essential evidence to be preserved for reuse by others, so that, in the case of more widely dispersed information, corporate knowledge – however 'corporate' is defined – is captured. For the specialist librarian, the adoption of and implementation of this principle is almost a dream come true, for the basic tenet of librarianship (whether it be special librarianship or more 'traditional' librarianship) is that the information being sought be available when it is needed. For centuries, librarians have been thwarted in their attempts to provide information on demand, simply because the artefacts in which information was captured meant – usually – that its use was limited to the number of copies that could be made available. That has changed now and with the adoption of this third principle of the integrated digital environment and the utilisation of enabling technology, specialist librarians can provide information for their users, as it is required (or, if the second principle is applied as well, simply direct the users to the information). The days of the librarian as one who simply 'fetches' information – usually in the guise of fetching the container in which the information is captured – are finally gone.

Other characteristics of specialised librarianship and information management in the 21st century influence employers as they seek to staff a special library. For example, the focus on customer service (now – appropriately – generally referred to as 'client relationship management' in most businesses and organisations in which special librarians are employed) is not a new phenomenon, but the amount of attention being given to the subject demonstrates that special librarians are expected to think about how the information that users seek is valued by the users. We may have left behind the days when the customer was 'always right', but we have also left behind the days of the librarian as the intellectual arbiter of information services and the professional arrogance that such attitudes engendered. Today, as special librarians see themselves as part of a 'team', as members of the same organisation as the people who are seeking information through the use of their skills and competencies and as fellow stakeholders (albeit with specific expertise in information management) in organisational success, the role of the special librarian in the organisational effort is considerably enhanced.

Similarly, as alluded to earlier, special librarianship is less about collections and more about information delivery. The emphasis for today's information customers is on obtaining and using mission-specific information, and the gathering of 'just-in-case' information is no longer appropriate. So special library staff must routinely be prepared to deny information services when the information being sought is not mission-specific but, on the other hand, must be particularly adept at understanding the organisational mission so that appropriate information delivery can be implemented, even when – as is the case in many specialist libraries – the information being delivered was not specifically sought (or known about) by the user.

What all this portends, it seems, is that we are essentially seeing in specialised libraries a move to a collaborative workplace, a workplace and a workplace *style*, if you will, that is based on a new attention to collaboration, to the idea that working together, whether in person or in an integrated digital collaborative workspace, is better than working in a hierarchical management environment. This is a workplace ambiance whose time has come, according to Edward M. Marshall (1995):

> Collaboration is a principle-based process of working together, which produces trust, integrity, and breakthrough results by building true consensus, ownership, and alignment in all aspects of the organisation.

Marshall reduces that formula to one that everyone, regardless of the type of special library in which he or she is employed, can understand and relate to. 'Put another way,' Marshall writes, 'collaboration is the way people naturally want to work.'

This is a totally new way of looking at the workplace, but it is one with which specialist librarians are comfortable. While the history of management in the most organisations has been – and frequently continues to be – based on hierarchical principles, the basic tenets of work in the collaborative workplace veer drastically from the hierarchical and provide the specialist librarian with a unique opportunity to participate more directly than librarians ever have in the achievement of the organisational mission. In fact, Marshall has also written, in the same book, that 'collaboration is the premier candidate to replace hierarchy as the organising principle for leading and managing the 21st-century workplace,' and while such a drastic separation of management methodologies is not expected to take place in every organisation, in those in which it does occur, the work of the staff in the special library will be markedly different, and better (from a professional service-providing point of view). People work differently in a collaborative workplace (regardless of the institution or organisation under discussion), and the very foundation of the collaborative workplace is that it is an environment in which mutual respect and association permeate the flow of work. People at all job levels take their work more seriously, work more responsibly, work together to resolve joint questions of mutual importance and, particularly, identify themselves as being part of a collaborative team or group whose workplace responsibilities are, without question, mission specific. This is the kind of environment in which a special librarian – with his or her determination to contribute seriously to organisational success – can thrive.

As Marshall has described it, the workforce in the collaborative workplace has as its attributes effective work relationships, respect for people (both within the workforce – at all working levels – and among the customers and stakeholders in the external environment with whom these knowledge workers interact), honour and integrity, ownership and alignment, consensus; full responsibility and accountability, trust-based relationships, and specific reward, recognition, and growth applications. Knowledge work in the organisation – and particularly that of the special library – is built on training, development, and strategic/performance-centred learning that results in faster decision making, decisions that are of higher quality, and decisions that are customer driven (regardless of how the term 'customer' is defined).

In this respect, the role of collaboration in the information workplace has been succinctly stated in a statement from Ann Wolpert, Director, Massachusetts Institute of Technology Libraries. 'The issue,' Wolpert (2000) says, 'is not print versus electronic resources, but rather the shape of the new intellectual "package" that contains information in different formats, originating from different sources.' Wolpert goes on to suggest that 'by providing a gateway to this diverse world, and the skills to navigate it, the MIT Libraries share their information expertise, and integrate the research experience for students.' Simply by substituting the term 'identified clientele' for the word 'students', Wolpert's recommendation that the library provide a 'gateway to this diverse world, and the skills to navigate it' could well define the work of today's special librarian.

In the academic community (even in academic research institutions as specialised as the Massachusetts Institute of Technology), the role and the function of the library is established. In the specialised library community – and in the organisations in which specialist libraries are to be found – the role and function of the library is not so clearly established, and much effort goes into developing the organisational relationships that will result in a better understanding of what the special library can provide. The key to the success of this effort is collaboration.

Knowledge management and the special librarian

When you stop and think about it, the basic activities and functions associated with knowledge management are what special librarians have been doing all along. For the manager seeking to employ appropriate staff for working in a special library, it is a wise step to give attention to knowledge management and the skills required for the successful organisation and implementation of a knowledge management programme.

In fact, within the profession of specialised librarianship, the concepts and ideas connected with what we now call 'knowledge management' were being given serious thought long before Thomas Stewart (1993) identified the capture and application of an organisation's intellectual capital as a valuable corporate function (and thus called startling attention to the importance of managing that intellectual capital, a function that became known as 'knowledge management'). As early as 1916, only seven years after the founding of the Special Libraries Association, *Special Libraries* editor Dr John A. Lapp defined the purpose of the special library as being 'to put knowledge to work'. (The phraseology stuck, of course, and went on to become the Association's motto, used throughout its history (SLA, 1999).) So, even in its earliest days, specialist librarianship recognised that its function was to do more than simply organise and disseminate information.

James Matarazzo and Suzanne D. Connolly (1999) find the same historical link, observing, in the introduction to their anthology of articles about specialist librarians and knowledge, that for librarians, providing information for users has always been part of what we would call today a 'knowledge' focus in the delivery of that information:

> Libraries have always existed for the sole purpose of serving patrons and providing information. Librarians have always been considered the experts at navigating through countless information sources and finding the correct answer to a request... We have taken on the role of internal consultants to our clients when they sought specific information... Providing information is our most important contribution to the field. When we discuss information, this includes not only third party vendor information but also internal company information. This includes understanding our company and identifying the most important activity it performs, which can be as simple as reading our company's mission statement or having a conversation with coworkers. It's building networks and leveraging them when necessary to provide our end-users [with] critical, much-needed information. It includes making our libraries the crossroads within our corporations. End-users will look to us as liaisons between different parts of the organisation.

For most of us, we have become very aware that the terms 'information' and 'knowledge' have become interlinked and in many cases appear to be used synonymously in today's management environment. While we are all quick to recognise that it is crucial in an integrated digital environment to make a distinction between information and knowledge, there is still, within the wider societal framework, a tendency to confuse the two terms.

Obviously the terms do not mean the same thing. In fact, although there are accepted definitions for each (that is, accepted in the terminology of whatever field of study or interest is being discussed), the meanings vary and, in some environments, using the terms synonymously would be inappropriate and confusing. Despite these different meanings and usage, however, in the larger management community the phrase 'knowledge' has become part of the effort to identify and capture an organisation's intellectual capital (as when the phrase 'knowledge management' is used to refer to an organisation's efforts to capture both tacit and explicit information). While such 'loose' terminology might be regrettable in a strictly controlled environment, in the larger management arena, this 'looseness' is something with which most observers have come to terms. While many are not comfortable with the substitution of 'knowledge' for 'information' (or vice-versa) such casualness in the management community is now something that most people accept.

Certainly this battle over the distinction between 'information' and 'knowledge' is one that has been raging for a long time, and it will probably continue. In their book on the role of information in society, John Seely Brown and Paul Duguid (2000) recognise that to attempt to discuss the distinction is to move into dangerous territory: 'We do this with some trepidation,' they write. But they overcome their trepidation, and plunge in with a very reasoned and very useful approach to making this important distinction:

> On the one hand, epistomology, the theory of knowledge has formed the centrepiece of heavyweight philosophical arguments for millennia. On the other, knowledge management has many aspects of another lightweight fad. That enemy of lightweights, *The Economist*, has pronounced it no more than a buzzword. We may then, be trying to lift a gun too heavy to handle to aim at a target too insubstantial to matter.

> Certainly much about knowledge's recent rise to prominence has the appearance of faddishness and evangelism. Look in much of the management literature of the late 1990s and you could easily believe that faltering business plans need only to embrace knowledge to be saved. While it's often hard to tell what this embracing involves, buying more information technology seems a key indulgence.

> Nonetheless, people are clearly taking up the idea of knowledge in one way or other. From within organisations come sounds of fighting between the IT (information technology) and HR (human resources) factions over who 'owns' knowledge management. Similarly, technology giants have entered the propaganda war over who best understands knowledge. Elsewhere, the management consultants are maneuvering for high ground in the knowledge stakes.

> In the process, *knowledge* has gained sufficient momentum to push aside not only concepts like reengineering but also *information*, whose role had previously looked so secure. To be, in Peter Drucker's term, a 'knowledge worker' now seems much more respectable than being a mere 'information worker', though for a while the latter seemed very much the thing to be. Similarly, pundits are pushing 'information economy' and the venerable 'information age' aside in the name of the more voguish 'knowledge economy' and 'knowledge age'. . .

> Beyond the buzz, however, is there any bite to the uses of *knowledge*? When people talk about *knowledge*, are they just clinging to fashion (as many no doubt are), or might some be feeling their way, however intuitively, toward something that all the talk of

information or of process lacks? Is there, we begin by asking, something that *knowledge* catches, but that *information* does not?

Twenty-five hundred years of unresolved epistomological debate from the Sophists to the present argue that we would be unwise to seek the difference by [poring] over rigorous definitions. Moreover, whatever differences abstract definitions might clarify, persuasive redefinition now obscures. People are increasingly eager that their perfectly respectable cache of information be given the cachet of knowledge. Such redefinitions surreptitiously extend the overlapping area where *knowledge* and *information* appear as interchangeable terms.

Brown and Duguid (2000) then offer three generally accepted distinctions between knowledge and information (but not before suggesting that 'we check the language of knowledge management at the door'):

- Knowledge usually entails a knower (information is independent, but knowledge is usually associated with someone).

- Knowledge appears harder to detach than information (information is 'a self-contained substance').

- Knowledge seems to require more by way of assimilation. ('Knowledge is something we digest rather than merely hold').

In the more 'traditional' special library community, defining knowledge takes on a very practical perspective, according to Andrew Berner (who manages the largest private club library in the world, the University Club Library in New York City). 'Knowledge,' says Berner (2000), 'is information which is used.' As a practical application, Berner's definition is not very different from what Stewart calls 'intellectual capital', so perhaps 'traditional' librarianship and the more *moderne* (or even futuristic) information delivery we give so much attention to are not so far apart after all. Stewart, in his 1997 book, refers to intellectual capital as 'intellectual material – knowledge, information, intellectual capital, experience – that can be put to use to create wealth,' a definition that puts 'intellectual capital' very close to what we call 'knowledge', but gives it a practical twist so that the term describes what is done in the corporate world – where most special librarians work.

Then there is the necessity to think about which *kind* of information/ knowledge is to be managed, and it is important to note that there are, in fact, two 'sides' to the same 'coin' of information/knowledge management. It is now recognised that the success of any collaborative effort in an information- or knowledge-based environment runs the risk of falling too much on one or another 'side' of the knowledge 'definition'. In an article in one of the popular information magazines, an important distinction is made between 'communication-centred knowledge' and 'storage-centreed knowledge', a distinction which has some influence on how knowledge workers think about their work, particularly as organisations (and special libraries) attempt to move more in the direction of an integrated digital environment:

> Verbal or communication-centred knowledge is information that passes between people for urgent or tactical purposes, such as conveying the answer to the question: 'How many generators do we have in overstock?'

> Without IT intervention, you could transmit that knowledge through a conversation or by leaving a note or voice message. Historically, IT hasn't been able to do much about this kind of knowledge.

> Storage-centred knowledge, on the other hand, is filed away somewhere, perhaps as a physical or electronic document, in a file system, in an Email, or buried with thousands of other entries in a data warehouse. It sits in structured files, such as forms or database reports, and in unstructured ones, such as word-processing files. Most IT knowledge efforts have been aimed at making use of storage-centred information.

> Both kinds of knowledge are quite necessary in most companies. . . (Angus, 2000).

Knowledge management as an organisational management methodology has been defined on many different occasions, and a brief sample of these definitions demonstrates that the role of the special librarian as a knowledge manager is an appropriate one indeed. In the corporate world, Lois Remeikis (St. Clair, 1996) says that knowledge management is the organisation's effort to '...define, create, capture, use, share, and communicate the company's best thinking....' In the RIM community, the records and information management field, Bruce Dearstyne (1999) writes that knowledge management is '...cultivating and drawing on tacit knowledge; fostering information sharing; finding new and better ways to make information available; applying knowledge for the strategic advantage of the organisation'. In the world where high technology and big business combine, the folks at Microsoft have their own take on knowledge management. 'Knowledge management,' they say, 'incorporates systematic processes of finding, selecting, organising, and presenting information in a way that improves an employee's comprehension and use of business assets' (Brown and Duguid, 2000).

By alluding to the thinking of the information technology and software development community, we are left to ponder the question that all specialist librarians must deal with:

Does knowledge management necessarily require technology? In today's workplace, and in the thinking of today's business and organisational leaders, it probably does, since it is the enabling attribute of technology that has permitted the working community (and society at large, of course) to come to the point where it is possible to work, unencumbered, with data and information in such quantities and with such sophistication. In fact, in the quotation from Microsoft, which Brown and Duguid (2000) use in their discussion of knowledge management, the paragraph quoted is preceded by another:

> Knowledge management is the use of technology to make information accessible wherever that information may reside. To do this effectively requires the appropriate application of the appropriate technology for the appropriate situation.

For specialist librarians, then, one of the basic questions has to do with distinguishing between information and knowledge, since the special library must deal in both. In the general scheme of things, information management might be said to be concerned with the acquisition, documentation, arrangement, storage, retrieval and use of information to produce knowledge; and knowledge management is the process or technique of making relevant information available quickly and easily for people to use productively. It is a process, certainly, and it is a management methodology through which the company is able to transform its intellectual capital into enduring value. It is a methodology, involving the connection of people with the knowledge they need, when they need it and we employ information technology as the tool for managing information to produce knowledge.

In today's competitive business and organisational environment, the successful players are the businesses that are what we might refer to as 'knowledge-centric'. In fact, recent descriptions of this business environment as a 'network-centric, integrated digital environment' are now being revised, for the commonly accepted phraseology for today's successful business is to refer to itself as a knowledge-centric business and it is the staff of the special library who have the skills and the abilities to manage that knowledge.

There are any number of reasons why knowledge management is vital in today's workplace, and for the specialist librarian, assuming the role of knowledge manager is not simply a step in wish fulfillment. It is assuming a role that brings significant benefit to the parent organisation. If we are seeking to enumerate just how important knowledge management is, it might be useful for the manager of the special library to think about how knowledge management:

- facilitates the leveraging of organisational knowledge – bringing the right information to the right people in an understandable context

- permits the company to meet business / mission goals

- permits the company to achieve knowledge superiority over adversaries or competitors

- focuses on customer needs, in order to drive the organisational effort and improve relationships with customers

- provides an infrastructure for electronic and social networking to develop new products and services; fosters and provides access to rich pools of ideas so others can use them

- increases collaboration opportunities to enrich the exchange of tacit and explicit knowledge between people

- permits the sharing of best practices within the company

- provides a platform for knowledge reuse and innovation

- establishes benchmarks for internal and external performance, for both individuals and teams

- facilitates and accelerates learning at all levels within the company, creating opportunities for individuals and groups to put new knowledge to use.

In a knowledge centric competition-focused business, the chief knowledge officer (CKO)[1] has responsibility for ensuring that the company's commitment to knowledge management contributes to the successful achievement of the company's mission, but an examination of organisational expectations for this senior management role provides a striking resemblance to what a specialist librarian does. For example, in terms of organisational management, it has been suggested that the CKO has a variety of responsibilities, and special librarians do many of these things, and do them well:

- leads the corporate KM strategy, creating and selling the KM vision and helping other organisational leaders drive the company in the desired direction

- promotes an organisational culture that facilitates tacit and explicit knowledge development and knowledge sharing; recognises and promotes enterprise-wide knowledge development/ knowledge sharing contributors

- champions the development of a KM budget and serves as an advocate for keeping KM resources available

- evaluates the effectiveness of KM projects and their contribution to the corporate mission

- benchmarks with other organisations (public and private)
- develops strategies, in co-operation with the established training and development operation (usually through the company's human resources unit), to facilitate training and education of knowledge workers
- champions cross-organisational communities of practice
- establishes relationships with related leaders in departments such as human resources, organisational learning, IT, records management, corporate archives, etc.

All of these are roles which, in the successful specialised library, the staff (or at least the senior staff) have expertise and ability.

Competencies for special librarians

Much has been written about the famous list of competencies that the Special Libraries Association produced in 1996. While it is true that the concept might have been developed as an ongoing project, to ensure continuation and regular updating, even in its singular form this important document has proven to be a valuable contribution to the management of specialist libraries, particularly in terms of management expectations for staff. Formally titled *Competencies for Special Librarians for the 21st Century*, the effort was intended to be a handbook providing specific and codified direction for those who would be employing specialist librarians (Spiegelman, 1997).

Published in a monograph that provided much excellent background information about competencies and the value of competency-based management, the list of competencies was also published in an executive summary format, as an electronic document on the SLA web site, and, as demand from non-English speaking information professionals around the world grew, translated into several languages other than English. (The list of competencies from the document is appended to this chapter.)

Seeking to ensure that all who used the document understood the concept of competency-based management in the contemporary workplace, Barbara Spiegelman (1997), who edited the monograph, in a chapter she wrote turned to Gary Hamel and C.K. Prahalad (1990) for a general definition of core competencies: 'sets of integrated skills and technologies that are unique to a specific company'. In the list itself competencies are defined as 'the interplay of knowledge, understanding, skills, and attitudes required to do a job effectively from the point of view of the performer and the observer' (Spiegelman, 1997).

There is no doubt that the list is a valuable management tool for those who must staff a specialised library, since it does, indeed, codify those qualities and skills required for the successful achievement of the special library's objectives. Using this list, the manager of a special library can identify where staff strengths are, and, whenever possible, build on those strengths. More important, the manager can identify and address weaknesses that might hamper or interfere with the staff's work in the library, and these deficiencies can, when it is appropriate to do so, be turned around so that they do not interfere with the library's progress in performing its mission.

The list of competencies serves another, equally valuable purpose in the management of the special library, and that is in the larger organisational context. As mentioned, the list also provides those who have management responsibility (from a senior management level) for the library function in the organisation with an important description of what a specialist librarian is expected to do, and of the environment in which he or she is expected to work. A persistent complaint in all professions is that the professionals who work in an environment not specifically connected with their profession must suffer misunderstanding about their work, simply because the people who surround them (and frequently make judgments about their success) are not practitioners themselves in the same profession. These 'outsiders', it is thought, simply do not 'understand' what the professionals do, and cannot understand the more intricate elements or the 'mystique' of the work. Such complaints are heard from accountants who do not work in accounting firms, corporate or organisational lawyers who do not work in law offices, and of course from librarians who do not work in libraries. While there is perhaps some validity to these complaints, the beauty of the competencies list that was developed by the Special Libraries Association is that it can be used by managers who know nothing or little (or who have incorrect perceptions) about the specialised library function for an organisation. In and of itself, the document provides important background and reference for those managers.

As it turns out, while the 24 listed competencies are useful, even that list might be too comprehensive for some, and it can be condensed to five broad component issues. The condensed version, with the five keywords: resources, content, media, manager (or management), advocate (or advocacy), is also useful, and provides a practical introduction to the larger description of what a special librarian does. In the condensed list, the special librarian:

- has expert knowledge of information *resources* within a specific subject field or fields
- has specialised knowledge of the *content* of these resources
- understands and implements information delivery *media*
- performs as a *manager* within the organisational entity
- serves as an information *advocate* within the organisation or community at large (St. Clair, 1997).

For some library managers, it might be easier to think about staff competencies and their relationship to the success of the special library in these broader, perhaps less daunting terms. In either case, however, it is generally acknowledged that this list of competencies for success as a special librarian is a good list, and one that should be on the desktop of every special library manager, as it will be referred to with some frequency in the management of the library.

Conclusion

It should be mentioned that two subjects of importance in the consideration of staffing for a specialised library are not discussed here, although both of these subjects have been more fully explored in other works by this author[2] and are discussed in other essays in this collection. Both the role of the specialist librarian as a change agent within the parent organisation, and the educational, training, and development requirements for qualification as a successful practitioner in specialised librarianship are critical staffing considerations, and must be given much thought by those who employ professional workers in this field.

As for future prospects for special librarians and the future of this branch of the information services profession, it is clear that staffing these operational entities will continue to be a challenge for many of those who have senior management responsibility for information and knowledge management. This branch of librarianship continues to change (and *will* continue to change), and if this chapter were an attempt to *predict* what will happen, it seems likely that the work of specialist librarians will move further and further away from librarianship, *per se*, and more to the management and delivery of information *as information*. As a result, those whose function is to perform such management and delivery roles will rely less on the skills and competencies generally associated with librarianship and will be required to understand the organisation of information, the value of information and the delivery of information in an organisational, mission-specific context. While they may be required to manage a collection of artefacts containing the information their users need, they more than likely will be required to understand how to identify and access information more directly, and to route it more directly, in an electronic format. This does not mean that their work as librarians is without value; it simply means that specialist librarians will do (as they do now, to some extent) a *different* kind of work. Whether it will be appropriate to refer to this work as 'librarianship' remains to be seen.

In any case, as direct and intimate participants in the larger business and organisational management community, specialist librarians will be required to understand and to relate to a workplace that is not connected with the educational/library community, and the work systems in which they participate will be those of the larger working environment. This idea has already been noted in the literature, and librarians – particularly special librarians – will benefit from understanding how the workplace is changing and how their roles will change. If they do, those who hire employees for working as special librarians will be able to plan how those people will fit into the larger organisational workplace:

> Work systems will be more participatory than hierarchical. The Internet has freed up communication systems inside and outside work. Downsizing and reengineering have made it clear that job loyalty is an outdated concept. The challenge then becomes how to retain the best people, when many of the structures and supports for doing that are no longer present. The best people will move from project to project and expect far higher levels of freedom (Lubans, 2000).

The challenges are there, and it is now up to those who manage special libraries to recognise that the challenges exist, that there is a different workplace, and to understand that both management and user expectations have changed. If those who want to practise in specialised librarianship are willing to accept these challenges, they – and the organisations that employ them – will be successful.

Notes

1. These concepts about the role of the knowledge manager were developed by the author from a variety of sources, and particularly from two presentations: *Knowledge Management and the Role of the CKO in Public Organizations*, presented by Dr. Robert E. Neilson, CKO, Information Resources Management College, National Defense University (at *http://www.ndu.edu/ndu/irmc/km-cio_role/km-cio-role.htm*) at the US Department of the Navy Knowledge Fair 2000, 1 August 2000, and *Building Capability Through a Comprehensive Knowledge Strategy*, presented by Hubert Saint-Onge, Senior Vice-President, Clarica, Montreal, PQ, Canada, at the Chief Learning Officer Conference, 25-28 October, 1999 at (*http://www.linkageinc.com*).

2. St. Clair, Guy. Ann Lawes. Thinking about the information manager as change agent. *InfoManage: the international management newsletter for the information services professional.* 2(1) December 1995, *Change Management in Action*, op cit., and Qualification management in information services: my grand design *Information Outlook*, 4 (6) June 2000. A book on the subject of qualification management, *Beyond Degrees: professional learning in the information services industry*, is currently being written by the author. It is scheduled for publication in 2002.

References

Angus, Jeff. Harnessing corporate knowledge. *Information Week*, 7 August 2000, 54.

Barrier, Michael. Small firms put quality first. *Nation's Business*, **80**(5) May 1992.

Berner, Andrew. Interview with the author, 12 August 2000.

Brown, John Seely, and Duguid, Paul. *The Social Life of Information*. Cambridge, MA: Harvard Business School Press (2000) 117-120.

Dearstyne, Bruce W. *Records management of the future: anticipate, adapt, and succeed*. The Information Management Journal. October, 1999.

Hamel, Gary, and Prahalad, C.K. The core competencies of the corporation. *Harvard Business Review*, May / June 1990; and *Competing for the Future*. Cambridge, MA: Harvard Business School Press (1994); both quoted in Spiegelman, Barbara M. Using competencies as a performance appraisal and compensation tool. In: Spiegelman, B.M. (ed.) *Competencies for Special Librarians in the 21ˢᵗ Century*.

Lubans, John, Jr. On managing: 'I borrowed the shoes, but the holes are mine' – management fads, trends, and what's next. *Library Administration and Management*, **14**(3) Summer 2000, 134.

Marshall, Edward M. *Transforming the Way We Work: the power of the collaborative workplace*. New York: American Management Association (1995).

Matarazzo, James B. and Connolly, Suzanne D. *Knowledge and Special Libraries*. Boston: Butterworth Heinemann (1999), vii-viii.

Orna, Elizabeth. *Practical Information Policies: how to manage information flow in organizations*. London and Brookfield, VT: Gower (1990), 46.

St. Clair, Guy. *Change Management in Action*. Washington, DC: Special Libraries Association, 1999.

St. Clair, Guy. David Bender at the Special Libraries Association: visionary leadership for the information industry. *InfoManage: the international management newsletter for the information services professional*, **7** June 1997, 1-5.

St. Clair, Guy. Exceptional information delivery: the TQM / QIM / SLA competencies connection. *Information Outlook*, **1**(9) August 1997.

St. Clair, Guy. *Entrepreneurial Librarianship: the key to effective information services management*. London and New Providence, NJ, (1996), 5.

St. Clair, Guy and Berner, Andrew. Insourcing: positioning the information function where it counts. *InfoManage: the international management newsletter for the information services professional*, **3**(12) November 1996, 6-7.

St. Clair, Guy. Knowledge management: the third 'era' of the information age? Lois Remeikis at Booz-Allen & Hamilton thinks that it is. *InfoManage: the international management newsletter for the information services professional,* **3**(10) September 1996.

Schweitzer, Martha P.B. Interview with the author, 4 August 2000.

Special Libraries Association. Historical highlights. *Who's Who in Special Libraries, 1999-2000.* Washington, DC: Special Libraries Association, 1999, 19.

Special Libraries Association. *A Visionary Framework for the Future* (The Strategic Plan of the Special Libraries Association). Washington, DC: Special Libraries Association (1997).

Spiegelman, Barbara (ed.) *Competencies for Special Librarians for the 21st Century.* Washington, DC: Special Libraries Association (1997).

Stewart, Thomas. *Intellectual Capital: the new wealth of organizations.* New York: Doubleday (1997), x.

Stewart, Thomas. Welcome to the revolution. *Fortune,* 13 December 1993, 66ff.

United States Air Force. Integrated Digital Environment Project . *Transforming the Work Culture: project executive report,* September 2000. Available at *http://www.ide.hq.af.mil* .

Wolpert, Ann. From the Director. *Massachusetts Institute of Technology MIT Libraries News,* **12**(1) Spring 2000, 2.

Appendix

Special Libraries Association

Competencies for Special Librarians of the 21st Century

Competencies are defined as the interplay of knowledge, understanding, skills, and attitudes required to do a job effectively from the point of view of the performer and the observer. These include both professional and personal competencies. This set of knowledge and skills unique to special librarians allows us to function in a variety of environments to produce a continuum of value-added, customised information services that cannot be easily duplicated by others.

Professional Competencies

The Special Librarian...

- has expert knowledge of the content of information resources, including the ability to critically evaluate and filter them
- has specialised subject knowledge appropriate to the business of the organisation or client

- develops and manages convenient, accessible, and cost-effective information services that are aligned with the strategic directions of the organisation
- provides excellent instruction and support for library and information service users
- assesses information needs and designs and markets value-added information services and products to meet identified needs
- uses appropriate information technology to acquire, organise, and disseminate information
- uses appropriate business and management approaches to communicate the importance of information services to senior management
- develops specialised information products for use inside or outside the organisation or by individual clients
- evaluates the outcomes of information use and conducts research related to the solution of information management problems
- continually improves information services in response to changing needs
- is an effective member of the senior management team and a consultant to the organisation on information issues.

Personal Competencies

The Special Librarian...
- is committed to service excellence
- seeks out challenges and sees new opportunities both inside and outside the library
- sees the big picture
- looks for partnerships and alliances
- creates an environment of mutual respect and trust
- has effective communication skills
- works well with others in a team
- provides leadership
- plans, prioritises, and focuses on what is critical
- is committed to lifelong learning and personal career planning
- has personal business skills and creates new opportunities
- recognises the value of professional networking and solidarity
- is flexible and positive in a time of continuing change.

The Author Guy St. Clair is Senior Systems Analyst, Knowledge Management and Learning at Dynamics Research Corporation, New York, NY, USA. A Past-President of the Special Libraries Association, he is the author of many books and articles on information services management and the role of special libraries in the information industry.

Chapter 3

Organising access to information by subject

Stella G. Dextre Clarke

Introduction

The focus for this chapter is the information manager facing choices on how to organise her or his collection(s) for access by end users. The 'collection' may be real or virtual, composed of books; paragraphs or sections in a book; articles, patents, videos, images, records in a database, an incoming news feed, sites or pages on a network. Despite the variety, we shall consider all the items as 'documents', rather broadly defined. Some virtual collections may seek to integrate internal with external resources. Sometimes they will be used to 'push' unsolicited items to users; at other times they will serve as resources for answering queries.

The organisation of information presents challenges that have exercised the minds of great thinkers for more than two millennia. We shall use an approximately chronological sequence (a) to remind ourselves of key developments now manifested in today's techniques for organising access to information, and (b) to highlight the factors that will influence our choices among those techniques. Then we will ask how the different options may be evaluated. We shall have space only for the subject approach to access, ignoring other retrieval concerns.

Aims of organising and accessing information

A traditional assumption in the design of information storage and retrieval systems is that users will want to find all and only the relevant items, in response to a particular query. Similarly, with alerting services, only wanted items should be routed through to the user. Another long recognised user need is to be able to browse through a collection (or a news bulletin), perhaps straying over the boundaries of the usual field of interest, perhaps making a serendipitous find.

As we shall see later, 'relevance' of retrieved items is not universally favoured as the criterion by which system performance should be judged. However, it still seems a good starting point to assume that the main reason for organising information is to be able to find it – and the needle, when found, should preferably emerge cleanly from the hay in the stack.

Basic types of approach

The most fundamental way of organising any collection is to put like things together and separate the unlike ones. This is the basic technique of classification. We apply it when locating pickled walnuts in the supermarket as well as for tidying our sons' bedrooms. It is good for browsing as well as for finding specific items. Classification is useful, not just for the order of books on library shelves, but sometimes for the sequence of chapters within the books or for the presentation of electronic search results. At its simplest it implies taking objects and putting them into pigeon-holes or slots. The pigeon-holes are often subdivided, and those subdivisions sub-subdivided and so on, until we have an elaborate hierarchy of slots for accommodating our objects.

The method works splendidly while the slots are clear, visible, unambiguous, and mutually exclusive, and the objects nicely fit the shape of the slots; but particularly with document collections the following problems can arise:

- Some items may legitimately go into more than one slot.
- Chapters of a bound volume may each belong in different slots.
- No prearranged slot exists for a document on a new subject.
- The hierarchy is so elaborate that it actually separates related things (It's a bore navigating all the way to the bottom of a hierarchy, drawing a blank, then having to find somewhere else to start.)
- The hierarchy is so elaborate that users cannot find their way round it.
- Subject expert users may disagree fundamentally on the legitimacy of the slots, i.e. how knowledge in their own areas should be presented.
- The collection is specialised and certain slots accumulate so many items that they need to be subdivided…again and again.
- The labels on the slots are inadequate to describe the contents.
- Items may not be found because they are temporarily missing from their slots, e.g. while someone is using them.

All these problems can be overcome, but not without thought and effort.

Contrasting with classification is the approach of indexing. Instead of placing whole documents (books, articles, images, electronic documents or whatever) in slots, what if we analyse the contents of the documents and set up pointers to them, via an alphabetical index? After all, when people look for a non-fiction item, they are usually seeking the information inside rather than the document as a whole. The documents can be arranged in any determined order (by author, by accession number, and so on) so long as an accompanying index points to all the documents in the collection which deal with a particular matter. We overcome the problem of choosing the one best place for a document, because we can set up as many index entries to a given document as we like.

An index can relate to any feature or aspect of a document, such as its author or even its colour (not trivial in the case of image collections) but in this chapter we shall be focusing on subject indexing. So what we really want to index are the concepts in the documents. Indexing can be done at any chosen level of detail. In some systems an average of just two or three key concepts per item may be picked out for indexing. In others, 15 or more index terms may commonly be assigned to each item.

Now that so many documents are available in machine-readable form, stored and managed with very powerful hardware and software, it has become commonplace to 'index' every word in every item, enabling free-text retrieval. That is to say, we can search for every occurrence of a given word in the text. Notice the subtle difference in what is meant by 'indexing'. Here the computer is noting and finding the *words* in the document, not the *concepts*. This distinction (and our terminology!) can be confusing, because words are what we use in speech and in writing to convey concepts; but isolated words rarely coincide unambiguously with concepts. In this chapter, the term 'indexing' will normally be used as shorthand for 'subject indexing', that is, the intellectual process of selecting the key concepts in a documentary item and recording these in an index.

Another general means of subject access is via pointers from one document to another. The author may expressly cite other documents, or, in electronic collections, hypertext links may be the pointers. Hypertext and citation navigation are both very important techniques, particularly for browsing, but space limitations prevent us from covering them in this chapter.

Thus we are still left with at least three approaches to information management: classification, indexing, and free-text options where there is no human intervention at the time of input. Each of these will be discussed in the next three main sections, respectively. Many scholars would object to making a fundamental distinction between classification and indexing. Lancaster (1986), for one, maintains that, 'Classification pervades information retrieval activities. Indexing is obviously a classification process.' Foskett (1982) treats classification and indexing as different aspects of the same topic. As this chapter progresses, we shall indeed find that in a working system of any complexity, classification and indexing are inextricably complementary, as inseparable as the proverbial love and marriage. Initially, however, it is helpful to approach them separately. We shall view classification at its simplest as a top-down method, in which items are assigned to the subject areas or disciplines to which they belong. In contrast, subject indexing takes a cross-cutting approach, identifying concepts at the level of specificity in which they occur in individual documents and search queries.

Classification: key issues

The vast literature on classification, dating from the time of Plato, reflects the intense intellectual challenges that a working system must still confront. Key aspects include:

- *Subject content* – the scheme must be sufficiently comprehensive and detailed for the collection
- *Dimensionality* – the need to place books in a unidimensional array on shelves poses a huge artificial constraint, which does not reflect the way we mentally classify things
- *Representation/navigation* – communicating the structure of a classification scheme to users demands a raft of devices – notation, an index and perhaps other forms of representation
- *Continuing development* – every classification system must evolve if it is to serve its users well. Arrangements for maintaining and developing a scheme should be in place from the outset.

We shall use these aspects as headings under which to discuss the issues and compare key features of some of the well-known general classification schemes on offer.

Subject content – the analytical component

Subject hierarchies, generally composed of headings and relationships between the headings, are fundamental to every classification scheme. The great Dewey Decimal Classification Scheme (DDC) demonstrates the 'enumerative' style of classification, in which the whole of knowledge is divided into classes, these classes into sub-classes, and so on. For users of the DDC, every allowed class position must exist already enumerated in the scheme. Unfortunately, not everyone agreed with the way Dewey analysed knowledge (Berwick Sayers, 1962), either in 1876 when the scheme was first published, or now in its 21st edition.

Working from the 5th edition (1895), Otlet and Lafontaine adapted and greatly expanded the DDC tables in work that would eventually lead to the Universal Decimal Classification (UDC) (McIlwaine, 1995). With universality as a guiding principle, this scheme aims to serve specialised collections, not just public libraries. Since the time of its second edition (1927-33) the UDC has always been multilingual.

The Library of Congress Classification (LC) had a more empirical foundation (Foskett, 1996; Berwick Sayers, 1962), which can be viewed either as a weakness or a strength. Its basis was not an overview of the universe of knowledge but the stock of books actually present in the eponymous library at the turn of the 20th century – an immense collection by the standards of the time. First the books were arranged in what seemed the most helpful order; then the arrangement was studied, adjusted and recorded. The schedules for different subject areas were developed rather independently of each other, leading to discrepancies in approach that persist even today (Foskett, 1996; Chan and Hodges, 2000).

Dissatisfied with anomalies in all the existing schemes, Henry Bliss set out to develop a classification that would be more stable, scientifically acceptable and consistent, than any of its fore-runners (Berwick Sayers, 1962). His efforts to establish the underlying order in nature, in consultation with the foremost thinkers in each field, led to the publication of his much respected *Bibliographic Classification* (BC1) in 1940.

The historical foundations of all the schemes mentioned are still reflected in their modern schedules. All are discipline-based, their shape conditioned by the long-established fields of science and humanities. All face difficulties when coping with today's problem-oriented or mission-oriented fields, such as 'environmental studies', or 'genetic engineering'. From these latter perspectives, close collocation may be required between concepts that traditionally were seen as far apart.

Dimensionality, synthesis and faceted classification

The earlier classification schemes strove to provide better or more detailed analysis and enumeration of each subject area. But analysis alone proved not to be enough. Books or journal articles are typically not about just one subject but about combinations of ideas. Does a work on 'Computing for farmers' go with the computing books or the farming books? Even if we decide which is the best place for the purposes of one collection, the opposite choice might be better for a different collection, with different users. Imagine trying to classify the household linen and clothing in your home. You might decide to put all the socks together, or perhaps you separate them by owner: Mary's socks go to her cupboard and Tom's socks to his. But equally you could classify them by state of usage – all the dirty clothes go in the laundry basket, whether they are socks or shirts. Then you take them out for washing and put all the white items in one heap; all the coloured ones in another; later on, you classify all the clothes by fabric for ironing: the polyester clothes for the cool iron and a heap of cottons for the hot iron. When packing for the Bahamas, into one suitcase go all the clothes for a tropical climate, whether yours or your spouse's, whether skirts or swimming trunks. All of these classifications for the *same set of objects* are valid on different occasions, and there is no right or wrong, except in the context of a specific need.

'Faceted classification' is the name of a technique which recognises that one class of objects may be subdivided in different ways, using different characteristics of division: by function, by material, by colour and so forth. Or as Vickery (1960) puts it, 'The essence of facet analysis is the sorting of terms in a given field of knowledge into homogeneous, mutually exclusive facets, each derived from the parent universe by a single characteristic of division.' Figure 4 illustrates the use of facet analysis in the classified section of the *BSI ROOT Thesaurus* (1981). Being a thesaurus it does not demonstrate the full complexity of a faceted scheme for use in arranging books, but does show how long lists of concepts can be organised into meaningful groups by facet analysis. The phrases in italics and parentheses are the facet indicators, naming the characteristic by which each facet is governed.

Classifying by multiple mutually exclusive facets is simple enough with the household clothing, because you can do it one way today and a different way tomorrow. The challenge is much greater with a collection of books in the library, because when you classify the book you have to provide for all the useful ways, simultaneously. Ideally, we would use a multidimensional classification, where the book may appear in five or six places, but we have to avoid cutting it up or buying multiple copies. Thus, as well as analytical schedules laying out the headings and characteristics of subdivisions etc., faceted classification schemes for libraries need a notation which allows synthesis of a composite class code, and a set of rules for locating the composite class codes in a unidimensional array. The rules include deciding on a 'preferred order' of the facets in the schedules, designed to give a 'citation order' for the combination of the class codes of individual facets within composite class codes, that will ensure optimum retrieval performance.

Bliss recognised that any one part of the field of knowledge could act in some way on any other, and provided for synthesis or 'composite specification' in BC1. Similarly the UDC used symbols such as + : and = for combining two or more class codes into one composite one. (Such schemes are often described as 'analytico-synthetic' because class codes need not all be enumerated in advance.) Inspired by a Meccano set (Berwick Sayers, 1962), Ranganathan developed the idea of facet analysis and used it to apply synthesis more pervasively throughout his 'Colon Classification' (CC) (1960). If we view the CC's tables as inventories of mechanical parts, then the colon symbol takes the place of nuts and bolts, allowing the construction of a class mark to represent any subject. The most complete manifestation of the principles of faceted classification is now to be found in the second edition of the Bliss Bibliographic Classification (BC2). In the 1950s the Classification Research Group (CRG) in London had further developed Ranganathan's ideas. Then Jack Mills took on the editorship of BC2 and, still supported by the deliberations of the CRG, has been bringing out the separate volumes, class by class, until today 13 volumes have been completed and the remaining nine are close to publication.

Representation/navigation via notation

The prime function of notation is simply to locate a given subject matter on the shelves (or in the filing cabinet, or among the pages of a bibliography, etc.). For this purpose it could simply be a running number, but in practice it usually takes the form of a 'class code', intended to represent the desired subject. This secondary function – representation – is not essential but may contribute to the user's understanding of how the universe of knowledge is being laid out in the scheme. Hence many classification schemes try to have an 'expressive' notation. Complexity then inevitably arises from the challenge of converting our multidimensional way of thinking about subjects, to a unidimensional array. To add to the complications, the notation system must allow for hospitality, i.e. the capacity to accommodate new topics at almost any point in the schedules, in response to advances in human knowledge or user interests. Expansion is difficult to accommodate without straining either the user's ability to understand the intended filing sequence, or the expressiveness of the way codes represent their subjects, or both.

Dewey's decimal notation looks obvious enough now, but when it first appeared it was a breakthrough, in that the numbering applied to subjects rather than to shelves. Having divided the whole of knowledge into nine classes, he assigned a numerical digit to each. The digit zero was reserved for 'General works', covering matters too general to go into any one class. Each main class was subdivided into nine divisions; each division into nine sections; these into nine sub-sections, and so on indefinitely to whatever level required. Thus 5 represented Natural Science, 51 Mathematics, 512 Algebra, and so on. Once the scheme has been applied to every book, all you have to do is arrange the books in numerical order (you have to imagine a decimal point before the first digit) and Bingo! All the books on the same subject will be brought together.

Plainly, the idea that knowledge will naturally divide into nine at every level is a straightjacket, imposing artificiality on the real intellectual job of analysing the subject in question. Some other schemes use letters instead of numbers, so up to 25 slots are available at every level. (In most schemes, one slot at every level is generally reserved for the 'general' category.)

Some schemes, e.g. LC, use a mixture of letters and numbers, which can be 'friendlier' for a user to remember. UDC follows DDC with a basically decimal arrangement, but nowadays incorporates some special devices to escape from the 'rule of 9' straightjacket. UDC class marks also use punctuation marks to allow for synthesis. Thus the notation 649.1:616.28-008.13/.14-053.2 represents domestic care for deaf and hard-hearing children (Riesthuis, 1998). It is built up from:

649.1	Domestic childcare
616.28	Ears. Otology
-008.13	Distorted hearing
-008.14	Deafness
-053.2	Children

The facility for synthesis is admirable, but the penalty is a class mark so complex that shelving books in the right sequence becomes a new intellectual challenge.

The synthetic class marks generated with faceted classification schemes can look equally off-putting to the unfamiliar user, and any long string of characters fails the test of memorability – an essential characteristic if a user is to carry the mark in his head all the way to the shelves. To assist memorability (at the risk of some loss of expressiveness) the sequence of headings in BC2 is carefully arranged so that redundant characters can be omitted from the corresponding notation, making it exceptionally short.

But move from the traditional library to an electronic collection and there is light at the end of the notation tunnel. Pollitt (1998) has pointed out that, 'The need to maintain a single relative position on a bookshelf is the major source of complexity in classification.' He goes on to say, 'If we remove the need to produce a notation to act as a relative location for a book we can work on the idea of retaining the original multi-dimensional universe of knowledge and use a faceted classification-based interface to manipulate it.' The electronic medium brings liberation from notation (Svenonius, 1988). Provided entries are placed in the right relative position, correctly indented with respect to entries for broader concepts, users do not need to see a class mark (unless they choose to). Optionally, class marks can still be present behind the scenes. In some systems the computer will generate its own housekeeping notation, useful for driving the sequence of outputs; but the user should not be obliged to memorise or key in one of those notoriously unmemorable strings of characters.

A further benefit of the electronic medium is the ease of accommodating new subjects. Provided that users are not required to use or remember class marks, the marks do not need to be stable. The notation can ignore the need for hospitality and the whole collection can be renumbered automatically every time it is updated. For an example, see the notation used in hierarchical displays of the *Art & Architecture Thesaurus* (1994).

Navigation via an index

Finding things in a large classified collection can sometimes be done by starting top-down through the schedules and/or following the class codes, but users very often think first of *words* to describe the subject they want. An index is needed to convert those words to the corresponding class code(s), which may then be used to locate relevant documents. In some systems, headings in the index point directly to the documents, saving users any difficulty in manipulating class codes that can be cumbersome and easy to forget.

To provide for the multiplicity of ways a subject can be expressed, a comprehensive index can be longer than the schedules themselves. In the first edition of the DDC, for example, there were 18 pages of 'Relativ Index' to accompany 12 of tables (Berwick Sayers, 1962), and now at the turn of the millennium, the addition of yet more index entries is one of the activities being undertaken to fit Dewey for the Web (Mitchell and Vizine-Goetz, 2000). LC schedules have individual indexes, but the scheme as a whole is unusual in not having an overall index. A trial merger of the schedule indexes showed up too many inconsistencies and incompatibilities, traceable right back to the foundations of the scheme (Chan and Hodges, 2000). The existence of the *LCSH* (*Library of Congress Subject Headings*), which lists all of the headings in the LC together with subheadings and a number of *See / See also* entries, is another factor reducing the need for a full index. The development of a general index remains an aspiration, but not an immediate prospect.

Riesthuis and Bliedung (1991) describe taking an index a step further, in the 'Thesaurification of the UDC'. Their project, for just one UDC schedule, 'translated' each class into one or more preferred terms or non-preferred terms. The idea was to develop an information language that could be used both as a classification and as a search tool. Whether or not this idea proves generally popular, it reflects a general trend of complementarity and convergence between classification schemes and thesauri. We shall see this trend reappear, following our discussion of thesauri.

Continuing development

Even before we choose and implement a classification scheme we must have an eye to the future, for our needs will not stand still. Technology changes, user interests change, expectations change, and the whole environment in which our chosen scheme is to function will change. The most obvious need is for updating the schedules. Major schemes, such as DDC (Mitchell, 2000) and LC (Chan and Hodges, 2000), benefit from well-resourced agencies with vigorous maintenance programmes. The slow but immaculate process of revising BC2 has already been described. CC, widely used in India, is maintained by the Documentation Research and Training Institute (Foskett, 2000). The UDC Consortium, with its scarce financial resources, has a struggle to issue timely revisions. Even so, as McIlwaine (2000) recounts, updates are not popular with all users. Adoption of changes creates substantial work for an established library and makes it hard or impossible to retrieve earlier classified materials. A responsible maintenance policy has to find the right compromise between stability and dynamism.

There is, however, more to the future than just revising the schedules. Increasingly, classification systems are having to adapt to the needs of networked users and resources. Some of the demands and trends already in evidence include:

- electronic versions (e.g. *Dewey for Windows* (Mitchell, 2000)) to support cataloguing efficiency
- electronic versions built into search interfaces
- customisability of interface, presentation and language
- cross-mapping from one scheme to others
- provision of multiple access routes, including multiple class headings for one document.

Special schemes

So which classification scheme to choose? If any? One of the big general schemes mentioned above, or one of the many existing special schemes? All the candidate schemes need to be assessed under the headings discussed above and probably other requirements specific to the application.

There is much to be said for choosing an existing scheme that is:

- widely used, and thus familiar to some of one's own users
- ready-made, obviating the huge work of building one' own classification
- at least moderately well adapted to one's own subject area
- supported by a maintenance agency to keep it up to date
- supported by electronic tools to improve cataloguing and searching efficiency / effectiveness.

On the other hand, none of the ready-made schemes ever reflect exactly what an information manager would ideally like for a specific collection. One option is to adopt and adapt parts of an existing scheme. Another is to develop one's own scheme; some of the arguments (and techniques) for this are set out by Vickery (1960).

Today's electronic environment adds an additional dimension. There is a huge demand for delivering information electronically to the user's desktop, presented within a frame of reference adapted for his working needs. Typically within a large organisation different functional groups of users (e.g. marketing, research, finance) require very different styles of presentation. Typically also, users want things to look simple. So there may be a case for developing a rather simple classification, perhaps just two or three levels deep, and customisable for different user groups. More will be said later in this chapter about developing a 'taxonomy' for intranet use.

If a special scheme is to be developed, whether big or small, faceted classification copes well with interdisciplinary subjects and appears to be particularly well suited to application in the electronic medium (Svenonius, 1988; Foskett, 2000; Broughton, 2000). But with the exception of Pollitt's view-based searching software (1998; 2000), remarkably few examples may be found of search interfaces designed to exploit the power of facets. Scope here for some imaginative developments!

Indexing and controlled vocabularies

Pre- and post-coordinate indexes

An index offers an approach to subjects going straight to the specific concept, rather than navigating top-down. Many printed indexes are pre-coordinate, that is, their index entries combine more than one concept in an articulated string, such as 'Lampshades, design' or 'Drying, simulation models, tobacco'. Some library catalogues present pre-coordinated strings of headings, often drawn from a list of subject headings such as *LCSH*. Such lists usually show the 'subheadings' which may be attached to a given heading. Some printed indexes have elaborate structures of headings and subheadings, designed to bring like subjects together and to let the user discriminate between similar topics. Figure 1 shows a brief example.

Figure 1: Brief extract from a pre-coordinate index

Rice
aflatoxins, contamination *425*
composition
fats *302*
polysaccharides *303*
cultivars
storage life *153, 154*
storage quality *157*
stored products pests *291*

Items in a collection of research literature can often merit 10 or more index terms or phrases. Few pre-coordinate indexes list more than four or five terms in any entry and few seek to present all the possible permutations of any four terms selected from the 10 (or so). Otherwise the index could get very long indeed, and many of the combinations would fail to reflect appropriate concept groupings. The printed indexes of serial publications such as abstracting journals are typically produced by teams of indexers, with a set of house-rules to ensure consistency. Design of the index should take into account the order in which terms should be presented and strings conflated, to ensure intelligible entries under all useful access points, without inordinate length. Some producers have devised systems that will generate the desired index entries automatically from rather complex coded strings entered by the indexers. The most sophisticated system to be widely adopted was PRECIS (PREserved Context Index System), developed by Derek Austin (1984) and used for two decades in the printed *British National Bibliography*. This and other pre-coordinate systems are described in Lancaster (1998) and Wellisch (1995).

The permuted index is a much cheaper alternative. The first and simplest (Wellisch, 1995) was the KWIC (KeyWord In Context) index, invented by Luhn in 1958, based on titles and providing an entry point at every significant word in the title. A brief extract from a KWIC index is shown in Figure 2.

In response to perceived problems with the KWIC index, (e.g. arbitrary truncation at the end of the line; stopwords which are sometimes significant; the difficulty of reading wrapped-around titles) variants were soon developed, notably KWOC (KeyWord Out of Context) and KWAC (KeyWord And Context) indexes. All are cheap to produce, but all suffer from the same problem – only *words* are being indexed, not concepts or subjects.

Figure 2: Extract from a KWIC index of journal titles

Acta	Anatomica.
Anatomical	Record.
Journal of	Anatomical Sciences.
	Anatomy.
Annals of	Anatomy.
Clinical	Anatomy.
Journal of	Anatomy.
Surgical and Radiologic	Anatomy.
of Surgical and Remedial	Anatomy.
Journal	Anatomy and Embryology

Computer-produced indexes have by no means supplanted the traditional intellectually prepared pre-coordinate index, still the favourite for the back of a book. BS ISO 999 (1996) provides guidance on the organisation and presentation of such indexes. In the British Isles, the Society of Indexers keeps the art of indexing very much alive with a web site, training courses and materials.

For many applications, however, pre-coordination is an unacceptable limitation. Predicting all the concept combinations that a user might want to search for is difficult. The alternative is a post-coordinate system, in which any number of index terms may be assigned to an item, in no particular sequence. Co-ordination occurs only at the time of retrieval, when any combination of index terms may be sought.

Before computers became widely available, post-coordinate systems were implemented using 'feature cards'. Typically, there was a card for each allowed index term. On the card was printed a grid with up to 10,000 positions. When document 1234 was entered, all the cards for index terms assigned to that document were withdrawn from the pack and a hole was punched in position 1234. Later, when searching, you could pick out the cards for any desired combination of concepts. When you held them together up to the light, a hole would show through for each document combining all the concepts. Simple but effective. The same principle is used nowadays when we search inverted computer files using the Boolean 'And'.

Aims of vocabulary control

All subject indexes, pre- or post-coordinate, suffer from a huge problem: the difficulty of matching words reliably with concepts. One word can have a multiplicity of meanings; one concept can be expressed using a variety of words or word combinations. A searcher looking for 'wood' combined with 'knots' will not immediately find items indexed with 'timber' and 'defects'. And the items he does find may include some concerning the knots in cord for tying wooden slats. Pre-coordinate indexes address the problem by inserting *See / See also* references, which direct the reader to the entries he should consult instead of, or as well as (respectively), the term he or she first thought of. Even greater consistency can be achieved by adopting a controlled vocabulary.

The aim of vocabulary control is to guide indexers and searchers to use the same terms or term combinations for describing the same concepts. The very simplest form of controlled vocabulary is a straightforward list of all the terms (single words or multi-word phrases) which are allowed for indexing. But how do you find a wanted concept if the list is longer than a few pages? Look under 'Wood' and the term 'Timber' may be too far away to spot. We have already noted the *See / See also* entries used by

Subject Headings lists, which are controlled vocabularies for choosing pre-coordinated headings. Controlled vocabularies for post-coordinate systems are usually called thesauri, and these should provide more extensive guidance.

As well as listing all the 'preferred terms' which are allowed for use in indexing, a thesaurus provides lead-in entries from corresponding 'non-preferred terms'. That is to say, it directs the user from the term(s) he or she first thought of to those used in indexing. Furthermore, it alerts the user to additional terms, either broader than, or narrower than, or otherwise related to, the first terms identified. The links pointing to other terms can be used as an elaborate semantic network, allowing the user to navigate through the terminology in the system. Term linkages come in three main types (Dextre Clarke, 2001): equivalence relationships (USE/ Use For, linking preferred and non-preferred terms) hierarchical relationships (between Broader and Narrower Terms) and associative relationships (linking one Related Term to another).

In the early days of manual retrieval systems, one of the objects of controlling vocabulary was to limit the number of preferred terms and corresponding cards to manageable numbers. Nowadays computerised systems can cope with more extensive vocabularies. Some thesauri have 100,000 terms or more, although any number above about 10,000 may be considered large.

Styles of thesaurus

The word 'thesaurus' has been used (Roberts, 1984) since long before 1852, when the first edition of Roget's famous work was published. He and his fore-runners used the word (derived from the Greek, meaning 'treasure-house') for a semantic map which laid out words and phrases in a conceptual framework, as a source of inspiration for writers seeking just the right phraseology for their ideas. He was not thinking of controlling vocabulary; rather of expanding it! Only in the 1950s did researchers begin to apply the word to vocabulary lists for information retrieval systems. At about this time Mortimer Taube developed the famous 'Uniterm' system of feature cards with a controlled vocabulary of single-word terms (Lancaster, 1986). 1959 saw the completion of the first fully operational thesaurus, for information retrieval in the Dupont company (Roberts, 1984; Krooks and Lancaster, 1993). In those experimental days, quite a few different types of vocabulary resource were confusingly given the name 'thesaurus'. The thesaurus of the Engineers Joint Council published in 1964 (and later revised to become the 1974 *Thesaurus of Engineering and Scientific Terms* (1967) published by the US Department of Defense) profoundly influenced the layout of subsequent thesauri. Another milestone was the English Electric Company's 1969 *Thesaurofacet* (Aitchison, et al.,

1969) showing how an alphabetical thesaurus could be derived from and integrated with a faceted classification. In 1974 official standardisation of thesauri began, with the first edition of ISO 2788, 'Guidelines for the establishment and development of monolingual thesauri'.

The current edition of ISO 2788 (1986) was published in 1986. It has been adopted as a national standard in several countries, including Britain, France and Germany. ISO 5964 (1985) is a sister publication, for multilingual thesauri. The United States has its own national standard, ANSI 39-19 (National Information Standards Organization, 1993), rather more prescriptive than ISO 2788 but entirely compatible with it. The standards give advice on the form of terms, the relationships that should be shown between the terms and the way terms and relationships should be displayed. They are intended principally for the controlled vocabularies of post-coordinate information retrieval systems, although other applications are not excluded.

Standardisation has not brought uniformity. A taster of the immense variety among the thousands of thesauri in use today is illustrated in Figure 3, showing some corresponding entries in the alphabetical sections of five widely used and respected thesauri.

In limiting itself to the alphabetical displays, Figure 3 shows only the tip of the varietal iceberg. Good thesauri commonly supplement the printed alphabetical display with any or all of the following:

- a systematic or hierarchical display
- a permuted index (KWIC or KWOC)
- graphical displays.

In addition to the printed thesaurus, an electronic version is nowadays indispensable, and this may not correspond exactly to any of the printed formats. Availability of a searchable electronic thesaurus should incidentally remove the need for a printed permuted index.

The key to evaluating a candidate thesaurus lies in study of its systematic display, for without this the relationships shown in other sections are unlikely to be complete and consistent. When preparing the entry for one term in an alphabetical sequence among thousands of others, how could the thesaurus compiler possibly bear in mind all the other terms with which relationships should be established, if he cannot view them in a subject-systematic sequence?

Thesaurofacet in 1969 was just the first in a lineage of thesauri that demonstrate the systematic techniques progressively developed by its editor and compiler Jean Aitchison. Figures 4 and 5 show two pages from the first edition (1981) of the English version of the *BSI ROOT Thesaurus*, which was compiled under her guidance. Relationships are shown by means of

Figure 3: Sample entries from five well-known thesauri

Source: Macrothesaurus (OECD, 1985)	Source: Thesaurus of ERIC Descriptors (Houston, 1995)
AUDIOVISUAL AIDS **MOYENS AUDIOVISUELS / MEDIOS** **AUDIOVISUALES - 06.05.03** *FILMS, TAPE RECORDINGS, POSTERS, CHARTS, BROADCASTS, ETC. USED FOR TEACHING AND RESEARCH* *TT:* EQUIPMENT *BT:* TEACHING AIDS *NT:* EDUCATIONAL FILMS EDUCATIONAL RADIO EDUCATIONAL TELEVISION *RT:* AUDIOVISUAL MATERIALS	**AUDIOVISUAL AIDS** *Jul. 1966* CIJE: 3167 RIE: 3955 GC: 720 SN Nonprint instructional materials and the equipment required for their display (note: prior to mar80, the instruction 'nonprint media, use audiovisual aids' was carried in the thesaurus – corresponds to pubtype code 100 – do not use except as the subject of a document) UF Audiovisual Equipment Audiovisual Materials Audiovisual Media

****

Source: CAB Thesaurus (Wightman, 1999)
 	
 audiovisual aids
 CU00007
 uf   *audiovisual equipment; instructional media; visual aids; audiotapes*
 BT   equipment
 rt   communication
       extension
       films
       radio
       tape recorders
       teaching
       television
	NT Instructional Films
	      Protocol Materials
	 BT Educational Media
	 RT Audio Equipment
	      Audiodisks
	      Audiotape Recorders
	      Audiotape Recordings
	      Audiovisual Centers
	      Audiovisual Communication
	      Audiovisual Coordinators
	      Audiovisual Instruction
	      Autoinstructional Aids
	      Bulletin Boards
	      Cartoons
	      Chalkboards
	      Courseware
	      Display Aids

****

Source: INSPEC Thesaurus (1995)
 	
 audio-visual aids
 USE audio-visual systems
 	
 audio-visual systems
   UF   audio-visual aids
   RT   audio systems
        educational aids
        interactive video
        technical presentation
   CC   B6430; B6450; D2020
   DI   January 1989
   PT   audio systems
        television systems
	Documentaries
	      Educational Equipment
	      Educational Technology
	      Electromechanical Aids
	      Electronic Equipment
	      Filmstrips
	      Instructional Materials
	      Learning Resources Centers
	      Mass Media
	      Microphones
	      Multimedia Materials
	      Nonprint Media
	      Optical Disks
	      Photographic Equipment
	      Photographs
	      Programmed Instructional Materials
	      Projection Equipment

****

Source: BSI ROOT Thesaurus (1985)
 	
 Audiovisual aids
   →   Audiovisual materials LBQ.B
 	
 Audiovisual materials LBQ.B
   =   Audiovisual aids
   <   Non-book materials
   *<   Teaching aids ZBL.L
   *>   Films (cinema) ZWW.CWW
   *-   Recording media LNC
	Screens (Displays)
	      Sensory Aids
	      Slides
	      Talking Books
	      Three Dimensional Aids
	      Transparencies
	      Video Equipment
	      Videodisks
	      Videotape Recorders
	      Videotape Recordings
	      Visual Aids

language-independent symbols (see figure 6) instead of abbreviations, since the thesaurus is multilingual. Figure 4 is an extract from the Hierarchical Display, a sort of master classification of terms which drives the whole thesaurus. While working on the hierarchies, the editor builds in equivalence and associative relationships as well as the hierarchical ones. Scope notes are developed at the same time. Facet analysis is used to organise the sequence of terms in the hierarchies. Since the thesaurus is designed for post-coordinate indexing, a consistent 'preferred order' of facets is not so important as it would be in a classification intended for pre-coordinate class codes and shelf arrangement. When all the intellectual work is complete, the entries for the alphabetical section may be derived automatically from the hierarchical master database (Dextre and Clarke, 1981). The entries for 'Insulated cables' and 'Insulated wires' in Figures 4 and 5 show the dependence of the Alphabetical List on the Hierarchical Display section of the Thesaurus.

Figure 4: Extract from the *BSI ROOT Thesaurus (1981) – Hierarchical Display

K	**Electrotechnology**

KB/KO	**Electrical engineering** (continued)
KN	**Electrical components** (continued)
KNN	**Electric conductors** (continued)
KNN.L	Electric wires (continued)
	(By insulation)
KNN.LB	Non-insulated wires
KNN.LC	Insulated wires
	= Insulated conductors
	* – Electrical insulating materials KNY
KNN.LCC	Textile-covered wires
KNN.LCH	Enamelled wires
KNN.LCM	Sheathed conductors
	= Metal-sheathed conductors
KNN.N	Electric cables
	[A collection of wires]
	= Cables (electric)
	* > Floor-warming cables NES.T
	* – Bus-bars KNN.B
	* – Cable junctions KNV
	* – Cable laying RXC.K
	* – Communication transmission lines LLP.D
	* – Electric cable systems KNN.P
	* – Electric power transmission lines KDS.J
	(By property)
KNN.NC	Flexible cables
	= Flexible wires
KNN.NE	Rigid cables
	= Non-flexible cables
	(By construction)
KNN.NG	Single-core cables
	* – Cable cores KNN.NW
KNN.NH	Multicore cables
	* – Cable cores KNN.NW
KNN.NK	Coaxial cables
	* – Communication cables KNN.NS
	* – Telephone lines LLG.NC
	* – Waveguides LLP.K
	(By insulation)
KNN.NM	Insulated cables
	* – Electrical insulating materials KNY
	(By material)
	[Synthesize, for example]
KNN.NMH	* * Polyvinyl-chloride-insulated cables
	—Insulated cables
	+ Polyvinyl chloride
KNN.NMI	Sheathed cables
	= Metal-sheathed cables
KNN.NMP	Mineral-insulated cables
	* – Fire-resistant materials TLN
	* – Non-flammable materials TLT

Figure 5: Extract from the *BSI ROOT Thesaurus (1981) – Alphabetical List

•<   Personnel   YNC

Installation   AUN
=   Installing
<   Common terms

Installing
→   Installation   AUN

Instant coffee
→   Coffee   IHD.D

Instant foods   IGG.RG
<   Convenience foods

Instantaneous water heaters   NCD.RF
=   Flow heaters
<   Water heaters

Institutional facilities   RBD.D
<   Construction works
•–   Health and welfare facilities   RBD.H
•–   Residential facilities   RBD.N

Instruction
→   Teaching   ZBH

Instruction control units
→   Computer control units   MPF.M

Instruction handbooks
→   Handbooks   LBM.H

Instructions (computers)
→   Programming instructions   MVS.TM

Instructions for use   YWS.EN
–   Consumer-supplier relations
•–   Care labelling   LBH.MGL
•–   Handbooks   LBM.H

Instrument cases   BZS
–   Instruments
•<   Cases   QSM
•<   Cases   QSM

Instrument jewels   BCD.D
–   Measuring instruments
•<   Precious stones   DNN

Instrument scales   BCC.B
=   Scales (measuring instruments)
–   Measuring instruments

Instrument shunts   KNJ.T
=   Shunts (instruments)
<   Resistors
>   Precision resistors
•–   Ammeters   BJG.GJ

Instrument transformers   KGP.M
<   Transformers
>   Current transformers
>   Potential transformers

Instrumental methods of analysis   BWB/BWI
<   Chemical analysis and testing
>   Spectroscopy
•>   Mass spectrometry   BJP
•–   Instruments   BZ
•–   Laboratory equipment   BP
•–   Measuring instruments   BCB/BCD

Instrumentation
→   Instruments   BZ

Instrumentation recording   BZB.R
–   Instruments
•–   Analogue recording methods   LNF.L
•–   Data recording   LNF.H
•–   Recording instruments
       (measurement)   BCB.K
•–   Recording paper   WFL.P

Instruments   BZ
=   Instrumentation
>   Gamma-ray apparatus
>   Optical instruments
>   X-ray apparatus
–   Instrument cases
–   Instrumentation recording
•>   Measuring instruments   BCB/BCD
•>   Medical instruments   FF
•–   Instrumental methods of
       analysis   BWB/BWI

Insulated cables   KNN.NM
<   Electric cables
>   Mineral-insulated cables
>   Sheathed cables
•–   Electrical insulating materials   KNY

Insulated cables
+   Polyvinyl chloride
=••   Polyvinyl-chloride-insulated
        cables   KNN.NMH

Insulated conductors
→   Insulated wires   KNN.LC

Insulated wires   KNN.LC
=   Insulated conductors
<   Electric wires
>   Enamelled wires
>   Sheathed conductors
>   Textile-covered wires
•–   Electrical insulating materials   KNY

Insulating boards   WDJ.FJ
<   Fibre building board
•<   Acoustic insulating materials   NMR.NMR
•<   Thermal insulating materials   NEV.E

Insulating coatings   KNY.E
<   Electrical insulating materials
•<   Coatings   VT

Insulating enclosures   KNX.CC
<   Electric enclosures

Figure 6: Key to symbols from the *BSI ROOT Thesaurus

6   Key to symbols

Symbol	Meaning
<	Broader term
>	Narrower term
−	Related term
*<	Broader term in an alternative hierarchy
*>	Narrower term in an alternative hierarchy
*−	Related term in an alternative hierarchy
=	Non-preferred synonym or quasi-synonym
	Use. (The term or combination of terms following the arrow should be used instead of the term preceding it)
+	This symbol appears between terms which are used to synthesize a given concept
**	Synthesized term. (The term which follows the symbol is a non-descriptor which should be represented by a combination of terms, as indicated)
=**	The term (a non-descriptor) following the symbol should be represented by the combination of descriptors preceding it
[. . . . .]	Scope note or instructional note. This clarifies the meaning of a term in the context of the thesaurus or gives guidance on the use of a term
(By . . . . .)	Facet indicator. This is a device used in the subject display section to group together terms having a common characteristic

Space does not allow us to illustrate or even describe the diversity of styles and formats of other thesauri available today. The 1993 Eurobrokers EU Thesaurus Guide (1993) lists more than 600, and Aslib has a large thesaurus collection in its library. The University of Toronto maintains a North American Clearinghouse of classification schemes, subject heading lists and thesauri, comprising over 2,500 titles. At least two directories (Koch; Lutes) of electronic thesauri are currently available on the Web.

Choosing a thesaurus

Why all this variety? Would retrieval not be much easier for the user if every system used the same indexing language with the same conventions and style of display? There is always a huge pressure on information providers to adopt common standards, especially a common thesaurus. Efforts have been made by some international bodies such as UNESCO and the OECD, to provide vocabularies of worldwide applicability. The aim of the OECD's *Macrothesaurus* (1998), first published in 1972 and still actively maintained, was to 'create a documentary language for processing information in the broad field of economic and social development, while striving for compatibility with sectoral thesauri serving agriculture, industry, labour, education, population, science, technology, culture, communication, health and the environment'.

The pressure to standardise, however, is often outweighed by the pressures to improve performance and differentiate – adapting the vocabulary to the needs of a specific collection and its user base. The factors that have led to publication of hundreds of different thesauri are the same ones that a manager will bear in mind when evaluating thesauri for a specific application:

- *Level of specificity*. For a specialised collection, much greater specificity is required in order to discriminate among perhaps hundreds of articles on an aspect that would be considered very minor in another collection. Conversely, for a broad-based collection, the availability of too many specialised terms in the vocabulary confusingly multiplies the search options that have to be explored for any one query.

- *Terminological usages*. Move from one subject field to another, and many terms take on completely different meanings. Subject experts among the users do not take kindly to terms with the 'wrong' meaning. The narrower the scope of a thesaurus, the easier it is to avoid ambiguity in assigning terms to concepts.

- *Language*. A multilingual tool may be needed if the information system serves users in several countries.

- *Historical factors*. However much an information provider may wish to adopt a standard vocabulary, he or she may be tied to a large archival collection indexed some other way. The current thesaurus must provide access to older as well as new documents entering the system.

- *Integration factors*. Gone are the days of systems working in isolation. On the searching side, users want tools that will allow them to select and apply search terms with a minimum of mouse clicks. The thesaurus must integrate with the database(s) to be searched, or else be invisible (Milstead, 1995), invoked automatically by the user's query. Efficiency is vital for indexing/cataloguing too; while preparing catalogue records or tagging an input document with metadata, the indexer needs to be able to call up the thesaurus, navigate rapidly to the right term(s), click on them and see them instantaneously copied to the right index field.

If scrutiny of the available thesauri does not reveal one ideal for the application in hand, it will still provide copious raw materials. The construction of a new thesaurus is enormously eased by borrowing ideas and even large sections of hierarchy from existing vocabularies, including classification schemes (subject to respecting copyright, of course!). Practical advice on construction techniques is available in several guides (Aitchison, et al., 1997; Batty, 1989; Miller, 1997) and training courses, and of course the standards (ISO 2788 – 1986; ISO 5964 – 1985; ANSI / NISO Z39.19 – 1993).

Convergence?

We referred earlier to the growing trend of giving classification schemes thesaurus-like features. Conversely, many thesauri look rather like classifications, as we saw with the *BSI ROOT Thesaurus*. Subject heading lists, which are designed mostly for selecting pre-coordinate entries in library catalogues, tend to be somewhere in between. For example, *LCSH* was derived initially from the LCC, but its most recent edition shows Broader Terms (BTs), Narrower Terms (NTs) and Related Terms (RTs), almost in the style of a thesaurus. Although its title suggests otherwise and its alphabetical list does not explicitly show BTs, NTs or RTs, *MeSH (Medical Subject Headings)*, is usually considered a thesaurus rather than a subject headings list. Weinberg's 1995 comparison of classifications and thesauri concludes that the distinction is likely to blur in future. Despite the blurring, we can still note some differences in the outcomes of using these tools. Keyword indexes are very helpful for going straight to specific, known concepts. Pre-coordination of keywords is vital in printed search tools; post-coordination is more powerful with computer-assisted searching. For the fuzzy concept or the serendipitous find, a classified arrangement of documents is much more supportive of browsing. There seems no doubt that, when building tools to support an increasing variety of information retrieval (IR) tasks, we have to be prepared to pool what we have learned from the separate indexing and classification schools of thought. The evolving tools will combine elements of both in highly integrated systems.

Controlled vocabulary *v* free-text searching

As noted above, the reason for using a controlled vocabulary is to match terms unambiguously with concepts. A searcher does not then have to think of all the different ways the concept he seeks may have been expressed in source literature, and he does not retrieve a welter of documents using his terms to mean different things. That is the hope, anyway. And does the method work?

Between 1959 and 1964 the Aslib-Cranfield Research Project (Cleverdon and Mills, 1963; Cleverdon et al., 1966; Cleverdon, 1967), under the direction of Cyril Cleverdon and Jack Mills, ran a ground-breaking series of tests on 'indexing languages', including the UDC, a faceted classification, an alphabetical subject catalogue and the Uniterm system. The first round of tests showed little significant difference in performance between these four. One conclusion was that there were too many variables at play: each indexing language was its own amalgam of recall devices (designed to increase the number of relevant items retrieved) and precision devices (designed to decrease the number of irrelevant items retrieved). The objective of the second round of tests was to isolate some of these devices and analyse their effects on performance. This time the documents were indexed in three different ways:

- key concepts, humanly selected and recorded as phrases occurring naturally in abstracts of the documents
- those same concept phrases, separated into single natural language words
- main 'themes', derived by combining the concepts in various ways.

Variants of the above three were also developed by grouping synonyms and by confounding word forms. Controlled terms were applied, and again varied by such devices as including narrower terms, then broader terms, then related terms. Another set of variants was based on key words in titles and abstracts, with and without word forms confounded. Altogether there were 33 'different' index languages in the test. The results were compared over 221 queries applied to a test collection of 1,100 documents. Comparison and a final ranking of the 33 were obtained using a normalised recall ratio.

The broad conclusion, to most people's surprise, was that single natural language words did best, controlled term languages in the middle range, and natural language phrases the worst. The only devices that significantly improved on single words were the confounding of word forms and synonyms.

Argument has raged ever since. Perhaps the Cranfield setup was too far removed from operational reality; perhaps the controlled language was not as good as it might be, maybe the document abstracts bore little resemblance to full-text natural language, etc.; but proving which retrieval techniques and languages work best is not easy. There are just too many variables, starting with the subjectivity of the user. As Svenonius (1986) remarked, 'An experiment sophisticated and large enough to control all of the above variables [concerning effectiveness of controlled vocabularies] has never been conducted and probably never will.'

To this day our profession divides into two faiths: the believers and the unbelievers in systems of vocabulary control. In between are a great many experienced searchers (Henzler, 1978; Calkins, 1980; Dubois, 1984; Tenopir, 1985; Betts and Marrable, 1991; Milstead, 1994) who agree that *both* free-text and controlled index terms are needed. Different types of query benefit from a different mix of search techniques (Svenonius, 1986; Markey et al., 1982). As noted by Rowley (1994), their views are based as much on experience and case studies as on conclusive evidence. Figure 7, reprinted from Aitchison et al. (1997), sets out some of the pros and cons.

Figure 7: Comparison of natural and controlled language

Natural language	Controlled language
Stengths	*Weaknesses*
○ High specificity gives precision. Excels in retrieving 'individual' terms – names of persons, organizations, etc.	○ Relative lack of specificity, even in detailed systems.
○ Exhaustivity gives potential for high recall. Does not apply to title-only databases.	○ Lack of exhaustivity. Cost of indexing to level of natural language prohibitive. Also terms may be omitted in error by indexers.
○ Up-to-date. New terms immediately available.	○ Not immediately up-to-date. Time lag while terms are added to thesaurus.
○ Words of author used – no misinterpretation by indexer.	○ Words of author liable to be misconstrued. Errors in indexing terms can cause losses.
○ Natural language words and phrases used by searcher.	○ Artificial language has to be learned by the searcher.
	○ High input costs.
○ Low input costs.	○ Incompatibility a barrier to easy exchange.
○ Easier exchange of material between databases – language imcompatibility removed.	
	Strengths
Weaknesses	○ Eases the burden of searching:
○ Intellectual effort placed on searcher. Problems arise with terms having many synonyms and several species.	- controls synonyms and near-synonyms and leads specific natural language concepts to the nearest preferred terms to broaden search
	- qualifies homographs
○ Syntax problems. Danger of false drops through incorrect term association.	- provides scope notes
○ Exhaustivity may lead to loss of precision.	- displays broader, narrower and related terms
	- expresses concepts elusive in free text.
	○ Overcomes syntax problems with compound terms and other devices.
	○ At normal levels of indexing, avoids precision loss through over-exhaustivity (i.e. retrieval of minor concepts of peripheral interest).
	○ An asset in numerical databases and multilingual systems.

Both natural and controlled language systems offer the same powerful search aids – truncation, word proximity, etc.

The free-text world

Full-text electronic resources have been around for decades, either as in-house databases or as commercially available products. The earlier ones were often bibliographic databases, in which the text was not really 'full', consisting only of titles, citations and usually abstracts. Then followed products such as the *Federal Register*, with the full text of US government regulations. The early generation were orderly in comparison with the flood of resources washing around us today. Now that almost all working documents are originated in machine-readable form, the entire documented resources of an organisation can easily be loaded on a network and made accessible to all staff. The Internet provides them with an additional, unimaginably vast resource pool. Information right at their fingertips – if they can find it, that is.

The aspiration of the last 50 years of text retrieval research is to be able to extract from any free-text corpus the information relevant to a user's need, by entirely automatic processes. The benefit is not just the potential saving in costs of human processing. A fundamental objection to human classification/indexing is that all future retrieval attempts will be constrained by the indexer's judgement at the time of input. The indexer has to select the key concepts, and has to express them in the available indexing language. But different users, and especially the users five or ten years on, could have very different views of what is important and how it should be expressed. Automatic methods could potentially overcome this problem (Luhn, 1961).

A 1997 anthology from Sparck Jones and Willett (1997) presents classic papers charting the progress of probabilistic indexing (Maron and Kuhns, 1960; Robertson and Walker, 1994; Vechtomova and Robertson, 2000), vector space modelling, syntactic analysis and other key developments. Some of the results, for example Porter's algorithm for suffix-stripping (1980), have been widely adopted in commercially available search software. Others are generating still more research papers (*Proceedings of the BCS-IRSG*, 2000). No doubt automatic retrieval solutions will continue to benefit from the research, but perfection is still a long way off, and meantime, managers must find some way of extracting information from vast amounts of disorderly free text.

When weighing up the merits of free-text searching, we have to remember that much of the early research was conducted in the environment of relatively well-structured sources, in which there was at least some uniformity of document format. Sometimes document abstracts were treated as though they were full text. The Internet is a much less sheltered environment. On a good day, one distinctive keyword can lead straight to the few relevant documents on the World Wide Web. But other searches can be much less fruitful, as every Web user knows (Bates, 1998). With in-house networks, information managers frequently hear the cry of 'Help! – We can't find anything on the intranet.' What options are available?

The search thesaurus

One option is to give the user more search tools, in particular a 'search thesaurus' (Piternick, 1984; Gillman, 1997; Johnson and Cochrane, 1997). This is not a controlled vocabulary but aims to provide inspiration as to the many ways a given concept may be expressed in a mixture of source literature. Figure 8 shows an excerpt from Sara Knapp's *Contemporary Thesaurus of Social Science Terms and Synonyms* (Knapp, 1993), one of very few published search thesauri. Notice that it does not and need not conform to ISO 2788, since the whole context of vocabulary control is absent. The search thesaurus has in common with *Roget's Thesaurus* the aim of providing inspiration, not control. The example illustrated differs from *Roget* in that entries are listed in alphabetical order only. But there is no reason why a systematic layout could not be devised.

Figure 8: Sample excerpt from a search thesaurus

Attitudes, work. See *Attitudes toward work; Employee attitudes.*

Attitudes, worker. See *Employee attitudes.*

Attitudes toward aging. See *Age discrimination, Attitudes toward the aged.*

Attitudes toward computers. Attitude(s) to(ward) computer(s). *Choose from:* attitude(s), bias(es), preference(s), reject(ed,ion,ing), resist(ed,ing,ance), accept(ed,ing,ance), opinion(s), belief(s), fear(s), reaction(s), expectation(s) *with:* computer(s, ized,ization), microcomputer(s), automation. *See also* Attitudes, Computer anxiety, Computer illiteracy, Computer literacy.

Lykke Nielsen (1998) describes a very different style of search thesaurus, intended for use with a mix of internal and external databases. One electronic vocabulary resource already available on the Internet is the Princeton WordNet, not designed specifically for information retrieval but still potentially useful. The Plumb Design site (1998) shows one imaginative way of implementing the WordNet so as to give users inspiration for possible search terms. Many other thesauri (Koch; Lutes) are now becoming available on the Internet. Most of them are structured (more or less!) in line with ISO 2788, so not specially adapted to the uncontrolled environment. What these stand-alone thesauri lack is integration with the resources to be searched. Some of them have good browse software, so navigation via the relationships is easy. But few of them let you select more than one term at a time, and the process of building up a complex search statement, with the syntax needed for a particular set of resources, is unsupported.

Powerful search facilities

A second option, which can be combined with the first, is to improve the software. The early breeds of search software were much criticised for being limited to 'exact match' techniques. With only the Boolean operators AND, OR and NOT, either a document matches the search criteria or it does not; all matching documents have equal rank among the results. In response, packages like STATUS introduced weighting techniques, so that the documents retrieved could be presented in ranked order. The need for presenting the 'best' or 'most relevant' documents first has become all the more pressing in the age where a Web search can retrieve 50,000 hits or more, and there is a huge demand for precision devices of all kinds.

Some of the operators and other devices now commonly available in full-text search software include:

- ACCRUE. This is a sort of hybrid between AND and OR, backed by an algorithm which counts the number of occurrences of terms in the retrieved documents, in order to rank them. If the search statement includes, say, five terms to be ACCRUEd, then those with all five rank highest; those with four next and so on. Multiple occurrences of the same term contribute in a lesser way to the ranking, and the density of occurrences within the document (a factor to compensate for the variable length of documents) may also be taken into account.

- Proximity operators. These allow the searcher to specify how close to each other the search terms must occur, e.g. separated by up to 10 other words, or both in the same sentence, etc.

- Phrase searching. This is an extreme case of the proximity operator, in which the search terms must occur adjacent to each other, in the given order.

- CASE. This operator can be used to specify the occurrence of upper and / or lower case characters among the search terms.

- STEM. This operator automatically stems the search terms entered, and also the terms found in documents, so that all variants will be retrieved, e.g. 'walks' retrieves walk, walking, walked, etc.

- WILDCARD. A character such as * or ? is used to represent one or more characters, e.g. 'ioni?ation' retrieves ionisation and / or ionization; 'resist*' retrieves any word beginning with the stem given.

- Field limitation. The search may be limited to a particular sector of the metadata applied to the document, such as the document title, or the URL.

The above facilities include a mix of recall and precision devices, available with slightly different flavours and nuances in the various software packages available today. For the trained searcher they offer very powerful means of refining a search, especially in an interactive environment. But two important limitations apply. Firstly, it is hard to persuade users to learn and become fluent in use of the operators. Even when online help and / or personal training courses are available, the users who progress beyond single-term searches are still a minority. To some extent the problem may be addressed by designing an intuitive interface with pull-down menus, selection boxes and pre-set syntax, etc., but these features can also limit the capabilities of the syntax and operators. The second big limitation is that the occurrence of a term in full text says nothing about the significance of that term. It may or may not have the meaning the searcher wishes; it may be present as an exclusion ('.. this document will not address the question of XYZ'); it may appear as a minor mention rather than the main subject of the document, etc. None of the above substitute for the intellectual process of selecting the main concepts in a document and recording them, either as a class code or as a set of index terms.

Pre-established search strategies

Acknowledging that building a good search statement is a skill beyond the range of most end users, one approach may be to set up some standard searches for frequently wanted topics. Some software vendors, notably Verity, provide sophisticated facilities for building complex, structured families of searches called 'Topics' (Dextre Clarke, 2000). Verity's software includes all the operators mentioned above, and more. A trained information professional can use these to construct and test elaborate search statements in key business areas of the company. The Topics can be attuned to reflect the special meanings of buzz-words, abbreviations and so on that every large company develops inhouse. A user interface can present them on a pick-list, so that users can apply them with minimum effort. Even if the user wants something more specific than the pre-arranged Topic, he can AND the Topic with his more specific keyword and thus narrow his search to an area in which his keyword functions well.

Constructing the pre-arranged searches is a skilled job, and is sometimes compared with building a small-scale thesaurus. But the product is not a thesaurus in the ISO 2788 sense, or even in the Roget 'inspirational' sense. It is simply another type of search vocabulary tool to help users in the environment where vocabulary control is not available.

Categorisation of networked resources

We finally come to the classification option. The Internet portal Yahoo! has become, if not a household name, at least an office byword. Yahoo! subdivides the resources at its disposal, presenting them in 14 main categories, which in turn are subdivided into subcategories. The user still has to apply keywords like a fisherman casting a line, but at least he can fish within a smaller pool. The classification is said to be done by real human people, working rather hard to assign all the Web resources they find, to appropriate categories.

Not so most of the emulators of Yahoo! Since categorisation has proved so popular, the vendors of intranet software want to offer the same facility, but without needing human classifiers. The answer is automatic classification, which different vendors tackle in different ways. Some of them follow a pre-established classification, aiming to assign correct class codes or groups automatically to the incoming documents. Others examine the incoming documents to detect patterns or clusters, and define the output clusters according to what they have found.

Bright Station (previously known as Dialog) takes a rule-based approach, using its InfoSort technology. A rule-base is constructed for each wanted category. A particular rule-base looks for the frequency of occurrence of particular words, sometimes in combination with, or in proximity to, or not in combination with, other words. Sometimes a rule specifies the field in which the word must occur. The various criteria are weighted, and if enough of them are met, the incoming document is assigned to that category. Note that this gives a capability for multiple classification of one document. The rule-bases can be developed manually, or by providing the system with a set of correctly classified documents, analysis of which leads to inference of the required rule-bases.

Verity offers several different classification alternatives. The 'Topics', described above for use in direct searching, can equally be used as rule-bases for categorisation. In fact, their structure somewhat resembles the InfoSort rule-bases. The resulting categorisation can be applied to an incoming news feed, or for splitting up the results of a search query into clusters. Alternatively, automatic ad hoc clustering may be used. The retrieved documents are analysed and grouped according to the word patterns that emerge from those particular documents.

An extensive classification scheme underpins the Northern Light portal, comprising around 23,000 class 'nodes' or subject headings. Each node has specimen documents to represent the subject, and a classification query associated with it. Again, the words encountered are used to classify the vast majority of new documents, leaving only the problem cases to be resolved by staff. For intranets, Northern Light's public access classification scheme may be customised to meet specialised needs.

Design of classification schemes for networks

There is no doubting the popularity of categorisation schemes in network portals, but how well designed are they? Van der Walt (1998) has analysed the classification schemes of 10 popular Internet search engines / portals from the point of view of library classification theory, showing considerable room for improvement. Hudon (2000) finds similar inconsistencies in the knowledge organisation schemes of a number of virtual libraries on the Web. Some librarians are exploring the use of the established schemes such as LC for Internet resources (Cyberstacks). Others are developing their own schemes or taxonomies for inhouse use. Work is under way at OCLC Research to adapt the DDC for use as an Internet guide (Vizine-Goetz, 1998). In tandem with her criticisms of new schemes found on the Web, Hudon (2000) questions whether the traditional schemes have proved themselves as suitable for this medium.

Illuminating detail on the construction and implementation of an in-house scheme for the Weyerhaeuser Company is provided by Doran (1999). Despite having the use of a powerful search engine, company personnel were having difficulty finding things on their own intranet. Library managers opted for the principle of using metadata fields for tagging individual documents, rather than relying on automatic classification. This sounds like retrogression to the old days of library staff toiling to index and/or classify every document in a very large collection, and in effect it is, but with the difference that the authoring interface supports entry of the metadata by web page owners (in most cases not library staff) at the time of input. Drop-down pick-lists make it easy for authors to select terms from a controlled vocabulary. Since the subject metadata fields are mandatory, all new documents must acquire at least rudimentary indexing before they can be loaded on the intranet. The search interface makes it similarly easy to pick out controlled terms for searching.

In order to develop the controlled vocabulary, Weyerhaeuser Library staff were invited to suggest lists of terms. Interestingly, some contributed lists of headings and subheadings suitable for a classification or categorisation scheme; others suggested keywords more appropriate to thesaurus indexing. In the end, the project adopted both types. The scheme of category/subcategory pairs was implemented to make possible a Yahoo!-like browser; the thesaurus terms were intended for direct searching.

'Taxonomy' has become a fashionable word in the sales literature of the purveyors of knowledge management software and consultancy services. The hype leads us to believe that a 'corporate taxonomy' is essential for organising knowledge. And this may well be right. But what is a taxonomy? For some it is a classification; for some a thesaurus; for others a hybrid. A variety of solutions is on offer, and new ideas are still pouring in. As of summer 2000, there is no consensus as to what works best. In the fullness of time we will probably find that different techniques are needed for different applications and circumstances. However, many of the techniques will be based on some form of classification and/or indexing. The information manager who understands the strengths and weaknesses of these approaches is well positioned to make a judgement on the merits of solutions offered for the case in hand.

Evaluation

People may argue about the conclusions of the Aslib-Cranfield Projects with respect to controlled languages, but few deny their influence in establishing measures that could be used for evaluating retrieval performance. In response to a given query, the Recall ratio is defined as $100R/N$ and the Precision ratio as $100R/T$, where R is the number of relevant items retrieved; N is the total number of relevant items in the collection; T is the total number of documents retrieved. Precision and Recall are found to be inversely related. To use either measure, it is necessary first to make a judgement on the relevance of every item retrieved. To measure Recall, it is further necessary to establish how many relevant items exist in the whole collection – an extremely laborious task! The performance of a given system will obviously vary from query to query, and so an overall evaluation has to repeat this incredible labour for a representative sample set of queries, and average the results.

Forty years on, the measures of Precision and Recall are still very much relied on in quantitative IR research. An annual series of experiments known as TREC (Text REtrieval Conference) (Harman, 1995, 2000) now applies them to collections comprising gigabytes of data. An essential part of the method is to involve many participants (the number has grown from 25 in 1992 to 66 in 1998) who must both compete and collaborate. Each participating institution is given the test collection and the same set of queries. Each processes them with its own retrieval system. The results are pooled, and all the documents retrieved by all the systems are assessed for relevance. The set of all those judged relevant is assumed to be the total set of relevant items in the collection, and so it becomes possible for all participants to compute their own Recall/Precision results.

Thus the Cranfield methodology has been an important aid to IR research, for example in allowing the OKAPI team at City University to progressively refine their algorithm for probabilistic ranking (Robertson et al., 1997). And some of the research results do feed eventually into commercially available products. But for the practical information manager wanting to assess the merits of some alternative retrieval packages, to apply the Cranfield method is hardly the answer:

- As noted, the task of assessing relevance is so large that it can usually only be attempted in rather artificial circumstances (for this reason, the Cranfield test collection with its set of queries and relevance judgements, even though rather small by comparison with today's databases, is still used in some retrieval experiments).

- Relevance judgements are always subjective.

- The method ignores the variability of users and user behaviour, in particular it ignores the way a user's definition of his query can evolve as an interactive search proceeds.

- The method ignores other performance criteria that may be important to the user, such as speed of response or friendliness of interface.

- Selecting a representative sample of users/queries is not straightforward.

The fundamental nature of these objections has led some to reject the whole method. Ellis (1984, 1989), for example, dismisses Relevance as a useful measure and proposes that evaluation should be based on 'the quality of the interaction between the system and the user or the degree of "systems transparency"'. Warner (2000) advocates 'an enhanced capacity for informed choice' as evaluation criterion. Harter and Hert's thorough review (1997) describes a range of alternative user-oriented measures that have been proposed for system evaluation, including: utility, usefulness, usability, informativeness, impact, satisfaction, frustration, perceived value. Some evaluations include stakeholders other than the user. For today's researchers, the big challenge is to devise evaluation measures appropriate to the interactive environment (Robertson et al., 1997; Fowkes and Beaulieu, 2000).

So where does all this research, and the vast literature on evaluation of IR systems, leave the information manager who simply wants a method for comparing the performance of various systems? Disappointingly, there is no standard method; there is no simple yardstick. First principles, common sense, a good knowledge of one's users and their needs, a trial run based on the particular collection; these are the methods the manager must deploy.

Summary and conclusions

We have looked at classification and indexing as two fundamental, complementary approaches to the organisation of information. We have noted some of the issues a manager needs to consider before adopting one of the ready-made classification schemes, or developing a home-grown scheme. We looked briefly at pre-coordinate indexing as an approach to production of printed indexes. Then we considered post-coordinate indexing, and the merits of adopting a controlled vocabulary. We noted the variety of thesauri on offer, and the converging trend of thesauri and classification schemes. We observed the power of facet analysis for building classification and / or indexing tools.

Turning to the world of electronic networks, we considered some of the software tools that can be bought to organise information without human intervention, and we saw how the automatic functions, often rather rudimentary, can be boosted by complementing them with various types of knowledge structure, including our old friend classification.

Always thinking of how an information manager is to choose between the options, we skimmed the top of the long evaluation debate to note that there is no easy way of proving what is best. All of the methods, manual or automatic, have weaknesses. There is no universal panacea. Such a panacea is unlikely to emerge, when we recall how variable are users and their wants.

So we are thrown back to the old adage of not putting all our eggs in one basket. To satisfy most of our users most of the time we need to provide a variety of options, such as full-text searching with powerful search software, categorisation options, controlled language indexing, intermediary help available on request, and let's not forget the good old-fashioned library along the corridor. We need to have a good feel for what our users want and how they will apply it, so that the search interface integrates well with their other desktop tools, and we must keep our eye on new products incorporating new techniques.

Acknowledgements

Many thanks to Jean Aitchison, Martin van der Walt and Murtha Baca for their helpful and constructive comments on a draft of this chapter. Notwithstanding their assistance, any errors, omissions or unorthodoxies are entirely the responsibility of the author.

*Extracts from The BSI ROOT Thesaurus are reproduced with the permission of BSI under licence number 2000SK/0427. Complete British standards can be obtained by post from BSI Customer Services, 389 Chiswick High Road, London W4 4A, United Kingdom (tel UK 020 8996 9001).

References

Aitchison, J., Gilchrist, A. and Bawden, D. *Thesaurus Construction and Use: a practical manual.* London: Aslib (1997).

Aitchison, J., Gomersall, A. and Ireland R. *Thesaurofacet: a thesaurus and faceted classification for engineering and related subjects.* Whetstone, Leicester: English Electric Company, Ltd (1969).

Art and Architecture Thesaurus. Oxford and New York: Oxford University Press (1994, 2nd ed.).

Austin, D. and Dykstra, M. *PRECIS: a manual of concept analysis and subject indexing.* London: British Library (1984).

Bates, M.J. Indexing and access for digital libraries and the Internet: human, database and domain factors. *Journal of the American Society for Information Science,* **49** 1998, 1185-205.

Batty, D. Thesaurus construction and maintenance: a survival kit. *Database,* **12** 1989, 13-20.

Berwick Sayers, W.C. *A Manual of Classification for Librarians and Bibliographers.* London: Andre Deutsch (1962, 3rd rev. ed.).

Betts, R. and Marrable, D. Free text vs controlled vocabulary – retrieval precision and recall over large databases. *Online Information 91. Proceedings of the 15th International Online Information Meeting: December 10-12,*

1991; London. Oxford and New Jersey: Learned Information (Europe) Ltd (1991), 153-65.

Broughton, V. Structural, linguistic and mathematical elements in indexing languages and search engines: implications for the use of index languages in electronic and non-LIS environments. In: *Dynamism and Stability in Knowledge Organization. Proceedings of the Sixth ISKO Conference: July 10-13, 2000; Toronto, Canada.* Wuerzburg, Germany: Ergon Verlag (2000), 206-12.

BSI ROOT Thesaurus. Milton Keynes, England: British Standards Institution (1981; 1985, 2nd ed.; 1988, 3rd ed.).

Calkins, M.L. Free-text or controlled vocabulary? A case history step-by-step analysis. . . plus other aspects of search strategy. *Database,* 1980, 56-67.

Chan, L.M and Hodges, T.L. The Library of Congress Classification. In: Marcella, R. and Maltby, A. (eds) *The Future of Classification*. Aldershot: Gower (2000), 105-27.

Cleverdon, C.W. The Cranfield tests on index language devices. *Aslib Proceedings,* **19** 1967, 173-92.

Cleverdon, C.W., Mills, J. and Keen, E.M. *Factors Determining the Performance of Indexing Systems.* Cranfield: College of Aeronautics (1966).

Cleverdon, C.W. and Mills, J. The testing of index language devices. *Aslib Proceedings,* **15**(4) 1963, 106-30.

Cyberstacks(sm). Available at: *http://www.public.iastate.edu/~CYBERSTACKS*.

Dextre Clarke, S.G. Thesaural relationships. In: Bean, C.A. and Green, R. (eds) *Relationships in the Organization of Knowledge*. Dordrecht: Kluwer (2001), 37-52.

Dextre Clarke, S.G. Thesauri, topics and other structures in knowledge management software. *Dynamism and Stability in Knowledge Organization. Proceedings of the Sixth ISKO Conference: July 10-13, 2000; Toronto, Canada.* Wuerzburg, Germany: Ergon Verlag (2000), 41-7.

Dextre, S.G. and Clarke, T.M. A system for machine-aided thesaurus construction. *Aslib Proceedings.* **33**(3) 1981, 102-12.

Doran K. Metadata for a corporate intranet. *Online,* **23** 1999, 42-50.

Dubois, C.P.R. The use of thesauri in online retrieval. *Journal of Information Science,* **8** 1984, 63-6.

Ellis, D. A behavioural approach to information retrieval design. *Journal of Information Science,* **45** 1989, 171-212.

Ellis, D. Theory and explanation in information retrieval research. *Journal of Information Science,* **8** 1984, 25-38.

Eurobrokers. *Thesaurus Guide: analytical directory of selected vocabularies for information retrieval, 1992.* Luxembourg: European Communities (1993, 2nd ed.).

Faculty of Information Studies Inforum, University of Toronto. Subject analysis systems collection. Available at: *http://www.fis.utoronto.ca/resources/inforum/sas.htm.*

Foskett, A.C. The future of faceted classification. In: Marcella, R. and Maltby, A. (eds) *The Future of Classification.* Aldershot: Gower (2000), 69-80.

Foskett, A.C. *The Subject Approach to Information.* London: Clive Bingley (1982, 4th ed.; 1996, 5th ed.).

Fowkes, H. and Beaulieu, M. Interactive searching behaviour: Okapi experiment for TREC-8. *Proceedings of the BCS-IRSG 22nd Annual Colloquium on Information Retrieval Research: April 5-7, 2000; Cambridge, England.* Cambridge, England: British Computer Society Information Retrieval Specialist Group (2000), 47-56.

Gillman, P. Thesauri to aid retrieval from very large text bases: subject retrieval from large text resources, and the problems of ambiguity. *Knowledge Organization for Information Retrieval. Proceedings of the Sixth International Study Conference on Classification Research: June 16-18, 1997; London.* The Hague, Netherlands: FID (1997), 113-19.

Harman, D. What we have learned, and not learned, from TREC. *Proceedings of the BCS-IRSG 22nd Annual Colloquium on Information Retrieval Research: April 5-7, 2000; Cambridge, England.* Cambridge, England: British Computer Society Information Retrieval Specialist Group (2000), 2-20.

Harman, D.K. The TREC conferences. *Hypertext – Information Retrieval – Multimedia: Synergieeffekte Elektronischer Informationssysteme, Proceedings of HIM '95.* Konstanz, Germany: Universitaetsverlag Konstanz (1995), 9-28.

Harter, S.P. and Hert, C.A. Evaluation of information retrieval systems: approaches, issues and methods. In: Williams, M.E. (ed.) *Annual Review of Information Science and Technology.* Medford, New Jersey: Information Today Inc. for the American Society for Information Science (1997), **32**, 3-94.

Henzler R.C. Free or controlled vocabulary? Some statistical user-orientated evaluations of biomedical information systems. *International Classification,* **5** 1978, 21-6.

Houston, J.E. (ed.) *Thesaurus of ERIC Descriptors.* Phoenix, Arizona: Oryx press (1995, 13th ed.).

Hudon, M. Innovation and tradition in knowledge organization schemes on the Internet, or, finding one's way in the virtual library. *Dynamism and Stability in Knowledge Organization. Proceedings of the Sixth ISKO Conference: July 10-13, 2000; Toronto, Canada.* Wuerzburg, Germany: Ergon Verlag (2000), 35-40.

INSPEC Thesaurus. London: Institution of Electrical Engineers (biennial).

International Organization for Standardization. *Information and Documentation – Guidelines For the Content, Organization and Presentation of Indexes.* Geneva: International Organization for Standardization (1996, 2nd ed.) (ISO 999:1996(E) [=BS ISO 999:1996]).

International Organization for Standardization. *Documentation – Guidelines for the Establishment and Development of Monolingual Thesauri.* Geneva: International Organization for Standardization (1986) (ISO 2788 – 1986 [=BS5723:1987]).

International Organization for Standardization. *Documentation – Guidelines for the Establishment and Development of Multilingual Thesauri.* Geneva: International Organization for Standardization (1985) (ISO 5964 – 1985 [=BS6723:1985]).

Johnson, Eric H. and Cochrane, Pauline A. A hypertextual interface for a searcher's thesaurus. 13 May, 1997. Available at: *http://csdl.tamu.edu/DL95/ papers/johncoch/johncoch.html.*

Knapp, S.D. *The Contemporary Thesaurus of Social Science Terms and Synonyms: a guide for natural language computer searching.* Arizona: Oryx (1993).

Koch, T. Controlled Vocabularies, Thesauri and Classification Systems available in the WWW. Available at *http://www.lub.lu.se/metadata/subject-help.html.*

Krooks, D. and Lancaster, F. The evolution of guidelines for thesaurus construction. *Libri*, **43** 1993, 326-42.

Lancaster F.W. *Indexing and Abstracting in Theory and Practice.* London: LA Publishing (1998).

Lancaster, F.W. *Vocabulary Control for Information Retrieval.* Arlington, Virginia: Information Resources Press (1986).

Luhn, H.P. The automatic derivation of information retrieval encodements from machine-readable texts. In: Kent, A. (ed.) *Information Retrieval and Machine Translation.* New York: Interscience Publication (1961), vol. 3, part 2:1021-8.

Lutes, B. Web Thesaurus Compendium. Available at: *http://www-cui.darmstadt.gmd.de/~lutes/thesauri.html.*

Lykke Nielsen M. Future thesauri: what kind of conceptual knowledge do searchers need? *Structures and Relations in Knowledge Organization. Proceedings of the 5th International ISKO Conference: August 25-29, 1998; Lille, France.* Wuerzburg, Germany: Ergon Verlag (1998), 153-60.

Markey, K., Atherton, P. and Newton, C. An analysis of controlled vocabulary and free text search statements in online searches. *Online Review,* 1982, 225-36.

Maron, M.E. and Kuhns, J.L. On relevance, probabilistic indexing and information retrieval. *Journal of the Association for Computing Machinery,* **7** 1960, 216-44.

McIlwaine, I.C. UDC in the twenty-first century. In: Marcella, R. and Maltby, A. (eds) *The Future of Classification.* Aldershot: Gower (2000), 93-104.

McIlwaine, I.C. *Guide to the Use of UDC.* The Hague, Netherlands: International Federation for Information and Documentation (FID) (1995).

Medical Subject Headings (MeSH). Bethesda, Maryland: National Library of Medicine (annual).

Miller, U. Thesaurus construction: problems and their roots. *Information Processing and Management,* **33** 1997, 481-93.

Milstead, J.L. Invisible thesauri: the year 2000. *Online & CDROM Review,* **19** 1995, 93-4.

Milstead, J.L. *Needs for research in indexing. Journal of the American Society for Information Science.* **45** 1994; 577-82.

Mitchell, J.S. and Vizine-Goetz, D. DDC taxonomy server. *Dynamism and Stability in Knowledge Organization. Proceedings of the Sixth ISKO Conference: July 10-13, 2000; Toronto, Canada.* Wuerzburg, Germany: Ergon Verlag (2000), 282-7.

Mitchell, J.S. The Dewey Decimal Classification in the twenty-first century. In: Marcella, R. and Maltby, A. (eds). *The Future of Classification.* Aldershot: Gower (2000), 81-92.

National Information Standards Organization. *Guidelines for the Construction, Format and Management of Monolingual Thesauri.* Bethesda, Maryland: NISO Press (1993) (ANSI / NISO Z39.19-1993).

Northern Light. Available at *http://www.northernlight.com/.*

Organization for Economic Co-operation and Development. *Macrothesaurus for Information Processing in the Field of Economic and Social Development.* Paris: OECD Development Centre (1985, 3rd ed; 1998, 5th ed.).

Piternick, A.B. Searching vocabularies: a developing category of online search tools. *Online Review,* **8** 1984, 441-9.

Plumb Design. Plumb Design Visual Thesaurus. 1998. Available at *http: //www.plumbdesign.com/thesaurus/.*

Pollitt, A.S. and Tinker A.J. Enhanced view-based searching through the decomposition of Dewey decimal classification codes. In: *Dynamism and Stability in Knowledge Organization. Proceedings of the Sixth ISKO Conference: July 10-13, 2000; Toronto, Canada.* Wuerzburg, Germany: Ergon Verlag (2000), 288-94.

Pollitt, A.S. The application of Dewey Classification in a view-based searching OPAC. In: *Structures and Relations in Knowledge Organization. Proceedings of the 5th International ISKO Conference: August 25-29, 1998; Lille, France.* Wuerzburg, Germany: Ergon Verlag (1998), 176-83.

Porter, M.F. An algorithm for suffix stripping. *Program,* **14** 1980, 130-7.

Princeton WordNet. Available at *http://www.cogsci.princeton.edu/~wn/ w3wn.old.html.*

Proceedings of the BCS-IRSG 22nd Annual Colloquium on Information Retrieval Research: April 5-7, 2000; Cambridge, England. Cambridge, England: British Computer Society Information Retrieval Specialist Group (2000).

Ranganathan, S.R. *Colon Classification.* Bombay: Asia Publishing House (1960, 6th ed.).

Riesthuis, G.J.A. Decomposition of UDC numbers and the text of the UDC Master Reference File. In: *Structures and Relations in Knowledge Organization. Proceedings of the 5th International ISKO Conference: August 25-29, 1998; Lille, France.* Wuerzburg, Germany: Ergon Verlag; (1998), 221-8.

Riesthuis, G.J. and Bliedung, S. Thesaurification of the UDC. *Tools for Knowledge Organization and the Human Interface. Proceedings of the 1st International ISKO Conference: August 14-17, 1990; Darmstadt.* Frankfurt/Main: Indeks Verlag (1991), Part 2, 109-7.

Roberts, N. The pre-history of the information retrieval thesaurus. *Journal of Documentation,* **40** 1984, 271-85.

Robertson, S., Walker, S. and Beaulieu, M. Laboratory experiments with Okapi: participation in the TREC programme. *Journal of Documentation,* **53** 1997, 20-34.

Robertson, S.E. and Walker, S. Some simple but effective approximations to the 2-Poisson model for probabilistic weighted retrieval. *Proceedings of the 17th International Conference on Research and Development in Information Retrieval.* London: Springer Verlag (1994), 232-41.

Rowley, J. The controlled versus natural languages debate revisited: a perspective on information retrieval practice and research. *Journal of Information Science,* **20** 1994, 108-19.

Society of Indexers Home Page. Available at: *http://www.socind.demon.co.uk* (accessed 3 July, 2000).

Sparck Jones, K. and Willett, P. *Readings in Information Retrieval.* San Francisco, USA: Morgan Kaufmann (1997).

Svenonius, E. Design of controlled vocabularies in the context of emerging technologies. *Library Science with a Slant to Documentation,* **25** 1988, 215-27.

Svenonius, E. Unanswered questions in the design of controlled vocabularies. *Journal of the American Society for Information Science,* **37** 1986, 331-40.

Tenopir, C. Full-text database retrieval performance. *Online Review,* **2** 1985, 149-64.

Thesaurus of Engineering and Scientific Terms (TEST). New York: Engineers Joint Council and US Department of Defense (1967).

Van der Walt, M. The structure of classification schemes used in Internet search engines. *Structures and Relations in Knowledge Organization. Proceedings of the 5th International ISKO Conference: August 25-29, 1998; Lille, France.* Wuerzburg, Germany: Ergon Verlag (1998), 379-87.

Vechtomova, O. and Robertson, S. Integration of collocation statistics into the probabilistic retrieval model. *Proceedings of the BCS-IRSG 22nd Annual Colloquium on Information Retrieval Research: April 5-7, 2000; Cambridge, England.* Cambridge, England: British Computer Society Information Retrieval Specialist Group (2000), 165-77.

Vickery, B.C. *Faceted Classification: a guide to construction and use of special schemes.* London: Aslib (1960, reprinted with additional material 1970).

Vizine-Goetz, D. Dewey as an Internet subject guide. *Structures and Relations in Knowledge Organization. Proceedings of the 5th International ISKO Conference: August 25-29, 1998; Lille, France.* Wuerzburg, Germany: Ergon Verlag (1998) 191-7.

Warner, J. In the catalogue ye go for men: evaluation criteria for information retrieval systems. *Aslib Proceedings,* **52**(2) 2000, 76-82.

Weinberg, B.H. Library classification and information retrieval thesauri: comparison and contrast. *Cataloging and Classification Quarterly,* **19** 1995, 23-44.

Wellisch, H.H. *Indexing from A to Z.* New York; Dublin: H W Wilson (1995).

Wightman, P. (ed.) *CAB Thesaurus.* Wallingford, Oxon: CABI Publishing (1999).

Yahoo! Available at *http://www.yahoo.com/*.

Additional reading

Hjorland B. Nine principles of knowledge organization. *Proceedings of the 3rd International Society for Knowledge Organization (ISKO) Conference: Knowledge Organization and Quality Management: June 20-24, 1994; Copenhagen, Denmark.* Frankfurt / Main: INDEKS Verlag (1994) 91-100.

Keen, E.M. The Aberystwyth index languages test. *Journal of Documentation,* **29** 1973, 1-35.

Maltby, A. and Marcella, R. Organizing knowledge: the need for system and unity. In: Marcella, R. and Maltby, A. (eds) *The Future of Classification.* Aldershot: Gower (2000), 19-31.

Marcella, R. and Maltby, A. *The Future of Classification.* Aldershot: Gower (2000).

McIlwaine, I. UDC - into the 21st Century. *Aslib Proceedings,* **50**(2) 1998, 44-8.

Milstead, Jessica L. and Feldman, Susan. Metadata: cataloging by any other name. January, 1999; accessed March, 1999. Available at *http://www.onlineinc.com/onlinemag/OL1999/milstead1.html.*

Mitchell, J.S. Challenges facing classification systems: a Dewey case study. *Knowledge Organization for Information Retrieval. Proceedings of the Sixth International Study Conference on Classification Research: June 16, 1997-June 18, 1997; London.* The Hague, Netherlands: FID (1997), 85-9.

Raitt, D.I. Recall and precision devices in interactive bibliographic search and retrieval systems. *Aslib Proceedings,* **32** 1980, 281-301.

Chapter 4

Information needs assessment

Jan Sykes

An information needs assessment is a component of the information audit process described in greater detail in a separate chapter of this Handbook. A much more detailed picture of organisational investments in a range of information resources and user behaviours will emerge from a comprehensive information audit. However, the complexity of some organisations may make full audits complex and time consuming. And, as the global business environment becomes more competitive and as pressures increase to speed up product development and reduce time to market, there simply may not be time, resources, or management support to pursue a full-blown information audit. This chapter focuses on understanding information needs of users. The latter part of the chapter examines how to evaluate new information resources that are being considered as a result of what is learned from the information needs assessment.

If we believe that information is a strategic asset that must be managed in order to help organisations improve their productivity, their competitiveness, and overall performance, then we need current, reliable indications of the types of information required by knowledge workers in our organisations. Given the changes occurring in the business world and the pace of change, it is almost certain that information needs of an organisation are changing and evolving as well. The fast moving business environment and the increasing number of information purchasing decisions being made across the organisation argue for a streamlined information needs assessment as a means of gathering basic data for buying decisions. There is some urgency to have quantitative and qualitative user data to justify enterprise information purchasing decisions.

With increasing organisational investments in desktop information resources, intranets, and portals, it is critical for information professionals to step up to the task of helping the organisation make the wisest investments in information resources for the desktop, intranets and / or portals. It is imperative that information resources being made available are actually those that will provide the expected productivity and decision support advantages within the context of work objectives. Knowledge management initiatives may have higher visibility than information management initiatives at this point in time in many organisations. However, managing information resources is a critical part of the broader knowledge management activity and this part must be handled well in order for knowledge management activities to be successful.

An information needs assessment will determine what information employees need in order to perform their work at an optimal level in terms of:

- internal content
- external content
- timeliness
- format.

The scope of the information needs assessment must be determined in advance and may be influenced by budget and manpower resources. The information needs assessment can be focused on the entire organisation or specific departments or functional groups. It may also be organised around understanding needs for particular classes of information, such as for business and news information or for scientific and technical information.

Why should an information needs assessment be performed?

Information gleaned from the needs assessment should become the core of the information centre's strategic and operating plans. It should also be fed into the planning process for departments or functional units closely aligned with the information centre to emphasise the partnership and the information centre's objective to provide information critical to business processes.

Many information centres are now compelled to redefine their roles and responsibilities as they witness departments hiring their own researchers and competitive intelligence professionals, departments managing their own information investments, a proliferation of individual subscriptions to paid online or web information services, and an increase in web surfing for research. The information centre can showcase the expertise of its staff in these areas through a carefully orchestrated needs assessment process followed by strategic communication of results and recommendations. The process should also help information professionals rethink their roles and work priorities to keep in sync with expectations of the user community.

An information needs assessment may also be required for rationalising information services following reorganisations, mergers, acquisitions or takeovers. A more comprehensive information audit would be of most value in these circumstances, but if that is not feasible, an information needs assessment is in order. The outcomes of the study can help personnel affected by the organisational changes, as well as the information professionals, modify, expand, or change information tools and resources so that they are aligned with work objectives of the new units.

When should an information needs assessment be performed?

Periodic needs assessments should be standard operating procedure for a proactive, progressive information centre striving to be in tune with, and anticipating needs of, users. Results of an information needs assessment study are valuable when:

- a catalyst is needed for making major changes in information handling practices (such as eliminating certain information products or moving subscriptions from print to electronic format)
- there are complaints about any aspect of information services
- it is learned that information being delivered is not meeting needs of the target audience.

With the proliferation of new and repackaged information products and changing pricing models, an information needs assessment can help with buying decisions. Are there new products which more closely match user needs at better prices? Results of the needs assessment will show current user requirements which can be matched with vendor offerings. If the needs assessment project is led by the information centre, a tangential benefit is increased visibility for the information centre and reinforcement of the expertise of information centre staff in making decisions about information products for the organisation.

Who should perform the information needs assessment?

The answer to this question depends on resources available within the organisation. Possibilities include:

- information centre personnel
- information centre personnel with assistance/support from other departments
- external consultants
- combination of the above.

It is critical for information centre personnel to be involved in the information needs assessment process because of their:

- understanding of the culture and business model of their organisation
- sense of internal politics
- insights into current information seeking, using and sharing behaviours
- general understanding of internal and external content resources
- knowledge of commercial information products for their industry segment – including content, format, pricing, and access models.

If information centre personnel do not have experience with conducting a needs assessment, they can find valuable assistance within the organisation. The information centre might choose to partner with the marketing or market research departments; statisticians and demographers can provide expertise in defining the user segments to target and in collection, analysis, and interpretation of data. Some organisations have internal consulting groups that can provide additional personnel resources for constructing the framework, including tasks and deliverables, for the needs assessment and also for interviewing, leading focus groups and later formulating recommendations. Information technology departments are likely to have survey tools to automate the survey administration process. When the needs assessment is limited to specific areas of the organisation, representatives from those areas should also be included in the planning and follow-up phases to extend the partnership with the information centre. These representatives will have an interesting perspective on the needs assessment data and can be enlisted to champion changes that will be implemented as a result.

A key reason for considering external consultants is that they bring an objective point of view. While it may be advantageous to have knowledge of the organisation and current information seeking behaviours, it may be just as advantageous to have an outside, unbiased viewpoint. An external consultant who has experience in conducting information needs assessment studies will be able to advise on what works and what should be avoided in the process, drawing from his or her experience with other organisations. Because of time and staffing constraints for information centre personnel, it may be necessary to bring in external consultants to take the lead in a special project such as this.

The ideal scenario is a team approach with a team comprised of information centre personnel, external consultants, and internal representatives from other departments – each with expertise needed for specific aspects of the information needs assessment. With the team approach, tasks must be clearly delineated and assigned so that the process moves forward on schedule. Regular debriefing sessions and meetings of the team will keep the project on track.

How does one perform an information needs assessment?

There is no single accepted methodology for conducting an information needs assessment. The approach should be based on the strategic objectives of the business and alignment of information resources with those objectives. For example, if globalisation is one of the strategic objectives of the organisation, the needs assessment study should uncover or confirm what kinds of information users require in order to help them understand and operate in the global marketplace. If the needs assessment is targeted to a particular department or business unit, the approach should be based on knowledge of that unit's strategic objectives and how it fits into the whole organisation.

The needs assessment can be accomplished via:

- direct observation
- one-to-one interviews
- focus groups
- written surveys
- online surveys.

The best results are likely to be obtained with some combination of the above. If the needs assessment is being conducted by someone not familiar with the usual information-seeking behaviour of the group being surveyed, one-to-one interviews or direct observation will set the stage for understanding how users typically find answers, what resources they use, and where they have difficulty finding information. Focus groups work well for getting users to brainstorm about ideal information resources to meet work needs. Focus group discussions can easily get out of hand if the person leading the group does not have a clear agenda. It is important to stick to an agenda, to keep the discussions positive and constructive, and to record the essence of the discussion for analysis. Interviews may also be required following analysis of survey results to validate findings or to obtain additional qualitative information.

It is possible to gather input from a larger audience with print and online surveys. The decision to mail print surveys or to send online survey forms depends to a large extent on resources available for distributing and analysing the survey results.

The survey process

Designing the survey instrument or questionnaire, if one is to be used, is a specific step in the user needs assessment process. In advance of writing the survey questions, the team administering the survey must:

- articulate what it wants to learn from the survey
- determine the target audience
- identify time frames and cost considerations
- prepare a communications plan
- craft survey questions
- plan for testing and refining the survey instrument
- plan for data collection and analysis.

To encourage the greatest number of responses, the survey should be brief. Multiple choice questions or questions which ask users to rate a variable according to a given scale are typically easiest to answer and easiest to analyse. Open-ended questions require more time for analysis, but often provide the most insightful, qualitative data.

Articulating what is to be learned from the survey helps to keep the survey activities focused on business objectives – not initiatives that the information centre wishes to launch. An example of a narrowly defined survey objective is to learn what types of company information are required by the sales organisation. An objective of a broader survey could be to learn users' expectations for 'push' news feed services. Survey questions can then be written to obtain meaningful responses in the light of business objectives. This also makes it easier to launch crisp, clear communications about the survey.

Target audience

The target audience for the survey depends on what is to be learned from the survey – whether it is information needs of a particular department or user group or a broader analysis of user needs at the enterprise level. Collecting demographic data from survey respondents is critical for cross tabulation of the survey results and subsequent determination of information service offerings by user segment.

Organisation charts are helpful in determining whom to target when a representative sampling of levels and departments is to be included in the survey. Human resources departments may provide assistance when setting up the target survey population – especially in large organisations. Using labels established by human resources for departments or business units and job categories assures consistency in identification of users. For balanced input, consider including thought leaders and change agents, people who are information advocates, key users of information resources (directly or via the information centre), and departments or individuals who are not using information resources.

Time frames and budgets

Time frames and budget considerations will vary depending on the extent of the survey and personnel resources available. It is not practical to expect immediate turn around of the survey questionnaires given busy work schedules, travel schedules, and vacations. Asking for responses within a two or three week period is respectful of users' schedules. Budgets should be set in advance; costs to be considered include possible cross charges to other departments for support in survey design and administration, external consultants, and materials, such as software for web-based surveys.

Communications plan

The communications plan informs the target community about the survey and also promotes participation in the survey. Communications regarding the information needs assessment should stress that the overall objectives of the survey are to provide access to information tools that allow knowledge workers to be more productive in their work, and thus, improve performance and competitiveness of the organisation. Sponsorship from senior management increases the visibility of the activity and generally increases the response rate. The team administering the information needs assessment can draft messages for the sponsor to send. Marketing tactics appropriate to the corporate culture, such as posters, brief broadcast voice mail and email announcements, and contests (e.g. a drawing for gift certificates to be used at an e-commerce site) should be used to generate more awareness and enthusiasm for participating in the survey. The communications plan might also include:

- message to be sent out a week or so after the survey has been delivered, reminding users to complete and submit the survey
- follow-up messages thanking participants and providing highlights of the assessment results
- articles for company or departmental newsletters describing the survey and results.

Survey questions

Survey questions must be crafted for individual situations – depending on the objectives of the survey, types of information being considered, and makeup of the user group. For a general information needs assessment, a suggested sequence is as follows (with one or two questions for each area):

- demographics (location, department or division, and functional area)
- current situation – how users are getting information now (personal journal subscriptions, consult with a colleague, hire a consultant, Web research, etc.)
- future possibilities for information access – exploring new options for broader access (desktop information products, information professionals in business units, satellite libraries)
- checklist of categories of information (e.g. news publications, trade journals, management journals, patents, scientific journals, etc.) which users might need to accomplish their work objectives
- frequency of use for items in checklist (daily, weekly, monthly)
- subject areas of greatest interest
- format preferences (e.g. Web, online, print)
- cost allocation preferences (centralised, departmental, project allocations)
- return on investment (ROI) (hours saved per week, number of days product development cycle could be shortened, estimate of additional sales) – if appropriate information were always available
- text boxes for general user feedback (e.g. open-ended questions about difficulties experienced in obtaining the information or suggestions for enhancing the service).

Survey participants may view questions about demographic identifiers as a survey within a survey. As respondents move through demographic questions, they typically become easily fatigued so it is important to limit this section to a few critical questions, e.g. division, location, and functional area. Survey experts recommend capturing demographic information at the beginning of the survey.

Testing and tweaking

Prior to distribution of the survey, it should be tested with a few people. If it is possible to observe this process, it quickly becomes clear which questions are most difficult to understand or answer, and the observer can also elicit feedback about the length and flow of the survey. This is an opportunity to eliminate any jargon that might have crept into the survey and to re-word questions so that they are clearer to the user.

Survey analysis

As noted earlier, the decision to mail print surveys or to send online survey forms depends to a large extent on resources available for analysing the survey results. Analysing responses to print surveys can be time-consuming and tedious. Before embarking on a print survey project, consider whether scanners can be used to aggregate the survey responses or if the data compilation tasks can be outsourced. For online or web-based surveys, it should be possible to capture survey feedback in a spreadsheet at a minimum, or in a database program, if you have access to more sophisticated tools. It may be worth investigating services of web survey companies who host the survey and automatically aggregate and display data as surveys are returned.

Answers to survey questions should be calculated as percentages and displayed in tables and graphs. Charts and graphs help with interpretation and are valuable for presentations to project sponsors and management.

Interpretation of information needs assessment results

It is extremely important to approach the analysis and interpretation phase with an open mind. The results of the information needs assessment survey (or interviews and focus groups) are a snapshot of information needs at the present time and do not necessarily reflect satisfaction or dissatisfaction with the way information services have been delivered in the past. It is critical to be open to the possibility that radical changes in the way information resources are managed may be needed. Users should be made to feel comfortable expressing what they actually think and experience vs. what they think the survey administrators want to hear. The desire for openness and honest, direct answers can be encouraged in the communications announcing the survey. The persons analysing the response must actively 'listen' to what users / data are communicating. This is especially important advice when the information centre staff is involved in interpreting the data. It is difficult not to be defensive when a user reports via the survey that he or she really needs access to a certain type of information – when the information centre has been announcing availability of exactly that type of information for months. For whatever reason, the message has not reached that individual.

How well users are able to express their information needs in a survey may depend on their level of familiarity with information resources typically used by practitioners in certain disciplines, a certain level of information literacy. Follow-up interviews will help to clarify ambiguous or confusing survey data.

Recommendations and action plans

The analysis of gaps between what exists and what is expected or needed provides the basis for actionable recommendations in a written or verbal report. The report will make recommendations regarding information services/products per market segment or user group. Cost–benefit calculations and projected ROI for the services and products being recommended should be included.

After making their recommendations, the team leading the information needs assessment project will draft an action plan, setting measurable, actionable goals based on company objectives and the information needs assessment data. Results of the needs assessment should be used to make strategic changes in the way information services are delivered in the organisation. The needs assessment findings should be shared with information centre management, and the data should be used to recommend and implement change. The team will benefit from 'thinking big' – while still setting realistic goals to be accomplished during the next quarter, next six months, and next 12 months.

Reviewing the needs assessment data provides an opportunity to think long and hard about who are currently information centre customers and which user groups should be targeted for specific products and services. Saying 'no' to certain groups of customers or certain types of user requests may be a new strategy for growth. Establishing and adhering to service level standards for specific market segments can make the information centre more vital and more valued; and, with the wealth of end-user information products available, no market segment within the organisation should be without access to some information resources.

High level summaries of needs assessment findings should be shared with those who participated in the survey and focus groups and findings should be used to cement partnerships with other departments. The team will enjoy additional visibility by offering to contribute extracts of the needs assessment as well as action plans for improving information services to the strategic and operating plans of other departments.

Information needs assessment outcomes

What can be learned from the information needs assessment? The outcome of an information needs assessment should be an understanding of users' information needs related to their work goals and organisational business objectives. At a more granular level, the assessment should provide insights into information needed for background research, to support business decisions, to spark creative insights, to aid in the innovation process and to monitor activities related to business intelligence by defining:

- questions which need to be answered by specific demographic groups
- types of information needed by these groups
- decision points in project cycles at which information is critical
- quantity and authority of information users expect
- referred formats
- 'push' versus 'pull' preferences
- willingness to pay
- frequency of information needs
- business impact of not having access to appropriate information in a timely fashion.

Business benefits

Business benefits resulting from adjusting information services to meet the needs identified in the survey include:

- better business decisions
- quicker decision-making
- increases in productivity
- quicker response to competitive pressures
- higher ROI for information purchases or licensing
- data justifying particular decisions regarding investments in information resources
- information centre staff who are more attuned to the information needs of organisation.

Raw information has only potential value – it must be made available for the right application by the right individual or group for its potential to be realised.

Secondary benefits that may be realised include:

- formalised standards and processes for acquiring and deploying information resources
- increased awareness of information resources as a business asset
- increased appreciation for skills and expertise of information professionals.

Informal needs assessment opportunities

As information professionals are involved with project teams, cross-functional teams, and special projects, they have an opportunity to be continuously assessing the information needs expressed on an informal basis and in the context of team initiatives. This participation in activities at the project or business unit level provides a general sense of information needs related to specific work activities which is valuable background when undertaking the formal needs assessment. In addition, it helps knowledge workers learn more about information resources available to them via information professionals.

User profiles

Another way in which some information professionals are documenting user needs is by preparing client profiles and client databases, along the lines of customer relationship management databases for key individuals or clients in key market segments. The client profiles consist not only of typical questions that people ask of the information centre, but information gained from announcements of a person's background when they join the firm, their publications, quotes in the press, etc. This enables information centre personnel to share knowledge about clients, detect information seeking patterns, and proactively design or acquire products and services to meet the needs of target clients or user groups.

Advisory groups

Establishing an advisory board comprised of representatives from information-intensive departments throughout the organisation and meeting with them periodically to discuss projects and changing information needs is another way for information professionals to keep their fingers on the pulse of information needs in the organisation. This interaction will help information professionals to be more closely integrated with the rest of the business, informed about strategic initiatives, and in a position to consult with information users about management of internal and external information. As with other outreach activities, working with an advisory board increases visibility of the information centre personnel and their initiatives.

Information needs assessments for information professionals

It is important that information professionals do not neglect to assess their own information needs. Information professionals tend to focus on

the information needs of their client communities and may not systemati-
cally evaluate their information needs – in terms of resources for ongoing
professional development, resources to help them keep aware of developments in the industry in which they are working and information analysis
tools. In order to recommend and manage high-quality information and
knowledge services for their organisation, they must equip themselves
with appropriate tools to keep on the cutting edge themselves.

Product trials and evaluations

Once the information needs assessments activities are complete and action plans agreed upon, there is an assumption that new information
products and services will be introduced to the organisation – some being online or web-based services available at the desktop for direct user
access. Users may not know what information services will best meet
their needs until they actually use and evaluate them in the course of their
work. For better or worse, user expectations are changing as a result of
their experience with searching the Web for information. Based on content and functionality requirements the information centre can narrow
down the field of appropriate services and then arrange with the vendors
for hands on testing by the target user groups.

Some guidelines are given here for managing product trials so that the
process is straightforward and convenient for the user, vendor, and information centre team overseeing the trials. This is an extension of the needs
assessment – now at a practical, hands-on level to see which products
users find most valuable in the context of their work.

Products and services

There is a wealth of information services available – with similar (or the
same) content being packaged in many different ways. It is the responsibility of information professionals to use their professional judgement to
narrow the list of options for direct user access based on their experience
with the products, conversations with vendors and a deep understanding of user requirements. Limiting the product evaluation to two or three
information products produces the best results; users do not have time for
thorough testing of many products and the features of each product easily become blurred – particularly if their need to use the products is
sporadic.

Vendors

Vendors of information products are typically willing to offer some evaluation period – at the best rates that can be negotiated and in some cases, at

no charge – to market their products to a larger audience. Before embarking on the trial, it is critical to confirm trial parameters with the vendor, including:

- number of participants
- password handling procedures
- documentation requirements (if any)
- time span of trial
- support (phone and email) during trial
- training program (if necessary)
- vendor expectations regarding feedback
- fees (if appropriate)
- plan for transition to paid use.

Target audience

Choosing participants for product evaluations requires thought, planning, scheduling and negotiation with vendors. For broad-based information products, the more people who can provide feedback, the more likely the most appropriate product will be selected. The extent of the participation depends on the deal negotiated with the vendor for cost and distribution of passwords. For niche information products most appropriate for specialised applications, the feedback will be more meaningful if it comes only from the people who are going to be using them regularly. If a limited number of passwords or seats are available for a trial period, it is advisable to select a few individuals who can be counted on to put a product through its paces and report on how well it fits their needs.

Information professionals should be included in the trials if the products being evaluated are for their use as well as for direct users or end users. Also, if information professionals will be asked to support users after the trials conclude, they should be included in the trials so they have a better sense of the level of support that might be required. Their observations should be considered in the purchase decision along with feedback from the user groups.

Communications

The person(s) managing the product trials will want to generate enthusiasm among trial participants in order to encourage maximum participation. Vendors can provide invaluable support by customising brief descriptions of their products, value statements and search tips to be sent to the target audience. Kick-off or launch meetings introducing the information service and the trial process help build enthusiasm; this is particularly effective if the users are in a single location. If the users are scattered around the globe, videoconferences, teleconferences, and web broadcasts are effective ways of communicating with users; if these resources are not available, focused email messages can communicate essential details in an enthusiastic way. Vendors with representatives around the world typically call on local staff to support product trials in global organisations.

In addition to communications required for the target audience, it is a courtesy to plan communications to managers of persons or groups evaluating new resources, and to information professionals – especially where the products under consideration will impact on their workload. For these groups, brief messages about the services being evaluated, the trial process and potential impact to them are sufficient.

Prior to the beginning of the trial (preferably within a week of the start of the trial), users should receive information on the parameters of the trial, product descriptions, and tips for how and when to use the resource being evaluated.

At the outset of the trial, another message should be sent to participants announcing the launch of the trial, availability of the product, passwords (or instructions for generating a password online), information on how to get help using the product, and expectations regarding user feedback.

Depending on the length of the trial and the level of use or activity (as reported by the vendor), it may be advisable to send additional messages – suggesting applications, reminding users of support / training options, and that the trial is of limited duration.

At the close of the trial period, participants should receive a brief message thanking them for participating in the evaluations and explaining how the products to be introduced will be selected and approximately when they will be available.

Vendors should also receive thank-you messages at the close of the trial. Communications with vendors at this time should confirm plans for deployment and promotion to specific groups if the product is to be introduced to the organisation.

Feedback

While it is important to be respectful of users' time and the fact that they may feel bombarded with surveys, the only way to collect feedback is through some sort of survey – whether it be in-person interviews, phone surveys, or a survey form. It should be made clear from the outset of the product trial, that one of the expectations is that users will provide feedback in exchange for the opportunity to evaluate the resource in question. The feedback form should be brief and should cover essential information regarding:

- ease of use
- value of the content in the context of their work
- satisfaction with training and support
- impact on their productivity.

This feedback is critical to the purchasing or licensing decision and ultimately to the success of the product within the organisation. If users report a positive experience during the evaluation period and see that the product brings new value to their work processes, it will likely be well received by their colleagues.

Conclusions

Businesses today are increasingly focusing on establishing effective customer relationships. Information professionals are also well advised to pursue every opportunity to learn more about their customers and the information that is critical to the success of the organisation. The concept of an information needs assessment, while surely not new to information professionals, deserves renewed attention as the role of information professionals in the knowledge-based economy evolves to incorporate more of the attributes of a guide or consultant. Information professionals can most effectively contribute to the business objectives of the organisation and provide guidance and leadership in information and knowledge management activities as they understand work goals of specific user segments. An information needs assessment continues to be a useful tool for gaining a more comprehensive understanding of user needs and how users apply information to making business decisions.

Selected readings

Cortez, Edwin M. and Kazlauskas, Edward J. Information policy audit: a case study of an organisational analysis tool. *Special Libraries*, Spring 1996, 88-97.

DiMattia, Susan S. and Blumenstein, Lynn. In search of the information audit: essential tool or cumbersome process? *Library Journal*, 1 March 2000, 48-50.

Kennedy, Mary Lee. Positioning strategic information: partnering for the information advantage. *Special Libraries*, Spring 1996, 120-9.

Ribbler, Judith. Delivering solutions for the knowledge economy. *Online,* **20**(5) 1996, 12-19. (Highlights some interesting needs assessment questions and cites several economically priced questionnaire software packages.)

Special Libraries Association (ed.) *The Information Audit.* Washington, DC: Special Libraries Association (1995).

Stanat, Ruth. *The Intelligent Corporation: creating a shared network for information and profit.* New York: AMACOM (1990).

Chapter 5

Information audits

Steve Thornton

Introduction

Although the concept of the information audit has been around since the 1960s, and the term used since at least the early 1980s, there is no single accepted definition of what it is, nor an agreed methodology of how it should be carried out. Some of the written definitions amount to little more than slightly extended information needs analyses, while others take a far more global organisational information structure approach. It is taken for granted that the reader is aware that information should be considered a major strategic asset in any organisation, and that business strategy and information strategy need to be linked if optimal success is to be achieved. The information audit provides an important link between those strategies.

This chapter will review the elements of major existing audit methods, outline some of the potential problems inherent with each, and the obstacles which can prevent successful conclusions. For that purpose, I have adopted the following definition: 'Information Audit is the process of discovering and evaluating the information resources of organisations with the aim of implementing, maintaining or improving information management systems' (Buchanan and Gibb, 1998).

Why?

It has long been held that information technology is one of the major factors that affect the competitive advantage of organisations. Without a comprehensive information technology (IT) strategy to support the business strategy of the organisation, it must be at a competitive disadvantage with its rivals. Yet an IT strategy alone is not enough. There needs to be an overall information strategy aligned with both the business and the information technology strategy of the organisation. Without such a strategy, without identified sponsors and/or owners of information there must by default be duplication, gaps in services, waste of resources and inefficient decision making. This is not to say that organisations cannot run without such strategies, merely that they will not be run as efficiently as they could be.

The information audit, in its truest sense, is a mechanism which should allow the mapping of an organisation's information processes and flows, showing the links between the communications process, the users of information within the organisation, and the means by which information is transferred and used. This map allows identification of current implementations, responsibility for maintenance of the data, and (hopefully) areas in which improvements can be made or duplication eliminated. However, the success of an information audit lies not only in the efficiency and skill with which it is carried out, but ultimately with the way that any results and conclusions are implemented by the parent organisation, turning its observations on information handling and processes into an effective support for the information strategy, and ultimately the business strategy itself.

Among the benefits often identified with information audit are that it:

- provides a comprehensive listing of existing information sources
- permits a better appreciation of the costs involved in creating, maintaining and accessing these resources
- allows an appreciation of the value of these resources within the organisation
- improves (or at least changes) user expectations
- may lead to changes in way information is handled and utilised (sharing practices, knowledge creation and individual creativity).

The very linkage of information audit, to information strategy, to business strategy, highlights one very major problem from the start. The information strategy is just one component of business planning. In addition, any organisation will also have its human resources strategy, financial strategy, information technology strategy and so on. Such business planning comes from the highest levels in the organisation. Unless there is support and championing from the highest levels (and more than just token support at that) a proper information audit will fail at its inception. It needs co-operation, resources and time to carry it out, and senior management support and financial backing for implementation.

General principles

In Chapter 4, Jan Sykes has provided an excellent breakdown of what information needs analyses are, and how to carry them out. The prime differences between the two are scale and scope. Information needs analysis, by default, tends to be aimed at analysis at a limited or local level. Information audit is aimed at a pan-organisational level. The differences are summarised below.

Information needs analysis	Information audit
• Information needs	• Information resources
• Information Centre (Library) point-of-view	• Organisational point-of-view
• Linked to the business strategy of the Information Centre (Library)	• Linked to the business strategy of the organisation
• Departmental or Business Unit basis	• Pan-organisational basis

There is a tendency for librarians and other information professionals to limit their horizons to the information centre point-of-view and to believe that their competence is in fact limited to that arena. I know. This is how I used to think. As a consequence, many librarians tend to limit themselves to an advisory (if asked ...) rather than an influencing (you should be doing this ...) role.

As David Snowden (1999) points out, when discussing the knowledge economy in the modern organisation:

> Librarians are worth their weight in gold. They are human processors within a more complete 'word' system... Librarianship is also a profession; it is not a resting place for secretaries or under-utilised analysts.

Librarians are information specialists and experts, but have too often hidden their lights (very efficiently) under a bushel. The development of intranets and the growth of knowledge management (KM) as a favoured organisational policy, have both often been implemented in organisations without the direct involvement of information professionals, missing out on both their skills and their talents.

In many organisations, recent changes in information delivery mechanisms have been approached from the technological side. Intranets, for example, have often been installed and operated by technology experts in isolation. Knowledge management has also been seen as a technical problem that can be solved by the introduction of bigger, better, faster machines and software, without any real appraisal or understanding of the underlying information structures they are required to support. In a recent interview, Nigel Oxbrow (2000), Managing Director of TFPL Ltd, who carry out and advise on information audits, is quoted as saying:

> The two main drivers for information audits at the moment are intranets that don't deliver benefit – because they have been designed without proper thought to the information and knowledge flows and resources needed – and knowledge management initiatives, where the KM team is trying to get a handle on the very complex array of information available from inside and

outside the organisation, and on where and when that information is needed.

One major UK organisation instituted a multi-million pound KM programme, initially ignoring their library and information professionals until it became obvious that it was achieving far less than it was supposed to be.

> It wasn't until it became obvious to them that the technical approach was not the sole solution to the KM problem that they finally started to listen to what we had to say – 18 months too late! But we should have made our voice heard a lot earlier, and we didn't.[1]

For all that, information audits must not be seen as purely librarian/information professional-based exercises. To carry out the task effectively, the audit needs to utilise a widely diverse set of skills, talents and expertise. A mixture of staff with information, IT, finance and interviewing experience should to be brought together, a partnership of representatives of interested parties and departments throughout the organisation. Failure to get these associates on board at an early stage can lead to serious problems later on.

> … I entered the project with a great deal of enthusiasm, … and helped get it pushed through our Board of Directors. What I didn't do was get … (the IT Section) … on board. I'd rather ignored them, largely because (the IT Manager) and I had never got on. When push came to shove, he managed to block and delay me at every turn, and his crew were no better. They saw this as another 'Library fad' and were as obstructive as could be. … We got round this eventually, but (only by using) the Finance Director as a bludgeon to make them comply. I don't think that he was too impressed with my management skills![2]

Full and comprehensive information audits will take time to carry out properly. In most organisations there are rarely staff with the time to commit themselves full-time to such projects. The alternative is to employ consultants: they can devote themselves to the task, although the overall cost to the organisation will be seen to be higher than attempting to do it all inhouse. Somewhat perversely, the presence of consultants in an audit may also raise the status of the audit in the eyes of senior management and give greater credence to any proposed recommendations. Probably the most effective solution is to use a mix of both internal staff and consultants; the internal staff will have a comprehensive awareness of the internal dynamics of the organisation, while the consultants can supply the time and specialist expertise. To this end, make sure that any consultants selected are information management specialists, rather than general management consultants.

Methods

As indicated earlier, there are as many methods as there are definitions of what an information audit is. Pete Dalton (1999) identified between 14 and 16 reported versions 'which made the most significant contribution', and he was being selective! Many of those reported are aimed at specific organisations, at specific information types or to meet a very specific purpose. Nor are there any methods which have been accepted as a standard or promulgated by any of the professional bodies. There are, however, three major generic methods:

- InfoMap
- Information Flow Analysis
- Integrated Strategic Approach.

I will only give a brief description of the first two methods. Buchanan and Gibb's (1998) Information Strategic Approach consolidates all of the current thinking about the audit process, and provides guidance on a wide range of necessary tools and frameworks. As such, they provide an almost complete method which can be followed step-by-step by any team needing to conduct an information audit from scratch. I have therefore shamelessly taken much of the following section directly from their article, adding to it only where necessary.

InfoMap

Burk and 'Woody' Horton's InfoMap (1988) has been around for some time now. First published in 1988, as 'A complete guide to discovering corporate information resources', it proposes a structured approach to identify all of the information resource entities (IREs) which make up the total inventory of an organisations information resource pool.

The approach has four main phases:

- survey
- cost/Value
- analysis
- synthesis.

The purpose of the survey is to list all of the IREs currently in use within the organisation, either from a preliminary audit or from discovery by a selection of paper surveys or interviews with those who supply, handle, manage or use information. This approach depends on individual users identifying what they use, rather than how they use the information.

Although it will produce a comprehensive list of those IREs currently used, the dependence on the users' perspective can create a serious problem in the analysis phase. The relative importance to the organisation of a particular IRE may be unclear as the context of its use, value and importance may vary from user to user.

The values and benefits of each of the identified IREs are then related to their cost (based on a variety of measures) a technique that allows a degree of cost/benefit to be defined per IRE. While this does create a hook on which to assess value, the results can vary from the arguable to the spurious; such results, though attractive, should only be considered a rough guide to value, and should not be relied upon as a cornerstone of decision making – to do so can open the audit to criticism and discredit.

The results obtained from the survey and assessments of value are then analysed, using a variety of mapping techniques linking the IREs to the management and structure of the organisation. This allows the identification of which elements are corporate information resources, and which relate to much more local needs fulfilment. The final stage reviews all of the identified IREs, their strengths and weaknesses, as supporters and adjuncts to the overall objectives of the organisation. In theory this will allow management decisions to be made about each IRE, whether to continue to support it, increase investment in it, merge it with another, or scrap it altogether.

InfoMap has come in for more than its fair share of criticism, not the least of which is the lack of tools or techniques for identifying the context of an IRE's use from an organisational viewpoint. That lack of agreement on value and use of IREs from within an organisation can almost negate the value of the audit. The audit can have been conducted, the results analysed, and conclusions reached, but the lack of any significant buy-in from users across internal organisational boundaries may prevent any useful, worthwhile benefits coming out of the exercise.

A case study has been presented in detail by Underwood (1994), who, using InfoMap as the audit method, identifies serious deficiencies in the process. However, as he points out, the organisation audited was only three years old, and in a relatively immature stage of development. InfoMap's bottom-up approach is far more likely to be of value to mature and stable organisations, where a common viewpoint on the value of particular information is more likely to have developed.

Information Flow Analysis

The Information Flow Analysis model developed by Liz Orna (1999) is a top-down approach, taking as its starting point an analysis of the organisation's corporate objectives, its structure and culture, with the emphasis on information flow and interactions between individuals and groups of people. Although the model asks 'what is?' it also asks 'what should be?'

The audit itself has elements similar to those outlined by InfoMap, but also includes mapping of information flows, the influence of the IT structure on that flow, and the human element involved in the flow mechanisms. The information flow mapping covers what resources are created/generated within the organisation, and by whom; who are the users, why and how they use them; who are experts in particular areas, who should be knowledgeable about them, and who have no real need to know. This flow map should enable the identification of the whole information flow chain, gaps and duplication, and highlight where links in that chain are missing or weak.

There is now a growing acceptance that the human element is a critical factor. Orna (2000) has recently said: '…librarians in research organisations are equally foxed by encounters with the communications habits of research scientists, and their failure to see either obligation or potential benefit in contributing 'their' information to the organisation's store of knowledge for present and future use … I now look at the problem … as a central rather than an incidental one, because if you can't find a way to deal with it, you might as well not go through the motions of "doing an information audit."'

The human problem is cultural – sharing information (rather than keeping a tight grasp on it), openly reporting failures and problems (rather than hiding them), can provide massive benefits for the organisation but very little for the individual. Attempts are being made in some organisations to tackle this issue, by rewarding sharing and disclosure, rather than penalising lack of success or downright failure. However, if such attempts are unsuccessful or the corporate ethos cannot be changed, the following experience of mine will continue to repeated in one form or another.

> One of my scientists had had major problems with data gathering using a five-hole yawmeter, and asked me to see if anyone else had reported similar difficulties. I followed the design, which is still in international use, back through several text-books and other publications to its origins, only to find it had been designed by two of our own scientists twenty years before! Although their formal report fails to mention any such difficulties, when I spoke to one of the original designers, and described the problems that had been encountered by his colleagues in the next building, he nonchalantly explained that although they had experienced exactly the same hysteresis problems, 'you never reported failures, only successes.' What was probably more disconcerting was that of 75 international papers I traced which

used the same design of probe in their research, and which must all have experienced the same problem, only one had the honesty to report it.

Finally, a balance sheet is then created, comparing the 'what is' situation with the 'what should be' ideal, and highlighting the positive and negative factors. From this can be developed a strategic corporate information policy, and the guidelines and policy instructions that will be necessary to turn a theoretical study into effective practical day-to-day operations.

Like InfoMap, Orna's method has been criticised for a lack of detail in the tools and techniques to carry out the various elements of the audit, but there is no denying that her flow mapping technique is one of the most powerful and essential tools in any current audit process.

Integrated strategic approach

Buchanan and Gibb (1998) propose a far more integrated strategic approach to the audit (Ref 1). Consisting of five major steps, it is an attempt to create a universal model for information audit, although they have predicted that it will have to be amended/customised to local needs. They recommend that the audit is carried out by an information auditor – either an internal or external information professional – with the support of a working group drawn from senior information-related representatives within the organisation. The steps are:

- promote
- identify
- analyse
- account
- synthesise.

Promote

The preliminary stage is aimed at developing an awareness and support of information audit as a concept within the organisation, thus creating and fostering an understanding that information management has a critical strategic importance to its success. Another major target at this stage of the process is to 'reduce suspicion and hostility among staff members'. It is therefore important that the selection of the working group members be comprehensive, in order to avoid the potential problems that have occurred in some organisations before. An awareness drive using, for example, seminars, workshops and internal quality newsletters, can force home the message and encourage participation. There can never be too much publicity at this stage.

It is very important that the working group not only has the power and authority to make changes, but that it is seen and promoted as a body that *will* make changes, rather than as 'just another committee'. They recommend that this preliminary stage is supported by a passport letter from the CEO, outlining what the audit is about, and – perhaps more importantly – giving their full support to the project. In different organisations such support may take different forms (an internal global email for example) but it is very important to get visible support from the highest level, with the implied threat that this support contains. This stage concludes with a preliminary assessment of the awareness of the value of information from a series of walk-rounds, allowing the auditor or auditing team (depending on the size of the organisation) to determine the structure of the audit itself, which will vary according to the nature of the organisation and possibly several other factors.

Identify

Buchanan and Gibb specify six separate steps in the identify stage, with the intention of building up a picture of the organisation's structure, avowed mission, ethos and environment, the available information resources and information flows.

Step 1: What is the organisation's mission? This is seen as key to the whole audit philosophy, providing it with its strategic direction. It is essential to understand what the organisation is there to do in order to assign appropriate values and priorities to its information resources. They recommend the use of three framework tools to carry out this step: Abell's (1980) business definition framework; Synott's (1987) portfolio analysis and Pellow and Wilson's (1993) critical success factor (CSF) approach. There are a large number of alternatives to these tools, but these were favoured because of their widespread use in the business analysis world.

To some it may seem that this particular step is superfluous. Many businesses already have a comprehensive internal strategic analysis of their structure, mission, portfolio and CSFs. However, it is probably worth revisiting all of these statements and conclusions, especially if the view of the organisation as a whole differs from that of the avowed mission.

Step 2: What is the organisation's environment? The recommendation is to carry out a PEST analysis (Johnson and Scholes, 1993) – to find out what political, economic, social and technological influences impinge on the organisation. 'Best fit' information solutions will vary from one organisation to another, often according to their different environments. In addition to PEST they recommend the use of Porter's (1980) model of competitive forces to identify the organisation's competitive position, and use this to assess the role and value of information in relation to corporate competitiveness. It is in this area that you may find significant differences between the corporate view of the environment and the view from 'the factory floor'. What the Board believes to be the current environment, based on reports from its senior management, may differ greatly from the real situation as seen by those who have to get the system to work on a daily basis.

Step 3: What is the organisation's structure? The actual structure of an organisation can aid or hamper information flow and transfer, or be neutral and passive. Any information strategy ultimately proposed has to be compatible with the existing structure: it is all too easy to put forward a plan which has no chance of success because it cannot be made to work with the organisation's existing framework. In most cases, the standard functional model of the organisation should be perfectly adequate, although there are growing trends towards less formal internal structures which may require more in-depth analysis. Buchanan and Gibb then recommend using Mintzberg's analysis (1988) of the structure to examine the closeness of its fit to the already identified organisational strategy, followed by an initial information flow mapping exercise as described above.

Step 4: What is the organisational culture? The very culture of any organisation affects the way information is generated and used, and what value is placed on that information. A stakeholder analysis (Pickering et al., 1996) can be used to identify important stakeholders within the organisation, and to what extent they will influence any future information strategy. It is important to remember that position in the organisation's hierarchy does not necessarily equate with importance as a stakeholder. This should then be followed by an analysis of the various elements within the culture that will affect, either positively or negatively, the information strategy.

Step 5: What are the information flows? A general information flow map, as described by Liz Orna, can now be created from, and overlaid on, the functional and structural maps and models created during the earlier steps.

Step 6: What are the information resources? A fairly comprehensive database of information resources in use within the organisation will have been gathered during the earlier steps. This database will be further refined and greater detail added throughout this phase of the study, largely through face-to-face interviews with users of particular resources, either nominated by the working group champions, or selected by other means. Those interviewed can be asked to place a figure, according to a fixed scale, on each resource they use according to its value, ease of use, functionality etc., together with details of any particular problems associated with using it.

During the interviews additional resources appear out of the woodwork: unofficial systems, work-arounds and separately purchased tools all abound in any organisation. Often, corporate systems which are supposed to be fundamental to the organisation information base – according to management – are found to be so cumbersome and unreliable by the end users that a sub-culture of alternative systems thrives under the surface. In fact some of these systems have been known to replace the official system as the preferred corporate one. If there are too many of these 'revealed' systems, it may be necessary to redo the interviews from the beginning as part of an iterative process, in order to provide as comprehensive resource and value map as possible.

Although each of the above steps is identified as a discrete process, several of them will in fact be carried out at the same time.

Although Buchanan and Gibb conclude the Identify stage at this point, thought should be given to widening the scope of the interviews; having created a comprehensive resource map, it may be advisable to carry out a survey of all of the information users within the organisation. In the past such surveys would have been considered too expensive and time-consuming to justify, but the proliferation of intranets and the availability of easily created electronic questionnaires which dump the results directly into databases have now made the process much more viable. Using the resource map as a template, a wider range of users can be asked to rate each of the separate resources in a similar way to the face-to-face interview, providing a more comprehensive estimate of their value and impact, usability etc. Text boxes might also be included in the survey and could help reveal even more unofficial systems, although there is a possibility of opening too many cans of worms (Stewart and Thornton, 2000).

Analyse

This stage consists of four steps to evaluate and analyse the discovered information resources, identify required remedial actions and produce an initial report. This report will form the basis for a recommended action plan sponsored by the working group.

Step 1: Evaluation of the information resources. The evaluation can be broken down into three separate viewpoints:

1. Strategic importance: what is the resource's relationship to the tasks it is meant to support, and thence to the strategic relationship between tasks, critical success factors and organisational objectives? What was its value score as identified by the interviews and survey?

2. Utility: is it being used by all of the people it was designed / created for, and is it being used to its full potential by those that do? If not, why not? When the full appraisal has been carried out, they recommend using McFarlan and McKenney's (1984) strategic IT/IS grid technique to show its current importance and its planned potential importance to the organisation's overall strategy.

3.   Problems: what are the problems associated with each resource? Do the potential users know it is available; is it accessible by them; is it comprehensive or does it have to be used in conjunction with another disparate system? Is it user friendly or so cumbersome and complex that most users just give up? By identifying these problems, it should be possible to reach an assessment of whether they are easily soluble, would require significant rework to make them useful or accessible, or whether the costs and time involved far exceed the potential value of the resource itself.

> We carried out a limited information audit – I'm not sure that it was really grand enough to be called that – of the resources used by x Faculty. We got surveys completed by a sample of all of the stakeholders, from the Head of Faculty to the students, and asked them to put a value on each of them, 0 to 10, 10 being the best, and 0 if they didn't use it at all … Although the [Department Library catalogue] rated fairly high in usefulness (more for the students, less for the Professors) it also came out with a very low usability score, which surprised us at the time. Compared to [the new catalogue system], in retrospect it probably was unfriendly and archaic; but we still miss it![3]

Step 2: Production of a final version of a detailed information flow analysis. This is created by overlaying the full information resource map onto the general information flow diagram, showing who is using what and why.

Step 3: Produce an interim report. This should be a summary report of the audit process so far, its findings and recommendations, highlighting areas of concern and including a series of action plans to resolve those concerns.

Step 4: Initiation of action plans. The report should be presented to the working group, who can then discuss and agree the proposed action plans, and recommend their adoption and action. It is therefore imperative that the working group has teeth, and can see changes through. Recommendations for action, without any power to see they are carried out, is just a waste of time. They recommend the use of the Checkland soft system (1990) method to deal with poorly defined problem areas.

Account

The account stage attempts to identify the costs in information resource creation and maintenance, and thus to allow a cost/benefit analysis to be carried out, something which should be core to the development of any form of information strategy, but which – in my experience - is rarely carried out at the time a resource is created or introduced.

This is one of the biggest problem areas in any information audit. Orna stresses the importance of only attempting to carry out this particular

task with the full co-operation of the organisation's accounting department. This will allow the exercise to fit in with existing costing practices,
but few organisations actually have experience in costing information as
a resource, and there are relatively few accepted models which you can
follow. Buchanan and Gibb (1998) identify three which may be suitable.
They are:

1. *Activity based costing (ABC).* Turney's ABC method (1996) is based
    on the causal relationship between the cost of the activity and the
    use of the nominated information resources . This is a very detailed
    approach, which may preclude its use for more than just a handful
    of selected resources.

2. *Output based specification (OBS).* 'OBS is a quality performance meas-
    urement system that also provides, where required, a mechanism
    to link payment to quality performance by identifying the mini-
    mum quality standards and quality indicators for each information
    resource (rather than costs). ABC and OBS can be usefully com-
    bined to provide a rigorous analysis of inputs and outputs to a
    process' (quoted in Buchanan and Gibb, 1998, 45).

3. *Glazier's model (1993).* This model identifies the delivered value of
    individual information resources where they assist in improving
    revenue, reduce costs, and aid customer demand.

These are not the only methods which can be used, and the surveys by
Keyes (1995) and Koenig (1992) of various techniques may provide alternatives, although usually aimed at library type information resources.
Nevertheless, whatever approach is used, this still remains the most problematic area of information auditing, and the one where senior
management may dispute the final results. Personally, I cannot help but
feel that the account stage needs to be carried out prior to the formulation
of action plans. If resources no longer have value to an organisation, there
seems little purpose in including them in an action plan.

Synthesise
The final stage consists of the production of two reports. The first is the
comprehensive report on the audit, how it was conducted, what it found,
and its recommendations. The second is the creation of an overarching
information strategy based on the audit's findings. This will link the
organisation's business strategy, its objectives and future plans with the
means of providing the optimum information resources to support those
targets.

Two further points need to be raised. Is an information audit a one-off
snapshot, or should it be seen as a continuing process? While a single
audit represents the situation in an organisation at a given point in time,
it is expensive and time consuming. If the full benefits of proper

information management in support of the organisation's aims is to be achieved, it needs to be part of an on-going information strategy. New information resources are continually being designed, created or purchased to meet newly identified needs and old resources are being updated, and even occasionally improved.

By monitoring new resources and improvements to the existing ones, the information resource map can be kept up-to-date, and snap surveys of value and usability estimation carried out. The results of this monitoring exercise can be used to refresh the audit results, leading to modifications of the information strategy if necessary. However, after a while a full information audit will need to be repeated to maintain the currency of the information strategy it supports. Secondly, unless the results of the audit and strategy are implemented and integrated into the organisation's culture, the whole thing just becomes a pointless theoretical exercise. Mechanisms need to be put in place for ensuring the recommendations are implemented.

Is it worthwhile?

To be successful, an information audit has to have:

- full commitment from senior management
- adequate resourcing
- the right blend of skills, talents and representation
- adequate power and authority to overcome internal opposition
- ongoing commitment within the organisation to see recommendations implemented.

If you lack any of these, you are probably doomed to failure from the outset.

> Now, I'd spent a lot of time on (the audit report), a lot of my time – not just the firm's, and we presented the results to ... the Finance Manager, who had overall responsibility for IT. And there it stayed.[4]

Nevertheless, a successful audit can reduce wasted effort, highlight duplication and shortages, and become the cornerstone of an organisation's effective information strategy, ultimately leading to improvements in business success.

> 'The experience has been very positive from a number of points of view:
>
> • The definition of the organisation's information policy

- The increased awareness of personnel, as the audit supported this and got them involved in the discussion of results and proposals

- The improved perception of the Information Service as a key element in the work of the organisation' (Soy and Bustelo, 1999).

References

Abell, D.F. *Defining the Business: the starting point of strategic planning.* Englewood Cliffs, NJ: Prentice-Hall (1980).

Buchanan, S. and Gibb, F. The information audit: an integrated strategic approach. *International Journal of Information Management,* **18**(1) 1998, 29-47.

Burk, C.F. and Horton, F.W. *InfoMap: a complete guide to discovering corporate information resources.* Englewood Cliffs, NJ: Prentice-Hall (1988).

Checkland, P. and Scholes, J. *Soft Systems Methodology in Action.* Chichester: John Wiley (1990).

Dalton, P. Investigating information auditing. *Library and Information Research News,* **23**(Summer) 1999, 45-50.

Glazier, R. Measuring the value of information. *IBM Systems Journal,* **32**(1) 1993.

Johnson, G. and Scholes, K. *Exploring Corporate Strategy: text and cases.* Englewood Cliffs, NJ: Prentice-Hall (1993, 3rd ed.).

Keyes, A.M. The value of the special library: review and analysis. *Special Libraries,* **86**(3) 1995, 172-87.

Koenig, M. The importance of information services for productivity 'under-recognized and under-invested'. *Special Libraries,* **83**(4) 1992, 199-210.

McFarlan, F.W. Information technology changes the way you compete. *Harvard Business Review,* **62**(May-June) 1984, 62.

Mintzberg, H. The structuring of organisations. In: Quinn, J.B., Mintzberg, H. and James, R.M. (eds) *The Strategy Process: concept, contexts and cases.* New York, NY: Prentice-Hall (1988), 278.

Orna, E. The human face of information auditing. *Managing Information,* **7**(4) 2000, 40-2.

Orna, E. *Practical Information Policies.* Aldershot: Gower (1999, 2nd ed.).

Oxbrow, N. Quoted in: Dimattia, S.S. and Blumenstein, L. In search of the information audit: essential tool or cumbersome process? *Library Journal,* 1 zMarch 2000, 48-50.

Pellow, A. and Wilson, T.D. The management information requirement of heads of university departments: a critical success factors approach. *Journal of Information Science,* **19**(6) 1993, 425-37.

Pickering, H., Crawford, J.C. and McLelland, D. *The Stakeholder Approach to the Construction of Performance Measures: a report to the British Library Research and Development Department.* Glasgow: Glasgow Caledonian University (1996) (British Library Research and Innovation Report 31).

Porter, M.E. *Competitive Strategy: techniques for analysing industries and competitors.* New York, NY: Free Press (1980).

Snowden, D. Liberating knowledge. In: Reeves, J. (ed.) *Liberating Knowledge.* London: Caspian Publishing (1999), 6-19.

Soy, C. and Bustelo, C. A practical approach to information audit: case study. *Managing Information,* **6**(9) 1999, 30-8 and **6**(10) 1999, 60-1.

Stewart, C.D. and Thornton, S.A. The use of an impact survey as a measure of special library performance. In: *Proceedings of the 3ʳᵈ Northumbria International Conference on Performance Measurement in Libraries and Information Services.* Newcastle upon Tyne: Information North (2000), 243-6.

Synott, W.R. *The Information Weapon: winning customers and markets with technology.* New York, NY; London: John Wiley (1987).

Turney, P.B.B. *Activity Based Costing: the performance breakthrough.* London: Kogan Page (1996).

Underwood, P.G. Checking the Net: a soft-systems approach to information auditing. *South African Journal of Library and Information Science,* **62**(2) 1994, 59-64.

Private communications

1.   Anonymous senior librarian, UK government department. 1999.

2.   Anonymous industrial special librarian, European pan-government organisation. 2000.

3.   Academic librarian, UK university. 1998.

4.   Former special librarian, UK chemical company. 2000.

Chapter 6

Performance measurement and metrics

Sandra Parker and Marshall Crawford

Introduction

Measuring performance is a key management activity. Measures are needed to provide an indication of the effectiveness of a library or information service – however, services are notoriously difficult to measure. A service is intangible and depends on an act that is often variable, lacks consistency and depends on the interaction between the client and the provider. The production and consumption are simultaneous and transitory; special libraries and information services offer intangible services directed at peoples' minds. The staff often have a membership relationship with their clients and usually provide services in discrete transactions. The services themselves are customised, the staff are specialised in meeting individual needs. Services can be delivered in person or through electronic means and may be offered from single or multiple sites, therefore measuring effectiveness is complex. Performance measurement can be seen merely as a reactive mechanism, responding to the need for accountability. Information service managers however should welcome the process, as above all they need to account for their services to their stakeholders and clients. It is they who will decide if the information service lives or dies, is worthy of investment or starved of resources. The indicators will tell the story of the service and it is by this means, by having an effective Information Strategy, that decisions on future strategic developments will be made.

Information strategy

Meeting the information needs of an organisation will be made easier if it has information policies that clearly relate to the strategic goals of the organisation. Because there is no single agreed system for expressing such information policy, a review of Information Strategy may help in understanding the context in which the performance measurement is taking place. Positive support from top management is more likely to be gained when the goals of an information unit are expressed, at least in part, in terms that are used in strategic planning for the organisation.

Elizabeth Orna (1999, p.10) defines it thus:

> Information strategy is the detailed expression of information policy in terms of objectives, targets, and actions to achieve them, for a defined period ahead. Information strategy provides the framework for the management of information. Information strategy, contained within the framework of an organisation policy for information and supported by appropriate systems and technology is the 'engine' for:
>
> - maintaining, managing and applying the organisation's information resources
> - supporting its essential knowledge base and all who contribute to it, with strategic intelligence, for achieving its key business objectives.

Most academic and government agencies have developed and published an Information Strategy. These are valuable within their context but do not translate easily into the private sector with its focus on revenue/income generation and competition. Indeed, some of the dissemination policies of academic and government agencies are the exact opposite of the confidential commercial environments of private organisations. There is no single method of developing an Information Strategy which could be all embracing, but there are several useful models which should help communication with senior management, because these methods are generally stated in management terms rather than purely information terms. A better understanding of Information Strategy can be derived from studying the guidelines for developing Information Strategy.

JISC

The Joint Information Systems Committee of the Funding Councils for Higher Education *Guidelines for Developing an Information Strategy* is expressed as a set of attitudes in which:

- any information that should be available for sharing (and most will be) is well defined and appropriately accessible (allowing for necessary safeguards)
- the quality of information is fit for its purpose (e.g. accuracy, currency, consistency, completeness – but only as far as necessary)
- all staff know, and exercise their responsibilities towards information
- there is a mechanism by which priorities are clearly identified and then acted upon.

Reuters guide to good information strategy

This guide gives many case studies of how Information Strategy has been developed and cites 10 steps to a good Information Strategy:

- Appoint a senior person with overall responsibility for information management.
- Conduct an enterprise wide information audit.
- Conduct an enterprise wide technology audit.
- Pinpoint information dearths and excesses and define an overall strategy for rationalising these.
- Ensure the Information Strategy is championed at board level.
- Communicate the strategy and its importance to all members of the organisation and gain their buy-in.
- Train staff in effective information management and systems operation.
- Clean corporate data to maintain its veracity.
- Provide incentives for information sharing.
- Implement procedures for continually monitoring the strategy's effectiveness.

Donald Marchand (2000) reflects the business school background and views information as a means for creating competitive or entrepreneurial opportunities. This does not restrict its use to those of 'high flying businesses' and it is possible to relate the Strategic Information Alignment (SIA) framework outlined in this book to many information activities. SIA states that information can be seen to support one of four activities: minimise risk, reduce costs, add value or create new reality.

With a better understanding of the Information Strategy, it is possible to measure performance against each of these activities. Marchand's book provides excellent examples of benchmarking. Each of these facets is described in detail and benchmarking indicators provided for measuring activity across the organisation (the organisational culture and structure, personnel and skills development, brand perception, marketing and customers, innovation, information systems). There is one more step in this process of relating to strategy and that is establishing the scope of activity to be measured. Information is rarely the responsibility of one person or department, and particularly with the rise of Knowledge Management, the borders have been blurred with many people making claim to being the gatekeeper for information. Marchand's book presents this framework:

This should clarify which aspects of information are being measured and assist in identifying those areas of overlap with others where some negotiation may be required to establish who is measuring what (and against what criteria). Knowledge Management often sets out to deal with 'all the information' within an organisation and this proves too ambitious (or possibly too threatening) in many cases. It may be best to demonstrate how an effective Information Strategy operates within the immediate scope of information services. If this is seen to be a success it can be built on and then there may be the possibility of acting as consultant to other business areas (financial information, marketing information, etc.).

Information is power and while others in the organisation may be happy for the library to be managed in this way they may feel threatened when a wider view is taken on information in the organisation. This leads back to the most important rule: there needs to be a strong supporter from management on the team. If not it may not be possible to gain access to the management information required, to delineate the business strategy of the organisation and later, in the implementation phase, this strong supporter may be able to enforce the Information Strategy when that is required.

Regardless of the scope of the content, it is important to consider all sources of information when developing an Information Strategy. Information managers are often seen as being in the business of acquiring and managing external information, yet some of the most valuable information in an organisation is internal information. Similarly the information services must not be restricted to 'library' materials – in addition to journals and books, there is the whole multimedia world of information which does not fit so easily into the traditional view of information management. In it simplest terms, Information Strategy is the application of technical and human resources to information resources in order to produce results which support the goals of the organisation.

It is critical that there is a thorough understanding of the need for, and value of, Information Strategy before embarking on its development. There are at least two reasons for this. Firstly, it must be possible to keep sight of the higher level goals of the exercise. There are examples of Information Strategy which are nothing more than lists of information resources or IT facilities (email, WWW, video conferencing, etc.). Secondly, when dealing with senior management it is necessary to be able to explain the value of the exercise in strategic terms or there is a risk not gaining their co-operation.

If the organisation has a well-documented business strategy it is a fairly straightforward exercise to review these in terms of information needs. Internal and external inputs and outputs must be considered together with any processing of the information, and what is achieved with the output. A checklist should be used which spans all the activities of the organisation (management, research and development, marketing, production, distribution, administration). Even if some of these are not within the sphere of influence of the information service, it can be noted which are being handled by others and those that appear to be 'falling through the net'.

Information Strategy can often identify the information needed within an organisation and highlight ways in which this information (and the information resulting from processes within the organisation) can be used to best effect in pursuing the business goals of the organisation. It is inevitable that owing to the prevalence of discussion on the Internet and the value of IT, that management may be looking for the IT component of the Information Strategy. It must be remembered that traditional information management skills are not as widely known as they should be and they should not be overlooked. Indeed, they may need explanation (in a diplomatic fashion, of course). Information identification, acquisition, assessment, evaluation, processing are all tasks which may need to be undertaken before it is provided to the user. Similarly, information management skills are useful in developing strategies for long term archiving and maintenance of information.

Measures

Each workplace library or information service is different in terms of markets, products, organisational structure, corporate culture and maturity in terms of process management and quality management. They are diverse in terms of subject and funding, geographical location, size and lack of focus. Thus measuring their performance and providing benchmarks has seemed to be an impossible task. There is none of the cohesive nature of the public library sector or higher education. This often makes meaningful measurement and comparison very difficult to achieve, except within the organisation and in time lapse mode. Organisations need a balanced group of measures which provide a well-rounded view of their purpose and function. A single measure such as cost of the service per employee can be very misleading. Measures which only focus on internal activity can also be distorting, thus measure are needed which represent data on customers and competitors.

Measures should satisfy the following criteria: relevance, helpfulness, validity, reliability, practicality, comparability, affordability and sensitivity. They should include measures of inputs, outputs and service effectiveness. Examples of measures for traditional print based services could be:

Output measures:

- library membership/visits per capita

- circulation/loans per capita
- stock turnover rate i.e. library stock, annual issues.

Input measures:

- How much does it cost to catalogue a book?
- How much per loan?
- How much per interlibrary loan?

Service effectiveness measures:

- enquiry satisfaction rate
- document delivery rate.

Performance indicators are measures put into use and are the relationship between two or more measures.

- Operational performance indicators relate input to outcome measures to examine the internal effectiveness of the service (e.g. average number of loans per item per annum).
- Effectiveness indicators relate outputs to outcomes (e.g. cost benefit to clients of the enquiry service).
- Service indicators relate inputs to outcomes (e.g. user satisfaction).

Measures for the electronic environment are much more difficult to determine. For example, in order to provide services the library or information service needs to have intelligence or information about both the user population and the information 'record'. Traditionally in the print environment the former has been met by collecting registration data, while the latter has been the catalogue and related bibliographies and indexes. In an electronic environment this is not possible or sufficient, and imaginative alternative measures must be used. They may usefully include the following:

- *Technical infrastructure*: the hardware, software equipment, communication lines and technical aspects (e.g. workstations, modems, servers)
- *Information content:* the resources available on the network
- *Information services*: the activities which users can access on the system such as online applications
- *Support:* the assistance and support services provided to help users (e.g. training, help desks)
- *Management of the network:* the human resources, planning and finance .

The following types of criteria evaluate web-based use and services:

- *Extensiveness*: how much service the network provides (e.g. number of hits per day)
- *Efficiency:* the use of resources accessing networked information services (e.g. cost per session, or number of times access fails)
- *Effectiveness:* how well the service meets the objectives of the provider/user (e.g. enquiry/helpline success rates)
- *Impact:* how a service made a difference in some part of the organisations activities (e.g. demonstrable savings in researchers time)
- *Usefulness:* the degree to which the services are useful or appropriate for individual users (e.g. the range of users within the organisation)
- *Adoption:* the extent to which organisations or users integrate and adopt electronic networked resources or services into individual activities (e.g. answering queries on requesting interlibrary loans).

An excellent example of the evaluation of a web site can be found on the ICEnet: The Institution of Civil Engineers Homepage (ICEnet, August 2000). The Monthly Statistics pages cover the total accesses, most popular date, most accessed page, busiest time, top three accessed pages, top three domains, top three countries. It also includes the most accessed resource centres and graphs covering the statistics by the hour: average requests per hour, by date and hits by day. Output measures or indicators should be complemented by assessments of user satisfaction with the service that can be achieved by: discussion with users, focus groups, self-administered questionnaires and by observation. The user or client should be central to the process.

Mechanisms – techniques and tools

There is a wide range of mechanisms which enable managers to organise performance measurement data in order to produce informed indicators. These are often then seen as management fads and can be the product of a passing fashion or the obsession of the moment. Others have become integrated and embedded in to good management practice.

Qualitative measures

- *Case studies* – in-depth exploration of selected service areas and target audiences in branches or groups of the organisation. The findings would be used to inform broader quantitative data collection activities such as mail and electronic surveys
- *Content analysis* – gather documentation and reports to review historical development and evolution of network related activities
- *Focus groups* – explore key issues areas of content, service, management and performance.

Quantitative measures

- *Mail/electronic surveys* – to explore identified key issues of content, services, management and performance with a broader population base
- *Traffic measures* – to collect network/terminal traffic use statistics such as number of users, user access points, information and service content use, network server and router load
- *Web Log File Analysis* – to measure web-based services by the analysis of the web server log
- *Individual interviews* – to undertake in-depth exploration of content, services, management and performance with key project administrators and users to assess the development of the print and network environment.

Benchmarking

Benchmarks provide a route to determining appropriate standards for a service, which are based in practice rather than aimed at excellence (which can rarely be achieved). It is a continuous and systematic process of studying and evaluating similar services in order to establish 'best practice' and therefore rational performance goals.

The purpose is to identify areas for improvement and to stimulate change by:

- *Competitive analysis* – the systematic analysis of competitor activity so that performance can be matched and improved; data can be difficult to acquire in competitive environments
- *Best practice* – looking for best practice associated with the way that information services perform
- *Performance comparison* – comparing organisational and functional performance to identify areas for improvement and innovation
- *Standard setting* – a means of providing guidance on setting and appropriate performance standard; the Department of Culture Media and Sport is currently setting standards for public libraries.

Much work has been done in this area. Particularly important for the sector are LISU's invaluable publications *TFPL Survey of UK Special Library Statistics* (Creaser and Spiller, 1997) and *Libraries in the Workplace* (Spiller et al., 1998). The latter supplies benchmarking material on: number of libraries, reporting structures, corporate Information Strategy, target users, outsourcing, space, automation systems, budgets, staff, electronic and print materials, use and performance, document delivery and automation. The main findings are presented by sector with a comparison of the sectors.

Benchmarking is carried out as follows:

- *Planning* – decisions need to be made about what is to be benchmarked, focusing on those areas which are most important and will deliver greatest returns e.g. measuring the usage of electronic information services to justify investment.

- *Collecting data* – decisions need to be made on the sources of the data; appropriate organisations and people can be approached; the right questions need to be asked and the information provided evaluated.

- *Analysing the results* – compare figures and solutions to ensure that like is compared with like; what can be learned needs to be assessed.

- *Implementing changes* – the improvements need to be made need to be established; the change needs to be planned and executed; appropriate people should be involved in the planning, analysis and decision making.

- *Evaluating progress* – the changes need to be reviewed and corrective action taken if necessary; it may be necessary to gather new information from different sources, or to check the validity of the initial data.

Balanced Scorecard

The importance of not relying on single measures or indicators was recognised by Robert Kaplan and David Norton (Kaplan and Norton, 1992) when they developed the Balanced Scorecard approach. They developed the system to translate an organisation's mission and strategy into a comprehensive set of performance measures, which provide the framework for a strategic measurement and management system. There are two key objectives: to convert strategy into specific goals for different sections of the organisation (e.g. information services) and to communicate that strategy to all parts of the organisation. They advised the use of a limited number of key measures from each of four critical perspectives:

- *Financial* – How do we look to our stakeholders?
- *Customer* – How do our customers see us?
- *Internal business* – What must we excel at?
- *Innovation and learning* – Can we continue to create value?

The Balanced Scorecard is a comprehensive framework to translate organisations' strategic objectives, which would include those of the library and information services, into a coherent set of performance measures. In addition, Judy Broady warns 'Developments such as the increasing use of score cards models require all strategists to be expert at information retrieval and analysis. Therefore unless information strategists equip themselves with the requisite knowledge of such models, they may find themselves marginalised increasingly within their organisations' (Broady, 2000).

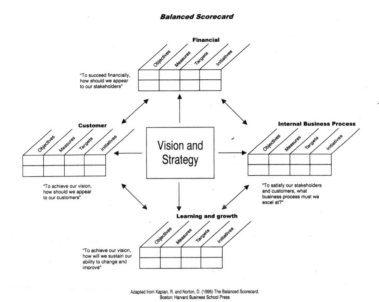

Adapted from Kaplan, R. and Norton, D. (1996) The Balanced Scorecard. Boston: Harvard Business School Press

Management measures

F.W. Taylor, the father of Scientific Management, was fascinated by the inefficiencies of much of the work that he observed (see Handy, 1993, 21). To counteract this he suggested that managers should plan ahead, count things and movements, allocate tasks and responsibilities, limit the span of control and review results. This was and is common sense and much of it prevails. However the 'span of control' is now vastly greater than it was even in the 1980s because of the perceived need to reduce management costs and the current approach to motivation of such theorists as McGregor and Peters. They emphasise the motivational qualities of creating opportunities for individuals to work independently to agreed goals and not within a narrow span of control. However, performance measurement in terms of productivity remains important and much discussion is available on discussion lists on the average time it takes to catalogue a book and so on (see the mailbase discussion list, lis-perf measures).

For example, employee absenteeism is a problem faced by all service managers as it erodes both salary budgets and productivity. It can have an undermining effect on staff morale, and it may be an indicator of low staff motivation levels. Morale is part of the culture of organisations and as such can be difficult to measure in any quantitative form, thus any indicators in this area must be valued. Maslow (1954) indicated that insecurity and change can cause increased sickness and absence rates, increased turnover of staff and poor industrial relations. As information and library workers live in the greatest period of change in 200 years, staff may succumb to greatly increased pressure and managers must have accurate methods of recognising and responding to any changes. It may be possible to predict stress in some change situations and thus be able to take appropriate action ahead of the problem. Managing a service industry where the quality of the service depends directly upon the effectiveness, efficiency and tacit knowledge of well-trained and motivated staff is much more difficult if those staff become unreliable in attendance. In *Absent from Work,* a survey by recruitment consultants Alfred Marks, 40 per cent of companies say that high levels of absenteeism were caused by poor management and 35 per cent low job interest or motivation – both issues which could be addressed by an effective change in management (Bolton, 1993).

Sickness and absence rate measurements must be easily obtainable and accurate. Analysis by managers can reveal trends and patterns that can quickly indicate areas that need to be addressed. In the UK at present, the average number of days of absence is eight per annum, but in Japanese owned companies it is much less (Employee, 1993). This would indicate that the culture of the organisation and management response to the problem could significantly affect performance.

How should an organisation define and measure absenteeism? It falls into two distinct groups. The first is *unavoidable absence* that employees and employers believe to be legitimate under the terms of their contract. This includes illness, bereavement, jury service for example. *Avoidable absences* involve some kind of individual choice, which employers would not see as justifiable and where motivation is seen as playing a part.

A firm's personnel policy document must address the grey areas which might be thought to belong to either category such as doctor or dentist appointments, driving tests, or the death of a non-family member. Such absences must be firmly allocated in a classification system so that meaningful and useful performance measures can be developed. These may not be universally applicable and may lose their viability over time, for example what may be acceptable during slack time may not be acceptable during busy time. Any measurement of the problem – 'an essential precursor to effective action' – is dependent on access to accurate information; ' . . . the number of companies that don't have the right picture is amazing' (Bolton, 1993).

Lost time rate is the most common form of measurement. This shows the percentage of the total time available which has been lost because of absence from all causes in a given period.

Total absence (hours or days) x 100 = Lost Time Rate

Possible total (hours or days) available

For example, if the total absence in the period is 124 hours, and the possible total working time is 1,550 hours, the lost time rate is:

124 x 100 = 8 per cent

1550

Use of this type of measure, benchmarked against other organisations, departments or previous years will determine the scale of the problem and highlight specific areas which need attention. Where absenteeism becomes a focus of management attention and the process is measured there can be very tangible improvements. One organisation claimed that it experienced a 50 per cent reduction in absenteeism from 8 per cent to 4 per cent over a three year period (Parker, 1996).

Service quality

Service quality is a judgment about the ability of a service to fulfill its task. Parasuraman, Zeithmal and Berry refer to it as 'a form of attitude, related but not equivalent to satisfaction, (it) results from a comparison of expectations with perceptions of performance ' (Parasuraman et al., 1994). Customer satisfaction refers often to a specific transaction, whereas service quality is more generalised, long term and enduring based on previous encounters.

The major approach to measuring service quality during the last 20 years has been based on the work of Parasuraman, Zeithmal and Berry, who in 1988 devised the SERVQUAL instrument (Parasuraman et al., 1988). It measures quality in terms of the gap between the expectation (E) of the customer and the performance (P) of the service, and is commonly thought of the P-E approach. The associated Gap equation is therefore Q=P-E. In a SERQUAL exercise the client responds by questionnaire to the same 22 questions twice. First to establish their expectations of the ideal service and then to record their perceptions of the actual service provided by a particular library or information service, for example. Each response is recorded on a seven point Likert scale. The different scores are computed by subtracting the score for expectation from the perceptions, so scores can range from - to +6, thus the higher the score, the higher the perception of quality.

As a service provider the Gap model is appealing to librarians and information service providers, as there have always been difficulties in assessing meaningful outcomes. The skill in using the system lies in the identification of the questions asked to the clients to ensure that the scores are valid and reliable. There are obvious gaps that exist in service quality and the questions will focus on those areas, but some questions must be asked to ascertain the weight or relative importance that the client awards to the differing aspects of the service. Questions which were identified as being the most important in an academic environment (see Cook, 2000) were:

- providing services as promised
- convenient business hours
- employees having the knowledge to answer questions
- willingness to answer questions
- maintaining error free customer and catalogue records
- providing service at the promised time.

Over a period of three years the question with the highest perceived mean score was 'Convenient business hours' and this would provide the basis for entering into discussion with management to move towards the now relatively common 24 hours a day opening.

The evidence seems to be that Servqual provides the best tool available to identify best practice. 'The instrument introduces a mechanism to shift the assessment of the quality of a library from the traditions of measuring collection size and counting incidents of its uses, to begin investigating how the provision of services relates to library users service quality perceptions' (Nitecki, 1996).

Conclusion

Although 'What gets measured gets done' is a favoured management stance, it is important not to assume that only that which is measured is important or valued. Effectively measuring performance in the virtual library will bring a different set of challenges. However the principles remain the same: the strategies and policies must be paramount, and increasingly imaginative measures and indicators will need to be developed. The challenge has only just begun.

References

Bolton, L. Absence makes the company poorer. *Accountancy*, **11** January 1993, 44-6.

Braithwaite, Kenmore. *Information Engineering*. CRC Press (1994).

Broady, Judith. Scorecards and their use in measuring performance: UK retail banks: a case study. In: *Proceedings of the 3ʳᵈ Northumbria International Conference on Performance Measurement in Libraries and Information Services*. Information North (2000).

Cook, Colleen. SERVQUAL: a client based approach to developing performance indicators. In: *Proceedings of the 3ʳᵈ Northumbria International Conference on Performance Measurement in Libraries and Information Services.* Information North (2000).

Creaser, C and Spiller, David. *TFPL Survey of UK Special Library Statistics.* Loughborough: LISU Department of Information and Library Studies, Loughborough University (LISU Occasional Paper no. 15).

Employee absence: industrial society CBI chart patterns and policies. *Industrial Relations Review.* May 1993.

Guidelines for Developing an Information Strategy: a report prepared by Coopers & Lybrand and the JISC's Information Strategies Steering Group. (1995). Available at *http://www.jisc.ac.uk/pub/infstrat/.*

Handy, C. *Understanding organisations.* Penguin (1993).

ICEnet. The Institution of Civil Engineers Homepage, monthly statistics. Available at *http://www.ice.org.uk* (August 2000).

Kaplan, Robert S and Norton, David P. Putting the Balanced Scorecard to work. *Harvard Business Review,* **70**(1) 1992, 71-9.

Lis-perf-measures. Available at *http://www.mailbase.ac.uk/lists/lis-perf-measures/.*

Marchand, Donald. *Competing with Information.* John Wiley (2000).

Maskell, B. Performance measurement for World Glass Manufacturing. *Management Accounting,* **67**(5) 1967, 32-3.

Maslow, A. H. *Motivation and Personality.* Harper and Row (1954).

Nitecki, D.A. Changing the concept and measure of service quality in academic libraries. *Journal of Academic Librarianship,* **22**(3) May 1996, 181-90.

Orna, Elizabeth. *Practical Information Policies.* Aldershot: Gower (1999, 2ⁿᵈ ed.).

Parasuraman, A., Zeithmal, V.A. and Berry, L.L. Reassessment of expectations as a comparison standard in measuring service quality: implications for further research. *Journal of Marketing,* **58**(1) 1994, 111-24.

Parasuraman, A., Zeithmal, V.A. and Berry L.L. SERVQUAL: a multiple-item scale for measuring consumer perceptions of service quality. *Journal of Retailing,* **64**(1) Spring 1988, 12-40.

Parker, Sandra. Performance indicators: sickness and absence rates as indicators of staff morale. In: *Proceedings of the 1st Northumbria Interna-*

tional Conference on Performance Measurement in Libraries and Information Services. Information North (1996).

Powell, Alan. Management models and measurement in the virtual library. *Special Libraries,* Fall 1994, 260-3.

Reuters Guide to Good Information Strategy. Note: Reuters are now known as Factiva and the document is no longer available on their web site. It may be possible to access this document by contacting Factiva or via a search on Northern Light through its Special Collection.

Spiller, David, Creaser, Claire and Murphy, Alison. *Libraries in the Workplace.* Loughborough: LISU Department of Information and Library Studies, Loughborough University (1998) (LISU Occasional Paper no. 20).

Chapter 7

Knowledge management: working at the speed of 'e'

Neil Munn

Introduction

Knowledge management (KM) is a topic that has captured the attention of senior management in the commercial world over the past five years. Numerous books, journals, articles, conferences and web sites have been produced discussing the concepts that make up KM, highlighting the fact that managing knowledge is a vital activity in an increasingly knowledge-based global economy. In a recent survey produced by KPMG Consulting (2000), KM was recognised as an essential business tool with some 79 per cent of respondents regarding it as playing an 'extremely' or 'very significant' role in improving competitive advantage.

As commerce is increasingly knowledge-driven, the explosion of ready access to external information, fuelled by cheaper technology and widespread take-up of the Internet, has ignited a parallel interest in managing internal knowledge 'assets'. With external information being plentiful and often free, competitive advantage for organisations lies in the ability to access and exploit the information and experience stored in their employees' heads. Companies are spending large sums of money on enterprise-wide KM programmes in an effort to enhance their performance as the rapid rise of e-business continues. Knowledge is increasingly at the 'heart of the business'.

Managing information and knowledge are key aspects of many information specialists' work and the rise of the dedicated 'knowledge manager' within the ranks of information professionals has been very noticeable. It is a rapidly evolving job and this chapter seeks to examine the key skills required for performing this role in today's fast changing corporate environment.

What is knowledge management?

There are numerous definitions of KM, usually involving some distillation of the idea that an organisation seeks to identify, capture, disseminate and exploit the knowledge it possesses for the benefit of both its employees and clients. Knowledge guides actions and informs decisions – it is personal to an individual, based on their unique experiences and associations.

Managing knowledge is important for the following reasons:

- People need knowledge to make change happen.
- Knowledge encourages the cross fertilisation and cross contribution of ideas.
- Knowledge capture creates an organisation that remembers what it knows.
- Knowledge sharing gives people a sense of belonging.
- Lack of knowledge breeds uncertainty and anxiety, which in turn interferes with focus and productivity.

Creating a knowledge management strategy

Many organisations have already developed, or are in the process of creating, a KM strategy. It is very important that the aspiring information specialist looking for a role as a knowledge manager seeks to involve him or herself in this strategy creation at the earliest possible stage. KM is an increasingly competitive environment, and competition for leading internal roles will come from other internal functions within an organisation such as IT (information technology), Marketing and HR (human resources). IT is often the major rival as the success of a KM programme often depends greatly on a reliable technological solution. But IT is predominantly an enabler, the foundation infrastructure that supports a successful KM programme – it should not be the driver.

The aim of any KM strategy is to set out clearly the activities necessary to integrate knowledge management into the business processes of an organisation in order to benefit performance and support the overall aims of the organisation. The strategy will need to consider the people, technology, processes and cultural aspects that will be required to produce a successful cohesive programme. Senior sponsorship is essential to drive a KM programme – those KM programmes that have failed have often suffered from a lack of executive sponsorship and have consequently delivered little value to an organisation. Information specialists need to identify who the key senior KM champions are within their organisations and develop strong relationships with them.

A KM strategy must be closely aligned with the business. This requires a detailed understanding of the challenges facing an organisation and the marketplace within which it operates. Given the rapid changes currently affecting all markets the KM strategy will need to be flexible and quick to respond to the needs of the business. Understanding the context of the organisation is crucial to identifying correctly the most important knowledge issues.

KM involves connecting people to people, and people with information. Information may be external or internal, tacit or explicit, and the KM strategy needs to set out how these connections will take place. Knowledge sharing is enhanced when staff can readily identify sources or colleagues who can assist with queries – a clear example of exploiting what the organisation knows.

Many organisations have appointed a Chief Knowledge Officer (CKO), who has the responsibility for co-ordinating the KM programme across the enterprise. Sometimes this is a member of senior management given a new or additional role, or it may be a specialist brought in from outside. The CKO will usually seek to devise a central team to support and implement the programme and this gives information specialists the opportunity to be involved – their expertise can be extremely valuable in developing the mechanisms that will support knowledge management activities. Failure to become integrated within any proposed KM programme heightens the risk of the information specialist becoming marginalised within the organisation and may ultimately lead to their role becoming redundant.

Much of KM depends heavily on the organisation's culture and staff behaviour. The aims of whole enterprise collaboration and the sharing of knowledge are laudable and relatively easy to write down in a plan – they are much harder to implement effectively. Any KM strategy needs to pay careful attention to the existing culture to sense how change (assuming it is required) may be instigated. Staff will instinctively wish to understand the reasoning behind any proposed change in behaviour and most obviously need to understand the benefits that they will experience. Attention to possible incentives to promote knowledge sharing may be required – these could be tied closely to performance appraisal evaluation mechanisms or may be remuneratively driven. Rewarding and highlighting good examples of knowledge sharing are essential to send clear messages to the whole of the organisation that this type of behaviour is not only encouraged, but also expected.

Visible senior management support will be essential here but any change in management effort should seek to employ both a 'top-down' and 'bottom-up' approach. The aim should be to create a momentum and enthusiasm for knowledge sharing from all parts of the organisation that spreads, virus-like, through the corporate body and infuses staff positively. Ultimately, continued momentum will depend on whether an individual experiences benefits from the programme or makes a conscious effort to share knowledge – anything that makes it easier for staff to perform their daily work and improves the overall productivity of an organisation should be generally welcomed.

In addition to positively altering culture and behaviour, improving flows of knowledge across the organisation and capturing the most important material and making it readily available is also of paramount importance. Good content management will require support from technology but it is important to be able to distinguish between the two – technology should be focused on the tools that will enable efficient search and retrieval of knowledge. Content management seeks to provide the right information to the right person at the right time. In order to develop the correct content management strategy, the KM strategy has to examine what types of information and knowledge staff require, depending on the role they perform. Making tacit and explicit content from both external and internal sources available to staff is a complex task, best approached initially through a knowledge mapping exercise.

Knowledge mapping offers the opportunity to discover key aims of different operating units within an organisation, the type of information they most often require and, most importantly, whether they have problems accessing such information currently. This exercise will highlight where the organisation is suffering from gaps in information provision and steps can be taken to resolve the weakness.

Organising and distributing information across an organisation is a major challenge, especially if the organisation is global. Actively managing knowledge stored in databases is often crucial to a successful KM programme, especially in an 'e-speed' corporate world where information can be quickly out of date or redundant. Gerry McGovern (Chief Executive Officer of Irish based Internet consultancy Nua) refers to information as being 'like milk' – rich, relatively plentiful and accessible but with a short life-span before it sours. Proactively managing content on a regular basis will help the success of any KM programme – repositories that are allowed to expand with old or poor quality material will quickly stagnate (or sour) and be ignored by staff. In addition to new material being identified, acquired and classified, existing entries must be constantly updated and refreshed, redundant material deleted or archived and staff encouraged to contribute and populate available databases. Quality far outweighs quantity in this environment – users are increasingly only interested in material relevant to their roles – they wish to find this material quickly and with a minimum of time and effort involved.

Technology will always have a major role to play in any KM strategy – relatively cheap systems now enable organisations to communicate and transfer vast quantities of information across the world with ease. Any KM solution will require a familiarity with the organisation's IT strategy and architecture. The knowledge manager must aspire to understand the technical landscape within which they perform, in order to better understand the possibilities as they relate to KM. Typically, one would need to explore the following:

- groupware/collaborative tools
- internal/external repositories
- automated classification tools
- search engines
- existing intranet capability
- electronic content feeds
- browser capability.

Components need to be integrated so that their capabilities meet the needs of the organisation. Most KM solutions feature the following at minimum:

- *collaborative environment* – providing the ability for individuals, teams and communities to share and communicate
- *content management* – supporting the collection and organisation of a wide variety of content
- *portal design* – to minimise user effort, a unifying entry point to the knowledge base is created acting as the front door to the 'House of Knowledge'.

Most systems are now Internet/intranet technology based, exploiting the standard web browser interface with which users are increasingly familiar.

The knowledge manager needs to be aware of all these aspects in order to be able to 'sense and respond' to the needs of the business. KM needs to provide enduring value to an organisation, hence it is logical to seek to apply the KM process in areas of greatest strategic importance. Understanding the business is crucial to be able to identify these areas. An enterprise may concentrate particularly on research and development or customer service in order to be successful – whatever these key areas are, they provide the knowledge manager with targets with which to focus the integration of their services.

All organisations contain groups of staff with like-minded interests. These are often informal groups of people forming natural knowledge sharing communities. They may well be cross-functional and widely dispersed but are strong networks which provide existing knowledge conduits which can be exploited. They are often the most receptive to early KM initiatives and their knowledge requirements provide another good starting point for the knowledge manager to target. Offering to facilitate a community may be a good introduction to integrating the services a new knowledge manager is able to offer the organisation.

In many respects, knowledge management is a journey with no ending. Because it is a dynamic, constantly evolving environment, new challenges and obstacles will constantly emerge and need to be faced. Whether the journey is worthwhile depends on the benefits the KM programme is able to deliver along the way.

KM and the corporate environment

One has only to glance at the business pages of any newspaper today to perceive a sense of how dramatically the corporate landscape is changing. The spread and connection of computer and telecommunications technologies, seen most obviously in the rise of the Internet, has created a huge shift in corporate structures. Business is increasingly conducted in a global marketplace where larger, long-established organisations find themselves increasingly challenged by smaller, virtual firms who are often able to move more quickly in the marketplace and innovate faster.

Knowledge is increasingly the most important asset an organisation possesses. In all sectors of the economy, organisations are focusing on their knowledge assets producing a reassessment of what actually constitutes value in the context of the organisation. Increasingly, companies are valued by assessing their intellectual assets. Knowing what a company knows, and being able to exploit it, therefore becomes essential to its continued prosperity.

KM has a critical role to play in supporting this shift in focus as it supports several key elements which will provide an organisation with competitive advantage in the new millennium. It:

- encourages innovation
- facilitates enterprise-wide learning
- enhances new product and service development.

The rise of the dot-com organisation and the virtual stampede towards e-business demands a different approach to how an organisation is structured. Many 'old economy' organisations have completely reassessed their identities. E-business requires fundamental changes to the way a firm operates and how they do business with their clients and partners. Speed and flexibility are increasingly crucial to corporate survival. What will the successful future business look like? It seems highly likely that it will demonstrate the following characteristics. It will be:

- flatter, less hierarchical in structure
- global in outlook

- flexible
- learning-focused
- client-focused
- networked
- individual and group empowered
- knowledge sharing
- technology smart.

These characteristics offer invaluable signposts for any information specialist seeking to become a successful knowledge manager. Consider, too, that information is now more plentiful and readily accessible than it has ever been. Whereas access to information used to be the preserve of only a few employees in the largest, best resourced organisations, the Internet alone now provides a constant flow of new information to everyone with a computer and Internet connection. Figures from Nua reveal that since 1998, the number of documents on the Internet is estimated to have doubled from 400 million to 800 million with little sign that this explosion will slow down – it would require over 200,000 years to spend just 30 minutes reading each document. Add to this the amount of internally generated information increasingly being made available via corporate intranets and it is clear that a new challenge has been created as organisations increasingly face problems of information overload. Many organisations would recognise author John Naisbitt's comment that 'we are drowning in information, but starved of knowledge'.

Just as organisations have to evolve at a rapid rate in the knowledge economy, so too must the information professional. In this environment knowledge managers must demonstrate all of the generic characteristics of the business and understand how they can integrate their services to best support the business process. It will be crucial, however, for information specialists to be prepared to relinquish the notion that they perform a narrowly focused job. Instead, the successful knowledge manager performs a wide variety of roles, many of which draw on traditional information specialist skills, such as indexing and research, but allied with non-traditional characteristics, like project and risk management. This broad canvas of skill requirements means that non-information specialists are able to compete for the same positions – just as organisations face new competition in the e-business world, so too do information specialists. The good news, however, is that as KM shows few signs of being a management fad, there should be relative security in the role – a recent article in *Management Today* (1999) identified knowledge management as one of five major careers with a future.

What makes a good knowledge manager?

So what are the roles and characteristics that an information specialist has to perform and demonstrate in order to become a good knowledge manager? One thing is clear, 'You can't be what you must be by being what you have been' (Jim Clemmer, The Clemmer Group). Opportunities for the information specialist are now in different contexts – each context demands that we perform a different role.

Leader

The KM environment is increasingly as competitive as the general commercial marketplace. Ownership of KM does not pass by divine right to the information professional (although we may like to think it should) and many organisations place the responsibility for their KM programme with the IT department, Communications or HR function. Given this competition, how does the information professional differentiate themselves from their internal rivals? One key area is in basic leadership. KM as a formal discipline remains a relatively new idea for most organisations which means 'territory' can be claimed by those who can demonstrate commercial understanding, innovation and a strategic approach to implementing new ideas. Think of all the leaders that you may have come across, either in history books or as part of your working life – what made them successful? What characteristics do you require to stake your claim to be a leader of your organisation's KM programme? Consider the following list for some ideas:

- Leaders build the future – but don't necessarily predict it.
- Leaders make meaning – by creating the context and environment which allows people to perform successfully.
- Leaders make connections – they sense and respond to their environment, always seeking to influence actions.
- Leaders listen and learn.
- Leaders know that leadership is a 'team sport' – they seek and value other peoples' opinions.

Above all, leaders focus on the issues and opportunities and *get the job done.*

Leaders require a deep understanding of the organisation and how it functions and the external environment in which it operates. Sensing and responding to change enables the organisation to evolve and survive. Being a KM leader will also involve the ability to sell the KM message, persuade those who may be reluctant to participate and, above all, create relationships based on trust that you are able to deliver results.

Strategist

Knowledge managers should expect to be involved in decision-making and strategy creation. In order to meet this expectation, it is essential that an individual has the ability to make informed comments that will help develop successful strategies. Failure to achieve this involvement results in being part of an environment that is controlling you, rather than the reverse. Having opinions means being able to identify key drivers of any situation, analysing appropriate responses, crafting strategies which offer solutions to those issues, while fully understanding the impact of anything proposed and being able to articulate the justification for so doing. It takes courage to offer contrary views to those who may be senior to yourself in the organisation's hierarchy, but you will be respected for your opinions providing they are well reasoned and sensibly communicated. Ultimately, the knowledge manager should seek to have their opinion sought on any matter relating to KM – that is the best indicator that they are valued and are at the heart of the business.

Technologist

The importance of IT cannot be under-estimated, particularly in an e-business environment. As organisations increasingly develop databases, intranets, web sites, and individuals have access to sophisticated personal computers, cellular phones and handheld devices, the knowledge manager must have a good understanding of how the technology works. Creating strong relationships with your organisation's IT group, which are mutually beneficial, should be a key tactical aim. Each needs the other if you are to successfully deliver a broad KM solution.

Consider the users' perspectives at all times – they are your customers and they value simplicity, reliability and accuracy. Can staff access knowledge repositories while they are out of the office? Does the search engine require knowledge of complex search strings or will it support natural language? Is your classification designed to match how the business operates or written in terms that staff can understand? Creating a simple, easy to use system is not straightforward, but the more you understand about how technology can work, the more effective your solutions will be.

Change manager

As we increasingly find ourselves operating in an e-business world, knowledge managers must accept the notion that disruption has become a fact of life. The days of safely established, routine information units are receding quickly and it is essential to be at ease with the rapid changes occurring in the enterprise and the wider marketplace. The dynamic revolution occurring across the business world has seen a number of landscape altering shifts:

- the rapid rise of new, virtual organisations (e.g. Amazon.com) that quickly become major players in their chosen markets
- convergence as companies realise they can enter new markets with relative ease (e.g. UK supermarkets increasingly offering financial services)
- the stellar growth of people having access to, and using, the Internet – breaking down the barriers of distance and time in communicating across the globe.

Change can be disorienting, especially when you are a passive recipient, uninvolved in determining new directions or ways of working. Knowledge managers should always seek to influence the strategic changes that affect them – seek to run the KM function as if it is a business within a business. This requires a mission statement, business objectives (always linked to the overall organisation's goals), strategic plan and key initiatives.

Change management works best by 'contagion' – top-down and bottom-up. Much has been said about the need for visible senior support for your KM initiatives being essential and this cannot be underestimated, but creating momentum among all levels of staff is equally important. If enthusiasm and momentum for knowledge management can be generated throughout the organisation, it should be easier to persuade those who may at first seem reluctant that your plans are a good idea with demonstrable benefits for them as individuals. Consider the communication channels you will require to deliver your messages, prepare a long-term communications plan to support your efforts and exploit examples of success or where the KM programme has made a difference to the organisation. Most structured change programmes involve creating a vision, building commitment, and sustaining change – all supported by strong leadership and management of the programme.

Maintaining the momentum is equally as challenging – this may involve devising long-term incentives such as incorporating aspects of good KM corporate 'citizenship' into formal performance appraisals and skills development. As the corporate environment changes increasingly quickly, so too must the knowledge manager be prepared for, and welcome, the upheaval. Look for opportunities to support those who face shifts in their ways of working and guide them through the transition.

Ambassador

A key skill requirement that has emerged is the ability to manage relationships internally, externally and across borders. In a connected age, the art of networking is paramount – the need to create strong relationships at all levels throughout an organisation is vital to being successful. Developing your sphere of influence, range of contacts and delivering valued services will ensure that the position of the knowledge manager is recognised as being important. This requires the ability to sense and respond to the needs of different individuals. Taking the time to understand different user's roles and information needs will enable you to personalise the service you can offer, making your support that much more precise. Providing assistance that helps to maximise people's attention span and learning capacity will be a key asset in the future development of KM programmes. Looking outside the immediate organisation is also an important activity – communities of interest are increasingly developing, stimulated by the spread and easy access that the Internet offers. Knowledge of these resources, which may include staff from competitors, is essential. Partnerships and alliances, for however short a period, are the secret to solving a myriad of knowledge-based problems. Participation, promotion and contribution to such communities should be regular goals of the knowledge manager.

Increasingly, knowledge managers need to manage relationships with outside vendors. This requires strategic understanding of the organisation's requirements, awareness of what is available in the marketplace and the ability to conduct successful negotiations. Developing a productive relationship with vendors requires creative dialogue that benefits both parties – establishing fair pricing for either enterprise-wide or *per seat* models requires intimate knowledge of what best serves the needs of users.

Awareness of inter-cultural issues will be essential for anyone working in an international organisation or who deals with global organisations. Whilst knowledge of additional languages is obviously invaluable, understanding the best way to communicate to non-native speakers of English can be the difference between smooth operations and chaotic miscommunication. Cultural sensitivity is essential for any knowledge manager who travels overseas – taking the time to understand local customs and ways of working ensure that you are respected and that unfortunate misunderstandings are avoided. Some countries have linguistic problems with the notion of 'knowledge management' as no direct translation exists, others traditionally do not ask questions in formal presentations – these are all potential pitfalls to avoid. There are a variety of guidebooks and training courses for improving cultural awareness that are well worth investigating.

Being an 'ambassador' requires you to promote (and sometimes defend) the KM programme but also requires you to listen and sympathise with the feedback from users. Acting as someone who can understand and resolve individual issues demonstrates that you possess the ability to sense and respond to users sensitively. Making a difference on a global stage is immensely fulfilling but can be a considerable challenge.

Promoter

Many information specialists finding themselves in positions where they have an opportunity to become involved in knowledge management often face difficulties in being able to gain attention from internal senior management. Their services are often undervalued which leads to being under-resourced and held in low regard. Often, this may be a result of ignorance on the part of senior staff who are unaware of the attributes information specialists can offer. However, it is essential that anyone seeking a career within knowledge management develops strong marketing and self-promotional skills – and it is often the skill most commonly lacking amongst our community.

Being able to market the services that a knowledge manager has to offer across an organisation is vital. Successful knowledge management requires the activity to be integrated throughout the daily routine and business process of an organisation. Being able to communicate the benefits of KM to all grades of staff, from boardroom to mail room, will enable a knowledge manager to be held in high regard and influence decision makers.

There are two aspects to the marketing role – publicising the services the knowledge unit has to offer, such as research, facilitation, content management and training; and championing the KM 'cause', acting as an evangelist for the uptake and participation of staff in knowledge sharing exercises. Each of these requires a familiarity with the concepts of good promotion and advertising, understanding individual circumstances and requirements, and being able to communicate clearly and persuasively the messages you wish to impart. Good writing and presentation skills are essential – being able to articulate your messages in the business 'language' of the audience will boost your chances of successfully conveying your argument. Much of this requires strong self-confidence and awareness that you, as the information specialist, are the 'expert' in many aspects of KM. Do not be readily intimidated by those who you assume know more than you do, just because they hold a more senior position or have been with an organisation for a long time. This is your territory and you must demonstrate that you are the person who understands the issues best and has practical solutions and benefits to offer.

Content manager

Avoiding information overload is one of the main problems organisations now face. The knowledge manager has a fundamental task to guide and direct the knowledge that is captured and made available to the communities they support. Typically, this involves:

- proactively identifying and evaluating internal and external sources of both explicit and tacit content
- creating, maintaining and evolving the knowledge system's taxonomy
- facilitating contributions from staff
- updating content and removing redundant information
- monitoring trends in usage.

These are traditional strengths of the information specialist and are probably of more value today than ever before. Organisations must cope with large volumes of information that they must make readily available to their staff – to do so requires clear classification and organisation of material in such a way that the non-information specialist can readily understand and intuitively interrogate. The user is not interested in seeing the skill that goes into developing a successful taxonomy scheme, but they will recognise the benefits of it instantly, particularly when faced with the relatively chaotic experience of searching the Internet.

Communicator

Building respect and credibility requires the ability to communicate skilfully. Typically, this includes writing, presenting, facilitation and coaching. They all require good levels of self-confidence and the belief that you are the expert who can best assist the user.

Writing may involve formal reports, training manuals, policy documents, marketing brochures, advertising posters, presentations and require the ability for producing documentation that will be read by non-native English speakers. For example, mastering the art of 'offshore English', the use of clear, simple language, is particularly valuable for anyone working in an international organisation.

Few people can genuinely declare that they enjoy standing up in front of an audience delivering a presentation. However, it is a standard activity in corporate life and developing skills in public speaking are critical in enhancing the perception of the knowledge manager. It is an essential skill, especially if the knowledge manager has to operate at senior management level where they will be expected to deliver presentations on a regular basis, often at short notice. Mastering the art of being comfortable in such situations will provide enhanced confidence in other aspects of the job.

Facilitator

Facilitation skills are another invaluable asset the knowledge manager needs to develop. Being able to assist project teams and subject experts in discovering hidden knowledge through capture exercises or brainstorming sessions places the information specialist at the heart of the business – exactly where they should aim to be. Facilitation requires good listening skills, and the ability to keep discussions moving whilst capturing key points throughout and allowing everyone to have their say. Critically, it enhances the perception within the organisation that the knowledge manager is an enabler, helping staff to learn key new skills for themselves, rather than acting as a support person performing the task on their behalf. Facilitation is a generic skill which will enable you to be involved in a range of other events, not necessarily directly connected to KM.

Trainer

Increasingly, corporations are recognising that learning and knowledge should be closely integrated. KM is valueless unless staff learn from the experience that is captured and made available to them and apply that learning to their own situations. Noticeably, we are beginning to see the merger of KM and training departments, where there is a logical fit. For the knowledge manager, this stimulates a need to develop a broader understanding of training needs, curriculum development, delivery channels and learning support functions. Training may be classroom based, technology-based (e.g. CD-ROM), web delivered or involve self-help via a learning resource centre. All offer additional opportunities for knowledge managers to increase their influence. Web delivery of learning courses seems poised to escalate. The Internet enables organisations to distribute courses globally at low cost while, with regular updates of material, offering staff the latest available thinking and knowledge.

A knowledge manager could seek to be involved in developing learning support services, such as staffing help desks or researching the latest developments, so that course material can be updated. Analysing feedback from users is an important element to future course development and monitoring new content is vital to keep on top of the subject. There will always be a place for classroom or one-to-one training, and indeed some 'soft-skills' are better delivered in this way. Being a good trainer requires: confidence in the topic you are delivering, good presentational, communication and listening skills and a willingness to invest time in the knowledge transfer process.

The future of knowledge management

Far from being a management fad, KM would seem to have survived its infancy and is now growing quickly to maturity. The recent KPMG survey into KM would support this assertion – the majority of large organisations across the world are actively involved in a KM programme. While benefits are being realised, there are still major challenges which remain. What are the key emerging trends that we can observe in the evolution of KM?

A key aspect of any successful KM programme is the ability of the organisation to integrate the positive aspects of knowledge sharing into daily activity. However, altering the behaviour of people is a slow process and perhaps we should not expect to see dramatic sudden changes in this area of KM, however critical it remains. As benefits accrue on a consistent basis and increasing numbers of staff experience the many positives a KM programme can deliver, so should the evolution of knowledge sharing into a routine way of working be fulfilled.

Personalisation is a growing feature of the e-business world, with the promise of 'markets of one' becoming a reality. Logically, any KM programme has to exploit the technologies delivering this ability to create a highly personalised KM experience for the user. The more pertinent and relevant material offered via KM services and systems can be, the greater the impact any such programme should have on an organisation and its staff.

A growing concern has been the amount of time staff have to devote to knowledge sharing activity. As the world moves seemingly ever faster, the new economy appears increasingly based on temporal considerations. The scarcest resource today is people's time and many KM programmes have identified this as a serious impediment to their implementation. Accordingly, it seems probable that a key aspect of future KM will be an emphasis on what has been termed 'attention management'.

Nobel laureate Herbert Simon outlined the reasons behind this in 1995, based on three simple facts: there are only 24 hours in each day, people have a limited capacity to pay attention, and increasingly people are overwhelmed by the amount of information they receive. Attention management solutions begin with the premise that it is undesirable to try to aim for every member of staff knowing everything that the organisation collectively has learnt. This may sound somewhat at odds with the common wisdom of making access to information freely available but experience is beginning to show that many organisations who have created unlimited access have actually 'drowned' their staff in information. Faced with a seemingly never-ending deluge of emails, news alerts, and web pages, staff feel overwhelmed and are choosing to ignore material (some of which may actually be very valuable to them). Staff have an individual tolerance level for paying attention and capacity to learn and sensitivity to this will be increasingly important.

It has become more and more apparent that contributions to shared, global, electronic repositories are often neither of the quality nor quantity expected. Reasons offered to explain this failure usually involve a combination of unfriendly technology, lack of incentives and resistance to knowledge sharing. Perhaps we will see a realignment of KM strategies that emphasise filtering services which enable the individual to access and receive only the precise information they require. Providing just enough knowledge on a just-in-time basis assists the majority of staff who only require enough information to solve a current problem.

For information specialists, acting as human 'filters' (or intermediaries) provide clear opportunities. Being able to access, package and interpret internal and external information enables staff to save valuable time. Much depends on the ability to add value and create strong relationships, where they are trusted to produce this material reliably. Despite the apparent rise of disintermediation technologies, human judgement is still in high demand. Knowledge managers may increasingly characterise their work as delivering 'just-in-time, just-for-you' solutions to users.

Most organisations have concentrated their KM programmes internally up to now, but as e-commerce opportunities expand, we may see commercialisation of these knowledge assets in the external marketplace. Most of the major management consultancies now offer online advisory services and e-commerce payment systems are enabling a number of new, micropayment based knowledge markets to be created, such as Knexa and Knowledge Shop. Despite the failure of iqport.com, these markets should thrive over time.

The boundary between knowledge and learning will become increasingly blurred. The need for lifelong learning is vital as the rate of change demands we all learn new skills and competencies on a regular basis. There will be a huge growth industry based on the delivery of training via the Internet. So called e-learning services are considerably cheaper than traditional classroom-based delivery and they also permit the learner to choose the most appropriate study time and location. Improvements in technology will allow live video streaming of lectures, the ability to interact with peers across the world and the opportunity to pose instant questions to tutors. Courses can be constantly updated, links to related content made readily available (irrespective of location) and publishing material in multi-language versions should become standard. While unlikely to totally replace classroom-based training (some skills are better delivered in this environment, such as learning how to give presentations), e-learning is poised for hyper-growth in the next five years.

Knowledge managers should examine the potential for e-learning in their organisations and initiate or integrate with any such programmes.

As the world of commerce becomes increasingly dependent on e-business, KM will have a significant role in assisting organisations to become e-businesses. Working in markets where prices change by the minute, where competition can emerge from anywhere in the world at short notice, where alliances and partnerships are made only for the duration of a single transaction, requires access to reliable, timely, relevant information. Knowledge will be the key differentiator for organisations. KM can be a key enabler for e-business, helping the organisation to transform to new ways of working.

So how can the knowledge manager best support this transition? Perhaps the answer lies in the idea that all of an organisation's staff need to become knowledge managers in order to create a knowledge-based organisation. Effectively, all of the skills and behaviours the information specialist as knowledge manager needs to display, are exactly the ones organisations wishing to become knowledge-based require – how to structure information and knowledge, and the ability to find, interpret and utilise information. All staff will require information literacy skills to some extent throughout all levels. Who better placed to provide that knowledge than the information specialist? It is your specialism that everyone else needs to learn which offers you major opportunities to make a real difference to your users.

In his excellent 1995 work, *Entrepreneurial Librarianship*, Guy St. Clair ended his book with a rallying call to all information professionals based on the image of joining a train awaiting departure, bound for the 21st century, the dawn of which he viewed as a 'golden age for information services'. Six years on, the train is now moving at e-speed – are you?

References

How to ageproof your career. *Management Today*, March 1999, 56-7.

Knowledge Management Research Report 2000. KPMG Consulting.

Further reading

There are now many sources of useful material available on various aspects of knowledge management – listed below are those which I have found most valuable.

Books

Botkin, Jim. *Smart Business: how knowledge communities can revolutionize your company.* The Free Press (1999).

Bukowitz, W. and Williams, R. *The Knowledge Management Fieldbook.* The Financial Times / Prentice Hall (1999).

Dixon, Nancy. *Common Knowledge: how companies thrive by sharing what they know.* Harvard Business School Press (2000).

Nonaka, I. and Takeuchi, I. *The Knowledge Creating Company.* Oxford University Press (1995).

St. Clair, Guy. *Entrepreneurial Librarianship: the key to effective information services management.* Bowker-Saur (1996).

Stewart, Thomas. *Intellectual Capital: the new wealth of organizations.* Nicholas Brearley Publishing (1998).

Journals

Journal of Knowledge Management (MCB University Press)

Knowledge Management (Learned Information)

Knowledge Management Review (Melcrum Publishing)

Web sites

There are many web sites now devoted to the topic of KM. A good starting point is *http://www.brint.com*, which has masses of information, articles and links. Additionally, Martin White wrote an invaluable summary of KM resources in issue 60 of the excellent Free Pint newsletter at *http://www.freepint.co.uk/issues/130400.htm#feature*.

Chapter 8

Records management

Julie McLeod and Catherine Hare

Introduction

Many organisations, particularly large ones, recognise records management as an important, if not a core, activity and consequently employ specialist records management staff to manage, both strategically and operationally, the information they create and receive in conducting their business; equally many do not. Where there is no such specialist, the responsibility for records management often becomes the domain of the information or library professional, especially in the case of special libraries. This is because they are seen as the person with the expertise in managing and organising published information, activities which share some common principles with managing records. This chapter is written for those information professionals who are not records specialists but find themselves wanting or needing to manage some or all of the records of their organisation. It aims to help them to draw on their existing expertise but to recognise the key differences when dealing with records.

It is not possible in a single chapter to cover the discipline of records management in any great detail. Instead, the aim is to provide an overview of the subject with further readings, contacts and other sources of information. In doing so we consider records in all phases of their existence and irrespective of their format, whilst recognising the reality of the hybrid, multiple media environment, and we do so across different sectors.

After setting the context, we begin by looking at what records management is and then answering the question 'why manage records?' Then we look at key models and techniques, in an attempt to highlight essential records management principles and practice. The chapter ends with a look at current research in the subject and the major challenges facing records management professionals.

The context for records management

Organisations have always recognised the role that information plays within business but no more so than today. However, as the importance of information has grown, the way in which it is viewed within organisations has evolved, from being the product of business processes to being a key driver for business success. An important step in mapping this process of evolution was the establishment, in 1995, of the Hawley Committee under the auspices of the KPMG IMPACT programme (Hawley Committee, 1995). This Committee set out to discover whether organisations have information, which constitutes a strategic asset and, if so, whether they understand their information assets and manage them appropriately. The outcome of the Committee's work was the publication of a checklist of guidelines and explanatory notes on managing the information asset. Crucially for information professionals these guidelines were written for boards of directors – the senior management whose support is vital for information policy, system and service development.

This recognition of the importance of information in business for efficiency, effectiveness, quality, accountability and competitive advantage has continued to grow and strengthen. At the dawn of the 21st century, it is not just information assets which must be managed but also organisations' knowledge assets. The information society is metamorphosing into a knowledge driven economy (UK government's white paper *Our Competitive Future,* 1998) underpinned by the effective management of information.

Much of this development has resulted first from the growth in electronic information as personal computers have become standard office equipment. But secondly, and perhaps more importantly, during the latter part of the 20th century, the world witnessed an information revolution, facilitated by the rapid expansion of the Internet, which has taken us into a global information society. This revolution has resulted in dramatic increases in the volume of information created and distributed as well as in the speed of access and delivery. The whole approach to doing business, for example in manufacturing, has moved from stocking components on a basis of having them 'just in case' they are needed, to ordering them 'just in time' to be able to complete and deliver.

The outcome of these developments has been the emergence of the end-user culture where the user wants direct access to the right information seamlessly, whether internal or external, thus potentially bypassing the traditional role of the information professional. In this new environment, the trend from the mid-1990s has been one of integrated information services and professions. The proposed merger for 2002 of the Library Association and the Institute of Information Scientists and the successful establishment of the Information Services National Training Organisation to oversee and plan training across all of the information professions are two examples of how the professions are coming together. There has been consolidation of the well-established roles of the information and library professional but with a change of focus from intermediary to navigator. New roles, such as webmaster, have appeared to meet the particular needs of the new electronic information and communication environment, and the role of records manager has emerged, as the importance of internally produced information has been recognised.

All of these factors have resulted in, and driven forward, the development of records management. In specific industrial sectors, for example the pharmaceutical industry, the potential savings to be made in getting a drug to market as quickly as possible or, in government, the advent of new legislation relating to freedom of information and protection of personal data, have impacted on the practice of records management. There has also been a growth in the provision of academic and professional qualifications for records managers and records management is now a topic of academic research; 2001 should see the ratification of an international standard for records management. From this brief introduction we can see that much is happening in the world of records management but now it is time to focus on what exactly it is.

What is records management?

To answer this question and therefore establish what records management is and how it relates to other information management domains, we need to begin with some key definitions.

Records

The first definition we need to establish is that of a *record*. Eminent writers in the field have defined records in slightly different ways but two of the most useful and complete definitions are given by Emmerson (1989) and Cox (1998):

> ... those documents, in whatever medium, received or created by an organisation in the course of its business, and retained by that organisation as evidence of its activities or because of the information contained. Records ... are products of the activities of which they form a part. Indeed records have no existence other than as a product of business activity, without which they have no context or meaning (Emmerson, 1989).

> Records ... document a specific activity or transaction and ... this documentation has a particular content (information), structure (form), and context (relationship to a creator, function and other records). A record is a specific entity. Records are transaction oriented. They are evidence of activity (transaction), and that evidence can only be preserved if we maintain content, structure, context. Structure is the record form. Context is the linkage

of one records to other records and to the originating process. Content is the data or information, but content without structure and context cannot be data or information that is reliable (Cox, 1998).

While neither definition is 'short and snappy' and suitable for sharing with a senior business manager perhaps, for the information professional charged with the responsibility for managing an organisation's records, they capture the three essential characteristics of a record which make it different to other kinds of information. Those characteristics are content, structure and context. Like other documents in your office, such as the local yellow pages or the latest management textbook, records contain information and they have a structure or form which is captured in some medium, be that paper, electronic or something else. But most records managers would not be concerned with the management of these information resources because they have no business context. The creators of the local yellow pages or the latest management text book are not usually your organisation's employees, customers or business partners, and these documents are not usually an output of one or more business processes within the organisation. In other words they do not provide evidence of a business activity or transaction – at least not to most organisations. They may of course be considered to be records, or at least copies of records, by the organisation which publishes them.

If you are a librarian or information officer then you will be familiar with the management of information resources that have the first two of these three characteristics – content and structure. The additional dimension you need to consider if you find yourself managing records is that of *context* which serves to demonstrate their legitimacy or authenticity, their evidential value.

Records series

There is a direct relationship between records and business processes or operations which means we can consider records not as individual entities but in groups. These groups are commonly referred to as *record series* and a series may contain tens, thousands, perhaps even millions of records. The advantage of recognising records series is that records, generally, can be managed at the level of the series rather than the individual record.

Some record series are universal, that is common to all organisations. Such record series relate to generic business activities, for instance financial and human resource management, policy-making. Other record series are peculiar to the organisation and relate to its core activities as in, for example, the clinical trial records of a pharmaceutical company, the patient records of a general practice or hospital, the student records of a school or university and the artists' contracts in a film, television or radio company.

Records management

Having defined both a record and a record series the final definition or concept we need to consider is that of records management itself. Records management is not a new concept although it is often regarded as a product of the 20th century, particularly the second half of the century. But it was in 1934, in fact, that the concept of managing records from birth to death – throughout their life – was developed by the National Archives of the USA. This concept, known as the *lifecycle concept*, became the fundamental principle on which 'modern' records management was based until the end of the last century. And it is this concept which is encapsulated in many of the textbook definitions of records management, including the following two:

> …the systematic control, organisation, access to and protection of an organisation's information, whether it be on tape, disk, paper or film, from its creation, through its use, to its permanent retention or legal destruction (Records Management Society of Great Britain, s.d.).

> … the discipline of applying well-established techniques and procedures to the control of those sources of information which arise internally within an organisation as a result of its own activities. The objective of the control is both to provide efficiency and effectiveness and to ensure the maintenance of corporate memory (Newton, 1985).

In essence then, records management is concerned with the consistent and cost effective management of records – internal / proprietary not published information, throughout their useful lifecycle, and this implies that:

- only those records which are necessary are created
- they are kept appropriately according to their value to the organisation
- they are destroyed when they are no longer needed

within the context of business, legal, fiscal and other regulatory or statutory requirements.

From these key definitions the nature of records management is clear but we need to explore in more detail why we do it.

Why manage records?

The trite answer to this question perhaps is that we manage records for organisational efficiency and effectiveness and, particularly for anyone operating in the public sector, for the future development and posterity of society, but we need to break these generic reasons down into more specific reasons to be able to answer this question fully.

Records as information

As we have seen, records are information carriers and the output of a business activity. They are unique to an organisation and play a key role in the way it operates. They assure its ongoing activity and play a vital role in its continued operation in the event of a disaster. They are therefore an organisational asset and, like an organisation's other key assets (money, people and property), they need to be managed if their value is to be maximised. But, unlike some other assets, their value is not diminished through use. A record may be created by one person and used by another, it may be created for one purpose and used for another purpose later and hence its value to the organisation is increased. And, whilst some records will be destroyed because they are no longer required, the value of the records resource is not diminished. In fact it usually grows because only those records with potential future use will be retained and will be more readily accessible when not overwhelmed by records that have reached the end of their usefulness. Records capture information about what has worked well and perhaps, more critically, about what did not work and thus provide an invaluable source of information to aid decision-making.

Records as organisational and collective memory

By their very nature records are unique to the organisation, they cannot be replaced by placing an order at the local bookshop for instance. They are the organisational memory, particularly in the recent climate of right-sizing, outsourcing and employee turnover. Therefore, if records are not managed, the corporate memory and the history of society are in danger of being lost. Writing about managing the corporate memory in the electronic age Megill (1997) shares some powerful examples of the potential consequences of both losing and unnecessarily recreating information. Estimates of the cost of lost information, often contained in records include the following:

- 'executives spend an average of 150-200 hours a year looking for misplaced, misfiled or lost documents

- ... a user working in Windows spends an average of 7 per cent of their working time looking for files

- in 1991 the average cost of a misfiled record is $126.81. This figure refers to a paper record, but we might assume that the cost of a misfiled electronic record may be equally as great' (Megill, 1997).

Information from records can be lost in different ways. Again Megill (1997) shares some examples. These include the pharmaceutical company which had no system for accessing previously prepared responses to enquiries, and was therefore repeating work in creating new responses to every enquiry, and the near failure to migrate the first computer-held census data in the USA in the 1960s.

In today's highly competitive environment superior customer service and being first to develop and market a product are crucial. Both depend on efficient and effective access to information, much of which is contained in records. Managing a merger or acquisition successfully so that the benefits can be gained sooner rather than later has implications for information and knowledge sharing and therefore for records management. These situations can apply both in the public (Hinton, 1999) and private sector (Marsh, 2000) and embrace a whole range of cultural, organisational and technical issues thus reinforcing the interdependence of the business activities and the records they produce.

Not only do we need to manage records as the corporate or organisational memory but also as the collective memory of society. A proportion of the records created for some initial administrative, legal or audit purpose may have a secondary value for historical purposes. This is particularly true of records created within the public sector, though of course not all records whose ultimate destination is an archive, are from the public sector. The Public Record Office (PRO) stores the national archives for England, Wales and the United Kingdom but also advises government departments on records management.

In contrast to this view of records being an asset which, if properly managed, can be used for competitive advantage and societal good, some, particularly in the corporate world, consider records to be a potential liability. Whilst citing litigation in the United States tobacco industry as a good example of this, Dietel (2000) suggests that a systematic examination and evaluation of records management practices can, in fact, avoid records being a liability. On the contrary the application of sound records management practice will help to maintain them as an asset.

Records as evidence

Earlier we said that a key characteristic of a record is its context and that it is this factor which means a record has evidential value. We therefore manage records as evidence of an organisation's policies and activities, in case of litigation, and of its compliance with regulations and procedures. The latter reason for managing records is particularly important in heavily regulated sectors such as pharmaceuticals but also applies across sectors.

By law all organisations are required to create and maintain certain records. These might include records relating to incorporation, employment, health and safety and finance, for example, the payment of salaries and tax, the purchase and/or sale of goods. A very good source of guidance on the retention of these common groups of records is the guide by Hamer (1996). In addition to these there will be sector-specific legal requirements. In the United Kingdom examples include the Public Records Act 1967 and the Local Government (Records) Acts 1962, the Charities Act 1993, Health Circular HC (89) 20 1989 relating to the retention of patient records, and the Financial Services Act 1986.

But as well as laws, there are regulations and guidelines which have records management implications and where compliance may be a legal, i.e. mandatory, requirement or just good practice. The consequences for failing to comply may be more or less serious depending on the status of the requirements and the nature of the environment in which the business operates. The price of embarrassment is often very difficult to quantify.

Two pieces of legislation or near legislation worthy of special mention here are the new Data Protection Act 1998 and the Freedom of Information Bill 1999. The Data Protection Act 1998 came into force on 1 March 2000, superceding the 1984 Act and implementing a European Directive on data protection (95/46/EC). It relates to the automatic processing of personal data – data about living, identifiable individuals, and applies to anyone holding such data on computer and now also in some manual records. It therefore applies to virtually all organisations. Organisations must register their use of personal data with the Data Protection Registrar and must comply with eight data protection principles identified in the Act. These include:

- fair and lawful processing of the data, which now includes processing only with consent, with certain exceptions
- strict conditions for processing 'sensitive' data
- retention of the data for 'no longer than is necessary' and capture of data which is relevant, adequate but not excessive, accurate and up to date.

The rights of data subjects – those to whom the data relates – have been extended. Data subjects continue to have the right of access to the data that has been retained on them but also can object to this data being processed and used for certain purposes, for instance direct marketing. Because of the significant changes relating to manual records and data subjects' rights there is some transitional relief, i.e. that the specifications within the Act are not in force for all instances immediately. Further information is available from the Registrar's web site (*http://www.open.gov.uk/dpr/*) and the BSI publication DISC PD 0012 (1999).

The draft Freedom of Information Bill was published in 1999 (Cmd 4355) following the 1997 White Paper *Your Right to Know* (Cmd 3818). It aims to provide wide statutory access rights to a broad range of official records and other information and therefore relates to openness in government. Members of the public will have the right to be informed about whether information is held, and this is not just personal data and, if so, then the information can be given to the requestor. There are some exemptions relating to preservation of confidentiality where disclosure would be against public interest, for instance national security or commercial interest. This bill will apply to the public sector and therefore cover government departments, nationalised industries, the National Health Service, the Police Force and other public bodies. The Lord Chancellor's Department has issued a Code on the Management of Records under Freedom of Information Clause 45 of the Freedom of Information Bill which is available from the PRO web site (*http://www.pro.gov.uk/*).

The key records management implications of these pieces of legislation are the need to have ready access to records and information, to have an integrated approach to handling records (for example the need for guidance on keeping and destroying records) and a process for managing requests for information access.

The role of records as evidence, however, does not just relate to specific legislation or regulations but is based on the principle of proof of a business transaction. In the past records were paper-based and therefore had a physical dimension which, by its very nature, had the potential to confer and confirm authenticity and reliability. We now however live in a world which is dominated by technologies with records being reduced to strings of bits and bytes. Everyone is talking about e-commerce and e-business, which rely on systems such as electronic data interchange (EDI) which is 'the process by which business documentation is transmitted electronically through computer links' (Kennedy and Schauder, 1998).

EDI systems rely on standards for data exchange and initially there were different standards within individual business sectors, for example SWIFT for banking. Two universal standards, EDIFACT and ANSI X.12, subsequently were developed and are now used by major vendors. Nevertheless it remains a costly system because of the need to set up and operate the necessary, often dedicated network services. However the emergence of XML as a web-standard has lead to the establishment of a project to map the X12 standard to XML which will allow EDI to be web-enabled (Wiggins, 2000).

This ever-growing proliferation of records in electronic format has raised the issue of the admissibility of electronic records in a court of law. The main area of concern is the ease with which electronic records can be altered without leaving any trace. In a legal system based on case law, legislation can only provide some of the answer, although it is very important to remember that key generic principles from the paper world remain valid. Most evidence is judged to be admissible but the crucial issue relates to the weight attached to it by the judge (Smith, 1996). For the records manager the aim must be therefore to develop record systems which maximise the weight of records. Guidance on this is available in PD 0008: 1999 *Code of Practice for Legal Admissibility and Evidential Weight of Information Stored Electronically.*

Business continuity and risk management

The final aspect of why we do records management relates to the fundamental principle which drives all organisations – the goal of survival. In order to survive organisations need records, whether in the form of customer orders, policy documents or the formulae for their medicines. These records need to be available not only in normal operating circumstances but also in case of a disaster. Some disasters cannot be foreseen but it is possible, by identifying potential risks and minimising their effects through contingency planning, to improve the chances of uninterrupted operation if an incident occurs. Classically the three stages are prevention, preparation in case a disaster does occur and recovery after the disaster, if it is unavoidable. Some information to help plan for business continuity is available via the Home Office web site (*http://www.homeoffice.gov.uk/epd/publications*).

And so, to summarise, the major reasons for managing records are for:

- information
- organisational or collective memory
- evidence
- business continuity.

Key models and techniques for managing records

Having considered the what and the why, we now need to look at how we manage records and in this section we highlight the main models and methods used.

The lifecycle and records continuum models

There are two key models for approaching the management of records – the lifecycle model and the records continuum model. The former is well established and has its roots in the paper environment. The latter is more recent and takes account of the more complex hybrid environment of both paper and electronic records.

Despite its much earlier development, the concept of the lifecycle model is well captured by Linton (1990), who said:

> records are rather like people. They are created during a moment of inspiration; are born in a typewriter or computer printer; are very active when young; are often given inappropriate names; are married together into files; reproduce themselves via photocopiers; occasionally get lost; and are finally retired to inactivity to be looked after with tender care (or total neglect) until death when they are buried or burnt. As with people, some die young, some are of sufficient importance to live in conditions of high security, receiving special care and attention.

Several authors have tried to depict the lifecycle in diagrammatic form (Couture and Rousseau, 1987; Linton, 1990; Ricks et al., 1992; Penn et al., 1994). Interestingly, the first two of these depict the lifecycle in a linear form whilst the other authors use different variations on a closed circle. Irrespective of the detail of the diagram the lifecycle model is based on the principle that records are created or received (and that some form of planning goes into their creation), they are distributed, used and maintained, and they are disposed of. The latter may mean destruction but it may also mean transfer to inactive or archival storage which may be in paper, electronic or some other form. If the lifecycle is truly a cycle then at least some of the records will be reused once transferred.

The strength of the lifecycle model, namely the simplicity of viewing records as having discrete phases with a beginning, middle and end, is also its weakness, particularly in the dynamic and complex electronic environment. The records continuum model looks at four major aspects of records management and archival science represented by four axes: identity, evidential, transactional and recordkeeping. These are the aspects of records management we need to consider. On each of the axes are four points or co-ordinates which, when linked together, form four dimensions relating to the recordkeeping system. These four dimensions are: creation, capture, organisation and pluralisation. So there are more aspects to consider (see Figure 1). In particular there is the separation of the creation and the capture process which take place simultaneously in the world of paper records. In the electronic world however the operation of capture needs to be undertaken explicitly to ensure that the context of the record is established. Crudely one might say that the continuum model focuses on records management processes and systems whereas the lifecycle model focuses on the records per se.

Figure 1: The records continuum based on diagram in Upward (2000)

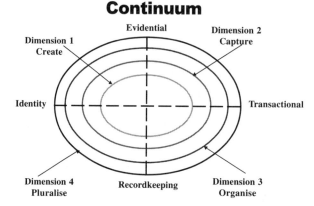

Policy and programme

The lifecycle approach to records management has typically provided a framework for a records management policy and, in particular, a records management programme. But the continuum model could also be used as a framework for developing a policy and programme or records management strategy, systems and procedures.

An organisation's records management policy, like any other policy, should be a statement of intent – what the organisation aims to do. The policy should be brief and not contain the operational detail. It should be in the same style as other organisational policies and typically would contain:

- scope
- policy statement or aim
- objectives
- how the policy will be implemented, e.g. via a records management programme
- responsibilities
- review mechanism
- sign-off or approval.

The records management policy is then implemented via a programme or series of programmes supported by procedures and systems.

The elements of a records management programme might include:

- design and creation of records particularly for core or commonly used records such as forms, appraisal documents, financial documents, client files
- design and development of recordkeeping systems, e.g. filing systems
- records storage
- records retrieval systems
- records protection and security
- disaster plan or business continuity plan
- retention schedule
- disposal and destruction
- evaluation and performance measurement.

Both the policy and the programme need to be documented and maintained in some form of manual, in paper or electronic form. Increasingly the details and procedures for managing records are being maintained on organisational intranets providing easier access and maintenance (Gibbons, 1999).

But neither the policy nor the programme can operate without an effective system for identifying the value of records.

Assessing the value of records

Assessing the value of records is one of the most challenging aspects of records management. Although some records have easily defined operational value to an organisation and precisely defined legal value, as in the case of many financial records, the majority do not.

All records have *primary* value which relates to the reason for their creation and immediate use. Some records also have a *secondary* value which relates to their potential use in the future. A record's primary value can fall into one or more of three categories:

- *administrative* – this relates to their value in the day-to-day business operation; examples of records with this value are routine correspondence, staff timekeeping, sickness
- *fiscal or audit* – this relates to their value in financial or audit matters; examples of records with this value are income and expenditure records
- *legal* – this relates to their value as proof of compliance with statutory requirements; examples of records in this category are deeds and contracts, health and safety records.

The secondary value of a record falls into one of two categories:

- *evidential*
- *informational or historical.*

In addition to having a value in terms of what they prove and the information they contain, records also can be classified according to their importance. McKinnon (1977) identified four classes: vital, important, useful and non-essential. Vital records are those which are essential to the organisation's continued operation and which are irreplaceable. These are the ones which are crucial for business continuity planning and must be secured in case of a disaster and might include, for instance, accounts receivable, that is money owed to you, ownership records and client details. At the other end of the scale, non essential records are those which have no current value and should be destroyed, for instance staff memos or agendas relating to events which have passed. Assessing the value of records is known as *appraisal*.

Appraising records

There are different approaches to appraising records:

- the traditional, records-based, approach
- the functional approach
- the business process-based approach.

The traditional records-based approach centres on determining the values of groups of records and is associated with paper records. In the past, when organisations were more hierarchical and structures were more static, this was a valid approach although labour intensive. However, nowadays organisational structures are continually changing and tending to grow as mergers and acquisitions become the norm in the global economy and more and more records are created and stored electronically.

The first alternative to be proposed was that based on functional analysis which was proposed as early as 1941 by Edward G. Campbell who was then Head of the National Archives of the USA. The emphasis shifts from what is actually produced by the organisation to what needs to be recorded. The focus is on the functions and processes of the organisation, working from the principle that the record has no intrinsic value but takes its value from the function which produces it (Campbell, 1941). The great strength of the functional approach comes from the fact that organisations tend not to change what they do but will almost certainly change how they do it. Schellenberg (1956), the pioneer of functional analysis, identifies three levels of operations: functions, activities and transactions. He also differentiates between substantive functions which are specific to a particular organisation such as manufacturing for a car company and facilitative functions such as financial management which are common to all businesses. From the framework it is then possible to place a value on the business function and hence on the records associated with it.

The third approach shares characteristics with the functional approach but focuses on business processes as the context through which to examine the records. This approach begins with an analysis of the processes, using business modelling techniques, and the identification of related data stores and has been successfully implemented in a number of large organisations (Morelli, 1999).

Records audits and retention scheduling

The purpose of appraisal is to establish a system for ensuring that records are kept for as long as they are needed and no longer. Traditionally, with paper records a first and very important step is to determine what records exist and how they are used. The methods, which are well documented in all of the standard texts, are questionnaires and physical surveys, either separately or in combination, with the possibility of also conducting interviews with the records users during the physical survey. This audit methodology fits very well with the records-based approach to appraisal but is less appropriate when dealing with electronic records. Because of the need to ensure that electronic information is not only correctly captured as records but also that their value is determined at the point of creation, it is very important to incorporate the rules for appraisal into the recordkeeping system at the point of design. Hence the focus on the business process rather than on the records per se.

The appraisal decisions determine the periods for which the records need to be retained. This is the process of retention scheduling and takes into account the primary and secondary values of the records in the context of organisational need and legal or other regulatory requirements. The format and content of the schedule will be affected by the appraisal approach but should indicate:

- what the records are
- what their status is, for instance, vital
- where they are located
- for how long they need to be kept in total
- the storage medium
- why they are being kept
- who the official copy holder is
- how they will be destroyed.

Nowadays the schedule is usually created by a computer, ideally in the form of a database. This facilitates maintenance and publication with a master copy to cover the whole organisation or separate listings by department. Publication needs to be complemented by a process of implementation which involves staff training and it is very important to keep the schedule up to date by establishing a review programme and procedures for authorising revisions.

Records storage

The physical storage of records initially was a prime concern of records management and remains an important aspect of managing paper records. Different storage equipment is required when the records are in daily use in offices where they tend to be stored in filing and other types of office cabinets. Once they no longer need to be consulted frequently but still need to be retained, they are often stored in records centres which operate like warehouses. The emphasis at this stage is to pack the space as densely as possible. Some organisations have their own centres but many outsource the operation to data storage companies who specialise in this service.

There is, however, a second aspect to storage. This is logical storage and relates to the intellectual content or the message of the record. It provides a means of grouping records together into a logical order by classifying and indexing them to aid both storage and subsequent retrieval. Unlike published information which can be classified and indexed according to universal schemes, it is often necessary to devise customised schemes and thesauri since the records are by their very nature unique to the organisation. Groupings may relate to subject content as with published information but may equally be geographical or chronological, depending on the records.

Standards for records management

While it may be necessary to design individual classification and indexing schemes there are a number of standards available to the records manager. The ISO 9000 (ISO, 1994) suite of quality standards in the manufacturing industry, impose requirements in terms of keeping records to demonstrate the operation of quality systems but equally provide a valuable tool to support and drive forward records management practice. A new version of ISO 9001:1994 is planned for 2000 and will apply to records and information management more widely than the manufacturing sector (Van Houten, 2000).

The ISO 46/SC11 Committee is using the ISO 9000 requirements as a benchmark. It is currently working on the conversion of the Australian Standard AS 4390 Records Management (1996), the first ever national standard for records management, to an international standard, ISO 15489, for scheduled release in May 2001.

While focusing on public records and with a prime interest in those records which will survive to be retained permanently, the PRO has developed a range of standards and guidelines which have many generic elements, covering both paper and electronic records. These documents are available via their web site (*http://www.pro.gov.uk/*).

Other sectors, such as the pharmaceutical and allied industries, operate according to guidelines such as Good Laboratory Practice, Good Clinical Practice and Good Manufacturing Practice (GLP, GCP and GMP). Finally there are standards which relate to specific aspects of records management and a number are listed at the end of the chapter.

We have reviewed the nature and the role of records management and examined the key principles and practice. To conclude we will examine the developing trends and key challenges ahead.

Current research and trends

Development

Records management is now taking its place alongside the established discipline of information and library management. It is recognised as a topic for academic research with national projects in Australia at the National Archives and Monash University, in the USA at Pittsburgh University, in Canada at the University of British Columbia and an international project, InterPARES, which brings together many of the key researchers in records management across the world. Important work is also taking place in Europe under the auspices of the DLM Forum and in the UK by the PRO. Relevant web sites are listed at the end of the chapter.

Electronic recordkeeping

The focus for much of this research is the challenge of managing information in the electronic world which means the hybrid environment of paper, electronic and other media (Horsman, 2000). Electronic document management systems are operating in many organisations driven by one of the many software packages available. Such systems focus on information access and can be very effective at achieving this important goal but need the extra dimension of functionality offered by records management software. TFPL and the Records Management Society on a regular basis publish a review of records management software (Winterman, 2000).

In order to achieve the creation, capture and management of authentic electronic records it is necessary to develop electronic recordkeeping systems which ensure that all three elements for a true record – content, structure and context – are bound together into a discrete and inviolable object. Building rules into the recordkeeping system at the design stage can do this. The purpose of these rules is to capture the metadata which will link together over time the bits and bytes of the message of the record with details of its structure and of its context, both in terms of the business process and additionally the software which produced it. Some of the metadata can be captured automatically by using the technology and is then encapsulated within the document itself. You will perhaps be familiar with the metadata tags incorporated into an HTML web document which can be readily displayed by viewing the source document. To enable effective and efficient management over time and over different systems, the use of standards or models is recommended.

Metadata models

Within the context of the World Wide Web there are a number of possible models including Dublin Core, RDF (Resource Descriptor Format) and TEI (Text Encoding Initiative) but there are also specific records metadata models, notably BAC (Business Acceptable Communications) and RKMS (Recordkeeping Metadata Schema) (Duff and McKemmish, 2000).

Professional development

As a result of these developments and trends, the work of the records manager has changed. The role is now one of facilitator within a hybrid environment and requires a combination of technical, interpersonal, informational and management skills. There is evidence of a significant professionalisation of records management. There are a variety of specialist records management educational initiatives. They range from the MSc in Records Management by Distance Learning and the Advanced Diploma in Lifelong Learning (Records Management) for Document Archives initially designed for staff at the BBC, both offered by the School of Information Studies (SoIS) at the University of Northumbria (UNN), to National Vocational Qualifications in Records Services and also a Certificate/Diploma in Records and Information Management for government records staff, provided by the rm3 partnership of Liverpool University Centre of Archives Studies (LUCAS) and SoIS at UNN.

It is significant to note that at the moment the demand is for qualification opportunities for people already working in records management who wish to study in the workplace. However the number of vacancies for professional posts is growing and in the future this will result in records management being viewed as a path for aspiring information professionals alongside the established library management courses, particularly at masters level. These educational opportunities are complemented by short training courses for people new to records services, offered by Aslib and TFPL and the professional societies.

Conclusion

If the old roots of records management lie in administration and facilities management, with efficient storage and resultant cost savings as the main drivers, then the new roots surely do not. They lie in the effective and efficient management of the organisational 'memory' for competitive advantage and accountability as well as for the future development of society based on an understanding of the past. This no longer means simply taking care of what has already been created but includes facilitating the creation of records, specifying systems which will support the use, protection and long term access of records which have been created in the dynamic electronic environment.

Records management is at a crossroads in its development and for records managers or other information professionals with records responsibilities the challenges and opportunities are there to be met.

References

Campbell, E.G. Functional classification of archival material. *Library Quarterly*, **41** 1941, 433.

Charities Act. Elizabeth II Chapter 10. London: HMSO (1993).

Couture, C. and Rousseau, J.-Y. *The Life of a Document: a global approach to archives and records management* (translated by David Homel). Véhicule Press (1987).

Cox, R.J. Why records are important in the information age. *Records Management Quarterly*, **32**(1) 1998, 36-52.

Data Protection Act. Elizabeth II Chapter 29. London: HMSO (1998).

Department of Health and Social Security. *Health Service Management: preservation, retention and destruction of records: responsibilities of health authorities under the Public Records Act 1989.* (Health Circular HC 89/20). London: DHSS (1989).

Dietel, J.E. Improving corporate performance through records audits. *Information Management Journal*, **34**(2) 2000, 18-26.

Duff, W. and McKemmish, S. Metadata and ISO 9000 compliance. *Information Management Journal*, **34**(1) 2000, 4-16.

Emmerson, P. (ed) *How to Manage Your Records: a guide to effective practice.* ICSA Publishing (1989).

Financial Services Act. Elizabeth II Chapter 60. London: HMSO (1986).

Freedom of Information. Consultation on draft legislation. Cm 4355. London: HMSO (1999).

Gibbons, P. Casting the 'Net: the records management intranet pages. *Records Management Journal,* **9**(1) 1999, 21-32.

Hamer, A.C. *A Short Guide to the Retention of Documents.* Institute of Chartered Secretaries & Administrators (ICSA) (1996, 2nd ed.).

Hawley Committee. *Information as an Asset: the Board agenda. Checklist and explanatory notes.* KPMG (1995).

Hinton, C. Promoting records management in a hostile environment – a case study. *Records Management Bulletin,* **92** (1999), 3-4.

Horsman, P. Through the looking glass: the intelligent management of hybrid record systems. *Records Management Bulletin,* **97** (2000) 13-20.

ISO 9000. *Quality Management and Quality Assurance Standards: parts 1-4.* ISO (1991-4).

Kennedy, C. and Schauder, J. *Records Management: a guide to corporate recordkeeping.* Longman (1998, 2nd ed.).

Linton, J.E. *Organising the Office Memory: the theory and practice of records management.* Sydney: Centre for Information Studies Publications, University of Technology (1990).

Local Government (Records) Act. Elizabeth II Chapter 56. London: HMSO (1962).

McKinnon, G. *Fire Protection Handbook.* National Fire Protection Association (1977, 14th ed.).

Marsh, M. Records in mergers and acquisitions: the records management perspective – turning a threat into an opportunity. *Records Management Bulletin,* **97** 2000, 9-12.

Megill, K.A. *The Corporate Memory: information management in the electronic age.* Aldershot: Gower (1997).

Morelli, J. Process-driven retention scheduling. *Records Management Bulletin,* **94** 1999, 3-8.

Newton, C. Information and malinformation: records management in information systems. *Information '85. Using Knowledge to Shape the Future,* 1985, 75-86.

Our Competitive Future: building the knowledge economy. London: HMSO (1998).

PD 0008. *Code of Practice for Legal Admissibility and Evidential Weight of Information Stored Electronically.* BSI DISC (1999).

Penn, I., Coulson, J. and Pennix, G. *Records Management Handbook.* Aldershot: Gower (1994, 2nd ed.).

Public Records Act. Elizabeth II Chapter 44. London: HMSO (1967).

Records Management Society of Great Britain. (s.d.). Membership form.

Ricks, B.R., Swafford, A. and Gow, K.F. *Information and Image Management: a records systems approach.* South-Western Publishing (1992, 3rd ed.).

Schellenberg, T.R. *Modern Archives: principles and techniques.* Chicago: University of Chicago (1956).

Smith, G.J.H. PD0008: a lawyer's view of the legal admissibility of document images. *Records Management Journal,* 6(2) 1996, 71-4.

Upward, F. Modelling the continuum as paradigm shift in recordkeeping and archiving processes and beyond – a personal reflection. *Records Management Journal,* 10(3) 2000, 115-39.

Upward, F. Structuring the records continuum. Part One: post-custodial principles and properties. *Archives and Manuscripts,* 24(2) 1997, 268-85. Also available at *http://www.sims.monash.edu.au.rcrg/.*

Van Houten, G. ISO 9001:2000: a standard for all industries. *Information Management Journal,* 34(2) 2000, 28-37.

Wiggins, B. *Effective Document Management: unlocking corporate knowledge.* Aldershot: Gower (2000).

Winterman, V. *UK Records Management Software Survey.* Records Management Society of Great Britain 2000, Issue 5.

Further information

Books

Best, D.P. *The Fourth Resource: information and its management.* Aslib / Gower (1996).

BSI DISC PD 0012. *Guide to the Practical Implementation of the Data Protection Act 1998.* British Standards Institute (1999).

Diamond, S.Z. *Records Management: policies, practices, technologies.* Amacom (1995, 3rd ed.).

European Commission. *Proceedings of the DLM-Forum. European Citizens and Electronic Information: the memory of the information society. 18-19 Octo-*

ber, 1999, Brussels. Office for Official Publications of the European Commission (2000).

Hare, C.E. and McLeod, J. *Developing a Records Management Programme*. (Aslib KnowHow Guides). London: Aslib (1996).

Kennedy, C. and Schauder, J. *Records Management: a guide to corporate recordkeeping*. Longman (1998, 2nd ed.).

Lord Chancellor's Department. *Code on the Management of Records under Freedom of Information Clause 45 of the Freedom of Information Bill*. Available at *http://www.pro.gov.uk/*.

Orna, E. *Practical Information Policies*. Aldershot: Gower (1999, 2nd ed.).

Parker, E. *Managing Your Organisation's Records*. London: Library Association (1999).

Schellenberg, T.R. *Modern Archives: principles and techniques*. Chicago: University of Chicago (1956).

United Nations Advisory Committee for the Co-ordination of Information Systems. *Management of Electronic Records: issues and guidelines*. United Nations (1990).

Wiggins, B. *Effective Document Management: unlocking corporate knowledge*. Aldershot: Gower (2000).

Your Right to Know: the government's proposals for a Freedom of Information Act. Cmd 3818. London: HMSO (1997).

Journals

Informaa Quarterly: official journal of the Records Management Association of Australia. Records Management Association of Australia. Available at *http://www.rmaa.com.au*.

Information Management & Technology. The journal of Cimtech, The Centre for Information Management and Technology, containing document and records management case studies and product reviews.

Information Management Journal (formerly Records Management Quarterly). The journal of the US Association of Records Managers and Administrators (ARMA) Inc. Available at *http://www.arma.org*.

Records Management Bulletin. The journal of the Records Management Society of Great Britain containing articles from practitioners and news of forthcoming events. Available at *http://www.rms-gb.org.uk*.

Records Management Journal. A journal publishing material on current research and practice and including reviews of recent publications. Available at *http://www.aslib.co.uk*.

Society of Archivists – Newsletter and Journal. These contain, respectively, news and in-depth articles or reviews of recent publications; free to Society members. Available at *http://www.archives.org.uk.*

Standards

AS 4390 / 1-6. (1996). *Records Management.* Standards Australia.

BS 4783. (1988). *Storage, Transportation and Maintenance Media for Use in Data Processing and Information Storage.* BSI.

BS 5454. (1989). *Recommendations for Storage and Exhibition of Archival Documents.* BSI.

BS 7768. (1994). *Recommendation for Management of Optical Disk WORM (write once read many) Systems for Recording of Documents that may be Required as Evidence.* BSI.

BS 7799. (1995). *Code of Practice for Information Security Management.* BSI.

ISO 9000. (1991-4). *Quality Management and Quality Assurance Standards: Parts 1-4.* ISO.

PD 0008. (1999). *Code of Practice for Legal Admissibility and Evidential Weight of Information Stored Electronically.* BSI DISC.

Public Record Office. (1999). *Management, Appraisal and Preservation of Electronic Records: Standards for the Management of Government Records.* 2 vols. 2nd ed. PRO.

Web sites and list servers

ARCHIVES – Archival theory and practice list server, available at *archives@miamiu.muohio.edu.*

Data Protection Registrar, available at *http:://www.open.gov.uk/dpr/*

DLM Forum, available at *http://www.dlmforum.eu.org*

ERECS-L – Management and preservation of electronic records list server, available at *erecs-l@uacsc2.albany.edu*

International Council on Archives, available at *http://www.ica.org/*

InterPARES, available at *http://www.interpares.org/*

National Archives of Australia, available at *http://www.naa.gov.au/National Council on Archives or http://www.archives.org.uk/*

Public Records Office, available at *http://www.pro.gov.uk/*

RECMGMT – Records management list server, available at *recmgmt@suvm.syr.edu*

Records Continuum Research Group, Monash University – Developers of the records continuum model, available at *http://www.sims. monash.edu.au.rcrg/*

Records Management Research Group, School of Information Studies, University of Northumbria at Newcastle, available at http://www.imri.org/rmrg/

University of British Columbia, available at *http://www.slais.ubc.ca/*

University of Pittsburgh School of Information Sciences – Developers of the *Functional Requirements for Electronic Record keeping*, available at *http://www.lis.pitt.edu/~nhprc/*

Organisations

ARMA. The US Association of Records Managers and Administrators Inc, available at *http://www.arma.org*

Records Management Association of Australia, available at *http://www.rmaa.com.au*

Records Management Society of Great Britain, available at *http://www.rms-gb.org.uk*

Society of Archivists, available at *http://www.archives.org.uk*

Chapter 9

The enquiry service

Declan G. Kelly

Introduction

The enquiry service has seen rapid change and development in recent years as technology has revolutionised the amount of information available, the way it can be accessed and how it can be delivered to users. There is also far more information that users can directly access for themselves. This means that the user now has a much greater choice, not just about sources of information, but whether or not to use an enquiry service at all.

In this chapter I will describe the core skills needed in enquiry work, with reference to examples taken from the BBC. These include the reference interview, search strategy and sources. I will also address other aspects of the enquiry service that I believe are becoming more important as users have greater choice, and the ability to bypass the library and do research themselves. These are primarily issues of access and customer service. The BBC Information & Archives Department is an interesting case study as the changes in our services are pointing us towards a rather different, but very interesting and rewarding future for the enquiry service.

The BBC employs over 23,000 people mostly based in the United Kingdom, but with bureaux around the globe. It has the largest newsgathering operation in the world. In the UK it operates seven television channels (plus the UKTV channels), five national radio networks, and 39 local radio stations. The BBC has a major presence on the Internet, and the BBC World Service broadcasts in 43 languages to over 150 million radio listeners. Additionally the World Service is available via the Internet.

BBC Information & Archives employs approximately 500 staff who provide research, information, and archival services to the BBC. The department is responsible for archiving and cataloguing the output of the BBC – television, radio, online and text records of the Corporation. There are also libraries in all of the major regional sites.

Access

Access is a key issue for the enquiry service. Access to the service must be appropriate to the needs of the users. This can be viewed as: *when* are the services available; *where* are the services located; and *how* easily can they be accessed?

When are services available?

While it might seem obvious to state that services must be available when users need them, it is important to know who uses the service, when they need it to be available, and to keep abreast of organisational or other changes that might affect patterns of demand.

For the BBC, where programme makers operate around the clock every day of the year, there is a demand for 24 hour access to key enquiry services. This is achieved in two ways – opening hours that match user needs, and delivering online services that can always be accessed. BBC Information & Archives have services that are open 24 hours a day seven days a week, all year round.

Where are services available?

The location of an enquiry service can be critical to its success – for organisations spread over more than one site one needs to know from where in the organisation the bulk of the work will emanate, and consideration may have to be given to operating more than one enquiry unit. The BBC is geographically spread over several sites across the UK. Enquiry services are located close to users in these major sites. In London, there are enquiry services in Television Centre, which is home to television and most news programmes; Broadcasting House, home to radio programmes; and Bush House, home to the World Service and BBC Online. There are also services in key regional sites – Belfast, Birmingham, Bristol, Cardiff, Glasgow, Manchester and others.

Location within buildings is equally important. The business maxim 'location, location, location' is just as true for an enquiry service as a retailer. The enquiry unit hidden away in an obscure, difficult to find location, can easily become the forgotten enquiry unit, then the former enquiry unit. Similarly, the enquiry unit that appears welcoming and inviting will attract more work than one which is inhospitable to users. It is interesting to note the increase in enquiry work that occurred at the BBC World Service Research Centre after it moved to a location in the heart of the site and close to the canteen. Much of this increased workload was mid-afternoon, just when the canteen had its busy 'tea time' period.

How do users access the service?

Face to face, by telephone, and by letter or fax are common, and each has advantages and disadvantages for both users and enquiry staff. Email is becoming more common, and in the BBC it is being encouraged, particularly for ordering materials. New methods of access bring new challenges, for example the email reference interview.

Internet and intranet technology has made organisation-wide access to information much easier. The BBC Information & Archives have responded to user demands by embarking on a programme to put its major catalogues onto the BBC's intranet. Online ordering from these catalogues is a natural progression, and for some material the BBC already offers not only a catalogue, but also content online. Users within the BBC can now access from their desktop the content of major newspapers and magazines online; over 100,000 news photographs; anniversaries and future events information; the catalogue of archival radio and television content, and the library book catalogue. Other catalogues and services are being developed for intranet access, including a database of World Service news output and an online pronunciation system. The development of online ordering from library catalogues cannot be far away.

Another major development made by BBC Information & Archives has been the introduction of an online, or virtual library – Research Central. This service offers not only a route to library and organisational information and resources, but a trusted guide to the Internet as well. In addition, it is offering BBC-wide access to commercial databases and reference sources by negotiating site licences to key sources. As the site develops, it also offers another channel of communication between libraries and users over and above traditional communication methods. Such service developments not only improve access to key library materials, but also serve to raise the profile of the library or information unit.

The reference interview

The *Concise Dictionary of Library and Information Science* (Keenan, 1996) defines the 'reference interview' as a 'discussion between an enquirer and information staff to determine the exact requirements and formulate a search strategy'.

There is an extensive literature on the reference interview and the skills necessary to do this well. It has traditionally been seen as a face-to-face or telephone dialogue, but the advent of electronic mail means that the reference interview is also an email dialogue as well, and this brings its own issues which are now being addressed (e.g. Abels, 1996; Haines and Grodzinski, 1999; Abels et.al., 2000). The email reference interview does not have the immediacy and interactivity of a telephone or face-to-face interview. Early research by Abels (1996) suggested that a systematic approach was needed. Her research project concluded that a structured approach worked well, and went so far as to formulate a search request form. Presentations by Abels and others to the US Special Libraries Association conference in June 2000 on the email reference interview take this further, and the web site has examples of a number of online enquiry forms (Abels, 2000).

Some key issues that have emerged so far concerning the email reference interview are:

- use of structured online forms to capture data – often with a number of compulsory fields
- use of structured forms for specific enquiry types, e.g. document requests
- knowing when to switch from email to another media – particularly when clarifying requests
- knowing what technical resources and *technical ability* your users have
- electronic delivery of results - copyright implications.

However the enquiries arrive, dealing with them requires a good deal of skill and tact, as users' questions can be unclear, incomplete, misleading, unrealistic, or simply plain daft. (BBC libraries have in the past been asked for film footage of dinosaurs, photographs of the *Titanic* sinking, and a recording of an event that occurred in the 4th century AD – though in this instance the customer accepted that it would not be an 'original recording'!). Enquirers can of course be incredibly easy to deal with – precise, clear and easy to understand. Whatever the nature of the enquiry, the approach is still the same and there are a number of steps to go through and some key things that need to be established in a reference interview:

- What does the customer want?
- What is the context and what does the customer already know?
- What are the deadlines?
- What does the customer really need?
- What will it cost?
- What has been agreed?

First – what does the customer want?

A few real examples will serve to illustrate some of the potential problems:

I need to know everything about AIDS.

There is an awful lot of information on the subject, is there any particular aspect of the disease you are interested in?

Well I want to know all about AIDS but particularly the way it spreads.

When you say 'the way it spreads' are you after information about the incidence of the disease, or about how individuals develop AIDS?

Oh – how people get it.

Right. In that case, I can get together some information of various ways in which individuals are known to have contracted the HIV virus. This is the virus that causes AIDS.

OK. Can I get statistics as well?

Do you mean statistics regarding the various ways people become infected with the HIV virus or statistics on the incidence of the disease?

Initially I want statistics on the way people become infected – something that I can use to show the various risks.

I can get statistics. You mentioned using the data to show risks – can I ask what the information is for?

Yes – I am doing an item in a programme about young people and AIDS in Britain for part of our 'World AIDS Day' coverage.

In terms of the statistics we discussed – would it be useful to have statistics relating just to the UK or not, and would some statistics on incidence of HIV infection in the UK be useful as well as statistics on means of infection?

Yes.

OK – I will get you some UK statistics on ways in which people contract the HIV virus, and the incidence of AIDS in the UK. How soon do you need the information?

As soon as possible.

Or another example:

Could you supply me with a list of all composers who have set words from The Bible to music?

That is a very broad question, could you tell me something about the programme you are working on?

I am working on a television programme on Jerusalem and need background music.

Are you looking for settings of particular Biblical texts?

Yes, ideally I would like settings of The Lamentations of Jeremiah.

OK – I will get you a list of all the settings of The Lamentations of Jeremiah which might be useful as background music for a television programme on Jerusalem. How soon do you want this?

As can be seen from the examples above, the process can require probing questions to establish what the enquirer really wants (and tactful handling when the enquirer appears to want the impossible, or has an impossible deadline). The aim is to lead the enquirer through a process whereby the initial question is clarified to the point where there is a common understanding of what the customer wants. Part of this process may involve helping customers to understand what they want, especially if they only have a limited grasp of the topic they are enquiring about. Patient questioning and clarification is necessary to get to this point.

Second – context and customer knowledge

It is important to find out as much as possible about the context of the enquiry – what the customer already knows, what research he or she has already carried out, who or where else he or she might have approached for help and information. (Before the introduction of an internal market to the BBC, it was not uncommon to discover that an enquirer had dealt with their own urgent need for information by calling several people in different parts of the organisation and asking them all the same question – in the belief that this would somehow speed up the answer.) Questions about the context will often help to clarify what the customer actually wants. In addition, understanding how the information is to be used and the level of knowledge of the customer, helps one start to plan a search strategy that will pitch the answer at an appropriate level, and can also give pointers to the best method of delivering the results.

Another AIDS related example was the query that began 'I need to know all about AIDS, especially in Africa.' With further probing, particularly about the enquirer's knowledge and about the context of the enquiry, the reference interview ended with the enquirer explaining that they knew very little about the topic but had to write a short 10 minute feature about AIDS in Africa aimed at a global radio audience, most of whom would not have English as a first language. This enabled the information staff to provide a response that included a range of material, beginning crucially with some simple factsheets, but avoiding complex research literature, and including a glossary of terms to enable them to provide simple explanations or to use jargon-free terminology.

Knowing context can also explain what might otherwise seem to be odd or unusual enquiries, and will then help to formulate a response. One such was the enquiry that started with the question 'Why do Jews hate Nazis?' By asking questions about the context of the request - what did the enquirer already know about the topic, how the answer was to be used, it was established that the question had come from a listener who had heard some reference on a radio programme to enmity between Jews and Nazis but was from a part of the world where it would not be unusual to be unaware of modern European history. The broadcast had therefore sparked a question, which naturally had been directed to the broadcaster. With this context, the question is obvious rather than unusual, and an answer was provided that included the appropriate historical context the enquirer would need.

Third – deadlines.

It is important to establish the deadline exactly. All too often the customer asks for information 'as soon as possible' a phrase that rapidly becomes meaningless. Does 'as soon as possible', mean today, tomorrow, next week? For someone on a news programme with a script to be on air in a few minutes it means now. For the customer who asked what was the correct form of address for an archbishop it meant right now – as illustrated by what they said next: 'Quickly, quickly, he's coming into the studio now.' One news customer once responded to the deadline question with 'Oh it isn't urgent – this afternoon will do.' On the other hand, to a researcher on a long term series 'as soon as possible' can mean next month.

What is really important is to remember that deadlines are to be negotiated and agreed. There is no use agreeing to deadlines that you will not be able to meet, even if the customer demands you do. If deadlines are genuinely very tight then it might be possible to negotiate what is to be provided rather than the timescale. One might also need to negotiate quality – for example if the enquirer wants the answer to an urgent enquiry immediately then they might have to accept that speed of response will equate to checking fewer sources than would normally be the case. It is far better to explain honestly why a proposed deadline is unrealistic than to agree it and fail. The enquiry service will be judged in part by its ability to meet deadlines, so they must always be realistic.

Fourth – what does the customer need?

I include this because experience suggests that this can often differ from what a customer wants. For example; *I want the book by Friday* turns out to mean that I need it by the following Wednesday but by giving a false deadline it will definitely arrive in time; or *I want a reply today* may mean I need to know before my 10.30 meeting tomorrow morning. In the AIDS and Bible music examples, the enquirers began with a very general enquiry, which with probing turned out to be quite specific. Such customer behaviour may be a lack of knowledge, may reflect lack of confidence in the service, or the enquirer may be exercising caution. Whichever, it is worth establishing the exact needs of the enquirer as these will govern how the enquiry is to be handled.

Fifth – cost

This is a factor often overlooked in reference enquiry work, but has increasing importance as information services are asked to justify expenditure and demonstrate value for money, and customers want to be assured they are getting the same. Where services are provided on a fee paying basis, then this may be an added element to negotiation as the information staff must establish cost parameters. Increasingly, the information staff may be asked to provide estimates at the outset of the cost of work to be done. In the BBC internal market, library enquiry staff currently charge their time in 15 minute units. Self research and loans are free at point of use as are online catalogues. This may itself distort the enquiry as enquirers endeavour to reduce cost by prescribing what sources may or may not be used in answering the queries.

For some types of enquiry, for example those involving sourcing books and journal articles, there is a direct trade off between cost and speed. The customer needs to be made aware of such trade offs so that they can make an informed choice about how best to proceed with an enquiry. The role of the enquiry staff is to provide enough information and advice to the customer to enable them to make appropriate choices.

Sixth – playback

At the end of the reference interview the enquirer ought to know exactly what the enquiry service is going to deliver, when and how it will deliver and, if applicable, what it is likely to cost. The enquiry service may even have helped the enquirer identify what it is he or she wanted. The enquirer will hopefully be confident in the abilities of the service to deliver and to keep him or her updated on progress. The information staff member ought to know exactly what they have to do and to have confirmed this clearly with the enquirer. It is the responsibility of the library or information worker to confirm this back to the enquirer – this not only clarifies and confirms that both sides understand what has been agreed, but is important in imparting confidence in the enquiry service. If customers are not confident in the ability of the enquiry service to deliver results, then they are more likely to doubt the results or be dissatisfied with what is delivered.

The search strategy

Whereas only a few years ago this might have been limited to what books and journals would be consulted, it will now encompass an ever increasing range of sources of information – printed, CD-ROM, online, Internet, intranet, contacts. For library staff in the BBC there is in addition a breaking down of old media barriers which increases the range of material one might wish to access. Whereas radio journalists might in the past have focused on audio material only when searching for material, nowadays they are far more aware then ever before of the alternatives – for example taking the audio track from a television item. Similarly the programme maker looking for something visual might combine radio output with still pictures or library footage. Whilst there has always been an element of this mixing of media the convergence of technology and the development of 'bi-medialism' makes it simpler and easier. With the rapid expansion of online, it is likely that the programme maker of today is not just preparing the television or radio programme but probably planning the web site as well. As this material is archived the amount and type of material available to the programme maker increases.

This explosion of information is nothing new to library and information workers, and it is reassuring to know that the response is not new either. A good search strategy relies on a systematic approach. Start by identifying the sources most likely to provide the answer and deciding the order one will use them. Think about how up to date, relevant, and appropriate the sources are to the enquiry one has to answer. Be prepared to change the strategy if it does not deliver what you need. Ask colleagues if possible – if in a large team then there is likely to be a variety of experience and knowledge that can be drawn upon. (One enquiry that once stumped most of a team was 'Do any individuals own their own railway lines?' Then one of them remembered that a colleague was a railway enthusiast and realised that he would either know the answer or know where to look.) An extension of asking colleagues for help are the 'virtual communities' that have grown up on the Internet. Examples include the Free Pint site and the Association of UK Media Librarians site. These can be especially useful for those working solo or in small teams as they give access to a wider community of information professionals. Finally, be prepared to trade completeness for speed. Particularly with complex and difficult enquiries a partial answer now may be worth far more to the user than a complete answer later.

Sources

I do not plan to give exhaustive lists of reference sources – readers will be aware of these themselves, or will know how to find them. Instead, there are two areas I want to refer to briefly in relation to sources in enquiry work - the impact of the Internet and internal sources of information.

Impact of the Internet

Previous editions have listed a range of basic sources for a good reference collection (*Whitaker's Almanac, Directory of British Associations, Willing's Press Guide*, etc.) or else have pointed the reader to guides to reference sources (such as *Walford's Guide to Reference Sources or Current British Directories*). Tim Owen's 1997 edition of *Success at the Enquiry Desk* includes a list headed 'Twenty five multipurpose reference sources you can't afford to ignore'. It is interesting to see in a list of key reference sources published as recently as 1997 how few are available in any other format except print; 14 of the 25 in Tim Owen's book were only available in hard copy, and only five were online. No web sites were listed. Contrast that with the situation in mid-2000, where many of the key reference sources that librarians and information workers have used for years are now available online, not just to libraries but to their users as well. In addition, there are many reference sources which are only available online.

I conducted a straw poll in July 2000 across three BBC Research Centres and asked staff for their top 25 reference sources. The types of sources listed included many of the key reference titles that librarians and information workers will recognise and be familiar with such as *Whitaker's Almanac, Europa Yearbook, Directory of British Associations, Who's Who, International Who's Who, Vachers; Dods Parliamentary Companion, Social Trends, Benns, Willings* and so on. What was most interesting though was that everyone who responded included a number of web sites in their list, and some included search engines as well. The sort of online reference sites listed fall into the following categories, with examples for each:

- popular reference books online
  Encyclopedia Britannica
  Oxford English Dictionary
- online reference collections
  Know UK
- specialist web sites
  UK Open Government web site
  Houses of Parliament
  The Internet Movie database
- catalogues
  The British Library
  Library of Congress
- portals
  RDN – The Resource Discovery Network

> BUBL – National information service for the higher education community
>
> SOSIG – Social Science Information Gateway

- search engines

> Google

- virtual communities

> Free Pint – Library network
>
> AUKML – Association of UK Media Libraries.

That there has been such a dramatic change in a short time shows how rapidly the Internet has developed, and how quickly organisations have responded to the opportunities it offers. Other chapters in this book cover the Internet in much more detail, but in terms of enquiry services there are two points worth noting. First, the Internet sources that enquiry staff use have been subject to just the same sort of analysis and assessment that library staff have traditionally applied to printed reference sources. Secondly, Internet sources are far more transient than printed reference sources. The Pantos *State of the Web* survey of the Internet showed that 6 per cent of links given are dead, and 30 per cent of web pages include a dead link. This makes the job of the library worker more difficult - imagine a library where between 6 and 30 per cent of the reference sources simply were not available year on year and had to be sought out, checked and verified all over again.

Internal information

It is easy to overlook the information that is readily available in one's own organisation, and this is particularly true of large organisations which may have staff spread not just across the country but worldwide. A useful source of information internally is the marketing department – regardless of their use of the library, they will often have their own information collection. Likewise, Legal, Training and Human Resource departments are all likely to house information that can be useful in enquiry work, and are worth remembering as potential sources of information.

Monitoring enquiries

Monitoring enquiries provides extremely valuable information, which can support the enquiry service in many ways. The usefulness of the information will depend on what is collected but I suggest that the following basic data needs to be gathered:

- topic or subject details of enquiry
- number of enquiries handled

- date and time of enquiries
- sources used to answer enquiries
- enquirers' details – name, department (if internal), company (if external), address or contact details; charge or billing details.

There are a number of ways of logging this data. Tim Owen's excellent *Success at the Enquiry Desk* (1997) gives a very good example of a paper enquiry form which collects all of the above data and also aspects of the success of the enquiry and marketing needs. BBC Information & Archives currently log the above data into electronic systems. These were originally designed to capture data to enable enquiries to be charged within the BBC internal market. They do, however, provide useful data on customer usage and usage patterns. The ability to manipulate and analyse this type of data is increasingly valuable, and logging electronically will become more important.

What can be achieved with this data?

First of all, one can collect the income generated by the work. In the BBC where research is nearly all done on a 'pay per use' basis, this is essential. Beyond that one can, over time, analyse the use of the enquiry service gaining useful information on the sources used (and not used) to answer enquiries; the numbers of staff needed to satisfy enquiry demand; the times of day or night and days of the week staff are needed; the cost of enquiries; trends in usage; enquiry service productivity; utilisation of resources, and so on. Such information can also be used to identify who the key customers and stakeholders are, and who uses which elements of the service (and therefore who needs to be consulted about possible changes).

Monitoring success of enquiries can be a useful way of identifying where the enquiry service fails. What types of enquiry does it have difficulty with? What sort of information is hard to find? This can be used to pinpoint improvements – such as more or better sources of information, better training, more effective use of the resources available. Examples of how enquiry monitoring has been of value in the BBC's enquiry services are:

- Analysis of overnight workload across two 24 hour enquiry units, on different sites, demonstrated that the service could be provided from one unit, resulting in cost savings.
- Analysis of usage of audio news clips downloaded by enquirers showed that 97 per cent of use occurred within three days of issue. This enabled the unit, in conjunction with the IT department, to plan for the most cost effective level of server capacity needed to support the system.

- Analysis of usage by user department of audio news clips downloaded by enquirers pinpointed which part of the service needed expansion and enabled system expansion to be clearly based on user needs.

- Usage data has identified how costs of services are to be shared among users.

- Analysis of trends in time of day of enquiriues helped in planning changes to staff rotas to meet changed demand.

- Analysis of sources used in answering enquiries provided evidence to justify the need for particular information sources, or to demonstrate they are no longer needed.

- Data gathered about enquirers was used to identify key users for consultation regarding service developments.

Monitoring the customer environment

Changes in the customer environment can also be important – in one instance in the BBC the move of a key user out of the same building as the research centre led to a dramatic increase in the demand for enquiry results to be faxed. This increased the fax bills by several thousand pounds per annum. At the time desktop electronic delivery of selected material was being considered. The increased fax bills not only spurred on the development, but became a saving to be factored into the finance case for developing the desktop electronic delivery.

Organisational change may be important. A move of a BBC department from one part of London to another necessitated a move of an information unit with it, with all the planning, organising and cost that entails. In another case, the move of a group of staff from offices to open plan resulted in significant reductions in subscriptions to library information bulletins, reducing library income. I have already referred to the effect seen when a research service relocated close to the canteen.

Within the BBC the introduction of online services aimed at the end user have opened up choices to enquirers. They can now choose to do their own research, using the resources on their desktop provided by the library. Whilst this has led to a reduction in the use of the enquiry service, it has also had an interesting effect on the time of day enquiries arrive. The mornings are less busy than the afternoons and early evenings. Some of this shift can be explained by analysing programme output – there has been an increase in dawn programming in some areas; but much of the shift cannot be explained this way. Early conclusions are that users are trading time and money – when they are far away from a deadline (in the morning) they are happy to do the research themselves, investing their own time to save money that would be paid to the library to do the work.

As deadlines approach, they trade again – this time investing money (paid to the library to do research for them), to save their own time. By understanding not only changes in the usage, but the reasons for them, the library can react in way that best meet customer needs.

To summarise, monitoring enquiries and customers gives the enquiry unit the information necessary to be able to demonstrate the usefulness of the enquiry service; the value it adds to the organisation; and its cost effectiveness. It also helps the service to identify how it needs to develop if it is to continue to provide useful, value added services to its users. Finally, on the topic of monitoring enquiries, always ask yourself why you are gathering any particular data – what is it for and what will you do with the information? Monitoring and logging all take up valuable time, and there is no point in measuring unless you are going to use the information gained to good effect. Well chosen data, properly recorded and analysed will deliver real benefits to the enquiry service. Anything else is just wasting time.

Customer service

At the heart of the enquiry service should be the objective of helping the organisation to achieve its aims. To this end the enquiry *service* should be just that – a service. It is vital for the enquiry service to operate with a customer service culture. For those information services that charge their users at point of use, satisfying the customer has an added edge as it translates directly into income.

When the customer has easier access to information than ever before it follows that they have real choice as to whether to use the enquiry service at all. Enquiry services need to respond to this by emphasising their commitment to high standards and by engaging with their users to make sure their needs are met. BBC Information & Archives now have a 'service charter' defining enquiry service standards and, interestingly, the standards the library expects of their customers:

Information & Archives professionally manages the BBC's archive and collections by:

- Promoting high quality research and information services
- Selecting, obtaining, indexing, preserving and providing access to material
- Ensuring that our services meet our customers' needs
- Fulfilling the BBC charter and statutory requirements

Our responsibilities to you, the customer
We will:

- Deal promptly with your enquiries to agreed deadlines

- Help you to get the best from our services by providing access to systems, information and materials
- Be professional and courteous

Should we ever fail to meet our responsibilities, we will find a solution and keep you informed of progress.

What we ask of our users

To help current and future users of the archive by:

- Depositing material according to agreed BBC policies
- Taking care of materials now to ensure they survive in good condition
- Letting us know when you have a problem
- Enabling us to deal efficiently with your requests by providing contact details and a valid programme number, charge code, account number or credit card

Feedback

We want to make our services even better. We can do this with your help. Please speak to any member of staff, or send comments and suggestions regarding our service to:

Information & Archives Customer Services Team
phone: 020 857 **67743**
address: B250 television Centre
email: I&A Customer-services

For more information about our services, visit our web site.

In addition to the service charter, BBC Information & Archives operate a service recovery system. When things do go wrong, customers are offered refunds, or the enquiry service may pay for a courier to deliver an item to meet that all important deadline. Sometimes we send flowers, or a bottle of wine – a useful way of apologising for less than excellent service. This approach to customer service has also been extended back into the enquiry service, and from time to time library staff are the recipients of flowers or wine or chocolates if they have been nominated by customers for providing excellent service.

The future of the enquiry service

There is no doubt that the role of the enquiry service is changing rapidly. In a few years it has developed from a largely book based service to a research service that spans books, databases, and a vast range of information from the Internet. There has also been a much greater emphasis, particularly with the Internet, on end-user access and searching. In some ways this makes the job of the information professional easier – as users do more of their own basic searching, valuable time is available to spend on the more complex work that really does add value and makes best use of information skills. However there is a real possibility that the end users will abandon the enquiry service and choose to do it all themselves. Ever easier access to information presents challenges and opportunities to the information professional.

The challenge is to be able to continue to demonstrate the need for professional information skills, and the benefits these skills bring to the organisation. There are many opportunities. As many organisations encourage their staff to go online and do it themselves there is an opportunity for information professionals to be the guides and trainers, helping users to get the most out of the variety of online systems available to them. In the BBC teams of 'floorwalkers' have gone out into user departments to train staff to search for information and to get the best out of what is available to them. With the development of the 'Research Central' site, BBC librarians have evaluated and organised the best of the intranet and the Internet and presented it to users in a clear easy to use package, backed up with on-the-spot training. Within a few months of launching the site in the BBC, it is now used by 600-700 people per day, accessing approximately 5,000 pages per weekday and using the site as their gateway to both BBC and external information resources. Developments such as these not only demonstrate the value of information skills, but raise the profile of the library or research service within the organisation, and also bring library and information staff directly into the users' workplace. My opinion is that this partnership with the user should be at the heart of the enquiry service. If it is, then we have an interesting and exciting future.

Acknowledgements

Thank you to all of my colleagues in BBC Information & Archives who have provided advice, help and research, in particular Kate Arnold, Research Central Editor; Joan Redding; and Margaret Katny.

References

Books and articles

Abels, A. et. al. Presentation at the USA Special Libraries Association 91st annual meeting, Philadelphia June 10-15 2000. Available at *http://www.library.nwu.edu/transportation/slatran/philadelphia.html.*

Abels, A. The email reference interview. *RQ (Reference Quarterly)*, **35**(3) 1996, 354-8.

Benn's Media : 2000. Miller Freeman Information Services (2000, 3 vols).

Current British Directories. Beckenham: CBD Research (1999, 13th ed.).

Directory of British Associations & Associations in Ireland. Beckenham: CBD Research (1998, 14th ed.).

Dod's Parliamentary Companion. London: Vacher Dod (2000).

Europa World Yearbook. London: Europa (2000, 2 vols).

Haines, A. and Grodzinski, A. Web forms: improving, expanding, and promoting remote reference services. *College & Research Libraries News*, **60**(4) 1999, 271-91.

International Who's Who, 2000. London: Europa (1999).

Keenan, Stella. *Concise Dictionary of Library and Information Science.* London: Bowker Saur (1996).

Matheson, Jil and Summerfield, Carol. *Social Trends.* London: Stationery Office (2000).

Owen, Tim. *Success at the Enquiry Desk.* London: Library Association Publishing (1997, 2nd ed.)

Vacher's Parliamentary Companion. London: Vacher Dod (2000).

Walford's Guide to Reference Material. London: Library Association Publishing (1995-7, 3 vols).

Whitaker's Almanack. London: Stationery Office (1999).

Who's Who : an annual biographical dictionary. London: A. & C. Black (2000).

Willing's Press Guide. Teddington: Hollis (2000).

Web sites

Association of UK Media Librarians, available at *http://www.aukml.org.uk*

Britannica online, available at *http://www.britannica.com*

British Library catalogue, available at *http://opac97.bl.uk/*

BUBL, available at *http://www.bubl.ac.uk/*

Free Pint, available at *http://www.freepint.co.uk*

Google search engine, available at *http://www.google.com*

Houses of Parliament online, available at *http://www.parliament.uk*

Internet movie database, available at *http://www.imdb.com/*

KnowUK, available at *http://www.knowuk.co.uk/*

Library of Congress catalogue, available at *http://www.loc.gov/catalog/*

Oxford English dictionary online, available at *http://www.dictionary.oed.com/*

Pantos 'all things Web', available at *http://www.pantos.org/atw/*

RDN – The Resource Discovery Network, available at *http://rdn.ac.uk/*

SOSIG – Social Sciences Information Gateway, available at *http://www.sosig.ac.uk/*

UK Open Government, available at *http://.www.open.gov.uk/*

Chapter 10

The use of the Internet in special librarianship

Mary Ellen Bates

Special librarians have been online since the dawn of the Internet, using professional online services such as Dialog, DataStar and Lexis-Nexis, consumer services like CompuServe, and email on proprietary networks as well as directly through the Internet. Some of the first gophers – the precursors to web sites – were built and maintained by librarians. And telnet was used to facilitate remote access to libraries' online catalogues as well as to dial in to online services. But the real impact of the Net was not felt by most librarians until browsers, hypertext transfer protocol and the Web came on the scene in the mid-1990s.

This chapter will look at special librarians' use of the Net and the impact of the Net on the special librarian profession. While much of the focus of the popular press has been on the Web and on information accessible through search engines and portals, there are also vast repositories of information outside the reach of what most people think of as the Web. One of the challenges of information professionals is educating our clients about the extent of information available online *beyond* the open Web.

Strengths and weaknesses of the Net

One of the clear advantages of the information available on the Net is that it is often inexpensive or free. Government web sites often house valuable collections of reports, statistical information and policy papers. Company sites have annual reports, product information, financial data, and background information on the company. Non-profit organisations make available information on their mission, and often sell or publicly post reports and other materials that they publish. Newspapers, magazines and scientific and academic journals often make the full text of articles available online; archival material is less often available.

Special librarians particularly value the Net for the access to information that simply was not previously available in electronic format. We can download annual reports, look up the organisation chart of a government agency, read an article from today's newspaper – the local paper or one from half way around the world – and search archives of photographs, video clips or interview transcripts. Looking up an address and telephone number is now simply a matter of finding the appropriate directory on the Web.

Moreover, the Net provides access to information in formats beyond the plain ASCII text of most professional online services. Adobe Acrobat (PDF) documents can be published on the Web with the formatting, charts, graphs and typesetting of the original document retained. Recordings of speeches, music and other audio material can be indexed, searched and downloaded. Spreadsheets and databases can be posted on web sites.

Of course, there are similar benefits for intranets maintained within organisations. Materials such as product specifications, operating manuals, and employee handbooks are searchable via intranets. Special librarians have taken on the role of content managers, evaluating the information needs of their organisations, negotiating contracts with information providers, training users on the use of their intranet and the Internet, and developing new information products and services for their clients.

Special librarians are uniquely qualified to acquire, develop, maintain and distribute information on intranets, and this technology now enables them to extend the reach of special libraries beyond the geographic limitations of a traditional library. (There are many issues related to the 'virtual library', which go beyond the scope of this chapter. Keep in mind that virtualising library services is neither a substitute for professional reference services nor a way to save money in the provision of information services. It may seem obvious to librarians, but this insight is sometimes lost on management outside the library.)

While the Web has been a tremendous boon to our profession, it has its weaknesses as well. One of the most significant and least understood limitations of the Web is that search engines, the principal way in which most users look for information on the Web, cover only a fraction of what is available. Search engines are not, as their name suggests, actually searching the Web each time a user types in a key word. Rather, they continually 'spider' the Web (and, in some cases, other areas of the Net as well), indexing sites and collecting new links. Some search engines index every word from an accessible page on a web site and others do not; some search engines only drill down a few levels into a site whereas others drill down as far as possible; some track down all links contained on a site and others ignore links. And search engines cannot index material that is not in plain text on a web page. As a rule, they ignore:

- PDF and word-processed files, spreadsheets, and other binary files
- text embedded within a graphic, such as a table or image
- information within a database, such as Amazon.com

- the content of audio files
- web sites that require registration for access.

They can capture any textual description of non-ASCII material provided by the web site, but are of course dependent on the quality and depth of indexing supplied by the site manager.

Forrester Research, a market research firm that focuses on the Internet, estimated that 1.5 million web pages are added *daily*. Given the pace at which information on the web changes, it is impossible for any search engine spider to maintain a current index of Web sites. In fact, according to a study reported in 1999 (Lawrence and Giles, 1999), no search engine covers more than 16 per cent of the open Web and only 40 per cent of the open Web appears in a combined search of a number of search engines. (The 'open Web' means the information that could be indexed by a search engine, excluding information contained within databases, sites that require registration, non-text files, and so on.) Imagine offering your clients a library catalogue that excluded 85 per cent of the collection. Once your users caught on to the fact that the catalogue covered such a small amount of the collection, they would create an uproar, or at the least would demand a better way to access the information within the library. Now imagine what those users would say once you explain to them that a Web search cannot be considered comprehensive, and much of the information on the Internet will only be retrieved if they know exactly where to look. This offers excellent opportunities for special librarians, who are expert in knowing *where* to look as well as the most efficient techniques for searching.

In addition to the impossibility of any search engine keeping up with the information on the Web, using the searching tools available is not always a straightforward process. Every Web database, such as a magazine's archive or a company web site's search utility, and every search engine operates differently. Some support Boolean logic, some offer truncation, some have automatic (and non-optional) truncation features, some allow adjacency and phrase searching, some offer the ability to limit the search to specific languages, domains, or geographic regions. Some search engines sort the results of a search by calculated relevance based on the frequency of the search terms; some sort by the frequency that other searchers have clicked on the sites, and some use other methods of calculating the relative 'popularity' of web sites and sort accordingly. The techniques useful when using one search engine may result in very different, and unintended, results when used in another search engine. Developing and maintaining a proficiency in several Web search tools is akin to learning the ins and outs of DataStar, Reuters Business Briefing and Lexis-Nexis - some principle remain the same but many of the power search tools are different and do not carry over from one service to another.

Unfortunately, determining the search features and limitations of each search engine is not always a simple process. This information is sometimes found under a link for [Advanced Search] or [Power Search], or it may be in a FAQ (Frequently Asked Questions) file. Because the advanced search techniques may still not have the power that an information professional needs, special librarians find that for many searches it is more efficient to use one of the professional online services to retrieve information, even if it is also available on the free Web.

While considering the benefits and limitations of Web search tools, it is important to remember the distinction between search engines and Web directories. Alta Vista (*http://www.altavista.com*), Google (*http:// www.google.com*), and HotBot (*http://hotbot.lycos.com*), for example, are all *search engines*. They attempt to crawl the entire publicly-accessible Web and index the sites found. Typing in a search term in a search engine will almost inevitably retrieve thousands of web sites. Fortunately, they are sorted by calculated relevance, so the searcher need not review more than the first 50 or 100 before the relevance drops off significantly.

Yahoo! (*http://www.yahoo.com*) and Open Directory Project (*http:// www.dmoz.org*) are examples of *Web directories*. Rather than attempting to index all the Web, these are human-built catalogues of selected web sites, organised in hierarchical categories. They include only a fraction of the publicly accessible Web, but they are designed to include the best of the Web. Note that some search engines include directories as well. For example, the main page of the search engine Google has both a search box (for searching its index of spidered web sites) and a link to 'browse web pages', which takes you to a catalogue of web sites, based on the Open Directory Project.

The distinction between search engines and directories is an important one. If you want to cast a wide net and retrieve as many potentially relevant sites as possible, or if you are looking for a very specific or unusual topic, use a search engine. If you want to find the key web sites on a subject, if you are looking for the Web address of a specific organisation, or if you want to browse a number of listings in a general category such as fishing or genetic engineering, you will be better served by a directory, with its selective coverage and hierarchical structure.

In addition to search engines and Web directories, there are a number of *meta-search engines* – sites that allow you to run your search through a number of Web search tools simultaneously. These meta-search sites are useful in determining the relative likelihood of retrieving useful information from one search engine or another. The limitations of meta-search sites are significant, however. Since they must execute the search on a number of search engines, each of which has its own functionalities and advanced features, meta-search engines tend to reduce a search to its simplest form. Usually, you are not able to use nested logic, Boolean connectors or truncation, for example. In addition, meta-search sites usually return a maximum of only 15 or 20 results from each search engine. Given the imprecision of most relevance ranking algorithms, this means that the most useful web site may not appear in the abbreviated search results from a meta-search engine. These tools are best used as a quick verification that a search term is valid or to decide which search engine to use for a more sophisticated search.

The open, gated and professional Web

When Reva Basch and I wrote the second edition of *Researching Online for Dummies* (Basch and Bates, 2000), we divided the Web into three categories – the open Web, gated web sites, and the professional Web. Understanding the distinction among the three groups, and knowing when and how to search each, will make the difference between a successful Web search and an exercise in futility and frustration.

The 'open Web' comprises those sites that are accessible to anyone, require no registration or payment, and – perhaps most importantly – do not put their information in databases that must be searched to be retrieved. Because the contents of open web sites are simply other web pages, search engine spiders can troll the site and index the contents. Open web sites can be retrieved via search engine searches (unless the web site has specified that search engine spiders not index the site).

The open Web includes corporate web sites, personal web pages, and many academic and government sites. They do not require users to register before accessing the information, and the pages within the site can usually be retrieved without needing to conduct a search within the site – that is, the user can simply drill down or click one link after another to get from page to page. Most of the sites retrieved from a search engine search are on the open Web.

The next category of web sites is what Reva Basch and I have called 'gated sites'. Think of those houses in communities that have entrance gates and guards who require identification before granting entrance. By the same token, gated web sites have some kind of gatekeeper at the site. For some of these sites, you simply need to provide your name or email address in order to proceed. At others, you need to pay a subscription fee, or you are charged when you wish to view information. Many gated sites have much of their information within databases, which means that you use a search box to retrieve material. Perhaps most significant, gated web sites are not spidered by search engines; their material is not indexed by any of the major Web search engines.

Examples of gated web sites include newspapers' sites, government sites that provide access to databases of companies' annual reports or regulatory files, or online telephone directories. Amazon.com, (*http://www.amazon.com*), the *Financial Times* (*http://www.ft.com*) and Moreover (*http://www.moreover.com*) are also gated sites; while some or most of their material is available at no charge, the information must be retrieved through a search box within the site.

One of the frustrations of gated sites is that, while they are often excellent research tools, they are difficult to locate, since their contents are not included in search engines. Fortunately, there are directories of many of these sites which, while they do not search the gated sites directly, do provide pointers to likely resources. Direct Search (*http://gwis2.circ.gwu.edu/~gprice/direct.htm*) is a directory of hundreds of database sites on the Web, arranged in broad categories. Invisible Web (*http://www.invisibleweb.com*) is a similar site, but has a more polished user interface. For listings of newspaper and magazine web sites, most of which are gated, check out *http://ajr.newslink.org*, maintained by the respected *American Journalism Review*. It includes print and broadcast news sources, and has good coverage outside the US, despite the 'American' in the title.

The third category of web sites is the 'professional Web' – the high-powered online services accessible through the Web, such as Reuters Business Briefing (*htp://www.business.reuters.com*), Dialog (*http://www.dialogweb.com*), and Lexis-Nexis (*http://www.nexis.com*).These resources, also known as professional online services, have been in existence for years; before the popularity of the Web, subscribers accessed these services through packet-switching networks and proprietary software. As with gated sites, contents of the professional Web are not spidered by search engines. One of the principal distinctions between the professional Web and gated sites is that the former offer far more – and more powerful – search tools, more sources, and more output options. The tradeoff for this higher value is, not surprisingly, a higher price tag.

Some material on professional web sites is also available on gated web sites at no charge, particularly recent articles from newspapers and general interest magazines. So why would a researcher ever pay the high price of a professional online service? One of the primary reasons is time. To conduct a search in 10 or 15 publications takes minutes in a professional web site. An equivalent search in gated web sites could take half an hour or more, as the researcher goes from one publication's site to the next, building a new search at each site depending on the search features of that site. Another reason for using a professional online service is that many of its resources are not available online elsewhere. And experienced searchers find that more complex searches cannot be constructed with the limited functionality of most gated web sites.

Implications of end-user Web research

The Internet has had tremendous impact on special librarians. One of the more noticeable changes is that many clients now do much of their research on their own; every desktop with Internet access is now a personalised research centre. That is good news in that special librarians are now freed from some of the ready reference questions that can be so time-consuming – looking up a company address, retrieving a copy of an article from yesterday's newspaper, or finding the correct citation of a particular book. We are now seeing more complicated requests, as our clients have higher expectations of what information is available.

One of the pitfalls of the increase in do-it-yourself searching on the Web was outlined in a study by the NPD Group (*http://www.npd.com*). According-ing to a 9 May 2000 press release, a study of end-user searchers found that 82 per cent said they find the information they want and that 39 per cent rate their favorite search engine 'excellent'. This suggests several trends to special librarians:

- Most end users are conducting fairly simple research – the kind that usually has a definite yes or no answer, such as yesterday's sports score, a current stock quote, or a summary of today's news.

- We are competing with 'good enough' – the attitude of end users that if you find *something* on the subject being researched, the search was successful.

- End users may not know what resources they are missing when they search; in particular, they probably do not know that search engines only cover a small percentage of the information available on the Web.

In order to differentiate ourselves and our information services, special librarians are challenged to emphasise added value, to demonstrate our ability to dig deeper, to access information sources not available or not easily retrieved on the open Web, and to provide the information in the most convenient format for our clients. That may mean providing an executive summary of search results, or delivering the material in a spreadsheet or presentation format. In all our research, we need to be mindful that we have competition, from the 'good enough' mentality that is satisfied with Web search results that only scratch the surface of the available information, and from outside firms that offer direct access to online databases. Our responsibility as special librarians is to determine the most appropriate and cost-effective mix of inhouse, customised research, desktop delivery of high-quality information sources and a well-designed intranet portal with pointers to the best of the open Web for our organisation.

Trends in Web research

Prior to the Web, most special librarians relied on the professional online services for research. The information was almost invariably in plain ASCII text, and the most sophisticated delivery option was to provide the material via email. The Web has changed all that. Now, we have to be able to deliver information from both Web searches and the professional online services in a multitude of formats – word-processed documents, PDF files, graphic images, HTML, and so on. In addition, we have to accommodate the varying needs and technological capabilities of our clients, some of whom may be sophisticated users of the latest technology and some of whom may prefer the entire package in hard-copy format.

We are seeing the rapid emergence and rising popularity of portals – web sites that provide an organised entrance into subject- or industry-specific subsets of the Web. Some of these portals focus on a single vertical market such as industrial chemicals or agriculture, and are often referred to as *vertical portals* or *vortals*. ChemConnect, for example, provides a business-to-business exchange for the chemical and plastics industry (*http://www.chemconnect.com*). And AgDomain (*http://www.agdomain.com*) includes directories and links on agricultural topics ranging from breeders of Jersey cattle to the 'corn cam', a web camera with a live feed of a corn field for those who want 'an opportunity to watch the progress of the crop from seedling to harvest'.

Industry Click (*http://www.industryclick.com*) and Vertical Net (*http://www.verticalnet.com*) are two sites that host a number of different industry portals. For an example of a very wide-ranging collection of portals, check out About.com (*http://www.about.com*), formerly known as The Mining Company. This site has over 700 'guides', each of whom is responsible for maintaining a portal on a specific topic. These range from anesthesiology to daycare to, yes, Web searching itself (*http://websearch.about.com*).

We are also seeing more of a focus on what is sometimes called the hidden or invisible Web, and what I have referred to as gated sites. Web site developers are building more sophisticated sites, and more of the information is being hidden behind search boxes. As a result, resources such as Invisible Web and Direct Search, which catalogue Web-based databases, are becoming more important research tools.

We are being forced to become more sophisticated in our search techniques. The number of web sites is growing exponentially and the Web search engines are striving to differentiate themselves by size, search functionality, extra features, or personalisation. As a result, special librarians cannot assume that the finding tool that was most useful six months ago will still be the best choice today. Imagine if we had to re-evaluate our selection of periodical subscriptions or cataloguing systems every six months! Fortunately, there are several web sites that provide running commentaries on the current state of the art in search engine functionality, size, timeliness, and usability.

- Search Engine Watch (*http://www.SearchEngineWatch.com*) is maintained by Danny Sullivan, a consultant who provides guidance to web site owners on how to optimise their sites for search engines. This site includes tips on how to best use each of the major search engines, ratings of the relative popularity of various search engines, and a free monthly newsletter about search engine trends.

- Search Engine Showdown (*http://www.SearchEngineShowdown.com*) is developed by Greg Notess, a librarian at Montana State University, Bozeman. He regularly analyses a dozen search engines and produces charts showing features, size, estimated overlap with other search engines, number of dead links, and so on.

- The Web Search Guide (*http://websearch.about.com*) is the section of the About.com portal that focuses on Web searching in general. Chris Sherman, the Guide responsible for this area of About.com, writes a weekly newsletter about trends in Web research, has interviews with expert Web searchers, and maintains links to sources of information about Web research.

Web research tips

One of the biggest challenges for information professionals is the need to shift between search techniques that work well for the professional online services such as Lexis-Nexis or Dialog and those that are appropriate for the Web. The heavy-duty vendors justify their costs by providing value-added search tools that enable users to efficiently sift through tremendous quantities of data, such as:

- structured databases of material

- uniform record types – company directory entries, the full text of patents, bibliographic citations, chemical formula, the full text of articles, and so on

- field indexing down to the level of title, lead paragraph, author, company address or postal code, and subject indexing with a controlled vocabulary

- system commands that allow you to construct complex search requests

- a variety of display options, including ones that show just a bibliographic citation, the full text, or the key search terms and subject indexing.

Web searching, on the other hand, requires an entirely different set of techniques and skills. While entire books have been written on how to do Web-based research, this section will cover a few of the core proficiencies that any special librarian should have.

First, learn the advanced search techniques of whatever tools you use. Virtually every major search engine has an [Advanced Search] link or something similar – a separate search screen that shows you how to use the available power tools, letting you construct more finely tuned searches, use Boolean logic, limit your search to the title or URL, indicate terms that must or must not appear in each retrieved site, and take advantage of truncation and adjacency searching. Note that you will often see different search results depending on the *order* that you type your terms in the search box. Many search engines use the order of the words as an indicator of relative importance. So, for example, the search results of *backpacking Montana* may display web sites pertaining to backpacking in general higher in the list, whereas the results of *Montana backpacking* may have among the top of the list web sites that cover any outdoor activities in Montana.

Many search engines have added directories or catalogues to their search options; if imitation is the most sincere form of flattery, Yahoo! should be feeling very flattered these days! Become familiar with the directory of each of your favorite search engines and keep in mind that your search results will be more limited and often more focused if you restrict your search to a directory.

Learn to use the specialised search engines that, while perhaps not as comprehensive, may handle some searches better than the larger search engines. Some examples of these niche search engines include:

- Those that focus on disambiguation, or sense-making, such as Oingo (*http://www.oingo.com*) or SimpliFind (*http://www.simpli.com*). Both of these sites specialise in figuring out which of several meanings of a word you want. If you type in the word *record*, for example, you are prompted to indicate whether you mean *phonograph album, a document, an achievement, a criminal record* or *to register*.

- Those that build collections of commonly-asked search questions, such as Ask Jeeves (*http://www.ask.com*). If you are looking for something that you think others often ask for, start with one of these so-called answers databases.

- Those that sort results in a certain way. Most search engines use proprietary algorithms that look at frequency of search terms and relative position of terms within the web site. However, there are other ways of ranking results. Direct Hit (*http://www.directhit.com*), for example, keeps track of how often a particular URL in a search result is clicked on, and ranks frequently clicked sites higher in a search result list. Other sites, such as Google (*http://www.google.com*), look at how many web sites link *to* a particular site, and rank frequently linked-to sites higher. Sometimes this kind of ranking is useful; keep in mind, though, that it tends to favour more established and older sites, i.e., those that have established presences and a long history of being clicked on. A newer but possible more relevant site may be ranked lower simply because it has not been in existence long enough to be linked to or clicked on.

Develop an expertise in several search tools – a catalogue or two, a couple of search engines, and a few portals that pertain to your industry or subject area. No one can stay on top of every finding tool on the Web; you are more likely to get good results if you learn how to use a few tools very well than if you try to use 10 or 15 different tools for every search.

Remember the 'hidden Web'. Much of the information on the Web is never captured by search engines. Newspaper archives, buyers' guides and directories, statistical databases and files of government documents usually do not appear in search engine indexes, because search engine spiders cannot drill down into and 'read' a database. These databases are often tremendously useful and, almost by definition, they are structured collections of information designed for more sophisticated searching. Use the catalogues and directories of Web databases to identify these treasure troves of information, such as Invisible Web (*http://www.invisibleweb.com*) and Direct Search (*http://gwis2.circ.gwu.edu/~gprice/direct.htm*).

Keep your search simple and straightforward. Your search strategy in a professional online service such as DataStar may be very complex, including several phrases for each aspect of your topic. This approach simply does not work with the Web. Instead, identify the most important aspect of your search, and the most uncommon search terms, and start your search with those words.

Take advantage of the ability of the Web to unearth links among organisations, individuals, and ideas. One of the less known but powerful tools of Web research is *link analysis* or *reverse link look-up*. This technique identifies web sites that link to a particular web site or domain. Why would you use this tool? You can learn about a company by seeing what its suppliers or vendors are saying about it; you can find out what organisations an individual is active in; you can see what companies have established partnerships with the company you are researching. Several search engines support this kind of search. To look for any web sites that reference the web site *http://www.acme.com*, for example:

*   In Google or Alta Vista, type *link:www.acme.com* in the search box

- in HotBot (*http://hotbot.lycos.com*), type *http://www.acme.com*, pull down the 'Look For' menu and select [links to this URL].

Know what you are looking for. The Web is often jokingly referred to as a time sink, for good reason. There are always tangentially related sites that might be useful; each of those sites points to five other sites that might be worth going to; oh, yes, and then maybe there's that other aspect of the research project that you should look into too… Before you know it, you have spent more time than you intended on the question at hand. Reference interview tools are more important now than ever before. If you do not have a clear idea of what your client wants and what would best answer the question, then you are much more likely to spend far too long surfing – rather than searching – the Web. The time you invest in a thorough reference interview pays off when you can quickly retrieve and recognise relevant information.

And speaking of time, remember to value your time. It is easy to focus on the direct expenses associated with using a professional, fee-based online service; it is more difficult to quantify the value of your time if it takes three times as long to find the same information on the Web. Along this line, I wrote a white paper for Factiva, the producer of Dow Jones Interactive and Reuters Business Briefing, examining the true cost of online research. I calculated the direct cost of a number of typical business research projects, using the free Web, the low-fee online services, and Dow Jones Interactive, a professional online service. Then I factored in the hourly cost of a typical corporate researcher, to calculate the *total* cost of the research to an organisation. To my surprise, I found that virtually all business research projects cost the most on the 'free' Web and the least when using a professional online service, once the researcher's time is included in the calculation. You can read the full text of the white paper at *http://www.factiva.com/infopro/BusIntellletter.pdf*.

Staying Current

It is often said that an Internet 'year' is three or four months long. Given this pace of change, it is important for special librarians to re-examine their Web research tool kit at least every six months. Not only are the most appropriate resources likely to have changed, but we also must stay ahead of our clients in terms of Web research. I am reminded of the Red Queen in *Through the Looking Glass*, who told Alice, 'Now, HERE, you see, it takes all the running YOU can do, to keep in the same place. If you want to get somewhere else, you must run at least twice as fast as that!' How do we modern-day Alices stay up to date on Web research tools and trends?

The best resources we have for keeping up on developments in our profession are … our colleagues. Librarians have always shared resources, collaborated in finding information, and valued continuing education. The Web has greatly expanded our ability to participate in collective brain-storming with the development of electronic discussion lists, sometimes known as listservs. (Note that **LISTSERV** is a registered trademark of L-Soft international Inc.) For starters, identify the email discussion lists frequented by librarians and information professionals in your field. For business librarians, that might be **BUSLIB-L**. (To subscribe to **BUSLIB-L**, send email to **LISTSERV@LISTSERV.BOISESTATE.EDU**, with the following in the body of the message: *subscribe buslib-l your-first-name your-last-name*.) For US law librarians, it would probably be **LAW-LIB**. (To subscribe to **LAW-LIB**, send email to **listproc@ucdavis.edu**, with the following in the body of the message: *subscribe law-lib your-first-name your-last-name*.) If you do not know of an appropriate list, ask other librarians in your field. There are also web sites that attempt to catalogue all publicly-available lists, although maintaining such a list is roughly equivalent to trying to sweep the beach of sand. Given that caveat, you can try looking for [*librar** and your subject area] in Liszt (*http://www.liszt.com*), one of the premier web sites for indexing of mailing lists.

There is also a growing number of information portals and Web-based discussion forums for information professionals. Rather than getting individual postings delivered to your email, you have to remember to go to these sites to read the latest buzz; this can be seen as either an advantage for those whose email box is overflowing or a disadvantage for those who prefer the push technology of email. One of the better-known discussion forums is Free Pint (*http://www.freepint.co.uk*). The professional online services are also beginning to set up information portals. See, for example, Dialog's portal at *http://library.dialog.com/infopro*.

Likewise, subscribe to at least one list that your clients or key users read. Yes, some of it may be esoteric, overly technical, or downright boring. But just as you need to read the key print publications that your clients read, so you need to monitor the electronic information sources that your clients rely on. This is how you stay on top of trends in your industry, hear about cutting edge developments early in the process, and get exposed to the same industry news and gossip your clients hear.

The impact of the Web on our profession

Some librarians have looked at the Web as a tremendous asset, enabling them to provide research services and information products that would have been impossible before the advent of the Net. Other information professionals see clients relying on the information they find on the open Web, and they worry that their clients are being short-changed and, indeed, misinformed.

Both perspectives have validity. There is a lot in the business-to-consumer (also known as b2c) arena that we probably do not have to worry too much about. A number of ask-an-expert sites, both free and fee-based, have sprung up over the last year or so. Examples include *http:// www.keen.com, http://www.exp.com,* and *http://www.answers.com.* While they all appear to compete with the typical reference librarian, the questions that they are designed to handle tend to be those that are asking for advice – What should I feed a baby bird? What kind of printer should I buy? Should I pursue a career in MIS? – rather than true research. In fact, they may be a boon to special librarians. We all have the occasional clients who want help planning a vacation, researching possible schools for their children, or selecting a car with a good repair history. Referring these clients to the ask-an-expert sites frees special librarians to spend time on the more in-depth, work-related, value-added research projects.

One thing that the Web has undoubtedly done is turn information into a commodity. If clients are looking for late-breaking news, or company press releases, or background information on an organisation, they can head over to the Net and find what they want from their favourite news site or search engine. Virtually any search, including fairly complex research topics, will retrieve *some* results. It is true that many library clients – and non-clients, for that matter – do not appreciate the value that information professionals bring to the research process, and do not recognise the limitations of and enormous gaps in the information available on the free Web. Since it is so easy to retrieve something at least marginally relevant for any research topic, our challenge is to raise the information expectations of our clients. We need to remind them of the resources we special librarians have *beyond* the Web, as well as our ability to sift through, organise, synthesise and package the information we retrieve. What special librarians bring to the table is the added value of understanding the industry in which we work, our organisation's goals, competitors, and priorities, and the internal as well as external resources that would best meet our clients' needs.

Evaluating information quality

More than ever, special librarians need to educate their clients on how to evaluate web sites for usefulness, reliability, accuracy and timeliness. While material in newspapers, trade journals, industry newsletters, and scholarly publications is subjected to editorial review, much of the information on the Web is not. Following is a list of the general types of material commonly found on the Web and some of the information quality issues of each.

- *News*: this includes newswire stories, video clips and photographs, audio files of interviews and speeches, and archives of newspapers, magazines and journals. Newswire stories are sometimes inaccurate, due to the pressures of getting the news out quickly. Archived material and articles are generally reliable, as it is presumed that they have been reviewed by an editor.

- *Corporate information*: information found on companies' web sites, including annual reports, advertising, product information, job listings and so on. Financial information from publicly traded companies can be assumed to be reliable, as they are regulated by a government agency. Advertising and product information should, of course, be viewed with a more skeptical eye. Clients should be cautioned about judging a company solely by its web site; a well-designed site does not necessarily indicate that the company behind it is stable, established or reputable.

- *Grey literature*: this includes material such as white papers, pamphlets and reports, published outside the traditional media stream. The reliability of this information varies widely, depending on the source and motivation of the publisher. Since much grey literature is self-published, it is important to contact the writer to get additional background information before relying on the material.

- *Editorial material*: this includes commentary, editorials, product reviews and web sites intended to advocate a particular point of view. It is usually clear that editorial material is written with a certain perspective. Special librarians should help clients recognise advocacy information; some web sites are designed to obscure the fact that they are, in fact, not sources of impartial information on a topic.

- *Factual material*: this includes sites such as the British Library online catalogue, the National Library of Medicine's databases and a site built by an expert on raising and training Old English Sheepdogs. Note that factual sites are not necessarily sources of accurate information. Most are, of course, particularly those maintained by government agencies or non-profit research organisations. However, a site about medieval architecture built by someone passionate about that topic, for example, may include unintentional historical inaccuracies.

- *Commercial sites*: this includes sites designed for commerce, such as Amazon.com, Hoovers.com and Travelocity.com. Reliability is usually not a problem; users generally are not using commercial sites as sources of research-related information.

- *Discussion forums*: this includes sites that provide online bulletin boards, Usenet sites, and other web sites that consist primarily of person-to-person communication. Some discussion forums can be useful sources of information; others are full of less-than-reliable commentary. Sites that encourage non-anonymous posting, that foster a sense of long-term, stable community, and that focus on a particular industry, profession or subject tend to be more reliable. The peer-review aspect of these virtual communities should not be underestimated. With a little patience, researchers can usually identify the community expert and, yes, the village hot-head within any virtual community.

  There are a number of general criteria that information professionals commonly – and often almost subconsciously – use to evaluate the quality of information, both on the Net and in other media. The questions that you ask yourself when looking at a web page will vary with the type of material being reviewed. Use the following pointers as general guidelines for evaluating the source.

- Is it clear who has written or created this material? Can you contact the author directly, via telephone or mail? An email address by itself does not necessarily indicate credibility. What credentials does the author have?

- If this is a company web site, does it include a street address and telephone number for the company? Look up the domain name in one of the look-up services in which domain name owners are listed, such as *http://www.NetworkSolutions.com*. Is the name of the owner of the domain the same as the company name?

- Does the material have spelling or grammatical errors? If so, that indicates a lack of quality control and editorial review, not to mention the possibility of errors due to transposed numbers or mistyped words.

- If there is advertising or editorial material on the site, is it clearly differentiated from factual material?

- Is the point of view clearly stated? If, for example, you are reviewing a site that discusses possible treatments for a disease, does it appear that the web site is promoting a particular treatment modality or product?

- If the site describes research or quotes from other sources, are those sources fully identified? Can you verify that the sources are being represented accurately?

- How does the information provided correlate to related sources? Is it at odds with most other information sources? Can you find other sources that confirm what this site is saying?

- Does the site indicate the date when the information was last updated? If it is several years old, do you think that the content is too dated?

For an excellent tutorial, see Jan Alexander's and Marsha Ann Tate's *Evaluating Web Resources* (Alexander and Tate).

Special librarians in the age of the Web

As challenging as the Web is for our profession, special librarians are in perhaps a unique position. Never before has there been so much information, in so many formats, with such varying quality, available to so many people. The commonly heard complaint about information overload is a valid one, but it misstates the problem. The issue is not *information* overload but *data* overload. Anyone with a Net connection and a browser can download more data than could be read in a lifetime. What users need are information professionals who can start with data, comb through it for the valuable intelligence contained within, distill it down and present it in a format that can be understood and acted upon by the user.

It used to be the case that special librarians thrived by being information retrievers – the people with access to computers and databases and Boolean logic and reference books. Now, none of those things set us apart from our peers and colleagues. Instead, what we bring to the table is our ability to be information analysts, providing added value and intelligence to the information. We understand how information is created, gathered, formatted, organised and retrieved. Using that expertise, we can provide that invaluable link between data and intelligence.

References

Alexander, Jan and Tate, Marsha Ann. Evaluating Web Resources. Available at *http://www2.widener.edu/Wolfgram-Memorial-Library/webeval.htm*.

Basch, Reva and Bates, Mary Ellen. *Researching Online for Dummies*. IDG Books (2000, 2nd ed.).

I Lawrence, Steve and Giles, C. Lee. Accessibility of information on the Web. *Nature*, 8 July 1999.

Chapter 11

Selecting information resources for the special library

Susan Henczel

Introduction

A library exists within an organisation to provide the information resources that employees need to do their work, therefore the resources
collected and maintained by that library must consist of those resources
that support the work of the employees in that organisation. The person
who is selecting the information resources for the library collection must
have a clear understanding of the ongoing needs of information users
right across the organisation. This involves understanding the structure
of the organisation, the functions of each group, section or department
and the relationships between them. An understanding of the external
environment in which the organisation is operating is also important in
that it enables a level of proactivity to be incorporated into the provision
of information resources.

The selection tasks undertaken by the special librarian are becoming more
complex with the exponential growth in the number of products and the
multitude of formats (hard copy, CD-ROM, online dial-up, online Web-
based etc.), the increasing levels of overlap between products, the
complexity of licences and the range of options available for delivery of
the information. By understanding the nature of the work carried out by
each section of the organisation, the selector can ensure that better decisions are made regarding new products and formats and that the
appropriate delivery methods are used for existing and new resources.

This chapter will cover all of the issues that need to be addressed during
the selection process, beginning with the identification of user needs and
the development of the appropriate policies to minimise subjectivity and
to ensure comprehensiveness and consistency. It will cover the selection
of books and serials as well as the evaluation and selection of electronic
products including web resources.

There are two main steps that must be completed to ensure that the most
appropriate resources are selected for inclusion in a special library, or
that the most appropriate information is delivered to the clients of a

special library. The first is to identify the needs of the clients, and the second is to develop a collection development policy and a selection policy to ensure objectivity and consistency in the selection process.

Identifying the needs of information users

Before selecting resources for a special library collection it is important that you have a clear understanding of the information needs of the organisation's employees. There is no point adding to an existing collection if the current resources are not meeting the needs of the users or if the resources are not in an appropriate format for delivery to the user. User needs can be identified by conducting a *needs analysis* or an *information audit* (Henczel, 2001). A *needs analysis* will tell you what information people need to do their jobs, whilst an *information audit* goes beyond that and will also tell you how they use the information and how strategically significant it is in relation to the achievement of the organisation's objectives. New products and requests received from users can be matched against the findings of the information audit, and a decision made as to whether they should be purchased according to their level of strategic significance.

As well as understanding the information needs it is also important to determine the information seeking behaviour of the users – do they head for electronic sources, prefer paper, think everything they need is on the Web, or do they generally bypass the corporate resources and use personal sources? Because of the nature of their jobs, some information users have specific needs, for example employees in the field are not always able to access electronic information. It is important to know this, as it will determine which formats and delivery methods are appropriate. Information needs analysis and the information audit are covered in more depth in separate chapters of the Handbook.

The collection development and selection policies

Once the needs and behaviours are identified, collection development and resource selection is a much simpler process. A collection development policy will ensure that the resources that are selected match the needs of the clients by ensuring that selection is done objectively, consistently and in accordance with established guidelines.

A collection development policy is a written document that is ideally an appendix to an organisation's information policy. A collection development policy:

- identifies the client groups to which the library provides resources and services
- states the goals to be met by collection development, and the resources and services to be provided to meet those goals
- identifies the staff responsible for selection and acceptance of client requests
- outlines methods for dealing with donations and exchanges, controversial items, weeding and discarding.

The use of a collection development policy ensures accountability as it assigns responsibility for making selection decisions (Whitehead, 1989). It also assists with the information explosion by providing boundaries for the material to be added to the collection.

Many special libraries may act as a central ordering point for all information resources required by an organisation and in these cases the library collection may have a specific purpose rather than an all-encompassing one. The scope of the library's responsibility from an organisational perspective must be clearly stated in the collection development policy to minimise gaps and duplication in the supply of information resources. This will ensure that the selection librarian has a clear understanding of the parameters in which he or she must work.

Some libraries may have separate *selection* and *acquisitions* documentation that contain the procedures for selecting and acquiring resources. These documents contain much more detail than the collection development policy and include specific selection criteria for resources and the procedures for acquiring them.

A *selection policy* must include a breakdown of the collection according to the level of strategic significance of the needs that it supports. Resources that support tasks that are rated at the highest level of strategic significance, in other words that are critical to the achievement of organisational objectives, must receive the highest priority. These resources form the 'core' collection. This process can be worked through the 'not essential but adds value', 'desirable but not essential' and 'nice to have but rarely used' resources that constitute the supporting and peripheral collections. It consists of books, serials, internal and external reports, online services, grey literature, electronic documents, encyclopedias, glossaries and directories.

The 'supporting' collection consists of the resources that add value to the core collection. Rather than providing the critical information, they provide the additional information that adds to the value of the organisation's function. Again all formats must be considered. This collection can contain all of the formats of the core collection as well as access to online databases 'as required' and interlibrary loans and document delivery.

The 'peripheral' collection includes resources that are the 'luxury' items that should be provided if the budget allows. Many of these will be expensive online services that may only be used every once in a while and 'fringe' publications that do not focus on the core needs but that cross their boundaries in some way. This collection also includes materials obtained from other library collections or purchased through commercial document suppliers 'as required'.

The selection policy must also incorporate a procedure for project-based selection. Every organisation at some point in time embarks on projects that require supporting information resources. These projects may be radically different from the everyday operation of the business and may require information resources that are beyond the scope of the selection policy. The procedure for dealing with the provision of resources for projects must be clearly stated in the selection policy. Often there are multiple projects that are competing for supporting resources and the selection policy must contain a method for prioritising so that the available resources are used to support the most strategically significant activities. The selection policy must include specific guidelines for selecting books, serials and electronic resources.

Selecting books

The selection process for books is less complex than either serials or electronic resources due to the nature of books in that they are generally singular publications that have an evident scope, level and coverage. The downside of selecting books as an information resource is that the information that they contain can be out of date before they are published. The significance of this feature will depend on the subject area of the information required and the importance of the currency of the information.

Publishers, vendors, organisations and associations are developing a variety of print-based, electronic and web-based tools to assist the selection librarian. Tools for the selection of books include publicity material (catalogues and flyers, both in print and electronic form), magazines and journals (for reviews), web sites, CD-ROMs and online services.

Blurbs, catalogues and magazines can be delivered directly to selection staff or to the appropriate people throughout an organisation. In some cases, the information users are the most appropriate people to select information resources, and the distribution of publisher and bookseller material throughout an organisation can minimise headaches for selectors. If this is done however there must be some means of validating their selection to ensure that it is within the parameters of the selection criteria set out in the selection policy.

Many publishers' blurbs and catalogues contain details of resources prior to their publication, which can be both an advantage and disadvantage for the selector. The advantage is that orders can be placed for items that may have a very short print run which can ensure that a copy will be supplied on publication. It allows the selector to budget for purchases ahead of billing and enables him or her to promote the publication prior to receipt. Disadvantages include the fact that not all pre-publication is correct. Titles can change which can create difficulties with order records in acquisitions systems and possibly result in duplicate orders. The expected date of publication can vary dramatically with delays resulting in some publications being released months or even years after their initial promotion. Some are never published at all.

Booksellers and publishers who have their catalogues on their web site enable selectors to generate periodic searches by subject or author to locate details of books that meet their selection criteria. Details of the selections can be delivered electronically to information users for validation prior to ordering. Profiles can be established with many online booksellers to generate periodic alerts containing details of new publications. Alerts can also be set up for individuals or groups within an organisation who can then pass on their selections to the library. Searching publisher and bookseller catalogues via a web site can also enable you to locate similar material once you have found a relevant item. Many allow you to continue your search for additional items that are similar in content to the item you have selected or have the same author or publisher. This enables you to review a range of items and is particularly useful when establishing a collection in a new subject area.

Many of the vendors and some of the larger publishers offer books on approval to libraries. This process allows the information user or the selector to assess the value and relevance of a book prior to purchase. It is particularly useful for expensive books, books where the content and level is unknown, books on the fringe of a subject area or a new subject area and when there are many similar books to choose from. The books must be returned in an unmarked condition and must be returned within a specified timeframe. Not all publishers and vendors offer this service and some may not offer it for all of their books.

Another service offered by vendors is a profiling service that enables you to periodically receive items that match predefined criteria. A profile is established for your library based on your answers to a number of questions that relate to the subject coverage, level, type and price of the items you require. As the vendor receives items that match your profile they are delivered to you to review. You are able to return those that you don't wish to keep provided they are in 'as new' condition and are returned within a specified timeframe. This process has advantages in that the vendors may provide items that you would not have known of otherwise and less time is spent 'shopping around' and interrogating web sites and booklists. If it is used exclusively however it can exclude material published by the smaller publishers and items that do not fit neatly into the predefined criteria. The objective for both the vendor and the library is to minimise returns and provided the profile is adjusted by the vendor as unwanted items are returned it should not take long to have the process working efficiently. It is important to review the profile regularly to ensure that it is resulting in the provision of items that meet the information needs of the organisation. The frequency of the review will depend on the rate of change of the information needs in the organisation.

Specialist publishers, organisations and associations often produce their own printed blurbs, catalogues and magazines. You may have to subscribe to receive them and some will incur a charge. Many have web sites that contain details of their publications and often allow you to place an order for a listed item or register to receive details of forthcoming publications. Once you have registered you may find that you are inundated with mail or email from them as they only have one general mailing list and not a specific one for publications. It can become time consuming to sort through the material they send you but it is often the only way to learn about their publications.

Many publishers are offering electronic books, or e-books, although at present they are particularly aimed at the academic market. Some specialist publishers are producing books in electronic form and in hard copy, with the electronic copy being provided only if the hard copy is purchased. Many electronic books are sold in 'collections' and incur a purchase price as well as an ongoing access cost. There are stringent copyright, distribution and access restrictions on some while others include all copyright, distribution and access rights in the purchase price. Some current collections do not allow concurrent users and require users to 'sign out' an e-book as if it were a library loan which means that the next user is unable to access the book until it is returned. When buying an e-book it is important to have a clear understanding of what it is you are purchasing and what you are allowed to do with it once you have purchased it.

You will undoubtedly be visited regularly by sales representatives from book vendors, publishers and even local bookstores. Rather than view these visits as an inconvenience, use them to work for you. If these people all have a clear understanding of the material required by your organisation they can pass details of new and existing publications, special offers (discounts, package deals etc.) as well as networking opportunities such as social activities, exhibitions, forums and conferences.

Selecting serials

Selecting serials to add to a library collection or to make available to departments or individuals within an organisation differs from books in that it is not a single purchase and it requires management and administration to ensure that what is purchased is received over the period of the subscription.

The selection policy for serials must include:

- coverage of subject area, price limitations and formats
- consideration of who pays for the subscriptions
- consideration of whether issues are circulated or not
- annual review of subscriptions prior to renewal
- retention policy and discard decisions, what gets bound, archived, etc.
- policies for handling gifts and donations.

Serials are very different in nature from books and because they are ongoing it is a common mistake to renew subscriptions year after year without reviewing their content, prices, number of copies, format and levels of usage.

The content or focus of a serial can change dramatically over time and if a title has been subscribed to for a few years it may be necessary to look at how heavily it is used and whether or not it still matches the selection criteria. Also the information needs of the organisation may have changed since the title was first purchased. For both of these reasons the review of serial subscriptions must be included in the selection policy.

The review process must include:

- assessing the relevance of existing subscription titles
- assessing the number of copies of each subscription title
- assessing the appropriateness of the subscription price in relation to the strategic significance of the tasks or activities supported by each subscription title.
- assessing the alternative means of accessing the content of the serial (alternative formats)
- identifying other titles that may be more useful.

Internal statistics such as interlibrary loans and document delivery can be used to identify serial titles that should be added to the collection. Where multiple articles have been acquired from one title or where articles from a particular title appear frequently in search results it may be more cost effective to subscribe to the title. Establishing a balance between ownership and access is difficult but by comparing the cost of the subscription with the costs (both direct and indirect) of acquiring articles from other sources it should become clear which titles should be owned. Owning a title will also ensure faster delivery of articles when required by information users.

Selection tools for new serial titles are similar to those for books. Publishers, vendors, organisations and associations use printed or electronic blurbs, alerts, magazines and catalogues to inform you of the details of new titles. Sample copies for new and existing titles are available from publishers and vendors and your sales representative should be able to organise this for you. Once again, let the sales representatives work for you to acquire samples, liaise with publishers, keep you informed of new and relevant tiles and provide networking opportunities.

Many serials are being produced in varying formats and decisions must be made on the most appropriate format in which to purchase a serial. Choices often include hard copy, CD-ROM, online dial-up or web-based. With the electronic formats there may be several products that include a particular serial title so further choices must be made based on the relevance of the additional material included in the product, the price or in the case of CD-ROMs the frequency of the updates. As with e-books, it is important to know exactly what you are getting for your money when purchasing e-journals. How long will you be able to access the content of previous years issues that you have paid for, what restrictions are placed on copying, distribution and access, and is the content of the electronic version identical to that of the hard copy are all questions that must be asked. As with e-books, access to the electronic version is often provided free or at a reduced price for a specified period of time when the hard copy is purchased. This may only be on a trial basis, so be wary of establishing online access for information users if access to the product is only short-term without making them aware that it is a trial. It is a good way, however of allowing the information users to evaluate a product and to assess its usefulness in comparison with the hard copy.

Research reports, government material, grey literature

If the selection process was simply a matter of choosing books and journals for a library collection it would be fairly straightforward. Most organisations, however, have a need for resources that are not so easy to find out about, locate and purchase. These are the challenges for the selection librarian.

Many publications cannot be supplied by vendors and in these cases it is necessary to go directly to the organisation or association that produces them. Finding out what is available is often a matter of registering to be included on a mailing list or email list, or bookmarking a web site and checking it periodically to see if anything new is available. Research organisations can fall into this category, as they do not always publish their research results or interim reports. Direct contact with the organisation is the only way to find out they exist. Other organisations may publish material but only make it available to members so taking out an organisational membership may be the only option you have to enable your organisation to have access to the material.

Fewer publishers are accepting scholarly material for publication and much of it is being 'self-published' by the authors or associations either in hard copy or electronically. The web sites of associations and individuals contain a huge amount of self-published material. Locate the web sites of significant associations and individuals and bookmark them. Details of material that has been self-published in hard copy can be found by contacting the authors, the author's institution or from the author's web site.

Accessing information about government publications varies from country to country but most have established some degree of web access to the details of official government publications. The web sites often include ordering facilities. Vendors are usually able to supply details of the more significant government publications and often include them in their blurbs, alerts, magazines and catalogues. Details of government reports that have not been released into the public domain, and reports from countries other than your own are often more difficult to locate.

Selecting electronic resources

Many resources are available in hard copy as well as in electronic form on CD-ROM or online via web or dial-up access. There are many things to consider when deciding whether to purchase the hard copy or the electronic version of a resource such as the methods of access, content, and of course the cost.

Whether you select resources in electronic format or hard copy will depend on the technical infrastructure that exists to enable information users to access the information. Existing networks, intranets, Internet access, telephone communications and the capacity of computers all impact on the electronic delivery of information and before selecting electronic resources you must be sure that it is the best interests of the information user. Some may be unable to access the appropriate telephone facilities and computer networks to make the access to electronic resources feasible.

As well as the technical infrastructure there are also 'people' and workflow issues that need to be considered. Users have different abilities and information preferences. Some who are used to printed books and journals may not adapt quickly and easily to electronic products unless they can see the immediate benefits of doing so. Also bear in mind that changing from print-based to electronic information resources can mean significant changes to workflows and procedures. A change from print to electronic may have significant negative impacts on workflows, productivity and attitudes towards the library.

There may be some users who are unable to access the resources they need if they are only available in electronic form. For example, fieldworkers and others who work offsite may be unable to access electronic resources due to network limitations. Employees who rely on access to resources while visiting their customers may not always have dial-up or web access, or they may have downloading difficulties. It is therefore important to gain a good understanding, not just of information needs but the nature of the work so that the best decisions can be made regarding format of resources.

When considering a change from a print version of a resource to an electronic version, or even when changing from CD-ROM to online, there are several things to consider:

- *Content* – print, CD-ROM and online versions of a product may have differing content. In some cases this is insignificant, whilst in others there are dramatic differences in quality, scope, indexing, referencing and illustrations.

- *Cost* – the cost of each format will vary and may not relate to the quality and scope of the content. Does the cost vary according to the time of year that you purchase the product? Are compilations of CD-ROMs available at reduced charges? Are there any other additional charges, for example postage and handling on CD-ROMs?

- *Bundling* – to purchase a resource in electronic form you may be obliged also to take the print or CD-ROM version, sometimes at an additional cost. You may receive the print version for a limited time when subscribing to the electronic version, or you may not be permitted to buy both print and electronic. When purchasing one title in electronic form you may have also to take a variety of other titles or modules, 'bundled' together as a product, whether you need them or not.

- *Access and distribution* – are you able to make the resource available to the people who need it? This includes consideration of licences that restrict distribution, access and copying as well as the technical infrastructure required. In the case of electronic serials, archiving must also be considered. Will you always have access to the material you have paid for, even if you do not re-subscribe? Are copies archived to enable access to back issues? What is the retrospective coverage? Is the archive searchable? In the case of electronic books, how long will you have access to the resource and how can the vendor guarantee this access?

- *User behaviour* – will the same users that currently use a resource in print form use it in electronic form? It seems that when moving from print to electronic resources there is a high incidence of users moving away from material they previously 'couldn't do without' to others that they would never have looked at in print form. This is particularly related to electronic products purchased in aggregated collections, or suites, and is a consequence of the ability to search across titles in an electronic environment and to source information from titles that were not previously purchased. It is also related to the ability to browse across titles and to jump from one title to another via hyperlinks.

Choosing appropriate electronic databases is one of the most difficult tasks facing a selection librarian as there will inevitably be competing products on the market. There are however a number of selection criteria that can be used to rate the suitability of electronic databases. These include:

- *Full text / Abstract / Citation.* Is full text required? If the database does not contain full text does it have a document delivery option? If not, are the citations complete enough for ordering?

- *Coverage.* To what degree is the subject area covered adequately at the required level? Is the scope clearly stated, are the limits clear and are any omissions clearly stated? What is the retrospective coverage of the database? Is the coverage unbiased (for example, are both sides of controversial issues presented equally), or if not, are the biases clearly stated? Are there links to further sources of information?

- Are there *different versions* of the database and is the information the same in each one?

- *Currency.* How current is the information and how regularly is it updated? What is the time delay between the print version and the electronic version?

- *Reliability.* Is it well compiled with information from a valid source? How accurate is the information and what is its authority? Is it technically reliable?

- *Quality.* Is it well indexed using synonyms etc.? Is the updating of the product frequent and regular?

- *Format.* Can documents be viewed and downloaded in a variety of formats (for example, text and PDF)?

- *Speed of retrieval and relevance of output.* Does it include efficient and effective search facilities? Are both searching and browsing catered for?

- Does it *overlap* with other databases and products? If so, is the level of overlap acceptable?

- *Ease of use.* Is end-user training required?

- What level of *support and backup* is provided by the producer in the form of online help, support documentation, help desk and training? Is local support available?

- How much does the product *cost*? There are many different ways in which vendors charge for access to their electronic products. These include, but are not limited to:
  - free to search, with charges made for viewing or downloading of documents from the search results
  - subscription, with either limited or unlimited access to documents
  - subscription for a limited number of users, with additional charges for users over and above that number
  - prepaid searches
  - timed access.

- The ability to *purchase independently* of other products.

- Is a *free trial* offered to allow a complete evaluation of the product by the people who will be using it? (A note of warning here from a trusted colleague – be very wary of vendors who insist on processing an invoice in order to provide you with a password. If you do not go ahead with the subscription it is often difficult to get your money back.)

- *Terms of the licence.* What restrictions are placed on copying, access and distribution? For example, how many concurrent users can access the product and can they print or download documents?

- *Technical suitability?* Is the product compatible with the existing technical infrastructure? Is specialist software required to access it?

- *Statistics.* Are usage statistics collected and stored in a usable format? If so, what data are collected and what statistical reporting and analysis can be done?

Current awareness services

Current awareness services (CAS), or alert services, have their own set of selection criteria including:

- *Coverage.* Subject coverage, level and depth etc.
- *Profiling.* Does it have flexible profiling features that enable tailored profiles to be submitted to increase the relevance of alerts/ reports? How many profiles can be established? How specific can they be? What limitations are there on the number of alerts.
- *Reputation/validity.* What is the reputation and expertise of the organisations involved in the production of the service?
- *Accuracy.* What is the likely accuracy of the information extracted?
- *Currency.* How frequently is the service updated?
- *Accessibility.* How is the service accessed and how are reports/ alerts delivered? Can they be delivered directly to the users, or must they come through a central point such as the library?

Selecting Web resources

In selecting Web resources you can use the same criteria as for choosing other electronic products. There are however some important differences. It is important to bear in mind the dynamic nature of the Web and the fact that web sites are constantly changing.

- URLs change and sites can become 'lost'.
- Is the information on the site current, and is it updated frequently?
- Do you have to register to access the site? Does it involve a charge? If so, can a corporate or group registration be arranged?
- The content and focus of web sites change more rapidly that that of print or commercially produced electronic products
- The authority of the products must be examined. Where has the information come from? Are the authors or compilers recognised authorities on the topic? Is the author affiliated with a university, government agency or other reputable organisation related to the topic?

- The validity of the document must be examined. Has it been linked to or referenced by a recognised authority? Does the author cite references to confirm the accuracy of the information? Is the document a primary or secondary source? Does a university, government agency or other reputable organisation maintain the site?

All of the above criteria for selecting books, journals and other information resources for a library collection, regardless of their form, must be included in the selection policy.

Frequency of review of policy documentation

Many special librarians may have inherited a selection policy from a previous regime or they may have one that has not been looked at or changed since it was first written. The selection policy must be a living document and must change as the organisation changes and as the nature of information resources change.

All organisations are undergoing change in some way, however the scale of the changes and the rate in which they are happening varies from organisation to organisation. Some are more dynamic or static than others. These characteristics impact on the selection processes established by the library and also on the frequency that collection development and selection policies must be reviewed.

A periodic review of both the collection development policy and the selection policy will ensure that the guidelines to be followed reflect the current state of the organisation, not how it used to be. As the technical infrastructure changes, and policies concerning the distribution of information change, then so should the selection policies.

Having given all of the selection criteria, and emphasised the importance of having a clear, objective and well-written selection policy I would like to say that even with the best written selection policy and the most experienced selection staff, there will still be occasions where it is impossible to choose between products that are seemingly the same. In situations such as these, defer to the subject experts within the organisation, particularly those who will be using the resource. In many cases it is the users who will be able to identify a feature or characteristic that distinguishes one particular resource from another.

Managing print and electronic collections

When faced with a resource that is available in print or electronic formats, the information seeking behaviour of the clients, the technical infrastructure that is in place and physical size of the library are the three main determinants of which format of a resource must be chosen. The size of the library budget is a constraint that often forces trade-offs where there are significant price differences or where there are additional costs involved in providing access to a resource.

Much has been said already about alternative formats and how to choose between them. Some further issues are raised here that may impact on those decisions.

Firstly, the currency of the information required is critical. There are significant differences in the currency of information provided in online resources, CD-ROMs, serials and books. Even within online resources the currency of the information can vary significantly. The resource chosen must match the need – for example if daily current information is required, then it is inappropriate to choose CD-ROMs, serials or books as the resource.

Secondly, the information seeking behaviour of a client group determines the most appropriate format for their needs, but these behaviors are also limited by the technical infrastructure. Client preference for print or electronic resources is largely determined by what is available to them and how they are able to access it. Many client groups have specific needs, for example an organisation with large groups of employees working off-site may or may not have the technical infrastructure in place to allow them to access electronic resources. Field workers may need hard-copy resources which they can carry around with them.

Physical space is at a premium in many organisations and the cost of expanding a library may be higher than the additional value to the organisation gained by the expansion. Combined with this is the commonly held view that all information is available electronically and therefore physical space for books and journals is no longer necessary. Many special libraries are being downsized to the point where they are only able to offer access to electronic resources, others are being closed and their clients told to source their own information.

Print collections require physical space, maintenance (covering, processing, binding, repairs, shelving), administration (loans, returns), as well as management (weeding, development, archiving).

Electronic collections require the technical infrastructure to be in place to store, access, distribute, manage and administer the resources. Rather than buying the resource itself you are buying the right to access the resource for a given period of time. Electronic resources are usually more expensive than their print counterparts, and often come as part of a 'bundle', which means that you have to buy them as part of a package that may contain resources you do not want or need.

Both print and electronic collections require cataloguing; however, experience has shown that they are treated differently. Electronic resources are still considered transient and are often not given the same attention by cataloguers. There are many reasons for this with the main one being the continually changing content of many of the electronic products and the subsequent difficulties in maintaining catalogue records.

Outsourcing selection

There have been a number of highly publicised examples of selection outsourcing, but it seems that the general consensus amongst librarians is that the selection of information resources for a library collection and for delivery to information users within an organisation is the role of the librarian within that organisation. The main reason for this is that it is the librarian who is in the best position to match user requirements with the resources that are available, make decisions regarding alternative products and prioritise selection according to the strategic significance of the tasks that the information resources support.

Profiling is a 'partial' outsourcing of selection as it enables the vendor to supply resources that match predefined criteria. It remains the responsibility of the librarian however to make the final decision as to whether the items supplied meet the current needs of the organisation. Profiling does facilitate the selection process by allowing the librarian to examine the resources more closely and to see a range of resources that are available. Having said that though, it is important to remember that no one vendor will be able to supply a 'complete' range of publications due to their relationships with publishers. It is important to be aware of what each vendor is not able to provide, and to fill those gaps by other means.

Collaborative selection

It is becoming more common for groups of special libraries to work together to purchase electronic resources that they would not be able to justify the purchase of on an individual basis. Vendors are facilitating this process by allowing libraries to form unofficial 'consortia' to enable them to purchase a product and spread the cost across the group. By paying one subscription charge and a user license for each library in the group, the cost for each library is dramatically reduced without having to compromise on access or user rights. For example a product may have a subscription charge of $10,000 (for one user) and $2,500 for each additional concurrent user. A group of five libraries would pay $10,000 plus $2,500 x 4. This allows five libraries to access the product for $20,000 instead of them each having to pay the $10,000 subscription charge. Libraries are also working together by each selecting a different resource for purchase, and then offering reciprocal access to the other libraries in their group.

Recent and future developments

Recent developments in the selection of library materials are mostly related to the increased use of electronic means by which to communicate with vendors and publishers, and the ways in which promotional material such as alerts, blurbs, magazines and catalogues are distributed. Vendors are able to tailor their products to suit the needs of each librarian, and deliver them simultaneously to librarians and users.

The use of publishers' and vendors' web sites enable librarians to browse, to initiate tailored alert services to meet specific short or long term needs, to direct potential users to information about resources and to create 'wish lists' of resources. Many web sites store information relating to items selected previously and will alert you to the addition of similar new material. I expect that these developments will become more sophisticated in the near future to the point where the product information you receive matches your selection criteria more and more precisely.

The publishing and bookselling environment, like most others, is volatile at present with continual mergers and acquisitions. Consequently many vendors have changed the way they do their business including their products, the formats that they handle and the publishers with whom they deal. You need to keep up with developments in publishing and bookselling by reading trade literature (such as *Managing Information, The Bookseller, Information World Review* and *Against the Grain*).

Conclusion

The role of the selection librarian is becoming more difficult with the exponential increase in products, formats, delivery options and charging schedules. To make matters worse, many library budgets are declining. For these reasons it is necessary for the selector to have a clear understanding of the information needs of their organisation so that they can make the best decisions regarding which products to buy and in which format. This involves not only knowing which resources are needed, but understanding why they are needed and how they are used. This is important because print needs do not necessarily transfer neatly to an electronic environment, and because of the variations in content between the different formats of a resource.

Underlying the selection process is the selection policy that sets out the criteria by which resources are chosen and the rules by which decisions regarding alternative resources are made. A comprehensive selection policy will ensure a level of consistency and, provided it is reviewed on a regular basis, it will also provide the assurance that the money being spent on information resources is being used in the best way possible to meet the information needs of the organisation.

Acknowledgements

I would like to thank the following people who contributed to this chapter by giving of their knowledge and experience in special libraries and in the information industry: Patricia Burke (ALDIS, a division of Geac Computers), Kerryn Callaghan (Gas Industry Information Centre), Ralph Godau (RMIT University) and David Tan (Coles Myer Research).

References

Henczel, S. *The Information Audit: a practical guide.* London: Saur (2001).

Whitehead, D. Why have a collection development policy? *Acquisitions: newsletter of the Acquisitions Section of the Australian Library and Information Association,* **6**(2) 1989, 20-3.

Chapter 12

Acquiring information resources for the special library

Susan Henczel

Introduction

Over the past few years the nature of acquisitions in special libraries has changed significantly. This is due partly to the declining resources available to many special libraries, but is primarily because of the diversity of resources that have become available and the ways in which they can be acquired. A brief scan of the environment in which most organisations operate identifies huge economic, political, social and technological changes over the past five years or so. These have all impacted to some degree on the type of information resources that are required, how publishers make them available and the ways in which libraries can acquire them for use within the organisation. In many cases now special librarians are buying 'access' rather than 'ownership' and consequently the procedures they must follow are changing.

Buying more with less, and satisfying the full range of information needs within an organisation is the challenge faced by acquisitions librarians. This challenge is made more complex by the constantly changing publishing and vendor environment. This chapter will examine some of the issues to be addressed when dealing with the intricacies of acquisitions such as choosing a vendor and using different purchase methods for different items.

The role of the acquisitions librarian

The role of the acquisitions librarian is to locate and acquire the resources required for the library collection and for distribution to information users. These include hard-copy resources such as books and serials, electronic resources such as books, serials, CD-ROMs, databases, online services and multimedia resources such as videotapes and audiotapes. They can also include microfiche and microfilm although these are becoming less common in special library environments.

The costs associated with adding a resource to a library collection are significant and in fact when all indirect costs are taken into account the cost of acquiring and processing an item can be equal to or greater than the cost of the item itself. The acquisitions librarian has the responsibility therefore, to choose the most efficient means of supply in terms of his or her time, administrative procedures and item cost. This involves knowing the vendors and how they operate, understanding what they can supply and what they cannot and recognising their limitations in terms of service and efficiency. It also involves understanding the implications of local and international currency fluctuations, taxes and duties, and how different payment methods can impact on the total price of the items ordered.

The acquisitions librarian must:

- develop a knowledge of the book trade and vendor environment
- develop a working relationship with publishers and vendors
- monitor the expenditure of funds, maintain the required records and produce reports regarding the expenditure of funds.

The flexibility that an acquisitions librarian has within an organisation can vary dramatically. In some cases the acquisitions librarian must submit all orders through a central ordering system, with the advantage of saving library staff time. The main disadvantages of this system include:

- the library being unable to select its own suppliers
- the orders department being unable to change the status of orders if they become urgent
- when the supplier has questions regarding the item requested it must then be referred back to the library
- the need for the library to maintain duplicate order records
- general delays as the central ordering system may have other priorities.

Often a preferred list of suppliers is developed using a tender process. It is critical that the library participates in the development of the list to ensure that all potential vendors are listed so that the most appropriate can be chosen in each circumstance.

If the library is able to manage its own orders, a suitable order management system must be put into place to ensure that orders are handled efficiently and claims for outstanding items are processed regularly. Regardless of whether the system is manual or automated it must fit neatly with the other workflows and processes in the library and fulfil the requirements of the procedures set out in the Acquisitions Policy.

The Acquisitions Policy

The Acquisitions Policy, along with the Selection Policy, is a 'sub-policy' of the Collection Development Policy. The Acquisitions Policy is a statement that details how the resources identified by the selection process are to be acquired for the library or for access by the information users within the organisation. It sets out the procedures that are to be followed and who does the work. Designed to be an 'inhouse' document it must be a 'living' document and must be regularly reviewed and updated. When changes are made to how things are done in practice, they must be reflected in the Acquisitions Policy.

The policy can be as detailed as to list individual vendors that are to be used for specific types of material, or it can be a general statement that allows the acquisitions librarian to make informed choices according to the material type, urgency and cost.

Acquiring books

By their very nature, books are possibly the least complex resource to acquire for a library collection. Provided you have sufficient information about the book you can order it directly from the publisher, from a vendor or bookseller or from a local bookstore usually directly from their web site. How you choose a supplier will depend on the procedures outlined in your Acquisitions Policy. Using a smaller number of suppliers will reduce the number of invoices to be processed and also the time spent chasing outstanding orders.

Most special libraries have preferred vendors that they use for standard book orders, serials and electronic products. Some use the same vendor for all orders while others use different vendors for different types of resources or for material that is produced in particular countries. An example of this is a library that uses one vendor for US material, one for UK and European material and one for Australian and Asia-Pacific material. If you are able to choose your vendor, be careful not to spend too much time searching for the 'best deal' on any particular item. This is not cost effective as after factoring in your time, and the cost of telephone calls, faxes and web access, you may not have saved any money.

Many special libraries use a local bookstore for urgent items that are likely to be on the shelves such as popular management books, computer books and general reference material. Bookstores will often offer discounts to corporate customers but as this is a discount off the retail price it is still likely to be higher than the vendor's discounted price.

The three main types of orders for books are firm orders, blanket orders and approval plans:

- *Firm orders* are placed for books where a specific book is required. Books supplied on firm orders can usually not be returned unless faulty.

- *Blanket orders* are placed when a library requires all books by a particular author, association or organisation on a particular subject.

- *Approval plans* can be established with a vendor for the supply of books that match a predefined profile. To define the profile the vendor works with the librarian to define the library's requirements in specific subject areas and levels, material types and budgetary limits. The vendor then selects and regularly supplies resources that match the defined parameters. The library evaluates the resources supplied and returns any unwanted items. The goal for both librarian and vendor is to continually review and amend the profile until returns are minimised.

Specialist vendors are often used for out of print and secondhand books.

Out of print books

The Internet is transforming the out of print market with searchable lists from hundreds of dealers that included price and availability. Books can be ordered online and the order tracked until the book is received. Many major booksellers such as Amazon.com also offer an out of print service and will search for specific titles for you.

Secondhand books

Many secondhand and antiquarian bookdealers have searchable catalogues on their web sites that include details of price and condition. Many will also search for a particular item for you and notify you when they find it.

E-books

Access to electronic books (e-books) and web-based reference resources is usually arranged directly with the publisher.

Collections of electronic books are being promoted by vendors and publishers as electronic library collections. E-books can be purchased individually or collectively with an initial purchase charge plus ongoing access charges. Some of the important issues related to e-books are:

- *Ongoing access* – how long will access to the books last? Where will they be stored in the future? How can ongoing access be guaranteed?

- *Access restrictions* – what restrictions have been placed on access, downloading, copying etc. Can concurrent users access a particular book? Some allow only one user at a time, with that user having to 'borrow' the book for a specified period. During that time, no one else can access it, and the 'loan' cannot be cancelled.
- *Additional titles* – if a collection is purchased and additional titles become available can they be added later?

Web-based reference resources

Dictionaries, encyclopedias, directories and other reference resources that were previously only available in print format are now available on the Web. They are often free for a defined period then incur a charge for ongoing access. Often the charges are similar to the cost of the print resource, but with the advantages of being more up to date and easier to search. Disadvantages include the uncertainty of continuity, restrictions on copying and access, and the cost of access such as Internet and telecommunication charges.

Acquiring serials

Very few special libraries order their serials directly from publishers as the advantages of using serial vendors (subscription agents) far outweigh the disadvantages. Some use one vendor, while others use different vendors for serials from different geographical areas.

Using vendors can reduce the problems caused by the complexity of serials, as they take over the responsibility of dealing with the publishers. They provide advice on changes of title, variations in content or frequency, supplements, associated publications and handle subscription renewals. When ordering a new title it is important to provide sufficient information for the title to be identified by the vendor. The minimum requirement is title, ISSN and publisher. Some serials have different editions for different audiences. These may be geographically based (UK, US or international editions). Sometimes different editions will have the same ISSN so it is important to inform the vendor as to the edition you require. The vendor must also be told which issue you wish to begin your subscription with, how many copies of each issue you need, and where they are to be mailed (if not the library).

The two main types of serial orders are subscriptions and standing orders.

Subscriptions

Regular or irregular serials for a specific period of time or a specific number of issues. These must be renewed in advance at the end of the specified period of time or number of issues.

Standing orders

These cover annuals, yearbooks, conference proceedings, supplements, and are also used to acquire continuations, which are sets that are published over a period of time with a planned conclusion in mind – monographic series or multi-volume sets. Once established a standing order continues until it is cancelled.

Access to electronic journals, or e-journals, is usually arranged directly with the publisher, although it is becoming more common for vendors to handle subscriptions to e-journals along with hard-copy subscriptions.

E-journals

Many journal titles are now being published in both print and electronic format, with electronic versions being made available via the publisher's or vendor's web site. As with e-books there are concerns about the transient nature of some of them, and other important issues such as:

- *Archiving* – will back issues be available in the future and if so will you be able to access them without additional charges?
- *Content* – is the content the same as the print version?
- *Access restrictions* – who can access it, and how? What restrictions are placed on downloading and copying? Are concurrent users allowed, and if so, how many?

Many serial vendors offer consolidation services that include serials ordering and receipt, cataloguing, accessioning and end processing. Issues are received by the library in a 'shelf-ready' state – stamped, with circulation slips attached, security tags in place, labelled and covered. The vendor claims all missed and outstanding issues and ensures that issues are delivered in batches to the library at agreed intervals (weekly, fortnightly or monthly). Many vendors allow the librarian to access their online system to review holdings and update circulation slips. Because the vendor is able to order multiple subscriptions for their clients, the discount they receive from publishers enables them to offset some of their processing costs. Consequently the direct cost to the library of using a consolidation service is not as great as you might think. There are disadvantages, however, and these include the use of standardised cataloguing and processing methods – you may not get a label printed in exactly the way you'd like, and the format of the circulation slips may be different. You need to consider whether this is an acceptable trade-off for reducing staff time and costs.

Acquiring electronic products

Acquiring electronic products for use in a special library or to allow access to organisational information users is an area that requires planning, coordination and good management to ensure that information users are able to access the resources they need. The most important issue to be addressed when planning to introduce electronic information resources is whether the existing technical infrastructure is suitable. Most require only web access, but some corporate networks have security systems and firewalls that prevent access to particular sites or types of sites, and the downloading of certain files. Always request a trial of the actual product, not a sample product, so that any problems can be identified and resolved as appropriate.

I've mentioned electronic books and serials briefly in the sections above. These can often be acquired from the same vendor to facilitate their management and to minimise the time spent in solving problems and processing invoices. This enables common passwords to be used so that you do not end up with different passwords for each product, and often they can be set up so that they are accessed directly from the vendor's web site.

A major problem faced by special librarians is the fact that many electronic products (books, serials and databases) are sold in 'bundles' that contain an assortment of resources. They often cannot be separated which makes it difficult for the library which has very narrow information needs and limited money as they are unable to acquire the resource they need without taking (and paying for) the accompanying resources that they do not need.

Licensing and copyright are both major issues that often conflict when purchasing electronic products and it is the responsibility of the acquisitions librarian to understand how the terms of the licence impacts on how the product can be used, and how they correspond with the current local copyright legislation.

Using vendors or buying direct from the publisher

Once resources have been selected for a library collection, you need to decide the best place to purchase them. Whether you buy directly from the publisher or from a vendor can be a difficult decision and can mean significant variations in cost and efficiency.

Advantages of ordering directly from the publisher include:

- *Lower price* – usually the publisher price is lower than the vendor price, unless the vendor offers a significant discount.

- *Faster service* – if the publisher has the item in stock it is more likely to arrive more quickly that it would if ordered through the vendor. This is particularly so if the publisher has a retail outlet or online ordering from their web site. In some cases the publisher may offer immediate download of a document from their web site on acceptance of credit card details.
- *Exclusivity* – some publishers will not deal with vendors.
- *Efficient problem solving* – dealing directly with the publisher facilitates problem solving rather than dealing through a third party.
- *Mailing list* – once you have ordered an item from a publisher you will more than likely be added to their mailing list to receive information about their other publications. (This may or may not be an advantage!)

Disadvantages include:

- more invoices to process, as each publisher will supply an invoice with the item ordered
- some smaller publishers not being geared up to sell books direct to users, preferring to deal with vendors, agents or retailers.

If you make the decision to purchase an item from the publisher and the publisher is located overseas, find out who has the local distribution rights and make some enquiries regarding the price of the publication. There will often be significant variations in the price charged in the country of publication and the local price because of fluctuations in the exchange rates.

Using a vendor to supply your information resources also has advantages and disadvantages, but the more difficult task is choosing the right vendor. There is a vast number of vendors who are selling the same products and the prices can vary dramatically from one vendor to another as can service levels both prior to and after the sale. To be competitive vendors often offer additional resources or services with a purchase such as 'buy one get one free' deals, or 'buy the electronic version and get the print version free' or at a 'reduced cost'. These deals are fine if you can actually make use of the extras, but if not, then it is a matter of choosing the vendor who can provide the best service for a reasonable price.

Advantages of using a vendor include:

- negotiation of contracts with the publisher on behalf of the library
- discounts and ancillary services
- tailoring of services to suit libraries – ordering, invoicing, delivery, reporting, end processing, cataloguing.

To maximise the advantages it is important that there is a high level of co-operation between the vendor and the library:

- The vendor must take the time to understand how the library's ordering systems work and to understand the needs of the library (what are the priorities – cost, time, service).

- The library must understand how to get the best out of the vendor – what information does the vendor need to get the order right?

- Prompt payment and timely feedback is important to ensure a healthy vendor – library relationship.

Choosing a vendor

Vendors exist in a dynamic business environment. We regularly hear about mergers and takeovers with many of them changing the nature of the vendors. Most are becoming larger with many now having multinational coverage. Many are changing their focus – some from serials to books or books to serials, others from print to electronic, while others are diversifying to cover all materials in all formats. Some are broadening their subject scope while some are narrowing it. Keeping up with the changes is difficult and to a large degree we rely on the sales representatives themselves to keep us informed about how their services are changing.

As a consequence of the dynamic environment, there is currently a high level of competition between vendors. This benefits librarians in that reasonable discounts are being offered, with frequent 'special deals', added extras and improved levels of service.

Choosing the wrong vendor can result in a high level of user dissatisfaction, and higher overall costs. High error rates (wrong books, faulty books, supply delays) lead to higher costs overall (time spent chasing, postage to return items, staff time, more records to keep, letters to write) and higher user dissatisfaction (delays in receiving items).

Unfortunately (or fortunately?) there is often very little to differentiate one vendor from another in general terms. It is up the special librarian to establish which characteristics are important to them and to choose their vendor or vendors accordingly. As a starting point ask other libraries with similar requirements which vendors they use, why they use them and what they consider to be the good and bad characteristics of the vendor. Library meetings, conferences and other functions are the best place to hear about which vendors are doing a good job and which are not, but keep in mind that people are more likely to complain about bad service than praise good service. The vendor will provide details of current customers if you are unable to find someone. Bear in mind that the individual sales representative may have developed a particular rapport with his or her customers and if sales personnel change, the quality of the service may vary too. You need to find out if service quality has been consistently good over a period of time, as well as finding out about current experiences. Use any comments you receive from other customers as a trigger for further investigation rather than as the sole reason for selecting a particular vendor.

The following checklist contains the main characteristics of a vendor to help you consider all of the important issues and to make an informed decision.

Range of subjects offered, types of material and range of publishers represented

Most say that they can supply all publications from all publishers. This is often not the case. Ask for a list of publishers that the vendor represents. Which major or significant publishers does the vendor not deal with?

Overseas publications

Do they handle items from overseas publishers? If so, in which countries? Are there any exclusions, and if so are the exclusions likely to be significant to your information needs? Do they handle foreign language material? If so, which languages?

Subscriptions and books?

Some vendors handle books and serials while some only handle one or the other. If a vendor handles both books and serials are they handled by the same people or do they have separate departments?

Electronic and print-based formats

Do they handle both print and electronic items?

Government and grey literature

Do they handle government publications? From which countries? Do they handle orders for grey literature? Can they source self-published resources?

Materials published by bodies other than commercial publishers?

Do they handle materials published by non-commercial publishers such as organisations, associations, universities, individuals etc.?

Approval service

Do they offer an approval service? If so, how do they develop the profiles? How often can they deliver books? Do they expect a minimum number of books to be purchased or books to a particular value?

Standing orders

Do they handle standing orders?

Returns policy

Do they have a reasonable returns policy? Are faulty books, for example books with missing or blank pages or improperly collated pages, able to be returned? What is their policy regarding duplicate serial issues received and duplicated book orders (when either the library or the vendor is at fault)?

Account options

Do they offer deposit account options, credit card payments, periodical invoicing (quarterly etc.)? What currencies can they invoice in, and can this be varied if exchange rates fluctuate significantly?

Invoicing

Do they offer tailored or electronic invoicing? What facilities do they have in place to handle subscription price rises when the subscription has already been paid in advance?

Ancillary services

What additional services do they offer? Do they have a bookstore or online retail outlet? Do they offer bibliographic searching? Do they offer ancillary services such as catalogue records, end-processing? If so, what level of cataloguing and what processing options are offered?

Postage and handling charges

Do they charge per item or per delivery? Do they charge for both handling and postage? Do they waive postage charges on bulk orders or once a certain volume of material has been ordered?

Discounts

What level of discount can they offer? From what base price is the discount offered (publishers list price, wholesale price, retail price, etc.)? Is the level of discount reliant on a particular level of purchases? Does the level of discount vary according to the source of the publication?

Delivery time and urgent order options

Does the vendor send individual requests to the publishers, or do they wait until they have a batch of orders for the same item before sending to the publisher? (If they wait it can result in significant time delays.) What options do they offer for urgent orders?

Type of orders accepted

Can orders be placed by phone, fax, or email? Is written confirmation of the order required? Can the vendor accept orders electronically directly from the library's acquisitions system?

Special reports and price analysis
Does the vendor offer regular and comprehensive status reports, reports of outstanding items, cancelled orders, recent shipments etc? Is an order cancelled when an item is out of stock? After what period of time do they cancel unfulfilled orders? Can they supply reports such as order turnaround time, cost changes over time, currency and exchange rate variations, total expenditure for a specified period?

Can they handle memberships?
If a membership is required to obtain a publication, can the vendor initiate a membership on behalf of the library?

Monitoring vendor performance

Having chosen a vendor it is important that you monitor their performance and match it against predefined and realistic benchmarks. Many are able to provide you with reports that detail item turnaround time (from order to delivery) and cost variations over time. If it is not possible to get this type of data from your ordering system, then it is important to choose a vendor who can supply them. This enables you to support your decisions with proof of efficiencies such as prompt supply, consistency of charges and discounts.

If you are dissatisfied with a vendor's performance, or have concerns about the processes or procedures they use, raise it with them as soon as possible. Provide immediate feedback on both the good and bad aspects of their service as this lets them know what works and what does not and if a vendor is unable or unwilling to conform to your needs, do not be afraid to change to another vendor.

Pre-order checking

Before submitting an order to a publisher or vendor it is important to ensure that you have sufficient bibliographic information to enable the supplier to identify the item you want. The minimum requirement for a book is usually title, author, publisher, edition, date and ISBN. The minimum requirement for a serial is title, publisher and ISSN.

Other details that should be included on the order are:

- *Format*
  Many resources are available in a variety of formats such as hard copy, CD-ROM and electronic. The order must specify which format you want.

- *Version*
  For technical books be aware that there may be different versions such as metric or imperial.
- *Edition*
  Do you want a specific edition, or the latest edition? A new edition may come out after the order has been placed which means that if you order the fourth edition for example, you may still get the fourth edition even though the fifth edition has been released.
- *Edition (geographical)*
  There may be editions for different geographical areas – UK, US, Asia-Pacific, international, student. Geographical editions can also apply to serials.
- *Accompanying items*
  Ensure that accompanying items such as CD-ROMs and disks are included on the order if there is any concern that they may not be supplied with the book.
- *Type of cover*
  Unless the vendor is already aware of your requirements, your choice of cover (softcover, hardcover) should be stated on the order.
- *Duplicates*
  If you have an outstanding order for an item, and you are placing an additional order, you should indicate to the vendor that the order is an 'intentional duplicate'. If they are not told, they may contact you and ask you to check it, or they may cancel the order if it is in your agreement with them that they do not provide duplicates.

Tools for pre-order checking include online bibliographic tools such as *Global Books in Print* and *Ulrich's International Periodicals Directory*. Library catalogues (Library of Congress (US), British Library (UK), Kinetica (Australia)) are useful as are vendor's and bookseller's web sites such as YBP's, GOBI, Amazon.com, and Blackwell's Online Bookshop.

Be aware that publishers' and vendors' blurbs and catalogues can contain incorrect data, particularly for pre-publication items. In some cases the title, publication date and even the publisher can vary.

Ordering

When ordering resources for a special library collection there are a variety of types of orders that can be used. These include subscriptions, standing orders, blanket orders, approval plans and firm orders. Blanket orders and approval plans require detailed negotiation with a vendor to ensure that the most relevant items are supplied. Subscriptions, standing orders and firm orders can be initiated using either manual or electronic means.

Electronic ordering

Large volumes of orders placed by academic and large reference libraries are usually done by tape upload or file transfer protocol (FTP). Special libraries also use file transfer, but web-based ordering is more common. The emergence of web-based booksellers such as Amazon.com and the addition of online ordering forms linked to the web catalogues of most vendors and publishers allow librarians to place their orders electronically. To be able to order this way means having to use a credit card, or establishing an account with the vendor prior to ordering.

Unfortunately very few of the vendors have their web sites linked to their warehouses or stock control systems so it is not possible to identify whether or not the item is in stock without making a telephone call or sending a message by fax or email. Some include an indication of how quickly the item can be supplied, but they are often incorrect. The advantages of online ordering are that with most vendors you receive a confirmation of your order, usually by email within seconds of placing the order. Be aware however, that the confirmation is of you having sent the order, not of the order being accepted by the fulfilment department.

The increase in online ordering between library and vendor has moved libraries into the emerging e-commerce arena far ahead of many other industries and although it is still evolving significant advantages and disadvantages are becoming evident. These include:

- a reduced need for intermediaries (sales representatives)
- more flexibility in choice of suppliers (libraries are less likely to remain loyal to one specific supplier)
- the improved efficiency with which acquisitions staff are able to process and track orders; claiming for outstanding items is also made easier
- more accurate budgeting as price and availability can be confirmed prior to placing an order
- suppliers can automatically create selection lists and periodic email alerts based on the patterns of completed orders.

Most of the larger vendors allow files of orders to be submitted using file transfer protocol. The orders are transferred directly from the library system to the vendor's order system. They are then distributed to the appropriate departments or sections to be processed.

This process can also enable invoices and status reports to be directly transferred to the library.

The receipt of items from the vendor, bookstore or publisher involves:

- determining that the correct item has been supplied
- determining that the item is not faulty
- ensuring that the item is noted as received on the order record
- ensuring that invoices are processed and passed for payment.

Using credit cards

Many organisations are concerned about the security of their credit card details and prohibit the use of credit cards over the Internet despite the obvious advantages including:

- increased efficiency
- fewer cheques
- decreased use of petty cash
- fewer exchange rate issues
- less paperwork at point of order
- decrease in use of deposit accounts.

There are however a number of disadvantages:

- There is more work in reconciling accounts, particularly when goods are purchased overseas and the statement arrives before the order.
- An additional step is added to the process of receiving items.
- Policy issues need to be addressed and documented – who can use the card, when and where and for how much.
- You do not always receive a receipt from the vendor to enable you to reconcile the statement.

Budgets and prices

Because acquisitions budgets generally are not keeping up with the proliferation of products and formats it is essential that the acquisitions librarian make informed judgements about which vendors to use to achieve the most cost-effective and efficient service. The process of managing a budget for acquisitions is a continuous process of forward planning, prioritising and monitoring. Spending more than you have in your budget allocation implies poor management while having money remaining at the end of the financial year is an invitation to have your funds reduced next year.

There are three elements to managing an acquisitions budget:

- *Forward planning* will ensure that the implications of exchange rate fluctuations and price increases are minimised. Vendors can assist with this by passing on any information they have regarding anticipated price increases and details of possible changes in currency values. They may also be able to suggest ways in which currency exchange costs and other costs related to overseas purchases can be reduced.

- *Prioritising* the orders will ensure that those with the highest level of strategic significance are purchased first.

- *Monitoring* will ensure that funds are being expended at an acceptable level. Information on expenditure must include not only the value of orders that have been supplied but also the value of committed orders. Committed value will be an estimate only and should include all postage and handling costs. This is especially important when purchasing overseas publications because of the significant time delay between the time the order is placed and the time the item arrives. It is important to know the average time taken by suppliers so that you know which orders will be received and invoiced prior to the close of significant budget periods.

Currency

Dealing with currencies is becoming more of an issue as more and more acquisitions librarians are purchasing resources directly from overseas sources rather than through vendors. It is still an important issue when purchasing through vendors, but it is an issue that is largely invisible as it is handled by the vendor. When dealing directly with overseas vendors and publishers the main issues are:

- fluctuating exchange rates causing dramatic and often sudden price increases

- implications of internal tax systems such as VAT, customs duties, GST

- method of payment that established when the currency conversion takes place.

Duplicate or disposal lists

Duplicate (or disposal) lists used to be, and are again, a very effective means of disposing of unwanted items. I say 'used to be' because the preparation of duplicate lists was one of the first activities to be sidelined when libraries began to lose their staff and when their budgets were reduced. Preparing the list was time consuming in terms of staff time and distributing it was costly in terms of postage and telecommunication costs. With the advent of the Internet, and our increasing sense of social and environmental consciousness, duplicate lists are re-emerging as a cost-effective means of disposing of duplicates and other unwanted items.

Duplicate lists are appearing on listservs and email distribution lists to enable librarians to supplement journal collections, acquire additional copies of heavily used items or replacement copies of lost or damaged items. Items are generally offered free of charge, with the recipient library paying all freight charges.

Duplicate lists are an effective way to fill gaps in a collection and acquire items that otherwise would not be able to be purchased. Older books that are out of print, and peripheral and support material that is important but not critical can be added to the collection at little or no cost.

Gifts and exchanges

A valuable means of acquiring information resources is by exchange with other organisations. These are reciprocal agreements whereby each organisation sends the other a copy of selected publications. These are often publications that can not be acquired by any other means and usually are supplied free of charge.

Interlibrary loan and document delivery

Borrowing items from other libraries is a way in which librarians in special libraries are able to better satisfy the information needs of their users by providing resources that are not part of the core, supporting or peripheral collections of the library. These can include:

- resources required to fill short-term needs
- resources where the cost of purchasing the item cannot be justified because of low usage or low level of strategic significance.

Many acquisitions librarians will borrow an item from another library before making a decision to purchase it. Borrowing it provides an opportunity for the user to evaluate the resource prior to purchase if it is expensive or if its usefulness in uncertain.

Using commercial and web-based document delivery services is also a way to extend the information that can be provided by the library. Articles and complete documents can be supplied at a cost directly to the library or to the user's desktop. The 'ownership versus access' issue is forcing librarians to consider the total cost of acquiring, managing and storing serials. Many special libraries are cancelling their subscriptions to serials that have low usage, and acquiring any necessary articles from document delivery services. The cost of the articles is significantly less than the cost of purchasing, managing, circulating and storing a complete serial title.

Outsourcing acquisitions

The outsourcing of acquisitions is a way in which special libraries can allow their staff to focus on the core task of information provision. For many years we have outsourced much of the work involved in serials acquisitions by employing vendors to deal with the publishers on our behalf. More recently we have begun to outsource the management of subscriptions by extending the services that we ask the vendor to handle to incorporate accessioning, claiming, cataloguing and end processing. This consolidation service eliminates the need for libraries to maintain comprehensive order and acquisition records and provides the library with shelf-ready serial issues.

Special libraries are also beginning to recognise the many potential benefits of outsourcing their book acquisitions, not only to vendors but also to agencies that are able to provide acquisitions services as well as quality ancillary services. The benefits include:

* cheaper prices for books by drawing on the bulk purchasing power of vendors and agencies
* books received in shelf-ready state thus eliminating the need for cataloguing and end processing
* less time spent managing, controlling and maintaining acquisitions, cataloguing and processing systems – more time for library staff to focus on core tasks.

Collaborative acquisitions

Due to the exponential increase in the number of resources that are available, the rising costs of the resources and the declining purchasing power of individual libraries it is becoming common for libraries to work together and combine their purchasing power. This enables them to offer a wider range of resources to their information users and to offer resources that they would otherwise not be able to afford.

By their very nature, electronic resources lend themselves to collaborative purchasing, provided the publisher or vendor is willing to allow it. By forming a group or consortium, one library can subscribe to the product and acquire user licences for the other libraries. By working together in this way the libraries are able to spread to cost of accessing resources without restricting the way in which their clients are able to use the resources.

By pooling their purchasing power, libraries are able to negotiate with vendors for higher discounts and improved levels of service. Although more common in the academic sector this approach has been used successfully by a number of industry groups of special libraries with them achieving not only significant discounts on the prices of the books, but also discounts on ancillary services such as cataloguing and processing.

Acquiring resources from within the organisation

It is important that a special library collection within an organisation contains all of the significant reports and documents produced by the departments and sections within the organisation itself. It usually requires an official policy to be written to make this happen, and a great deal of effort on the part of the librarian to make sure that it does happen. A statement in the Information Policy is an appropriate starting point, with procedures in the Acquisitions Policy for collecting the material.

Future developments

There have been many significant developments over the past few years that have impacted on acquisitions practices and processes in special libraries. The Internet has changed the nature of acquisitions by enabling the provision of electronic resources directly to the users' desktops, facilitating communication between librarians and vendors and making the services offered by vendors more visible.

One can only imagine the changes that may occur in the next few years. Some suggestions might include sophisticated searching mechanisms to enable librarians to search across the catalogues of many vendors to find the item you need against selected criteria such as price and availability. These systems are already emerging in other industries such as the travel and real estate industries.

Collective purchasing may be facilitated by the development of global consortia established along the lines of Global Net Xchange which is used by the retail industry. This enables orders from all over the world to be pooled and submitted as bulk orders to suppliers, resulting in reduced prices and efficient delivery.

Whatever the developments you can be assured that they will be Internet-based and that they will enable us to work within a global marketplace.

Further reading

Against the Grain. Charleston, SC: Against the Grain, LLC, bi-monthly, ISSN 1043-2094. Available at *http://www.against-the-grain.com*.

Schmidt, Karen A. (ed.) *Understanding the Business of Library Acquisitions.* Chicago: American Library Association (1999, 2nd ed.).

Author's note

I would like to thank the following people who contributed to this chapter by giving of their knowledge and experience in special libraries and in the information industry: Kerryn Callaghan (Gas Industry Information Centre), Ralph Godau (RMIT University) and David Tan (Coles Myer Research).

Chapter 13

Current awareness services in an electronic age – the whole picture

Ina Fourie

Introduction

Timely access to appropriate, quality information is often associated with power, progress and prosperity. The need for people to keep up with the latest developments in their areas of interest has therefore long been recognised. Similarly the threat of information overload has been recognised. For a number of years libraries have been providing their users with current awareness services (CAS) to help them keep track of developments. Unlike retrospective search services, which search backwards for information published within a specific period, CAS cover information as it is published and then bring it to users' attention.

At first CAS were based on manual methods such as accession lists and indexing or abstracting bulletins. In 1958 H.P. Luhn was the first to propose the use of computers for CAS (Housman, 1973). Various CAS based on the use of computers, for example the selective dissemination of information (SDI) and the use of CAS in specific business sectors (e.g. accounting firms, charity organisations, engineering firms, insurance groups, pharmaceutical companies, management consultants, merchant banks, professional associations and public libraries) was reported on during the 1960s to 1980s (e.g. by Whitehall, 1985; Price and Burley, 1986; Jax and Van Houlson, 1988; Stenstrom and Tegler, 1989; Hamilton, 1995). In 1977 Martha Williams not only stressed the importance of CAS as part of the functions of a library, but she also argued that librarians should guide their users in the creation and use of personal databases — thus stressing the importance of personal information organisation and the need to prevent information overload.

The core methods for providing CAS and the procedures to follow are well documented (e.g. by Kemp, 1979; Whitehall, 1982; Rowley, 1985, 1994; Behrens, 1989 and Hamilton, 1995). Several editions of the *Handbook of Special Librarianship and Information Work* have also included contributions on CAS or the dissemination of information, namely Richards (1992), Trench (1997), and Whitehall (1982). Several review articles have appeared in the *Annual review of Information Science and Technology* (e.g. by Housman, 1973; Landau, 1969; and Wente and Young, 1969). In spite of the wide acceptance of the role and importance of CAS, they were, however, mostly offered only by special libraries and information services (henceforth referred to only as special libraries) and to a limited extent by academic libraries. One of the reasons for this was the high cost of CAS and especially of the SDI offered by commercial online services such as Dialog and DataStar. The use of SDI services also requires specialised skills in the selection of databases, the use of databases and the formulation of search strategies. More traditional methods such as indexing and abstracting bulletins, accession lists, newspaper clippings and displays were more widely used. However, not even all special libraries offer CAS to their users. In two LISU surveys (Creaser and Spiller, 1997) conducted in 1994 and 1996, it turned out that 68 per cent and 69 per cent of special libraries in the United Kingdom offered CAS. It is not clear why the rest of the libraries did not offer such services (lack of finances and staff time might be possible reasons). What I, however, would like to argue is that all information specialists should reconsider their use of CAS in the light of the renewed interest in such services and also the variety of new products and possibilities on offer.

Over the last 10 years various electronic methods for CAS have been reported on, for example the use of electronic tables of contents, SDI services using CD-ROM databases and the emailing of search results (Cox and Hanson, 1992; Mountfield, 1995; Hentz, 1996; Deardorff and Garrison, 1997). New terms have also been introduced, such as alerting services or alerts, to describe the former SDI services. Other new terms which have been coined include CAS-IAS (current alerting service – individual alerting service (Brunskill, 1997)) and current alerting service – individual article supply (Davies et al., 1998). The latter stresses the importance of linking CAS to document supply services, which has also added a new dimension to the provision of such services. The new terms do not, however, really indicate a serious change in the purpose of CAS. The only difference is that they are all electronically based. Since SDI services that have been used for many years are also electronically based, I have decided to retain the term current awareness services (CAS) in this discussion.

Although these electronic methods made CAS easier to access and to offer to users, many of them were (are) still very expensive and therefore out of reach for some libraries. The Internet on the other hand has not only reinforced the need to have access to information and to keep track of new developments, but has also introduced a number of interesting, affordable, easily accessible and user-friendly CAS to keep track of such developments. An additional benefit of the Internet CAS is that some of them are available free of charge, and that they are accessible to anybody with Internet access. A number of the former electronic services (e.g. the

SDI services of Dialog) are now also offered via the Internet. It has therefore become necessary for special librarians to reconsider the mix of CAS they can offer within their special environments. The challenge lies in combining the old and the new, and balancing the strengths and shortcomings of each. It should also be asked whether CAS are still the same concept as accepted 10 years ago. Are the reasons for offering CAS and the principles on which such services are based still the same? How should librarians prepare to offer CAS in the 21st century? How should they reach out to their users, and how can they employ the Internet in offering CAS?

The approach in this chapter will be to take an overall look at CAS: what is on offer and how does it affect librarians and library users. How can the traditional methods be combined with the newer methods and services offered via the Internet? To do this it is necessary to take a holistic view of the provision of CAS by libraries. Each library should consider CAS within its own individual environment and context. A framework of such a context is depicted in Figure 1. This framework will also serve as a guide for the rest of the discussion.

Figure 1: A typical environment for the provision of CAS

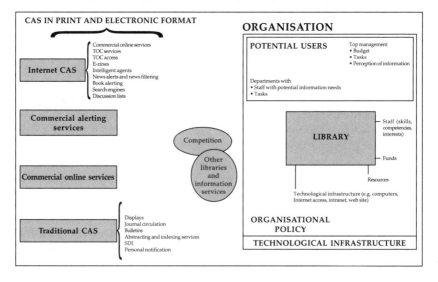

Reconsidering the concept of current awareness services

The point of departure for CAS is always the users' information needs, and especially their need to keep track of the latest developments. The information needs of users can be addressed on different levels. Firstly there are their needs as individuals. They can also have information needs as part of a group of people with similar interests (e.g. top management, a group of people working on a research project or people from a specific department or section of the organisation). Lastly there are the information needs of the organisation as a whole. These include aspects everybody working for the organisation should be interested in. The concept of CAS was formulated around such user groups and their needs. It also assumes that all users realise the need for CAS and that they want to keep track of new developments. This might not necessarily be the case since there are many people who fear information overload. Several examples of this can, for example, be found in *Secrets of the super Net searchers: the reflections, revelations, and hard-won wisdom of 35 of the world's top Internet researchers* (Basch, 1996).

In the past a current awareness service was described as

> A system, and often a publication, for notifying current documents to users of libraries and information services, e.g. selective dissemination of information, bulletin, indexing service, current literature. (*Harrod's Librarians' Glossary*, 1995).

It has also been defined as 'a service which provides the recipient with information on the latest developments within the subject areas in which he or she has a specific interest or need to know' (Hamilton, 1995). Based on such definitions CAS were planned and offered to library users.

With all the changes mentioned in the introduction, however, it has become necessary to ask whether CAS still mean the same thing. Within the context of CAS developments on the Internet, Fourie (1999), for example, defined CAS as

> 'a selection of one or more systems that provide notification of the existence of new entities added to the system's database or of which the system took note (e.g. documents, web sites, events such as conferences, discussion groups, editions of newsletters). CAS automatically notify users or allow users to check periodically for updates. The entities can be specified according to users' subject interests or according to the type of entity (e.g. books or newsletters).

The reason for looking at these definitions is not to embark on a theoretical debate about the meaning of CAS, but to show how changes in the meaning of CAS will require librarians to reconsider the aspects underlying the planning of CAS. From the afore-mentioned definitions it can, for example, be seen that librarians should pay special attention to the following:

- *The number of systems and publications available for use in CAS.* These include expensive commercial services, services available at more reasonable subscription fees and services available free of charge. This leaves librarians with more options to make a meaningful selection which will meet the users' needs and their budget constraints.

- *The variety of formats in which CAS can be offered.* These include printed and electronic formats (e.g. online, CD-ROM, the Internet and email). CAS can also use informal, oral methods and also audio and video. The variety of formats makes it possible for librarians to select CAS according to convenience, ease of use and cost considerations. In the past they often had to make do with whatever was available.

- *The different methods of notification, such as automatic and periodic updating.* For automatic notification, the user's interest profile is automatically run against the system or publication and he or she is automatically notified of any new documents of interest. This can be done by email, fax or the mailing of printed copies of documents or descriptions of documents. For periodic updating, the user's interest profile must be run against the system at regular intervals. Alternatively, the user must check the system or publication at regular intervals for new documents of importance (e.g. the latest table of contents). (Interest profiles will be explained in a later section.)

- *The variety of subjects and interest fields covered.* Nowadays CAS can be used to keep track of work-related interests and study and entertainment interests (e.g. sports, movies, music and even the latest offers by hotel groups!). (If it does not take up much extra time it is worthwhile bringing non-work-related CAS to users' attention.) There are also so many subjects and interests covered that it has become less important for libraries to develop their own, tailor-made, inhouse current awareness products.

- *The timeliness of CAS has gained a new meaning* (Rowley, 1998). In the early days of CAS it was quite acceptable to provide updates on a monthly or weekly basis. Newspaper clippings were about the only services provided daily. Many of the new CAS can now be delivered hourly or even more frequently.

- *The need to use a combination of CAS.* Although there is a greater selection of services available, no one service will cover all interests, and since a large number of services are available for free or at reasonable subscription fees, it is worth considering a combination of CAS. Another important aspect to bear in mind is the coverage of both formal and informal methods of keeping abreast of developments. This aspect also stresses the need to inform the user of the limitations of individual CAS, and the need to supplement any CAS with informal methods of keeping contact with people and professional societies.
- *The increased variety of documents and other entities that are covered by CAS.* These include journal articles, reports, theses, conference proceedings, books, videos, CDs, updates to web sites, news, weather reports, stock market prices, new web sites, conferences and meetings, and research and developments concerning individuals or organisations.

In the following sections it will be shown in more detail how these aspects can impact on CAS.

Reasons for providing a current awareness service – a point of departure for marketing

When carefully considering CAS developments, it becomes clear that not only the meaning of CAS has changed, but also the reasons for offering CAS. With users' needs as the point of departure, the traditional reasons for offering CAS have been well documented by authors such as Kemp (1979), Whitehall (1982) and Hamilton (1995). With the new range of electronic methods and CAS available via the Internet, it has, however, become necessary to reconsider these reasons. This is important for selecting appropriate services and for planning CAS. It is also important for marketing CAS to management and the potential users. CAS can even be turned into an important marketing tool! This in turn may improve the image of librarians. When marketing CAS their shortcomings should, however, also be noted and explained to users.

Benefits offered by CAS

When reconsidering the traditional reasons for offering CAS, the following list of potential benefits of CAS in an electronic environment can be identified. CAS can help users to:

- keep track of new developments in a particular field(s) of interest
- keep track of new web sites, discussion groups (listservs, Usenet groups), publications (e.g. books) etc.

- keep track of *trends* in a particular field of interest (e.g. by means of the tables of contents of journals); (In this case the profiles should not be too specific)
- keep track of new research projects in order to react timeously
- keep track of Internet-related developments (e.g. search engines, web browsers)
- take note of daily news events of interest (e.g. as reported in newspapers)
- take note of developments by competing markets (e.g. changes to a company's web site)
- take note of market developments (e.g. changes in stock market prices)
- have intelligent agents learn from their preferences and filter information accordingly
- heceive customised information on things like the weather report
- keep track of new documents added to a database, or of which the service took note (e.g. records in a database such as *ERIC* or new sites indexed by a search engine)
- support productivity in terms of research and publications
- keep track of forthcoming events
- keep track of specific document types (e.g. patents or standards).

Some of these benefits will become clearer when considering the available CAS methods in a later section – it might even be possible to add more benefits. Different CAS will also offer a different combination of these benefits.

Shortcomings and potential problems

CAS do not only offer benefits. There can also be negative aspects such as information overload, the time required to work through the information, the need to organise and manage the information provided by CAS, and cost implications. As already mentioned, some of the commercial services are very expensive. There are also no CAS that will cover all the information on a topic or subject of interest. If possible (and affordable) a combination of CAS should therefore be used. This can, however, lead to duplication of information, which again may waste users' time. Setting up an interest profile (explained in a later section), and evaluating and refining such a profile, can also take up a lot of time. Often a CAS will only provide descriptions of documents (e.g. announcements of new books or new journal articles), and users will still have to get hold of the full-text document. This can take up some time if interlending is used. If a document delivery service (e.g. Carl UnCover) or an online book ordering system (e.g. Amazon.com) is used, it can, on the other hand, become very expensive.

CAS methods

There are a wide variety of CAS methods and also specific products. The more conventional or traditional methods include accession lists, newspaper clippings, current awareness bulletins, displays, abstracting bulletins, periodical circulation, photocopies of the tables of contents of periodicals, indexing and abstracting journals, internally produced abstracts and indexes, press clippings, personal notifications and selective dissemination of information (SDI). To this can be added electronic tables of content, electronic newsletters, electronic news alerts, electronic notification systems, push services, pre-print archives and alerts offered by search engines. The traditional methods and how to implement them are well documented by Behrens (1989), Kemp (1979), Hamilton (1995) and Whitehall (1982). Kemp especially offers detailed notes on setting up CAS. More recently electronic current awareness methods and especially table of contents services have been discussed by, among others, Cox and Hanson (1992), Davies et al. (1998), Hanson and Cox (1993) and Mountifield (1995). To this can be added discussions on using methods available via the Internet such as those by Solomon (1999), Van Brakel and Potgieter (1997) and Yeats (1999).

Librarians planning CAS should first of all get an overview of the types of services and specific products which are available. There are different ways of looking at the types of CAS. One can, for instance, distinguish between external and internal services (the latter include inhouse CAS such as accession lists, journal circulation, inhouse indexing and abstracting bulletins, circulation of photocopies of tables of contents, and display boards). One can also distinguish between commercial services and services which are available at no charge (e.g. some of the services offered via the Internet). It is also possible to distinguish between formal and informal methods (the latter include personal notifications, invisible colleges, membership of societies, and attendance of conferences and meetings). CAS can also be classified according to the method of delivery, for example print-based services, electronic services (e.g. via CD-ROM, online services and Internet services). Even inhouse CAS can be print-based or electronic (e.g. services delivered by an intranet or internal network). It is not always possible to make clear-cut distinctions, but the above-mentioned considerations can still provide a useful point of departure.

In the following table a list of CAS methods, their delivery methods and specific examples are provided. Neither the list of methods nor the examples are exhaustive – although it was very tempting to keep on adding to these. The list serves merely as an indication of the possibilities available and can be supplemented with examples from Fourie (1999) and Davis et al. (1998). There are also many commercial services that are not dealt with here.

A few of the newer methods for CAS will first be briefly explained.

- *Book alerting services.* There are a number of book alerting services available on the Internet. Users mostly subscribe to broad categories of topics in which they are interested and are then automatically notified via email if there are new books that may be of interest.

- *News alerts or news filtering systems.* Newswire services provide filtered news services or personal web services. These services receive news and articles from many sources, for example newswires and trade journals. The services are normally delivered via their web site, or via email to the user's email address.

- *Notification systems.* Notification systems are based on the use of intelligent agents. These are programs that learn from what you do while you are on the Internet. They remember the topics you searched for, notice the types of information resources you prefer and so on. There are different types of systems based on intelligent agents, such as recommendation systems (e.g. Amazon.com which recommends books and music titles) and notifiers (e.g. The Informant and TracerLock). The agents can also search the Web (and other Internet resources) for information on one's topic(s) of interest.

- *Push services.* Push services are based on the use of push technology. This is software that sends (pushes) information directly to a user's desktop, rather than requiring the user to search for it him or herself on the Internet. Push services are mostly associated with the use of information channels, for which the user needs to load special software. The push services let the user decide on the content sent ('pushed') on a regular basis. Push technology can also be very useful on intranets for collecting information from third parties to push to users in topic-defined channels.

- *SDI services* (also known as alerts or alerting services). SDI services involve the automatic notification of users when new records are added to the database. The records are matched against a search strategy reflecting the user's interest profile. In the case of SDI services, the search strategy is often referred to as the search profile.

In the following list of CAS methods, the emphasis is mostly on electronic methods or methods for which more than one method of delivery can be used. Displays, for example, are not dealt with here, although a 'virtual display' might certainly be interesting. At the end of this chapter all relevant Internet addresses are listed.

Methods of CAS Method of delivery Examples

Methods of CAS	Method of delivery	Examples
Accession lists	Print	Printed lists of new documents added to the library collection can be made available to users.
	Intranet/internal network	Lists of new documents added to the library collection can be made available on the intranet or via email on the internal network.
Periodical circulation	Printed copies of journals to which the library subscribes	Copies of any printed periodical can be circulated as soon as the latest edition is available.
	Internet (e-journals)	Users can be notified as soon as the full text of e-journals to which the library subscribes is available, or users can check the sites on a regular basis.
Table of contents (TOCs)	Print	Photocopies of the table of contents of any printed periodical to which the library subscribes can be circulated.
TOC services	CD-ROM	Current Contents, Faxon-Finder
	Commercial online and Internet-based services	British Library Inside, Carl UnCover, Information Express, Information Quest, Institute for Scientific Information.
	Free Internet-based services	BUBL
TOC provided by journal publishers	These are made available via the Internet. They are based on:	
	Automatic email notification	Elsevier ContentsDirect, Ideal: International Digital Electronic Access Library, SARA
	Periodic updating where the user checks the web site at regular intervals	Cambridge University Press, Kluwer, Wiley-VCH

Pre-print archives		Pre-print archives sites and lists of sites can be found at *http://xxx.lanl.gov, http://dynatog.whoi.edu/docs/e-print/e-print.html* and *http://www.mastqueensa.ra~haht.aly.htm*
Bulletins One can distinguish between inhouse bulletins and commercial bulletins.	Print	Inhouse bulletins: printed copies of bulletins including bibliographic descriptions of documents and sometimes also indexing terms and abstracts can be made available to users. Commercial bulletins, such as Aslib's *Current Awareness Abstracts.*
	Intranet/internal network	Copies of inhouse bulletins can be made available on the intranet or via email through the internal network.
Newletters/e-zines	Print	Inhouse newsletters can be made available in printed format. If there are commercial newsletters they might also be circulated among users.
	Intranet/internal network	Copies of inhouse bulletins can be made available on the intranet or via email through the internal network.
	Internet	There are numerous newsletters available on the intranet or via email through the internal network. Only a few examples are mentioned here, namely: Search Engine Report, First Monday, The Internet Scout Project and Net-Happenings.
News alerts	Clippings (print)	Inhouse files with newspaper clippings can be circulated to users.
	Intranet/internal network	Inhouse files with newspaper clippings can be made available on the intranet or via email through the internal network. Such clippings can also be stored in an inhouse database.

News alerts	Commercial newspaper clipping services	Commercial services can provide clippings in printed or electronic format, e.g. the International Press-Cutting Bureau.
	News alerting/news filtering services (Internet)	There are numerous news alerting or news filtering services available on the Internet. Only a few examples are listed here, namely CRAYON, NewsAlert and Newspage. There are also news services such as: CNN Quick News, Daily Briefing and Reuters Business Briefing.
	Newspaper SDI services (online)	Online search services like Dialog offer SDI (or alerting services) which can be run against a wide variety of databases.
Book alerting services (Some of these also include book recommendations and other media such as CDs and videos.)	Accession lists (print)	Libraries can circulate printed copies of their accession lists of books and other publications.
	Accession lists (intranet/internal network)	Copies of inhouse accession lists can be made available on the intranet or via email through the internal network.
	Online (commercial)	Running SDI profiles against databases such as *Books in Print* or *British Books in Print*.
	Internet	There are a number of book alerting services available on the Internet, for example Amazon.com and UnCover Reveal.
SDI or alerting services	CD-ROM	Interest profiles can be compiled for users, saved and then run against each update of the database.
	Intranet/internal network	Inhouse files with newspaper clippings can be made available on the intranet or via email through the internal network. Such clippings can also be stored in an inhouse database.

SDI or alerting services	Online (commercial) (Many of these databases are also available via the Internet.)	Online search services such as Dialog have been offering SDI or alerting services for many years. More recently SilverPlatter and others have also been offering such services.
	Internet (search engines)	At the time of writing, I was only aware of Northern Light offering an alerting service.
Indexing and abstracting services	Printed inhouse bulletins	Inhouse indexing and abstracting bulletins can be compiled according to user needs and circulated among users.
	Intranet/internal network	Copies of inhouse indexing and abstracting bulletins can be made available on the intranet or via email through the internal network.
	Commercial bulletins: printed or electronic format	There are commercial indexing and abstracting services which make their bulletins available in printed format, for example Aslib's *Current Awareness Abstracts.*
	Internet	There are commercial indexing and abstracting services which make their bulletins available in electronic format on the Internet, for example Aslib's *Current Awareness Abstracts.*
Notification systems	Printed	Printed notes can be sent to users.
	Email notes	Email notes can be sent to individuals or groups; such notes can also be generated via the intranet or internal network.
	Electronic – based on intelligent agents	There are many notification systems available via the Internet. Only two examples are mentioned here: The Informant and TracerLock.
Push services	Commercial services (Internet)	Examples of push services available via the Internet include PointCast and BackWeb.

	Services available via the intranet	Push technology can also be used for internal alerting services.
Informal contact, informal discussion groups, Internet discussion lists and Usenet groups	Based on oral or electronic communication	There are numerous electronic discussion groups and Usenet groups available to keep in touch with new developments.

The following Internet resources can also be consulted to identify examples:

- Alert! A sampler of email services: *http://PowerReporting.com/alert.html*.

- E-journal: *http://www.edoc.com/ejournal*

- Infojump: information for the masses: *http://www.infojump.com/?ezdb,refresh*

- The Mining Company: *http://www.miningco.com* The Mining Company is a selection of subject guides. One can search for a topic and then combine it with a 'newsletter'.

- Anancyweb: *http://www.anancyweb.com/push_links.html* (provides links to push technology)

- Webcasting (push technology): *http://whatis.com/webcasti.htm*

- CataList: *http://www.lsoft.com/lists/listref.htm* (to keep track of discussion lists)

- Directory of Scholarly and Professional E-Conferences: *http://www.n2h2.com/KOVACS* (to keep track of discussion lists)

- IFLA: Internet Mailing Lists Guides and Resources: *http://www.ifla.org/ifla/I/training/listserv/lists.htm* (to keep track of discussion lists).

Selection of CAS methods and products

Once the librarian has taken note of the variety of CAS methods and products, it is also important to realise the possibilities for combining such services, and to select an appropriate combination. Although the electronic methods all seem very exciting, and offer tremendous possibilities, each library will have to take decisions according to its own unique circumstances. Such circumstances are depicted in the framework in Figure 1. According to this not only the library, but also the larger environment in which it operates, should be considered. This includes the financial budget and the allocation of funds, the availability of staff, the technological infrastructure, and the skills of library staff members and users. Such skills include computer skills, information literacy skills and network skills. All libraries complain about budget constraints. Although there is a perception that special libraries are better off, many have very limited funds. In such cases the Internet services offered free of charge or at reasonable subscription fees might be a good solution.

An analysis of the above-mentioned factors should of course also include an analysis of the users' information needs. Studies of user needs should be followed up by selecting specific CAS products according to a set list of criteria as explained in a later section. One aspect of the selection of CAS is the decision to compile inhouse products or to subscribe to external products. With the wide variety of products and media available, there may be a growing trend to use external services.

Consideration of information needs and users' expectations

There are a wide range of methods that can be used to determine users' information needs concerning current awareness services. There are, for example, formal interviews, questionnaires, focus group interviews, the checking of loan records and chats at lunch time. The needs of top management and the organisation as a whole, as well as the needs of groups of users and individual users, should be considered. Users' explanations of their information needs and an analysis of their tasks in the organisation should be considered. The first step is to get an overall idea of the information needs in order to decide on the CAS to which a library should subscribe. Such studies may also point to a need to compile inhouse products for CAS. Once this has been completed, and services and products selected, users must be interviewed to determine their specific information needs in order to compile their interest profiles (covered in a later section). One problem with studies of users' information needs is that their needs and expectations of CAS may be influenced by their knowledge of CAS or their lack thereof. It might therefore be a good idea to include a briefing on the reasons for offering CAS and the range of possibilities that exists. When questioning users about their needs, their technological skills and the computer technology (such as the Internet and database software to which they have access) should also be considered. CAS needs should also be seen in context with users' other information needs (such as for retrospective and ready reference services). One may even find that there are users who resist changing their search methods and information gathering behaviour (Brunskill, 1997).

Apart from learning about the users' information needs, the librarian should also consider the needs of the organisation as a whole. What is the core business of the organisation? What products does it deal in?

What services are offered, and what is the need for timely information? Richards (1992) states:

You must also acquire an in-depth knowledge of the products or services of your organisation, its actual and potential markets, competitors' products, product life-cycles, and new and emerging areas of development. A good understanding of your organisation's business and a sound knowledge of the people, their job functions, subject interests and existing sources of information is the first and very necessary step to enable you to develop useful services for everyone.

Criteria for selecting CAS

A number of articles have been published on comparisons of CAS and especially electronic products for CAS (e.g. Hanson and Cox, 1993; Hentz, 1996; Jaguszweksi and Kemp, 1995). These provide a good overview of the criteria that can be used for the selection of appropriate CAS methods and products. Solomon (1999) also provides an interesting list of criteria for push services. When considering the following table of criteria, one has to bear in mind that they apply mostly to electronic CAS methods and that most of the criteria applied will also depend on the type of CAS being evaluated.

The above-mentioned criteria can be used to select one or more CAS. First of all the CAS to which the library will subscribe, or which will be internally produced, need to be selected, and then a combination of CAS should

Criterion Importance of criterion

Criterion	Importance of criterion
Cost	Some of the commercial CAS are very expensive, and therefore out of reach of some libraries. Cheaper services, or services that are available free of charge, may however, be less sophisticated. (Such services may especially be useful to supplement shrinking periodicals' budgets.) If you do not pay for the services, you cannot, however, complain. Cost should also be considered when compiling inhouse products.
Subject coverage	CAS should be selected for the widest coverage of subjects within users' fields of interest.
Types of documents covered (e.g. journals, books, videos, web sites)	Users will probably be interested in a selection of document types. This can be catered for by selecting a combination of CAS (e.g. TOCs provided by journal publishers, SDI services for books and journals articles, and notification systems for web sites).

Amount of detail given (e.g. bibliographic descriptions, full text, tables of contents)	Detailed descriptions (e.g. including abstracts) are more useful; they are, however, also more expensive. If the service is available free of charge one should not expect added value and you will have to accept the information offered.
Frequency of updating	The importance of frequency as a criterion will depend on how urgent it is for the user to keep up with developments. In certain tasks and in certain disciplines currency may be very important.
Method of notification (e.g. automatic notification via email or periodic checking)	Automatic notification is of course more convenient. Decisions in this regard will, however, depend on the cost of the CAS.
Type of subscription (e.g. individual, corporate licence)	CAS offering site licences might be more convenient and cheaper for large organisations.
Availability of document delivery service	Users have grown accustomed to information on demand, and prefer immediate access to full-text document services.
Cost of document delivery service	Very convenient document delivery services may be too expensive for the library, or they may only be used occasionally.
User-friendliness. This includes ease of use, ease of access, and online help.	The ease with which the CAS can be used is important, especially if the users will be accessing the system themselves.
Search options. These include the availability of Boolean operators, options to search for an exact phrase, truncation, case sensitivity, options to limit the search to specific fields (e.g. author, title), options to specify the word position and the possibility of linking to related documents.	The search options offered by electronic CAS are very important since they determine how effectively the information searches can be refined. Once again, one cannot expect services available free of charge to be very sophisticated. Search options are, however, an important criterion when choosing between commercial CAS.
Ease of administration	This includes how much work the library has to do to run the CAS, for example the management of passwords and notifying users of their search results.
Customisation for individual users	Some CAS, for example Internet news alerting services, allow for customisation according to the needs of individual users.
Ease with which service can be integrated with existing services	This is important if a combination of services is used, which might easily be the case if a number of CAS are required to cover the different subject disciplines and interests.

Delivery options (e.g. HTML, text, etc.)	The options for delivering search results might be important if users want to incorporate the results in their personal information management systems.
Customer service and support	Good support services are very important when considering commercial CAS.
Quality of the documents	The quality of the documents delivered by the CAS is important. The users' time should not be wasted with documents of a poor quality.

be selected from these according to the needs of the individual user, user group, or organisation as a whole. In the case of the numerous services available on the Internet for free, users can also be encouraged to use these services on their own. The following is an example of a combination of CAS for a user interested in distance education in library and information science. (It is not an exhaustive list of possibilities.)

Services	**Specific titles**
Electronic journals offering access to their tables of content	*American Journal of Distance Education, Distance Education: an international journal* (There are many more examples.)
Tables of contents services	Carl UnCover, Elsevier ContentsDirect, etc.
Book recommendation services	Amazon.com, UnCover Reveal
E-zines	Distance Education Systemwide Interactive Electronic Newsletter (DESIEN), Net-Happenings, etc.
News filtering services	
Intelligent agents	The Informant, TracerLock
Push services	
News agencies	
SDI services	Dialog (ERIC, Library literature, LISA)
Search engines	Northern Light

Running a CAS

After selecting a suitable CAS method and product, or a combination thereof, the next step will be their implementation (the alternative of developing an inhouse service will not be dealt with here). This is followed by the running of the CAS, its maintenance and the very important regular evaluation and adaptation of the service. Once again this should be done within the environmental framework in which the library operates. Librarians should, for example, take into account not only the exciting possibilities offered by the CAS, but also the realities of their time and budget constraints. With the wider availability of CAS via the Internet, it is also important to consider constantly the new role that the users may play. Fourie (1999) deals in more detail with the empowerment of end users and CAS. Although this is one aspect that may be considered for running a CAS, librarians should, however, not expect that all users will be interested in such involvement.

In the following sections a number of aspects of running CAS will be discussed. These relate mostly to an electronic CAS, but do not necessarily apply to all types of such CAS. If traditional CAS are used, there are a number of other aspects, such as making photocopies, distributing journals and setting up displays. The purpose of the following discussion is merely to put the running of CAS in an electronic era into perspective by highlighting some of the most important tasks.

Compiling user interest profiles

A major component of the successful running of a CAS is the users' interest profiles. These are used as a basis for making decisions about CAS suitable for the individual user, groups of users, or the organisation as a whole, and for the formulation of search strategies. The latter is important for SDI services or any electronic CAS where you specify a topic or combination of topics in order to receive automatic notification of new information. For some CAS the 'search strategy' might simply mean typing in a single topic. In the case of groups of users or general profiles for the organisation, the librarian can also filter the information retrieved by such profiles before using push technology to disseminate the information to the users via the organisational intranet.

Interest profiles are also referred to as user profiles, and are still considered extremely important for a good CAS. The compiling of interest profiles will not be covered in detail here, since sufficient information can be found in standard texts such as Kemp (1979) and Hamilton (1995). There are, however, a few extra things to bear in mind in the electronic environment.

The compilation of a user interest profile is normally based on a reference interview and the completion of a request form. Email requests and electronic request forms can, however, also be used. A number of libraries are, for example, already providing request forms on their web sites. An example of a request form is provided in Appendix A. The form does not necessarily cover all options, but should provide a starting point for the development of such forms. The purpose of an interest profile is to collect as much useful information as possible from the user to assist in the selection of appropriate CAS, and for the formulation of the search strategy. This includes suggestions for search terms, the combination of search terms, and options for limiting the search strategy. Although it is standard practice to limit retrospective searches according to the language of publication, this may defy the purpose of a CAS where the idea is to keep track of new developments, and not just to identify documents for later reading.

With the wider range of document types covered, it is also important to establish Internet resources in which the user might be interested (web sites, electronic journals or electronic newsletters). Since there are many services available free of charge it can do no harm also to cover the users' non-work-related interests, especially if they take responsibility for them themselves. The addition of studies and personal interests is for example covered in the request form provided in Appendix A.

There are also a number of other aspects on which information should be collected. The preferred format for references should be established (e.g. titles only, bibliographic descriptions, abstracts included or full text). It should also be explained to users that the formats available will differ for CAS, and that commercial services charge more for the formats with value-added information such as abstracts and, of course, for the full text. It is also important to know the preferred format of delivery (print, email, PDF files, HTML). If the records are to be added to a personal database, the database management software in use might also influence the format selected for records.

It is important that users realise the impact of the interest profile on the success of the CAS, and why they need to spend some time on it. They should also realise the importance of regularly revising their interest profile and resulting search strategies as information needs change all the time. This is the theory for good CAS. I can, however, offer no advice on convincing a reluctant user to co-operate in this regard. Some users just want to get it over and done with as soon as possible!

During the reference interview the following aspects should also be discussed with the user: the concept of CAS, the reasons for using CAS, the variety of CAS available and the options as well as limitations offered by each. Users should also be informed of the value of organising the information and the use of database programmes and personal information management software. The copyright implications of saving electronic records should also be addressed, as should the necessity of complementing CAS with other methods for staying abreast (such as attending conferences or meetings). It is also very important for users to realise that there is no CAS that will cover all the information on a particular topic, and that if they use a combination of CAS they should also expect information to be duplicated.

Principles to consider when formulating search strategies

The search strategies are based on the information gathered for the interest profile. When formulating these strategies, all the principles of sound online searching and search heuristics still apply. It is, for example, important to use tools for vocabulary control if available and to use textbooks, dictionaries, and so on, to check the terminology when using natural language. The names of authors, journal titles and corporate authors should be verified to make sure that all variations are covered. The search result should never be limited to the latest year of publication, and other methods for limiting the search result should be used as available and as appropriate. To this can be added the correct and most effective use of Boolean operators, proximity operators, truncation, relevance ranking, sorting and so on. If applicable, the display format and method of delivery should also be specified.

When testing the search strategy it is especially important to check the relevance of the records retrieved and to ensure that careless mistakes have not been made (such as incorrect use of Boolean operators and neglecting to use parentheses to combine search terms when using more than one Boolean operator). The strategy should also be run against the latest update (the last week or last month) as well as the last year to ensure that the number of records retrieved will be acceptable to the user. When finalised, the search strategy should be saved for future use. A printed copy of the strategy should be kept on file to make it easier to revise the profile in the future. When using online or CD-ROM databases, a back-up copy should be made of the search strategy.

Administrative tasks

The management of a CAS involves a number of administrative tasks. These can be handled by a librarian or an administrative staff member. Such tasks include the management of passwords and of user accounts where applicable, the management of the delivery of search results, and notifying users of the search results where necessary and reminding them to revise their profiles. When notifying users of the search results (e.g. when running the profile against a CD-ROM database), users should be informed among other things about the database searched, the search strategy used, the frequency of update, and of course the name of a contact person in the library. If users are expected to pay for the CAS, this also needs to be dealt with.

Linking to a document delivery service

The value of CAS is greatly diminished if they cannot be linked to a document delivery service or full-text database. With shrinking budgets most libraries can only provide access to a limited collection of resources. There are many document delivery services available (e.g. Carl UnCover, Dialog and Ebsco). Although such services are extremely convenient, they can also be very expensive and therefore out of reach for a struggling special library. A search engine such as Northern Light also offers access to a selection of full-text articles. Document delivery services should also be evaluated in terms of their cost, convenience and services offered.

Evaluation of interest and search profiles

Interest and search profiles should be revised and updated at regular intervals. The users normally neglect to do this and it is therefore up to the librarians to take the initiative. Much has been published on the evaluation of IR systems and the measuring units to use, namely recall, precision and novelty. Novelty in particular has been associated with CAS. If a combination of CAS is used, users can, however, expect more duplication, which will also mean that novelty as a measuring unit will be less effective. The accuracy and quality of the records, the time it takes to use the CAS and also the time it takes to work through the search results, and the cost and the timeliness of the records should also be considered when evaluating search profiles.

Implications of CAS for the special librarian

CAS can offer exciting possibilities for special librarians to contribute to the welfare of an organisation. They can also involve a lot of work. Apart from appropriate knowledge and skills, enthusiasm is therefore an important factor. Depending on how a CAS is run, it might lead to more active user involvement, which in turn can strengthen the threat of disintermediation. To counter such a threat special librarians should stay alert of developments in their own field. They should for example:

- broaden their awareness and knowledge of existing methods of CAS
- increase their knowledge of commercial and informal methods of staying abreast of developments
- refine their knowledge of users' needs (in general as well as for individual users)
- streamline the time they spend on CAS by, say, considering new methods for involving users.

Above all, special librarians should keep track of developments in their own field. The following are two sources that may prove useful:

- Current awareness application of new technologies in libraries: *http://lib.ua.ac.be/WGLIB/ATTEND/index.html*
- NewsAgent for Libraries: *http://www.sbu.ac.uk/~litc/newsagent/*.

At the time of writing, the Faculty of Information Science of the University of Toronto was also offering an excellent online course on Internet CAS, which is an ideal point of departure for the interested special librarian.

Conclusion

The growth in electronically available CAS has made it essential for special librarians to reconsider the way in which they are offering CAS. Factors having an impact on the new possibilities include CAS available for free via the Internet, easier access to CAS via the Internet (this also includes commercial services), more user-friendly services, and a much wider array of topics and interests covered by CAS (including job-related interests, studies and entertainment). The concept of CAS and the reasons for offering such services have also seen a change in emphasis. This leaves the special librarian with exciting opportunities for offering a range of new services to users, to combine CAS, to market the library, to enhance the image of librarians and to empower the end users. It also leaves the special librarian with a new responsibility for picturing all the possibilities within the realities of his or her specific environment. Such realities include the constraints of time, funds, technology and skills. The electronic environment requires new insights into the concept of CAS, and it also requires renewed emphasis on the needs of individual users and the organisation in general.

References

Basch, R. *Secrets of the Super Net Searchers: the reflections, revelations, and hard-won wisdom of 35 of the world's top Internet researchers*. Winton, CT: Pemberton Press (1996).

Behrens, S.J. Current awareness services: inhouse methods and commercially available products. *Mousaion*, **7**(2) 1989, 58-75.

Brunskill, K. The issues surrounding the provision of CASIAS service in libraries. *Interlending & Document Supply*, **25**(2) 1997, 57-63.

Cox, J. and Hanson, T. Setting up an electronic current awareness service. *Online*, **16**(4) 1992, 36-43.

Creaser, C. and Spiller, D. *TFPL Survey of UK Special Library Statistics.* Loughborough: LISU (1997) (LISU Occasional paper, no. 15).

Davies, M., Boyle, F. and Osborne, S. CAS-IAS services: where are we now? *Electronic Library*, **16**(1) 1998, 37-48.

Deardorff, T.C. and Garrison, A.O. Developing an automated current awareness program using microcomputers and electronic mail. *Technical Services Quarterly*, **14**(4) 1997, 1-11.

Fourie, I. Empowering users – current awareness on the Internet. *Electronic Library*, **17**(6) 1999, 379-88.

Hamilton, F. *Current Awareness, Current Techniques.* Aldershot: Gower (1995).

Hanson, T. and Cox, J. A comparative review of two-diskette-based current awareness services: current contents on diskette and reference update. *Database*, **16**(3) 1993, 73-81.

Harrod's Librarians' Glossary: 9,000 terms used in information management, library science, publishing, the book trades, and archive management. Aldershot: Gower (1995, 8ᵗʰ ed.).

Hentz, M.B. Comparison and utilization of electronic table of contents delivery in a corporate library environment. *Journal of Interlibrary Loan, Document Delivery & Information Supply*, **7**(2) 1996, 29-41.

Housman, E.M. Selective dissemination of information. In: C.A. Cuadra and A.W. Luke (eds) *Annual Review of Information Science and Technology*, **8**. American Society for Information Science (1973) 221-41.

Jaguszweksi, J.M. and Kemp, J.L. Four current awareness databases: coverage and currency compared. *Database*, **18**(1) 1995, 34-44.

Jax, J.J. and Van Houlson, C. A current-awareness service for faculty and staff: The Stout Experience. *College and Research Libraries*, **49**(6) 1988, 515-22.

Kemp, A. *Current Awareness Services.* London: Bingley (1979).

Landau, H.B. Document dissemination. In: *Annual Review of Information Science and Technology.* (1969) 229-70.

Mountifield, H.M. Electronic current awareness service: a survival tool for the information age? *Electronic Library*, **13**(4) 1995, 317-20.

Price, C. and Burley, R.A. An evaluation of information sources for current awareness on occupational diseases. *Journal of Information Science*, **12**(5) 1986, 247-55.

Richards, D. Dissemination of information. In: P. Dossett (ed.) *Handbook of special Librarianship and Information Work.* London: Aslib (1992, 6ᵗʰ ed.).

Rowley, J. Current awareness in an electronic age. *Online & CD-ROM Review*, **22**(4) 1998, 277-9.

Rowley, J. Revolution in current awareness services. *Journal of Librarianship and Information Science*, **26**(1) 1994, 7-14.

Rowley, J.E. Bibliographic current awareness services – a review. *Aslib Proceedings*, **37**(9) 1985, 345-53.

Solomon, M. When push comes to pull: serving current awareness applications in your company's news cafeteria. *Searcher*, **7**(6) 1999, 70-6.

Stenstrom, P.F. and Tegler, P. Current awareness in librarianship. *Library Trends*, **36**(4) 1989, 725-40.

Trench, S. Dissemination of information. In: A. Scammell (ed.) *Handbook of Special Librarianship and Information Work*. London: Aslib (1997, 7ᵗʰ ed.).

Van Brakel, P.A. and Potgieter, H.C. Creating World-Wide Web bulletin boards to enhance current awareness services. *South African Journal of Library and Information Science*, **65**(2) 1997, 124-9.

Wente, Van A. and Young, G.A. In: *Annual Review of Information Science and Technology*. (1969) 259-95.

Whitehall, T. Current awareness in education: an evaluation of Trent Polytechnic's *Education News*. *Aslib Proceedings*, **37** 1985, 355-70.

Whitehall, T. Dissemination of information. In: L.J. Anthony (ed.) *Handbook of Special Librarianship and Information Work*. London: Aslib (1982, 5ᵗʰ ed.).

Williams, M.E. Online retrieval – today and tomorrow. *Online Review*, **24**(4) 1978, 353-66.

Yeats, R. Have you heard the library news? Personalized net alerts for librarians. *Aslib Proceedings*, **51**(5) 1999, 137-43.

APPENDIX A: EXAMPLE OF A REQUEST FORM FOR A CURRENT AWARENESS SERVICE (CAS)

Office use

Profile number:
Type of profile:
  Retrospective profile
  CAS profile: Individual Group General
Date received:
Date compiled:
Updated:
Profile compiler:

Personal detail of user

Name:.. Department / section / company:...........

Office: .... Position:...

Postal address:............................ Telephone: Office:............ Home:...........
.... Fax:...
Postal code:................................ Cell:..
Email address:............................

| **Interest profile** |
| You may need a retrospective search or CAS for your work, studies or personal interests. |

Work-related interests

1   Describe in a paragraph the **topics** you are interested in (e.g. distance education; distance education in South Africa; the use of instructional design in distance education). For CAS you have to list only those topics you would like to be informed about on a regular basis.

....
....
....

2   List the companies, organisations, institutions, etc. in whose activities you are interested.

....
....
....

3   List the names of people in whose work you are interested.

....
....
....

4   List any institution, product, etc. in whose financial details you are interested.

....
....
....

Study-related interests

1   Describe in a paragraph the **topics** you are interested in (e.g. distance education; distance education in South Africa; the use of instructional design in distance education). For CAS you have to list only those topics you would like to be informed about on a regular basis.

....
....
....

2   List the companies, organisations, institutions, etc. in whose activities you are interested.

....
....
....

3   List the names of people in whose work you are interested.

....
....
....

4   List any insititution, product, etc. in whose financial details you are interested.

....
....
....

Personal-related interests

1   Describe in a paragraph the **topics** you are interested in (e.g. wine tasting, stamp collecting). For CAS you have to list only those topics you would like to be informed about on a regular basis.

....
....
....

2   List the companies, organisations, institutions, etc. in whose activities you are interested (e.g. hotel groups, travel agencies).

....
....
....

3   List the names of people in whose work you are interested (e.g. movie or sport stars).

....
....
....

4   List any insititution, product, etc. in whose financial details you are interested.

....
....
....

Would you also like a retrospective search on any of the topics? Specify.

....
....
....

List all journal titles you would like to monitor on a regular basis.

Journal title	Journal title	Journal title

Why do you want to keep track of new developments? Tick the most appropriate option(s). (This information will help us to select a suitable type of CAS.)

❏   To keep track of new developments in my field of interest

❏   To keep track of trends in my field of interest

❏   To keep track of new web sites, discussion groups (e.g. listservs, Usenet groups), new publications (e.g. books), new CDs, new videos

❏   To keep track of new research projects

❏   To keep track of Internet-related developments (e.g. search engines, web-site design)

❏   To take note of daily events of interest (e.g. as reported in newspapers)

❏   To take note of developments by competing markets

❏   To have intelligent agents learn from my preferences and filter information accordingly

❏   To receive customised information on things like the weather report

Any other reasons (please specify):

....

....

Which type of service would you be interested in? Tick the appropriate service(s)

Interested	Type of service	Description of service
	Acquisitions list	Lists all new documents added to the library's collection
	Bulletin board/newsletter	Provides an overview of new developments concerning the organisation
	Tables of contents	Provides access to tables of contents of selected journals (sometimes abstracts and/or full text are included). Automatic notification; periodic updating
	Book alerting	Automatic notification of new books in your field of interest
	E-zines or electronic newsletters	Mostly available for free; mostly automatic distribution via email
	Push services	Information is automatically sent to your computer's desktop.
	Intelligent agents	Notify you of changes on web sites, or new web sites picked up by a search engine in your field of interest.
	Newspapers and broadcast news	
	Commercial SDI or alerting services	Your search profile is run against a commercial database. The information is well structured, but it is also expensive.

Cost of services (the cost of services varies greatly and can fall in the following categories). Indicate in which category you are interested and whether you would be willing to pay for the services:

Commercial services (sometimes very expensive)	Reasonably priced (between $20 and $40)	Free

Would you be prepared to pay for any of these services yourself?

....

Method of payment:

....

Prefered method of delivery

❑   Email: Text files   or   ❑   Email: HTML files

❑   Fax

❑   Printed copy

❑   Web site: would you be prepared to periodically check a web site?

Search profile(s)
A search profile consists of the topics or other aspects you are interested in, the terms describing these and the combination of terms

Title of search: (this will be based on the description of topics of interest you described in a paragraph):

....

....

Search terms and combination of terms (**there may be more than one topic involved**):

Concept	Concept	Concept

Search terms you specifically want to exclude:

....

In which broad category or categories will the topic fall (e.g. education, social science, medicine)?

....

Specify if you want to limit the search in any way (e.g. according to title, keywords, journal title). Tick the appropriate option(s).

❏   Keywords
❏   Titles
❏   Journal titles
❏   Authors
❏   Type of publication
❏   Other (specify) ....

Specify the languages in which you are interested. Tick the appropriate option(s).

❏   English
❏   French
❏   German
❏   Other (specify) ....

Format in which you would like information (this will also depend on what is offered by the service):

❏   Complete bibliographic detail
❏   Complete bibliographic detail and keywords
❏   Complete bibliographic detail and abstract
❏   Complete bibliographic detail, keywords and abstract

Repsonsibility for CAS. Tick the appropriate option.

❏   Librarian
❏   Librarian and user (specify the role of each) ....
❏   User

Office use

Combination of selected CAS services	
Service	**Specific titles**
Tables of contents services	
Book recommendation services	
E-zines	
News filtering services	
Intelligent agents	

Push services	
News agencies	
SDI services	
Databases covered	

Office use

Search strategies

Attach the search strategies for individual services.

Problems experienced:

APPENDIX B: LIST OF INTERNET ADDRESSES NOT LISTED IN THE TEXT

Amazon.com: *http://www.amazon.com*

BackWeb: *http://www.backweb.com*

British Library Inside: *http://www.bl.uk/online/inside*

BUBL journals: *http://bubl.ac.uk/journals*

Carl UnCover: *http://uncweb.carl.org*

Cambridge University Press: *http://www.journals.cup.org*

CNN Quick News: *http://www.cnn.com/QUICKNEWS/mail/*

CRAYON: *http://crayon.net*

Dialog: *http://www.dialog.com*

Daily Briefing: *http://eralguide.real.com*

De Gruyter: *http://www.deGruyter.de/journals/journals.html*

Elsevier ContentsDirect: *http://www.elsevier.com*

First Monday: *http://www.firstmonday.dk*

Ideal: International Digital Electronic Access Library: *http://www.idealibrary.com*

The Informant: *http://informant.dartmouth.edu/*

Information Express: *http://www.express.com*

Information Quest: *http://www.eiq.com*

Institute for Scientific Information: *http://www.isinet.com*

The Internet Scout Project and Net-Happenings: *http://scout.cs.wisc.edu/scout/report/index.html*

Kluwer: *http://kapis.www.wkap.nl/kapis/*

NewsAlert: *http://www.newsalert.com*

Newspage: *http://www.newspage*

Northern Light: *http://www.nlsearch.com*

PointCast: *http://www.pointcast.com*

Reuters Business Briefing: *http://www.reuters.com/rbb*

SARA: *http://www.tandf.co.uk*

Search Engine Report: *http://searchenginewatch.com/*

SilverPlatter: *http://www.silverplatter.com*

TracerLock: *http://peacefire.org/tracerlock*

UnCover Reveal: *http://www.uncweb.carl.org*

Wiley-VCH: *http://www.wiley-vch.de/contents/index.htm*

Chapter 14

Financial planning

Michael Maher

Introduction

The aim of this chapter is to provide a basic introduction to the task of financial planning within the library and information service (LIS). It has been written from a practical perspective, offering advice and examples based on experience rather than theory and is intended for whoever is responsible for managing the LIS financial planning process. For convenience, I have divided this process into the following parts – awareness; budget preparation; budget presentation, and financial control – each of which is treated as a separate unit. In reality they are intertwined and this needs to be borne in mind when formulating or carrying out any aspect of financial planning.

LIS departments cater for different work sectors – for example private, public, and academic. They provide services for many different users and business groups. They greatly range in staff resources and size, in categories and type of collection. Thus, what financial advice applies for one may not apply for another. My own experience is firmly rooted in the commercial specialist LIS sector and is the base for much of this chapter but, hopefully, most of what follows will be of relevance and interest to the wider audience.

So, what is financial planning? You have a budget and you try not to overspend it – that's it, isn't it? Well, it certainly is a part of it, but only a part, and herein lies the major hurdle that the library manager may well trip over – namely, that they do not utilise, or are expected to utilise, the full range of financial management techniques available to manage their department.

In the mid-1980s, Stephen A. Roberts (1985) wrote that '… the principles and techniques available to support the economic management of library and information services are one of the weakest areas in the repertoire of library management'.

Ten years later, Duncan McKay (1995) noted that '…significant progress has been made in ensuring that librarians and information workers are aware of the importance of financial management [but] it is still an area of weakness for many'.

This is still the situation today because people do not see any natural links between libraries and money, particularly making money. Very few specialist LIS units are independent corporate bodies subject to full public accountability or the wrath of their share holders. In the main, they exist as a part of a larger organisation which categorises them as a necessary cost centre to help achieve its goals, without offering them any real influence in its overall financial strategy. Also, a library's prime function is rightly perceived as the management of information, not financial planning. Yes, effective financial management should be part of the LIS manager's skill set, but as long as the library is successfully providing its designated user groups with the relevent information sources and services they require, then there will be little pressure from senior management to adopt any in-depth financial management techniques. In other words there is little opportunity or expectation for the LIS financial planner to develop financial expertise.

This said, financial planning has to be treated as more than a yearly cycle of agreeing a set of figures on a spreadsheet. At the very least the person responsible for managing it needs to monitor the current budget regularly and be planning the next in light of changing developments. This person also needs to appreciate that financial planning is a valuable communication tool, a way of integrating the LIS department into the host organisation's mainstream objectives and activities. This is important not only for profile raising but also for justification and survival. Certainly, in the commercial sector the technical information revolution over the last 20 years is raising questions about the need for traditional hard copy collection. End users are increasingly able to access directly the information sources they need to carry out their working responsibilities via their desktop screen, putting pressure on libraries taking up valuable office floor space. Thus, it is imperative that the library manager treats financial planning as an essential skill within their management portfolio. They need to be able to put across the true value that the LIS department adds to the organisation. To show how it helps fulfil the organisation's objectives and strategies. To make sure it is seen as proactive and dynamic, a vital part of the organisation's future plans. To do all this, the library manager has got to be aware of the organisation they are working for. And this awareness is the first part of the financial planning process.

Awareness

Awareness of the organisation and of the information marketplace are important criteria to be considered when financial planning.

Organisation

The person responsible for LIS financial planning needs to understand the parent organisation, to appreciate how it is structured and where the LIS department fits into this structure. What are its information needs? What are its strategies for the next few years? What impact do these have for LIS? These are essential questions and their answers will provide the foundation block on which to base financial planning. As Sylvia Webb (1995) has pointed out: 'Finance cannot be managed in isolation.' LIS budget requests and capital expenditure proposals need to be clearly linked to the LIS strategic plan which, in turn, should be based on the organisation's objectives. The following areas should be addressed.

The mission statement

What is the parent organisation's mission statement? What is its vision for the next three years? This will normally be presented as some broad statement, perhaps 'to become the largest corporate practice in the region' or 'to turn into a paperless office'. Whatever it is, it will be what the organisation's strategies and objectives will be based on. The LIS strategic plan and objectives should clearly derive from it, and this includes all financial issues. Bidding for resources to increase staff numbers, expand stock levels, or upgrade equipment, will have a better chance of acceptance if they can be shown to be an integral part of the organisation's direction. As Jim Basker (1997) rightly states: 'The vision of the organisation is very important to the information service because it confers legitimacy.' You cannot be planning a budget behind a closed door, oblivious to what is happening on the other side of it. It needs to be seen to be a necessary part of achieving the organisation's vision. Current services and resources should be constantly reviewed to make sure they are still relevant so that money expended on them can be justified.

Who are the LIS users and potential users, and what are their information requirements?

This may seem an obvious point, but user group(s) and information needs change. Let's take an example – in the mid-1980s a typical large UK law firm's library would be catering solely for the fee-earning departments. Now, the legal profession is operating in a more aggressive marketplace and in addition to the fee-earning departments the library is providing services to business development and human resources teams, inhouse support lawyers and, increasingly, external clients. These new groups require different information needs and so the library services have to adapt accordingly. Traditional information paper-based means of access and delivery have been joined by CD-ROM technology, email, the evolution of intranets and extranets, and the rise of the Internet.

These changes mean that LIS financial planning within law firms today is significantly different from 15 years ago. And these changes are reflected in many LIS departments catering for specialist work areas. What is critical for the financial planners is that they keep abreast of these changes and budget to make the needed alterations to services, collections and access collections.

What is the organisation's financial structure?

This covers a multitude of areas with which the financial planner needs to be familiar.

- *Financial set-up* – how is the organisation financially arranged? Is there a central finance department? If so, where is it located and how is it managed? Is the LIS department expected to directly report to it or to an intermediary such as a library partner or management committee?

- *Procedure* – read and understand any internal financial operations manual which will include details on how to process invoices, raise a cheque, bill a client and so forth, plus examples of purchase invoice vouchers, expense claims forms and the like.

- *Practical* – What accountancy system does the organisation use? Has the LIS department direct access to it? If not, how do staff check to see if an invoice has cleared or what the latest budget expenditure level is?

Where are the users located?

It is easier and certainly cheaper to plan services for users if they are located within the same building as the LIS department. The more spread out the users, the more complex the financial planning. For example, if there is a demand for immediate access to core hard-copy information material then it may be necessary to set up and maintain local libraries in different locations. This will inevitably mean extra resourcing to pay for duplication, and additional staff will be required. The same will be true for electronic information – if users do not have access to a networked IT system then it may be necessary to purchase additional copies of CD-ROMs for each local library. With an increase in remote and home-based working there may be a demand for personal copies of essential resources, access to CD-ROMs and commercial online information products.

Marketplace

As well as an awareness of the LIS department's parent organisation, it is important to consider the information marketplace itself. Key areas are discussed below.

Delivery of information

As already noted, the desktop screen has become a recognised platform for accessing information. This has opened up a new financial avenue for publishers who can now sell their products by hard copy, CD-ROM or browser access (or often a combination of all these). It has also created a new area of costs for the LIS planner who will need to budget for the necessary hardware and software technology to access and deliver the information as well as pay for the product itself. Often such expenditure will fall under the IT department's remit and so it is important to warn them if new CD towers, server space or communication technology is going to be required.

Pricing for required information products and services

There are a couple of points worth noting. Firstly, the inflation rate for books and journals is rarely the same as the standard RPI – in recent years the former has been much higher. Secondly, pricing for electronic information products is more variable than fixed. It is more difficult to budget accurately for pay-as-you-go online services than subscriptions for hard-copy products because you cannot calculate exact usage in advance. One way round this is to agree a standard monthly charge irrespective of usage. Not all providers are prepared to do this and those that do will set the charge at a very high level. Another financial headache is trying to agree licence costs with the provider (for electronic information products based on a regular number of users) because there are problems in trying to define precisely what constitutes a 'regular user'.

Employment market

There is a need to be aware of any changes in the employment market, not just for information workers but any general changes in terms and conditions. The 'Working Time Directive', ISO 9000 and Investors in People may well impact upon LIS staff costs. Some tasks may be better financially managed by being outsourced.

Competitor market

If possible, compare competitor information budgets to your own. If they are larger then are they able to provide better user services (thus providing an argument for raising your own)? Also, look internally at other support functions' budgets within the parent organisation to see how they compare. Find out if they have been increasing more sharply than the LIS budget and, if so, why.

Budget preparation

Budget preparation is the second part of the LIS financial planning process and has been split into the following sections: budget type, cost centres and profit centres, budget categories, budget headings and costings.

Budget type

Written budgets are basically requests for funding and how you approach preparing one depends very much upon the house style of the parent organisation. You may only be required to come up with simple, single line figure or, alternatively, have to produce an in-depth discussion document. You may not even need to prepare one because LIS expenditure will be seen as part of another department's budget. Or you may be expected to prepare several budgets, each relating to different types of expenditure or income. It is recognised that there are several standard types.

Operating budget

Probably the one most familiar to LIS departments and is based on day-to-day expenditure items such as staff wages, overtime, rent and rates, stationery, materials, equipment, utilities and any other standard item of expenditure LIS is responsible for paying for.

Capital expenditure

This covers one-off major items of expenditure such as a new library management system. It will normally be accounted for as a depreciated item spread over several years rather than a single cost item paid for in year one of purchase.

Internal recovery budget

This budget covers predicted internal revenue expected to be raised during the life of the budget from cross-charging other departments to recouping costs incurred by the LIS department in providing information to them. This is important, not just for the LIS department, but to the departments being charged so that they, in turn, can allow sufficient funding to cover such charges. Internal cost recovery may be seen by some as a meaningless exercise in that it does not actually generate any income, merely move it from one budget to another, but it has the benefit of placing a financial value on information and of keeping other sectors of the organisation aware of how much it costs to provide it. A variation on this is to include a mark-up to cover staff time working on dealing with the request or providing the particular information service (perhaps a specialist practice briefing).

Income budget

This covers expected income that the LIS department will generate. Traditionally, this has been raised by charging for photocopying, levying fines, sales of material, membership subscriptions and the like. To this may be added charging out LIS staff time spent on client files.

It needs to be agreed beforehand whether monies received from cross-charging and income generation will be used to offset LIS expenditure or to purchase additional LIS resources.

Cost centres and profit centres

Before preparing the budget it is necessary to confirm whether the LIS department is expected to operate as a cost or profit centre.

Cost centres

Most LIS departments run as cost centres, which means they are viewed as a necessary organisational overhead without a remit to make money. This is fine in that it removes the pressure of having to reach financial targets, but the down side can be a lack of status compared to, say, fee-earning departments. Fee-earner time spent on a client matter will normally be billed, while LIS time spent on the same matter may be treated as 'added value'. This makes placing a value on LIS staff time more esoteric when trying to calculate it in pure accounting terms. As Kate Hodgson (1999) has pointed out, 'It is always easier to promote the library or argue for funds when a monetary value can be attached to the performance of the department.'

Profit centres

This raises a different set of issues to those of cost centres. If the LIS department is expected to make a profit then it will be necessary to identify the licensing, copyright and liability positions of selling information onto a third party. Staff resourcing will need to be more flexible to allow for changes in service demand volume. Staff skill sets will be different. Financial accountability will be more to the fore because of the need to maintain full and accurate financial records. There will be a need to set up pricing structures, plus a policy on how staff time is monitored and charged out. The financial planner needs to be ready to react to competitor moves. Also, any information services that are to be charged will have to be effectively marketed and promoted beforehand. Finally, as LIS staff will be dealing with clients directly they will need to adhere to any organisational client relationship management programme. For a detailed explanation on charging for information services see Sylvia Webb's *Making a Charge for Library and Information Services* (1994).

Although the LIS department may not be expected to make a profit charging for its services, it should be using any opportunity it can to reduce overheads and increase income. In the commercial sector a LIS department needs continually to justify its existence and any attempt to reduce costs will help. The concept of charging has been around since the 1950s. However, it is since the 1980s and the advent of new technology that the possibility of charging for information has taken really off. It is not surprising to find that LISU's 1998 survey *Libraries in the Workshop* (1998) found many different specialist library sectors now implementing external charging policies for their services (see Figure 1).

Figure 1: Specialist library sectors that implement external charging policies (based on LISU's 1998 findings)

Sector	Per cent with external charging policy
Legal	41
Energy	28
Management and Info. Consultants	70
Pharmaceutical	7
Commercial and Financial	21
Trade and Learned Associations	71

Budget categories

There are several recognised budgeting preparation categories, each of which are covered in Duncan McKay's *Effective Financial Planning for Library and Information Services* (1995). Briefly, they are:

- line item budgeting
- formula budgeting
- program budgeting
- performance budgeting
- planning programming budgeting system
- zero based budgeting.

Which category to use depends upon the preferred methods of the parent organisation . It is not necessary to use just one category, two or more can be combined. By way of an example, Figure 2 shows a typical law firm line item budget, probably the simplest and most common style used by LIS departments.

Column A lists the expenditure units under the common headings they will be known as. The Law Books heading covers central LIS hard-copy purchases which, along with the specific departmental headings, comprises the expenditure for stock renewals and new acquisitions for the main library and departmental ones (another way to organise this might be to assign a heading to each type of publication, i.e. serials, looseleafs, reports etc.). There is an Electronic Costs heading to covers the library's CD-ROM and online subscriptions (again, this could be organised by type or, maybe, provider). Finally, there is a Recovery heading to cater for expected reimbursements such as cross-charges. Alternatively, this could be set-up as a separate budget.

Column B lists the actual nominal ledger codes assigned by the finance department for each of the headings. Column C contains the existing budgets for the current financial year and Column D the actual expenditure to date. This latter is important because the new budget will be prepared in advance of the year end and this is a useful way to show how the current budget is performing and to highlight any unexpected underspend or overspend. Column E shows the proposed budgets for the new financial year. Finally, at the bottom of the diagram is the *GRAND TOTAL* for each column.

Figure 2:

ABC & XYZ – LIS budget proposal 2000-01

A	B	C	D	E
Headings	Nominal Budget Code	1999/00 Budget	Expenditure To Date	2000/1 Proposed
Law Books	111111111111	£ 78,000	£ 53,615	£ 85,000
Commercial Book	222222222222	£ 2,500	£ 3,282	£ 3,500
Litigation Book	333333333333	£ 2,500	£ 1,524	£ 2,800
Corporate Book	444444444444	£ 2,500	£ 1,694	£ 2,500
Tax Book	555555555555	£ 1,500	£ 1,463	£ 2,000
Property Book	666666666666	£ 2,500	£ 822	£ 2,500
Planning Book	777777777777	£ 1,500	£ 1,245	£ 2,000
Employment Book	888888888888	£ 2,500	£ 2,216	£ 3,000
Administration Book	999999999999	£ 2,000	£ 482	£ 2,000
Total Dept Costs		£ 18,000	£ 12,728	£ 20,300
Online Costs	1234567891011	£ 48,000	£ 50,364	£ 60,000
Total		£ 143,500	£ 116,707	£ 165,300
Recovery	1110987654321	-£ 22,000	-£ 11,883	-£ 25,000
GRAND TOTAL		£ 121,500	£ 104,824	£ 140,300

Budget headings

McKay has produced a comprehensive list of headings to arrange the budget under:

- payroll costs
- books and monographs
- electronic services
- periodicals, newspapers and serials
- interlibrary loans
- communication costs
- training
- conferences
- office supplies
- accommodation costs.

What to use depends upon the type of library and organisation concerned. Public libraries will include most of these headings in that they are responsible for budgeting for staff, all service costs and stock acquisitions. Commercial LIS may well just use the stock acquisitions headings or, as in Figure 2, split the budget by user group type.

Costings

Assigning an accurate cost or recovery figure for each budget heading will require carrying out a cost analysis exercise for the particular items it covers. It should not be a case of current cost plus inflation. This exercise needs to include the organisation's plans for the forth-coming year or whatever time period the budget is expected to cover.

Communication is a crucial part of this exercise in that the LIS financial planner needs to be aware of user group opinion on existing services. This includes stock provision and changing information needs. Expenditure may well need to be redirected if current services are no longer required or failing to cope with demand levels. Similarly, what library holdings will be required, and how the user should best access them, will need to be considered.

This communication is two-way in that the LIS financial planner should be making other budget holders aware of any impact LIS may be making on their budget. For example, informing personnel about salaries and recruitment needs; the line manager about training needs; the IT section about new equipment requirements.

In the main, LIS departments are support functions and tend to be under threat in a cost cutting exercise. A cost analysis exercise should therefore be aiming to place a cost value on the continued existence of the service. A calculation should be made on the true cost of stopping or outsourcing particular information tasks to external agencies. Any 'value added' elements need to be clarified in financial terms – for example, if the LIS department provided information in a successful client pitch then there is every reason for this to be mentioned in the budget.

Speaking to publishers will provide a guide to expected cost rises in publications and any new services being offered for the oncoming year. Such information can be used as the platform to base any budget headings for stock acquisitions.

Finally, any cost analysis should cover not just the specific headings within the LIS budget but all other expenditure the LIS department incurs or income it generates. If the LIS financial planner is aware of this expenditure and income then it can be promoted (or hidden!) during the budget presentation.

Budget presentation

The third part of the financial planning process is the budget presentation. This should not be regarded as just a request for funding but an opportunity to promote the value of the LIS service.

Budgetary timetable

There will inevitably be a budgetary timetable to follow and it is important to be aware of it so that sufficient time is allocated to carry out any cost analysis exercises and write up the budget itself. Also, allow time to carry out any rewrites. Before presenting it to the budget committee or whoever is responsible for approving it, let the LIS department line manager look at it so they can make any final recommendations or changes. Once it has been presented, it may be returned to the financial planner to make further changes before being presented again. Even then it may still not be approved, particularly if other departments are presenting strong arguments for taking a bigger slice of the funding pie. Once the presentation merry-go-round is completed do not assume that the budget has been approved. If overall organisational costs exceed expected revenue then it may well be trimmed. Speak to the finance department to get confirmation for what the final approved budget is.

Written submission

How to present the budget depends largely upon what the organisation requires but the following sections should, if possible, be included.

Background information

This provides information on the LIS department and its role within the organisation; it should be concise and not too detailed. It should state the LIS objectives and how they relate to the parent organisation's objectives. This is a chance to promote the service and market its value to the organisation.

Plans for the period of the budget

Briefly highlight any LIS plans for the period of the budget, particularly if they represent a change from the current set-up. Continuing with existing arrangements can also be promoted – for example, the financial planner may have looked at what financial benefits could be accrued by outsourcing a particular service item and discovered it would be more cost effective to let it remain inhouse.

The budget proposal

This is the actual figures and headings themselves. Where necessary, background information should be provided. The figures may all be contained within a single, overall heading or separated out. Any capital expenditure proposals will normally be kept apart from the normal expenditure budget. This is the section to highlight any other LIS expenditure or income that has gone into another department's budget. For example, IT may have agreed to provide funds for a library CD tower, or human resources to pay for some vacation workers.

Phasing

It is important to include in the budget presentation any phasing of LIS expenditure. It is unlikely that expenditure will be evenly spread over the length of the budget. Therefore, if possible, provide a timetable for the finance department indicating expenditure high and low points so they can be prepared.

Budget presentation

The formal budget presentation itself is an opportunity to sell the LIS service. As already highlighted, it is important to provide relevant background information about the LIS department and to explain any changes to the budget. Equally, the budget and the department should be linked to the organisation. Show awareness of other departments' roles and how the budget covers their information needs. The presentation should not be just a request for funds but a means of marketing the service to the organisation.

Financial control

Financial control is the final part of the financial planning process and relates to the procedures that may be applied by the LIS department to record and manage its expenditure and income generation activities. What procedures to use will, again, be influenced by the expectations of the parent organisation but the following should be considered.

Book-keeping

The LIS department should have some formal book-keeping procedure to record all of its financial transactions. In most cases a simple spreadsheet will suffice. Financial details need to be entered for committed as well as actual expenditure so that a full financial picture can be produced. Committed expenditure covers standing orders, regular renewals and items ordered but not yet received. Exact figures for some of this cost information may not be available but if the spreadsheets are maintained over more than one budgetary period it is possible to make a reasonable guess based on previous charges. Spreadsheets can also be used to indicate inflationary trends and peaks and troughs in expenditure levels.

Figure 3 is an example of a spreadsheet used for monitoring expenditure for a library book budget. Columns C and D contain the publisher and title information. Columns A and F show corresponding invoice times and costs for the previous financial year. Columns B and E show times and costs for the current year. The current budget column automatically keeps a running total of costs, including predicted costs, to date. The actual budget for the year has been included along with the amount that remains to be spent.

Figure 3: Book budget 2000/01

A	B	C	D	E	F
1999/00	2000/1	Publisher	Title	Cost 2000/1	Cost 1999/00
Sept	Sept	Butterworths	*Yellow Tax Handbook* 1999/2000 for library x 1	£ 45.00	£ 45.00
Feb-00		CANS Trust	CANS – sub 04/00-03/01	£ 90.00	£ 87.50
Dec		CCH	*Absence Manual*	£ 242.00	£ 231.95
Jan	Jan	CCH	*British Company Law* – Ann Sub	£ 550.00	£ 520.50
Jun-99	June	CCH	British Personnel 5/00-4/01	£ 425.00	£ 404.72
	June	Waterlows	O'Brien's *Goodenough at Last*	£ 29.99	-
	Ordered	Waterlows	Smith's *Employment Law*	£ 50.00	-
			Current total (including predicted expenditure)	£ 1,431.99	
			Budget for year	£ 10,000.00	
			Remainder to spend	£ 8,568.01	

As well as keeping a track of expenditure, a benefit of keeping such a spreadsheet is that it reduces the likelihood of paying for the same goods twice. Finance departments often have just one invoice payment run a month. Meantime many suppliers operate a 30 day credit system and if they do not receive payment within time may send out a second invoice, sometimes with a different invoice number. This creates the risk of a busy finance department accidentally paying both the original and the chaser. By running its own spreadsheet of orders the LIS department should pick up the duplication and be able to cancel the second invoice.

Acquisitions policy

Written guidelines on what policies to follow when ordering material is a useful way of ensuring that LIS staff responsible for buying are aware of what procedure to follow. This is particularly useful for new members of staff still learning the job. Such a guide could include details on the titles and products that need to be ordered and renewed to maintain the LIS collection. These may well cover the full range of formats from books through to online, each of which may be ordered in different ways. There could also be information about the different types of orders that may exist, such as renewals for existing subscriptions, standing orders and new acquisitions. Details about suppliers could also be recorded.

Information could be added to clarify what level of authority is required to place orders, plus details on how and where to record orders once they are made. Other advice might be how to raise cheques and the process to follow to pass invoices through for payment.

Financial reporting

Regular financial reporting is a useful exercise in that it allows the LIS financial planner to see how expenditure is compared to budget. By using a spreadsheet they can be aware of how much is being spent over a particular time period, a particular service or user group. As well as providing actual information, reports can be used to analyse trends and conditions. For example, spreadsheets covering several years could be analysed to highlight pricing movements.

Reporting is an important way to monitor and control finance. Expenditure and income generation budgets need to be regularly looked at so that financial trends and concerns can be picked up early and dealt with. There are plenty of financial packages available to process financial information and generate a range of different reports. As ever, what is important is not how sophisticated the package is, but what is needed by the organisation.

Conclusion

I will conclude with two points. Firstly, libraries and financial planning do not sit well together. Libraries are not expected to make money but to provide information. The successful financial planner will be an excellent communicator, wide-focused, and proactive within the parent organisation – skills not traditionally associated with the library. Secondly, that IT is changing all of this. Much of this section has been based around personal experience acquired from working in the private commercial sector where strategies and objectives centre on the bottom line and libraries are treated as necessary overheads – a sort of second class citizen compared to the departments generating the income. Libraries are not expected to make money. Thus, financial planning is based around expenditure requests to pay for relevant information resources. However, IT has altered the image of information. It has moved it away from the books and journals and onto the screen. One financial consequence of this has been a shift in investment from bay units and binding to hardware and software. A second, possibly much more interesting consequence, has been the growing awareness that information services can be packaged and developed into financial opportunities. In the USA, the LIS financial planners in legal practices are expected to generate income and run their departments as profit centres (which are consequently, treated as assets rather than overheads). The UK is now moving in this direction and starting to look more seriously at the selling potential of information.

References

Basker, J. Resourcing the information centre. In: A. Scammell (ed.) *Handbook of Special Librarianship*. London: Aslib (1997, 7th ed.) 81-100.

Hodgson, K. Charging for library services: a commercial law firm perspective. *Law Librarian*, **30**(3) 1999, 173-7.

McKay, D. *Financial Planning for Library and Information services*. London: Aslib (1995) (Aslib Know How Guide).

Roberts, S. A. *Cost Management for Library and Information Services*. London: Butterworths (1985).

Spiller D. et al. *Libraries in the Workplace*. Loughborough: Library & Information Statistics Unit (1998) (LISU Occasional Paper no. 20).

Webb, S.P. The management portfolio: essential skills for the LIS practitioner. *Law Librarian*, **26**(3) 1995, 428-30.

Webb, S.P. *Making a Charge for Library and Information Services*. London: Aslib (1994) (Aslib Know How Guide).

Chapter 15

Project management

Barbara Allan

Introduction

This chapter is aimed at LIS (Library and Information Service) staff who are involved in project management. It will be relevant to LIS project managers working on either small projects where they are the only person working on the project or large complex projects where there is a project team made up of staff from different departments.

The ideas in this chapter originate from a number of different sources that include: the author's experience of project management in LIS (closing a LIS, moving a library, creating a new LIS, automating a library service, managing a collaborative project across four organisations for the development of multimedia learning resources); feedback from participants on Aslib's training programmes in project management; feedback from other information and knowledge management professionals; and the project management literature.

What is project management? Project management involves planning, organising and managing the activities and means which lead to the achievement of a defined objective. It involves taking into account time, staffing and financial resources. The project management process may take less than an hour or, for very complex projects, it may be a full time job. In all situations, the basic techniques are the same. All projects have a number of features in common. They:

- have a definite start and end date
- involve a new or innovative process
- are affected by limiting factors e.g. resources
- have a single point of responsibility
- normally result in change.

LIS projects can be classified according to their level: those that take place at a strategic level and those that take place at an operational level. Strategic change is very distinctive and changes the direction of the organisation. It may result in a changed mission and vision and will certainly result in new goals. Strategic change involves a major change and will have a far-reaching impact on the organisation and the staff (and possibly customers). This type of change normally takes place over months and years. Examples of strategic level projects include:

- merger of two distinct LIS services
- introduction of a no smoking policy
- introduction of a new appraisal scheme
- introduction of new working conditions and practices.

Operational change happens constantly and results in changes to a particular activity within an organisation. They may only have an impact on a small group of staff. This type of change normally takes place over days and weeks. Examples of projects at an operational level include:

- introduction of a new web-based service
- introduction of a new IT system into a department
- introduction of new team working arrangements in a department
- relocation of an office
- introduction of a new approach to answering telephone calls
- organising a conference.

This classification is not absolute and if you are involved in project management it is worthwhile identifying which level you need to be working at. This is important as projects that lead to achieve change at a strategic level tend to require a change in culture and attitudes. This involves a more in-depth management of change process than projects that take place only at an operational level. Project managers who are not aware of this difference may find that they are having to deal with a backlash to their project as a result of the cultural changes associated with the new strategy not having been addressed.

Projects vary in their complexity from relatively simple projects, such as organising a conference, through to very complex projects such as the development of multimedia archives by collaborative groups working across three or more European countries and funded by the European Union. Factors that affect the complexity of a project include:

- speed of the project
- speed of change
- level of innovation
- availability of key resources
- volumes of data involved
- connections with other projects
- involvement of different teams
- involvement of different organisations

- working across different national boundaries.

The more complex the project then the greater the potential for failure and the greater the need to use project management techniques to ensure that the project outcomes are delivered on time and within the available resources.

Project cycle

All projects involve the following cyclical process and this presents the structure for the next few sections:

- defining the project
- basic project planning
- planning the schedule
- staffing the project
- costing the project
- developing a communication strategy
- project management and reporting
- implementation
- management of change
- project completion.

Defining the project

An important first stage in a project is to define the project and its boundaries. It may be that you are an LIS manager who has a good idea and wants to go ahead and make it happen. Alternatively, you may have been given responsibility for a project and asked to deliver the project outcomes within a limited budget and timescale.

Defining the project involves identifying the basic project idea (or vision) and what the project must achieve – what the project outcomes are. These need to be clearly identified and compared with the LIS and the organisation's objectives. If the project does not support these objectives then the proposed project could result in a diversion of staff time and resources.

The scope of the project also needs to be identified. Many projects start off with a small scope and then, depending on the success of the first phase of the project, will expand its scope. For example, the scope of a project on the design and development of multimedia-based learning materials limited the project to the development of three basic resources. Once these had been produced and the project evaluated the scope was broadened to another subject area. Sometimes a project will exclude some aspect of work and this needs to be clearly identified with the rationale behind this decision.

The timescale of the project needs to be considered too. What are the proposed start and end dates? How do these fit in with the LIS service requirements? It is worthwhile identifying some project milestones which are important landmarks in the project process. Two obvious milestones are the project start and end. In a project involving moving a library, milestones could include: end of weeding of stock, end of changing catalogue records, all periodicals moved to new location, all books moved to new location. These provide useful measures for evaluating and celebrating the success of the project throughout the project process.

At the project definition stage you will also need to consider the resourcing requirements of the project. At this stage, there is no need to carry out a detailed staffing or financial analysis but there does need to be some indication of the staffing costs and also the financial costs of the project.

It is important to think about how you are going to manage the project and the systems and structures you need in place to both support you as project manager and also the project. This will depend on the size and complexity of your project.

If you are working on a large or complex project then it is well worthwhile involving two different groups of staff in the project process. The management group will be concerned with the overall project strategy and resolving significant problems. If you establish a management group then it is worthwhile including a few senior members of staff who are likely to be allies if the going gets tough. The project team is the group of staff who deal with the project operation, they resolve day-to-day problems and report to the management group. In a year-long project the management group is likely to meet quarterly while the project group is likely to meet on monthly.

In very small or simple projects the project team may be one person while in more complex and larger projects it may be a group of staff either in the same or different LIS. The scope for selecting team members is often limited in smaller LIS and it is often based on identifying people with specific knowledge and skills, interest and enthusiasm for the project. In many situations we have no choice as to who are members of the project team and the project manager may have to lead demotivated or unenthusiastic staff. In practice I have found it useful to include a couple of members of staff who take on a 'critical friend' role. These people often provide a helpful counter-balance to the positive enthusiasts who do not always see potential problem areas. The people side of the project management process is considered in more depth on page 338.

Example

In major projects there is often the need to develop a fairly complex project team structure. The University of Westminster used the following structure for the design and implementation of their new learning resource centre:

'There was an inner planning group (which had representatives from each group of staff,) who looked at the overall structure. This group then devised other planning groups (representatives from the whole of IRS across the whole university) in a brainstorming session and designated the project group leaders and other members. These groups fed their findings back to the inner planning group.

There were project groups on shelving, group study rooms, the exhibition area, the special needs area, the design workshop area, non-book material, the counter, furniture, the reception area, the clean and dirty workshop etc. So the project groups looked at specific functional areas and not overall policy.

A lot of the donkey work was done by these groups, although in some there was an enthusiastic leader who did most of the work, and the other members were apathetic. Some groups worked very well and it gave the people the chance to work on something quite different. Overall the response was very good.'

From: An interview by Bill Downey with Juliet Dye (1996) The learning resource centre, the University of Westminster, UK, *http://www.lgu.ac.uk/deliberations/lrc/westminster.html*.

One product from the project definition stage is the project brief which is a summary of the proposed project on one sheet of A4. This is likely to cover the following topics: project aim, project outcomes, project scope, timescale, resource requirements, proposed project team, other key issues. This brief can then be used at the initial project meetings and as a communication tool with other staff.

The team needs to come up with a project name. This can be dealt with as a team activity although care needs to be taken if cynical team members come up with less than helpful names. One project I came across was called the LIMP project while others had names that cannot be repeated!

Project definition

The project definition is an official document which can be used to obtain agreement from senior managers and directors on the project. It clearly defines the project, the project timescale and the resource requirements.

Different organisations use different forms of project definitions and it is worthwhile finding out if your organisation uses one. The project definition is likely to contain information under the following headings.

Project definition
Introduction
Purpose
Background
Goals and objectives
Scope and limitations
Strategy
Description of main activities
Project schedule
– GANTT, PERT, Critical path analysis
Resources and costings
List of staff and their involvement
Connections to other activities
Communication strategy
Management structure
Reporting schedule
Risks
Quality standards, processes and procedures
Intellectual property, patents and licenses
Insurance
Distribution list
Formal approval (signature, name, date)

Basic project planning

The basic project planning process involves the following steps:

- review of project brief
- analysis of work content
- planning the schedule
- staffing the project
- costing the project
- developing a communications strategy.

This information is then used to complete the project definition described in the previous section. In a small and relatively simple project this planning process may take less than an hour and involve tools no more complicated than paper, pen and calculator. In a complex project then you are likely to use the type of project management tools described below. There are many different computer software packages that will help you to manage the project and its information. These are described in a separate section on page 350.

Review of project brief

If you start the basic project planning process by reviewing the project brief then it will remind you and your team of the project's aims, outcomes and key features. This will set the scene and also the boundaries to the project.

As project manager you may find it helpful to review the project using the set of questions presented in Table 1. If there are a significant number of 'no' answers then it is worthwhile reconsidering your involvement in the project.

Table 1: Project review, adapted from Smith (1997)

Potential questions to ask	Responses
The project	
Is the project linked to the organisation's aims and objectives?	
Is the project concerned with a specific issue or problem within the organisation?	
Is the project linked to current organisational development and change?	
Is the project capable of solution?	
Is the project clearly defined?	
Has the project got clear boundaries?	
Does the project offer a challenge and provide a stretch, and is not a set of clerical routines?	
Within the timescale is it possible to make a real impact on the project?	
Will the project require involvement, co-operation and commitment of other colleagues?	
Does the project contain a 'technical' element?	
Does the project contain a 'people' element?	
Working in the organisation	
Will I be able to gain organisational support and agreement for me to undertake this project?	
Will the organisation invest in time be spent clearly defining the project?	
Will I be able to have access to the necessary information, resources, people to carry out this project?	
Will I have sufficient time to carry out this project i.e. as part of my normal working day?	
Will I be able to adopt new or innovative approaches to tackle this project?	
Will I have the support of my line manager?	
Will I have the support of my mentor?	
Is there anyone else's support that I need before I start this project?	
Working on the project	
Am I sufficiently interested in this project?	
Am I able to identify my likely personal outcomes from working on this project clearly?	
Does this project fit in with my long-term career plans?	

Analysis of work content

For all types of projects it is important to analyse the work content of the project and this involves the following processes:

* identification of specific outcomes (SMART)
* identification of tasks or activities
* identification of recurrent tasks
* identify milestones.

The specific outcomes of the project are best identified as SMART outcomes where the acronym SMART stands for Specific, Measurable, Achievable, Realistic, Timebound.

> Example
>
> An example of a SMART outcome when moving a library of 100,000 items over a three month period was:
>
> To move 100,000 items from their old to their new location and to have every book in the correct location with catalogue amendments by 1 September 2000.

A simple and practical way of analysing the work content is to ask the team members to identify the specific tasks or activities that will need to take place for the project to be completed. Each task is then written on a post-it note (see Figure 1). Next ask them to estimate how long each task will take. They need to write this down on each post-it note. Then ask them to arrange the tasks in logical order i.e. using the logic

$$A \quad \longrightarrow \quad B$$

where B can't take place until A is completed.

A simple way of carrying out this process is to lay the post-it notes on flipchart paper and to draw the arrows on the paper. Ask them to number each task and write this on the post-it note.

Recurrent tasks are those that are repeated at regular intervals throughout the project. Examples of recurrent tasks include regular project team meetings, sending out a weekly project news bulletin, updating the project spreadsheet. Milestones can be added by writing the milestone onto a different coloured post-it note and including these in the logic network. Examples of milestones include project start, project end, end of Phase 1. It is important to be aware that a milestone is a significant landmark in the life of a project and that a specific task or activity is not associated with a milestone.

Figure 1: Identification of tasks using post-it notes

Task number		Estimated time
	Name of task	
Earliest start date		Latest start date

Task number = 14		Estimated time = 2 hours
	Install software	
Earliest start date = 12/11/00		Latest start date = 18/11/00

The next step is to work through the activities starting from the beginning and identifying the earliest start date and earliest finish date for each task. Write these dates on the relevant post-it note. Then work through the activities starting from the latest finish date identifying the latest start date and latest finish date for each task. Write this on the relevant post-it note.

The critical path is the set of activities where the earliest and latest finish dates are the same. In other words, the timing is crucial if the project is to remain on schedule. Any time slippages across the critical path have a major impact on the project.

If you are working with a project team of six or more people then it can be fun to split them into two teams, ask each team to carry out this activity and to compare the results of the two teams. The best of both the models can then be used to create the final plan.

Planning the schedule 2

The previous task provides a useful insight into the project management process. Using post-it notes and flipchart paper is a useful way of planning relatively small projects. For larger or complex projects it is worthwhile using standard project management tools as a means of organising and working with the project data. These tools are now commonly available in project management software (see page 350) and they include two very important and useful tools:

- GANTT charts
- PERT charts.

A GANTT chart is a bar chart that shows the relationship between the project tasks and the timescale of the project. The name GANTT comes from their developer Henry Gantt (1861-1919). An example is shown below:

Figure 2: Example section of a GANTT chart

	January	February	March	April
Book conference facilities				
Book speakers				
Produce publicity materials				
Mail shot				

GANTT charts are easy to read as they can have a powerful visual effect of indicating the links between the project tasks and the life of the project. They provide a position statement that shows tasks in relationship to time, milestones and also tasks that take place in parallel. This can be very useful for identifying busy times in the project life. The main disadvantages of GANTT charts are that they do not show relationships between tasks and they do not show a critical path.

Another way of obtaining a clear picture and also detailed information about the project is to produce a PERT chart. PERT stands for Programme Evaluation and Review Technique and this type of chart was developed in the United States. A PERT chart shows the logic network of the tasks i.e. the chart produced in the post-it note activity. PERT charts:

- provide a critical path
- show relationships between tasks
- are similar to flow charts
- show milestones
- provide a view of the complexity of the project.

However, they can be large and difficult to work from. If you use project management software then it can be very difficult to see the whole view of the project on a single screen.

Most project management software packages will produce both GANTT and PERT charts automatically. Project management software is covered on page 350.

Staffing the project

Once you have planned the project and worked out the project schedule then you will know the tasks that need to be carried out and you will also have an estimate of how long each task will take to complete. This original estimate can be worked out in a more detailed way using the following standard project management calculation.

For each task you need to identify three different estimates:

t_o the most optimistic (i.e. the shortest)

t_m the most likely or probable

t_p the most pessimistic (i.e. the longest).

You then take these three estimates and calculate the expected time for each activity using the following formula:

$$t_e = (t_o + 4 t_m + t_p)/6$$

The next stage is to identify the staff required to carry out specific tasks. This step involves identifying the skills and knowledge required to complete each task successfully and then matching these with the staff taking into account their availability. In practice this will involve negotiating with their team leaders or managers so that you obtain the staff you require for the project and the LIS continues to function. One aspect that is worth spending some time on is the role the project will take in the staff development process. Staff may be involved in the project as a means of fulfilling their staff development needs as well as contributing to the project outcomes.

In some projects, such as those that are externally funded, resources are available to pay for temporary contract staff. These people will then need to be selected and recruited. This process, unless part of the original project plan, can add to the timescale of the project. One disadvantage of recruiting temporary contract staff is that, as a result of fears of unemployment or due to advertised opportunities, they may leave the project before it is complete. This can leave the project manager with a staffing shortage often at the vital implementation or evaluation stage of the project.

Some LIS projects are essentially summer vacation projects particularly in academic library and information services. In these LIS staff regularly move, close down or open new libraries during the long vacation. This can pose a particular problem for project managers as key team members may be on vacation during the crucial project phases. One way of overcoming potential problems caused by staff absence is to appoint pairs of people (who are taking their leave at different times) to be responsible for particular tasks. This provides cover during the leave and it can also provide a staff development opportunity for a less experienced member of staff.

Once you have identified the members of staff who will be involved in the project then it is time to allocate them to their specific tasks in the project plan. At this stage, it is important to make sure that their time is not over-allocated i.e. that they are not required to work more than a reasonable number of hours on the project each day and also that they have sufficient time to carry out their 'normal' activities. This process is called resource levelling and many project management software packages will carry out this function (see page 350).

Planning other resources

The resources needed to carry out the project also need to be taken into account in the planning process. They include:

- durable equipment
- software
- consumables
- external assistance, e.g. consultant, trainers
- printing
- travel and subsistence
- miscellaneous.

At the planning stage it is worthwhile identifying all the resources that are likely to be required for the project. Discussions with the project team and also the LIS administrative team will help you to produce a list of all the required items. In large and complex projects it is worthwhile bidding for a contingency fund to cover unexpected events and requirements.

Example

One library move project I was involved in was delayed by a week due to an outbreak of fleas that came to light when furniture was moved in the library. As well as the delay in the project schedule, money had to be found to pay for the area to be decontaminated!

Costing the project

Costing the project is a relatively straightforward activity. You will need to identify all the likely costs of the project and present them in a suitable manner. Many organisations have their own sets of guidelines and rules for costing projects and it is worthwhile contacting the finance department before you start this stage in the project. The list of headings that you will need to consider is likely to be similar to that considered in the resourcing section:

- staff
- durable equipment
- software
- consumables
- external assistance, e.g. consultant, trainers
- printing
- travel and subsistence
- miscellaneous
- VAT.

Staffing is likely to be a major cost and it is important to calculate it using the following type of standard equation:

Daily rate = (annual salary + on-costs)/days

Days = working days per year – (annual leave + weekends + statutory days + sick leave)

The on-costs are the costs to the organisation of employing a member of staff. This is likely to consist of employer-related National Insurance contributions and pension contributions and this is typically 20 per cent of the gross salary. In many externally funded projects a fixed overhead is also charged for labour and this may be as much as 20 per cent. This takes the on-costs to 40 per cent. It is important to know the rules of your own organisation before calculating the staff costs.

If your project is going to last more than a year then any likely pay rises (e.g. cost of living or performance-related pay rises) will need to be included in the costings.

The other project costs will need to be worked out and included in your project plan. An important detail is whether or not you can claim VAT on purchases. This is a grey area and very complicated so it is best to obtain specialist advice on this subject, perhaps from your finance department. The situation varies depending on the organisation you are involved in and the sources of funding for the project, for example European-funded projects are allegedly VAT exempt. The best solution is to obtain up-to-date specialist advice and to keep every piece of paperwork related to the project.

Monitoring costs

Once the project starts you will need to monitor the project costs and this is most easily managed using a spreadsheet and updating it regularly. You will need to keep a cumulative report which shows the actual and the planned costs. This will enable you to respond to unexpected changes in expenditure. Monthly reports can be used to show current situation.

Developing a communication strategy

This is an important part of the planning process and it involves identifying:

- Who will be working on the project?
- Who will be affected by the project?
- When do we need to communicate?
- Who is responsible for implementing the communications strategy?
- With whom will you communicate?
- What will you communicate?
- How you will communicate?
- What channels are required for feedback?
- Who is responsible for giving, receiving and acting on feedback?

It is worthwhile working through these questions with the project team and using your answers to develop a communication strategy.

Ideas from communication studies (O'Connor, 1990) suggest that people are convinced about new ideas in different ways. Each person has their own preferred style of receiving information and they are also influenced by the timing of this process. The preferred ways of receiving information are visual, auditory, or activity based, e.g. by doing it or reading about it. In addition, there is the time element to this process of being convinced about something: some people have an automatic convincer, others need to receive the new information or ideas a number of times (typically three); other people will need a few weeks; and a small number of people are never convinced!

This model offers some useful ideas about the communication process. In general, you will need to use as many different forms of communication as possible and this is likely to include: meetings, presentations, workshops, briefings, emails, newsletters, posters, memos, letters and reports. You will also need to repeat your message a number of times over the time period of the project.

Example

I was involved in managing a summer moving project in a university LIS department. One of the project team members convincer pattern was of the 'never' variety. Throughout the project he constantly pointed out that we would never meet our deadlines or targets. We did achieve them. He had to have the final word and chipped in to say that 'of course it was a fluke and we were just lucky, we will never be able to achieve that result a second time'. Words failed me!

For project managers (and indeed all LIS managers and team leaders) it is worthwhile being conscious of this pattern of taking on board new ideas. If you are working with someone who will never be convinced about something then it is a waste of time to put effort into convincing them.

If you want to find out how someone is convinced about something then the simple question 'What will convince you . . . ?' will produce the information you need to inform your communication strategy with that person.

Project management and reporting

The project management and reporting process involves a number of distinct activities:

- two-way communications between the project manager and the management group
- two-way communications between the project manager and team.

The project manager is likely to produce regular reports aimed at the management group, the project group and also interested external parties such as the funding agency. These reports may include:

- progress reports
- management reports
- milestone reports
- financial reports
- final report(s).

The number and content of these reports will depend on the type of project. Small projects may involve a reporting process no more complicated than a weekly email to a manager or team leader while externally funded projects may require reports written to a particular format at set times during the project life.

An essential part of the communication strategy is how project team members report to the project manager. The reporting process enables the project manager to identify:

- significant dates and milestones
- significant constraints
- potential problems
- existing problems
- creep in project time
- slack in project.

Nowadays much of the communication processes between a large or distributed project team is likely to take place electronically and this is covered on page 346.

> Example
>
> In a project that involved five LIS staff working together to produce multimedia resources the staff agreed to communicate via a discussion group on the organisational intranet. They each agreed to communicate progress (or lack of progress) by email every Friday before 11 am. This meant that the project manager didn't have to chase up individual team members to discuss their progress.

Implementation

Once the project starts then the project manager and team members are likely to be involved in a number of distinct activities:

- monitoring and controlling the project
- monitoring the communication strategy
- informing the team of developments
- supporting and encouraging the team
- networking with key staff, e.g. senior managers.

Monitoring the project involves monitoring a number of different aspects of the project's life. The first of these is staff motivation and morale and these can be monitored though written and spoken communications. This is where 'management by walking about' becomes important as informal conversations and joint coffee breaks can sometimes uncover problems that would otherwise be missed.

It is also important to monitor the project tasks or activities and to identify the tasks that have started and also ended. In the initial stages of a project it is important to check up the accuracy of estimates of staff time. These also need to be monitored as the project progresses and the project plan needs to be adapted accordingly, for instance, towards the end of a major project the amount of time it takes for staff to complete specific activities may rise or fall depending on their state of jubilation or exhaustion!

It is important to monitor the match of the plan with reality and also to identify any blockages. The importance of monitoring the expenditure has already been mentioned. If the monitoring process identifies significant changes to the project plan then it is important to act quickly. One of the advantages of having identified the critical project path is that this is the set of tasks or activities that must be kept to schedule if the project is not to overrun. This information provides clear guidance to the project manager on where to focus action if the project starts to deviate from its plan.

The communication strategy will include the processes whereby the project manager and team communicate to the stakeholders. The project manager will need to monitor the effectiveness of the communication strategy and also be responsive to any negative responses to the project.

The project team will need to be kept informed about progress of the project and any key developments. This can be achieved through a number of different activities: meetings; emails, project newsletter. These activities also provide a mechanism whereby the project manager can give positive feedback and support to the team .

In some projects it is worthwhile considering the importance of networking with key staff either through formal or informal channels. Being part of an active network can be very useful if you need information or advice at very short notice. The many email discussion groups indicate the importance of this information source.

The people side of change

When you are introducing major changes into the LIS then you are likely to be subject to pressures that will make this change process difficult. These pressures may be the result of the working environment, for example inappropriate organisational structures or a change-resistant culture. A major cause of resistance to change is the responses of individuals to the change process.

The actual response to the project and its resultant changes will depend on a variety of factors. Some changes may be viewed as positive, such as moving to a new building with fabulous resources, or negative, such as the merging of two units or departments. Some changes will be major, for example restructuring of a LIS with job losses, some will be relatively monir, such as changing over to a new IT system. In essence the more staff have invested in the old situation and the greater their need to change in response to the new scenario then the greater their psychological responses to the change. This means that the management of change becomes even more important in these situations.

Many people feel apprehensive about going through a change process and they may go through a psychological process that is similar to that experienced in bereavement. Individual responses to change typically involve a number of distinct phases:

- phase 1: shock
- phase 2: defensive retreat
- phase 3: acknowledgement
- phase 4: adaption and change.

The shock phase may be signalled by staff feeling overwhelmed by the news and responding with panic, feelings of helplessness, numbness and shock. This phase may last minutes, hours, days or weeks. This is then often followed by what is called a defensive retreat where staff may attempt to maintain old structures and avoid their new reality. This stage is sometimes accompanied by feelings of indifference, euphoria or anger. Again, this stage may last from minutes to weeks. The next stage is the one where staff begin to acknowledge the situation and begin to face reality. This stage may be accompanied by feelings of indifference or bitterness. The final stage is one of adaption and change and here staff begin to build their lives and gradually gain their confidence and self esteem in the new situation.

As a project manager an awareness of these responses to change is important as at different stages you will need to focus on different aspects of the change process. For example when staff are experiencing shock it is important to focus on the communication processes and to provide lots of opportunity to explain the current situation. You will need to remember that they may not remember everything that has been communicated to them and so you are likely to need to repeat the message, perhaps many times and give lots of reassurance. The different strategies required for managing and supporting people through change are summarised in Figure 3.

Figure 3: Managing and supporting people through change

Be adaptable	Provide a vision for the future
Delegate	Explain and keep on explaining
Monitor	Talk to individuals
Support	Communicate, communicate, communicate
Mentor	
Encourage flexibility of approach	Listen, listen, listen
Value considered risk taking	Give reassurance
	Put the change into perspective
	Do not give out too much information – keep it simple
	Handle people with great sensitivity
	Keep your feet on the ground
	Be available
Phase 4 **Adjustment**	**Phase 1** **Shock**
Phase 3 **Acknowledgement**	**Phase 2** **Defensive retreat**
Provide more detailed information	Don't panic!
Keep listening	Don't take staff reactions personally
Evaluate options	Keep listening
Support realistic ideas and strategies	Allow people to let off steam
You don't have to provide ALL the answers	Highlight the positives
	Keep meetings to the point
Provide direction not control	Don't get hooked into win–lose situation
Involve as many people as possible in the planning process	Don't get hooked into critical parent
Acknowledge positively people's efforts	Use a wide range of strategies

Project completion

The project completion process involves checking that the project has achieved all of its outcomes. The formal project reports will need to be written and also any informal reports or letters, for example informing interested parties of the successful achievement of project outcomes and the end of the project.

Decisions will need to be made about completing any loose ends and, if appropriate, handing the project over to another team. An important part of the project completion stage is evaluating and reviewing the project and this is covered in the next section.

An important final stage is to thank the people who have been involved in the project and to celebrate the project successes.

Project evaluation

The purposes of carrying out a project evaluation process are to:

* improve the performance of the current project
* improve the performance of future projects
* provide evidence of the impact of the project on services, products and people
* contribute to the development of the staff involved in the project.

Different projects will base their project evaluation process around different parameters

Example

The eLib project evaluation process identified six design principles and the main questions that needed to be addressed as:

Evaluation design principles	Key questions
Purposes of evaluation	What are the main purposes of evaluation?
Stakeholders	Who are the different actors who have a stake in the project and its evaluation?
Lifecycle	What evaluation activities are appropriate at different stages of the project life cycle?
Utilisation	How will evaluation be integrated into the project?
User involvement	How will users be involved in evaluation?
Methods and techniques	What kinds of evaluation questions will be asked and what assessment methods are appropriate?

Adapted from: Kellecher, J. et al. *Evaluation of the electronic Libraries Programme. Guidelines for eLib evaluation.* The Tavistock Institute (1996). (Available at *http://www.ukoln.ac.uk/services/elib/papers/tavistock/evaluation-guide/*).

The project review process may involve an evaluation and review of:

- overall project process
- use of project management tools
- effectiveness of project (did you achieve your project aims?)
- efficiency of project (was your project process efficient in terms of the use of resources?)
- impact on other people within your organisation.

This process may be carried out by external or internal evaluators who may involve LIS staff, project team members and other stakeholders including customers.

Working with the project team

A key factor in the success of project work in LIS is successful project team working. Nowadays LIS projects often involve teams of staff working within the same or different LIS . It may involve staff working in different LIS sectors, for example special LIS and public sector LIS. In addition, it may involve staff working within the same or different geographical locations and also virtual teams who rarely or even never have face-to-face meetings. This suggests that it is very important for LIS project managers to spend some time on working with and developing the project team.

Peter Honey (1991) has identified the following positive behaviours which contribute to effective team work.

Wanted behaviour	Unwanted behaviour
Asking questions	Acquiescing
Suggesting ideas	Rubbishing ideas
Exploring alternatives	Going for expedient, quick fixes
Taking risks/experimenting	Being cautious
Being open about the way it is	Telling people what they want to hear
	Filtering news
Converting mistakes into learning	Repeating the same mistakes
Reflecting and reviewing	Rushing around keeping active
Talking about learning	Talking about anecdotes (i.e. what happened not what was learnt)
Taking responsibility for self	Not taking responsibility
	Passing the buck
Admitting inadequacies and mistakes	Justifying actions
	Blaming others

Strategies for developing these behaviours to develop an effective team include:

- specific skills training
- team development workshops
- team appraisal processes
- individual appraisal processes
- role modelling of required behaviours
- rewarding wanted behaviours.

Initial project team meeting

A key factor for the success of the project is establishing a project team that will work effectively together. Once you have identified the proposed project team then you will need to invite them to an initial project team meeting. The outcomes for this team meeting are likely to be:

- introduce team members
- introduce the project
- agree the project vision and objectives
- agree team members and project manager's responsibilities
- agree the project brief and project name
- agree the production of a project definition.

The importance of the project vision and objectives is discussed in the next section. This initial meeting is all about getting to know each other and the proposed project. It is also about identifying and agreeing working practices. A useful way of establishing team member and project manager's responsibilities is to ask the meeting to split into sub groups and to for each group to identify the responsibilities of team members and the project manager. These can then be shared and written up on a flipchart. The final list can then be used as an informal contract for the project team. The project manager may find it useful to keep this flipchart paper then if people don't fulfil their responsibilities this activity can be revisited.

> Example
>
> When carrying out this activity during a LIS project the following suggestions were made:
>
> | Team members' responsibilities | Project manager's responsibilities |
> |---|---|
> | To attend project meetings | To organise, monitor and control project |
> | To agree realistic targets / deadlines | To keep the costs, meetings and administration to a minimum |

complete project tasks as agreed in meetings	To ensure that information about the project is communicated to the stakeholders
To inform team of current or potential problems	To keep the team informed of all developments
To provide or suggest potential solutions to problems	To give positive feedback and to support the team
To support team members and the project manager	To keep the project in line with LIS and organisation's policies and procedures
To manage their own time – for the project and routine LIS activities	To make sure the project complies with legal requirements
Not to whinge or whine	To provide tea and biscuits at project team meetings.

The project brief provides a useful starting point to ensuring that everyone understands the project and its boundaries. If necessary the brief can be edited in line with feedback from the team.

The final step is to agree who will produce a project definition and what this will cover.

Working across boundaries

The LIS profession has always had a tradition of networking and collaborative working either within an organisation, for example a LIS and IT department, LIS and training department, or across organisations, such as through professional groups, local, regional or national networks. Project managers are increasingly asked to lead project teams that involve LIS and perhaps other staff from organisations either within their sector or across sectors.

The benefits of this type of working include:

- enhanced quality
- increased diversity
- increased exposure to new ideas and approaches
- increased use of resources
- increased operational efficiency.

However, there are also some challenges to leading collaborative teams. These challenges to successful project team work may be the result of:

- long held rivalries
- different values and beliefs

- power struggles
- differing perceptions / perspectives
- potential commitment of large amounts of time, resources and energy
- differences in systems and procedures
- responses of people NOT involved.

As project manager it is worthwhile spending time helping to create effective partnerships. Teams that work across boundaries effectively are likely to display the following characteristics:

- synergy of culture and objectives
- shared vision
- commitment
- respect and honesty
- acknowledgement of the importance of effective teamwork.

This can be achieved by spending time in the first few team meetings on the following processes:

- surfacing expectations
- creating the vision
- building the objectives
- agreeing the action plan.

The process of surfacing expectations is a simple and yet very important one. Asking team members what they expect as part of being on the project team will enable similar, and also different, expectations to be aired and discussed. It will also help to prevent small issues becoming blockages to the project process.

> Example
>
> I was involved in a collaborative lifelong learning project which involved staff from six different organsiations. During the surfacing expectations activity it became very clear that different people had very different expectations as to the length of meetings that they would be involved in. For some team members it was very important to end meetings by 5 p.m. at the very latest while for other people they expected (and were quite happy about the idea) that meetings would run through until 6 or 7 p.m. As a group we agree that all meetings would end by 5 p.m. at the very latest. This discussion and decision helped to prevent conflict at a later stage in the project process.

Creating a vision involves creating a picture of our preferred future. A vision captures the hopes, desires and aspirations of a team. It is something that people will work towards and be motivated by. A vision inspires and captures the core values and beliefs of a team. A vision will enable a leader to inspire and motivate team members and enable them to translate the vision into reality.

A vision is an expression of hope and it is concerned with values and what really matters. We each have our own set of values – what is important to us, and examples of values include honesty, fairness, valuing people, excellence, innovative. By identifying a vision which matches individual and team values it is possible to inspire and motivate them.

To turn a vision into a reality we need objectives which are about strategy or how we will get there. The difference between vision and objectives can be expressed as:

- Vision is concerned with *values* – or what really matters.
- Objectives are about *strategy* – or how we will get there.

Once the project team has identified its objectives then it will need to develop and agree an action plan. This process of agreeing the vision and objectives is an important one and if the whole team are in complete accord with their vision and objectives then they will be able to work effectively together. Any conflicts or disagreements are likely to be easy to resolve as the basic foundations of excellent team working are there.

Managing virtual teams

There are two main types of virtual teams: those that use computer-mediated communications to supplement face-to-face meetings; and those that never meet face to face and whose whole life is carried out online. In LIS projects the former type of virtual team is more common than the later. Project teams are likely to use asynchronous web conferencing (e.g. using software such as FirstClass) or email as an important and significant part of the project process. As project manager it is worthwhile spending time and effort on getting the virtual team to work effectively in the same way in which you would get a face-to-face team to work effectively.

> Managing a virtual team meeting is not unlike managing a face-to-face team meeting; fruitful experiences don't happen by chance. There has been a lot of excitement about the potential of online networks to provide new environments for teams, communities of practice, and learning. But virtual meeting experiences can be frustrating and disappointing when interaction with others in the group results in information overload, topic drift, or conversations that are just not at all valuable (Kimball, 1997).

Working with a virtual team involves a similar process to working in face-to-face groups. Kimball (1997) identifies that, as with face-to-face teams, when you are working with virtual teams it is important to support them by:

- recognising team members and their importance
- encouraging members to explore questions that matter including questions about how they are working together
- supporting the creation of some kind of shared space (the feeling that there is an infrastructure where people are working together)
- facilitating the co-ordination of the technology, work processes, and the formal organisation
- recognising reflection as action and as legitimate work (getting the infrastructure of the organisation to support the learning process)
- supporting activities which make the virtual group visible.

In practice, as project manager you will find it helpful to:

- open and close the conference (at the start and end of the project)
- lead a round of introductions with, perhaps, an online ice-breaker
- welcome new team members or late arrivals
- provide a structure for getting started, e.g. agreement of group Netiquette
- allocate online group tasks to individual members, e.g. to provide a summary of a particular thread of discussion
- pose questions for the group to consider
- close off threads as and when appropriate
- wherever possible avoid playing 'ping pong' with individual group members and ask other people for their opinions and ideas
- encourage quieter members and 'lurkers' to join in
- if individuals break the agreed group netiquette then tackle them (either privately or through the conference)
- encourage the conference to develop it's own life and history; welcome shared language, metaphors, rituals and jokes
- encourage team members to post short messages with longer items sent as attachments
- provide summaries of online discussions; this is called weaving and involves summarising and synthesising the content of multiple responses in a virtual group
- thank team members for their contributions and work.

Effective online group work involves project team members agreeing to the following processes:

- check the conference at agreed intervals; this may be two or three times a day, daily, every few days or even weekly depending on the project.
- inform team members of any absences, e.g. due to annual leave.
- Keep messages concise and relevant.
- Keep one topic per message; this enables threads to develop.
- Encourage quieter members and 'lurkers' to join in.
- Acknowledge someone else's contribution and offer support.
- Ask for clarification about something you don't understand.
- Enhance acknowledgement by showing you understand what they say when you acknowledge; this is particularly important if you then want to disagree.
- If disagreeing then say first that you recognise that other opinions exist, then provide your own opinion; do not just disagree or, even worse, claim someone is wrong.
- Give a rationale for your opinion; allow others to see where you are coming from.
- Before posting your message think about how other people will read and interpret it, if in doubt then ask for another opinion.

The project manager

In this section we will discuss two topics: the knowledge and skills of the project manager and looking after yourself.

The knowledge and skills of the project manager

Successful project managers have knowledge of:

- the context of the project, e.g. LIS, organisation, sector
- the organisation structure and culture
- the people involved in the project
- the effects of change on individuals and organisations
- project management tools and techniques
- motivating and influencing people
- self management
- relevant legislation e.g. health and safety.

Project managers need a range of practical skills including:

- administration skills
- decision making skills

- delegation skills
- facilitation skills
- feedback skills
- information management skills
- information technology
- leadership skills
- listening skills
- negotiation skills
- presentation skills
- project management skills
- relationship skills
- team building skills
- time management skills.

In addition, the project manager needs a range of personal qualities and these include:

- a clear sense of direction
- awareness and management of own feelings
- awareness of own strengths and weaknesses
- emotional resilience
- ability to take other people's needs into account
- flexibility and adaptability
- decisiveness
- conscientiousness – deliver the goods, match words and deeds.

Looking after yourself
It is very important that you look after yourself during the project process (as well as in your everyday working life). This involves three different types of activities:

- healthy living
- time management
- support networks.

Healthy living involves good eating habits, exercise and reducing stress. This really means having a decent diet and managing your energy by having regular breaks and having lunch breaks. The habit of skipping lunch or eating at the VDU means that you are unlikely to be refreshed in the afternoon and this has a detrimental affect on the quality of your work. It is also important to have some physical activity (even if it is only walking up and down stairs instead of using the lift) during the day as this helps to energise the body. It is also worthwhile reducing or stopping bad work habits such as working extra long hours, long periods at the PC. There are many potential stressors in the workplace and, if you are particularly under pressure, it is worthwhile spending some time finding ways to reduce them. There are many useful guides to reducing stress at work, for instance Markham (1995) and Wilson (1997).

It is also important to manage your time and to include in your diary thinking and development time. It can be tempting to fill every second of the day with different activities and, as project manager, it is very important to make space for yourself. Again, there are many useful guides to time management, e.g. Godefroy and Clark (1989) and Maitland (1995).

It is important to have a support network of other professionals who will give you help, advice and ideas when you need it. It is very useful to have a small group of trusted colleagues with whom you can share ideas and concerns either face-to-face over coffee or via the email. It is also important to make time in your busy diary for these types of professional contacts.

Mentoring offers another route to gaining additional support for the project management process. You may already have a mentor who provides you with excellent support. Alternatively, your mentor may not be able to provide specific support in a project management context or you may not have a formal mentor. In this case you may want to consider identifying and working with a mentor during the project. Fisher (1994) has presented a useful guide to mentoring in LIS.

Project management software

Project management software enables you to store the project plan electronically and then edit and update the plan. Common project management packages will produce GANTT charts, PERT charts and automatically identify the critical path. These packages enable you to forecast and ask 'what if?' questions such as 'What will happen if the data input takes 25 days instead of the estimated 15 days?' Project management software enables you to allocate and level the resources and also monitor the progress of the project. This software is widely available either as shareware or for sale. Many of the most sophisticated packages, e.g. MS Project, are available as evaluation packages over the Internet.

If you use project management software then you will need to enter your project data – the tasks, their duration, the relationships between the tasks and the resources allocated to them; this was covered in the project planning stage. The software will then use this data to produce a range of views on the screen and these normally include:

- GANTT chart

- PERT chart
- resource sheet
- resource usage
- calendar
- resource graph.

The project management software will typically enable you to produce a range of reports or printouts and these may include:

- overview
- current activities
- costs
- assignments
- workloads
- customised, e.g. for individual team members.

There are a number of advantages to using project management software. It provides:

- a professional image
- and extensive range of reports
- the big picture – detailed views are possible
- easy identification of the impact of changes

There are some disadvantages too! These include:

- the time required to learn the software package
- time taken to input data
- garbage in garbage out (GIGO)
- the danger of not recognising that software provides a means of managing information–it is NOT the project!

Bibliography and References

Black, K. *Project Management for Library and Information Service Professionals*. London: Aslib (1996).

Burke, R. *Project Management. Planning and Control*. Wiley (2nd ed) (1992).

Dye, J. The learning resource centre, the University of Westminster, UK. An interview by Bill Downey (1996). Available at *http://www.lgu.ac.uk/deliberations/lrc/westminster.html*.

Fisher, B. *Mentoring*. London: Library Association Publishing (1994).

Gallacher, C. *Managing Change in Libraries and Information Services.* London: Aslib (1999).

Godefroy, C. H. and Clark, J. *The Complete Time Management System.* Piatkus (1989).

Harrison, F.L. *Advanced Project Management.* Aldershot: Gower (1992, 3rd ed.).

Honey, P. The learning organisation simplified. *Training and Development,* 1991, 30-3.

Kellecher, J. et al. *Evaluation of the Electronic Libraries Programme. Guidelines for eLib evaluation.* The Tavistock Institute. (1996). Available at *http://www.ukoln.ac.uk/services/elib/papers/tavistock/evaluation-guide/.*

Kimball, L. *Managing Virtual Teams* (1997). Available at *http://www.tmn.com/~lisa/vteams-toronto.htm.*

Leigh, A. and Walters, M. *Effective Change: 20 ways to make it happen.* IPD (1998, 2nd ed.).

Lock, D. *Project Management.* Aldershot: Gower (1992, 5th ed.).

Maitland, I. *Managing Your Time.* IPD (1995).

Markham, U. *Managing Stress.* Element (1995).

Maylor, H. *Project Management.* London: Pitman Publishing (1996).

O'Connor, J. and Seymour, J. *Introducing neuro-linguistic programming.* Thorsons (1990).

Pugh, L. *Change Management in Information Services.* Aldershot: Gower (2000).

Smith, B. and Dodds, B. *Developing Managers Through Project-based Learning.* Aldershot: Gower (1997).

Wilson, P. *Calm at Work.* Harmondsworth: Penguin (1997).

Chapter 16

Marketing the information service

Fiona Bell

Introduction

There have been occasions when I have sat at my desk and smiled to myself as colleagues from other departments come into the Information Service with customers on a whirlwind tour – 'And this is the Library. The information team here find information for us. Very handy' – and with that they are gone. I write this not by way of criticism of my colleagues but to illustrate that quite often the Information Service sits very quietly and modestly within the parent organisation with no one fully appreciating what the information team is capable of contributing.

Information overload is a recognised problem in today's business environment. In the Information Department we have a group of individuals uniquely skilled to assist their colleagues in filtering relevant information from the rubbish. With our help senior managers should be making informed decisions on company strategy. Every one in the parent company should be up to date on what is happening in his or her sector. In theory our colleagues should be beating a path to our door but how many of our users, or potential users, understand what could be available? The onus is on the Information Manager to open lines of communication between the Information Department and other departments and to organise the Information Service in such a way as to deliver services the customers want and which are going to make our customers' working life easier.

Information Managers working alone are worthy of a special mention. I have been in the position of being a one person information service myself and it is very hard work answering enquiries on a day-to-day basis without trying to develop other services as well. Trying to research and implement a marketing plan may not be as hopeless as it first seems. It might be possible to get low cost help. Is there a university in your area which offers courses on marketing, business or information? If so, speak to someone in the department involved: they will probably be grateful to have the opportunity to offer hands-on experience of marketing to one of their students. Even if there is not a college or university it is worth remembering that many students return to their parents' homes during the holidays. One advantage of using outside help is that they will have an unbiased view of the organisation and should be able to offer fresh comments and ideas. Both the student and the Information Manager should benefit from the arrangement.

In the following chapter I hope to give an overview of marketing techniques which will be of use to Information Managers. For those of you who are already well versed with marketing techniques there may be nothing new here except for a few observations I have made for myself over the years. For those who have never had a crack at marketing I hope this chapter is not patronising and provides enough detail to help you set the process in motion and give you the confidence to seek out further information on marketing.

I begin with a definition of marketing and its relevance to the information sector. I then move on to look at the environment within which the Information Centre operates; the process of carrying out market research; the pros and cons of various methods of data collection and what to do with the information when you have collected it. I then briefly look at the importance of marketing in the context of the long-term future of the information profession.

What is marketing?

What is marketing and what relevance does it have for the Information Manager? You may be surprised to read that marketing is not about persuading people to buy or use something which they do not really want or need. Marketing does not begin with a product or service and the marketer cannot create demand that does not exist. Marketing is not a magic formula for instantly increasing use of a service or product. The Chartered Institute of Marketing defines marketing as: '….the management process responsible for identifying, anticipating and satisfying customer needs profitably'.

Michael J Baker (1987) suggests that real marketing has four essential features. It:

1.	starts with the customer
2.	[takes] a long run perspective
3.	[makes] full use of all the company's resources
4.	is innovative.

Note that both descriptions have the customer at the heart of the statements. Marketing however is not just a management process, it requires a shift in priorities – it becomes a way of working. We might be surprised by the logic and simplicity of the four points listed in Baker's definition. Is there anything in these four points that an Information Manager in the context of the information service cannot do? I would suggest not.

Is information inherently difficult to market? The customer does not see what he or she will get prior to being presented with the information. On taking the enquiry, the information provider may not know for a fact that the information being requested is available. The information provider may not know whether he or she will incur any charges in getting the information for the customer or that he or she can get the information in the time required by the customer. In short there are many uncertainties involved here but it is not just information a customer gets when using the information department, it is a service. An information provider is unlikely to be able to answer *every* enquiry, absolutely accurately in the time span the customer requires. However, if customers believe that the service they have received is the best available then they will use it again. It is by adding value to information through service delivery that Information Managers can encourage usage of the Information Service. The marketing process will show where the service can be enhanced.

You will need to be clear about the reasons for marketing. For example it could be increased usage or income generation. Is recognition or validation from the parent organisation being sought in order to secure further resources? It could be a combination of all these aims. Without a sense of direction and without measurable outcomes to be able to monitor and control the marketing strategy, the effort could be futile. A note of caution: be careful to collect only the management information you need to meet your immediate goals. Anything else will be a waste of time and therefore money. Superfluous information could also cloud the real issues.

Situation analysis

Environment

The Information Centre does not exist as an isolated entity within the parent organisation. Whatever affects the parent organisation will surely have repercussions for the Information Centre. You will need to ask yourself whether there are any external factors influencing the success or failure of the parent company. Does the state of the economy have a bearing on the activities of the parent company? Would a shift in politics have an effect? Is there any legislation about to be implemented which might have an impact? What are the trends in that particular sector? I am not suggesting that you could do anything about such factors but forewarned is forearmed and preparations could be made to lessen the effects of these influences.

The alignment of the marketing strategy of the Information Centre with the long-term aims and objectives of the parent company could be a crucial step in gaining recognition and integration. Integration is important because it ultimately benefits the organisation's customer (Powers, 1995) who are also (whether directly or indirectly) your customers.

Is the culture of the parent organisation receptive to change? If not then the marketing process for the Information Centre could be made more difficult (though not impossible). If change is readily accepted then the marketing process and resulting actions should be comparatively easy to implement.

Does the parent organisation have a business plan, a marketing strategy and a corporate strategy which is available for staff to examine? If you are able to look at such documents you may spot opportunities for the Information Centre. Where does the Information Centre currently feature in this bigger picture?

Marketing strategy

Where would you like to see your Information Service in three years time (or even longer)? You might argue: 'I'd like to see the team doing X, but for all I know our funding may have been pulled by then / the parent organisation may have been taken over / our syndicate may have won the lottery etc. How can I know what's around the corner?' Of course you cannot possibly know what is going to happen but you can still plan ahead using educated guesswork. The marketing strategy is an overall statement of what you will do in order to achieve your aims and objectives.

A marketing strategy might begin as a set of objectives. For example, you know that in three year's time you would like the Information Service's income to increase by X per cent. You would like to know that Y per cent of customers express satisfaction with the service they have received and that Z amount of pounds was added to the parent company's overall income (directly or indirectly) through the involvement of the Information Service.

You will need to assess the strengths, weaknesses, opportunities and threats facing the Information Service (also known as a SWOT analysis). Strengths and weaknesses come from within the information team and perhaps within the parent organisation. Opportunities and threats could be external influences over which you may have little control, for example a change in Managing Director who takes a more (or less) favourable view of Information Services. A downturn in the economy could threaten your parent organisation and affect your own department. The marketing strategy document will refer only broadly to the measures which will need to be taken to meet these objectives. Marketing planning makes the strategy possible through more detailed, manageable and measurable processes.

Carrying out primary research

Product research

If the figures are available you might want to carry out a cost benefit analysis of the resources available to the Information Centre. You will need to know how heavily the information has been used and how much income has been generated for the company (not only the Information Centre in general but by each of the products offered). The technologies available for storing and organising information are evolving all the time. Is the format of the information held the most cost and time effective? Questions regarding the quality of service will have to be asked of users and non-users and action taken as a result of their feedback. You will need to know if your customers and potential customers get their information from other sources, meaning competition for the Information Centre. Many people have access to the Internet, professional literature and professional associations. Without knowing the source of the competition, however, how can you make your services more attractive? Later, this feedback will be useful in targeting customers and potential customers in order to pilot new or revitalised services.

Customer research

You will need to find out if there are any patterns in existing user behaviour. Are there any services which are more heavily used than others? If users are making repeat visits, which services are they using? If such data on usage is not readily available it will need to be monitored for a period of time. The sample has to be broader than existing users. The odds are that you will already have a strong sense of existing user habits but non-users are an unknown quantity. The answers may be unpleasant, but data on non-use of the service is vital if you are aiming to increase usage. The aim is not to make *all* potential customers use the Information Centre. Many Information Managers (mistaking marketing as promotion only) shy away from promoting the Information Centre for fear of stimulating an overwhelming demand (Brick, 1999). The aim is merely to gather information which will help to target activities better in future. The reason for not using the Information Centre could be something as simple as misunderstanding the nature of the services on offer, or even not being aware of it at all.

Service delivery and geography

Is the Information Centre located on the same premises as all its internal users? Are there any staff who work out in the field but still have information needs? Are there any satellite offices? In such situations consideration will need to be given on how you can make information services more easily accessible to such customers. Use of email could be one solution but the answer may not lie in technology: it could be something as simple as posting information, holding regular briefing meetings or visiting remotely located clients.

Advertising and promotion

What are the customers' preferred methods of finding out about the services on offer from the Information Service? Some people like to receive email, others prefer a personal approach. How much time is available for members of the Information Team to attend events being held by the parent organisation and present the services of the Information Department to delegates? Would this be welcomed by staff from the parent organisation? Members of the Information Team may need training in presentation skills. Some members of staff will not feel comfortable with presenting at all but others will become used to it quickly. You will need to harness the strengths of the individual members of your team and deploy people where they are most effective.

How much money will you have to promote products and services? Is there the possibility of having professionally written promotional literature? In most cases it is unlikely that money will be made available to promote the Information Centre and much of the promotional work will have to be done by the staff themselves. 'Do-it-yourself' does not have to equal 'amateur' and promotional activity can begin on a small scale until its value has been proven.

Other considerations

You will also need to be confident that your team is aware of the marketing process and what it will mean to them so that they are committed to the project and the resulting action which will be required.

You might need to consider going outside the Information Centre (and even the parent organisation) in search of other service ideas, networking opportunities and to share experiences and good practice. It may also be worth looking outside the information sector altogether, to other service providers, for examples of good practice and new ideas. Software suppliers provide a good example of customer service marketing (trial periods with a product, help desk support, assigned account managers). Is there any reason that information users cannot have an 'account manager' assigned to them? It is very easy to become focused on delivering an *information* service rather than delivering a service.

Actively gathering opinions

Choosing samples and information gathering

I have already alluded to the fact that you will need to involve non-users as well as existing users. The idea of a sample is to get a group of respondents', the characteristics of which reflect that of the total population being studied. This means that to have a representative sample you will also need to include a member (or several members of the parent organisation depending on its size) of the Senior Management Team. This could be rather daunting but it is important and while you are communicating with the senior manager you are raising the profile of the Information Service within the organisation. The sample also needs to be as random as possible. Tempting though it is, you cannot just involve people you *know* will respond to you, you need to go outside the known to learn anything new.

There are many methods of gathering information from respondents and not all of them need be formal. Useful titbits of information, which can aid research, are everywhere. Spontaneous communication such as conversations at the coffee machine, can add to your ideas although this is not an unbiased method of information collection and therefore could not be included in a research report, but it might open up an avenue to be explored formally. You will probably have observed certain behaviour amongst users over time but behaviour must be measurable if it is to be included. For example, if respondents were asked to find a past journal article with no assistance from an information team member some might choose to look through the journal physically while others will try to search on a CD or the Internet. If the expected behaviour was that the methods used would be split evenly, but in actual fact a high number of respondents chose to search electronically, what does this tell you about the preferences of the Information Centre's users?

Questionnaires

Formal methods could include questionnaires, face to face interviews or telephone interviews and a mixture of these methods can be used. Questionnaires and interviews need to be well constructed and you should avoid leading questions. Questionnaires might be better used to ask closed questions – those which require a yes or no answer and or questions where the questioner can limit the number of responses available. For example:

> How do you rate the usefulness of our current awareness service?
> Please give a score between one and five where one is not at all
> useful/never used, two is not very useful, three is occasionally
> useful, four is very useful and five is of great use/used all the time.

It is prudent to give the respondent a definition of the meaning of each
score to avoid him or her bringing his or her own subjective interpretation
of the values of each score but this can also make the questionnaire appear longer and therefore off-putting for the respondent. It can also be
useful to give only an even number of choices for the respondent to choose
from: that way the questioner *forces* a choice either side of 'average'. When
faced with a questionnaire how many of us have quickly ticked the middle box because we haven't got time to give the question the consideration
it might deserve or because we cannot decide? I certainly have done this.

Do the respondents have to identify themselves? It would depend on how
the questionnaire was to be used. If the questionnaire was used to collect
statistical data then it may not be necessary but if the questionnaire is to
be used to help choose respondents then you will need to know who they
are. One flaw of doing this research yourself is that if you are asking
colleagues for their opinion they may be reluctant to be honest if what
they have to say is unfavourable. Not a great deal can be done about this
except to remind respondents that without their honest feedback you cannot hope to improve the service.

Interviews

If your parent company does have satellite offices or fieldworkers, telephone interviews might be useful. Telephone interviews also need to be
reasonably brief and it's a good idea to give an indication of how long the
interview will take, to give the potential respondent the option of declining to take part. Again it could be difficult encouraging people to be honest
when you both know you will have to work together afterwards.

With questionnaires and with telephone interviews you do not *see* the
respondent when he or she is answering your questions. Personal interviews on the other hand require face to face contact and therefore careful
preparation and administration is essential. The interviewer will need to
try and behave in the same way with every respondent. For example, if
you carry out more than five interviews in a morning you may be flagging
a little by the fourth and losing the will to live by the fifth. Your body
language will probably say as much. You may slouch, show impatience,
or (heaven forbid) yawn. How will this make the interviewee feel? If the
respondent senses you can't be bothered, they will not be either. I was
once interviewed by a man who never made eye contact but looked around
the room all the time I was speaking. He yawned – a lot. He did this as
soon as we sat down to speak (so you cannot blame me for boring him).

He seemed to regain consciousness often enough to ask another question but then did not seem to be listening to the answer. When our little chat was over I felt rather demoralised. I had to work with him afterwards and I have to admit to feeling less than enthusiastic about giving any further input.

Try not to lead interviewees. You are trying to get their opinion not give them yours. Even emphasising a particular word or smiling when you offer a particular option on a multiple choice question might affect the response. The whole exercise will take a significant commitment of time and effort but the information accrued at the end is invaluable and vital if informed decisions are to be made as to the way forward for the Information Centre.

Using the information to create a marketing plan

Measuring success

I mentioned earlier that you will need to decide on what you are aiming to achieve by implementing a marketing plan for the Information Centre. In order to know whether the measures you are using are successful or not you will need to be able to assess them in some way. Often when marketing a product the aim is to get more sales and therefore increase profit but would this be a fair way of measuring the success of a marketing plan for an information service? Increasingly income generation is becoming important for many special libraries but I would argue that information services are better measured in terms of customer satisfaction. Custom for information services cannot be 'drummed up' in the same way it might be for a product. Some products can be sold using an element of persuasion. For example, have you ever been to your local supermarket and offered a taster of a new drink? You might enjoy it so much you end up buying some. You emerge from the supermarket with a product you did not even know existed let alone wanted.

Services are usually provided in order to meet a specific need at a specific time. A customer could ask for financial information on a company he is considering trading with; you sell it to him. He will seek you out to provide the information when he needs it. Income generation could be *a* measurement of the success of a marketing strategy for the information but not *the* measurement. Customer satisfaction is more important because it ensures repeat visits, perhaps new users through word of mouth recommendations. Monitor the value of the information and the impact it had on the user's situation. This in turn could result in greater recognition of the contribution of the information service, a by-product of which could be an increase in resources. Like marketing itself, monitoring customers' satisfaction will need to be an ongoing process. You will need to be able to prove the value of your activities and have evidence of the improvements that have resulted and be sure to promote your successes.

The 4 ps

Product (or in our case service)

Your research should have shown you which of your current services are used and why. Suggestions as to what other services you could offer should have emerged. Are some of these suggested services feasible to deliver? Do enough people want them? Would the benefits of offering the suggested service outweigh the cost or other difficulties which could be involved in delivering it (this is not an exercise in altruism)? Some of your existing services may still be appropriate but in need of some tweaking to make them a little more appealing.

The total product concept (and other theories)
Theodore Levitt (1986) argued that products need constantly to be kept one step ahead of customer expectations in order for the products to maintain their competitiveness. This is referred to as the total product concept.

The generic product	This is the basic product with nothing added to it to make it more appealing. Take for example a mailing list which is a random jumble of contact names and addresses of companies operating in different sectors in different towns, all in hard copy. The contact names and addresses are what the customer wanted and that is all he or she has.
The expected product	The customer was probably expecting to get the information in some kind of order to make it easier for him or her to use; perhaps in alphabetical order and divided into the sectors he or she was interested in and/or by town.
The augmented product	To add value to or augment the product the information provider may also offer the information in MS Word format on disk or by email so that customers can manipulate the data. Before long however this augmented service will become the norm and the information provider will have to think of a new way of

offering the service to keep it ahead of the competition. This leads to the notion of the potential product.

The potential product   Rather than just providing the information in MS Word so that customers can manipulate it themselves, the information provider could manipulate the data for them. The data could arrive with customers in a mail-merged format with a set of sticky address labels with the contact names on them already. Customer need to do very little with the information then to turn the raw data into a mail shot.

Just as products wax and wane in popularity, so too do services. For example, the current government has introduced a great deal of legislation which affects businesses. Both consultants within our organisation and the customers themselves need information on what current legislation entails and what other legislation is due to be introduced. A law alert is therefore produced by the Information Centre. If there is a lull in the legislation being introduced or if our customers can get the information from elsewhere, the popularity of the service may decline. The service goes through four phases in its life cycle.

Service introduction or launch There is a need for the service so it is provided and promoted.

Growth   More people become aware of the service and take it up.

Maturity   The service has been available for some time and many people are using it but the usage has reached a plateau.

There is little movement in terms of customers taking up the service and customers dropping out.

Decline   For whatever reason, existing users no longer want the service and there are few or no new customers for it.

Decline does not necessarily mean death because some services can be revitalised and offered in a different way (see augmented and potential products above). However, if the amount being spent on keeping the service going exceeds the amount being made on it, and there is no indication of an upturn, the service may have to be dropped.

The Boston Consulting Group produced a model which, although not the same as the product life cycle theory, has similar elements. The launch phase is similar to the 'problem children' phase, growth services are referred to as 'stars'. Services in the maturity phase are referred to as 'cash cows' and services in decline are 'dogs' (Henderson). If an Information Centre had only one service then the decline or dog phase would certainly be a disaster. The idea of product portfolio management, however, is that several services are available and are at different phases of their lifecycle so the Information Centre is never totally dependent on one product for its income. If a service is not generating much income but there is still a demand for it, it can be retained as long as there are a sufficient number of 'cash cows' to absorb the cost. The cash cows don't *have* to be those of the Information Centre. They could be those of the parent company. For example, if the parent organisation has services or products in its own portfolio which generate income this income could be used to offset the cost of providing a service elsewhere in the organisation. This is only good sense if the service from the Information Centre could be used as a 'loss leader' i.e. a service which will draw a customer in for more services from the Information Centre or parent organisation at usual prices.

Price

Price in the context of the Information Centre need not necessarily be a monetary value (although as mentioned previously income generation is increasingly becoming a concern in many special libraries). The cost of something could be in terms of time for example. In the case of CD and Internet subscriptions, up-front charges for a product can be very high and it is difficult to forecast how often the information from such products might be required. How much would the customer be willing to pay to get the information? If the charges are perceived by customers to be too high, they may decide they can cope without it. If the price is too low they may think that the information is poor quality.

Can the services in your product portfolio absorb the cost? If this is the case you could provide services which are expensive for the Information Centre but at a price the customer does not consider to be too high. They may then come back and use services which are making profit. I have had customers who don't want to pay for information at all. In such cases I have pointed out that the databases from which we will get their information costs thousands of pounds: suddenly £30 or £40 for a financial report does not seem so steep. It is more difficult to sell our time as information professionals. For example, if customers ask us to carry out some market research on their behalf we will often use the Internet for part of this search. Customers might say they are just as capable of using the Internet to find the answer. They are possibly capable of searching the Internet but they do not do this for a living (so we are likely to be faster) and it is not a good use of their time.

An investment in time may be required from the customer. If you were setting up a current awareness service for an internal staff member, for instance, you would need to spend some time with your colleague. He or she would need to tell you exactly what type of information will be required, perhaps where he or she has been getting the information from until now. The price being paid is given in time. It may seem obvious but once a price has been decided for a service make sure everyone in the organisation is aware of it.

Place , location and distribution

Earlier in this chapter I wrote of how customers will use services when they need them. When a customer needs a service it is important that the service is readily available and easily accessible. Physically speaking there is probably not a lot you can do about where the Information Service is located within the parent organisation, especially if there is a library attached to it. There are, however, ways and means of reminding customers where you are and getting the information to them so that your physical location is of less importance. Is the department well signposted? If you have a logo is it prominently displayed? Does the reception area of your building display literature from the Information Department? As it becomes easier and quicker to distribute information electronically it could be argued that where an Information Centre is, is becoming less important. I believe hard copy will always be with us because there is a sense of possession for customers when they look at (and can take) something in the printed format. People do not always trust technology either: have you ever lost an afternoon's work because your computer crashed and you forgot to save? Obviously it is better to be physically located near your customers. Do not forget you can always deliver enquiry results in person, giving you the opportunity to explain your findings face to face.

Promotion

All the communicating you have been doing in order to carry out your research has raised the profile of the Information Service. This is promotion in itself but there is much more which can be done, cheaply and easily, to promote the service. Building relationships with the people around you is possibly the best promotion work you can do as a service provider. Often, the tendency of information departments is to be reactive but proactivity is required for a marketing effort. The information team will need to get involved with the general activities of the parent organisation and be seen to be getting involved. Information workers are not particularly good at 'networking'. Attend events and meetings held by the parent organisation, so that you become aware of the issues affecting the whole organisation. Make presentations about the department to colleagues.

The Information Department will need to have a distinct image. It does not have to be a logo but do draw attention to any departmental literature by displaying 'Information Centre' on it, with full contact details. In my own Information Department we use the front sheet of completed enquiries to summarise the information and we sometimes list the sources we have used – it works better than a scribbled post-it note. Consider publishing case studies of some examples of where the information you have provided has made a real difference to the work of your colleagues in the host organisation. Why not write a mission statement of your own and display it prominently so that users can gain an understanding of your service ethos?

People

There is a fifth p: *people*. A service is only as good as the people delivering it. In my experience people working in the information profession are passionate about their work. In his article 'Marketing and promotion in today's special library' Guy St. Clair (1990) states:

> One of the hardest things for us to recognise as information specialists is that everyone in the organisation which employs us, does not think about us and our services as much as we do . . . we are so involved in what goes on in the library. . . . that it comes as a shock to us to have others in the organisation express surprise or wonder that we can provide a particular service.

I use this quotation because I think it indicates behaviour which is probably true of many working in the profession. Such is our passion for what we do (commendable though such passion is), we forget to promote ourselves. If just a fraction of this enthusiasm could be applied to telling other people about the Information Service think how much could be accomplished. I do not want to discuss the social skills (or lack thereof) of information workers here or commonly held perceptions about us as shy and retiring. Such assumptions are over generalisations. Perhaps as a profession we are just guilty of modesty.

Marketing the information service does require the information team to make sure that everyone in the parent organisation understands what the service is able to deliver. If you have customers outside the parent organisation, a dialogue needs to be opened with them too so that they also appreciate what is available. A huge commitment will be required from all the staff in the information team in order to make the marketing plan work and it will be an ongoing commitment.

Marketing is an ongoing, cyclical process. The exercise needs to be repeated regularly and progress monitored. Decide what you will be using as a measurement of your progress. For example, have you achieved a specific goal within a certain period of time and has this resulted in improved value? You will need to be prepared to make changes to your plan if monitoring shows that the desired results have not occurred. The marketing process and its monitoring needs to continue so that the customers are constantly offered services they really want and need and so that the Information Service is recognised as a thriving operation. In turn this will result in securing the future and ongoing development of the services. I made reference earlier in this chapter to the need for the Information Service to align itself with the goals of the parent organisation. In this way the the role of information as a support service can be changed to one of a driving force improving the competitiveness of the organisation overall.

Some final thoughts

Marketing involves a range of skills information professionals will need to master as we enter the new millennium, Sandra Ward (1999) argues that information professionals of the future will have to demonstrate qualities such as:

- self belief
- vision and creativity
- opportunism
- confidence
- willingness to take risks
- focus
- team playing and partnership
- ambition.

Because as a profession we must be prepared to:

- catalyse and drive change, visibly, in our own areas and in the business itself
- reinvent, change or even eliminate our current roles.

We are bombarded with more information all the time – some of it useful, a great deal of it not. Information overload threatens the competitiveness of businesses. In the 'information age', as information professionals we should be poised to reap rewards from our existing range of skills. We cannot assume however, that because we have these skills the profession will be exalted. We need to market ourselves and our services in order to reposition information services within our parent organisations making the presence of the information service a distinct competitive advantage to our parent companies. Above all we must always be in touch with what our customers want, or information professionals will cease to have a role.

References

Baker, Michael J. *One More Time – What is Marketing? The Marketing Book.* London: Heinemann (1987).

Brick, Laura. Non use of libraries and information services: a study of the library and information managers' perception, experience and reaction to non use. *Aslib Proceedings,* **51**(6) June 1999, 195-205.

Chartered Institute of Marketing. *Our Definition of Marketing.* Available at *http://www.cim.co.uk/libinfo/index.htp.*

Henderson, Bruce D. *The Product Portfolio.* The Boston Consulting Group. Available at *http://www.bcg.com/this_is_bcg/mission/growth_ share_matrix.asp.*

Levitt, Theodore. *The Marketing Imagination.* New York: FreePress; London: Colier McMillan (1986).

Powers, Janet E. Marketing in the special library environment. *Library Trends,* **43**(3) Winter 1995, 478-93.

St. Clair, Guy. Marketing and promotion in today's special library. *Aslib Proceedings,* **42**(7/8) July/August 1990, 213-17.

Ward, Sandra. Information professionals for the next millennium. *Journal of Information Science,* **25**(4) 1999, 239-49. (Presidential address to the IIS AGM and Members Day, 17 September 1999.)

Chapter 17

Library management systems

John Ross and Peter Evans

Introduction

Different types of information management package

Both the number and types of information management packages are still increasing; and they cover a wide range of information applications. This chapter concentrates on library management systems (LMS), sometimes called library housekeeping systems, although, as ever, the distinctions between categories become somewhat blurred.

Other types of information management systems that information professionals may well encounter include information retrieval packages (probably the closest relatives of library management systems if one was to construct a family tree), electronic records management, document management systems, geographical information systems (GIS), archives and museum documentation.

All these are, of course, in addition to the ubiquitous database management systems (DBMS) and relational database management systems (RDBMS) that are in use in almost every organisation, if only in the form of Microsoft Access. It is increasingly common for library management systems to be built using a standard DBMS 'under the bonnet'; but although it may be relevant to know which DBMS is being used, the information professional is not usually required to become au fait with its inner workings.

The last two types of package we shall mention are interlibrary loans (ILL) and serials management, which are special case of library management systems and fall squarely within the scope of this chapter.

What this chapter covers

The main objective of this chapter is to give the information professional who has the task of selecting and installing a new library management system a realistic idea of:

- types of package available
- the marketplace

- evaluation and selection techniques and procedures
- likely costs
- staffing implications
- timescales.

Package v tailored v bespoke

One issue that still raises its head from time to time is whether to go to the expense of buying in a package when one could get the IT Department to knock up a system virtually for nothing in the next few weeks, during a slack period. This is the same argument which suggests that, if the managing director cannot afford to buy a Rolls-Royce, then the company's maintenance department could build one for him in their spare time – at virtually no cost of course.

From time to time, someone does produce a new system. Despite consolidations at the top end, the market is still seeing new entrants coming in almost every year. However, building your own system is not for the faint-hearted and requires deep pockets and rock-solid commitment from senior managers and those who finance the organisation. It also usually involves several years' wait and is almost always the most expensive option – certainly not the cheapest. Even if a system is built successfully, it is highly unlikely that the original designers and programmers will be around in five years' time to maintain or extend it.

What is becoming common, and manageable with the right controls, is tailoring of a standard package to a particular customer or installation. There are two approaches to producing a tailored package. One is to write extra or additional code for specific customers, the other is to create options within the package, which the customer or supplier or a consultant can select by choosing various parameter settings. The one-off, ad hoc coding approach is simpler, cheaper, quicker – and usually a step on the road to disaster. Over time such systems often become unmanageable and unmaintainable. The parameterised approach, which has always been used to some extent in library systems, although more complex, is usually safer in the long term. Some suppliers will charge for bespoke development work and then incorporate it in their standard package. This may seem like having their cake and eating it, but it does make sense for the customer as well, because the supplier can concentrate on maintaining a standard product.

Market overview

Although there is consolidation amongst some of the larger and medium-sized suppliers, there are still quite enough suppliers to give prospective customers a range of choices – and headaches trying to make them. As more and more systems cover the basic library management functions, and conform to the same international standards, it becomes more difficult for the suppliers' sales representatives to differentiate their product. However, there are still 'horses for courses'. For the bemused potential customer, it is crucial to decide what type of course and then choose a horse to suit, rather than allow the selling process to convince them their requirement matches the product being offered.

We look at the market segmentation in more detail later, and some guidelines for going about the selection and evaluation process. Here we take a broad overview of the library management system (LMS) market and identify the key trends as the millennium changes.

Categories of systems

Library management system v information retrieval package?
Originally LMS packages contained very little to help end users retrieve information; and information retrieval (IR) packages were primarily concerned with extracting records from full-text databases. Nowadays, most LMS contain extensive information retrieval facilities such as OPACs and some text retrieval functions; and most IR packages contain more collection management functions. Some systems started out as an information retrieval package (CAIRS for example) and now have versions which are full library management systems. The distinction is somewhat artificial nowadays but the origins of a system (and its original target market) still tend to be reflected in its particular strengths. At a time when, in many organisations, the 'library' is being replaced by the 'information centre' or 'business intelligence centre' or 'knowledge centre' it pays to reflect on which is the top priority: automating the housekeeping functions or extracting the underlying information – or even knowledge?

The other main categories of system are the 'peripheral' library management facilities such as serials control and interlibrary loans. These are the last modules to be added to the 'integrated library management systems'. There are still separate packages for these functions and it is not absolutely necessary to have them incorporated in one single integrated system.

Different types of library will require different emphases, a public library for example requires more efficient high volume housekeeping processing. Special libraries often need more information retrieval emphasis while universities tend to have a requirement for interlibrary loans.

Recent developments

0   The integration of the interlibrary loans (ILL) facility is one of the main current developments. Soon it will be *de rigueur* for every integrated LMS to have an ILL module, which is not to say they will all do it equally well. The key development in this area is the general deployment of the ISO 10160/61 standard for ILL messaging. This standard enables ILL sub-systems to request from other conformant systems and to exchange standard messages about the status of a request or loan. Older ILL systems were built to communicate with central services, e.g. BLDSC, and cannot work 'peer to peer' – now seen as part of the future for ILL.

1

2   The other major trend is the web-enabling of library systems. At first this was simply making the OPAC compatible with a web browser so that the library catalogue (a) had a familiar 'look and feel' for many readers and (b) could, relatively easily, be made available over the corporate intranet to almost every desktop PC in the organisation.

3

4   Because of the ubiquity of the World Wide Web standard and the adoption of a common inter-communication format by most library system developers (Z39.50), this has led to two major developments. It is now relatively easy to link up separate library systems, not necessarily from the same supplier, to offer a 'virtual catalogue' of several institutions, and/or link an organisation's library system to other internal systems using the web-format interface. It also enables the library or information centre to accept requests and send responses, for example, to people in the rest of the organisation, even if they never set foot near the library.

5

6   The other big element of web-enabled library systems is that, increasingly, the items catalogued can be in other people's collections, potential requirements not necessarily in anyone's catalogue at present (except the supplier's), electronic resources or web locations. The technology is now commonplace to allow a catalogue item to refer to a web address and with one mouse-click to link across the World Wide Web to that resource, which is by implication, a dynamic resource, and so may be updated regularly.

7

The other key trend is the increasing use of 'object linking'. An 'object', i.e. an electronic resource – text file, image, video clip, sound recording or a computer program, can be linked to a catalogue record and then launched with its program so that the image is displayed or the sound heard. This gives library management systems a potentially much wider role as collection or resource management systems. Technical standards in this area are still emerging and suppliers may adopt one of several methodologies for implementing this kind of linking.

If this is an important feature for the library then it is wise to check that the object linking can work with those objects required in the organisation. Thus if the need is to be able to link to and play audio clips, then make sure the package can work with the specific file formats that are used in the organisation. A quick demonstration of an image being loaded and displayed does not demonstrate in-depth functionality or understanding of this complex area.

Trends

Three major trends are affecting the software industry:

- *Globalisation* – systems are now being sold in markets far from their physical origin. Libraries are universal and the basic management functions are much the same in any country; but language, technical support and user feedback become progressively more difficult as a company's market expands.

- *Modularisation* – software is becoming 'componentised' – smaller packages that link to another via inter-working interfaces and standards. A spin-off from this approach is that it is now feasible to personalise user interfaces such as OPACs, just as Windows and Mac users can personalise their desktop screens.

- *Web-based software* – more and more software is becoming re-designed for access over the Internet or an intranet using a web browser for the user interface. This has the advantage for the librarian with distributed sites that the system can be accessed worldwide, and the 'client' is a standard piece of software that needs little or no maintenance. It is also leading to ASP (Application Server Provider) distribution of the software – software and data residing on a server not owned by the organisation. Software is rented – leading to low initial cost of ownership, fewer maintenance and back-up worries and less 'tie in' to a specific piece of software.

Standards

Standards are touched upon in several places in this chapter. Their importance in the advancement of system interworking (allowing different systems to exchange data, etc.) and hence increase productivity, speed of response for the librarian are enormous. For practical purposes one can divide standards into two groups:

- those already established and implemented in the better systems – which, therefore, will be better able to communicate, exchange and store data, and retrieve and display search results, and so on

- those emerging standards which may not yet be fully defined or implemented; these are the standards that the better system suppliers will be aware of and possibly shaping via co-operation within the industry; these standards will shape the future interworking of systems.

There are also, of course, those standards that are peculiar to the information handling world and those that operate in the wider context of the IT industry.

Key established standards and their implications

Cataloguing: AACR2

Not a computer standard – but if a package claims to conform to, or allow cataloguing to AACR2 standards, then it should allow you to describe an item in the depth to which this standard expects. For example, AACR2 expects a publication statement to include multiple publishers, places and so on, if these are relevant. If a product cannot do this then it is not AACR2 compliant.

Cataloguing: MARC

MARC stands for MAchine Readable Catalogue. It defines both a format for the exchange of bibliographic (catalogue) records and, via national versions, the data that should be assigned to various tags. The important function for any library system is to be able to import a MARC format file of records of the particular national variant the library wishes to use, and also to export it again, thereby ensuring that one can move data easily to another system in the future. The ability to import records means that for many items in the library it will be possible to load records from the Internet. The most common national variants of MARC are USMARC, UKMARC and UNIMARC.

There was an attempt to merge the formats of UK and USMARC. This proved impracticable. So, instead, there has been a partial harmonisation and in future, the relevant UK and US standards committees will try to ensure that there is no more divergence.

Interlibrary Loans (ILL): ISO 10160/61 1997

This standard defines how ILL requests should be presented between systems. Any modern ILL system should conform to this. The standard

will enable a library system to send requests to any other conformant library system in the world.

Searching: Z39.50
This enables a library system to send a catalogue search request and receive responses from any compliant system. Version 2 has now been superseded by version 3. One should look for support of the 'Bath Profile' sub-set of the specification. This gives a system more consistent search results; if combined intelligently with MARC import, it will allow the librarian to search for and then download records from any other library.

Character sets: Unicode
Unicode defines a coding standard for representation of all the world's character scripts. It is very important to have compliance should your organisation require to store and catalogue material using more than one character set such as Chinese, Greek, Cyrillic, Arabic, Hebrew as well as Latin.

Thesauri: ISO 2788 (Z39.19) and 5964 (multilingual)
This standard defines how a thesaurus should be constructed. If implementing a structured controlled language then the library system should be capable of importing and maintaining a thesaurus to this standard.

EDI (Electronic Data Interchange): EDIFACT, BISAC, SISAC
EDI is the electronic interchange of commercial data – orders, invoices, etc. – and can speed transactions and substantially reduce paperwork, especially in larger libraries. Most European systems have moved to the EDIFACT standard – an international standard accepted by the UN. In North America, standards were developed by what is now BASIC (Book And Serial Industry Communications – *http://www.bisg.org*). BISAC defines book ordering and SISAC serial check-in barcoding, whereby a serial issue can be received simply by reading the barcode on the cover.

Electronic Mail: MAPI
Mail Application Programming Interface is a common standard designed to make linking to email systems possible. A MAPI compliant overdue system will enable a system to provide electronic overdues through a MAPI email system.

Database connectivity: ODBC (Open DataBase Connectivity)
Originally developed by Microsoft, ODBC allows desktop tools like Access and Excel to connect to and retrieve information from databases such as Oracle, Sybase and SQL Server.

Further information on relevant standards
ISO (International Standards Organisation)
http://www.iso.org.ch

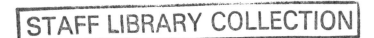

NISO (National Information Standards Organisation – USA)
http://www.niso.org
BSI (British Standards Institution)
http://www.bsi.org.uk

Pricing models

As the functionality of systems has converged, the pricing models they use have diverged. This complicates, of course, the task of comparing prices on a like-for-like basis at any given point in time. It also means that the comparison may well change over time. The customer will need to make some reasonable predictions as to how their 'configuration' will change over the next few years and compare the total cost of ownership over say a five year period. 'Configuration' in this sense means some-thing much wider than the hardware configuration. Factors that could have a disproportional impact on the cost of a particular system include possible retrospective conversion of records, availability of library sys-tems to corporate desktops, and mergers with other institutions.

Pricing models can be based on:

- size of the processor
- number of software modules installed
- number of potential users, and whether they have write access (staff or readers in essence, but perhaps less clear-cut)
- number of simultaneous users allowed
- size of database (e.g. number of catalogue records).

There will also be an annual maintenance charge for all except the small-est package. Quite often, the customer will have a choice of two or three levels of service, which mainly means speed of response. Furthermore, if the system uses a proprietary DataBase Management System (DBMS), Oracle or Sybase, there will be a licence fee for the DBMS, which may or may not be included in the LMS price.

The traditional pricing model for library systems and most large software systems, was comprised of:

- *Initial licence fee – annual maintenance.* The initial licence fee was the 'purchase cost' (although not normally a purchase in strict legal terms, just a licence to use the software). The annual maintenance was typically around 12 per cent per annum. Now there are two radically different models available from some suppliers.

- *Annual rental.* The annual rental model typically charges the same each year (perhaps with an inflation clause built in). This reduces the initial cost, which can sometimes be attractive (or crucial, depending on the library's budget and its influence in the organisation). For a long-term investment this can become more expensive or, to put it another way, it makes upgrading the system after a few years financially more attractive.

- *Application Service Provider (ASP)*. The Application Service Provider or ASP model is the one grabbing the attention in much of the IT press, perhaps because Microsoft seems keen to apply it. Here the supplier may charge for the software on a unit usage basis and / or run the system on their own computer on behalf of the customer; yet another example of out-sourcing a function from the purchasing organisation.

As well as software licences, costs should cover:

- hardware and software installation
- implementation consultancy (making it do what you want)
- training
- data conversion
- special services, e.g. bespoke functionality.

Key characteristics

Technical

- *System architecture*: most systems are variants on the client / server model but with a degree of variation within that model. Systems can be multi-tiered from two – five levels and beyond. Each tier represents a degree of separation of the elements of the application. The more tiers, the greater theoretical flexibility to adapt the system to different input devices, RDBMS, operating systems, network options, and so on, without having to change the other elements. This does not affect the functionality (the application layer) but longer-term development options are enhanced in multi-tier systems.

- *Operating system*: both client and server require an operating environment. Most clients require MS Windows variants for clients with UNIX or Windows NT / 2000 as the server or back-end. Java clients can run on any desktop O/S including Mac / OS, Linux, X Windows, MS Windows or on the server with a web browser as the user interface. Java is a programming language. Java-based clients run on a 'Java Virtual Machine' which can be implemented under many different operating systems and has become popular because it provides independence from any single operating system.

- *Database*: stores the data reliably for retrieval. The database architecture can be relational, inverted file (indexed), free form, object orientated, nested relational or proprietary. Relational can be inflexible if specific local variations in data structures are required. Proprietary systems can lag behind in latest technologies but are lower in cost. In practice, most database management systems combine some aspects of different architectures.

Application software

Application software can be split into general characteristics and library specific functions.

General characteristics and functions
General characteristics are:

- data import and export to MARC standards
- maintenance of MARC records and authorities
- web capability: OPAC and possibly administration - some systems are entirely web based.
- links with other corporate systems - e.g. Lotus Notes.
- CD integration
- electronic journal integration
- object integration.

Library functions
The main library functions usually included in an integrated library system are:

- *Cataloguing* – the heart of the system – enables the librarian to enter and update the catalogue records for the items in the library. It should provide the functions needed in your library and have MARC import and export capability. Useful new functions are direct download of records from the Internet.

- *Acquisitions* – the control of the purchase of materials. Check for capabilities for different material types (such as serials) and different order types (such as standing orders). Other factors to watch for are currency handling, linking to catalogue, multiple location and budget control.

- *Serials* – one of the most difficult modules. It should be linked to acquisitions and cataloguing. Watch for the capability of handling 'difficult' publication patterns such as multiple levels of enumeration.

- *Circulation* – control of the loan of material. It should have a loan policy dependent on a matrix of copy and borrower category for maximum flexibility. Production of notices for item pick-up and overdues should have email options.
- *OPAC* – the online public access catalogue. How the user views the catalogue. Modern features include local customisation by the library and the ability of users to view their own transactions and place reservations requests.
- ILL – interlibrary loan – should link automatically to the major document supply agencies (e.g. BLDSC) and allow peer to peer ILL via ISO 10160/61 – see section on standards.

Market segments

Library system suppliers tend to specialise in certain market sectors – usually because of size – the software will not scale beyond a certain number of records, users or response time, or because of special functional needs; for example special libraries need good routing control for serials. Bigger market systems have richer functionality but are expensive for small numbers of users. Thus a mixture of size and type characteristics defines market segments since sometimes the one defines the other.

By library type, in the UK sectors, sub-sectors, and their main characteristics are:

Library Type	Normal Size	Entry cost of systems
Public	Large	High
Academic		
HE	Large	High
FE	Small/Medium	Low
Schools	Small	Low
Special	*libraries which focus on a restricted group of users usually by subject, general function etc.*	
Corporate	Small	Low
Government	Medium	Medium
Research	Small/Medium	Small

Note that there are variations in other countries. There are many small public libraries in the USA, Ukraine and other countries, but very few in the UK.

There is a huge variation in the special libraries sector. The sector 'Research', for example, really covers any organisation involved in research activities and therefore shares problems with the HE (University) type library. Learned societies often combine this function with the archival function (usually absent in academic libraries).

Evaluating and selecting systems

Evaluating and selecting a new library management system is something that most librarians or information scientists will be heavily involved in only once or twice during their careers. It can be a lengthy and expensive process when done thoroughly. In addition, if the organisation has to abide by strict procurement procedures it will have to be done thoroughly.

Any public body making a procurement over a certain value must abide by World Trade Organisation (WTO) and European Union (EU) public procurement rules; and many large corporations have their own rules which are in essence similar, but usually a little more flexible. Furthermore, a private body using public funds (such as a Heritage Lottery Fund grant) is also bound by public procurement rules.

Sometimes the person who will be responsible for purchasing and running the new system will know exactly which system they want and, unburdened by any procurement bureaucracy, it may be just a matter of haggling a little over the price, dotting the 'i's and crossing the 't's. Even in this idyllic world, it is a worthwhile exercise to document exactly why 'WonderLib' (or whatever) is the only viable choice for you – and what you expect it to achieve.

In general, the process is an iterative one of defining requirements, surveying the field, refining the requirements, shortlisting, evaluating, negotiating and finally making a selection. Although this can be a fascinating process and an excuse to spend days looking at different library systems, it is usually a luxury that most organisations can ill afford. On the other hand, it is not a task that can be handed over lock, stock and barrel to an outside consultant, who will then unveil the chosen system in a few months' time. There is a strong case for using outside expertise in the form of an experienced consultant (as consultants themselves you are forgiven for thinking 'they would say that, wouldn't they' about the authors of this chapter) and/or any specification documents produced by colleagues in similar libraries.

At present there is considerable discussion in the profession and some of the consultants (including the authors) involved in evaluation and selection as to how the process can be simplified, made cheaper for all concerned and, in particular, how the information gathered for each procurement exercise can be re-used. Most consultants will have a template for defining the User Requirements Specification (URS) or an alternative document, as will some system suppliers.

The guiding principles of the evaluation and selection process should be:

- Start by defining what the organisation and users require.
- Define what is required, not how it is to achieved.
- Limit the number of systems looked at in detail.
- Produce an evaluation model that is flexible but demonstrably impartial.
- Do not waste suppliers' time – their customers, your colleagues, pay for it.

There is considerable disagreement in some circles as to the level of specification needed and at what stage it should be produced. The authors take the view, very strongly, that it is counter-productive to produce a detailed system specification in order to evaluate systems that already exist. They will not be changed in the light of your specification.

Problems and objectives

Let us begin at the beginning. Why upgrade or purchase a new system? What are the problems with the current one?

This should be documented, and ought to consist of a series of bullet points no longer than a page. From this it should be possible to write a slightly longer paper stating the objectives of the new system; this can then serve as an introduction to the User Requirements Specification.

User Requirements Specification

The User Requirements Specification (URS) is the main document. It should specify what functions the users need, but not how, so that two systems could present different ways of achieving the same result. Its initial sections should deal with the operational environment of the system, what sort of organisation it is, the type of service the library provides, the main priorities, and also the technical environment in terms of networks, computer architecture, hardware and operating systems. The URS also needs to indicate the number of users expected (library staff and readers separately), and the size of the catalogue or database. Later sections should address the functionality required of the main processes, Ordering and Acquisitions, Cataloguing, Circulation, etc.

The main purposes of the URS are to:

- give the supplier a good idea of whether to submit a proposal and, if so, what sort of configuration he or she should propose
- provide the library staff evaluating prospective systems with a reference point or benchmark.

The URS needs to draw out any special or peculiar features of the library in question, such as multilingual or multi-script requirements.

The URS will also be the basis for the Invitation To Tender (ITT).

Shortlisting criteria

The point of short-listing criteria is to reduce the list of possible contenders down to some predetermined and manageable number, ideally three or perhaps four and never more than five, which can then be evaluated in detail. Typically around half a dozen and no more than a dozen criteria should be needed. There is no point in having more criteria than are necessary to produce a manageable shortlist.

Price is usually a crucial shortlisting criterion. The technical environment may be another, for example, does the organisation insist on UNIX or Microsoft NT? Multilingual support or ability to manage non-book material may be another. The availability of reference sites or a large user base in the country is also a major element of the evaluation process.

Evaluation and selection

The evaluation process itself may well be guided or run by an outside consultant, but it is essential that library staff are closely involved. They should be involved in testing each system for their own particular function, so the librarian's fingers must be on the keyboard, not those of the sales staff demonstrating the system. Ideally the slowest or least competent typists should be involved because (a) it is easier to follow what they are doing and (b) they are more likely to make mistakes. A predetermined script should be prepared of typical transactions, and it should be ensured that some of these transactions are incorrect. Any fool can design a system that works, the skill is in designing a system that works when it goes wrong.

The evaluation model

A key element of the evaluation process is having a structured evaluation model so that the same judgement process can be made for each shortlisted system. This is why one needs to limit the shortlist to three systems, above that and it becomes more difficult to distinguish one system from another. The evaluation model also needs to allow for the relative importance of various features and functions. The evaluation process needs to look at a much wider range of issues than just the functionality and price of each package on offer. The quality of the support service, the availability of training courses, the development history and projections all need to be taken into account.

At the end of the process, one needs to be able to compare two or three systems that probably cannot, sensibly, be made to be exactly equivalent. So there will be, at least, two measures that need to be balanced:

- the relative evaluation score of each system
- the predicted cost of ownership.

There is a great temptation when testing and evaluating systems to concentrate on the 'special bits' of one's requirement and assume that all the standard functions must be OK because everyone performs them. Such assumptions can be dangerous! Hence, the need to undertake evaluation sessions with a script that includes the boring, everyday, standard functions as well.

The final stages of the selection process are to:

- select a system based on functionality and cost of ownership
- negotiate a detailed contract – without re-opening the whole evaluation procedure.

It can be tempting to think that 'negotiating' means screwing down the cost as far as possible – not necessarily so. A new library management system is likely to remain in place for several years and it is helpful if the supplier does too. Obviously no one wants to pay over the odds, but very often it can be mutually more beneficial to negotiate extra software or services for little extra cost.

Levels of maintenance and support need to be agreed – and accounted for in the budget. The question of implementation support is often crucial. Whatever existing system is in place will probably have to run for several months, usually at least three, perhaps six, in parallel with the new system.

It is at this final stage of signing a contract, that the argument about detailed specifications re-emerges. Are you sure exactly what the system will do? What if it all goes wrong? Part of the final contract should be a set of Acceptance Criteria and it is common for the system to be paid for in tranches, with the final one dependent on meeting the Acceptance Criteria.

Key evaluation criteria

Each library should produce its own evaluation model, but it is not necessary to start from scratch. Most consultants and some similar organisations will have produced evaluation criteria that can be tuned to a particular library. There are several alternative approaches but key principles are:

- Define as many criteria practicable.

- Allow different weights to be attached to different functions.
- Enable staff to contribute to evaluation.
- Have a mechanism for resolving disagreements.

What is not a good practice is to have a long list of very detailed mandatory and desirable requirements and then eliminate anyone who doesn't answer 'Yes' to every mandatory item. There may well be an acceptable or even better alternative for achieving the same objective. This approach will tend to eliminate the more honest responses and produce a shortlist of anyone who will answer 'Yes' to anything, and then 'clarify' their responses later, probably as late as possible, when time is running short and there is less room for manoeuvre. Customers can then find themselves reluctantly accepting a system that does not really meet their overall requirements in the best way.

Key evaluation criteria include:

- record import and export
- connectivity and networking
- standards
- supplier standing
- cost of ownership.

Record import and export

Record import and export should include the ability to input the previous catalogue, although this may be achieved by a separate retrospective conversion (ReCon) exercise. Import and/or export of MARC records will often be recorded. What happens if the same record is imported and then exported? Is it still identical? It may be necessary to exchange records with non-library systems in the organisation, such as email requests, accounting records, archives.

Connectivity and networking

Connectivity and networking are becoming the key features of library systems. The computer equivalent of an old truism: is 'IT's not what you know, but who you network with.'

Key points are:

- scalability of the system and its network connections
- network compatibility

Scalability

A library or information centre may have only one or two dozen terminals, but connection to the corporate network could give 5,000 or 20,000 people access, even though it is unlikely that many will be online at the same time.

Network compatibility

Library systems do not have to run on the same hardware and operating system as the rest of the organisation. They should be chosen on their merits, where network compatibility is definitely one of the key merits, but interconnection standards should make it easier to plug in different architectures. However there are several crucial factors which should be incorporated in the evaluation process.

Support skills
Life will normally be a lot easier for information professionals (who tend not to be computer 'techies') if they have the goodwill and technical support of the 'IT' staff (who tend not to know much about the 'I' in IT). This should give an advantage to a library system running on an operating system known by the IT Department.

Network suppliers
One of the iron rules of computer systems' maintenance is that if two machines are connected by a wire and something goes wrong, then it is the 'other suppliers' fault'. If two networks are connected, the situation is even murkier. In many ways, it is a miracle that the Internet works at all, a tribute to the peculiar breed of people who can actually understand and devise standards for the rest of us to follow. There will almost certainly be a significant cost saving in the long term if the networking used by the library system is the same as that for the rest of the organisation.

Security
Library systems now commonly connect to the outside world (presenting their OPAC to external viewers, sending requests to other libraries or suppliers, providing web access and perhaps providing an external email service). They will normally also be connected to the organisation's own internal network. Furthermore, libraries often provide PCs with floppy disc drives on which users can work or download references.

All these factors add up to a potential security hazard in these days when software viruses can flash around the world within a few hours and disrupt computer systems without warning. Libraries used not to think of themselves as targets in the same league as, say, military installations or bastions of international capitalism, but because of the random quality of software viruses and the open nature of library systems, libraries are in fact extremely exposed. It will therefore be necessary for the library system to include some security measures, or at least to connect to other systems via a computer which provides such security (often referred to as a 'firewall').

Although many library systems are moving on to the Windows NT and Windows 2000 platform, it should be noted that Windows NT has been criticised for poor security. UNIX is generally regarded as much more reliable and more secure. Many people will be under the impression that Microsoft and the Intel PC dominates the computer systems market and the Internet, with a fading contribution from Netscape. In fact, this is nowhere near true. Many web servers are Apple Macs and the commonest web server platform software is a package called Apache, usually running on UNIX, unheard of by many people.

Supplier standing and repuation

This can be a tricky one. Everyone has to start somewhere. Comfort factors for potential customers tend to include aspects such as a lengthy track record in the business, a large installed customer base, profitability, a healthy financial position (not necessarily the same as current profitability), size of the company or its parent group, current sales or a healthy share price. These are typically the points that a sales representative will emphasise to reassure a prospect. However, some of them can be a snare and a delusion.

> We are part of a £2 billion (or, increasingly, $2 billion) group; so
> we have financial security that competitor X can only dream of

When one hears this line it is as well to remind oneself that (a) unfortunately, it is true that large companies can go bust as well as small ones; (b) a stock market valuation has very little relationship to the worth of a company (merely to what people *think* it is worth); and (c) a £2 billion group can close or sell off a £2 million subsidiary without a blink of an eye. What is more reassuring is a list of existing satisfied customers. Most suppliers will furnish a list of reference sites and be happy for prospects to visit them unaccompanied by a company representative. Since librarians and information scientists are notoriously internationalist and use email at the drop of a hat, it would be rather difficult to stop them seeking out other users around the world anyway.

What is harder to discern, but more critical, is whether a supplier has the resources to continue supporting its existing customers while developing upgrades and new products. The age of the current product, the financial strength of the supplier and the size of the installed base are all part of this equation. However, satisfied customers who are happy to recommend the product are perhaps the most critical element. A well-established supplier will usually have a user group of existing customers and will often provide a contact point. User groups have varying degrees of independence (some are partly funded by the supplier) but they should be able to present a consolidated view of product development over the last few years.

Cost of ownership

Explicit costs
Explicit costs are relatively easy to identify, but some guarantee on future charges needs to be incorporated, for example, are annual maintenance charges inflation rates linked over the next, say, seven years? The main elements of the visible costs are:

- 'purchase' price
- implementation consultancy and assistance
- training costs
- retrospective conversion charges
- annual software maintenance
- database licensing charges
- upgrade costs.

Hidden costs
These are mostly time-based costs but may also involve additional training or bought in expertise, for example:

- database administration – advantages of self-maintaining databases
- client upgrade management – distribution of thick clients
- software component version compatibility – 'Will this work with that?' type problems.

The most difficult hidden costs are risk dependent, those for staff time that may or may not be needed. These could include: consequential costs of delays from not implementing the system, or a module, when planned; extra work required because of bugs and teething problems, and work-arounds because some function does not work the way it should. Since none of these scenarios should happen, it may seem perverse to cost them. Ideally, one should make a realistic estimate of what it might cost and as realistic an estimate as possible of the risk of it happening and multiply the two together. If the results are different for two suppliers, then this should be reflected in the evaluation comparison.

Total cost of ownership

The most critical evaluation criterion of all is usually the price. In the computer industry, the term being used increasingly is 'total cost of ownership' (TCO) The point of the TCO is that it reflects the real long-term price, not just what appears on the ticket. Since library systems are a much more complex purchase than, say, the purchase of a lorry-load of PCs, and they will probably have a longer life, the TCO issue is even more important – and harder to pin down. The two elements of the 'TCO' are the explicit costs and the hidden ones.

Electronic and hybrid library issues

Any modern library now offers its users at least some electronic resources. A library that comprises a mixture of print and electronic or digital resources is termed a 'hybrid' library. There are one or two corporate libraries which are now 'book-free' zones and completely electronic. Initially electronic resources were seen as additional services and often available on a separate PC, perhaps entered in the main catalogue (but probably not). Now that they are part of the core collection it is not enough that these resources are included in the catalogue: increasingly users familiar with the World Wide Web expect to be able to click on a catalogue entry and be taken direct to the appropriate item. The range of possibilities and, increasingly, of expectations includes:

- links to CD-ROM databases
- links to web sites
- links to other library systems:
  - of the same supplier
  - regional consortia
  - sector consortia
- ILL links
- online ordering
- links to electronic journal web services, such as SFX from Ex-Libris.

The issues that need to be addressed when managing and implementing the digital components of a library are both technical and techno-commercial (arising from the variety of methods used to control use of digital material).

Adding digital material to the library will soon add to the demands made on the network. Presenting catalogue records for printed material is one thing – transferring quantities of text and images is quite another. Suppliers must be able to provide figures on the bandwidth required for their services. Other technical issues to be addressed include the standards for communication across the network (many CD products for instance are not web-based and getting them to operate from a 'CD tower' is not always easy).

The commercial issues usually arise round the problems such as licensing and copy control. Publishers will place restrictions – usually on the numbers of people who have simultaneous access – on their products. Access outside certain IP (Internet protocol) addresses (and therefore for home-based users) may be problematic. Security firewalls may prevent access to externally held web-based products. There are products and techniques for getting round these problems but the best strategy is to include such issues in your assessment of products before a commitment is made.

The latest trends in digital libraries are the emergence of external online libraries and e-books. Services such as netlibrary and ebrary, provide complete resources for research including digitised books, serials and additional services all integrated into a package which can be subscribed to on a 'pay-as-you-go' basis. Although still in their infancy, and mostly general in coverage, they point the way towards specialist services which gather material from many sources and then sell on to special libraries.

E-books are small electronic reading devices which are pre-loaded and updateable that can carry around 10 to 100 books. Among the numerous advantages over traditional books, the text can be searched, annotated, copied (depending on copyright). Ideal for remote working and for practitioners requiring large collections of core material (such as a complete law library), e-books will become a key component of many library services.

Implementation issues

Phased implementation v big bang

The biggest difficulty in the implementation of the system is not technical – it is the management problem of absorbing the changes in service, procedures and training, the human and cultural factors. In deciding whether to go for a 'big bang' or a phased implementation, the technical issues certainly need consideration, not least whether it is actually *possible*. More importantly what are the 'knock-on' effects of implementation and will the other systems – manual and automated – continue smoothly?

An example is with serials implementation. The package can be installed and ready for use but the amount of effort in entering the relevant data to control checkin of issues will probably take some time since there is little standardisation in the area of publication patterns. Thus, a pragmatic approach whereby the manual system is used in parallel (as data is gradually added to the database) may be the only possible method. Each functional area should be assessed for the practicality of a big bang approach before the decision is taken. A pilot scheme on a small set of data, to simulate the effects, is an excellent way to reveal potential problems.

Phased implementation is less dramatic as there is generally less risk. However, make sure that phasing does not mean running two systems and doubling staff workloads, resulting in low morale.

Consultancy support

Consultancy support for the implementation phase can be a useful invest-ment – especially if you have not gone through the process before. Consultants have amassed much practical experience over many similar jobs and can make sure that expensive or embarrassing mistakes are avoided.

Data take-on

Database conversion
Main points:

• Learn and understand the data structures of the new system – restrictions, new features etc. (this is most important if this not a MARC to MARC transfer).

• Define the mapping of old system data fields to the new system.

• Clarify any issues when data needs to be split or merged.

• Define if data clean-up is required, e.g. upper to lower case etc.

• Do as many clean-ups on the old system as possible (if it is not possible to do on the new system or programming is expensive.)

• Create test data, either artificial or samples from real data, in order to test as many conditions in the specification as possible.

• Establish clear criteria for conversion acceptance and your own methods of checking sample data conversions.

• Don't forget the holdings data is not as standard as MARC biblio-graphic data.

ReCon

• Check out prices and services from a variety of companies. OCLC, BL, SLS Data Services, North West Data Services (Origin UK) and several Far East and American services that do an excellent job at very competitive prices.

• Decide on USMARC or UKMARC as some systems can only han-dle one sort; conversion between MARC formats is expensive on large collections.

Recataloguing

The recataloguing (manual entry of items) is not normally cost effective but may be unavoidable if the material being catalogued is unusual, such as video tapes or archives (where records cannot be obtained elsewhere). The opportunity to handle every item in the collection and assess its relevance is a side benefit – should it be catalogued or thrown away?

Acceptance criteria

System acceptance is a thorny issue and the rules for this should be established as part of the contract. The aim of defining acceptance criteria is to have a measurable test of whether the system meets the agreed objectives. To accept a system usually means that you are happy enough to pay for it. There are always some things about a system that are not quite as you expected and the acceptance rules should guide you as to what to do about them. A supplier will normally give a period for you to test and accept a system. If they do not provide system test criteria, then devise your own. Test each of the main functions and list any problems.

Classify the problems according to importance and define your acceptance in terms of these problems. For example, the system will be accepted if all class A (vitally important) problems are fixed and class B (important but not vital) problems are scheduled and contracted for fixing. Issues such as 'user friendliness', 'ease of use' and 'efficiency of input' are fine for evaluation criteria. They can be entirely subjective as long as the same test is used to compare all systems. As an absolute criterion for accepting or rejecting a particular system, such vague terms are no use at all. A throughput rate for certain transactions could be an acceptance criteria – but the supplier should have the option of being able to demonstrate it with their own staff.

Key acceptance criteria could include the conversion of old records, setting up of templates, completion of training courses and successful completion of a range of transaction types. Other typical acceptance criteria will include a list of transactions, with test data, which must be processed correctly. This list with the associated output definitions then becomes part of the contract. Hold back payments (agree this at contract time) if problems are not fixed. Note that when a system begins to be used and 'benefit' is gained from the software, however flawed it may be, then the supplier has a much stronger claim to be paid. If it is not 'fit for purpose' then do not use it.

Operational issues

'Operational issues' apply to the halcyon days *after* the period of selecting a system, *after* the implementation of the new system, *after* the database is taken on, *after* the initial staff training has been completed and *after* the period of parallel running of old and new systems. In practice, the operating phase for one part of the system will often overlap with the implementation phase of another part. For example, the Catalogue may be implemented first, then the Ordering and Acquisitions module, then Circulation Control, then Serials. Most operational issues can be grouped under one of four headings:

- support arrangements
- operating procedures
- system tuning and upgrading
- training and documentation.

Support arrangements

Support arrangements should have been a key element in the evaluation process. Normally the library system supplier will offer a range of support and maintenance options, usually varying from between 10 per cent and 15 per cent of the 'purchase' price (but this may be skewed if the pricing model spreads the 'capital cost' element over the life of the system). The main variables in support contracts are:

- whether upgrades are free (i.e. included in the maintenance contract)
- the speed of response to a call (typically between two and 48 hours).

Although it may sound fine to have a two hour response time to calls, that will usually come at a heavy premium. Is your library system that critical? It may also be necessary to have other support contracts in place, such as for the computer hardware, network and perhaps database management system, although usually one would expect the LMS supplier to be able to deal with database problems affecting their package.

Some support contracts are with third parties, perhaps the company responsible for putting together a 'turnkey' package of hardware and software; the company that was in charge of the evaluation and selection and/or implementation procedures. Less formally, the User Group may also offer a support network. To some extent mail groups such as LIS-Link, offer support, although not usually for system-type queries. Other useful (USA-based) mail-lists are:

- SYSLIB-L aimed at the general problems for systems librarians sorted – to subscribe, send :
  SUB SYSLIB-L your name to: **listserv@listserv.acsu.buffalo.edu**
- WEB4LIB – a useful list to get web access and other problems sorted out – to subscribe send :
  SUB Web4Lib your name to: **listserv@library.berkeley.edu**

Operating procedures

Certain operating procedures will be specific to an organisation (such as back-up, reporting, adding new users and deleting or suspending old ones). Most of these will concern only the systems librarian and perhaps one or two other staff. Nevertheless, any key procedures should be documented and consolidated into a procedures manual, 'cook book' or some other readily accessible single source. Moreover, despite being in the virtual age, these need to be recorded on paper; they are most likely to be needed when the computer has crashed.

Every library system needs a systems librarian
That is someone responsible for starting the system up, taking back-ups, ensuring there is paper in the printer, a tape in the tape drive, space on the disc etc. Even in a one-man-band library where the full job title may be 'chief cook, bottle washer and systems librarian', someone needs to have that responsibility. It may be that all the support functions are contracted out or delegated to the IT Department. Nevertheless, someone should be defined as systems librarian and have the prime responsibility for overseeing and co-ordinating this essential job.

The key operating procedures will usually involve:

* security
* back-up

and sometimes

* disaster recovery.

Part of the back-up cycle should involve one of the most recent back-up copies being stored off-site, or at least far enough away from the library system computer to ensure they will survive a major disaster in the computer room. Back-ups should be tested periodically by restoring their contents to a spare machine. Tapes should be retensioned often and replaced periodically according to the manufacturer's recommendations.

System tuning and upgrading

System tuning is something of a black art and not a skill librarians should normally need. If however, the catalogue database is expanded greatly from a small beginning (for example, as a REtrospective CONversion (ReCon) project takes effect) then some databases can become extremely inefficient. This is usually solved by running an overnight or weekend job to rebuild the database to optimise retrieval speed.

Upgrading a system to the latest release may be technically easy or it may require assistance from the IT department, supplier or external consultant. As any Microsoft user should know, the term 'upgrade' should be treated with some caution. Software upgrades are similar to wonder drugs for previously untreatable illnesses. They invariably have side-effects, and some are worse than the original condition.

There is much to be said for the traditional attitude of 'if it ain't broke, don't fix it'. However, staying with an old version of a software package almost invariably has deleterious effects in the long term – but not necessarily in the short or medium term. For those who don't want to be pioneers and trail-blazers, the best strategy is probably to wait for others to do the up-grade and report the faults, and then follow on when most of the bugs are fixed. In an ideal world, one should always be able to roll back a software upgrade if it results in unforeseen problems or unacceptable performance. It is also a good idea to upgrade software (and hardware) components one by one, with a suitable gap in between, to allow any problems to emerge.

Unfortunately, this step-by-step approach is not always feasible. In some cases an upgrade to one part of a system requires other software compo-nents to be upgraded, for instance the LMS version requires the latest operating system that needs the latest DBMS version and also a later version of the software in part of the communications systems. If this becomes necessary and something goes wrong, it can become extremely tiresome trying to identify which component (and supplier) is at fault.

In these days of very low disk costs, it is feasible to duplicate the whole system – a worthwhile practice run for back-ups in any case – and install and test any upgrades on the test system before releasing them on the main 'production' version. This is standard practice in most profession-ally run IT departments and is well worth emulating.

Training and documentation

It is relatively easy to cost in the initial training when the system is new. However, later versions of the software may mean that further training is necessary, or at least highly desirable. There will also be staff turnover, and therefore the need for repeat training. Inhouse documentation, how-ever informal, is part of the induction and training material for new staff, so any particular tricks or problems solved should be noted, rather like the Frequently Asked Questions (FAQs) listed on some web sites.

Further information

Any computer-related issues require constant updating as technology changes and trends emerge. An excellent source of both technical and commercial information about the library, information and IT industry is Biblio Tech Review: *http://www.biblio-tech.com* – posted each month and covering all the issues raised in this chapter.

Chapter 18

Intranets: the bigger picture

Paul Blackmore

Intranets explained

Intranets are now emerging from a recent history where they were commonly regarded as a cheap and cheerful means of meeting an organisation's information needs. The realisation now is that there is more to be gained from these enabling Internet technologies than merely reaping a quick return on investment (ROI) through savings on reprographic costs. Although intranets may initially appear to be inexpensive to implement, the ensuing operational and development issues become far more complex.

Five years on from when pioneering organisations first implemented corporate-wide intranets (Aslib, 1996) and claimed massive cost savings in reprographics and publishing, these same organisations are now realising that the technology can offer greater rewards. With the advent of more sophisticated technology and applications that greater reflect core business aims, the intranet has become recognised as a strategic tool to nurture the identification, sharing and creation of an organisation's intellectual and knowledge assets, known increasingly as the corporate memory.

This chapter aims to reflect how this transformation can be realised and the sometimes painful lessons learnt by these organisations in readdressing how best to exploit their intranets for greater business value.

So what is an intranet?

Due to the fact that intranets frequently cross organisational boundaries and 'touch' all functional areas and departments, even the process of defining an intranet can be more complicated than first envisaged.

An intranet may be seen to be different things, depending on the perspective held by each individual and their respective job function and department (or even their relationship to the organisation as a whole if they are a supplier or customer). An IT manager may well define an intranet as '...an IP-based network of nodes behind a firewall, or behind several firewalls connected by secure, possibly virtual, networks' (*Intranet*

Design Magazine, 1999). A knowledge manager may refer to an intranet as 'an organisation's corporate memory'. Both of these definitions are valid.

In trying to take into consideration as many differing perspectives as possible the context of this chapter will adopt the fairly wide definition for an intranet as prescribed by the Institute of Management (Irving and McWilliams, 1999):

> An intranet is a private, corporate network that uses Internet products and technologies. Access to an intranet is controlled by the organisation that established it, and is often restricted just to employees. Occasionally, however, suppliers and customers can also be given access to parts of it.

The latter proviso referring to suppliers and customers can also include remote employees in the field or at home. This form of access to an intranet is known as an extranet and will be examined later in this chapter.

KPMG (1997) have highlighted how organisations benefit most from implementing an intranet:

- releasing the latent value of the information it holds
- sharing the use of the information
- allowing expertise and intellectual skills to be exploited more widely
- encouraging teams to work and grow together
- removing departmental barriers
- improving cross-functional communications
- enabling greater collaboration between geographically distributed employees
- linking remote offices
- changing the nature of work and employment
- reshaping power structures and management.

Business applications and services

The following section highlights departments and functions that can benefit significantly from utilising an organisation's intranet in performing their core business activities. It does not, however, suggest that these are the only functions which are worthwhile in adding value to an organisation's intranet. The more appealing and useful the content is to a wide cross-section of the organisation, the more support it will have to grow and succeed.

Unfortunately, the scope of this chapter does not allow for a blow-by-blow account of how each business function can exploit the benefits offered by intranet applications. However, the following examples are given to show how central services may use an intranet to add business value to the range and delivery of their core services, many of which may be adopted in other functions across the organisation.

The personnel department

Content with instant appeal across all functions of an organisation is obviously a desirable asset to encourage the successful implementation of an intranet. One business area that provides such opportunities is the human resource (HR) department.

HR functions are often charged with the remit of publishing and distributing large amounts of documentation across the organisation. Such documents include organisational charts, telephone directories, newsletters, personnel policies and procedures, employee handbooks and training schedules. Having such currency-critical information on an intranet adds value because it is updated more regularly than hard copy and is more easily accessible. In addition to the cost benefits of electronic dissemination of such information, more significant gains are to be made by HR through the introduction of intranet systems that enhance the business process (Newing, 1997). Providing authenticated electronic access to individual personnel records for managers and employees to change details such as addressees, telephone numbers, marriage details, job descriptions etc., can significantly relieve HR personnel of these routine administrative tasks to pursue more proactive strategic remits.

Library and information services

Strong arguments are often made for the library and information service (LIS) to be at the centre of any programme to roll out new information management or dissemination technology (Blakeman, 1996; Blackmore, 1997). Based on the success of many case studies, the same argument can be equally applied to the introduction of intranets (Bevan and Evans, 1996; Blackmore, 1996; ISAC, 1998; Primich and Varnum, 1999).

A LIS will already possess knowledge of the salient issues and skills required to source, organise and disseminate information to an organisation. They will already have close business relationships with internal customers that span the organisation and have knowledge of their respective information needs. Indeed, a study of several corporate libraries highlighted that much inconvenience can be saved by involving the information management skills of the LIS at the outset rather than bringing them in to revamp and trouble shoot once the size of an organisation's intranet has become too unwieldy in later years (Hall and Jones, 2000).

Furthermore, the department will already hold large amounts of information, often in electronic format, ready to add instant and useful content to the intranet. The LIS may have responsibility for many of the remits described above for the HR department. However, services specific to the LIS which can add instant value to an intranet include: book catalogue databases, journal catalogue, new acquisitions databases, technical reports databases. Web-interfaced loan systems are able to provide loans and reservations for hard-copy resources whilst electronic resources can be quickly accessed through retrieval systems via established and meaningful controlled thesauri. CD-ROMs storing electronic journals and databases can also be launched and viewed via the web browser interface.

IT department

The department charged with the responsibility of supporting the needs of the end user and maintaining and repairing hardware (i.e. computer support, computing services or information systems and services) is a central service used by everyone in the organisation and thereby an ideal source of instant content and value-added services for the intranet.

Services can range from static content such as software manuals, workstation specifications and purchasing recommendations, frequently asked questions (FAQs), newsletters, lists of software availability, anti-virus alerts and advice, workstation and software configurations, corporate intranet templates, remote access instructions, security policies, training programmes, staff remits and contact details.

More dynamic content can include forms processing, 'backoffice' databases (for fault reporting, room and equipment bookings, general enquiries, etc.) and knowledge-based management systems for online help applications.

For multinational organisations simple scheduling systems can be used to reroute help-desk queries to IT support people as one shift pattern finishes and another shift begins on the other side of the world (Greer, 1998).

Implementing an intranet

As mentioned at the beginning of the chapter intranets are generally recognised as being fairly uncomplicated to initiate especially if the underlying network infrastructure already exists. However, it is at this point that many corporate intranets have been seen to stagnate and fail. So what are the reasons for this?

Following a field study of intranet implementation in large Danish and South African organisations, Damsgaard and Scheepers (2000) have prescribed a four-stage model which allows the organisation to reflect on each process used to implement their intranet and plan more strategically for its future development and therefore simultaneously planning to avoid its failure in the process.

The four stages of this progressive model towards organisation-wide acceptance are:

Initiation   ➔   Contagion   ➔   Control   ➔   Integration

The authors argue that specific objectives must be fulfilled during each stage of an intranet's implementation. If these objectives are not met the development of the intranet will not be able to move to the next stage, resulting in stagnation and its eventual regression to an experimental system.

The model from the Damsgaard and Scheepers study has been adopted below to list some of the objectives needed to be met at each stage of implementation and to highlight related issues raised elsewhere in the literature.

Stage 1: Initiation

Objective: identify and recruit a 'sponsor'
At this stage the intranet may be in the form of a feasibility study, a single experimental project or series of emergent 'child' or 'grey' (Ogg, 1997) intranets dispersed randomly across the organisation, each with its own respective 'champion' eager to promote its worth to those in their local environment.

Therefore, a 'sponsor' is required at this stage to 'adopt or grab' the intranet(s) to nurture and encourage its growth and usage. These will be prominent members of the organisation and will have the authority to secure funding and the resources to scale out and market the intranet to the rest of the organisation.

Stage 2: Contagion

Objective: achieve critical mass
The balance between content and the number of users is considered critical to aid self-proliferation and sustainability for the intranet. The sponsor's key role at this stage is to 'sell' the intranet to the organisation and its employees and encourage their own contribution to the expansion of the content.

In a recent benchmarking survey of intranets conducted by the Knowledge Development Centre at Cranfield University (Cap Gemini, 1999) evidence was found also suggesting that the existence of 'critical mass' is a key factor as to whether an intranet will provide increasing value to a business.

The three key areas in which 'critical mass' is purported to be required are:

- users (success can only come from people using the intranet)
- content (there has to be ever-more useful and relevant material available)
- utilisation (the extent to which potential users are connected per day).

The study estimates that at least 40 per cent of all potential users need to access the intranet to achieve this critical mass if real business value is to be generated.

Stage 3: Control

Objective: establish procedures and standardisation
Once critical mass has been achieved it is essential that relevance and currency of information and data can be guaranteed. If these policies are not in place the following problems begin to arise:

- 'dead' hyperlinks
- dated information becomes misinformation
- lack of cohesion and continuity between new and existing content
- information overload on the part of the end-user
- navigating and locating content becomes ever more difficult.

If this state goes unchecked the user-population will start to mistrust the integrity and value of the content, which in turn will quickly lead to ever decreasing states of stagnation.

Additional factors not yet considered as to why intranets sometimes fail may also include:

- lack of training – the remedy should not only include browser training but also provide employees with a basic awareness of HTML authoring, search engine use and content management issues
- unauthorised access (security breaches) to intranet content via external networks (extranets, virtual private networks, etc.)
- inefficient retrieval tools thereby creating time wasted through the process of retrieving information and then the problem of noise-to-relevance ratio whilst deciphering what is and what isn't useful
- bandwidth – don't overload the system and frustrate the end user with needless bells and whistles i.e. do not use multimedia formats where text will do!

- a misconception (or worse, the actual realisation) that the implementation of the intranet is in some way connected to downsizing initiatives by senior management
- failure to recognise up and coming technologies
- failure to control protectionist behaviour by knowledge holders or information gatekeepers.

Stage 4: Integration

Objective: seamless user-access to the corporate memory across the organisation
This is a point in time where the controls and procedures are now embedded within the quality assurance systems and culture of the organisation. The intranet becomes the 'definitive record' of all information, process, knowledge and therefore learning that takes place within the organisation.

This stage represents the required threshold of the intranet's evolution from that of the organisation's central information repository to become the 'corporate memory' (Kuhn and Abecker, 1999). The prevailing issue now is the continual improvement of processes that nurture the capture, sharing and creation of knowledge.

Filling the intranet

Regardless of any decisions which are finalised in how an intranet project is going to proceed, those involved previously in implementing projects will agree that for an intranet to succeed it must attract users.

There are generally considered to be two kinds of content: 'flat', also known as 'static' content and 'interactive' content. This simple method of categorisation generally reflects the level of technical sophistication of an intranet to relay this information. Research studies (August, 1999; Cap Gemini, 1999) have cited three stages in which an intranet often matures based on the following distinctive generations of development:

➜ Flat or static content (also known as the 'post-it generation')

   ➜ Interactive content (also known as the 'use-it generation')

      ➜ Extranet / e-commerce applications (a.k.a. the 'sell-it generation')

Flat content

Virtually any networking platform that is able to run a web browser on a workstation will support the dissemination of 'flat' or 'static' information. This kind of data is simply held in files (web pages or other standardised documents such as word-processed files or spreadsheets) on either a networked file or web server. It is then retrieved and viewed through the use of a web browser and hyperlinked, just like the World Wide Web. This simple framework is usually the way in which most intranets are initially implemented.

Examples of flat content include:

- travel aids, maps, service point locations, etc.
- the organisation's mission statement, aims and objectives, history of organisation
- internal contact directories: basic details such as job function, location and email addresses
- external contact directories: suppliers, other group businesses, industry-relevant organisations
- internal newsletters and related business information: share prices, major contract information, messages from the chief executive officer or managing director
- competitor information and market intelligence digests
- product information: specification and ranges of the organisation's products and services
- departmental pages: contact details, functions, remits and activities
- events calendars: relating to organisation and industry-related events and activities
- dissemination, compliance and maintenance of policy and procedures manuals e.g. Health & Safety systems, ISO 9000, BS5750 etc.
- FAQs (frequently asked questions)
- recruiting and internal job postings
- subject specific information may be mirrored from the Internet
- hierarchical subject menus, portals or quality filters providing organised signposts and live hyperlinks to relevant business sources available on the Internet.

Interactive content

Once you have identified or started to fill your intranet with static content and are satisfied that measures, policies and procedures are in place to continually improve the management of this information, you may then wish to examine how your organisation may capitalise from more interactive intranet applications such as:

- electronic mail
- education and training systems
- helpdesk systems

- search engines
- forms processing applications, i.e. resource reservation systems for conference rooms, pool cars and office equipment, etc.; feedback on official documents, reports and surveys; submission of expense claims, submission of internal order or purchase documentation
- discussion and conferencing boards, Community of Practices (CoP).

It is important to note here the additional technology required for an intranet to make the progression from 'flat content' to include interactive content. It is possible to implement a 'flat content' intranet on a client-server based network without using TCP/IP (Internet Protocol) (Blackmore, 1997) as long as it will support the use of web browsers on its workstations. To provide examples of the interactive content listed above, you will need to install a web server. This is software required to execute the various programs and 'scripts' required for the provision of interactive and dynamic content.

Commercial or externally sourced information

These resources may be:

- electronic databases
- electronic journals
- electronic newsfeeds.

These examples may fall into either category of flat or interactive content depending on the product or service purchased. You may find, however, that the provision of such resources provides an effective 'honey-pot' to attract users and to ensure they return frequently.

Information retrieval and document management issues

This next section highlights some of the technologies used to manage the storage and retrieval of the organisation's intellectual assets.

In a recent survey of IT users conducted by the UK National Computing Centre (1999) over half of the respondents regarded the keeping of intranet content up to date as a major problem and one-third also regarded the control of new incoming material submitted by users as a major problem.

As cited in the section describing the life cycle of intranet implementation, an intranet can easily become a 'victim of its own success'. Like paper-based systems, intranet content also needs to be organised and maintained effectively. This is essential to ensure the timely retrieval of information. It is just as important to maintain the integrity of information, and indeed this may be a compliance activity (for example when dealing with quality systems or customer projects which may be subject to stringent auditing procedures).

If the manual maintenance of information starts to become onerous, there may be a business case to support the purchase of an electronic document management system (DMS). DMSs were around long before the advent of the WWW and have been most commonly used in large corporate departments responsible for the creation and maintenance of manuals, reports, product specifications, marketing literature and related records. Today's DMSs have been further refined to help manage the additional complexities associated with web pages, namely the creation and maintenance of document hypertext links.

If your organisation is considering purchasing such a file management system, you may wish to evaluate whether it meets the following criteria as recommended by the 'Complete Intranet Resource' web site (2000):

- version control facility
- ability to store metadata
- security
- check-in/check-out facility
- search and indexing capability
- file interdependencies and groupings utilities
- interface (open standard solution preferred where no client-side installs needed)
- structure and organisational capabilities
- support for multiple file types
- maintenance file expiration dates.

Search engines

Just as search engines are one of the most popular ways of searching the Internet, by using combinations of keywords chosen by the user, so they have become one of the most popular retrieval technologies available to search an intranet. In fact the majority of search engine services on the Internet, including examples such as Altavista *http://www.altavista.com/* and Excite *http://www.excite.com/*, now also produce intranet versions of their WWW variants and can be expected to provide the same comprehensive range of search facilities including:

- natural language searching
- Boolean searching
- automatic root expansion

- proximity searching
- numeric searching
- term weighted searching
- thesaurus integration
- search by object, e.g. PowerPoint files, GIF images, Adobe Acrobat files
- search by metadata fields, e.g. function categorising, author, date
- concept searching, e.g. 'find similar to this'
- summarising facilities.

If you are considering using the above list as benchmarking criteria in selecting a search product for your own intranet you may also wish to consider asking some of the following additional questions (highlighted in an independently devised methodology suggested for evaluating intranet search engines (Stenmark, 1999):

- Is the product designed for [an] intranet?
- How large are the data volumes that can be handled?
- Can remote web servers be indexed?
- What is coming in the next 6-12 months?
- What formats other than HTML can be indexed by default?
- Are duplicate links automatically detected?
- How can the crawling be restricted [security issues]?
- Is the index updated in real-time?
- Is the full text or subset indexed?

Intelligent research agents

Agents are personalised pieces of software designed to search and re-trieve information for individual users who do not have the time to monitor regularly the wealth of information and knowledge resources available on the intranet or Internet. The word 'intelligent' is used to describe the software's ability to generate sets of rules which are used to refine the user's search criteria. This allows the agent to determine the context in which keywords are used to confirm a retrieved document's relevance and to dismiss those sources that are irrelevant to the user.

Portals

To a certain extent the previous retrieval technologies highlighted so far can be found in one generic information retrieval (IR) and management product, known as a portal. A more familiar example of a portal is the format used by web-based search engines and directories (such as

Yahoo!) providing indexed and 'in-context' keyword searching of Internet resources. The Enterprise Information Portal (EIP) is of interest here. The EIP, also described as a 'doorway into intranets' (Computer Technology Research Corporation, 2000), is a web-based interface providing a single point of entry or gateway to an organisation's electronic information resource. It uses a taxonomy common to the enterprise in order to classify and organise resources and make retrieval more precise. It can also include the integration of links to Internet resources relevant to the organisation's business needs.

Defining an EIP depends on the portal's functioning. Detlor (2000) takes a relatively broad view of its purpose and describes a corporate portal 'functioning as an underlying web infrastructure for information management' as a 'shared information space that facilitates access to information content, organisational communications, and group collaboration'.

The EIP is something that is new in name but not in concept. By 1995 Wirral Metropolitan College was already providing a hierarchical subject-based menu as the default page for 1,500 workstations installed with web browsers (Blackmore, 1997). This provided an optional filter providing access to several hundred web sites already inspected and deemed of suitable quality and relevance for the staff and students of the institution. This system of menus also provided a signpost to the more popular and multimedia enhanced sites mirrored on the College intranet servers.

Despite being easy to create inhouse (due to the intuitive nature of the underlying web-interface), maintaining such IR facilities in checking, adding new resources and expanding thesauri everyday can be extremely labour intensive and therefore costly. One solution is to buy a portal kit such as Autonomy's 'Portal -in-a-Box' or Verity's Portal Product Suite.

Common features of these products are the provision of automatic categorisation and hypertext linking of both structured data (i.e. Lotus Notes, ODBC databases, MIS systems) and unstructured data (i.e. PDF, word-processed documents, emails, PowerPoint presentations, newsfeeds and electronic journals). Other components include personalised portal interfaces which automatically generate profiles of user interests and complementary search routines so that they may be regularly alerted to new items of interest (or other colleagues with similar profiles) as and when the information becomes available.

Integrating knowledge management with your intranet strategy

It is now widely recognised that the intranet is an important tool in enabling an organisation's knowledge management strategy. It should be realised though, that an enabling tool is all an intranet can be at this stage. The existence of email clients, web browsers and any amount of static content cannot on its own exploit the benefits of knowledge management (although some managers would argue that the recording and making explicit of expertise and knowledge as static content, in itself, is a knowledge management system). Some hold the view that knowledge can simply be harvested and held as static content and that it is purely technology-led. However, others claim that the success or failure of a KM strategy will depend on cultural and people-centric issues (Hendriks and Vriens, 1999).

The definition

Whatever the standpoint, there is, however, complete agreement that a KM strategy is worth pursuing. So what is it exactly?

KM has been around as a concept for a long time. Part of the reason for KM enjoying such a renaissance can be attributed largely to the advent of the intranet as both a complementary and an enabling technology. This is certainly a view held by Ovum (1999), the independent research consultancy, who suggest in a recent report that 'intranets have been used by many user organisations to challenge and bypass existing barriers to communication' and '...forced organisations to think through their information content strategy, from the capture of ideas to the structure of data, and the storage and distribution of knowledge'.

For a more definitive explanation of KM, we first need to define knowledge. Knowledge is generally recognised to exist in two forms, namely in the form of *explicit* knowledge or *tacit* knowledge. Explicit knowledge is tangible information and is readily available for dissemination, scrutiny and examination by others. This knowledge may take the form of memos, emails, reports and other documented materials. Tacit knowledge on the other hand is not so readily available for capture and dissemination. It is the knowledge held within ourselves, combined with personal perspectives, experience, emotional intelligence and 'gut-feelings'. This is essentially the intellectual capital of an organisation. KM is principally concerned with capturing and sharing both types knowledge, in order to create new knowledge.

The use of technology to disseminate explicit knowledge is fairly transparent especially when this documented knowledge is available for storage and retrieval on the organisation-wide intranet and is obviously a product-centred view of knowledge management. However, the use of technology to make tacit knowledge more readily available to share, can be considered more of a challenge to an organisation and the knowledge manager. This process-centred management of knowledge uses technology to enable the social communication processes that exist when two or more people collaborate and work together. Known as Computer Supported Collaborative Working (CSCW) this utilises software known as groupware or Group Support Systems (GSS) (Dhaliwal and Tung, 2000). As work, discussions and projects progress, the group-decision processes and any related documents appear as digitised transcripts and available for reuse by anyone permitted access to this virtual workspace (or later, via 'archived' material if that specific project has been completed). Mechanisms can be built into CSCW to allow others to add comments or 'signposts' to other related information and knowledge. This will further enhance the intranet's ability to share and nurture the creation of new knowledge across the organisation.

Extranets

It is generally claimed that an extranet can improve communication between an organisation, its customers and suppliers and any geographically distributed employee. Extranet technologies and systems allow limited access to your intranet via the Internet.

A study by IBM Global Services (Poston, 1999) claimed the major benefits of internet or intranet deployment were:

- cost reduction by 36 per cent of the total number of respondents
- commerce revenue by 32 per cent of the total number of respondents
- productivity increase by 32 per cent of the total number of respondents.

Depending on the security systems employed, your extranet can provide varying degrees of access to internal information systems based on the identification of the respective user or user group. Security levels can vary from simple password authentication entered by the user, to more sophisticated levels of security requiring 'client-based' software to be installed on the external workstation. This further reduces the possibility of access by unauthorised third parties and provides greater control over which information, or areas of the web server, can be used. Systems that use this higher degree of security are often referred to as virtual private networks (VPNs).

So what is the value in providing access to an organisation's network and who are these users? There are three typical user groups:

1. Employees. These include home-workers, field workers, franchises, satellite locations (sales offices, etc.), providing access to the same business critical applications available to their corporate site-based counterparts.

2. Customers (corporate clients and individual clients). Facilities may include:
   - enabling customers to contact the organisation for information, complaints, feedback, etc., and even to facilitate collaborative working on issues such as joint ventures or QA compliance activities
   - enabling customers to make payments to the organisation
   - enabling customers to place orders and check their respective status or progress.

3. Suppliers. Facilities may include:
   - enabling suppliers to perform business activities, such as information exchange, joint product design or relevant quality assurance procedures
   - enabling the organisation to make payments to suppliers
   - to allow the organisation to place orders with its suppliers.

When building an extranet, Bradbury (1997) recommends the following should be taken into consideration.

What you should do:
   - Find a balance between the sensitivity of the data you want to expose and the security level you need. It is pointless spending tens of thousands of pounds on sophisticated security devices simply to protect basic marketing brochure information.
   - Think about maximising the function of the applications you offer to your partners using an extranet. Make sure, however, you protect yourself against illicit use of your services.
   - Replicate data to a dedicated server that manages intranet and extranet queries. If you are providing data from a core system, rather than having end-users putting it under additional strain, it would be better to have it replicated. Thus, if the system fails, the core information is still safe on a separate server.

What you should not do:

- Give people access to content without thinking. Anything you publish to external people is at risk, from both hackers and third parties who should not have access to confidential material.
- Underestimate the scale of traffic on your system or customer.
- Expect people to come rushing to your site unless your information is well presented and the site well publicised. Is the web address printed on every brochure and business card?
- Implement a 'fire-and-forget' intranet or extranet. Content should change to keep end-users coming back.

If your organisation has the ability to link one of its internal web servers to the Internet then it will almost certainly already have the technology to provide basic password authentication systems to restrict access to specific content. Most organisations do not have the resources to build their own VPNs (at least in the short term while the technology is still maturing). They do, however, still need the additional benefits and increased security associated with VPN technology (providing, for example, high-level encryption and digital signatures).

A cost-effective alternative to the high start-up costs required for building extranets is to lease the services of the new breed of ISPs (Internet Service Providers) known as extranet service provider (ESPs) (Bauhus, 2000).

Fears

Besides the usual anxieties felt as to whether a project or new initiative will be successful or not, the next major concern relating to extranets is the security issue.

A study conducted across 50 countries by *Information Week* and PricewaterhouseCoopers (Hobby, 1999) claims that organisations who have implemented web commerce, electronic supply chains and enterprise resource planning (ERP) experience 'three times more incidents of information loss and theft of trade secrets than anyone else'. However, the FBI suggests that 70 per cent of unauthorised access, data theft and damage to network infrastructure actually comes from within the organisation.

Costing your intranet

After careful consideration of the issues in the previous sections and the various options, applications and strategies open to your organisation, you may first wish to estimate the cost of implementing such a project. Costing the implementation of an intranet can be tricky. An organisation may already have many of the basic components necessary to construct an intranet and employees may already be unofficially supporting the development of existing 'grey' intranets. It is also useful to plan ahead for the almost certain demand for the integration of business-critical applications and legacy systems. These demands will also be accompanied by the costs for maintenance of ever-increasing volumes of information, requiring greater investment in both technology and human resources.

The most complex costing formula concerns human resources and this will depend largely on the culture of the organisation. It will also depend on the amount of expertise that already exists in the organisation, whether consultants and outsourcing is required and whether the day-to-day management and development of the intranet is managed centrally by dedicated teams or is devolved to individual departments. However, two rather more straightforward areas of costing are those associated with the technology and training. The following checklist, taken from the Complete Intranet Resource (1998) has been adapted as a method for identifying specific areas of cost. When identifying items of expenditure, initial and ongoing costs should both be taken into account for the following.

Client server, i.e. the workstation:

  TCP/IP stack

  browser software

  machine upgrades

    CPU

    memory

    hard disk

    operating system

    other components, such as multimedia

Server set-up:

  web server hardware

  web server software

    licensing fee

    installation

    support contracts

    other server software

    server management

    news server

    mail server

    proxy server

    access and user authentication

    search engine

    database support

    log analyser

    discussion and groupware

    chat and instant messenger software

    document management systems

    intelligent agents

    portal kits.

Networking infrastructure:

    increased bandwidth, routers, Internet Service Providers, cabling upgrades

Content creation:

    HTML editors

    graphics editors

    multimedia suites (including video streaming software)

Java tools:

    Javascript tools

    VBScript tools

    ActiveX components

    Perl scripts

    CGI scripts

    applications.

Training costs:

    intranet end-user training

    intranet publishing and authoring training

    application development

    server maintenance

    help desk

    other.

A final note

Predicting the future of technological developments (particularly any-thing related to the Internet) has always been a notoriously risky occupation. Areas that market analysts are confident *will* continue to grow are those closely related to e-commerce strategies. Datamonitor (1999) predicts that e-business intranet consultancy services in Europe will grow from its current market value of $728 million to $1.5 billion by 2003 as a direct result of extending the intranet [extranet] to their suppliers and strategic partners. This is also supported by research conducted for by the author (Blackmore, 2001) where managers of corporate intranets were surveyed regarding their plans to offer extranet services. This revealed that 34 per cent of respondents were already offering extranet access to customers and suppliers, 33 per cent had plans to provide related services within the next 12 months (with the remaining 33 per cent with no current plans).

There is one area of development (receiving less media attention) which holds the potential for revolutionising the way in which employees manage communication. Unified messaging (UM) provides technology to enable all telephone calls, faxes, emails, and voicemails to be managed and accessed through a single interface. This emerging market is expected to climb from $390 million (1999) to $2.2 billion by 2005 (Roberts, 2000).

It is clear that as the different networking topologies such as the Internet, intranets and extranets continue to merge so the navigation between them and their respective services will appear seamless to the end-user and be visible only as some kind of 'entire-net' rather than separate networking entities. Whichever technology, management strategy, fad or 'flavour of the month' is adopted next, it is almost certain the intranet will continue to be *the* key enabling tool. As the networking giant Cisco (1999) puts it: 'intranets, with their indisputable benefits and minimal start-up costs, clearly are here to stay'.

References

Aslib. *Proceedings from the Aslib conference, Evaluating the Intranet as Part of Your Knowledge Management Strategy*. London, 26th-27th September, 1996.

August, V. Intranets are failing business. *InformationWeek,* **73** 23 June 1999, 3.

Bauhus, D. *InformationWeek,* **781** 20 April 2000.

Bevan, S. and Evans, J. Managing the library intranet at Cranfield University. *Managing Information,* **3**(9) 1996, 38-40.

Blackmore, P. *Intranets: a guide to their design, implementation and management*. London: Aslib (2001).

Blackmore, P. Exploiting the Internet and related technologies as teaching and learning resources. *Broadcast: journal of the Scottish Further Education Unit,* **39** September 1997, 12-13.

Blackmore, P. Intranets: considerations for the Information Services Manager. *Information Services and Use,* **17**(1) 1997, 23-30.

Blackmore, P. The development of an intranet within a college of further and higher education. In: *Proceedings from the Aslib conference, Evaluating the Intranet as Part of Your Knowledge Management Strategy, London, 26th-27th September, 1996.*

Blakeman, K. The future role of intermediaries. In: *Proceedings from the UKOLUG conference, State-of-the-Art, Warwick, 17th-19th July, 1996.*

Bradbury, D. Extraordinary intranets. *Corporate Networks*, December 1997, 28-32.

Cap Gemini and Cranfield University. *Intranet Benchmarking and Business Value*. 1999. Available at *http://www.bnet.co.uk* [03 / 03 / 00].

Cisco Systems Inc. *Cisco Employee Connection: exploring the frontiers of intranet technology*. Cisco Systems Inc. (1999). Available at *http://wwwij.cisco.com/warp/public/cc/corp/mkt/gnb/gen/intra_wp.htm* [06 / 29 / 00].

Complete Intranet Resource. Intranet costs calculator, 1998. Available at *http://intrack.com/intranet/costs/index.shtml* [01 / 03 / 00].

Computer Technology Research Corporation. *Implementing Enterprise Portals: integration strategies for intranet, extranet and internet resources*. Computer Technology Research Corporation (2000).

Corporate Intranet Resource. *10 Requirements for a File Management System*, 2000. Available at *http://intrack.com/intranet/10_requirements.shtml*.

Damsgaard, J. and Scheepers, R. Managing the crises in implementation: a stage model. *Information Systems Journal*, **10** 2000, 131-49.

Datamonitor. *European Intranet Services: building the e-business pathway*. Datamonitor Inc. (1999).

Detlor, B. The corporate portal as information infrastructure: towards a framework for portal design. *International Journal of Information Management*, **20** 2000, 91-101.

Dhaliwal, J.S. and Tung, L.L. Using group support systems for developing a knowledge-based explanation facility. *International Journal of Information Management*, **20** 2000, 131-49.

Greer, E. HelpDesk Expert for customer support & service. *InfoWorld*, 23 November 1998.

Hall, H. and Jones, A.M. Show off the corporate library. *International Journal of Information Management*, **20** 2000, 121-30.

Hendriks, P.H.J. and Vriens, D.J. Knowledge-based systems and knowledge management: friends or foes? *Information & Management*, **35** 1999, 113-25.

Hobby, J. Special report: security. *InformationWeek*, **74** 30 June 1999, 35-43.

Intranet Design Magazine. IDM Intranet FAQ. 1999. Available at *http:// idm.internet.com/ifaq.html* [03.07.00].

Irving, R. and McWilliams, F. *Successful Intranets in a Week.* London: Hodder & Stoughton (1999) (Institute of Management Foundation).

ISAC. *Managing Information as a Strategic Asset: corporate intranet development and the role of the company library.* The Conference Board's Information Services Advisory Council. White paper no. 1, April 1998. Available at *http://www.conference-board.org/products/intranet-white-paper.cfm* [04.04.00].

KPMG Management Consulting. *Intranets: a guide for business users.* 1997. Available at *http://www.kpmg.co.uk/uk/services/manage/computer/index.html* [03.03.00].

Kuhn, O. and Abecker, A., Corporate memories for knowledge management in industrial practice: prospects and challenges. *Journal of Universal Computer Science,* 3(8) 1999, 929-54.

National Computing Centre. *Survey of IT users 1999.* Manchester: NCC (1999).

Newing, R. The virtual HR manager. *Information Age,* 1(16) 1997, 14-15.

Ogg, C. Grey intranets in the corporate underground. In: *The Corporate Intranet Forum.* London: Enterprise Events Limited (1997) (Report no. 3, 1-3).

Ovum. *Worldwide Market for KM Worth a Massive $12.3 Billion by 2004.* Press release for 'Knowledge Management: building the collaborative enterprise', 1999.

Poston, T. E-commerce to change view bottom line. *Computer Weekly,* 13 May 1999, p.8.

Primich, T. and Varnum, K. A corporate library making the transition from traditional to web publishing. *Computers in Libraries,* 19(10) 1999.

Roberts, I. Turning over a new leaf. *Computer Telephony,* 7(2) 2000, 36-8.

Stenmark, D. A method for intranet search engine evaluations. In: Käkölä, T. (ed.) *Proceedings of IRIS22, Department of CS/IS, University of Jyväskylä, Finland. Experiences made during evaluation, installation, and testing of several intranet search engines, 1997-99.* Presented at IRIS22, Keuruu, Finland, 7-10 August, 1999.

Chapter 19

The effective web site

Mark Kerr

Introduction

When the last Handbook was published, only three Earth years but many more 'Internet years' ago, the Web itself was barely seven years old. Windows-based browsers were still evolving rapidly, and the adventure for many special librarians was simply in getting information online, available to all and visible from anywhere.

That infant Web has matured considerably in the intervening years – although still far from adult, more an unruly adolescent, it is less of an adventure, instead it has become just another useful working tool. Netscape has lost its dominant position in the browser market to Microsoft's Internet Explorer; the Web itself is much more of an entertainment and shopping venue then previously; free connections – thanks in large part to Freeserve – are the norm; approximately 45 million US Internet users in early 1997 has become over 153 million by late 2000 and UK usage has grown from under one million in early 1997 to nearly 20 million by late 2000 (source: *http://www.nua.ie*). Whatever your views on the reliability and methodologies of such statistics, it is inescapably obvious that Internet usage is now quite simply normal, and no longer the exclusive preserve of those blessed with superior financial, technical or educational resources.

This brief background may only seem marginally relevant to the role of the special librarian, but with information on every conceivable topic now online, web publishing is no longer such a mystery. The emphasis has switched to optimising design, content management and customer service. Collection management and information management have always been a key element of the special librarian's role. To those must now be added web-site management – the supervision of the delivery mechanism for access to both the collection (whatever that might be) and to the information. Understanding the implications of digitisation, interoperability and accessibility are just a few requirements. Tools such as web page editors (like FrontPage or DreamWeaver) make web publishing more easily accessible to those without the time or inclination to master HTML. Databases and catalogues are not restricted to telnet access but are web enabled, indeed publishing from databases is the chosen method for many, even most, of the world's largest web sites.

The 21st century information professional is typically less concerned with deciding merely whether or how to publish: the issues now are what, to whom, and in what format. Jargon, abounds as ever, with terms such as 'sticky content', 'usability' and 'optimisation' just a few of the newer entries in the site manager's lexicon. Added to this is an ever present requirement to market effectively – to access those remote users, to reach new audiences, to feature prominently on search engines and directories, above all to demonstrate that the investment of time and technology is worthwhile.

All of these objectives can be achieved by following a realistic and continuing four-part strategy: Plan, Implement, Monitor, Improve. Each of these four elements includes a number of subsidiary activities of course, and the effective site manager needs to develop proficiency in all of them:

- planning: design, content selection, site creation
- implementation: testing, publishing and promotion
- monitoring: measuring and assessment
- improvement: content management, optimisation and generous design.

Planning the site

The planning process should not be limited to new sites. Every web site should be subjected to a constant process of evaluation by its management. While many leading commercial sites undergo total redesign every 12-18 months, this is often impractical or unnecessary for services whose style does not need to change with each new season's fashions. Nevertheless, the principle of continuous development is certainly one that should be applied to your site.

There are a number of design considerations that should be clarified prior to developing or redeveloping the site:

- Who is the core audience?
- What is the core content?
- How will the content be managed?
- What is the appropriate style and structure?
- How will the site be created and managed?

Who is the core audience?

Delivering information effectively requires an understanding not only of the information needs of your intended audience. It also requires an understanding of the audience themselves.

Internal or external

A captive audience of internal users may be easier to reach in marketing terms, but content still needs to be relevant to their needs and the style and structure appropriate for their skill levels. You would normally have a good idea of the technology available to this user group, so you can design around that to some extent. A largely external audience will have a wider range of skills, equipment and experience, and so you should consider either working to a lower common denominator, or more usefully, offering additional support for those with more need of assistance.

Educational and age range

This may affect your choice of colours and graphics, even style of language. A text-heavy page might be informative and convenient for committed and informed readers, while deterring younger, casual or less expert visitors. A service aimed entirely at experts or senior professionals can afford to use more jargon than a site designed to attract new users. Again, designing for the lowest common denominator is not the only solution – but you should consider adding extra information, such as a dictionary, tutorials or helpsheets.

Technical expertise

Will your users be familiar with the Web, comfortable with navigational metaphors and plug-ins such as Flash and Acrobat – or will they require very explicit instructions? If your site relies on documents in PDF format, or extensive database manipulation, will the users be able to cope? This may be solved simply by clear and well-signposted help pages. Dumbing-down the entire output is absolutely not a requirement, but aiding those less proficient most certainly is. If you decide to proclaim 'suitable for Version 4 or above of Netscape and Explorer' at least demonstrate that this choice is based on market and audience awareness, not laziness.

You can get an overview of the audience's technology from your server log files (see the later section on monitoring), which will give you information on the proportions of your visitors using different browser versions, screen resolution settings and operating systems. If your site statistics are not that detailed you can get an idea from the global statistics provided by The Counter (*http://www.thecounter.com* – follow the link to 'Global Statistics' in the third paragraph on home page).

What is the core content?

The specific purpose for your site – or a section of it – may include one or more of the following:

- to promote a product or service
- to deliver a product or service

- to provide service information
- to offer curriculum support
- to collect orders or enquiries
- to deliver printed materials
- to provide database access
- to act as a print depository
- to deliver training and support
- to provide a communications link
- to recruitment
- to a launch pad to wider resources
- to host community discussions.

Site content

There are certain obvious expectations from an organisation's web site. The least it should do is present the company or organisation effectively to its audience, outline its services or products, define and describe policies and provide a means of making further contact. Obvious though this may seem, many web sites do not provide easy access to essential information.

Contact details

A contact page should consist of more than just an email link. Postal address and phone numbers, location map and contact names, departmental contacts and email addresses all ensure that enquiries are directed to the appropriate destination.

Search

A keyword search facility adds a professional look to a web site and provides access to information. Some web server software creates a searchable index automatically and there are many UNIX tools such as Glimpse and Harvest that can do the job equally well, provided you have access to some programming expertise. There are also external solutions that will create your site's search tool for you – entirely free for up to 500 pages. Atomz (*http://www.atomz.com*) for example can be added to a site within minutes. Your web pages – and PDF documents – are searched and indexed weekly, and the search tool (simple or advanced search dialogue boxes) is provided as a snippet of HTML for simple copy-and-paste insertion in to your site.

Navigation

It is important to give visitors alternative routes through a web site. Keyword searching may be familiar to some visitors, but the new user may have no idea what topics the site contains. The two alternatives to the

keyword search are navigation buttons and a site map. Clear and consistent navigation buttons (or text links) on each page give the visitor some
context - both within and beyond the current section – guiding the next
click and illustrating the site structure. The BBC (*http://www.bbc.co.uk*) uses
its left-hand navigation column brilliantly, with top-level links combined
with links to related information from each page. A site map or directory
listing gives the visitor a snapshot of the total information on the site. The
British Library site index (*http://www.bl.uk*) is an elegant example of how a
straightforward page listing, colour-coded for each part of the site, provides clear direction and explains the site structure instantly. Similarly
the eBay auction site (*http://www.ebay.com*) has a clear site map that helps
users through an enormous amount of information about the services
offered, as well as the goods on sale.

Policies

Links to formal policy statements on copyright, secure payments, privacy
and data protection show that you understand their implications, but
also that you understand the concerns many users feel in these areas. If
your site is certified by one of the agencies that underwrite your policy
(Trust UK, Which WebTrader, truste.org or similar) then indicate this to
your users.

Disclaimers

It is often worth reminding visitors that you cannot be responsible for
content on external sites, that published information should always be
confirmed from independent sources, that individuals' opinions do not
always reflect organisational policy, that the technology itself cannot always be guaranteed to function. These disclaimers are especially important
for certain critical subject areas – such as health, legal or financial information.

News

The best sites include news appropriate for the subject of the site. This can
be culled from regular news sources and added to the site as and when
you have the time. You should distinguish between internal and external
news. Few visitors really care about staff changes at your organisation, or
minor service developments – they should of course be announced, but
perhaps more appropriately on the relevant service page, rather then
under 'news'. For a very effective means of adding 'live' news to the site,
try Moreover (*http://www.moreover.com*), which provides the code for you
to add headlines to your site – free. Select from around 300 different news
topics, drawn from 1,500 news sources, and within four clicks of the
mouse you are provided with a snippet of JavaScript and HTML to paste
in to your site. You then have the latest headlines at the moment your
visitor reaches that page – very powerful content that gives visitors a
reason to return regularly.

Other elements that are seen on many sites – particularly from non-commercial, educational and research organisations – are usually there for purely internal reasons. They have little to do with user expectations or customer service. Committee structures, organisation history, minutes of meetings, departmental relationships, constitutions and memoranda can of course be relevant, but perhaps within a discreet 'about us' section.

Page content

There are some elements each and every page on a site should include for the benefit of visitors:

- **A title (in the <HEAD> command)** is essential for every page – it is stored as the bookmark or favourite title, used by search engines as a record title, and needs to be a meaningful description of the page as it is used by the search engines in their indexing process.

- **A clear main page heading** allows the visitor's eye to fall easily on the topic of the page: this can be a graphic, or large font, or a simple HTML heading command. The important thing is that it is clear and unambiguous so the visitor knows instantly what the page is about.

- **Navigation links** take visitors to other relevant areas of the site – perhaps to every page in the current section, and to the main pages of each of the other sections of the site.

- **A signature** – an email address – allows visitors to respond or post queries to the site. It may have a statement of ownership or responsibility for the pages' content.

- **A date** is useful to demonstrate when the page was written, especially if the content is time-sensitive, however, it can also reveal your lack of attention if the date is not changed for a while! Think carefully before putting a date on a page that you know may not change very often.

The following elements, although important, are most often seen in the smallest font size as a navigation line at the bottom of the page – they need to be there, but they do not need to be particularly prominent:

home / copyright / disclaimer / privacy / contact / search / sitemap / about us

The guiding principle of web design should be that of usability. The only factor that really counts is whether or not your users can access the information easily, reliably and speedily. Jacob Nielsen, widely regarded as the guru of web usability, defines several mistakes often made by web designers. While some of these are more a matter of taste and choice, others are simply barriers to the information. The key consideration should be: 'If I remove this (feature, graphic, page) will it damage or reduce the usability of the site?' If the answer is no, then take it out!

The following are often listed as 'things to avoid at all costs'. But perhaps they should be better regarded as 'things to use only after careful consideration'. There are few absolutes in web design – the only true absolute should be the commitment to the user.

Frames

Although good for aiding navigation on complex sites, frames can cause problems with printing, saving and bookmarking. Badly designed frames can make a site unreadable. Best practice is to keep them to a minimum, allow scrolling and resizing where necessary, and offer a proper <NOFRAMES> alternative.

Standard clipart

Despite the millions of items available, there are some very recognisable items of web clipart on sites. Original graphics (or adapted clipart) gives a better impression for professional sites – and says something about the designer.

Under construction signs

A good site should always be under construction! If it is not ready for viewing do not publish it. If it genuinely is growing over time, say that, but make it a positive feature, perhaps inviting suggestions and contributions. If forced to launch a site, or section of a site, before it is complete, then make a virtue of its dynamic nature – 'coming soon, information about...' and give a launch date if possible.

Large files

No matter how fast the connection, faster is better: use optimised graphics where possible, to ensure the quickest possible page loading. Large files can be broken into sections and at the very least warn users of the size of a large download. Large images should be combined with thumbnail versions on a prior page, so that the user can get an idea of what they are selecting. Documents could be offered in different versions – multipage HTML, a single page printable version and PDF software – and larger files should be zipped.

Technical showcases

Advanced features must be sure to enhance the web site, not just the designer's ego. If they are appropriate, expected by the user, if the plug-in is provided or linked, if the audience is capable and interested, then the audience will be in a position to appreciate your efforts. But could that Flash movie, live Webcam or 3-D walkthrough be presented in a quicker or easier way?

Site creation

While this chapter is too short to contain a full HTML primer (see references for several of these), you will need to consider exactly how you are going to publish your information on to your web site. There are several format options, which are discussed below.

HTML

Most web sites are of course written in HTML, which ideally combines ease of updating, compatibility between browsers and platforms and quick page loading. Its limitations are that the end product is not absolutely fixed – the user can change resolution, colours, fonts and size – and that it lacks some of the finer layout control of other formats. Overall, this is seen as a positive feature, in that the document adapts its presentation to the user's preferences and the user's technology.

Database

Publishing via a database makes updating and consistency a good deal easier, but requires greater technical input at the design and planning stage. Most large retail sites and a good number of information sites are published via a database. It is also the preferred solution where a large number of contributors are involved as data entry via a form interface ensures that styles are preserved.

PDF

Typically used for republishing journals, reports and other pre-existing documents, PDF 'fixes' the style and layout and is perhaps most suitable for those documents which are intended for printing, rather than on-screen viewing. Although this requires the user to have the free Acrobat Reader plug-in installed, this is now so widespread that few users will be excluded from the information.

Flash

Some sites are developed entirely in Flash, with no HTML used at all in the page. Assuming your users all have Flash – and Macromedia claim some 75-80 per cent of browsers do have Flash installed – this allows a more dynamic, animated and interactive presentation. However, updating content is then limited to those with Flash development skills, and with access to the original files – hardly ideal for a multi-contributor environment.

In practice, the more sophisticated web site will use a combination of some or even all of these formats. The top level pages will be in HTML, with the content generated from a database. Downloadable PDF documents provide access to reports, articles and journals while selectively used Flash movies might provide micro-sites or navigational enhancements.

Which HTML editor?

While it is still important - and will remain important – for web site managers to understand the principles, potential and limitations of HTML, it is perhaps less important than it once was to create the pages using a basic text editor. HTML editors have developed to the stage where they can be relied upon to generate reasonably tidy and valid code, although there are still occasions where you will need to access the raw HTML in order to tidy up some small part of page. The most common are FrontPage and Dreamweaver. Both provide a fully featured means of designing and maintaining web pages, and of managing a web site. Each includes facilities for creating templates, checking links and exporting finished pages to a web server, but there are some key differences.

FrontPage is affordable* software that integrates with other Microsoft Office applications. A 'lite' version, FrontPage Express, is free with some versions of Microsoft Office and Microsoft Explorer. However, some of the more advanced features will only work if the web server hosting your site supports FrontPage Extensions. A useful task view lets you annotate and prioritise actions, and enables that tasklist to be shared over a network. FrontPage also makes connecting MS Access databases to the Web a good deal easier, creating a page that can browse the database – useful for smaller databases. Forms creation and simple search engines can be automatically undertaken, but again rely on the server extensions for full features. FrontPage is probably the most popular editor for use on intranets, where a number of individuals need to update different sections of a site's content quickly and easily.

Dreamweaver is considerably more expensive* than FrontPage, but also offers considerably more control and flexibility. Online help supplied with the software is very comprehensive, and Dreamweaver provides full support for XML, JavaScript and Cascading Style Sheets (CSS), all increasingly important on more advanced web sites. Dreamweaver also includes features such as 'clean up Microsoft Word HTML', ideal for those given the task to convert office documents for web use. Both editors let you write 'raw' HTML where desired, but Dreamweaver has less propensity to add its own HTML code when you're not looking. Most web design agencies use Dreamweaver for site design – in conjunction with other packages of course. Coming from the same design-focused software supplier as Flash (animation), Fireworks (graphics) and Drumbeat (database), Dreamweaver is seen as very much a designer's tool.

There are of course many other HTML editors – Homesite, HotMetal, HotDog, GoLive, to name but a few. The simplest advice is to try them out: trial versions can be found on the cover disks of most Internet or computer magazines, or can be downloaded from Tucows (*http://www.tucows.com*). Each web site manager has different aptitudes and preferences – pick the software that you feel most comfortable using, and of course software that your institution's IT team will support.

(*Prices on Jungle.com in September 2000 were £270 for Dreamweaver and £103 for FrontPage, both full versions, without any discounts.)

XML

One development that is getting more attention is that of XML (Extensible Markup Language). This provides a common syntax for expressing structure (as opposed to presentation, which is what HTML mostly does) in data. By separating structure and content from presentation, the same XML source document can be written once, then displayed in several ways: on a PC monitor, in a cellphone display, translated into voice on a device for the blind, and more. HTML is fine for web publishing, but if you want to prepare for automatic processing of data, you should think about incorporating XML into your publishing systems. More information can be found at CNET's 20 Questions on XML (*http://builder.cnet.com/Authoring/Xml20/*).

Implementation

Testing

It is essential that web sites are subjected to regular validation and testing. Few things undermine the professional image of a site than coding errors and spelling mistakes. Although most HTML editing programmes will normally ensure that the HTML is valid, a frequently changing web site risks causing irritation – and ultimately losing visitors – if the testing is not rigorously carried out after every update.

Confidence in your own web site's performance and reliability can be improved by ensuring that regular checks are carried out in the following areas.

The HTML
Ensuring the HTML meets the formal standards means that it will appear properly in all browsers – or at least the vast majority of them. Online validators such as NetMechanic (*http://www.netmechanic.com*) or WebSiteGarage (*http://www.websitegarage.com*) check the code, validate against the HTML standards and make suggestions for improvements.

Spelling

Spelling mistakes are easily overlooked, but appear very sloppy and ama-teurish. Try searching Google (*http://www.google.com*) or AltaVista (*http://www.altavista.co.uk*) for spelling mistakes – and then see what ostensibly professional pages they appear on! NetMechanic and WebSiteGarage do offer an online spellcheck, but of course they use an American dictionary, so expect to ignore some of their suggestions. Proof-reading your own work is notoriously difficult, so ask colleagues to scan your pages for you.

Test-drive

Invite someone with no knowledge of the web site – perhaps with little experience of the Internet – to try out the site. Can they understand your instructions? Can they find the key parts of the site? Are they confused? Do your instructions mean the same to a newcomer as they do to an experienced user?

If you are feeling brave, you might even offer a small prize (perhaps re-stricted to colleagues) to anyone who can find spelling, coding or linking errors on your site – a powerful motivator to avoid mistakes, and a good way to recruit enthusiastic site-checkers.

Promotion

Web site promotion is not a single event – it is a continuous process. As with 'real world' marketing activities, it is part of the ongoing life of the organisation. Your audience will determine which promotional strategy is most effective, but there are a group of actions that can be applied to almost all web sites, whether or not they have a marketing budget. Even if your service is not actively competing with similar sites, you are still competing with the rest of the Web for your audience's time and attention. Being easily found is as much about customer service as it is about com-petitiveness – the easier you can be found, the better the service to those who know about you, the better the impression on those who do not.

This section makes two key assumptions:

- more visitors are a good thing
- marketing budgets are minimal.

If these assumptions are not correct for your site, then you will need to adjust your strategy accordingly.

There are six key ways to attract attention to your web site. Some will be more effective than others, some more time consuming. All should be considered and perhaps implemented – as far as possible, practical or affordable.

Offline promotion:

- release
- include
- advertise.

Online promotion:

- design
- submit
- link.

Offline promotion

Include

The most simple, and the most overlooked: every communication, document, piece of stationery, report and publication should include your web site's URL. If it has the organisation's name and telephone number, it should have the URL.

You should also ensure that every email user within the organisation has an effective signature file combined with their email client, so that every outgoing message contains full contact details. Sending an email without a signature is similar to posting a letter written on plain paper – fine for personal use, but inappropriate for professional communication.

Active and appropriate participation in Usenet newsgroups or email discussion lists can keep your name uppermost in your audience's mind. This may not reach your user group directly, but by being a familiar name to sector colleagues you may win referrals, or even direct enquiries. Find relevant lists and groups by searching JISCmail (*http://www.jiscmail.ac.uk*), DejaNews (*http://www.deja.com/usenet*) or Liszt (*http://www.liszt.com*).

Release

Use the launch or significant extension of your web site as a marketing opportunity – press releases to existing and prospective users, the relevant trade or professional media, suppliers, trade associations and advice groups active in your area.

All the quality UK newspapers now have a technology or Internet supplement once a week. Each of these carries a few short notices or reviews of recently launched web sites or services. You may need to prove that your site has something extra – the elusive 'factor X' – to be included, but it is worth notifying the relevant columnist for the possible exposure to an Internet-friendly audience.

Advertise

Few special libraries can afford a serious banner advertising campaign, and research from the Internet Advertising Bureau (*http://www.iab.net*) shows declining effectiveness, as measured by clickthroughs, with response rates averaging as low as 0.5 per cent. However that same survey showed banner adverts to be very effective at raising awareness – a 20 per cent success rate. In other words, people notice banner adverts even if they do not click on them.

One strategy is to arrange direct banner exchanges, whereby your site hosts advertises for a complementary site aimed at a similar audience – and your advertiser hosts a similar advert for you. This need not be at the top of the home page, but on other pages in your site. It need not be a full banner – perhaps small adverts beneath your navigation buttons in the index column, or at the base of the page.

Online promotion

Design

Design 'searchability' into your site. It is not enough just to submit your site's URL to the indexing services – they need to be 'searchable'. When a potential visitor enters a keyword that is relevant to your activity, your site must appear at or near the top of the results listing. Appearing as result 500 out of 1,000,000 hits is useless. You need to be in the top 50, and preferably in the top 10.

Indexing search engines such as AltaVista or Google do not return hits at random, however it may seem at times. They compare the indexed contents of a page with the search terms entered by the user. The better the match, the higher the position. The web page designer can affect this 'matchability' by careful design and accurate selection of keywords.

Some services index the entire page. Others index just part of the page – perhaps the first 50 or 100 words. Most of the indexes give added weight to words in the <TITLE> or <HEADING> tags. Choose relevant keywords carefully and use them consistently – this should not just be your brand or organisation's name, but the word – any word – a visitor might enter when searching for your activity, product or service. There is in practice no limit to the number of keywords that can be placed in the META tags, but most indexing services will ignore deliberately repeated words.

<META> tags
Use the <META> tag in the HTML source code to provide the indexing services with the keywords and content descriptions that you choose, rather than the ones they generate automatically:

<META Name="description" Content="A concise and meaningful description of the site, that is presented as a search result.">

<META Name="keywords" Content="relevant, meaningful, numerous, words and phrases, essential, considered, well-chosen">

<ALT>
Most search engines index all the HTML code, so provide an ALT statement for each image. This is good design practice anyway, as it enables those without graphics to understand your page more easily, but it also provides another opportunity to insert your keywords in to the page without making it too obvious.

Beat the best
Perform a search using typical keywords relevant to your product or service. Look at the top 10 or 20 results in several of the main search engines. Use **View/Source** to see what they have put in their META tags, and try to work out why they are top of the list.

Frames
Indexing robots cannot access framed web sites unless there is a <NOFRAMES> alternative, because the framed home page has no links leading in to your site, just the FRAMESET layout. As with ALT tags, using NOFRAMES is more than just helpful design – ignore it at your peril.

Maintenance
Just as you should not abandon your web pages once they are published, so the same applies for the search engine listings. Re-submission every 2-3 months will allow you to update the index - new content, new keywords, new position on the results listings.

In order to ensure that you design to the requirements of the main search engines, check out which features they require or support on SearchEngineWatch (*http://www.searchenginewatch.com*), a comprehensive resource that compares search engines and provides a list of the features that you need to incorporate into your site design to ensure the best possible position in the search results.

Submit
To be found by those searching for information, products or services, but not specifically for your organisation, it is essential that you are 'searchable'. In other words you need to appear in the databases of the leading search services. Ideally you would feature in every database, but in practice the top six or seven account for some 80 per cent of searching activity, so focus on them first.

The top global search engines include Yahoo!, AltaVista, Infoseek, Excite, Google, Northern Light, HotBot, MSN and Lycos. Top UK search engines include UK Plus, Search UK and UK Max. Yahoo!, AltaVista, Excite and Lycos also have UK versions, subsets of their main global database.

Although most search services trawl the Web automatically, you can speed up the process by proactively submitting the URL to as many as possible. Each search service has a button or link on their main page which will provide information on doing just that – they make their money from advertising; they attract advertisers and users by having the most comprehensive collection of indexed pages, so they need to know about you, they really do.

Listings sites

There are a number of directory listings sites which will accept all relevant submissions – UK Directory and UK Index for example. Yahoo! is more selective. Lists of these can be found through the Yahoo! structure, and may be sector or country specific.

Submitting services

Submit-It (*http://www.submit-it.com*) or Broadcaster (*http://www.broadcaster.co.uk*) or BeSeen (*http://www.beseen.com*) will do the submitting for you, with varying effectiveness. Many offer a free service for a few major search engines, and then ask for payment for larger numbers. However as the top five or six search sites account for over 90 per cent of all searches – and Yahoo itself accounts for 45-50 per cent – the justification for paying submission services may be limited.

Link

Reciprocal links

A 'related links' page adds value to your site: you can request the webmasters of linked sites to place a return link on their pages. This is a favour not an obligation, so you cannot insist! Nevertheless if you can show that the content on your site is of direct relevance to their visitors (and is not in direct competition), then it is mutually beneficial to link the two sites.

Links are important for three main reasons:

- They add value to your site, giving visitors a reason to return and to use it as a useful jumping-off point to the rest of the Web. Do not worry about 'losing' visitors – they have to leave your site at some stage, better by far that they do so to somewhere useful, rather than simply hitting the Home or Back button.

- Links from busy, relevant sites will bring you visitors who have deliberately chosen your link because they are interested in what your site has to offer. Among those 'visitors' will be the automatic indexing tools run by the search engines: the more links to your site, the more often your site will be indexed.

- Increasing numbers of search engines, including AltaVista, Excite, FAST, Google, Go, Inktomi (which provides search results for AOL Search, HotBot, GoTo, LookSmart, MSN Search, Snap) and Northern Light use link popularity in the ranking process. They reason that if your site is popular, it must be good.

Use LinkPopularity (*http://www.linkpopularity.com*) or LinkCount (*http://www.linkcount.com*) to see how many sites link to you. More importantly, use it to see who is linking to your competitors or comparable sites: then contact them to see if they will also link to you.

Doorway or bridge pages

These are pages specifically designed to meet the needs of the search engines, and so are loaded (but not stuffed) with appropriate keywords. Each page however simply links to the existing home or menu page, and is not linked back, so is a one-way guide in to the site. You can create several of these, each focusing on a different aspect of your services, and therefore covering different groups of keywords.

Listings page – exactly the same as a site map, except this will include doorway or bridge pages as described above, and will not be used by your visitors: this is a 'private' page, simply listing all the pages with links. Use as above to ensure that the indexing search engines find and assess all your pages.

One grossly overlooked method of promotion is that of simply providing a good experience. A clear, easily-navigated web site that does what it promises and makes it easy for the visitor to accomplish their goals is worth hundreds of clever promotional techniques.

- Make it clear.
- Make it work.
- Make it worth returning.

Monitoring

Measuring and assessment

Your site design and its effectiveness is ultimately determined by your desired outcomes. In other words, just what do you want your visitors to do, find, learn? The effectiveness of your site can be measured in any of a number of ways:

- number of visitors, 'page hits'
- volume of feedback and enquiries
- sales and orders
- downloads of software
- completion of online tasks
- internal (i.e. within your organisation) approval.

One key measure to watch out for is 'hits'. A web page with 10 images will register as 11 hits, in other words, the server has delivered 11 files over the network. As a measure of performance that is irrelevant – what you need to measure is page views, unique visits or visitor sessions. The server measures everything, but you need to know what the numbers actually mean.

What you can determine from your site statistics:

- views for each page
- how many individual users visit each site
- average time that each page is looked at, and how often
- whether site changes increase or decrease traffic
- what resolution, browser and operating system your users have
- which advertising works (from source of traffic)
- busiest times, and days of week
- paths through the site taken by a visitor
- users' Internet domains (mostly academic, or UK)
- errors delivered to visitors as '404 Page Not Found'
- which keywords are used on which search engines.

And why?
To ascertain the effectiveness of your design, your content and your marketing activities; whether you need to focus more on a part of your site; whether an expected audience is simply missing; or whether part of your content is simply unread.

Software
The raw log files need analysing, usually by a software package such as net.Analysis (*http://www.netgenesis.com*), WebTrends (*http://www.webtrends.com*) or Hit List (*http://www.marketwave.com*) which are fully featured analysis packages. Extreme (*http://www.extreme-dm.com*), Ipstat (*http://www,ipstat.com*) and Nedstat (*http://www.nedstat.com*) are simple

graphic trackers and counters that do not require access to the server log files.

Improvement

Content management

Full-time editorial staff maintaining and developing a site are a luxury few information services can afford. In many cases, the web site is an addition to the range of services and needs to be resourced from within existing limits. There are some practices which can minimise the workload.

Share and delegate responsibility for sections of the site, but make it easier by developing both templates and style sheets. The template is the basis for each web page, providing the background and colours, the styles (if you are using CSS) and the head and footer for each page. It may also include the navigation index column, and the basic links for each page, leaving the contributor merely to add new content. Most web sites have only three or four basic page layouts, so fixing these in template form reduces the risk of inconsistent design.

A style sheet describes both the template and the overall site design specifications, with colours defined. Typographical formats are outlined: font size, spelling and capitalisations provided (CD-Rom, CDROM or CD-ROM for example). File naming conventions are explained, along with the authorities and permissions – who can add new pages, or new directories. A sample page is provided with annotations explaining each feature. Uploading instructions are specified. The site structure is mapped, showing the relationship between different sections. A graphics library can be provided with all the approved images available, along with their dimensions, file size, suggested ALT text. Similarly all colours used are specified in their HTML Hex codes.

Optimisation

Accessibility

Accessibility in web design provides usability for people with disabilities. Mostly based on general design principles, with some specific extra facilities, accessible design ensures that you do not deliver a restricted or exclusionary message. The Disability Discrimination Act 1995 includes requirements for information services to make themselves accessible to disadvantaged users – this need not be expensive or technically difficult, but it does need to be planned carefully. Providing a 'text alternative' utilising some of the available technology such as the BBC's Betsie script (*http://www.bbc.co.uk/education/betsie/*) can ensure an inclusive approach. The World Wide Web organisation provides formal accessibility guidelines (*HTTP://www.w3.org/WAI/*).

Interoperability and compatibility

Ensure that your site works in all the main browsers, not just the latest version of your current favourite. You cannot tell in advance what your visitors are using, so you need to ensure that your site works for the vast majority of the likely audience. Sites should be tested on Macs and PCs, on 15" and 17" monitors, at 640x480 and 800x600 resolution, and in Netscape 4.x, Explorer 4 and 5 and Opera – at the very least. Designing to the HTML standard should ensure that your site is seen and accessed by all users.

Speed and usability

Ensuring that your images are optimised for fast loading, and that all the elements on your site cannot confuse visitors will guarantee happy visitors. Jacob Nielsen provides a regular web column on usability called Alertbox (*http://www.useit.com/alertbox/*) which covers all these issues in great detail, and is archived back to its origins in June 1995.

Conclusion

Effectiveness and generous design

The effective web site is the one that takes your users quickly and painlessly to the information they are seeking. Generous design takes that one stage further, making the visit not just painless, but actually pleasurable, either because of the simplicity and clarity of the site, or because of the added-value provided in terms of extra information, links and services. Generous design takes the needs and expectations of the users and makes them the focus of the site design. Whether your site is a major portal, a specialist database or a simple guide to your library service, the principles of effective design provide an essential benchmark against which to measure your site's performance.

References

Web

This chapter makes several references to HTML commands. These web sites will provide the answers to almost any technical questions you might have:

- About.Com (*http://html.about.com/compute/html/*)
- Builder.Com (*http://cnet.builder.com*)
- HTML Compendium (*http://www.compendium.org*)
- Tips and Tricks for Web site Managers (*http://www. webtipsandtricks.com*)

The ADV-HTML discussion list – and its archive – is an invaluable source of expertise and assistance with web page creation (*http:// www.netsquirrel.com/adv-html/index.html*).

Moreover.com (*http://www.moreover.com*) has news sections on HTML, web site management and web development, providing current news and articles on these and related topics.

Books

Kerr, M. *How to Promote your Website Effectively.* London: Aslib (1999).

Lynch, P. and Horton, S. *Web Style Guide.* New Haven: Yale University Press (1999).

Nielsen, J. *Designing Web Usability.* Indianapolis: New Riders Publishing (2000).

Chapter 20

Copyright

Paul Pedley

The *Encyclopaedia Britannica* (*http://www.britannica.com*) defines copyright as 'the exclusive, legally secured right to publish, reproduce, and sell the matter and form of a literary, musical, dramatic, or artistic work'.

In the United Kingdom, copyright is primarily seen as a property right. Indeed, section 1 of the Copyright, Designs and Patents Act 1988 begins with the words 'Copyright is a property right...' Copyright entitles the copyright owner to five main economic rights:

- copying the work
- issuing copies of it to the public
- performing it or playing it to the public
- broadcasting it or including it in a cable progamme
- adapting it.

But an area which is often overlooked is the moral rights which authors have:

- the right of paternity – the right of the author to be identified as such
- the right of integrity – the right of the author to prevent or object to derogatory treatment of his or her work
- the right of false attribution – the right of a person not to have a literary, dramatic, musical or artistic work falsely attributed to them
- the right of disclosure – the right of the author to withhold certain photographs or films from publication.

The United Kingdom's copyright regime has to balance two conflicting sides. On the one hand there is the need for access to information, whilst on the other hand there is the need to protect the moral and economic rights of authors. Library and information professionals often find themselves in the difficult position of trying on the one hand to provide access to information for their users whilst at the same time wanting to respect the rights of authors and publishers to prevent exploitation of their works.

The Universal Declaration of Human Rights (*http://www.unhchr.ch/udhr/lang/eng.htm*) was adopted by the United Nations General Assembly on 10 December 1948. Article 27 says:

1. Everyone has the right freely to participate in the cultural life of the community, to enjoy the arts and to share in scientific advancement and its benefits.

2. Everyone has the right to the protection of the moral and material interests resulting from any scientific, literary or artistic production of which he is the author.

At times, these two human rights can conflict with one another. On the one hand access to material is seen as being a basic human right and such access is considered to be necessary in order to create an environment in which creativity and innovation can flourish. Whilst on the other hand, copyright exists to protect an author, publisher, or other owner against any unauthorised copying of his or her works.

Inevitably these two conflicting pressures mean that copyright is a controversial issue. Throughout history, technological advances have been a cause of concern to authors who do not wish to have their work exploited by others. But whilst their concerns may date back many centuries, it is quite clear that the pace of change has been speeding up, and that is why copyright has a much higher place on the agenda.

Technological environment

It is important to consider technological developments when one tries to put copyright law into perspective. Rightsholders are understandably wary about technological developments, since they often lead to new uses of protected material in ways which are not authorised by and which were not foreseen under the existing legislation.

Some key technological advances

- 1476 – introduction of the printing process in England by Caxton
- 1950 – first commercial use of xerography
- 1989 – development of the World Wide Web by Tim Berners-Lee.

Over the years, these and many other technological developments have been a cause for concern amongst rights owners. These include the use of online databases and CD-ROMs, the shift from information professionals being information intermediaries towards much wider end-user access to sources of information, and the use of email, which makes it possible through the use of file attachments to disseminate large amounts of information to huge numbers of recipients at the press of a button. There has been a dramatic change to the way in which information is handled and distributed, and rights owners have become understandably concerned about protecting their interests. Collective licensing agencies such as the

Copyright Licensing Agency and the Newspaper Licensing Agency have come up with licences that cover the use of digital information; and there have been many projects to investigate ways of being able to record the sale of information electronically. These include, for example, the INDECS project (*http://www.indecs.org*), the Digital Object Identifier (*http://www.doi.org*), and various research projects looking at electronic copyright management systems.

The current legislative framework for copyright in the United Kingdom is made up of a number of different elements – UK legislation, EC directives, and international treaties and conventions. The main statute is the Copyright, Designs and Patents Act 1988 which took effect from August 1989 and the many statutory instruments which interpret and modify it.

As one of the member states of the European Union, the United Kingdom is obliged to implement EC directives through UK legislation. Recent amendments to copyright law in the UK have been made in order to implement various EC directives. Examples include:

- SI 1992/3233 The Copyright (Computer Programs) Regulations 1992 which implement council directive 91/250/EEC on the legal protection of computer programs
- SI 1995/3297 Copyright Rights in Performances: the Duration of Copyright and Rights in Performances Regulations 1995 which implement council directive 93/98/EEC harmonising the term of protection of copyright and certain related rights
- SI 1996/2967 Copyright and Related Rights Regulations 1996 which implement council directive 92/100/EEC on rental right and lending right and on certain rights relating to copyright in the field of intellectual property
- SI 1997/3032 The Copyright and Rights in Databases Regulations 1997 which implement council directive 96/9/EC on the legal protection of databases.

There is a limited amount of discretion given to national governments concerning the way in which they implement the directives. But the aim of the European Commission is to harmonise copyright laws in the member states 'in order to achieve a level playing field for copyright protection across national borders to allow the Internal Market to become a reality for new products and services containing intellectual property' (European Commission, 1997). The proposed European Parliament and council directive on the harmonisation of certain aspects of copyright and related rights in the information society – which was originally published as COM(97) 628 final, with an amended version subsequently being published as COM(1999) 250 final – has proved to be extremely controversial, and it has taken much longer than expected for the member states to reach political agreement. Indeed, the copyright directive has proved to be one of the most controversial of recent directives which has seen extensive lobbying by rightsowners, users and other interested parties.

The Copyright Directive implements a number of new international obligations under the WIPO Copyright Treaties within Europe, and it also seeks to harmonise copyright laws across Europe. The Copyright Directive went through the European legislative process at roughly the same time as what is known as the Electronic Commerce Directive; and it was the intention that both of these directives should complete their passage through that legislative process at roughly the same time. Indeed, the Electronic Commerce Directive says 'It is important that the proposed Directive on the harmonisation of certain aspects of copyright and related rights in the Information Society and this Directive come into force within a similar time scale with a view to establishing a clear framework of rules relevant to the issue of liability of intermediaries for copyright and related rights infringements at Community level(European Commission, 2000).' As it turned out, the Electronic Commerce Directive received final adoption before the copyright directive. On 4 May 2000, the European Commission welcomed the European Parliament's approval of the Electronic Commerce Directive, clearing the way for this measure to become law within the next 18 months. Later in May 2000, the United Kingdom's Electronic Communications Act 2000 received royal assent.

Copyright legislation – history

The legal framework for copyright in the United Kingdom has developed over many years.

A major milestone in the history of English copyright was the Star Chamber Decree of 1556. This granted a charter to the Stationers' Company. The motivation for this decree was not the protection of authors or publishers, but rather the system of royal patent grants which was designed to raise money for the government.

The Stationers' Company was one of the livery companies of the City of London whose membership covered bookbinders, printers and booksellers. The Star Chamber Decree of 1556 stated that only members of the Stationers' Company were entitled to practise the art of printing and the charter gave the Stationers' Company a number of powers to enforce their monopoly. Despite the fact that the Star Chamber was abolished in 1640 and all its decrees therefore lost validity, it would seem that the Long Parliament continued the statutes regulating printing, and indeed, after the execution of Charles in 1649, strengthened the censorship regulations (Mead).

Whilst the Star Chamber Decree of 1556 was a major milestone in the history of English copyright, it was not the first British copyright statute. The 1556 decree did not give copyright protection to the entire country, but only to members of the Stationers' Company. It covered only specific works; and it was almost entirely used for the works of authors who had long since died. The golden age of the Stationers' Company had come to an end with the expiration of the censorship laws in 1694.

The first copyright statute was the Copyright Act of 1709, also known as the Copyright Statute of Anne. Indeed, this is seen as the world's first true copyright Act, as opposed to censorship act. The full name of the Act is 'An act for the encouragement of learning, by vesting the copies of printed books in the authors or purchasers of such copies, during the times therein mentioned.' The Act was dated 1710, but it is commonly known as the Copyright Act of 1709, 8 Ann. c. 19. The Copyright Act of 1709 gave statutory protection to rightsowners. The 1556 decree had stated that only members of the Company of Stationers might print and import books; but under the Copyright Act of 1709 copyright was no longer the exclusive privilege of the Stationers' Company.

In the Copyright Statute of Anne, copyright protection was given for new books for a period of 14 years. In 1814 an act 'to afford encouragement to literature' was passed which substituted for the previous term of 14 years, with a reversionary 14 years to the author (if then living), a term of 28 years, to begin from the first day of publication and, if the author should be living at the expiration of that term, for the remainder of his life. The Copyright Act 1842 provided a statutory protection period of 42 years from publication, or until seven years from the death of the author, whichever was the longer.

The Copyright Act 1911 codified the statutory law of copyright, abolished common law copyright and rendered it unnecessary to obtain registration at Stationers' Hall as a condition for bringing an infringement action. The passage of the Copyright Act 1911 saw British copyright governed by a single, integrated piece of copyright legislation for the first time since 1709. The Copyright Act of 1911 abolished the common law right in unpublished works and replaced it with a set of rights which were clearly defined by statute.

In 1951 the Gregory Committee was set up to advise on the revision of the Copyright Act 1911. This led to the Copyright Act 1956 which essentially represented a revised version of the 1911 Act. Broadcasting was specifically protected under the 1956 Act, but there was no specific mention of computer programs in the Copyright Act 1956.

During the 1970s and 1980s there were moves towards overhauling UK copyright legislation, largely due to the development and widespread use of new technologies. In 1973 the government set up the Whitford Committee on Copyright Law because of publisher pressure for the licensing of photocopying, and this led to the Whitford Report of 1977 (Copyright and Designs Law, 1997). There then followed the green paper of 1981 (Performers' Protection, 1982) and the white paper of 1986 (Intellectual Property and Innovation, 1986) leading ultimately to the publication of the Copyright, Designs and Patents Act 1988, which differs substantially from the Copyright Act 1956.

Copyright is international in nature, and the international protection of authors' works was firmly established among most of the developed countries with the foundation in 1886 of the Berne Copyright Union, whose Conventions are revised from time to time. Other international instruments of copyright protection have also been adopted, in particular the Universal Copyright Convention of 1952.

Berne Convention

In 1886 the Berne Union was founded. Countries belonging to the Berne Union undertook to grant reciprocal protection to each other's works by signing up to the Berne Convention for the Protection of Literary and Artistic Works of 9 September 1886 (*http://www.wipo.int/eng/iplex/wo_ber0_.htm*). Berne is the main copyright convention to which most countries are signed up. The original agreement was drawn up in 1886 and since then there have been a number of revisions. Under the convention authors are entitled to some basic rights of protection for their intellectual output. Berne recognises the need for people to have access to protected works and so it allows exceptions and limitations to the exclusive rights.

Universal Copyright Convention

The Universal Copyright Convention was adopted in 1952 at a conference sponsored by Unesco in Geneva. It established the copyright symbol ©. The Convention was revised in Paris on 24 July 1971.

World Trade Organization

The World Trade Organisation (WTO) signed an agreement in 1994 which had an annex known as TRIPS – Trade Related aspects of Intellectual Property (*http://www.wto.org/english/tratop_e/trips_e/t_agm0_e.htm*). This is designed to ensure that intellectual property rights do not themselves become barriers to legitimate trade.

The TRIPS Agreement, which came into effect on 1 January 1995, is to date the most comprehensive multilateral agreement on intellectual property. The areas of intellectual property that it covers are: copyright and related rights (i.e. the rights of performers, producers of sound recordings and broadcasting organisations); trademarks including service marks; geographical indications including appellations of origin; industrial designs; patents including the protection of new varieties of plants; the layout designs of integrated circuits; and undisclosed information including trade secrets and test data.

To facilitate the implementation of the TRIPS Agreement, the Council for TRIPS concluded with the World Intellectual Property Organisation (WIPO) an agreement on co-operation between WIPO and the WTO, which came into force on 1 January 1996. As explicitly set out in the Preamble to the TRIPS Agreement, the WTO desires a mutually supportive relationship with WIPO. The Agreement provides co-operation in three main areas, namely notification of, access to and translation of national laws and regulations, implementation of procedures for the protection of national emblems, and technical co-operation.

WIPO

In 1967 the World Intellectual Property Organisation (WIPO) was established. WIPO is a United Nations body which is responsible for the promotion of the protection of intellectual property throughout the world through co-operation among states, and for the administration of various multilateral treaties dealing with the legal and administrative aspects of intellectual property.

In December 1996 around 100 countries signed the WIPO Copyright Treaty (treaty on the protection of authors, *http://www.wipo.int/eng/diplconf/distrib/ 94dc.htm*) and the WIPO Performances and Phonograms Treaty (treaty on the protection of performers and phonogram producers, *http: //www.wipo.int/eng/diplconf/distrib/95dc.htm*).

Licences

What the law does not allow can often be done with the copyright owner's consent through an appropriate licence. The Copyright Designs and Patents Act (CDPA) 1988 allows for the setting up of collective licensing bodies such as the Copyright Licensing Agency (CLA) or the Newspaper Licensing Agency (NLA). Where there are disputes, these can be referred to the Copyright Tribunal.

Some years ago the Copyright Licensing Agency's then Chief Executive, Colin Hadley said: 'Illegal copying is the most common crime in the UK today. Eight out of 10 people admit to copying illegally in the workplace. As a consequence authors and publishers are being deprived of millions of pounds in royalties and lost sales' (Copyright Licensing Agency, 1996).

A major problem with copyright law is one of awareness – something which was recognised by the Intellectual Property Group of the government's Creative Industries Task Force. The group considered ways of improving awareness of and education about intellectual property, and came up with five main recommendations. Their report (Dept of Trade and Industry et al., 2000) was published in Spring 2000, and is available on the Patent Office's web site (*http://www.patent.gov.uk*). It said that the language for intellectual property should be made more accessible; that there should be an awareness campaign; that there should be more co-ordination of the provision of information about intellectual property; that appropriate material should be included in the school curriculum, and relevant higher and further education courses; and that there should be better training for those involved in enforcement work.

I believe that one of the main reasons why there is an awareness problem is that there is not a clear message. Copyright law is complex. The legislation seems to be deliberately vague in places, which means that there is then a dependence upon case law to rule upon what is and is not permitted. For example, the Act does not define 'fair dealing'. It is amazing the number of disagreements that have occurred over the years between copyright experts who interpret the legislation in different ways. What librarians always ask is how much they can copy, is there a certain percentage that the legislation specifies, but this is something that the legislation does not specify; we have to rely instead on custom and practice, and guidelines from organisations such as the British Copyright Council, rather than anything which is enshrined in legislation. It is no wonder that library and information staff are often confused about what is and what is not permitted.

Electronic copyright

If we first look at UK statute law, this says that the owner of the copyright in a work has the exclusive right of reproduction and that this includes storing the work in electronic form (CDPA 1988, sections 16-17). So, works which are 'published' in electronic form such as literary works contained in electronic journals, PDF documents on the Internet, CD-ROMs, online databases, or floppy disks are protected as are their printed equivalents.

Section 17 of the CDPA 1988 says 'The copying of the work is an act restricted by the copyright in every description of copyright work … This includes storing the work in any medium by electronic means.' Section 17 clause 6 goes on to say that 'Copying in relation to any description of work includes the making of copies which are transient or are incidental to some other use of the work.' In other words, having a copy of a work on your computer cache is regarded as reproduction.

A recent Patent Office leaflet asks 'Is material on the Internet protected by copyright?', and goes on to answer this, saying 'Yes. Under UK law (the position in other countries may differ) copyright material sent over the Internet or stored on web servers will generally be protected in the same way as material in other media. So anyone wishing to put copyright material on the Internet, or further distribute or download such material that others have placed on the Internet, should ensure that they have the permission of the owners of the rights in the material' (Patent Office, 1999).

A single web page may well contain a number of different copyrights. For example, textual articles would be literary works, the graphics would be artistic works, and the sound files would be sound recordings containing separate musical works. You need to look at the site to see if there is a copyright notice which explicitly states what is permitted. But if there is no copyright notice, or if the copyright notice does not cover the copying which you want to undertake, then I would advise that you email the webmaster of the site for permission.

As far as hyperlinking is concerned, webmasters may well be happy for you to link to the homepage; but they may be far less happy to let you link to a lower level within their site, also known as 'deep linking'. This could be the case because the homepage contains advertising which helps fund the development and maintenance of the site, or because the use of frames technology could mean that people using your site do not realise that some of the information which appears on your site is actually coming from the site of another individual or organisation. If you do set up a web site which draws upon other people's web pages, then the source should be acknowledged; or it should be made clear that the information is coming from another site. As a matter of common courtesy, it is best to let the webmaster know that you want to hyperlink to his or her site. The Web is all about hyperlinking, and by letting someone know that you want to link to their site you may well find that they are happy to link to your site in return, which will almost certainly help to increase traffic to your site.

The Copyright and Rights in Databases Regulations 1997 came into force on 1 January 1998; they implement Council Directive 96/9/EC on the legal protection of databases, which harmonises the laws of member states relating to the protection of copyright in databases. It is important to distinguish here between 'electronic information' and 'databases'. Regulation 6 defines 'database' as a collection of independent works, data or other materials which:

- are arranged in a systematic or methodical way
- are individually accessible by electronic or other means.

With that definition, one could argue that this includes hard-copy reference directories, or even newspapers; hence the reason why I said that we need to distinguish between 'electronic information' and 'database'.

Under the Copyright and Rights in Databases Regulations 1997 (Regulation 20) fair dealing with a database is permitted so long as:

- the person extracting the material is a lawful user of the database
- the purpose is illustration for teaching or research or private study and not for any commercial purpose
- the source is indicated.

These regulations are significant because they represent the first piece of UK legislation to make a distinction between copying for the purposes of research for private study, and research for a commercial purpose. Indeed, the regulations say that: 'The doing of anything in relation to a database for the purposes of research for a commercial purpose is not fair dealing with the database' (Regulation 8(3)).

Where databases (compilations) represent the author's own intellectual creation by virtue of their selection and the arrangement of the contents, these are afforded full copyright protection. But where this is not the case, databases may qualify for a new right which is introduced by the 1997 Regulations – database right – which subsists if there has been a substantial investment in the obtaining, verifying or presenting the contents of the database (part III of the regulations covers database right).

Period of protection

If a database has full copyright protection, then the protection is for 70 years from the end of the year of death of the author, if there is one, or the end of the year of first publication if there is not a personal author.

If the database does not have full copyright protection, but qualifies for database right, then the period of protection is for 15 years from creation or its being made available to the public if this occurs during the 15 year period. However, any substantial new investment would qualify the database for a new 15 year term of protection. Bearing in mind the nature of many databases, and the way in which they are continually modified and/or updated, the idea that substantial new investment qualifies the database for a further 15 year term of protection means that these could be said to have their 15 year period of protection continually renewed. Regulation 12 does give a definition of 'substantial' as follows: 'substantial, in relation to any investment, extraction or re-utilisation, means substantial in terms of quantity or quality or a combination of both'.

Database Market Strategy Group

When the Copyright and Rights in Databases Regulations 1997 were going through their legislative process, the then minister of state at the Department of Trade and Industry, Ian McCartney, announced the setting up of a Database Market Strategy Group which would monitor the impact –including the economic impact – of the new regulations on the education, library and publishing sectors (Dept of Trade and Industry, 1997). Membership of the group is made up of both database producers and users. But at the time of writing, this group had met only once.

Exceptions to exclusive rights

The CDPA 1988 has a number of exceptions – also known as permitted acts or statutory permissions – which do allow copying under certain circumstances. For the library world the main exceptions are fair dealing and library privilege. The key question is whether the exceptions apply to digital information.

Fair dealing

Fair dealing is not a right, but rather a defence that might be used by an individual or an organisation which is taken to court for infringing activity. We have already seen that the fair dealing defence has been watered down, so that as far as 'databases' are concerned, research for a commercial purpose is not fair dealing with the database.

In the higher education sector the Joint Information Systems Committee and the Publishers Association (JISC/PA) set up a working party to identify any possible areas of agreement between representatives of JISC and the PA on a practical definition of fair dealing of materials in electronic form and, if possible, the necessary mechanisms that might be used to provide a workable monitoring system. Their final report dates from November 1998 (see *http://www.ukoln.ac.uk/services/elib/papers/pa*) and represents a set of fair dealing guidelines which contain practical points and useful lessons which can be applied across other sectors.

Library Regulations

The Library Regulations (Copyright Regulations, 1989) apply only to prescribed libraries, and these are not for profit libraries.

Copyright declaration forms have to be completed and signed by the requester. With the use of electronic information, there has always been the practical problem of getting the user to sign a copyright declaration form. This has been a problem because UK law does not as yet recognise electronic signatures for use on copyright declaration forms. But there have been some recent developments in this area: at a European level, there has been Directive 1999/93/EC of the European Parliament and of the Council of 13 December 1999 on a community framework for electronic signatures (L13/12, 19.1.2000); and at a national level, the Electronic Communications Act received royal assent in May 2000 and it contains a section (section 7) on electronic signatures and related certificates.

Copyright Licensing Agency (CLA) and digitisation

In January 1998 the CLA announced that representatives of authors and publishers had endorsed in principle their plans to license the digitisation of existing print material. Then in February 1999 they launched their digitisation licensing programme. Initially, the first licences offered were for the higher education and pharmaceutical sectors.

Calling this initiative their 'digital licensing programme' is a little bit misleading because the licence does not cover any electronically published material such as CD-ROMs, multimedia or online publications. Rather, 'the rights licensed [are] non-exclusive and restricted to those necessary to produce an exact electronic facsimile of an existing printed page, but permitted versions include a 'locked' version of Adobe Acrobat's .pdf format, as well as page images such as .bmp and .tiff' (Copyright Licensing Agency, 1998).

The CLA was set up in 1982 to represent publishers (through the Publishers Licensing Society) and authors (through the Authors Licensing and Collecting Society) and their whole purpose is to collect copyright royalties on behalf of the PLS and ALCS for onward distribution to publishers and authors. The CLA can only do what the publishers and authors have given them a mandate to do, and what was agreed was a programme which is based upon four key principles:

- transaction only, managed and cleared via CLARCS
- exact representation of the original page
- rightsholders opt in
- rightsholder-determined fees.

The scheme is therefore a transactional one, where users pay per view; it is for rightsholders to decide whether to 'opt in' to the scheme and the CLA offers rightsholders the opportunity to opt into the licensing schemes on a non-exclusive, sector-by-sector basis; and, finally, it is also for rightsholders to determine the fee charged.

Newspaper Licensing Agency (NLA) – electronic extension

The NLA has arrangements in place to allow licensees to make newspaper cuttings available following digitisation. They define digitisation as an 'electronic' process, which is intended to be distinguished from conventional photocopying and faxing. The phrase 'electronic process' would cover the distribution of cuttings by email, or by making them available on a server or by storing them electronically for access on a web site (either an internal web site or that of the end user's press cuttings agency).

An 'electronic extension' to the basic licence is required, i.e. a basic licence (in Form A, Form PA or Form HEA) is required before then setting up the electronic extension. Cuttings can be retained electronically for up to seven days from their scan, otherwise an *archive extension* is also required.

The electronic extension does not cover all the papers that are covered by the photocopying licence. *The Times, Sunday Times, Sun, News of The World* and *International Herald Tribune* are all excluded; as are all titles in the foreign repertoire such as the *Wall Street Journal*.

Initiatives towards standard licences

In practice, copyright matters concerning digital information are largely governed by service agreements and contracts. This can be quite difficult because you could easily end up with different contracts for each product, and this makes it very hard to guarantee that you are complying with these agreements. Can you really be expected to know what the small print in each of these contracts means? Indeed, in many instances even the suppliers themselves can be quite vague about what is and what is not permitted under the agreement for their product. You can end up having to spend a considerable amount of time negotiating individual contracts with suppliers, and coming up with a form of words which is acceptable to both parties which encapsulates the essence of what you think you have negotiated. This whole process can involve your in-house legal team or external legal advisers. It is for precisely these reasons that a number of initiatives have been undertaken which attempt to come up with a standard licence that could be adopted throughout the information industry.

John Cox Associates

John Cox Associates (*http://www.licensingmodels.com*) has produced a number of model standard licences for use by publishers, librarians and subscription agents for electronic resources. The licences have been sponsored by and developed in close co-operation with five major subscription agents: Blackwell, Rowecom, EBSCO, Harrassowitz and Swets. Designed for the acquisition of electronic journals and other electronic resources, these standard licences contain the words needed to express most of the variables publishers and librarians will meet in negotiating licenses. There are four licences, which cover:

- single academic institutions
- academic consortia
- public libraries
- corporate and other special libraries.

The licences are in the public domain. They have been placed there by the sponsoring subscription agents to help publishers, subscription agents and libraries to create agreements that express what they have negotiated.

The intention is for the licences to be updated when there are new requirements, products or business models to deal with and each licence is therefore given a version number and date.

Other initiatives towards standard licences include:

- JISC/PA (*http://www.ukoln.ac.uk/services/elib/papers/pa*) – the UK's PA/JISC model licence, jointly developed by publishers and librarians from the Publishers Association and the Joint Information Systems Committee of the Higher Education Funding Councils.
- the International Coalition of Library Consortia (ICOLC), which produced *Statements of Current Perspectives and Preferred Practices for the Selection and Purchase of Electronic Information* (*http://www.library.yale.edu/consortia/statement.html*)
- European Copyright Users Platform (ECUP) (*http://www.eblida.org/ecup/licensing/*), which has four sample licences – one of which is for company libraries, plus a section of clauses favourable to librarians.

Copyright will continue to be a controversial issue, all the more so because of the higher profile resulting from the increasing usage of digital information. As changes are made to UK statute law to take into account technological developments, there is a need for copyright experts to try and interpret what the legislation means, giving practical examples of what they believe to be fair and reasonable. Without that, information workers understandably tend to over-compensate for the lack of clear guidance by being too cautious.

References

Copyright and Designs Law. Report of the Committee to consider the Law on Copyright and Designs. London: HMSO (1977) (Whitford Report, Cmnd 6732).

Copyright (Librarians and Archivists) (Copying of Copyright Material) Regulations 1989 (SI 1989/1212).

Copyright Licensing Agency. *Rightsholders support CLA moves to License Digitisation.* CLA News Release, 23 January 1998.

Copyright Licensing Agency. *Major Crackdown on Illegal Copying Launched.* CLA News Release, 5 December 1996.

Department of Trade and Industry, Department for Culture, Media and Sport and the Patent Office. *The Report from the Intellectual Property Group of the Government's Creative Industries Task Force.* (2000).

Department of Trade and Industry. *Ian McCartney announces Database Market Strategy Group.* DTI Press Notice P/97/805, 3 December 1997.

European Commission. *Common Position adopted by the Council with a view to the Adoption of a Directive of the European Parliament and of the Council on certain legal aspects of Information Society Services, in particular Electronic Commerce, in the Internal Market ('Directive on Electronic Commerce').* 98/0325 (COD). 28 February 2000. Available at *http://europa.eu.int/comm/internal_market/en/media/eleccomm/composen.pdf.*

European Commission. *Proposal for a European Parliament and Council Directive on the Harmonisation of Certain Aspects of Copyright and Related Rights in the Information Society. Explanatory memorandum.* (1997). COM(97) 628 final. 2.

Intellectual Property and Innovation. London: HMSO (1986) (Cmnd 9712).

Mead, Dale. *History of Copyright.* Available at *http://www.jps.net/dcm/copyright.*

Patent Office. *Copyright: basic facts.* London: Patent Office (1999, rev. ed.).

Reform of the Law Relating to Copyright, Design, and Performers' Protection: a consultative document, presented to Parliament by the Secretary of State for Trade, July 1981. London: HMSO (1982) (Cmnd 8302).

Chapter 21

Data protection

Amanda McKenzie

Introduction

The aims of this chapter are to provide a general overview of current UK legislation and consider how such legislation may impact upon the working practices of library and information services (LIS) and information professionals. It is essential that LIS and information professionals understand the basic concepts of data protection and consider the implications in order for them to ensure that operations are conducted within the law.

This is not intended to constitute legal advice and the author is not responsible for any omissions or inaccuracies. You are advised to seek further advice from the Office of the Information Commissioner (formerly Data Protection Registrar and Office of the Data Protection Commissioner) or legal advice if you are unsure of your position under data protection legislation.

The Office of the Information Commissioner is also responsible from freedom of information.

History of data protection

There are two fundamental ideas that need to be balanced within the concept of data protection. On the one hand there is the right to freedom of information and expression and on the other the right of the individual to privacy.

The idea of data protection embodies the right to protect personal privacy. The concept of personal privacy was firstly considered within a legislative arena when the Council of Europe, set up after World War II to help unite Europe and to encourage 'common action in economic, social, scientific, legal and administrative rights and fundamental freedoms', specifically mentioned the individual's right to privacy.

There was a feeling with the growth of computerised processing of data, in particular personal data, that safeguards were needed, especially in view of the fact that data could be easily transferred internationally. Whether there was justification for such concerns is debatable, but as a result a number of countries initiated studies on the subject and between 1968 and 1970 the Council of Europe undertook a survey of human rights and modern scientific and technological developments which concluded that existing laws did not provide sufficient protection for individuals. As a result the Council of Europe produced two resolutions on privacy and databanks. In 1976 a Committee of Experts was established to prepare a Convention and the result was the Council of Europe Convention for the Protection of Individuals with regard to Automatic Processing of Personal Data (Council of Europe, 1981).

In the UK the Younger Committee was established in 1970 to investigate the subject of privacy and produced its report in 1972 (Younger Committee, 1972). In 1978 the Lindop Committee published a report on data protection (Committee on Data Protection, 1978). These reports, together with the Convention and the publication of Guidelines (OECD, 1981) from the Organisation of Economic Co, operation and Development, resulted in the Data Protection Act 1984 (DPA 1984), which covered the processing of personal information by computer in almost every area. The passing of the DPA 1984 enabled the UK to endorse the OECD Guidelines and ratify the Convention.

EC and data protection

The EC Commission, having been pressurised to produce a directive on data protection, recommended that all member states ratify the 1981 Council of Europe Convention. This was taken up by some and not others resulting in little uniformity. In 1992 only seven countries had ratified the Treaty.

As a result the Commission issued Directive 95/46/EC (European Union, 1995) (the Directive) after a certain amount of criticism, debate and a whole range of changes along the way.

The Directive applies solely to 'personal data', as did the DPA 1984 and as does the Data Protection Act 1998 (DPA 1998). However, the Commission commenced a study in 1998 to consider whether the protection under the Directive should be extended to data about 'legal persons'. The study compared countries which already extended their data protection laws to legal persons and to those that did not.

The study concluded : '…it is recommended that consideration be given to extending specific elements of the protection of the Directive to legal persons in specific areas'.

Direct marketing and the processing of business information by credit reference agencies were two areas considered. It is conceivable, therefore, that the Commission may extend the Directive at some future date in a limited number of areas, to legal persons rather than just natural persons.

Article 1 of the Directive embodies the proposals and objectives of the Directive:

'1.   In accordance with this Directive member states shall protect the fundamental rights and freedoms of natural persons and in particular their right to privacy with respect to the processing of personal data.

2.   Member States shall neither restrict nor prohibit the free flow of personal data between member states for reasons connected with the protection afforded under paragraph 1.'

The Directive applies not only to automated data but also to personal data contained in certain manual files. The preamble states that it covers situations where: '...the data processed are contained or are intended to be contained in a filing system structured according to specific criteria relating to individuals, so as to permit easy access to the personal data in question'.

Personal data therefore can be in the form of computerised or manual data. This extends to sound and image data. In regard to manual data, the Directive in its preamble states that manual processing is to '... cover only filing systems not unstructured files' and 'in particular the content of a filing system has to be structured according to specific criteria relating to individuals allowing easy access to personal data...'. Manual data therefore extends to personal data filing systems, which is defined in the directive as meaning: '...any structured set of personal data which are accessible according to specific criteria, whether centralised, decentralised or dispersed on a functional or geographical basis'.

Other important requirements under the Directive are that the data subject's consent to data processing must be specific, there can be no implied consent, for example, by absence of any objection. The consent has to be informed – the data subject has to be clearly told in advance all about the proposed processing of data. There can be no coercion in obtaining consent from the data subject, which is consistent with the approach taken by the then Data Protection Registrar under DPA 1984. The data subject's consent is defined as any '...freely given specified and informed indication of his wishes by which the data subject signifies his agreement to personal data relating to him being processed'. There is nothing in the Directive that states that consent has to be obtained in writing so a fully informed oral consent would probably be acceptable in most areas.

The other major areas under the Directive are:

•   the specific requirement that data subjects be informed of activity

- the right of data subjects to be able to object to lawful process of personal data if it impinges on the data subject's right to privacy under Articles 1(1)
- rigorous rules regarding the processing of sensitive data such as that relating to race, religion and politics
- the introduction of an exemption relating to journalism and artistic or literary expression.

Under Article 25 of the Directive personal information from the EU can only be passed to countries which provide an 'adequate level of protection'. EU countries are given the right to halt the transfer of data to countries not offering enough protection.

Very few countries will have the level of protection found within the EU and alternative safeguards are being considered. One possible solution to transfer data legitimately is the use of model contract clauses to guarantee the protection of personal data. However, concerns have been raised about whether such guarantees will be sufficient and whether such a contract can be enforced. Article 25 has been the subject of a dispute between the EU and US as this could have severely disrupted the free flow of information between the two environments. The EC Commission has recently adopted a Decision determining that an arrangement put in place by the US Department of Commerce, known as the 'safe harbour' rules, provides adequate protection for personal data transferred from the EU. At the same time, the Commission has adopted similar Decisions concerning Switzerland and Hungary and has recently stated that it is considering whether Canada's new privacy laws provide adequate protection. The US 'safe harbour' deal involves US companies signing up to give data from EU citizens similar levels of protection to those they enjoy in the EU. However this is a voluntary signing up system and some are concerned that the scheme would not be adequately policed. See European Commission Memo/00/47, and Press Releases IP/00/301 and IP/00/865 (European Commission, 2000).

UK Data Protection Act 1998

Introduction

The EU Data Protection Directive had effect in member states from 24 October 1998. Many member states including the UK did not have all the necessary domestic legislation in place at that time. Germany, France, Luxembourg, the Netherlands and Ireland as of January 2000 were the subject of a notification from the European Commission prosecuting them for failing to implement in time. A previous notification included the UK but was dropped in the January notification, presumably because the

Commission was satisfied that all the UK law would be in force by 1 March.

The UK Data Protection Act 1998 received Royal Assent on 16 January 1998. The Act and the supporting secondary legislation were brought into force on 1 March 2000. DPA 1998 has repealed and replaced DPA 1984 in its entirety. It should be noted that for the purposes of the DPA 1998 the UK does not include the Channel Islands or the Isle of Man.

The new Act carries over elements from the DPA 1984 in regard to the data protection principles of good practice; the registration system; an independent supervisory authority; data subjects' rights to access to their personal data and to correct it where it is wrong. The additional requirements imposed by the Directive are reflected in the DPA 1998.

Data and data subjects

Introduction

The DPA 1998 states that personal data must be processed 'fairly and lawfully' (Schedule 1 Data Protection Principles) as was stated under the DPA 1984. Personal data are not to be treated as processed fairly unless one of the conditions in Schedule 2 is met, which includes informing data subjects of the identity of the data controller and informing the data subject of the purposes of which the data is to be processed.

Processing may only be carried out where one of the following provisions is met:

- the individual has given his or her consent to the processing
- the processing is necessary for the performance of a contract with the individual
- the processing is required under a legal obligation
- the processing is necessary to protect the vital interests of the individual or to carry out public duties
- the processing is necessary in order to pursue the legitimate interests of the data controller or certain third parties (unless prejudicial to the interests of the individual).

In the case of sensitive personal data stricter conditions apply and where such data is being processed not only must the controller meet the requirements of the Principles, and one of the conditions under Schedule 2, but also one of the conditions under Schedule 3. This section includes information relating to racial or ethnic origin, political opinions, religious or other beliefs, criminal convictions, health and sex life. Explicit consent is required in order for sensitive personal data to be processed unless the data controller can show that the processing is necessary, based on one of the conditions under Schedule 3.

As stated earlier, 'explicit' consent appears in the Directive; however, explicit consent is neither defined in the DPA 1998 nor the Directive, but obviously obtaining such consent has to be more onerous than the consent required under Schedule 2. In October 1998 the Data Protection Registrar, as she was then, published an Introduction (the Introduction) (Data Protection Registrar, 1998) to the DPA 1998, which provides additional guidance on this point, as well as comprehensive guidance in other key areas.

Data controllers are still required to take security measures ('technical and organisational') to prevent loss or damage to personal data and to protect data from being processed unlawfully or without authorisation (Principle 7, Schedule 1 Part I) but the Act states explicitly what precautions data controllers should take (Part II). Data controllers should consider whether their existing security measures meet the requirements under the new Act.

Data

Under section 1(1) the definition of 'data' is information which:

(i)   is being processed by means of equipment operating automatically in response to instructions given for that purpose;

(ii)   is recorded with the intention that it should be processed by means of such equipment;

(iii)   is recorded as part (or with the intention that it should form part) of a relevant filing system (i.e. any set of information relating to individuals to the extent that, although not processed as in (i) above, the set is structured, either by reference to individuals or by reference to criteria relating to individuals, in such a way that specific information relating to a particular individual is readily accessible); or

(iv)   does not fall within any of the above but forms part of an accessible record as defined in section 68.

Data includes data held in a computer, on tape, video, compact disc and includes manual records. 'Personal data' under the DPA 1984 meant information which related to a living individual who could be identified from the information. The DPA 1998 goes a step further to cover not only information which is in the possession of the data controller but also information which is likely to come into his or her possession.

The definition of data under the new Act has been extended so that it now covers information which is recorded as part of a 'relevant filing system' where the records are structured, either by reference to individuals or by reference to criteria relating to individuals, so that 'specific information relating to a particular individual is readily accessible'. It is clear that this section will cover certain types of structured manual or paper filing systems, though unclear how far this will extend. The Commissioner has provided an interpretation in the detailed guidelines available from the web site, which LIS and information professionals who consider themselves data controllers should consult if they are unsure of whether their filing system would fall within the definition. The introduction states that it is not wholly clear how this definition translates in practical terms in all situations. Ultimately in cases of dispute it will be a decision for the courts.

The definition of data in the Act is also extended to cover information forming part of an 'accessible record'. An accessible record is described as any health record or any accessible educational or accessible public record as defined in Schedule 11 and Schedule 12.

Data subject

A literal interpretation of data subject under Article 2 of the Directive would have extended to individuals who had died ('personal data shall mean any information relating to an identified or identifiable natural person...'), however the DPA 1998 only applies to 'data subjects' – living individuals who are the subject of personal data.

Under Part II of the 1998 Act the subject access provisions have been enhanced. Under the DPA 1984 the data controller was obliged only to provide a copy of any data processed by reference to the data subject. The new Act states that the data subject is also entitled, on making a written request, to a description of the data being processed, a description of the purposes for which it is being processed, a description of any potential recipients of the data subject's data and, except in limited circumstances, any information as to the source of the data. Note that the obligation is initially only to provide a description rather than the actual data, though we will have to wait to see how this is in fact interpreted in practice.

Under the DPA 1984 the data controllers were only obliged to register their sources as opposed to revealing them to the data subject under the new Act and this may prove problematic for some sectors such as the media. However, there should be some protection under section 7(4) regarding restrictions on disclosure of data relating to third parties, thereby ensuring that only categories of sources need to be named, rather than individuals.

Under section 7(2) of the DPA 1998 the data controller is only obliged to provide access to data if the data subject pays a single fee (with some exceptions) as opposed to payment of one fee per entry as under the DPA 1984. This ensures that the data controller receives payment before having to initiate a potentially costly and lengthy search.

Other important rights under the new Act for the data subject is the right to require a data controller to cease, within a reasonable time, or not begin, processing any personal data which is likely to cause damage or distress, and a specific right for the data subject to prevent processing for the purposes of direct marketing. For the purposes of this section 'direct marketing' means: '...the communication (by whatever means) of any advertising or marketing material which is directed to particular individuals' (section 11(3)).

Under the DPA 1998 the right to compensation has been extended to allow the data subject the right to claim compensation for damage caused by any breach of the Act and also for distress in certain circumstances. Under the DPA 1984 data subjects were only allowed to claim compensation through the courts where they had suffered damage as a result of inaccuracy or unauthorised disclosure.

Transitional arrangements

24 October 1998 is when the EU Directive had effect in the UK. This means that under the new Act (Schedule 8) personal data that was already being processed before that date will not in most instances (but not all) have to comply with the new Act until 24 October 2001 ('first transitional period'). Some data which was held in manual filing systems prior to 24 October 1998 need not comply with some aspects of the new Act until 2007.

For the purposes of Schedule 8, personal data are 'eligible data' at any time if, and to the extent that, they are at that time subject to processing which is already under way immediately before 24 October 1998. This may cause some confusion and, according to the Commissioner, new data added to an existing system after 24 October would fall within the meaning of 'processing already underway'. LIS and information professionals who consider themselves data controllers should consider whether or not they can take advantage of the transitional provisions and whether or not the exemptions will apply. See the Commissioner's introduction to the Data Protection Act 1998.

All manual data forming part of a 'relevant filing system' and, subject to certain conditions, back-up data, data processed only for the purposes of payroll and accounts, and mailing lists or data produced by unincorporated members' clubs will be exempt from compliance with the Data Protection Principles and Parts II (Rights of Data Subjects) and III (Notification by Data Controllers) of the DPA 1998. All eligible automated data will be exempt until 23 October 2001 from many of the additional requirements of the new law – manual data which was held in a 'relevant filing system' prior to 24 October 1998 will also enjoy a more limited exemption from some of the Principles until 2007. Schedule 8 defines the period after 23 October 2001 but before 24 October 2007 as the second transitional period.

Registration and notification

The old registration system is replaced with a similar system of notification, though it is slightly less formalistic and sources of personal data no longer have to be registered. The Commissioner maintains a public register of data controllers. Each register entry includes the names and addresses of the data controller and a general description of the processing of data. Individuals can consult the register to find out what processing of personal data is being carried out by a particular data controller.

Every data controller who is processing personal data is obliged under the DPA 1998 to notify unless they are exempt. A data controller is a person (or entity) who determines the purposes for which, and the manner in which, any personal data are, or are to be, processed. Data processors (any person, other than an employee of the data controller, who processes data on behalf of the data controller) are not required to notify.

Exemptions are available for certain non profit making organisations, for data controllers processing data for personal, family or household affairs and for those processing data for staff administration, advertising, marketing or public relations purposes, and for accounts and records. Individuals who are processing personal data for personal, family or household affairs are exempt from notification and the other provisions under the DPA 1998. Other data controllers who are exempt from notification must comply with the other provisions of the Act.

Under the 1984 Act the Registrar could not enforce the Data Protection Principles against those who were exempt from registration, however, under the new Act the Commissioner will be able to enforce the Principles against those who are exempt from notification.

The Data Protection (Notification and Notification Fees) Regulations 2000/118 deal with the arrangements for organisations using personal data to notify the Commissioner of the use they make of that data, for example, in respect of partnerships a single notification is required under the new Act as opposed to every partner having to register as under DPA 1984, and a single notification is required for schools as opposed to head-teachers and governors having to register separately as under the DPA 1984.

Data controllers will not be required to notify under the new system until their current register expires or until 24 October 2001 whichever is the earlier. An amendment to the Freedom of Information Bill, now Freedom of Information Act 2000, will allow registrations made during this period to run their full three-year course. The fee for notification is £35 and the period of notification is one year.

Exemptions

There are certain exemptions under the DPA 1998, as there were under DPA 1984. These are detailed in Part IV and are either exemptions from the 'subject information provisions' or from the 'non disclosure provisions'. The subject information provisions are defined in section 27(2) as:

'(a)   the first data protection principle to the extent to which it requires compliance with paragraph 2 of Part II of Schedule 1, and

(b)   section 7.'

The non disclosure provisions are defined in section 27(4) as:

'(a)   the first data protection principle, except to the extent to which it requires compliance with the conditions in Schedules 2 and 3,

(b)   the second, third, fourth and fifth data protection principles, and

(c)   sections 10 and 14(1) to (3).'

Exemption under the non-disclosure provisions is available where the Act considers that, although such a disclosure of personal information would be in breach of DPA 1998, the public interest requires it.

The exemptions are either full or partial and provide for non disclosure of data where they relate to national security; crime and taxation; health education and social work; regulatory activity (which covers exemption under the subject information provisions by reference to numerous different categories of regulatory function exercised by public bodies concerned with the protection of the public, of charities, or of fair competition in business); journalism, literature and the arts.

The last exemption (where data is used for journalistic, literary or artistic purposes) is new to English law. Personal data which is processed within this area is exempt from any provisions under the DPA 1998 relating to: the Data Protection Principles (except the 7th Principle); subject access; the right to prevent processing likely to cause damage or distress; prevention of automated decision taking; rights to rectification, blocking, erasure and destruction.

The exemption only applies if the processing is undertaken 'with a view to the publication by any person of any journalistic, literary or artistic material'. The exemption only applies if the data controller 'reasonably believes that publication would be in the public interest having regard to the importance of public interest in freedom of expression and that compliance with the provisions of the DPA 1998 is incompatible with the 'special purposes''. Guidelines exist in the Data Protection (Designated Codes of Practice) Order 2000/864. This exemption only appears to extend to the media industry and therefore is only likely to affect those information professionals working within the media sectors.

Section 33 of the DPA 1998 extends the exemption which existed under the DPA 1984 in respect of the processing of personal data for research purposes (including but not limited to statistical or historical purposes) provided that the processing is exclusively for those purposes. Conditions have to be met, namely that data is not processed to support measures or decisions relating to particular individuals, nor processed in such a way that substantial damage or distress is likely to be caused to a data subject. A disclosure of personal data to any person for research purposes does not prevent the exemption from applying, nor does disclosure to a data subject or to a person acting on his or her behalf.

Transborder data flows

The new Eighth Data Protection Principle interprets the restrictions relating to cross border transfer under Article 25 of the EU Data Protection Directive. As this is part of the Principles, breach of the provisions is not immediately a criminal offence but is subject to the procedure for enforcing the Principles, including enforcement notices and appeal, if appropriate.

There are no restrictions on the transfer of personal data between European Economic Association (EEA) countries (Norway, Iceland, Liechtenstein and the 15 EU member states). Transfer of personal data to third countries may occur if those countries ensure an 'adequate level of protection for the rights and freedoms of data subjects'. As mentioned earlier the Directive contemplates model contracts and so does the DPA 1998 and it appears that there is general support for this. Data controllers when considering whether protection is adequate should consult the Commissioner's 'legal analysis' and suggested 'good practice approach', including consideration of the issue of contractual solution and the 'safe harbour' rules.

Schedule 4 sets out the circumstances where, despite the fact that the transferee country provides inadequate protection, the transfer could still proceed; these include where the data subject has agreed to the transfer; where the transfer is necessary for the performance of a contract; where the transfer is necessary for reasons of public interest; and where the transfer is necessary to protect the data subject.

Data controllers who transfer data outside the EEA should consider whether or not they will be able to benefit from the transitional provisions which provide an exemption until 2001 from compliance with the Eighth Data Protection Principle for data which is subject to processing already under way. The criteria set out in Schedule 4 should also be considered, though this is subject to the overriding general obligation to process data fairly and lawfully under the First Data Protection Principle.

Data protection and library and information services

There are a variety of areas where the DPA 1998 will impinge upon the working practices of information professionals. LIS need to assess whether they would potentially be considered data controllers and what information they hold would be considered personal data under the DPA 1998 and whether some areas would be covered by the narrowly defined exemptions discussed earlier.

Some examples of data which would need to be considered are:

- public and internal directories – membership records
- circulation records
- personnel files
- payroll files
- accounts and invoice files
- data held on publishers' databases
- electronic mailing lists
- web sites and intranets which hold personal data.

For those information professionals and LIS unsure about their position under the DPA 1998 certain questions need to be asked in order for there to be an understanding of the obligations. Is the LIS unit (or librarian or information professional) a data controller? Is the unit processing personal data?

The Data Protection Principles under the DPA 1984 were probably the most fundamental parts of the Act and this remains so under the DPA 1998. If it is concluded that personal data is being held and processed then the LIS team must ensure compliance with those Principles. Therefore the information unit must consider whether the data is processed fairly and lawfully and whether it is being processed for limited purposes. It should be adequate, relevant, accurate and not excessive in length; it should be processed in accordance with the data subject's rights, be secure, and not transferred to countries without adequate protection. Once assessed, then consideration needs to be given to the conditions under Schedule 2 and 3. Are there legitimate reasons to process – has consent been obtained?

Processes may need to be set in place within LIS in order for data protection policies to be established. Such policies would have to ensure awareness of all the obligations under the Act and related legislation (for example the Regulation of Investigatory Powers Act 2000 and the Freedom of Information Act 2000). A policy of transparency and openness is key to all such policies.

Those who are already considered data controllers need to check whether they can take advantage of the transitional provisions and whether any of the exemptions will apply to them. The Commissioner has provided further advice and guidance on what will be considered 'eligible data' and 'processing already under way' in the introduction to the DPA 1998.

Data protection laws are equally applicable in cyberspace. Therefore, for those information professionals dealing with web site management, it is important to assess the position under the DPA 1998 and consider whether the web site is providing access to personal data and/or whether it is gathering personal data from visitors. Examples of areas that would be covered include:

- public and internal directories
- staff biographical information pages
- web front-ends to management databases
- mandatory or voluntary online registration forms which require the user to add their email address or postal address or other contact information
- online research surveys
- email subscription lists.

The other area for concern is the use of profiling technologies such as cookies or spyware, the former being created by the web site's server and stored in the visitor's computer to record browsing patterns, the latter being any technology which collects data about the visitor without their knowledge. Such profiling techniques need to be disclosed. The Eighth Principle on transborder data flow will be extremely important to web site managers and effectively prevents transfer without consent, though as mentioned earlier it is prudent to consult the Commissioners' guidance on this area and the EU's 'safe harbour' arrangements.

The Commissioner's First Annual Report (Data Protection Commissioner, 2000) highlights the potential problems with protecting an individuals privacy with the emergence of further internet related technologies:

> As information technology develops at an exponential rate and organisations continue to exploit the business benefits this presents, individuals must be aware of their privacy rights and given the confidence to exercise them.

Conclusion

The Data Protection Act 1998 and the Directive are such important pieces of legislation it is difficult to ignore the impact they have (and will have) upon working practices for those dealing with personal data in all spheres. It is extremely important for information professionals and LIS to be proactive in their approach to data protection and to assess whether they are potential data controllers and if they are to adopt appropriate policies to ensure compliance with their obligations under the Act. In this ever developing area awareness is key to any data protection policy whether for the data controller, the potential data controller or the data subject.

References

Committee on Data Protection, *Report of the Committee on Data Protection*. HMSO, London (1978) (Cmnd 7341).

Council of Europe. *Convention for the Protection of Individuals with Regard to Automatic Processing of Personal Data*. Strasbourg: Council of Europe (1981) (European Treaty Series no. 108).

Data Protection Act 1984. Elizabeth II. Chapter 35. London: HMSO (1984).

Data Protection Act 1998. Elizabeth II. Chapter 29. London: The Stationery Office (1998).

Data Protection Commissioner. *First Annual Report 2000*. Available at *http://wood.ccta.gov.uk/dpr/dpdoc.nsf*.

Data Protection Registrar. *The Data Protection Act 1998, an Introduction*. October 1998. *Available at http://www.dataprotection.gov.uk/*.

European Commission. *Data Protection: Commission adopts decisions recognising adequacy of regimes in US, Switzerland and Hungary*. 27 July 2000. (Press Release IP/00/865). Available at *http://europa.eu.int/rapid/start/cgi/guesten.ksh?p_action.gettxt=gt&doc=IP/00/865 | 0 | RAPID&lg=EN*.

European Commission. *Data Protection: Commission endorses 'safe harbour' arrangement with US*. 29 March 2000. (Press Release IP/00/301). Available at *http://europa.eu.int/rapid/start/cgi/guesten.ksh?p_action.gettxt= gt&doc=IP/00/301 | 0 | AGED&lg=EN*.

European Commission. *How Will the 'Safe Harbour' Arrangement for Personal Data Transfers to the US Work?* 27 July 2000. (Memo/00/4T). Available at *http://europa.eu.int/rapid/start/cgi/guesten.ksh? p_action.gettxt=gt&doc=MEMO/00/47 | 0 | RAPID&lg=EN*.

European Union. *Directive 95/46/EC of the European Parliament and of the Council of 24th October 1995 on the Protection of Individuals with Regard to the Processing of Personal Data and on the Free Movement of such Data*. Brussels: EU (1995 OJ L 31 23 November 1995).

Organisation for the Economic Co-operation and Development. *Guidelines for the Protection of Privacy and Transborder Data Flows*. Paris: OECD (1981).

Younger Committee on Privacy. *Report of the Committee on Privacy*. London: HMSO (1972) (Cmnd 5012).

Further Reading

The European Commission Internal Market Directorate General, Media Information and Data Protection web site. Available at *http://europa.eu.int/ comm/internal_market/en/media/index.htm*.

Hammonds Suddards. *Data Protection*. Institute of Personnel and Development (2000).

Mullock, J. and Leigh-Pollitt, P. *The Data Protection Act 1998* (1999).

Office of the Data Protection Commissioner web site. Available at *http:// dataprotection.gov.uk*.

Rowe, H. *Data Protection Act 1998*. Tolley (2000).

Chapter 22

Liability for information provision

Amanda McKenzie

Introduction

In recent years information professionals have paid more attention to issues of professional liability. There are many reasons for this, not least the increased value which has been placed upon 'information' generally. Librarians and information professionals (and I use the terms interchangeably in this chapter to encompass all professionals working within the information sector) are increasingly being relied upon for their skills and knowledge in this process.

A consequence of the growth of the information market (and value placed upon information as a commodity) is that users and clients of library and information services (LIS) have greater expectations. This is especially so where charges are introduced, thus placing a greater emphasis on the client–customer relationship and the duty of care that may result. As LIS become more involved in the role of 'advisors' in regard to the retrieval of information, questions can be asked as to what extent information professionals could be held liable for the information they provide.

This chapter is aimed at librarians and information professionals who need to consider issues of liability for information provision. It provides an overview of how liability arises under both tort and contract law. It will also address how librarians and information professionals could minimise the threat from legal action.

This is not intended to constitute legal advice and the author is not responsible for any omissions or inaccuracies. You are advised to seek further advice from a solicitor if you require specific advice on the liability of information provision for information professionals.

Liability

Contract

It is impossible to provide a definitive definition of a contract, however the most accepted definition is 'a promise or set of promises which the law will enforce' (*Halsbury's Laws of England*). To constitute a valid contract there must be two or more separate and definite parties to the contract. There must be an offer, acceptance, intention to create legal relations (and capacity to do so) and consideration supporting those promises. There has to be a mutual exchange of promises for a contract to arise.

Where a LIS accepts an offer from a user to provide information and a fee is agreed, then a contract exists. Where information is provided free of charge no contractual relationship exists between the librarian and the end user or the employer and the end user. Such a contract can be made either orally or in writing or partly orally and partly in writing. Of course though it may be legally acceptable to have an oral contract a written contract would specify the terms and conditions of that agreement and would offer greater protection for both the LIS and the client, providing substantial evidence in case of dispute. A written contract would provide express terms and define the obligations and rights of the parties and hopefully prevent a dispute occurring.

The obligations for the parties will depend upon what had been agreed – whether it be oral, written or both. If it is agreed that information shall be supplied at a certain date or that payment is to be made by a certain date, and such obligations are not met, then there will be a breach of contract.

While it can be argued that many transactions occur within the information world based on oral agreements (with few repercussions), it is advisable that if information is being provided to external clients for a fee that a contract be drawn up to protect all parties. In the absence of a written contract, and in the event of a dispute, the court would have to determine the obligations and the nature of the contract. Additionally, during pre-contractual discussions, statements made by the parties may be considered by a court to be statements made to induce a party into the contract, though the parties may have intended them not to be part of a legally binding agreement, i.e. mere representations.

The law also implies terms into a contract and the most important of these for LIS are the statutory obligations under the Supply of Goods and Services Act 1982. For example, the Act implies terms into a contract that the service must be carried out with reasonable care and skill and this is probably the most important aspect for the information professional. Additionally, in the absence of a term whereby a completion date is expressly set or a specific payment is agreed the Act inserts an implied term that the service be carried out within a reasonable time and that a 'reasonable fee' be paid. This is limited to services provided in the course of a business, which includes professions, government departments and local or public authorities. These provisions apply where a contract exists; that is, there has been a mutual exchange and promises, therefore the implied terms would not apply to services that are provided for free.

Breach of the implied terms, or the express terms, of a contract could lead to litigation (though where express terms exist there is less likelihood of litigation occurring in the first place). If held to be in breach of contract, the librarian or information professional may have to pay damages. There are other remedies available where a contract is breached (*Halsbury's Laws of England* is a good starting point if further reading is required).

Tort

Basically, rights in tort are civil rights of action which are available for the recovery of unliquidated damages by persons who have sustained injury or loss from acts or statements or omissions of others in breach of duty or contravention of right imposed or conferred by law, rather than by contract.

Liability in tort is wider than that in contract as there is no requirement for a mutual exchange of promises. There are distinct areas within the domain of the term tort; however, the main areas which will principally concern information professionals are negligence, and to a lesser extent defamation.

Negligence

Negligence as a tort is the breach of a legal duty to take care which results in damage, undesired by the defendant to the plaintiff. Its ingredients are:

- the existence in law of a duty of care, i.e. that the defendant owed a duty of care to the plaintiff
- the careless behaviour of the defendant breached that duty of care
- foreseeability that such conduct would have inflicted on the plaintiff the particular damage of which he or she complains
- as a consequence of that breach the plaintiff suffered damage – the plaintiff has to establish that the damage suffered was as a direct consequence of the defendant's action or failure to act, i.e. proximate cause.

For example, when applied to LIS, if inaccurate information is carelessly supplied to a user who it is established is owed a duty of care and they, as a consequence of that carelessness, suffer loss, then the information professional who provided that information (or, as is more probable, their employee) may be liable for damages.

Of course before an action in negligence can proceed it has to be established that a duty of care did indeed exist. The principles of negligence have developed through well-established case law, decisions of which have been based on legal and policy considerations.

Donoghue v Stevenson (1932) established the modern law of negligence by defining general principles which could be used to determine the existence of negligence. Lord Atkin established the 'neighbourhood principle', which defines classes of persons to whom a duty of care is owed. Summing up Lord Atkin defined a 'neighbour' as 'persons who are so closely and directly affected by my act that I ought to have them in contemplation as being affected when I am directing my mind to the acts or omissions which are called into question'. The scope of this test was limited, however, because the duty of care was not extended to cases of pure economic loss.

However, the duty of care was extended in the case of *Hedley Byrne & Co Ltd v Heller & Partners* (1964) to include economic as well as physical damage. Though the plaintiff, Hedley Byrne, lost their case it was established that 'a duty of care could arise to give careful advice and failure to do so could give rise to liability for economic loss caused by negligent advice'. This is significant for information professionals as in the majority of cases information provided is more likely to cause economic loss than physical harm.

Anns and others v London Borough of Merton (1978) further developed the 'neighbourhood principle' and considers the circumstances in which the scope of the duty of care should be limited. Lord Wilberforce established proximity and stated that public policy considerations should be taken into account when considering the scope of liability. For example, though in theory an information provider may be sued for negligence, whether or not they are charging for that information, it may not be in the public interest to set such a precedent as it would have a major impact on those organisations providing information freely such as, public libraries and Citizens' Advice Bureaux.

An important decision defining duty of care in the area of information provision was in the case of *Caparo Industries plc v Dickman* (1990), which involved the liability of auditors to potential investors. In this case it was stated that the concepts of duty of care existed where the advice or information is for a purpose; the purpose is made known at the time when the advice is given or when the information is sought; the advisor knows that his or her advice or information will be communicated to the recipient; it is known that the advice or information will be used for a specific purpose. Though auditors were involved it is arguable that it could easily be an information professional within a special library or information centre providing information for a fee. The case distinguishes between those standards applied to general information providers such as newspaper publishers and those applied to professional information providers.

In assessing whether a breach of duty had occurred, a court would consider whether that person had exercised reasonable skill and care in carrying out their duties. Both in contract and tort the standard test of whether a breach has occurred is 'reasonableness'. In *Donaghue v Stevenson* (1932) Lord Atkin states: 'You must take reasonable care to avoid all acts or omissions which you can reasonably foresee would be likely to injure your neighbour.' An information professional's actions would be judged against those of their fellow professionals. Therefore the onus is on the LIS and individual librarians to ensure that they meet expected professional standards. Relevant in this regard are the standards of professional practice at the time (often embodied in codes of professional practice and procedures of appropriate professional bodies). Different spheres within the information profession may be afforded different levels of professional expectation.

For freelance information specialists, the Code of Practice for Information Professionals (EUSIDIC, 1993), produced jointly on behalf of the European Information Industry Association (EIIA), the European Association of Information Services (EUSIDIC) and the European Information Researchers Network (EIRENE), may be beneficial for setting an initial benchmark for professional standards. Information professionals should consult the codes of practice of the professional bodies to which they belong and also check their own employment contracts.

Vicarious liability

In terms of professional negligence employers could be found liable for the acts or omissions of their employees, that is be 'vicariously' liable. For example, where a librarian has been negligent (and as a result a third party suffers loss) the employer could also be found liable, despite the loss being as a result of the individual librarian's negligence. This only applies where the employee is directly employed by the employer, in that there is a contract of employment. This would not therefore apply to freelance information professionals.

Defamation

This is an area which is increasingly important to information professionals especially in light of the development of 'cyber-libel'. Most cases have arisen because of libellous or potentially libellous statements placed on bulletin boards or created via emails. Many librarians and information professionals act as 'list holders', administering bulletin boards, discussion lists or newsgroups, intranets and web sites.

In the first defamation action involving the Internet within the UK – *Godfrey v Demon* (1999) – a newsgroup, carried by the defendant's Internet service provider (ISP), posted material which was defamatory of the plaintiff and which purported to come from the plaintiff. On 17 January 1997 the plaintiff sent a letter by fax informing the defendant that the posting was a forgery and requesting that it be removed. The posting was not removed immediately but remained available on the defendant's server until its expiry on or about 27 January. The plaintiff claimed damages for libel in respect of the posting after 17 January. The judge held that an ISP is a publisher of all material contained on its server. It was immaterial that the material was not posted by the ISP's customer, that the material was posted to a newsgroup which was not run by the ISP, and that the individual defamed was not a customer of the ISP.

The effect of this decision is that an ISP will always be deemed to be a publisher of material on its server and will be liable for defamatory material posted by third parties to any newsgroup which it carries, whether or not it is within its control, unless it can rely on the defence in section 1 of the Defamation Act 1996 of 'innocent dissemination', or on the defence of justification, fair comment or privilege.

The section 1 defence applies where an ISP's role is only as a carrier of the offending newsgroup (that is where it exercises no editorial control of any kind) and it has taken reasonable care and does not know, and has no reason to believe, that it has contributed to the publication of the defamatory statement.

To rely on the section 1 defence, the ISP will now have to remove an allegedly defamatory posting immediately if it is put on notice that it exists. The ISP is not entitled to investigate first whether any of the other defences outlined above may apply, or whether the allegation has any merits, unless it suspends access to the posting while it does so. This case was eventually settled and the defendant paid damages to the plaintiff.

This decision has potentially far-reaching consequences and although it may be disputed in time, information professionals involved with discussion lists should take reasonable precautions to ensure that any offending material is quickly removed.

Minimising the risk

Obviously it is better to minimise any risk of being sued by having set practices and procedures in place.

Exclusion clauses and disclaimers

Exclusion clauses are statements which are either expressly incorporated into a contract, or notified orally to the client or displayed by way of a public notice, which seek to limit responsibility for certain errors or omissions. For example, the Dun & Bradstreet exclusion clause states that:

Whilst D&B attempts to ensure that the information provided is accurate and complete by reason of the immense quantity of detailed matter dealt with in compiling the information and the fact that some of the data are supplied from sources not controlled by D&B which cannot always be verified, including information provided direct from the subject of enquiry as well as the possibility of negligence and mistake, D&B does not guarantee the correctness or the effective delivery of the information and will not be held responsible for any errors therein or omissions therefrom (D&B).

Exclusion clauses are limited in law by the Unfair Contract Terms Act 1977, section 2(2), which states that such exclusion clauses are subject to a test of reasonableness. The courts will consider certain factors when considering whether an exclusion clause is reasonable or not, including bargaining power of the parties and whether the supplier was operating in a monopoly situation. Obviously a blanket clause limiting liability for everything is unlikely to be viewed as reasonable and is likely to prove counterproductive. However, a reasonable exclusion clause can be extremely useful for setting out the limits of responsibility, especially if a dispute arose. A librarian could not reasonably be expected to verify all the information obtained from a well-known source nor provide a guarantee that research conducted produced all relevant information and such a clause stating this is likely to be viewed as being reasonable.

The Unfair Terms in Consumer Contract Regulations 1994 (SI 1994/3159), now revoked and replaced by the Unfair Terms in Consumer Contracts Regulations (SI 1999/2083), implemented the EC Unfair Terms in Consumer Contracts Directive 93/13 into English law. The Directive and hence the Regulations apply only to consumer contracts, whilst the 1977 Act applies to business-to-business dealings. These Regulations state that unfair terms should not be binding on consumers. Unfair terms are defined as '…any term which contrary to good faith causes a significant imbalance in the parties' rights and obligations…'. Terms that are regarded as unfair include clauses that attempt to exclude liability for death or physical injury due to negligence.

Insurance

Professional indemnity insurance has been a standard requisite for many professions to date and obligatory for others. Increased attention to insurance for information professionals reveals the growing awareness within the sector of the increased commercialisation of their work. Such insurance would include protection against actions for negligence which involve errors or omissions and could be used as a means of limiting the damages payable in cases of breach of contract. Information professionals who would be considered more susceptible to allegations of negligence or breach of contract, for example, those working in special libraries or commercial research centres, and independent information professionals, would benefit by taking such cover. In most situations employers would be vicariously liable for the negligence of their employees, therefore LIS managers should ensure that their employer's insurance policy is amended to cover their service.

In 1997 the Library Association announced that professional indemnity insurance could be arranged with the Royal SunAlliance 'to provide a suitable professional indemnity policy for members in consultancy...'. It is therefore worth contacting professional bodies to consult them about the type of insurance that could be obtained.

Training and continuing professional development

It is imperative for information professionals to stay abreast of developments generally and within their particular sphere and to continual enhance their skills and knowledge. In an age of rapid technological change and the increased appetite for information the librarian's role is continually developing and it is important that professional standards are maintained. LIS managers should ensure that staff are encouraged to attend courses to update and enhance skills and knowledge, and that they are made aware of the potential risks associated with information provision. It is also worth adopting policies and practices whereby research requests are well documented to ensure evidence exists of exchanges between the LIS and clients. Although information professionals are under no obligation to participate formally in a programme of continuing professional development (CPD) professional associations can assist in an informal programme. The Library Association has published a CPD framework for members to utilise when seeking to develop their knowledge and expertise.

Conclusion

Although there have to date been no specific cases brought against a librarian or information professional for negligence or breach of contract (or liability for defamation) that does not mean there never will be. Information professionals, though traditionally viewed as performing an essential role as intermediaries in the information chain, are now increasingly involved in publishing and intranet and web site management. Responsibility for the accuracy of web site information or the administration of an acceptable use policy is likely to be assigned to individuals who need to be aware of the risk associated with such responsibility.

LIS need to assess whether the service they provide places them at risk from being sued. Is the service fee based? If so is there a written contract in existence? Is it a specialist unit? Are the clients relying on the information being provided? Once these questions have been asked and answered then the information service, if required, needs to undertake measures to minimise those risks.

References

Anns and others v London Borough of Merton [1978] A.C. 728, [1977] 2 W.L.R. 1024.

Caparo Industries plc v Dickman [1990] 2 A.C. 605, [1990] 2 W.L.R. 358.

D&B. *Risk Management Agreement Contract*. One of the Terms and Conditions of Service.

Donoghue v Stevenson [1932] A.C. 562, [1932] All E.R. 1.

EUSIDIC. *Code of Practice for Information Brokers*. Brussels: EUSIDIC (1993).

Godfrey v Demon [1999] 1 All E.R. 342.

Halsbury's Laws of England. **9**(1) (4th ed. reissue).

Hedley Byrne & Co Ltd v Heller & Partners [1964] A.C. 463, [1963] 3 W.L.R. 101.

Further reading

Hannabus, S. Being negligent and liable: a challenge for information professionals. *Library Management*, **21**(6) 2000.

Moyat, M. *Legal Liability for Information Provision*. London: Aslib (1998).

Oppenheim, C. *The Legal and Regulatory Environment for Electronic Information*. Infonortics Ltd (1999, 3rd ed.).

Chapter 23

Freedom of Information Act 2000

David Haynes and Fran Huckle

Introduction

The Freedom of Information Act 2000 will have a considerable effect on public rights of access to information. It will affect all public authorities from central government departments to regional bodies, local councils, non-departmental public bodies, local health authorities and local education authorities. It will affect the way in which they handle information and records. Experience in other countries suggests that an industry will grow up to service the needs of freedom of information applicants and the requirements of authorities to organise their systems to handle requests for information. It will change the way in which information professionals go about getting hold of official information.

The purpose of this section is to review the main provisions of the Freedom of Information Act 2000 and its likely impact on users of information, library and information staff who act as intermediaries for users, records managers, and those responsible for describing the information content of documents produced by public authorities.

There has been a lot of debate and comment about the Freedom of Information Act 2000 and this section does not aim to discuss the relative merits of the different positions that have been put forward. However, we should mention the Campaign for Freedom of Information, which has played a leading role in the development of thinking on this subject and is likely to continue to be a focus for discussion of issues surrounding freedom of information. The Library and Information Commission, the Library Association and the Data Protection Registrar have all issued policy papers or direct responses to the bill prior to Royal Assent of the Act in 2000.

Background

In December 1997 the Government published its proposals for an Act on freedom of information in a white paper, *Your Right to Know* (Cm 3618). A draft bill was published in May 1999, which after considerable debate and public commentary was enacted in December 2000.

Main concepts

The Freedom of Information Act 2000 provides the right of access to recorded information held by public authorities. It clearly defines exemptions from the duty to disclose information and it establishes arrangements for enforcement and appeal. The Act is arranged in eight parts:

Part 1:   Access to information held by public authorities

Part 2:   Exempt information

Part 3:   General functions of the Secretary of State, Lord Chancellor and Information Commissioner

Part 4:   Enforcement

Part 5:   Appeals

Part 6:   Historical records and records in the Public Record Office or Public Record Office of Northern Ireland

Part 7:   Amendments of the Data Protection Act 1998; amendments relating to personal information held by public authorities

Part 8:   Miscellaneous and supplemental.

In its summary of the draft Bill, the Home Office saw the main features as being:

- a wide general access right subject to clearly defined exemptions and conditions
- the requirement to consider discretionary disclosure in the public interest even when an exemption applies
- the duty to publish information proactively
- stronger powers of enforcement through an independent commissioner and tribunal.

The main concepts are:

- right of access to information
- the appointment of an Information Commissioner
- publication schedules
- exempt information
- enforcement
- codes of practice.

Right to information

The Act proposes a general right of access to information held by public authorities. Applicants for information have the right to be told whether the information requested is held by that authority and if not where it is held. The wording of the legislation is:

> 1. (1) Any person making a request for information to a public authority is entitled:
>
> > (a) to be informed in writing by the public authority whether it holds information of the description specified in the request, and
> >
> > (b) if that is the case, to have that information communicated to him.

Requests for information under the Act should be in writing and should state the name of the applicant, a correspondence address and a description of the information requested. However the applicant is not required to provide a reason for requesting the information.

The Act makes provision for a fee to be charged by the public authority. This is similar to the provision of the Data Protection Act 1998 and is intended to cover a proportion of the administration costs (up to 10 per cent) plus the direct costs of satisfying the request. The maximum level of these fees will be set by the subsequent regulations.

The Act requires a prompt response to a request for information. Public authorities will have 20 working days, after payment of the fee, to respond to any valid request for information under the Act.

Information Commissioner

The legislation makes specific provision for an Information Commissioner whose responsibilities cover both the Freedom of Information Act 2000 and the Data Protection Act 1998. There has been considerable debate about the boundary issues arising from the two Acts: one provides for access to information held by public authorities and the other is intended to protect the privacy of individuals. The Data Protection Commissioner (a role that will become a part of the Information Commissioner's remit) recently produced a flow chart of the provisions governing access to personal information held by public authorities. This is intended to map out the effects of the Freedom of Information Act 2000 on the Data Protection Act 1998.

Publication schemes

Under the Freedom of Information Act 2000, public authorities will have a duty to adopt a publication scheme in order to make information available to the public proactively. Each authority has considerable latitude on what classes of information it will publish or the manner in which it is published and whether or not there is a charge for that information.However, they must publish information in accordance with their publication schemes. The schemes should specify the classes of information to be published, the manner of publication, and whether it will be available free of charge or for a fee. The Information Commissioner will be responsible for approving proposed publications schemes. The Commissioner may also approve model publication schemes for specific classes of public authority.

Exempt information

Public authorities will not be required to make all information available to the public and there is an extensive list of exemptions in the Act. This has been the cause of considerable debate and the accusation that the Act is being watered down. The Act exempts the following classes of information from disclosure to the public under freedom of information:

- information accessible to the public by other means
- information intended for future publication
- information supplied by, or relating to, bodies dealing with security matters
- national security, where an exemption is required to safeguard national security
- information, the disclosure of which would prejudice the defence of the British Islands
- information, the disclosure of which would prejudice relations between the UK and any other state or international organisation
- information, the disclosure of which would prejudice relations between any two administrations in the United Kingdom
- information which could prejudice the economic interests of the UK
- investigations and proceedings conducted by public authorities
- information, the disclosure of which would prejudice law enforcement
- court records
- information required for audit functions
- parliamentary privilege
- information that relates to the formulation or development of government policy
- information that would be likely to prejudice the effective conduct of public affairs
- communications with the Royal family

- health and safety information, disclosure of which would endanger the physical or mental health or safety of any individual
- environmental information
- personal information
- information that may be disclosed under another Act, such as the Data Protection Act 1998
- information that would constitute a breach of confidence
- information covered by legal professional privilege
- commercial interests such as trade secrets
- information which is prohibited from disclosure under any enactment.

Specific mention is made in the Act of vexatious or repeated requests:

14. (1) Section 1(1) does not oblige a public authority to comply with a request for information if the request is vexatious.

(2) where a public a authority has previously complied with a request for information which was made by any person, it is not obliged to comply with a subsequent identical or substantially similar request from that person unless a reasonable interval has elapsed between compliance with the previous request and the making of the current request.

Enforcement

If a person seeking information is unable to obtain a satisfactory response from a public authority, he or she can refer the matter to the Information Commissioner. The Commissioner will make a decision and notify the authority and complainant. If the Commissioner rules in favour of the complainant, he or she can serve an information notice. The Commissioner can serve an enforcement notice, if an authority has failed to comply with any of the requirements of Part I of the Act. Failure to comply with a notice could result in a court hearing, although the Act does not confer any right of action against a public authority.

Home Office Code of Practice

The Act makes provision for a code of practice to be issued by the Secretary of State for the Home Office. The Information Commissioner will be responsible for promoting the code of practice with public authorities, but it will not be enforceable. The aims of the code are to:

- facilitate the disclosure of information under the Freedom of Information Act 2000 by setting out good administrative practice that should be followed when handling requests for information

- set out standards for the provision of advice
- ensure that the interests of third parties who may be affected by the disclosure of information are considered
- consider the implications for freedom of information before agreeing to confidentiality provisions.

Although the code is not mandatory, public authorities are encouraged to provide advice and assistance to those making requests for information. The procedures for dealing with requests for information should be published. Where an applicant is unable to make a request in writing, the public authority should provide assistance such as advising them on agencies that can help them (such as Citizens' Advice Bureaux) or by offering to take a note of the application over the telephone. Public authorities should offer to help the applicant to describe their information requests by providing an outline of the different kinds of information that might meet the terms of the request, providing catalogues and indexes, providing a general response, or where cost is a factor indicating what information could be provided within the cost ceiling. The Code of Practice also suggests that authorities should not make unreasonable requests for file reference numbers, or detailed descriptions of records sought.

Requests for information should be transferred to the appropriate authority if the original authority to which the request for information was addressed was unable to provide the information. Where a request for information may infringe on the rights of another person or organisation, the authority should consult the affected party promptly. Public authorities should refuse to include contractual terms, which restrict the disclosure of information held by the authority beyond the provisions made by the Act. All public bodies should have in place a procedure for dealing with complaints.

Lord Chancellor's Code of Practice

The Lord Chancellor's Code of Practice on the Management of Records under Freedom of Information provides guidance to all public authorities and other bodies subject to the Public Records Act 1958 on the discharge of their responsibilities under the Freedom of Information Act 2000. It is a supplement to the Act. Part 1 of the Code of Practice deals with the principles of good records management. It states:

> The records management function should be recognised as a specific corporate programme within an authority…It should bring together responsibilities for records in all formats, including electronic records, throughout their life cycle, from planning and creation through to ultimate disposal.

It recommends that public authorities should have a policy statement on how they manage their records, including electronic records. The policy statement should be reviewed at least once every three years. A designated member of staff should have lead responsibility for records management, normally the Departmental Record Officer. The code of practice then goes on to describe good practice for record creation, record keeping, record maintenance, disposal arrangements, record closure, appraisal planning and documentation, record selection and specific issues connected with electronic records.

Part 2 of the code of practice deals with the review and transfer of public records. It states:

> 11.3 In reviewing records for public release, authorities should ensure that public records become available to the public at the earliest possible time in accordance with the Freedom of Information Act 2000.
>
> 11.4 Authorities which have created or are otherwise responsible for public records should ensure that they operate effective arrangements to determine
>
> a) which records should be selected for permanent preservation; and
>
> b) which records should be released to the public.

The code of practice also provides guidelines on determining the circumstances under which records should be released to the public and when exemptions from the proposed Act apply.

Impact of the Act

The Act will primarily affect two different groups: public authorities that hold information, which will become available under the Act; and individuals and organisations that seek access to official information.

Getting hold of information – your rights

The Act does not specify who is eligible to apply for public information. This could be a person or an organisation. In its consultation document the Government has stated that it sees the Freedom of Information Act 2000 as a component in modernising British politics and that it is seen as a way to involve people more closely in decisions that affect their lives. It provides members of the public with a right of access to information held by bodies in the public sector, including schools, hospitals, education authorities, central government departments and non-departmental public bodies. The Act also mentions companies owned by public authorities, or providing services under contract on behalf of public authorities.

Public authorities are obliged to respond to a request for information within a reasonable time and, if they claim exemption, they have to provide reasons. They can also charge for information access to cover up to 10 per cent of the marginal costs of providing that information plus reasonable direct costs. It has been suggested that a fee of £10 (similar to the level recommended under the provision of the Data Protection Act 1998) should be set, but the maximum could be set at a much higher level (£500 has been mentioned).

The main exclusions to the requirement to provide information are institutional exclusions or functional exclusions. There are a number of major exceptions to the coverage of the Act, and in its current form it leaves a great deal to the discretion of the public authorities. The main institutional exclusions are the security and intelligence agencies. Functional exemptions include information the disclosure of which may prejudice the effective conduct of public affairs. This is seen as a catch-all which could effectively stifle any access to information, because it leaves invocation of this exemption in the hands of the public authority. Other exemptions include commercial information, personal information, information relating to criminal investigations currently underway. They can also exclude frivolous requests, those that are considered too expensive to fulfil and information due to be published (within a specified time frame).

An applicant can appeal to the Information Commissioner if an authority fails or refuses to provide information in response to a request, however, the complaints procedure of the agency must first be exhausted. The Information Commissioner may serve an Information Notice if he or she judges that a request for information is reasonable. If they disagree with the decision of the Commissioner, an applicant may appeal to a Tribunal. The public does not have the right to take a civil action against a public authority under the provision of the Act.

Providing information – responsibilities of public authorities

Government departments and many public authorities follow the current Code of Practice on Access to Government Information. This is less restrictive than the Freedom of Information Act 2000, but does not have the force of law behind it. The Government has stated in its consultation document that it sees the legislation as one strand in access to information and considers that culture change within authorities is also important. The Act covers the full range of public sector activity (with some significant exceptions), including health authorities, education authorities, local government and companies providing public services on behalf of public authorities.

The Act makes provision for two codes of practice. Drafts of both codes are now available: The Home Office Code of Practice for the Freedom of Information Act, and the Lord Chancellor's Code of Practice on the Management of Records under Freedom of Information, which deals specifically with records management in public authorities.

Public authorities are required to respond promptly to requests for information. They may charge to cover some of the costs of obtaining that information. Where they do not hold the requested information the authority must tell the enquirer and where possible pass the enquiry on to the appropriate body. If it seeks an exclusion or an exemption an authority must state its reasons for not complying.

Although not required by the Act, public authorities are encouraged to make information accessible to the public by describing the information that it holds in lay person's terms. The draft code of practice recommends that public authorities help enquirers to frame their requests in appropriate terms and help those who are unable or unwilling to submit requests in writing. Public authorities should be aware that in some cases public interest may outweigh other factors such as security or confidentiality.

In response to the Act it is likely that public authorities will have to consider the following measures:

- Develop or adopt a publication scheme. The publication scheme will provide prospective applicants with details of classes of information for which there is a publication programme, and which is therefore exempt from disclosure under the Act. The scheme should be reviewed periodically.

- Develop procedures for dealing with requests under the Freedom of Information. The procedures should include guidelines for dealing adequately with complaints.

- Provide accessible published lists or indexes of information that it holds. This measure is intended to ensure that access to information is a practical reality. It should also help to minimise the work involved in dealing with information requests.

- Have in place an effective records management system that allows for ready identification and retrieval of information. Fulfilling the requirements of the Act is likely to be a significant burden for many public authorities, and this may require special staff to handle the work. In order to minimise the impact on the work of each authority and to keep costs down there should be procedures in place to manage information so that it can be easily identified and retrieved in response to an enquiry. The Lord Chancellor's Department has issued a code of practice on records management in response to the Act.

- It is also advised to publish summaries of all key documents. This saves time dealing with routine requests for information held by the authority.

Further information

There are several key sources of information on freedom of information:

Campaign for Freedom of Information (*http://www.cfoi.org.uk/*)

Data Protection Commission (*http://www.dataprotection.gov.uk/foinfo2.htm*)

Home Office, Freedom of Information Unit (*http://www.homeoffice.gov.uk/foi/foidpunit.htm*)

Public Record Office (*http://www.pro.gov.uk/recordsmanagement/CodeOfPractice.htm*)

Bibliography

Draft Code of Practice on the Discharge of the Functions of Public Authorities under part 1 of the Freedom of Information Act 2000. Home Office, 2000.

Draft Freedom of Information Bill Summary. Home Office, 24 May 1999. Available at *http://www.homeoffic.gov.uk/foi/dfiosumm.htm*.

Freedom of Information Act 2000. Available at *http://www.legislation.hmso.gov.uk/acts/en/2000en36.htm*.

Freedom of Information Bill Explanatory Notes. House of Lords, session 1999-2000 (H L Bill 55), 7 April 2000. Available at *http://www.publications.parliament.uk/pa/ld199900/055/2000055.htm*.

Lord Chancellor's Code of Practice on the Management of Records Under Freedom of Information. Version 21a (21 June 2000). Public Record Office, July 2000. Available at *http://www.pro.gov.uk/recordsmanagement/CodeOfPractice.htm* [2 March 2001].

Response to the Draft Freedom of Information Bill and the Consultation on Draft Legislation. Library and Information Commission, 16 July 1999.

Your Right to Know: The Government's proposals for a Freedom of Information Act. The Stationery Office, 1997 (Cm 3818). ISBN 0 10 138182 4. Available at *http://foi.democracy.org.uk/*.

Chapter 24

Legal issues of the Internet

Peter Groves

From a legal perspective, the Internet is several different things:

- To the commercial lawyer, it is a new medium in which businesses may offer their goods or services, and in which consumers may buy them.

- To the copyright lawyer, it is a colossal copying machine and a new medium for publishing original material.

- To the trademark lawyer, it offers a rich vein of disputes at the interface between trademarks and domain names.

- To the defamation lawyer, it provides several new ways in which defamatory comments may be made available to the public.

- To the criminal lawyer, it presents enormous possibilities for committing new offences, or old offences in new ways.

How do these legal problems affect information providers? Firstly, anyone engaged in providing information over the Internet must take account of a new range of copyright issues. Not only must care be taken to avoid infringing other people's copyright, but steps must be taken to protect one's own copyright too.

Secondly, providers of information have to be careful about the accuracy of what they disseminate. Activities which in the real world may have no potential for liability may be considered on the Internet to be of a different nature altogether, and an information provider who publishes inaccurate information on the Internet may be liable in circumstances which they could not foresee.

Thirdly, information providers are often engaged in commercial activities in much the same way as other online merchants. When they engage in selling information, they are dipping their toes into the experimental field of electronic commerce and they will have a significant interest in questions about contract formation and payment.

Copyright considerations

In one sense, there is nothing new, as far as copyright is concerned, in the Internet. Indeed the big revolution in recent years in copyright has been the advent of digital technology, but of course the Internet is the ultimate manifestation of this way of dealing with copyright material; and, while copyright law has managed to deal with these developments, the interests of all those – suppliers and consumers – who use the Internet, would be better served by tailored legislation than by rules written for the days of inks smeared on dead trees, bent into alarming new shapes by the judges.

The big difference between copyright in traditional media and copyright in the digital world lies in the way copyright material is used. Reading a book, admiring a picture or listening to a sound recording are not copyright events. Visiting a web site for any of these purposes is, in copyright terms, a different matter altogether. Digital technology gives us the tools to reduce every type of copyright work to a similar collection of binary digits. In this form, works can be transmitted through telecommunication systems and modified in a variety of ways. The Copyright, Designs and Patents Act 1988, written as it was in the very early days of the digital revolution, touches on some of these subjects but does not provide a coherent code for those who use the information superhighway.

As far as what copyright protects is concerned, there is little doubt that much of the material found on the Internet, particularly on the World Wide Web, is the stuff of copyright. Of course, there is material in which copyright has expired: the Bible and the complete works of Shakespeare can be found several times over on the Web, and now with the advent of e-books, out-of-copyright works are being made available for free download.

There will also be material which, for want of originality, is not protected by copyright. The question of whether a digital file made from, for example, an image long out of copyright, is itself protected remains a moot point. One day, perhaps, someone will have the nerve and sufficiently deep pockets to challenge an organisation like Corbis and find out whether the argument works that scanning and enhancing the resulting digital file is enough to create a copyright separate from that of the photographer.

So the World Wide Web is replete with copyright material. Every web page contains text and graphics, although whether a basic web page design or insignificant piece of text, like a copyright notice, would be protected by copyright would be open to some doubt. Scratch the surface of the web site, though, and you begin to find a wide variety of 'works'.

Sound recordings? The Web is rapidly becoming a (if not the) mainstream source of sound recordings, usually in MP3 form. Threatened by those, like Napster, who use the new technology to permit users to copy files from each others' computers, the music industry has embraced not only the technology but also many of the people whose use of it they took exception to in the first place.

Films? A broad, and technologically neutral, definition of a film in the Copyright, Designs and Patents Act 1988 included a film recorded as magnetic impulses on a tape. It also included a film recorded in binary digits from which a moving image can be reproduced. Of course, at present, films available on the World Wide Web are either short (to permit convenient downloading) and blurred and jerky, or in the case of material which is streamed (a copy of which is never made on the client computer's hard disk) just blurred and jerky.

Static web pages are becoming passé, with animation being a major component in web page design now, and databases providing a depth of content not available in pure text and graphics format. Visit an e-commerce site and you might be able to browse through a catalogue listing many thousands of items for sale. The catalogue is provided by a database underlying the web page. In a more prosaic situation, research tools like Lexis-Nexis and Westlaw in the legal field consist of databases, accessed these days through a (secure) web site. There may be copyright in the database if it meets the high standard of originality required of databases under the EC directive: even those that do not qualify for copyright protection will have the benefit of the new *sui generis* right, introduced in the UK as database right, invented by the same directive.

If it is fairly clear that copyright subsists in much of what is found on the Internet; the copyright owner's right to take action for infringement is rather less clear. Two types of copyright activity are central to what happens on the Internet: firstly, there are several different activities which fall within the broad restricted act of reproducing the work in any material form, which under the Copyright, Designs and Patents Act 1988 specifically includes at some point making transient and incidental copies. Secondly, copyright material is made available to the public, for example, by being posted on a World Wide Web site or newsgroup, or by being included in a web page. Finally (and much less obviously) using material on the World Wide Web may amount to including it in a cable program service.

It is not hard to see how, in the absence of authorisation, the reproduction right may be infringed by activities on the Internet. Consider the following:

- I visit the Ferrari – Shell Formula 1 web site and download a photograph of Michael Schumacher in action at last weekend's Grand Prix, which is provided specifically for use as wallpaper on my computer screen. Provided I keep within the terms of any restrictions placed on the download (for example, not to make it available to all the terminals on a network) I will not infringe because I am doing the act with permission. If I do exceed the permitted use, we have a nice argument about whether the terms posted on the web site actually bind me or not. That is another matter altogether.

- I visit the Home Office web site in the course of researching a talk about Internet law, find a copy of the Regulation of the Investigatory Powers Act 2000 and, discovering that it is far too long to scroll through on screen, I download a copy to my hard disk. In the course of doing this, I have reproduced the Act several times: the first time in the form of binary digits downloaded from the web site to my computer's memory (a transient and incidental copy, but a copy nonetheless); then as a copy of the image of the legislation on my computer screen (possibly reproducing the typographical arrangement of the statute as well as the text); and then as a permanent copy on the hard disk of my computer. There are also likely to be incidental copies made on intermediate servers through which the packets of bits which make up the file received by my computer travel. The Act has been made available on the World Wide Web for people to consult it: viewing it on a computer screen, and making transient and incidental copies on the computer's memory, as well as on intermediate servers, is all part and parcel of the reason for it being there in the first place. The copy I make on my hard disk may well go beyond what the Home Office was permitting me to do. However, I may plead in mitigation that left to its own devices the computer would have made a copy in its cache folder anyway.

- I visit HMSO's web site to find a copy of the Data Protection Act 1998, which I download to my hard disk in 48 convenient little files. The copyright implications are much the same as in the case of the RIP Act in the last example, but the permission situation is less ambiguous: if HMSO had wanted to let me get my hands on the complete text of the Act in this way, they would have allowed me to download it in one piece. The fact that it is so broken up means that it is clearly intended only for online viewing, not for downloading.

There are many other scenarios which could provide variations on these themes. Different web site proprietors offer their material on different terms, so what can be done with it varies from one to another. But, perhaps without exception, providers of information on the Internet do not wish to see it reused for commercial purposes. An information professional who downloads material from the Internet and sells it on to subscribers or clients will almost certainly infringe copyright in it.

Making information available on the Internet is another area of copyright interest. If you are providing an information service, it can be delivered very efficiently by means of the Internet, whether through a web site, a news group or a listserv. But if you collect the material from elsewhere, the rights of whoever owns copyright in it have to be borne very much in mind.

Clearly, anyone who makes the material available will unavoidably have made copies of it: if it originally existed only in analogue form, a reproduction in electronic form will have been made somewhere (a photograph must have been scanned, printed text converted into a computer file, a sound recording on tape digitally remastered). The copyright owner whose interests have been harmed by this can take action, as she or he can sue anyone who has downloaded a copy of the offending computer file to his or her computer: that act, and the incidental and transient copies made in the course of doing so, are infringements. But going against the perpetrators of these acts for these infringements does not hit the right target for the copyright owner.

What the owner of the copyright wants to do is stop the unauthorised copies being offered to the public. She or he could, it is true, obtain an injunction to stop the pirate making further copies, but the harm has already been done and, if damages are awarded, those available under this head will be tiny compared with the damage actually suffered by the pirated copyright owner.

Nor will copyright owners be anxious to pursue the home computer enthusiasts who have stored the material on their hard disks. A record company will not consider it good PR to be seen taking legal action against an army of teenagers, few of whom would be worth the damages and costs awarded against them if they are found to have infringed. Such a course of action could easily alienate precisely the people to whom the record company needs to sell its legitimate products.

But the 1988 Act does not make it an infringement to post copies of a copyright work on the Internet. It does deal with issuing copies to the public, an activity defined in terms that make it seem that Parliament never considered that sound recordings could be distributed otherwise than in some physical medium.

In addition to the long-established distribution right, copyright owners needs a communication right, enabling them to prevent unauthorised passive dissemination to the public of their material, by such means as uploading it to a server and allowing anyone who wishes to download copies from there. This is one of the most important areas dealt with in the EC's directive on copyright in the information society, which should become law later in 2001 and then appear in the national laws of member states some time later.

The directive will ensure that all member states protect copyright works against unauthorised reproduction, distribution and communication to the public. It is based on international treaties agreed under the auspices of the World Intellectual Property Organisation (WIPO) in 1996, which should ensure that this minimum level of protection is available to copyright owners throughout the world.

A final type of restricted act is including a copyright work in a cable programme service. Although this restricted act has been brought to bear against copyright infringements in the infamous Scottish case of *Shetland Times v Willis* in 1997. There, the editor of the Shetland Islands' establishment newspaper fell out with the proprietor and set up his own publication, the *Shetland News*, taking advantage of Internet technology to enable him to do so. He created a front page for his virtual paper, filling it with headlines that linked to underlying news stories: but the headlines were taken from the *Shetland Times*, and the stories to which they were linked were on the *Shetland Times'* site. The concept of a virtual newspaper had been taken to its logical extreme.

On the *Shetland Times'* application for an interim interdict to stop infringement pending trial, the judge (Lord Hamilton) considered there was the necessary arguable case that this constituted infringement of copyright in the headlines. They were substantial enough to enjoy copyright protection in their own right, and they had been included without permission in a cable programme service.

That the *Shetland News'* web site could be considered a cable programme service was a surprising development, but the judge considered it lacked the essential interactive capability to disqualify it from the statutory definition. Although it had an email facility, that could be severed from the main purpose of the site and was not essential to the operation of the service: it did not make the site an interactive cable programme service, inclusion of material in which would be excluded from the restricted act.

Unfortunately for lawyers looking for legal certainty, the case never came to trial and we are left with this preliminary decision as the basis for applying copyright concepts to the Internet. But it still has considerable weight, notwithstanding its Scottish origins: substantive copyright law is the same north of the border as it is in England.

If copyright protects much of the stuff that is found on the Internet, how then can one get permission to use it? In many cases, permission simply will not be needed, or (not quite the same thing) it will have been given when the material was posted on the web site. In the latter case, of course, the user will have to ensure she or he stays within the scope of what the owner allows. Perhaps you are allowed to do things with the material on the web site for your own personal use only, in which case copying it to a friend would require the copyright owner's consent, and posting a copy on your own web site without permission would be an infringement. But merely putting in a hyperlink would infringe no copyright, though if the provenance of the site to which the link leads is not made clear there could be a passing off or a trademark infringement, and the linker may incur liability for wrongs such as defamation, copyright infringement or negligence (for example, in giving bad advice) committed by the linkee. If permission has not already been granted for what you want to do, you can either try to argue that permission was not needed (because what you are doing is a permitted act under the legislation, or for some reason such as the smallness of the extract reproduced it is not an infringement, or by invoking library privilege) or you can seek express permission, from the copyright owner or someone who has the right to give permission on his behalf, such as a licensing agency.

Getting individual permission from every copyright owner whose material you might wish to use could be a long process. I have a client who wishes to supply copies of articles from learned journals to professionals who have an interest in reading them, having first placed abstracts on the Web. There is nothing high-tech about the document distribution part of the exercise, but we have found it impossible to cover every eventuality with a CLA licence. The rapid clearance system (CLARCS) operated by the CLA is quick and efficient but naturally restricted to material within the CLA's repertoire, and while you can find out immediately the approximate cost of making a copy of an article if you can put the journal's ISSN into the box on the CLARCS web site, many works do not have ISSNs (or ISBNs). To be fair to them, CLA can still help in many cases, but at this stage anyway the system cannot cope with every request that might be made of it.

Contacting every copyright owner for permission would be impractical for my client, and for many information providers. Library privilege, if available, would be an answer (it would not avail my client, which is established for profit) but of course only covers certain activities by the end user. And how to go about getting a declaration from the user? It still has to be on paper with a proper signature, although (as we shall see) this could change in the future.

In time, clearance schemes aimed specifically at Internet usage will no doubt develop. As the Internet becomes more and more widely used for information gathering and dissemination, copyright owners will wish to find a way to tap the rich seams of royalties that it provides (if only there was a way to charge people for the use of the material).

Technical protection and rights management information

Digital technology poses two further challenges for the copyright owner which we should mention before moving on. First, it enables owners of web sites to restrict access to the information or other material placed on it. The operator of a legal research database allows only those who have paid the subscription and obtained a password to consult it: online banking services give only their customer access to their account information. Other visitors are excluded by the software that powers the site. Firewalls protect sensitive data, but what protects the firewalls?

Second, the Computer Misuse Act 1990 creates three offences that will often be committed if unauthorised access is gained. Hacking is the basic offence, with a further ulterior intent offence when the hacking takes place in the course of committing another crime (for example, taking money from another person's bank account). Interfering with a computer to deny the user access, by releasing a virus or simply changing someone else's password, also amounts to an offence. As a Lloyds Bank customer, I am (marginally) reassured to see a notice to the effect that anyone seeking access to my account information would be committing an offence.

My bank account details are not copyright, or if they are it gives the wrong sort of protection. Lloyds will own copyright in the database that powers their web site, but to sue hackers for infringement would be on a par with rearranging the deckchairs on the *Titanic*. Database right, introduced in the UK under the EC database directive, may provide more relevant protection but still does not quite hit the mark.

Web site proprietors rely instead on technical means to limit access to their sites. Where these means are used to protect copyright material, the proposed EC directive on copyright in the information society (building on international agreements also reflected in other countries' legislation, such as the *Digital Millennium Copyright Act, 1998* in the USA) will require that national laws give protection to the technical means involved: how, it does not specify but, if you want a model; the treatment under the Copyright, Designs and Patents Act 1988 of pirate satellite decoders may assist. It is an infringement of copyright in the satellite transmission to provide unauthorised means to receive it, just as much as if it were received by the person providing the means.

There is much in the copyright field to interest lawyers and information specialists on the Internet, but it is only one part of the legal picture. Electronic commerce, including dealing in more tangible products than the stuff of copyright, raises a host of problems which lawyers and legislators are beginning to grapple with.

Contracting on the Internet

Making contracts over the Internet, whether by email or visiting a web site, is a far from certain undertaking. The classical elements of a contract – offer, acceptance, intent to create legal relations – familiar to anyone who has ever been obliged to study even the smallest amount of law, can fairly readily be identified, along with the gloss added by the courts to deal with self-service pharmacies, the invitation to treat, a preliminary stage in which the merchant asks consumers if they would care to make an offer to buy his wares at the checkout. But Argos, IBM and others have come close to testing the validity of the old assumptions.

In the absence of a judgement of the court, it is hard to say how Argos' £3 television, offered on their web site for one mad afternoon, would have been regarded by a judge. Presumably, there was an invitation to treat when the article was posted on the web site; consumers visiting the site, after the initial shock had worn off, could offer to buy, and the last stage would be for Argos to accept. In fact, the system automatically sent acknowledgements to would-be buyers, but it is unlikely that these would have been regarded as acceptances. Even if they were incautiously worded and operated as acceptances of the offer, they would almost certainly be considered to have been made pursuant to a mistake, usually fatal to a finding that there was a meeting of the parties' minds. It would, however, be nice to hear all this from a judge.

At least the courts need not perform the acrobatics required of their Victorian forerunners who, faced with the advent of a postal service through which offers and acceptances could be communicated (though not instantaneously), were able to deem a communication final when the sender entrusted it irrevocably to the postal service. Such was the public's (then justified) faith in the service that no one thought this strange: how different had the case been decided in the late 20th century! But email communications are now usually as good as instantaneous, and such problems should not arise.

If something goes wrong with an electronic contract, interesting questions arise about where action should be taken to enforce it. The Civil Jurisdiction and Judgments Act, 1982 sets out rules to determine where a contract can be enforced, giving due weight to the parties' intentions (though they do not necessarily prevail). Commercial organisations engaged in business-to-business (B2B) transactions are generally able to look after themselves, but now that consumers have begun buying in quantity on the Internet the needs of business-to-consumer (B2C) transactions have assumed a greater importance.

The European Commission has therefore come up with proposals to modify the governing conventions in this area, designed to ensure that consumers have worthwhile rights by making them enforceable in the consumer's home court. As a consumer, I can see the sense in this: shopping online should not entail throwing myself onto the mercy of a Spanish court if I buy bad wine from a wine grower who has ventured onto the Internet.

From the small trader's viewpoint, however, the problem might look rather different. The Spanish wine grower will give up on the Internet the first time it lands her or him in legal proceedings in an English county court. The risk is that providing a remedy in the consumer's home court will stifle e-commerce from the start.

Credit card companies, who finance the majority of transactions on the Internet, may have the answer. In the event of a complaint they can (and do) charge back the merchant whose goods or services are defective. The loss falls on the merchant, who can take issue with the credit card company: too many chargebacks and the merchant loses the merchant ID which is the passport to electronic retailing.

Security and cryptography

Any sort of transaction carried out on the Internet must be secure. People are famously unwilling to divulge credit card details online although they routinely give the card to a waiter in a restaurant or give the number to a retailer over the phone. The Internet needs to provide means to assure consumers that their details will not fall into the hands of fraudsters.

In addition, merchants need to know that the person with whom they are dealing is who she or he claims to be, otherwise contracts will be avoided and the security of credit card transactions will be compromised.

While technical methods will provide this protection, there must be a legal framework to accommodate digital signatures and encryption technology, to which consumers will need access. International organisations such as UNCITRAL and OECD have begun to lay down guidelines in these areas, and the European Community has produced directives on digital signatures and on electronic commerce in general. In parallel to these initiatives, and drawing on them, the UK has pursued domestic initiatives which have recently matured into legislation.

The Electronic Communications Act 2000 was intended to establish a framework for the provision of the encryption services needed by electronic merchants and consumers, and to make digital signatures (which are not physically much like real signatures on paper, but which do the same job using encryption technology: for example, the authenticity of an electronic communication may be guaranteed by using an image of the sender's retina; more mundanely, public key cryptography uses small pieces of computer code unique to the sender). The Act sets up a register of cryptography service providers and an approval system for the services they offer, but both are voluntary. Consumer protection in this field is likely to be provided more by the fact that only large and reputable organisations (like BT, with its TrustWise service) will be able to participate in the market.

The Act goes on to try to encourage the use of electronic communications, first by dealing with the admissibility of digital signatures in legal proceedings (where, unadventurously, the government decided to let the courts decide what weight to attach to what purports to be an electronic signature). It also gives ministers the power to amend primary legislation by statutory instrument to facilitate the use of electronic communications, for example by permitting electronic filing of documents that must presently be on paper.

The legislation was originally intended to cover decryption for encoded electronic messages. Making encryption technology, which is strong enough to have been classified as munitions by the US government, available to the public raises obvious problems for law enforcement and security agencies. It was originally planned that there would be a legal obligation on every provider of encryption services to lodge a copy of the code with an escrow agent, so the police or security services could get instant access to it if needed.

This proposal, which was seen by the industry and by civil liberties groups as far too draconian, was first watered down and then moved from the Electronic Communications Bill to the Regulation of Investigatory Powers Bill (now Act). In the RIP Act, as it inevitably become known (the Internet services industry saw it sounding the death knell of electronic commerce in the UK) powers to require a plain text version of an intercepted message, or as a last resort to demand the decryption key, replace the hated key escrow provisions.

The RIP Act also updates the law on intercepting communications, embracing email for the first time and introducing a new power to obtain communications data, such as satellite phone billing information and other data that might show who has communicated with whom. The first power is exercisable only under a warrant issued by the Secretary of State, a safeguard that has existed in the Act's predecessors for years: the second, more sinisterly, can be exercised by holders of offices designated in a statutory instrument by the Home Secretary, including relatively junior police officers.

The legislation also allows the authorities to require Internet service providers (ISPs) to maintain a 'reasonable intercept capacity', and it is this threat of being forced to install black boxes that has created such a furore among ISPs. There has been talk of businesses moving their servers off-shore to a friendlier jurisdiction: Germany has been mentioned, and indeed it seems from what the critics say that a less friendly jurisdiction would be hard to find. Russia and Zimbabwe have been mentioned: the fact that Ireland, Australia and the United States have legislated for the same problem but found less draconian (in the cases of Ireland and Australia, much less) solutions should perhaps have informed the government's approach to the issue.

In any event, the effectiveness of the RIP Act is open to much doubt. If ISPs can move offshore to escape the legislation's reach, it is not beyond the bounds of possibility that criminals will do likewise. Even those who lack the resources to relocate might resort to techniques such as steganography, which involves burying text messages in large computer files – images, perhaps, or music files or computer programs – where the interceptors will never even notice them.

Defamation

Finally, anyone publishing material on the Intenet, whether they are the author or not, must take care to avoid uttering any defamatory statements. Web site proprietors and usegroup hosts must take particular care, but any user of electronic mail must be aware of the dangers lurking in the informal way in which messages are commonly composed.

ISPs and others involved in the operation of the Internet rather than the creation of content, should be able to invoke the statutory defence provided in the Defamation Act, 1996. They are not to be considered authors or publishers merely because messages pass through their servers or defamatory statements reside on them. But woe betide the ISP who, alerted to a problem, takes no steps to prevent it continuing.

Godfrey v Demon, so far the only significant English authority on Internet libel (and note that statements made on the Internet will be considered to have the necessary degree of permanence to constitute libels rather than slanders) is a salutary example. However, liability on the ISP only arose following consistent failures not only to take action to remove defamatory material, statements falsely attributed to Dr Godfrey, but even to acknowledge his solicitor's letters. Recipients of letters from lawyers may wish they could ignore them, but actually to do so is a high-risk strategy, as the Godfrey case illustrates: a fairly modest award of damages paled into insignificance beside the award of costs.

In the virtual world of the Internet, the roles of author, publisher and distributor become blurred. Defences which would run in the real world cannot easily be applied in the virtual one. Anyone engaged in putting any sort of material on the Internet, including a link to a site where defamatory material may be posted, must think about the content of that material, and if an objection is raised take immediate action to stop liability mounting.

Conclusion

To speak of law of the Internet is perhaps misleading, but there is a growing body of law directed to issues that arise in that environment. Perhaps in a year or two there will be no more need to speak of it as a separate body of law as there is a need to speak of the law of the real world, but for now it serves to remind us that this is a new area.

For all the new law that is evolving to take account of this development, however, it is largely a matter of applying old rules to novel situations. So far, the courts have proved to be a long way from the stereotypical anachronism that they are often perceived to be.

Chapter 25

Digital library research

Adrienne Muir

Introduction

There is an enormous amount of work being carried out worldwide under the banner of digital library research and development. It is difficult to extract a core body of research, because so many activities, as well as general Internet, e-commerce and knowledge management developments, have some relevance.

There are the various national publicly funded digital library research programmes, including eLib in the UK. Large libraries, such as national and research libraries, often run their own programmes. However, a lot of this work involves the digitisation of collections. Organisations are working on inhouse initiatives, but much of this will be development and implementation rather than genuine research.

It would be impossible to provide a comprehensive overview of all the research activities that will be directly relevant for the library and information science community. Therefore, the activities within some major research programmes likely to be most relevant to special libraries are highlighted. Inevitably, the focus of publicly funded programmes is public sector information services. However, a lot of the work that is being carried out will be transferable to other sectors. The focus is on UK and European programmes, and the major US research programmes are also covered.

This chapter begins with a discussion of what the term 'digital library' means. Whilst it is a widely used term there is a lot of confusion about what a digital library actually is. The main areas of research in digital libraries are then summarised. There is an overview of major research programmes, with projects of most interest highlighted. Finally, the relevance and implications of digital library research activity for special libraries are discussed.

Definition of digital libraries

There seems to be some confusion surrounding the precise meaning of the term 'digital library'. Several writers have discussed this confusion (Bawden and Rowlands, 1999; Brophy, 1999; Chowdhury and Chowdhury, 1999) in recent reviews of digital library research. The term is often used interchangeably with various other terms such as 'electronic library', 'library without walls' and 'virtual library'. However, these terms can actually have different meanings. To add to the confusion, terms such as 'hybrid library' and 'gateway library' have come into common use.

'Digital library' may also mean different things to different people. One example that is widely mentioned is the difference in perspective between the library and information science and the computer science communities (Marchionini, 1998).

The Digital Library Federation (DLF) operates under the aegis of the Council for Library and Information Resources in the USA. The DLF describes itself as 'a consortium of research libraries that are transforming themselves and their institutional roles by exploiting network and digital technologies' (Digital Library Federation, 2000). The consortium uses the following working definition:

> Digital libraries are organizations that provide the resources, including the specialized staff, to select, structure, offer intellectual access to, interpret, distribute, preserve the integrity of, and ensure the persistence over time of collections of digital works so that they are readily and economically available for use by a defined community or set of communities. (Digital Library Federation, 1999).

Bawden and Rowlands (1999) have defined a digital library as:

> … a library/information space, located in either a physical or virtual space, or a combination of both, in which a significant proportion of the resources available to users of that service exist only in digital form.

They add that this definition was decided on so that all research coming under the digital library banner is included within the scope of the definition.

Whilst the terms 'digital library' and 'electronic library' are used interchangeably, Bawden and Rowlands (1999) consider the electronic library to represent an old-fashioned or limited approach: 'the provision of a range of material in digitised form, within the framework of traditional library provision'.

Bawden and Rowlands (1999) and Chowdhury and Chowdhury (1999) respectively refer to the 'virtual library' as 'collections of web resources' and 'a set of links to various information sources on the Internet'.

The term 'hybrid library' became popular in the context of the Electronic Libraries Programme in the UK. This term recognises a 'continuum between the conventional and digital library, where electronic and paper-based information sources are used alongside each other' (Pinfield et al., 1998). The aim of the hybrid library is 'to encourage end-user resource discovery and information use, in a variety of formats and from a number of local and remote sources, in a seamlessly integrated way'. Seamlessness and integration are heavily emphasised in the hybrid library approach. Oppenheim and Smithson (1999) have developed a model of the hybrid library.

The computer science approach, on the other hand, is more focused on the digital end of the continuum. Marchionini (1998) says that for this community the digital library is a 'metaphor for the new kinds of distributed database services that manage unstructured multimedia data'. In this approach, there may be no physical or institutional aspect at all.

For the purposes of this chapter, the interpretation of the meaning of 'digital library' and hence digital library research is broad and includes hybrid and digital library work. Digitisation projects are not within the scope of this chapter.

Research areas

Early research in digital libraries focused on technology and content rather than people or communities (Marchionini, 1998, 129). There was a lot of work on the digitisation of collections and network access. This situation has moved on somewhat over the last 10 years or so, and work increasingly has a user focus. Researchers have also recognised the impact of digital libraries on organisations and societies, and vice versa, as legitimate areas of research.

Bawden and Rowlands (1999) have identified eight thematic clusters of research in the area covering:

* human factors
* organisational factors
* library management factors
* information law and policy factors
* systems factors
* knowledge organisation and discovery factors

- impacts on the information transfer chain
- futures studies and scenarios.

These categories provide a useful framework for summarising research strands. Readers should note that there is some overlap between categories, for example, work on human computer interaction could be more human focused, or more system focused.

Human factors

Work under this category focuses on psychological and social issues, or people as individuals or communities. Studying users is an increasingly important area. This includes information needs, information seeking behaviour and skills, and information use. A specific area that is currently receiving some attention is the needs of people with disabilities in the digital environment, especially visually impaired people. Evaluation of digital library systems and services and their impact on people and communities is another area of work.

Organisational factors

One perception of the digital library is that there will no longer be a need for the library as a physical place. There is interest in studying the impact of digital libraries on organisations and their structures and cultures. Another area of study is the organisational impact of digital systems and services on physical libraries. There is a people element to this in that resistance to change can act affect these impacts.

Library management factors

Organisational change in libraries is closely related to the impact of digital systems and services on the way libraries are managed and run. Traditional policies and procedures may not be relevant in the digital environment. Methods and criteria for selection, acquisition, processing, access and preservation may need to be changed. The roles of staff may change or disappear completely. Staff may need to acquire new skills. The costs of digital libraries is also an area for research.

Information law and policy factors

There are various legal and policy issues arising from the use of digital technology for information provision. The main areas of interest are intellectual property rights, security and privacy. There are questions on how current legal provisions can be enforced in the digital environment. Further, there are questions about the applicability to current laws in the digital environment. Security applies to systems and access to information; it also applies to the integrity and authenticity of documents.

Overcoming 'password proliferation' and the privacy issues arising from the desire to personalise information for individual users is currently an area of great interest.

Governments are pursuing policies of social inclusion and lifelong learning and there is research looking at how the use of digital technology can contribute to these aims. There is an increasing convergence between the so-called 'memory organisations', such as libraries, museums and archives in the digital environment. This trend is increasingly reflected in government policies and the agenda of research funders, including Re:source: the Council for Museums Archives and Libraries in the UK (*http://www.resource.gov.uk/*), and the Culturage Heritage Applications Network of the European Commission (*http://www.cordis.lu/ist/projects/99-11133/htm*).

Systems factors and knowledge organisation and discovery factors

These categories are taken together here, because in many ways systems work is dependent on requirements arising from the way information is organised and discovered. Interoperability and scalability are important factors (Bawden and Rowlands, 1999). Because of the distributed nature of networked information, interoperability between systems is crucial and scalability depends to a large extend on interoperability. The need for standards in communication protocols and metadata is widely acknowledged and is reflected in work contributing towards seamlessness and integration in digital and hybrid library services. Different systems have to be able to talk to each other. Current cataloguing schemes may not be adequate for the digital environment. They were designed to describe resources, but they do not cope so well with describing multimedia resources. They also do not necessarily provide the administrative data needed. This data includes ownership, rights, access and preservation data. There is a lot of work going on in these areas and a lot of this work is necessarily collaborative (CEDARS Project Team and UKOLN, 2000; Dublin Core Metadata Initiative, 2000). Information retrieval research is working towards providing better retrieval interfaces and systems. Historically, information retrieval research has dealt with text, but there is now much work being carried out on audio and visual information.

Impacts on the information transfer chain

It is not just the future of physical libraries and information professionals that is being questioned in the digital age. The development of digital information provision may have a serious impact on the traditional information chain. This impact includes the roles of members of the chain and relationships between them. There is also the question of business models. There is a great deal of interest in the future of serials and serial publishers, and whether the serial can survive in the digital age. Publishers and libraries are collaborating to investigate new ways of working together and to investigate new business models. Traditional tensions between rights owners and users are being reduced by such collaboration.

Futures studies and scenarios

The major US digital libraries programme is aiming to help develop the next generation of digital library technologies. The European Commission also has a research strand focused on the future. Other than this, it is difficult to identify futures projects. In the UK, the Arts and Humanities Research Board (AHRB) funds basic research in the information and library area. This may be a source for this type of research in future. So far, the AHRB has funded two projects related to digital library research. These are two user-centred studies in the information seeking and retrieval area (University of Sheffield, 1999).

Research programmes

eLib

The main research and development programme in the UK is dedicated to the higher education sector. The Electronic Libraries Programme (eLib) started in 1994 and is now reaching the end of its third and final phase. The Joint Information Systems Committee (JISC) of the UK Higher Education Funding Councils funds the programme.

eLib funded 59 projects over its first two phases. The projects have been widely documented and the first two phases of the programme have recently been evaluated (Whitelaw and Joy, 2000). The aim of the third phase of eLib was to bring developments together and build on previous successful work. Phase 3 had four strands of activity (Rusbridge, 1998) covering:

- hybrid libraries
- large scale resource discovery (clumps)
- preservation
- the turning of early projects into services.

Hybrid libraries
The phrase 'hybrid library' reflects the current reality in many libraries in that they are neither completely print based or completely digital. According to Rusbridge (1998),

The hybrid library was designed to bring a range of technologies from different sources together in the context of a working library, and also to begin to explore integrated system and services in both the electronic and print environments.

The five eLib hybrid library projects have been pursuing these aims, taking different approaches and focusing on different areas. However, they are often working with the same technologies and dealing with common problems, such as authentication, user profiles, interface design, the management of digitisation, interconnection of databases and staff development. (Pinfield et al., 1998). The projects are called AGORA (*http://hosted.ukoln.ac.uk/agora/*), BUILDER (*http://builder.bham.ac.uk/main.asp*), HEADLINE (*http://www.headline.ac.uk*), HYLIFE (*http://hylife.unn.ac.uk/*) and MALIBU (*http://www.kcl.ac.uk/humanities/cch/malibu/index.htm*).

While these projects are focused on the higher education sector, the solutions they come up with should be transferable to other sectors that have to deal with managing and providing access to information in a variety of formats.

Clumps

The rationale for the work on clumps is to 'solve the problem of access to (mostly print) scholarly resources anywhere in the UK' (Rusbridge, 1998). The clump projects are exploring the possibility of virtual union catalogues. Virtual catalogues, using standards such as Z39.50, have potential benefits over physical catalogues in terms of currency and accuracy of bibliographic and holdings data (Rusbridge, 1998).

There are four clumps projects covering different geographical areas and subjects. The Co-operative Academic Information Retrieval Network for Scotland (CAIRNS, *http://cairns.lib.gla.ac.uk/*) includes universities in Scotland and a public library, M25 Link (*http://www.m25lib.ac.uk/M25link/*) is in the Greater London area and RIDING (*http://www.shef.ac.uk/~riding/*) is in Yorkshire. Music Libraries Online (*http://www.musiconline.ac.uk/*) involves a group of music conservatories.

The clump projects are all using Z39.50 and are attempting to provide access to information in a variety of forms. They are all necessarily exploring interoperability issues and the design of interfaces. The CAIRNS project will also be exploring selecting sub-sets of material for specialist information needs and the linking of various clumps together. The project will consider the organisational aspects of clumping and required standards. A special feature of the M25 Link is that it will be exploring and addressing issues relating to serial holdings. In the RIDING project, Yorkshire universities are working with a public library service, the British Library Document Supply Centre and Fretwell Downing Informatics Ltd, a commercial partner. One of RIDING's objectives is to build costing models for collaborative options.

Preservation

There is one eLib preservation project, CURL Exemplars in Digital Archives (CEDARS). The aim of CEDARS is to 'address strategic, methodological and practical issues and provide guidance in best practice for digital preservation' (CEDARS, 1998). The project will produce demonstrators to test the strategy that the project comes up with. The project will also develop various guidelines for preserving different types of material, collection management policies, and recommendations for standards and techniques.

Projects to services

A number of early eLib projects received funding in phase 3 towards developing services. These include electronic journals, Ordnance Survey map data and document delivery. Some services of particular interest are summarised below.

Earlier eLib projects and studies in the areas of on-demand publishing and electronic reserves had demonstrated various problems related to setting these up as operational services. Two of these problems were the difficulties and costs of obtaining copyright clearance and the costs of digitising paper-based material. To overcome these barriers to development, eLib decided to fund a project to build up a centralised service, a 'resource bank of pre-cleared, pre-digitised material' (Rusbridge, 1998). This project is called Higher Education Resources On-Demand (HERON, *http://www.stir.ac.uk/infoserv/heron/*). As well as building up the resource bank, for the use of higher education institutions, one of the project's aims is develop a sustainable business model for this service.

A service of possible interest to all information professionals is NewsAgent for Libraries (*http://newsagent.sbu.ac.uk/about.html*). This is described as a web-based personalised current awareness service.

Work carried out under eLib has been brought together under new JISC initiatives: the Distributed National Electronic Resource (DNER) and the Resource Discovery Network (RDN). The DNER is the managed information collection available to the higher education community. Elib funded a number of subject gateways that provided access to a quality-assessed selection of networked resources. The work carried out is being taken forward in a co-ordinated way through the RDN. There will be a central co-ordinating body and a number of subject 'hubs'. There will be a facility to search across hubs. While the RDN is designed for learning and research, the hubs will be of use to other types of information service. For example, the BIOME hub will be of use to life sciences libraries and EEVL to engineering libraries.

In November 1999 JISC announced that it was to fund several new proposals to contribute to the development of the DNER. One of the areas
covered by proposals was the enhancement of services for teaching and
learning. Another focus was the implementation and development of the
DNER. Developments coming out of this area are more likely to be of
interest to the special library sector. Projects include portal development,
use of Z39.50, electronic books, and the pricing of electronic material. The
projects that were funded are listed at DNER development projects (2001),
available at *http://www.jisc.ac.uk/dner/programmes/projects* [visited 31/5/
01].

Library and Information Commission/Re:source

The now defunct British Library Research and Innovation Centre used to
fund research in digital libraries, mainly through its Information Retrieval
and Digital Libraries research programmes. These research programmes
moved to the Library and Information Commission in 1999. The Library
and Information Commission was itself dissolved at the end of March
2000. A number of new and ongoing information retrieval projects moved
to its successor body, Re:source. There was a call for proposals for digital
library research proposals towards the end of 1999. This call was over-
taken by developments in that Re:source has a cross-sectoral remit,
covering museums and archives as well as libraries. It seems that only
three new digital library projects were selected for funding.

This funding stream is modest compared to programmes such as eLib
and the US Digital Libraries initiative. Nevertheless, unlike eLib, the
BLRIC/LIC projects were not restricted to one sector and the information
retrieval programme has been an important source of funding in that area
for many years.

The new information retrieval projects (Library and Information Commission, 2000) focus on retrieval from the Internet and multimedia
information retrieval. The digital library projects include a project that
will develop and test a toolkit of longitudinal qualitative survey methods
which will help understanding of changing user needs and behaviour.
This project is focused on the public library sector. Another project is
investigating privacy issues arising from the information collected by
automated library systems and digital library systems. This project covers various library sectors, including corporate and government libraries.
One of the deliverables from the project will be guidelines for best practice
in this area. The final digital library project will be looking at how people
with visual impairments cope with using digital library interfaces. This
follows on from an earlier project, REVIEL (Brophy, 1999).

Digital Libraries Initiative

The Digital Libraries Initiative (DLI, *http://www.dli2.nsf.gov/*) is a major US research and development initiative, now in its second phase. Phase 1 ran from 1994 to 1998 and the five-year phase 2 (DLI2) is now underway. The US National Science Foundation, the Defense Advanced Research Projects Agency and the National Aeronautics & Space Administration provided funding for six large-scale projects in the first phase of the DLI, (*http://www.dli2.nsf.gov/dlione/*). This was in contrast to the eLib approach, which involved funding a large number of smaller projects.

For phase 2, the National Library of Medicine, the Library of Congress, the National Endowment for the Humanities and the Federal Bureau of Investigation have joined the three original funders. There will apparently be $40-50 million in funding available over the lifetime of this phase.

The overall aim of DLI2 is to move digital library research on, to 'provide leadership in research fundamental to the development of the next generation of digital libraries'. Understanding of the 'long term social, behavioral and economic implications and effects' is seen as important. The initiative has a broad scope: it 'will address the digital libraries' life cycle from information creation, access and use, to archiving and preservation' (Digital Libraries Initiative, 2001). Research, education, commerce, defence, health services and recreation are singled out as areas of interest.

There are too many projects to describe here, but details of projects funded so far are available from the DLI web site (*http://www.dli2.nsf.gov/ international%20projects/nsfjisc.html*). Some of the new projects are extensions to projects funded in phase 1. Research areas covered include: organisation, capture and recording of provenance data of information; retrieval and manipulation of information in various forms; dissemination of scholarly information; conversion of material from analogue to digital form including workflow management; restoration of material using digital techniques; personalised access; reliability of information and security; intelligent agents; information seeking behaviour and privacy.

While this is a US–based initiative, the second phase has an international aspect. The International Digital Libraries Research strand will support the US portion of international projects. So far, this initiative has funded several joint US-UK projects with the Joint Information Systems Committee[21]. There are also plans to collaborate with Germany, Japan and the European Union.

European Commission

The European Commission has funded digital library research under its Libraries Programme. The Libraries Programme was part of the Telematics

Application Programme under the 3rd and 4th Framework Programmes. A list of the projects funded under this stream is available (European Commission, 2000).

Most of the Libraries Programme projects have finished. However, some projects that are still running are relevant to the special library sector. Controlled Access to Network Digital Libraries in Europe (CANDLE) is developing the CACTUS system to manage network users and resources. This project seems to be similar to the eLib hybrid library projects in that it will simplify access to customised information resources for users. However, this project is not focused on academic settings. The aim is that CACTUS will be usable in all sorts of environments, including special libraries. In fact the project team would like to work with special libraries that could test the software (European Commission). EQUINOX (*http:// equinox.dcu.ie/*) is building on previous work on performance measurement. The People and Resources Identification for Distributed Environments (PRIDE, *http://lirn.viscount.org.uk/pride/*) project is developing a directory-based system for locating resources. This will be capable of providing personalised access to resources for users. Libraries and Archives Collecting Newspaper Clippings Unified for their Integration into Networks (LAURIN, *http://laurin.uibk.ac.at/*) will develop a generic model for digitising news clippings.

The European Commission's Fifth Framework Programme does not have a dedicated libraries strand. This current programme has a much more cross-sectoral focus, including encouraging libraries, museums and archives to work together. Digital library research would come under the Information Society Technologies (IST) Programme. There are four main themes:

- systems and services for the citizen
- new methods of work and electronic commerce
- multimedia content and tools
- essential technologies and infrastructure.

There is also a future and emerging technologies strand. The multimedia content and tools theme is most closely aligned with digital library research interests. This theme currently has four work areas:

- interactive publishing
- digital heritage and cultural content
- education and training
- human language technologies.

Some of projects funded under IST so far are related to digital libraries. A few examples are:

- ALERT will develop a system for the automatic monitoring and selective dissemination of multimedia information using speech recognition, audio and video segmentation and automatic topic indexing (ALERT).

- COVAX will build a system that will allow access to documents in libraries, archives and museums regardless of their location. This work will be based on homogeneously encoded document descriptions based on the application of SGML and XML (COVAX).

- Personalised Services for Integrated Internet Information (PSI3) will investigate innovative techniques for personalising and integrating Internet information (PSI3).

- REYNARD will develop a European broker service to provide integrated access to national distributed networks of subject gateways and metadata repositories (REYNARD).

DELOS, a 'network of excellence on digital libraries', has also been funded under the IST programme. This will support digital library research in Europe by facilitating sharing of experience between projects and contacts with related sectors such as electronic publishing and archives.

Conclusions

There is a lot of interest worldwide in digital library research. Work in this area has moved beyond the retrieval of text-based documents and technology-based systems. The main thrust of work now seems to be on providing access to any type of digital information, whether it includes sound, still and moving images. The focus has shifted towards people, how they look for information and how they want it presented and delivered.

These two main thrusts and a global networked environment mean that systems need to be compatible to provide truly integrated and, preferably, personalised services. Another influence is the push toward the convergence between 'knowledge' or 'memory' organisations – libraries, museums and archives – which means that a lot of research is cross-sectoral. Research in this area is also multidisciplinary, involving researchers from disciplines such as information and library science, computer science, psychology, sociology and education. Funders such as the European Commission, the National Science Foundation and the UK's Joint Information Systems Committee also facilitate collaboration on an international scale.

A lot of digital library research is related to educational and scholarly needs. However, this does not mean that it is of no relevance to special libraries and it is worth while keeping a watching brief on digital library research projects. Libraries in learned societies especially may find value in the resources that are being created through digitisation programmes.

Academic and special libraries are facing similar issues. Both types of library are concerned with getting the best value for money. Academic libraries have increasingly been taking advantage of centrally negotiated deals for reduced subscriptions to services. This is an area currently being explored by the public library sector. This may be something that some special libraries could also explore. Academic libraries have been working with systems suppliers on requirements and the outcome of this work could benefit all libraries. The products of information retrieval research may also find their way into improved commercial products for workplace libraries.

Copyright and licensing are of concern to both sectors. While special libraries do not have the same privileges under the law, these privileges are under threat for all libraries anyway. Joint work carried out by bodies such as JISC and the Publishers Association as well as the contacts between projects and publishers has increased understanding between libraries and rightsholders on copyright issues in the digital environment.

The provision of desktop access to information and the integration of external digital sources into organisational systems are concerns of both special and academic libraries. Security, personalisation and privacy issues are also relevant to both sectors. Some of the output from projects developing hybrid library management systems will be applicable in other environments.

References

ALERT. Alert System for Selective Dissemination of Multimedia Information. Available at *http://www.cordis.lu/ist/projects/99-10354.htm*) [14 June 2000].

Bawden, David and Rowlands, Ian. *Understanding Digital Libraries: towards a conceptual framework*. London: British Library Research and Innovation Centre (1999) (British Library research and innovation report no. 170).

Brophy, Peter. *Digital Library Research Review*. London: Library and Information Commission (1999) (Library and Information Commission research report no. 17).

Brophy, Peter. *The Integrated, Accessible Library: a model of service development for the 21st century: the final report of the REVIEL (Resources for Visually Impaired Users of the Electronic Library) project*. London: British Library (1999) (British Library research and innovation report no. 168).

CEDARS Project Team and UKOLN. *Metadata for Digital Preservation: the CEDARS Project outline specification.* (2000). Available at *http://www.leeds.ac.uk/cedars/OutlineSpec.htm.*

CEDARS. *Project plan – Baseline, July 1998.* (1998). Available at *http://www.leeds.ac.uk/cedars/documents/ABA02.htm#DESCRIPTION.*

Chowdhury, G.G. and Chowdhury, Sudatta. Digital library research: major issues and trends. *Journal of Documentation*, **55**(4) 1999, 409-48.

COVAX. Available at *http://www.cordis.lu/ist/projects/99-11820.htm*) [15 June 2000].

Digital Library Federation. 2000. Available at *http://www.clir.org/diglib/dlfhomepage.htm.*

Digital Library Federation. *A working definition of a digital library.* (1999). Available at *http://www.clir.org/diglib/dldefinition.htm.*

Dublin Core Metadata Initiative. (2000). Available at *http://dublincore.org.*

European Commission. *Telematics for Libraries – project.* (2000). Available at *http://www.cordis.lu/libraries/en/projects.html.*

European Commission. ELVIL: the academic portal for European law and politics. Available at *http://elvil.sub.su.se/data1/home/home.html*) [14 June 2000].

Library and Information Commission. *Digital Libraries: current projects.* (2000). Available at *http://www/lic/gov.uk/awards/digit.html.*

Marchionini, Gary. Research and development on digital libraries. In: *Encyclopedia of Information and Library Science.* Marcel Dekker: New York (1998), 259-79.

Oppenheim, Charles and Smithson, Daniel. What is the hybrid library? *Journal of Information Science*, **25**(2) 1999, 97-112.

Pinfield, Stephen et al. Realizing the hybrid library. *D-Lib Magazine*, October 1998. Available at *http://www.dlib.org/dlib/october 98/10pinfield.html*) [26 June 2000].

PSI3. Personalised Services for Integrated Internet Information. Available at *http://www.cordis.lu/ist.projects/99-11056.htm*) [15 June 2000].

REYNARD. Academic Subject Gateway Service Europe. Available at *http://www.cordis.lu/ist/projects/99-10562.htm*) [15 June 2000].

Rusbridge, Chris. Towards the hybrid library. *D-Lib Magazine*, July / August 1998. Available at *http://www.dlib.org.dlib/july98/rusbridge/07rusbridge.html*) [26 June 2000].

Whitelaw, Alan and Gill, Joy. *Summative evaluation of Phases 1 and 2 of the eLib initiative: final report.* Guildford: ESYS Ltd. (2000). Available at: *http://www.ukoln.ac.uk/services/elib/info-projects/phase-1-and-2-evaluation/elib-fr-v1-2.pdf*.

University of Sheffield. *Department of Information Studies at the University of Sheffield: Information Management and Systems Research Group.* (1999). Available at *http://www.shef.ac.uk/uni/academic/I-M/is/research/imrg/imsrg.html*) [15 June 2000].

Chapter 26

The information 'player': a new and timely term for the digital information user

David Nicholas and Tom Dobrowolski

Summary

It is high time that researchers and practitioners gave thought to the terminology that they employ to study information use and information seeking in the digital environment. Existing (largely print) terminology is proving an impediment to understanding what happens when people go online to communicate and/or retrieve information (as they are doing in droves if the media are to be believed) and is probably also producing false readings. This chapter, based upon research into the behaviour of the digital information 'user', undertaken by City University's Internet Studies Research Group, evaluates the term and some related ones – information seeking, intermediary and end user, in the light of our knowledge of the new information order. A replacement term – the information 'player' – is presented for consideration and the significance of its adoption explained. It will be argued that the new term will enhance our understanding of what goes on in the digital information environment and will bring us closer to the information mainstream.

Background

This chapter arises out of the frustrations of many years of attempting to portray and evaluate information seeking behaviour in digital environments – and never really being able to do this accurately or to our own satisfaction.[1] Increasing sample sizes – something that is relatively easy to do thanks to web logs, or changing the methodology (focus groups being the latest flavour of the month) – never seemed to do the trick. Patently, what is required is a change in terminology, which would in turn bring about a change in thinking and hence produce more apt and understood descriptions of the information seeking process. In short, we need a new vocabulary that will help us understand what is going on in the new, but already ubiquitous, digital information environment. The vocabulary currently employed represents another age, and is proving an impediment to understanding and functioning in this one. In many respects the information profession is imprisoned by a Renaissance vocabulary, which represents a largely print-based world, yet increasingly works in a virtual world. New metaphors and a new language are needed if there is to be an improvement in our understanding of information seeking in cyberspace. There is especially a pressing need for a new vocabulary for evaluating networked services like the Web, intranets and WAP mobile phones. Without it there is a danger that information systems will develop a life of their own, irrespective of the actual needs of information consumers. Some would argue that this has already happened. The previous generations of information systems really took little cognisance of the user – despite the fact that they universally employed the dreaded phrase user-friendly (a distinctly systems-based term). But that has to change as we move rapidly towards personalised information delivery, bespoke information services and the like. We have moved to a dynamic, complicated and sophisticated information environment and our terminology, practices and thinking need to reflect this.

You might ask what is in a name, a word or a phrase? The answer must be, in today's communication rich environment: everything. Terminology is our thinking and the search for accurate terminology should drive our thinking. Terminology partly determines the perceptions of the people we serve. Consider, for instance, the extent of professional soul-searching associated with the term librarian[2] and the large number of dissertations that have been written on the topic.

The information user

Essentially, the argument is that the profession needs to change its vocabulary to change its thinking, and needs to start with what is probably the most central (key) word of them all – user (Julien, 1999). The word is generally used inaccurately because it is often used to describe non-users, too. The population being described by the term is a potential one, and an all-inclusive one. In reality it is used to describe anyone who might avail themselves of an information service. There are some hidden assumptions here that tell us much about the profession's psyche. The first assumption is that the term user embraces the majority of people – but frequently it does not. Despite the hype, Internet users still do not always constitute the majority of the population. The second assumption is that it is good to use, and this partly explains the evangelical approach of many information professionals towards their 'flock'. The implication is that use is *the* normal state but, of course, it is not always the case – the profession just wishes it were.

There is however a more general complaint that can be levelled at the word. User (and users), like information, has lost much of its meaning. It is a tired, over-used, cheap and misused word, which provides the information profession with a debased currency. It does not reflect the close and complex engagement that takes place between a person and today's interactive information systems. The word users paints a picture of a featureless mass, a homogenous body – people who are accustomed to being fed information through a batch-processing model. It is too passive and too mechanical for today's dynamic information environment. Users are in reality fast-moving individuals whose needs are constantly changing, depending on the problem, time, place and mood. Neither does the term recognise the fact that digital information systems create much greater information diversity than print-based systems. It is the wrong word, in the wrong place, at the wrong time.

The information player

Too much professional time has been spent complaining about the word user. There has been more than enough hand wringing. The time has come to abandon it, or to prescribe closely its meaning. What we really need is a more active and accurate term to replace it. The concept of individuality referred to above leads us very nicely to the term we need – *information player*. It is a term much richer in meaning, one that conveys both individuality and action. That is *player* used in the context of sport, meaning a football or cricket player. Players, of course, can be members of a team, but even then there are always the stars; or they can be truly individual, like tennis or golf players. Or we could use the term as it is used in the context of business, meaning someone who invests in, or plays, the financial markets.

- *Interactive.* Today's information consumer plays a much more important, complicated, creative and engaged role in the information seeking and retrieval process. The term user is one-dimensional and, if dynamic at all, that is only in a linear sense. Player on the other hand suggests a multidimensional, evolving relationship – the kind of relationship that is so much a feature of modern day information systems, like the Web. A player is constantly looking for new routes to a goal – evaluating options (information) as they go. Feedback from players is an essential part of search success. The player is part of the system while the user was all too often the person who stood outside the system, looking in. There is a good analogy to explain why a change of name is needed. Using traditional information systems was rather like going into an office canteen, at a specific time, asking for items on a restricted menu, having them given to you, you eating it and someone coming and taking away your plates (before you have finished your meal). Today's information systems are more analogous to the buffet lunch you order from an outside food caterer. You choose what you like, when you like, you take it to the table and you choose whether to return the empty plate to the trolley or leave it on the table. This plainly represents a fundamental change in behaviour. In the latter case you are much more involved and in control of the whole process. Determining the success or otherwise of the function – in this case the provision of food, but in our case the provision of information – will require us to examine different things. That is the point that is being made.

- *Recreational.* Today's information systems are now very much an extension of our life – and this will prove to be even more so as the digital mobile phone expands its horizons into the information systems and retrieval domain (Dobrowolski et al., 2000). The word player comes very much from the real world. Information seeking today is no longer just about professional problem solving; it can be recreational (and mindless) too.[3] Witness the phenomenal success of Yahoo!, Amazon.com and Lastminute.com, for instance. Or consider the widely held concerns over pornography on the Web. Indeed, the distinction between professional and recreational searching in the serendipitous and supermarket environment of the Web is becoming increasingly blurred. In a sense this has been partly recognised through the use of the term surfing (for information), but this word is rather too shallow a description for the process being represented.

- *Social.* Information gathering is often a social – and pleasurable, activity. The social context of the term player is very important. Players play with somebody else. Players have different social roles: you have, for instance, teacher and student, politician and voter, journalist and reader. This takes us close to the concept of virtual communities. Of course, one of the best ways to build a successful information service is to create a virtual community of players around it. AOL ICQ and Microsoft Netmeeting have done this. A combination of network-based information service with a communication program is the key to success here.

- *Competitive.* There are costs – financial and/or time costs, associated with finding – or not finding – information. You can win or lose in the information chasing and locating 'game'. Of course, players invest their time and money in every information journey or enterprise. With the migration of many communication, information retrieval, recreational and shopping activities to the Internet, the investment has increased enormously. Information services compete with each other to attract players. Amazon.com has been very successful in doing this.

The word player has other very important connotations. Firstly, it is a term that acknowledges the new economic and political realities of the new millennium. There has been a shift in power from information producer to information consumer. The information consumer now holds centre stage (another example of player power). This fact worries academic librarians and media moguls alike (indeed, anyone who manages large, centralised, inflexible batch-processing style information factories). Today's consumers have a wide choice and can quickly vote with their mice. Thus, as a patron of a university library you were always a supplicant – the Interlibrary Loans (ILL) librarian had particular powers to open (or not) the information gates to the wider world. Now the academic can go straight to the Web. The ILL librarian will have to undercut the opposition now (in terms of delivery times, cost or customer care) – the tables have plainly turned.

Secondly, the word player is closely connected with the term spectacle, a term once associated with pageants and tournaments. Today the Internet is the biggest capitalistic spectacle of our times. Witness how people pay fortunes for impressive Internet addresses. Witness, too, the amazing – and mythical – rise of e-commerce. There are fortunes to be had for the big players and games and adventures for the not so lucky. The Internet is part of the media world and not the information world

Thirdly, the term player is very much an Internet-type word. The Internet is part of the liberal world economy – the word user is most certainly not, and player most definitely is. There is an urgent need to get our words in line with the vocabulary of the Internet. The Internet has its own rich and picturesque language for describing itself. This cannot be ignored. It is only by employing this language that information professionals can address the much larger and more powerful audience that the Internet commands. We are dealing with a post-Modernist reality. The first goal of a new language is to facilitate narrative discourse. In a post-Modernist world it is discourse which creates and legalises vocabulary. Discourse also constitutes a research activity.

Perhaps the profession's notorious neglect of the user can be explained in some way by the term itself. After all, such a general and vague term hardly reminds us of the primacy of the individual and the need to investigate the individual's information needs. The term player demands such an investigation. It sends all the right signals. And that is what the Web is all about – sending (and receiving) the right signals. Maybe the solution to many of our professional ills lies with just changing one word. Now that begins to sound easy.

What the profession has not come up with yet is a term that describes success – not simply use, in the digital information environment. Interestingly, there really was no word for this in the print environment either. Of course, the terms references and records were often treated as synonyms for success, and the more records or references the higher the success levels – but the success being referred to here is really the success of the intermediary in finding the information, and not necessarily the success of the consumer in meeting their needs. Satisfaction – much beloved by questionnaire framers, is surely too remote, indirect and passé a term. In sports-speak it's all about what constitutes a score, what is the information equivalent of a goal or a wicket? Courtesy of the Web comes the word *hits*. Certainly it has directness and energy on its side, the only problem lies in measuring it (Nicholas et al., 1999). But you cannot have everything.

Re-assessing information seeking behaviour

The concept of a player is very helpful in understanding how people interact with information systems – and, also, re-visiting what we have said and learnt about them in the past. Continuing the sports analogy, few goals are probably scored in a textbook manner. Thus the Gascoines, Bergkamps and Zollas of the football world are famous for their ability to do the unconventional, the unusual, the creative. In any game of football, players do a lot of things that are not in the training and coaching manuals, but plainly they have received training. Similarly, a lot of information is collected by unconventional, unusual or serendipitous means. Thus, maybe, what was first seen as minimalist and idiosyncratic information behaviour was not so odd or strange after all – maybe it was just creative (Nicholas and Martin, 1993). Too often 'end-user' searching has been compared unfavourably with that of information professionals. But would you really expect a player to function always as the manager or ancillary staff has told them to? Would you expect all players (forwards or defenders) to operate in the same manner? Using the player concept helps us to get a closer and better understanding of what the web logs record – and what we witness – at the terminal, PC and mobile phone.

Of course, all players are subject to the rules of the game. The Internet has many rules associated with it – and these rules may be broken, of course. These rules can be social – that recreational searching at the office should only be conducted at lunch times or that visiting pornographic sites is strictly taboo – or they may be associated with searching – Boolean or proximity searching, for instance.

Maybe, too, the term player will help bury, once and for all, the myth that searching databases is a fundamentally academic exercise that requires high recall and is easily met by copious abstracts or bibliographic references of material (often well past their sell by date). The time has finally come to admit that consumers in the digital information environment have long superseded academics as the star players, and the latter should not be represented as *the* model information players. To determine satisfaction or success on the basis of the number of references found – or, for that matter, the amount of time spent online – must be wrong, but nevertheless it has been used as a quality metric for a very long time – too long a time.

Informobility

The advent of the mobile phone as an information retrieval system – connected, for instance, to the Internet and other specialist databases, will surely kill off the term user and herald the arrival of the player. With information on the move – or informobility, plainly the stress is now on action, movement and playing. The digital mobile phone offers a highly personal information service that is a much closer approximation to real life – and as far away from the traditional (four-walled) concept of a library as you can get. The mobile phone represents a genuinely popular (mass) platform for seeking and finding information. We are all players now. What will surely drive the use of the phone as an information retrieval medium will be the vast and ever-increasing amounts of real-time information becoming available. Playing too is a real-time activity: there is a natural harmony between these two words.

Other Renaissance terms

Getting behind the word is getting behind the concept. Getting behind the concept requires us to evaluate other obsolete, pejorative or 'loaded' words. We need to re-visit other terms, too: most importantly, information seeking, intermediary, and end user. Take information seeking – is this phrase not, also, redolent of a dim and distant past – one which featured fairy tales, perhaps? It is a phrase that implies timeless, mild and undirected action with no real end product. Clearly some searching is like that, but by no means all. *Information resolving* might be a more appropriate term for much of the searching conducted today.

Given that we are now dealing with a *player* then it is axiomatic that the role of the information professional must be revisited as well. After all it is largely a team game that we are talking about and intermediaries do search on behalf of others. If we have energised the concept of the user then, maybe, we have to energise the concept of the information professional too. Unless, that is, we believe that, as a direct result of user-empowerment, energy has flowed away from the information professional; and plainly that has happened in places, where information professionals have retired to the backroom – processing database feeds, as they do in the media for instance. In general, though, words such as intermediary and intermediation are far too passive, hands-off, words. They are in sync with the concept of user but out of sync with the concept of playing. As always the real issue is how dynamic a role should be adopted by the information professional. On the most general level, are information professionals *players* too? If they are players then what position do they play in? In football parlance are information professionals strikers or goalkeepers, or, maybe, player – managers? Perhaps, as we have hinted, some information professionals are not players at all, but ancillary staff – the chief coach or the groundsman, for example. The game is the same but the roles are quite different. If information professionals are to be coaches then that assumes that they are acknowledged authorities in the field – and maybe many of them would be deluding themselves if they believed this. To be coaches they would also need to understand their players intimately and that means having player profiles – information need assessments. This is also far from being anywhere near the truth. But maybe the change of vocabulary would lead to a change in their behaviour?

What then of the groundsman metaphor – someone who is responsible for the environment in which the players operate: the 'pitch' in sports terms and cyberspace in information terms. This is plainly a back-room operation, but nevertheless still one of importance. The involvement of many information professionals – incidentally one of the few terms that still fits, in intranet, web site and database developments would suggest that many are, indeed, ground staff. Traditionally the profession has very much played the role of the groundsman, but that was when much information gathering was conducted in the library, but today's pitches are found in cyberspace – and few information professionals can claim to have full territorial rights there.

What then should be done about end user – another very overworked, depersonalised term? End user is used to describe people who search information systems themselves – once a rare activity, now an extremely common one. The information profession is not alone in using this term; it has also become part of business-speak, too. Of course, the term is built around the concept of user – and shares all the same problems. It is also very inaccurate – many end users, for instance, pass on some information to others and do not consume it themselves. The term gatekeeper – another useful sports metaphor – is often used to describe these people. The distinction between searcher and consumer, that was once so marked, is now so blurred as to be meaningless. But having argued for the removal of the term, it should be re-introduced, but its meaning should be severely limited. Its use should be reserved for describing activities that involve the consumption of information canteen or batch-processing style, though not used in a derogatory sense but in a passive, uncomplaining sense. Sometimes just watching something – like TV – is all we want.

The term player also helps us in the marketing of end-user training programmes – something that appears to fall more and more in the information professional's domain. For instance, the latest 'buzz' term, 'information literacy', would be unsuitable as it is far too judgmental, prescriptive, and one-way. Players think they can play – even if they can't. E-training or i-coaching would be much more preferable terms. The concept of the personal trainer is also a useful one here.

Conclusions

These past few years information professionals have had to sit back and allow Internet 'nerds' to educate them in the ways and characteristics of the new information world order, that is the Internet. Starting from scratch as they did, they invented a brand-new vocabulary, full of live, popular, direct and apposite words. Very few of the words used – surfing, visitors, hits, navigate, and so on, have their origins in the information science field, which of course is significant in itself. The information profession should take a leaf out of their book and put some new words to work – starting, but not finishing, with the word player. If the term user already seems outmoded in connection with the Web, just think how even more outmoded it will appear in the context of the WAP or Internet connected digital mobile phone. A redundant and obsolete vocabulary is likely to divorce the profession from the wider information world to which it surely wishes to get closer.

In the information seeking area the last major change of vocabulary was when the term end user was introduced in the early 1980s. With so much change having taken place since then a major change is long overdue – the time has surely come to introduce the concept of the information player or, in its abbreviated form, the *i-player*. Such a change in vocabulary should help information professionals find their true role in the Information Society – and so far that role is unclear and slow coming. Clearly a major part of their role will be understanding, counselling, training and standing in for the *i-players*. The personal trainer could be a highly prized job. For that to happen, the whole profession has to move closer to the players and treat them all as individuals – something that many information professionals have been historically reluctant to do. Information professionals have to demonstrate their own player credentials (most of the successful football managers have been players) – and that is not simply about showing that they are better players, but also that they possess true team spirit.

At present no one is competing for this counselling–training role, but this should not make us complacent. The technology and the opportunity are there, but whether the interest and interpersonal skills are also there is much less certain. However, feet-dragging on the part of the information profession in terms of re-engineering will not slow the onward march of personalised information systems and services – and the information needs assessments that are such an essential part of them. We shall know whether this has all come to pass when an evaluation of an information unit is conducted in terms of player satisfaction and not by system performance, and when pride is shown in the quality and skills of the players and not just the quality of the systems.

Notes

1. This became most notable during the senior author's two recent projects *Web Log Analysis: case study newspapers* (1998-9) and *The Changing Information Environment: the impact of the Internet on information seeking behaviour in the media* (1997-8).

2. For instance, see Circle of State Librarians, Annual Study Conference, *Who am I?* Held on 7 February 2000, at the Institution of Civil Engineers, London.

3. Research has shown that peak use of web sites is at office lunch times. Nicholas, D and Huntington, P. Who uses Web newspapers, how much and for what? A log analysis of *The Times / Sunday Times* web sites. *NetMedia99 Conference: Proceedings,* City University, July 1999.

References

Dobrowolski, T. Nicholas, D and Raper, J. Mobile phones: the new information medium? *Aslib Proceedings,* **52**(5) May 2000, 197-9.

Julien, H. Constructing 'users' in library and information science. *Aslib Proceedings,* **51**(6) June 1999, 206-9.

Nicholas, D., Huntington, P., Williams, P., Lievesley, N. and Withey, R. Developing and testing methods to determine the use of web sites: case study newspapers. *Aslib Proceedings,* **51**(5), May 1999, 144-54.

Nicholas, D. and Martin, H. Should journalists search themselves? (And what happens when they do?) *Online Information 93: proceedings.* Learned Information, 1993, 227-34.

Index